Hemingway's
Death in the Afternoon

Dustjacket of Death in the Afternoon, *first American edition (Scribner, 1932).*
Courtesy Houghton Library, Harvard University.

Hemingway's
Death in the Afternoon

The Complete Annotations

Miriam B. Mandel

The Scarecrow Press, Inc.
Lanham, Maryland, and London
2002

SCARECROW PRESS, INC.

Published in the United States of America
by Scarecrow Press, Inc.
4720 Boston Way, Lanham, Maryland 20706
www.scarecrowpress.com

4 Pleydell Gardens, Folkestone
Kent CT20 2DN, England

British Library Cataloguing-in-Publication Information Available

Library of Congress Cataloging-in-Publication Data

Mandel, Miriam B.
　Hemingway's Death in the afternoon : the complete annotations / Miriam B.
Mandel.
　　p.　cm.
　Includes bibliographical references and index.
　ISBN 0-8108-3996-2 (alk. paper)
　1. Hemingway, Ernest, 1899–1961. Death in the afternoon. 2. Bullfights. I. Title.
　GV1107 .H4 2002 (Commentary)
　791.8'2—dc21　　　　　　　　　　　　　　　　　　　00-066124

♾ ™ The paper used in this publication meets the minimum requirements of
American National Standard for Information Sciences—Permanence of
Paper for Printed Library Materials, ANSI/NISO Z39.48–1992.
Manufactured in the United States of America.

Brindo por ti
Anthony Brand

If a writer of prose knows enough about what he is writing about he may omit things that he knows and the reader, if the writer is writing truly enough, will have a feeling of those things as strongly as though the writer had stated them.

Anything you know you can eliminate and it only strengthens your iceberg. It is the part that doesn't show.

Ernest Hemingway
Death in the Afternoon and Plimpton interview

The significant omission itself . . . Hemingway defines only vaguely. The thing eliminated that gives a story its "dignity of movement" can be "anything" the writer knows.

Susan F. Beegel
Hemingway's Craft of Omission

Contents

Preface

F. Scott Fitzgerald wrote of his subject Jay Gatsby that "he started as one man I knew and then changed into myself."[1] This book also wrought change, but not in its subject: it started out as an exercise in historical annotation, and it remained that thing to the end. The change occurred in myself.

I first approached the corrida with great ignorance and a faint distaste for it, but now I cannot read it as other than metaphor and poetry, allegory and philosophy. This change is not due to any mystical experience in the bullring: I have seen very few corridas, and none has moved me as, in concert halls and in front of *Las Meninas*, I know I can be moved. What has most impressed and liberated me, as I sat in libraries and pondered the bull, the bullfighter, and their ritual dance of death, has been the corrida's perfume of optimism, even gaiety.

The bullfight gets down to basics: it pits a fearsome aggressive beast against a human being armed with cloth, sword, knowledge, discipline, and character. It posits that in the normal course of events, this human being can and will dominate the beast bent on hooking and destroying him. Because the beast is huge and the danger real, the human triumph is necessary, the only outcome the imagination can countenance. It is in the confidence of this outcome that the corrida rests.

This is, clearly, a hopeful vision, a reassuring affirmation. But it depends upon a framework: a circle to contain it, a president to control it, an informed public to curb it, skillful performers who will come to each other's aid, and facilities to aid the injured. It is only in such a civilized world that the drama can be played out and catharsis achieved.

I have lived my life in a fairly civilized world, but my world has been haunted by that historical moment when reason crumbled and destruction was not contained. Displaced and fatally scarred by the Holocaust, my parents could not envision more than grim survival. But survive

ix

one must, both physically and culturally, and so I armed myself with education and ideology and, when the opportunity arose, went with my children to live in Israel. For twenty years I have educated Israeli students, supported the Israeli army, done my duty, and felt safe. I began to warm to the bullfight when I felt it speaking directly and reassuringly about survival and about the role of discipline and skill in achieving that aim; I recognized both the tools and the goal. But I fell in love with the bullfight when it took me one step beyond, to the vision that the fight against fear and extinction can produce beauty, even ecstasy.

No amount of art or optimism can bring back generations lost to genocide. But for the survivors and for the children of the survivors, art is liberating.

I began this book with the aloof intellectual curiosity and stern academic discipline that have ruled me most of my life. I got through the hard spots with a determination that bordered on grimness and teeth that I fear were often clenched (one often sees such grimaces on the faces of bullfighters). But generations of bullfighters have done more than survive: they have triumphed over mortal danger with passion and grace, creating beauty so poignant it becomes ecstasy. They have communicated this passion to their audiences, and they have convinced me too, that passion, perhaps even more than intellect, shapes us, shapes history, and makes art. I should have known, but did not, that the energy devoted to survival can produce beauty. For me, the fight against extinction had been grim.

I have studied Hemingway's bullfight and his long-dead bullfighters for the last dozen or more years, coming to love them in the libraries, thinking about what drove them into the dance with death, and starting to understand and change some of myself in the process. Now as I finish this book, I feel I have silenced most of the old fears and gathered new courage and energy, new openness to beauty.

For all that this study of Hemingway's bullfight has brought me, I am grateful.

Ra'anana, Israel

Acknowledgments

It took Ernest Hemingway nine years to produce *Death in the After-noon*, and it took me half again as long to research it. As my commitment to Hemingway and the bullfight grew, so did the number of people and organizations that it is an honor to acknowledge here. I take particular pleasure in acknowledging the generous three-year grant given me by the National Endowment for the Humanities, which freed me to research, think, and write with a concentration impossible to achieve while teaching. Such a grant has far-reaching implications in a scholar's life, and I shall be grateful for many years to come. Additional support was supplied by grants from the John F. Kennedy Library Foundation at Columbia Point in Boston, for work in the Hemingway Collection. Tel Aviv University graciously responded to these grants by allowing me to take an extended leave of absence. My thanks also to the *Journal of Modern Literature* and to *Resources for American Literary Study* for permission to reprint material that appeared in my articles "Hemingway Confirms the Importance of the Taurine Baptism: Fictional and Historic Case Studies" in *Journal of Modern Literature* 23.1 (1999): 145–57 and "Index to Ernest Hemingway's *Death in the Afternoon*" in *Resources for American Literary Study* 23.1 (1997): 86–132.

My publisher has presided over the expansion of my project from the one book they originally contracted to the multivolume encyclopedia this is turning out to be. It has been a reassuring pleasure to work with them.

Without Spanish libraries, archives, museums, and other depositories, my research would have been impossible. Spain's Biblioteca Nacional, my headquarters in Madrid, gave me extraordinary privileges, which made the months I spent in their archives much more comfortable and productive. The librarians at the University of Barcelona, at the National Library of Cataluña, and at the municipal and university libraries of Pamplona (Navarra) helped me launch my research well over a decade ago. I was also helped by the librarians and directors of specialized collections: Colonel José María Vega Fernández at the Servicio Histórico of the Biblioteca Central Militar, Madrid; Ana Rovira and the other helpful librarians at the Ilustre Colegio Oficial de Médicos de Madrid; Ana Corral, librarian at the Sociedad Rectora Bolsa de Madrid; and the officers of the Patrimonio Nacional, Dirección de Actuaciones Histórico-Artísticas, Monasterio de El Escorial.

In the United States, the John F. Kennedy Museum and Library at Columbia Point in Boston was my home away from home. The JFK Library houses the Hemingway Collection, whose curators, first Megan Desnoyers and then Stephen Plotkin, were always helpful and affectionate. In Boston, I was also well received at the Widener Library of Harvard University, and at the Boston Public Library. The librarians of Skidmore College in Saratoga Springs, New York, were remarkably efficient, and Patricia Plácido helped me find what I needed.

For technical information on bullfighting, bull breeding, and bullfighters, I thank Eduardo Gismera and especially Miguel Angel García and the late Don Manuel García-Aleas Carrasco, of the Unión de Criadores de Toros de Lidia in Madrid; Filiberto Mira of Seville; and Maestro José González (Pepe Dominguín), president of the Asociación de Matadores, Rejoneadores y Apoderados, Madrid. They were all very patient with me.

Elsewhere in Spain I was helped by Rosa María Malet, director of the Fundació Joan Miró in Barcelona; Dolores Miró and Joan Punyet Miró, Successió Miró, Palma de Mallorca; Jamina Castellnou Rovira, Ajuntament de Mont-Roig del Camp (Montroich); Rafael Gómez Díaz, municipal archivist at Ayuntamiento of Talavera de la Reina (Toledo); Fernando E. Furio Martínez, Jefe Sección de Archivos, Ajuntament de Valencia; Vicenta Peiro Guerrero, archivist at the Colegio Oficial de Médicos, Valencia, and Cruz Bespin, of the Biblioteca Pública de Zaragoza.

For information on the Spanish hotels that Hemingway mentions in *Death in the Afternoon*, my thanks to Ana López García and Natividad Caballero of the Hotel Reina Victoria, Ronda; Mauro Soler Arnau of the Hotel Valencia; and Simón Hernández Hernández, Hostal Aguilar in Madrid.

For information on alumni, special collections, and other matters relating to their universities and schools, my thanks to Rebecca J. Bates, curatorial assistant at the Harvard University Archives; Rick Ryan at the biographical section of the Office of Alumni Records, Princeton University; Sylvia Grinder and Eustace D. Theodore, Association of Yale Alumni at Yale University; Gould P. Colman, university archivist at Cornell University; Mary E. Foy, assistant dean and registrar at Johns Hopkins University School of Medicine; Adele A. Lerner, archivist at the New York Hospital–Cornell Medical Center; Carley R. Robison, curator of manuscripts and archives at Knox College in Galesburg, Illinois; Joan G. Caldwell, Louisiana Collection at the Tulane University Libraries in New Orleans; and Alesandra M. Schmidt of the Watkinson Library at Trinity College in Hartford, Connecticut.

For information on horses, my thanks to Doris Jean Waren, librarian at Keeneland Association in Lexington, Kentucky; Theresa C. Fitzgerald, librarian at The Blood-Horse in Lexington, Kentucky; Howard Bass at Thoroughbred Racing Communications in New York, and especially Thomas Gilcoyne, research librarian at the National Museum of Racing and Hall of Fame in Saratoga Springs, New York.

In England, I was helped by David J. Penn, keeper of the Department of Exhibits and Firearms at the Imperial War Museum in London; and T. A. Heathcote, curator, and Mrs. M. I. L. de Lee, acting curator, at the Sandhurst Collection of the Royal Military Academy in Sandhurst, Surrey. Further information on military matters was provided by Kapitänleutnant Sander-Nagashima of the Militärgeschichtliches Forschungsamt in Potsdam, Germany, and by Colonel Enrico Pino, Stato Maggiore dell'esèrcito, Reparto Affari Generali, in Pocol, Italy.

Anyone who has written a book knows that it cannot be done without the help of family, friends, fellow scholars, and those remarkable strangers who share information and, more often than not, become friends. Basic to this book were my husband and daughters. Although variously enamored of medieval dragons, martial arts, and the esoterics of literary theory, they encouraged enthusiasm they did not always share. For this and much else, I thank them. My relatives in San Juan, Cleveland, and Boston once again provided hospitality and humor. My family is small in number but large in understanding.

My friends, real and virtual, Hemingwayean and secular, have survived a decade of historical, political, linguistic, literary, and taurine excitements with much puzzlement and more kindness. I thank Judith

Abend, Susan F. Beegel, Nancy Bredendick, Gerry Brenner, Rose Marie Burwell, Alex A. Cardoni, the late Les Easterman, Muriel Feiner, Luca Gandolfi, Peter L. Hays, Stefano Illing, Allen Josephs, Deirdre Levi, Sean O'Rourke, Paul Montgomery, Andrew Moore, Beatriz Penas, Paul Preston, the late Michael Reynolds, José Gabriel Rodríguez Pazos, Patricia P. Trott and her family, and all the members of the Hemingway Society and the Hemingway List who helped me: you know who you are.

Many people read the manuscript. Gil Arruda, Albert DeFazio, Peter L. Hays, Jerome Mandel, Earl Rovit, Frederic Svoboda, and Arthur Waldhorn noted stylistic excesses, suggested entries, and gave pointed advice. I thank them all. Even with so much support, I greatly missed the mind of a generous and learned man who helped me through my last book and who encouraged me to persevere with this one: Paul Smith did not love the bulls, but he understood the need for annotation. He died in 1996, but he remains with me still.

One of the joys of working on *Death in the Afternoon* is that it led me to Anthony Brand—hispanist, practical aficionado, and taurine scholar par excellence. Tony read the entire manuscript five times; answered endless questions; noted oversights; clarified technical terms; tracked down out-of-print books, journals, and newspapers; and supplied most of the illustrations I present in this book. His encyclopedic scholarship, generosity and enthusiasm, appreciation of Hemingway, long experience of Spain, good sense, and passion for all aspects of the bullfight have made him the perfect partner for this enterprise.

User's Guide

This reference work is intended for readers who require information about the people, animals, and cultural artifacts mentioned in Ernest Hemingway's *Death in the Afternoon*. This book offers several hundred entries, which are arranged alphabetically to provide easy access.

TYPES OF ENTRIES

The book's single alphabetical list consists of entries that fall into three broad categories: People, Animals, and Cultural Constructs.

People

Most of the entries in this book refer to the people who are mentioned in *Death in the Afternoon*. *Death in the Afternoon* presents these people variously: sometimes by giving first and last names (Gertrude Stein, Virginia Woolf), sometimes by identifying relationships (Ortega, widow of), and sometimes by supplying just the first name (Rafael), initials (A. U., D. S.), a nickname (Alamendro), or other pseudonym. In almost all cases, I have been able to retrieve a fuller name, and the cross-references direct the reader to the main entry under the surname.

In addition to proper names, the reader will find entries for nameless characters who are identified only by their professions. They are grouped under headings such as Authors, Doctors, The Newspaperman, and the like. Readers interested in Hemingway's use of nameless, undefined background figures are directed to entries such as Narratee and Women and Girls. Nameless fictional characters, like the Adjutant and the Old Lady, are also listed, defined, and discussed.

Animals

Animals are listed only when they are mentioned by their own names (the horses Exterminator and Uncas, the bulls Comisario and Víbora), or are identified by the ranch that produced them (Murube, Villar), or the breed which defines them (Cabrera, Vistahermosa). For a discussion of the animal that dominates *Death in the Afternoon*, see the section in the introduction entitled "Bulls and Bull Breeding."

Cultural Constructs/Place Names

Individual or specific cultural constructs that are identified by name, title, or initials (e.g., the Madrid newspaper *ABC*, the poem *Snow Bound*, the book *Virgin Spain*, the YMCA) are listed and annotated. Events (Agrarian Reform), activities (Boxing), and objects (Drinks) that recur frequently are also annotated, as are more general concepts (Luck, Proverbs, Roman Catholic). Place names (e.g., of bullrings, cities, bars, cafés, hotels, the military academy at Sandhurst) are important signifiers in Hemingway's texts and are therefore fully annotated. For more information, see the section in the introduction entitled "Names of Places."

TEXT OF THE ENTRIES

The entries may be composed of some or all of the following elements:

Entry Heading

To facilitate access, the entry heading presents each item as it appears in the Hemingway text, even if that text presents the name in an incomplete, incorrect, or misspelled form.

Some variations in spelling are due to the instability of Spanish spelling in the 1920s, especially in terms of the consonants *j*, *g*, and *x*. Ignacio Sánchez Mejías, for example, appears on taurine posters as Megias, Megías, and Megeas. Other variants may reflect dialect or family tradition: the patronymic of Manuel Varé (Varelito) was also spelled Varés and Varest. A few variants result from Hemingway's ignorance or faulty memory, and additional errors and inconsistencies crept in as the manuscript passed through typists, editors, copy editors, and type-setters. Whatever the reason or the error, the entry heading reflects the text. Thus, the entries for the beer Aguila, for the bullfighter Manuel Jiménez (Chicuelo), and for the events at Vera are presented under the headings Aguilar Beer; Jiminiz, Manuel; and Deva, because *Aguilar*, *Jiminiz*, and *Deva* are the words that appear in the text. Although I re-tain the text's spelling and wording in the entry heading, I do indicate the correct spelling within the entry itself, and I also add or remove accents and capital letters to make Spanish words, phrases, and titles (of books, journals, and newspapers) reflect Spanish usage.

Body of the Entry

In the entry itself, I supply as much material as I think could be use-ful. For people, this includes full first and family names; nicknames, pet names, and pseudonyms; a paragraph presenting basic details such as nationality, profession, and birth and death dates; a biographical sketch that reviews education, achievements, and other relevant details; a sum-mary of critical evaluations of their careers; and, in the case of bull-fighters, instances when Hemingway saw them perform. The less familiar the historical figure, the more information I thought it proper to offer. Thus the entries for bullfighters and bull breeders are quite detailed; those for Cervantes, Hemingway, and Shakespeare are short.

For animals I trace the etymology or significance of the name (if any); the animal's breeding; the events or occasions that made the ani-mal well known; and, when possible, Hemingway's encounters with the animal.

For cultural artifacts like books, newspapers, and organizations, I offer dates of composition, first performance or publication, summary of contents, historical overview, and other relevant information.

Sources and Documentation

To make the entries as easy to read as possible, I have relegated most of the documentation to the notes at the end of the book. Information that is generally available (e.g., birth and death dates of Shakespeare, the titles of his works) is assumed to be common knowledge not requiring documentation beyond a listing of basic reference books (such as Webster's dictionaries, the *Encyclopaedia Britannica*, or the *Encyclopedia Americana*) in the list of works cited. The notes document information obtained from more specialized sources. When the entry is controversial, the note also summarizes the scholarly debate.

In the interest of saving space, short references are used in the notes section. Complete bibliographical information is provided in the list of works cited. For unsigned articles in daily and weekly newspapers, however, full documentation (newspaper, date, page and column numbers) is necessary in the note itself, and therefore newspapers are not listed in the Works Cited.

All direct quotations, even if they are from easily available sources like the *Encyclopaedia Britannica*, are documented immediately following the quoted material. Quotes in Spanish and other languages are followed by translations which, unless otherwise noted, are my own.

Hemingway's Use of the Item

Each entry ends with a short indented paragraph that identifies the occasion and context in which the item occurs in *Death in the Afternoon*, with page references to the Scribner edition.

Page Numbers

The pagination of *Death in the Afternoon* presents several problems. The first edition and all subsequent Scribner hardcover issues contain 517 pages, but the more widely available Scribner Library paperback editions, which present the same illustrations and text, number only 487 pages, the difference of thirty pages resulting from a more compressed presentation of the photographs and their captions. To make my book relevant to both the hardcover and paperback editions, I have adopted the following system: the first twenty chapters, which are similarly paginated in both versions (pages 1–278), appear without editorial comment. Page numbers higher than 278 refer to the hardcover edition and are preceded by *h*. To translate these into paperback numeration, the reader only needs to subtract 30. For references to details in Hemingway's Glossary, whose pages are unnumbered in some hardcover printings, I add Hemingway's entry heading to enable the reader to find the reference easily. Thus, to find Hemingway's remarks on the journal *La Fiesta Brava*, the reader is referred to *h:* 463, s.v. *Periódicos;* and to *h:* 475, s.v. *Revistas.*

Page Numbers Indicating Quoted Speech

Occasionally, Hemingway dramatizes a bullfighter (Diego Mazquiarán [Fortuna], Rafael Gómez Ortega [el Gallo]) or other personage (the Homosexual, the Newspaperman, the Old Lady). Page numbers presented separately at the end of the entry indicate direct speech as it occurs in monologue, dialogue, or general conversation. Free indirect speech, interior monologue, or dialogue presented without quotation marks is generally not indicated in this final section of the entry.

ORGANIZATION OF THE MATERIAL

Alphabetical Order

The entries appear in alphabetical order. Because the entries are geared to the published Hemingway text, the entry headings are capitalized, accented, and spelled just as they appear in the Scribner editions of *Death in the Afternoon*, even if these are incorrect or nonstandard. The alphabetization of the entries is governed by the spelling that appears in the Hemingway text.

Alphabetization is letter by letter, according to the English alphabet. Words beginning with the Spanish letters *ch*, *ll*, and *ñ* are listed under *c*, *l*, and *n*. Because Spanish is not a "foreign" language for Hemingway aficionados, I have alphabetized Spanish titles and names like English ones, according to the substantive and not the article: thus, *La Gaceta del Norte*, La Granja, and El Greco all appear under *G*.

Saints are alphabetized according to their names, not under San, St. or Saint. Names that include el, de, van, von, and the like are generally listed according to the substantive and not to the preposition or article preceding it: thus von Behr is listed under *B* for Behr, el Niño del Matadero under *N* for Niño, and de la Rosa under *R* for Rosa.

Cross-References

A generous sprinkling of cross-references leads the reader to either other, relevant materials in this volume or to an item in this book's companion volume, *Hemingway's* The Dangerous Summer: *The Complete Annotations* (cited as *DS*, as opposed to references to the text of Hemingway's *The Dangerous Summer*, which is cited as *TDS*). To differentiate cross-references, I use the abbreviation (q.v.) and the italicized words *see* and *see also* when referencing an entry in this book. See and see also in roman type reference either another section of this volume (the introduction or the notes); an entry in the companion volume (see also *DS*); or material in another book, journal, newspaper, or encyclopedia (see also Cossío). For example:

1. The entry on Philip II refers the reader to related entries in this same volume in two ways. Since Pius V is actually mentioned by name in the entry for Philip II, the insertion of (q.v.) after the Pope's name informs the reader that an entry exists for this person. The phrase, *see also* El Escorial, indicates that this entry is also relevant to Philip II.
2. The pointer (see *DS*) after a particular name or noun informs the reader that additional information on this person, animal, or cultural construct is available in a corresponding entry in the companion volume, *Hemingway's* The Dangerous Summer: *The Complete Annotations*. When the name or noun does not appear in the entry in this book, a more specific cross-reference, also in roman type, leads the reader to the relevant material in the companion volume (see also Dudley, Earl of, in *DS*).

A NOTE ON NAMES

I have alphabetized both Spanish and non-Spanish names according to the patronymic. English-language readers are accustomed to identifying the patronymic as the last word in the series (e.g., Ernest Miller Hemingway, John Greenleaf Whittier), but Spanish names are organized differently. Sometimes, only the patronymic is given, in which case it is the last word in the name. But in a full Spanish name, the patronymic is the penultimate word in the series, the final word being politely reserved for the maternal line. Thus, José Gómez Ortega (Joselito) would be alphabetized under *G* for Gómez and not *O* for Ortega, Ortega being his mother's maiden name—or, more accurately, his mother's father's name.[1]

In the bullfighting world, fathers, sons, grandsons, and nephews may share the same first name, patronymic, and nickname, so that generation after generation, we find the same names on bullfight posters. Aficionados will know from the *cartel*'s date (and from other details) which generation is meant, but for those who are less well informed, the maternal name helps us distinguish fathers from sons and uncles from nephews.

Although the full formal name gives precedence to the patronymic by presenting it first, occasionally a person will be known mainly by the maternal name. To reflect Hemingway's presentation of such instances, Andrés Leiva Mérida is alphabetized under *M* and Domingo López Ortega under *O*, although Mérida and Ortega are these men's mothers' names.

Women's Names

Countries like Spain and France did not need the Women's Liberation Movement to encourage married women to retain their given names. Married Spanish women have customarily kept their own names and nicknames for daily and even legal use, although their formal names acquire a prepositional phrase to acknowledge the new commitment. For example: when Carmen (Carmina) González Lucas, daughter and sister of the famous bullfighters known by the professional nickname *Dominguín*, married Antonio Ordóñez, her formal name became Carmen González Lucas de Ordóñez. In Spain, she could still be called Carmina González or Carmina Dominguín, although in British or American usage she would, at that time, be known exclusively as Carmen Ordóñez. Interestingly, a wife who becomes a widow is more likely to be known by her late husband's name than by her own.

The three women whom Hemingway includes among the best bull breeders of the 1920s and early 1930s exemplify the flexibility of the Spanish system: Enriqueta de la Cova married Félix Moreno Ardanuy but was not known by his name; Carmen de Federico married Juan

Manuel de Urquijo y Usía (or Ussía) and she too was known by her maiden name. But Mercedes Ugalde Bañuelos, who married Félix Gómez, is generally identified as the *viuda de* (widow of) don Félix Gómez; she lost even her first name when her husband died. Similarly, *la viuda de Ortega*'s maiden name, María Josefa Corrochano Sánchez, has been forgotten.

Nicknames

Because the same nickname can refer to several bullfighters, I have made separate entries for important nicknames, to explain their provenance and to identify the various individuals who used them (*see*, for example, the entries for Bienvenida; Gallo, Gallito; and Valencia). Such entries are cross-referenced to the main entry for each bullfighter, who appears under his patronymic. For more detail, *see* the entry for Nicknames.

A NOTE ON TAURINE STATISTICS

Since a number is only as reliable as its reporter, I have consulted as many authoritative sources as possible, reporting discrepancies and disagreements whenever these occur. I have relied heavily on Cossío's twelve-volume encyclopedia, *Los toros*, which is the standard work in the field, but I have also consulted other reference works as well as contemporary reports in newspapers, pamphlets, and journals. The detailed annual reports offered by *Toros y toreros en . . .* are invaluable not only for the wealth of detail they offer, but because Hemingway also relied on these books: he owned the volumes for 1925, 1926, 1927, 1929, 1930, and 1934, and their statistics and flavor are apparent in some of his thumbnail sketches and taurine opinions. Whenever possible, I read materials that I know Hemingway read, in Spanish, English, and occasionally in French.[2] I also worked with other taurine biographies, critical treatises, and theoretical and practical studies, the large majority of them still untranslated from the Spanish. Because changes in the legal codes that govern the bullfight are particularly instructive, I consulted various early local codes as well as the *Reglamentos* from 1917 (the first national code) to the present. Hemingway was well acquainted with the texts of the 1917 and 1923 *Reglamentos.*

My statistics are incomplete in two important respects. Because Hemingway's experiences with the bulls were limited to Spain, and because most reference books privilege the Spanish season and exclude all others, the numbers that I offer when describing a bullfighter's career reflect only those corridas he fought in any particular year in Spain. However, in the case of a foreign bullfighter or of a Spaniard who performed frequently in foreign bullrings, I mention the number of corridas he fought in those countries that also have a taurine tradition (Columbia, Ecuador, France, Mexico, Peru, Portugal, and Venezuela).

My statistics are incomplete in another respect as well: they reflect only the actual corridas fought (*corridas ajustadas*). One can argue that the number of contracts the bullfighter was offered or that he signed (*corridas contratadas*) is a more accurate indication of his standing. This number can be considerably higher than the number of *corridas ajustadas*, because a bullfighter may have to cancel many performances in a season. A serious goring might require weeks of convalescence, and rain, illness, accident, or some other factor could further depress the number of appearances. On the other hand, a few spectacular afternoons, especially if they occur in first-class rings and early in the season, may suddenly bring new contracts, so that a bullfighter can finish the season with many more corridas than he originally contracted for. When the discrepancies between *corridas contratadas* and *corridas ajustadas* are striking, I note them.

Statistics do not necessarily reflect an individual's contribution to his profession. A bullfighter might become a *figura* (an enduring presence) in the annals of *toreo* for reasons relating to personality, art, innovation, tradition, or other factors that cannot be measured with numbers.

For all these reasons, statistics must always be viewed with some skepticism. Still, the numbers do give a fairly reliable indication of the bullfighter's *temporada* (season), and a string of such statistics will reveal whether a bullfighter's star is ascendant. Generally speaking, thirty corridas mark a respectable season. A run of several years with forty, fifty, or more corridas means that the bullfighter is doing very well indeed. Most bullfighters maintain a precarious position, with ten or fewer corridas a season.

OTHER HEMINGWAY TEXTS

Some of the items mentioned in *Death in the Afternoon* appear in other Hemingway works as well. In noting these cross-textual incidences, I have used the following abbreviations, which are recommended by the Hemingway Society. All page references are to the Scribner editions:

ARIT	*Across the River and Into the Trees*	1950
TDS	*The Dangerous Summer*	1985
AFTA	*A Farewell to Arms*	1929, 1957
FWTBT	*For Whom the Bell Tolls*	1940
GOE	*The Garden of Eden*	1986
GHOA	*Green Hills of Africa*	1935, 1963
iot	*in our time*	1924
IOT	*In Our Time*	1930, 1958
IITS	*Islands in the Stream*	1970
MF	*A Moveable Feast*	1964
MWW	*Men Without Women*	1927
OMATS	*The Old Man and the Sea*	1952
SAR	*The Sun Also Rises*	1926
THHN	*To Have and Have Not*	1937
TOS	*The Torrents of Spring*	1926
WTN	*Winner Take Nothing*	1933

Introduction

ART, HISTORY, NOSTALGIA, AND THE LAW

Like any venerable art form, the bullfight retains traces of its past in its present. Striking historical markers, most clearly discernible in costume, ceremony, and terminology, make that past legible to the informed eye and ear. Indeed, one of the many pleasures of the bullfight is its respect for tradition, its historical consciousness, the insistent backward glance that informs not just the art but also the literature it inspires. Taurine journals, papers, and books commemorate dead bullfighters and vanished *suertes*; they keep the old days much alive in the present. But taurine critics do not insist, as Hemingway says they do, that the old days were always and inescapably better than the decadent present. The past affects us all differently.

For Hemingway, neither the past nor the present was a tool for constructing a brighter, more hopeful future. For him, the vanishing past was always replaced by a much diminished present. And that present was, in turn, threatened by the approach of the grimmer future. These attitudes emerged naturally from the experiences of his early years. As a child, he witnessed the destruction of Upper Michigan, when the loggers came, and of Oak Park, when urban development gobbled up open spaces. As an eighteen-year-old he went to war, was wounded in Italy, and lost, or so he said, his belief in his immortality. For him, change meant loss, and not a few critics have argued that his life and art were dominated by nostalgia.

That nostalgia dominates Hemingway's writing about Spain and the bullfight. Even in his early days in Spain, he knew that the country was changing. The 1920s were marked by military involvement in the north of Africa and rapid political change at home. Early in 1931, with Primo de Rivera gone, elections looming, and the growing desire for financial

1

and cultural Europeanization, it was clear that political upheaval was unavoidable and that the bullfight, like all of Spain, was condemned to change. Hemingway wanted to perpetuate the values expressed in the bullfights of the 1920s, to preserve the bullfight as he knew it, "for anyone who should ever be interested in knowing what it was like."[1] For as long as he could, until the very end of Chapter Nineteen, Hemingway clung to the present and to the past and avoided speculation about the future.

There is another, more practical reason for Hemingway's attempt to freeze the bullfight in time. Hemingway recognized that in offering such a foreign subject to readers indisposed to appreciate it, the most effective approach would be to focus on the corrida itself, not its past or its future. He offers only the briefest of historical detours as he guides his audience through the contemporary spectacle that they would see if they ventured into a bullring. Artistically, it was a wise decision. The corrida that Hemingway constructed for us is so vivid that for most of his audience it represents *all* corridas. We thus come across readers who, many decades after the publication of *Death in the Afternoon*, leave the bullring convinced they have seen exactly what Hemingway saw. They have not, just as Hemingway himself, when he came to Spain in the 1950s or even the 1930s, did not see what he had seen in the 1920s.

Hemingway saw his first bullfights in May, June, and July of 1923, and he returned to Spain's bullrings practically every year for the next decade. More precisely, he saw bullfights in 1923, 1924, 1925, 1926, 1927, 1929, 1931, and 1933. But his emotions were so powerfully stirred by his early experiences in the bullring that he accepted the corrida of the mid-1920s as the norm against which to measure all subsequent taurine events—even though, in the late 1920s, he witnessed drastic changes in the bullfight, and even though he knew, in 1931, that other changes were inevitable. Hemingway certainly understood that Belmonte and Joselito had irrevocably altered the style of bullfighting in that remarkable short period from 1914 to 1920 known as *la edad de oro* (the golden age of bullfighting), and that the bullfighting of the 1920s was still reeling from the changes introduced in those years.[2] But his nostalgic bent resisted further change. In 1931, returning to Spain after a year's absence, Hemingway found new bullfighters, new styles, and a different type of management—an altered bullfight, more aloof than the celebration of passionate, creative individuality that had flourished during *la edad de plata* (the silver age) of the 1920s. Holding new artists to an earlier standard, Hemingway misjudged them.[3]

In trying to hold on to what he loved, Hemingway sometimes became ahistorical or anti-historical, and such an approach necessarily distorts: the constantly evolving corrida cannot be fixed in time. If we read all of Hemingway's pronouncements on the bullfight, the bull, and the bullfighter as permanent "facts," we miss his taste, his judgment, his values, his art. And "facts" are, of course, inaccurate and sometimes false, especially so when the "facts" of one period are examined by eyes educated in another. Styles change; tastes differ. Hemingway confessed to us that "I know things change now and I do not care. It's all been changed for me. Let it all change" (278)—a defiant, painful cry. The corrida had changed, but *Death in the Afternoon* remains.

To understand Hemingway's stances, opinions, predilections, and predictions, the reader would be wise to understand the taurine norms of the periods during which Hemingway saw bullfights, as well as Hemingway's own attitudes at the time of writing. The point is not to establish the limits of Hemingway's taurine expertise, but to attempt to understand how he looked at a subject that passionately interested him, to understand how the artist interpreted and represented this subject in his own art. The relationship between what he saw in one period and what he saw in another, between what he read and what he saw, between the opinions he formed for himself and those he adopted from other sources, between accepted opinion and individual judgment, between fact and invention, biography and autobiography, fiction and nonfiction—these cannot be understood if we lack the relevant historical and intellectual backgrounds.

Intelligent discussion, whether focused on the author, his subject, or his artistic rendering of it, cannot be conducted in the context of historical ignorance. If we do not know how the corrida was conducted in Hemingway's day, and how it changed even as he observed it, we will not understand the power of his essay on it, the degree to which his art preserved his idea of the corrida. That corrida no longer exists, but historicizing the subject will enable us to study Hemingway's handling of it. Comparing his artistic rendition with statistics, with other contemporary accounts, and with the opinions of professional taurine critics and historians, we will see more clearly that *Death in the Afternoon* is a personal, impressionistic portrait, not a realistic reproduction, of one moment in the long history of tauromachy. The artist used his art to convince us to see as he saw, and we can use history to see the extent of that art.

There is, of course, no single "truth" about the bullfight, but there are facts and informed opinions to be considered. Dates and statistics, though not dramatic, are helpful guidelines for understanding not just the careers of bullfighters and the types of bulls they fought, but also the corrida's tempo of change. Perhaps the most important marker of change is the *Reglamento* (taurine code), which evolved significantly from its early version, drafted by Melchor Ordóñez in about 1847, to the increasingly detailed and prescriptive documents published in 1917, 1923, 1930, and, post-Hemingway, in 1962, 1992, and 1996.[4] These legal documents codify the changes in the corrida. They are very eloquent: their silences, their repetitions, the amount of detail they devote to any one item, and even the fines they impose for noncompliance—all these details reveal emphases, trends, and expected or accepted deviations. They help us understand the corrida as an evolving entity, a process.

Hemingway was aware of the importance of the *Reglamento*. In November 1931, he wrote his editor, "Everything is completed except this swell last chapter that I am still writing on [Chapter Twenty] and the translation of the 13,000 words of reglamento. Might get some one to rough out the translation to save me time and work—Then I will correct it and fix it up."[5] Hemingway did not include this projected translation because he knew that a new *Reglamento* (published in 1930) was replacing the one he was familiar with. In the Glossary, Hemingway wrote that a translation of the later *Reglamento* could be included "in subsequent editions of this book if there should be such editions."[6] This is the first study to follow Hemingway's suggestion that the *Reglamento* be read in conjunction with *Death in the Afternoon*.

Because changes in and additions to the taurine codes are so instructive, I refer to all the editions, from Melchor Ordóñez's local ordinances for Málaga (1847) and for Madrid (1852, 1868, 1880), to the national codes Hemingway knew. The first of these, the 1917 *Reglamento*, was still in effect when Hemingway saw his first bullfights in 1923. Indeed, several of its articles were reproduced on the *cartel* (poster or announcement) of the very first corrida Hemingway saw (illustration 2). The next *Reglamento*, adopted on 20 August 1923, was revised before it finally went into effect on 9 February 1924. This is the one Hemingway was going to translate and include in *Death in the Afternoon*. The codes of 1917, 1923, and 1930, then, ruled the bullfights Hemingway saw before the publication of *Death in the Afternoon* in 1932. The codes immediately preceding and following these three are interesting in that they reveal the trends and usages that required modification, criminalization, or legal acceptance. They help us identify the taurine topics that agitated Hemingway's contemporaries, the ways in which these questions were resolved, and the efficacy of those resolutions.

Changes in the rulings testify to the *Reglamento*'s flexibility. Sometimes, however, the *Reglamento* futilely insists on unenforceable norms (e.g., the spectators must remain in their seats) or attempts to outlaw well-entrenched practices. For example: the 1917 *Reglamento*, and all subsequent ones, expressly forbid the matador's *cuadrilla* to turn or dizzy the stabbed beast, or to push their matador's sword more deeply into its body.[7] Many *cuadrillas* performed these forbidden maneuvers while their matador stood by, but reprimands were seldom issued, fines were infrequently imposed, and the forbidden behaviors continue to this day. Here we see that the *Reglamentos*' repeated prohibition of a behavior merely registers its continued existence.

Interesting as these codes are, we must remember that, like any other legal document, they do not deal with morality, truth, or justice. They simply record society's response to a particular problem at a particular historical moment. And because they mediate between past definitions and present reality, or between tradition and current practice, they necessarily lag behind current practice. They give us the legal but not the actual definition of the corrida. The law cannot define or control the corrida, which, like any human endeavor, is always in the process of being negotiated.

Hemingway knew Spain and the corrida were changing. He did not like it, but he knew it. To be informed readers of *Death in the Afternoon*, we must know it too.

BULLS AND BULL BREEDING

The *toro de lidia*, the magnificent animal on whom the entire edifice of tauromachy rests, has been traced to "the wild cattle, called aurochs, that once roamed most of the ancient world."[8] The bull who is fought ritually in the ring, although frighteningly aggressive and unpredictable, is not wild in the same sense: he is the result of centuries of breeding. But unlike other domesticated or pedigreed animals, he is not bred for utilitarian purposes, to provide food, work, or protection for his human masters. Indeed, the *bos taurus hispanicus* (also called *ibericus* or *africanus*) may be unique among animals in that he is bred to provide art.

Life Cycle

Ganado bravo (literally, wild cattle) is a valuable property, carefully bred and expensively nurtured to maturity. When they are about two years old, female calves are tested for bravery in *tientas*, to see how they attack the picador's horse and how they respond to the cape and muleta; successful heifers are kept for breeding. Males are tested to see how they respond to mounted picadors.[9] Because they might end up in a bullring, these animals are not exposed to cape or muleta at a *tienta* or anywhere else. All care is taken to prevent their learning to distinguish between the lure and the person who wields it.[10] Fine specimens, whether they are destined for breeding or for corridas, must be kept in good health and strength. The *ganadero* (bull breeder), the *mayoral* (foreman), and the ranch's employees worry about the animals' health and pedigree, separating the males from the females in order to control breeding and separating adolescent males from each other as much as possible to prevent fights that could damage them.

Bull breeders are careful to provide optimum conditions for bulls that qualify for the bullring. En route to the bullring, these bulls travel in the company of the ranch's foreman, who ensures that no damage or discomfort comes to them. Cows and studs that remain behind on the ranch live long, comfortable, and productive lives. People who worry about the well-being of animals would be reassured if they were to see the vast acreage, carefully balanced feed, attention from professional veterinarians, and jealous protection that the *ganado bravo* enjoys throughout its lifetime. And the corrida itself, which draws so much disapproval from its opponents, is carefully designed to allow the *toro de lidia* to indulge his intense instinct to charge and to ensure that he is killed rapidly and skillfully. For all of its life cycle, up to and including its ceremonious death, the *ganado bravo* is carefully and even tenderly handled.

Age

The *ganado bravo* is so specific to the taurine spectacle that its age and size give their names to events such as *becerradas, novilladas,* and *corridas de toros.* This brings us to the complicated matter of nomenclature.

A bull is called a *toro* at the age of four and a *novillo* at the age of three. Animals younger than three years old are called by the generic name *becerro,* but a variety of terms exists, although demarcations between them are interestingly imprecise. The *Diccionario de la Real Academia de España* oxymoronically defines the *utrero/a* as "novillo o novilla desde los dos años hasta cumplir los tres" (*novillo* between the ages of two and three) although the *novillo* is generally defined as a three-year-old. In another dictionary, the *utrero* is defined as having "tres años cumplidos" (having passed its third birthday; this is the definition Hemingway gives [*DIA, h:* 488–89, s.v. *Utrero*]), although the *utrero/a* is more frequently defined as a two-year-old.

With this awareness of the slipperiness of language, we can review the variety of words, not all of them current today, which define the animal at various stages of its development. Generally speaking, then, the *choto* (also called *ternero* or *mamón*) is less than one year old, the *añojo* has passed its first birthday, the *eral* is about two years old, and the *utrero* or *utrera* is between two and three years old, although as they approach their third birthday they might already be called *novillos* or *novillas.* The *novillo-toro* is an animal thought unfit for a *corrida de toros* and therefore relegated to a *novillada*; he could be more than three years old. Such an animal might be physically imperfect (e.g., a deformed horn) or he might have been a *desecho de tienta* (rejected at testing as unfit for a *corrida de toros* or for breeding). Unimpressive or disappointing *novillos* and *toros* might be referred to pejoratively as *chotos* or *becerros*; Hemingway uses the term *half-bull* for a bull that seems too young or light to him.[11]

Although so much depends on the age of the bull, authorities disagree how age is most accurately to be determined. The stages of the animal's development (*becerro, novillo, toro*) are linked to weight in the *Reglamento,* but they can be determined more accurately by the rings (*anillos* or *rodetes*) on the lower part of the horn (*mazorca*), and by the animal's teeth. Doubts or disagreements about the animal's age are now settled after the fight. The carcass is weighed, sometimes whole, but more usually after it has been skinned and stripped of its entrails and head (*en canal*), and the teeth are examined.[12] *Artículo* 19 of the 1917 *Reglamento* was the first to call for a postmortem examination. It did not prescribe the method of examination, perhaps because dental development is so obviously the most reliable guide. The 1962 *Reglamento* specified that the teeth are the deciding factor in disputes about the bull's age.[13] In 1969, when the Registry Book was introduced, bulls began to be branded with the last digit of the year but not the month of their birth. This was clearly an insufficient indicator of age, and the year-brand was abolished in the 1992 *Reglamento*.

Corridas

As the bullfight developed, the emphasis shifted slowly from the mounted bullfighter to the one who fights on foot, and from the *suerte de varas* (the pic-ing) and the *suerte de muerte* (the killing) to the muleta work of the *faena*. But the animal itself necessarily and always remains the focus of attention, and perhaps nowhere more pointedly than in the *tientas*, which test young animals of both sexes, and the *corridas de prueba* and the *corridas de concurso*, which test the bulls. In the *corrida de prueba*, a sort of entrance examination for ranches aspiring to membership in the *Unión de Criadores de Toros de Lidia* (U.C.T.L., the bull-breeders' union), all the bulls are from the same ranch or *ganadería*. Five or six such corridas are required, to ensure that the ranch is been exposed to different sets of veterinarians and judges and thus to avoid charges of bribery, favoritism, or other wrong doing. The *corrida de prueba* features from three to six bulls and as many bullfighters.

The *corrida de concurso*, on the other hand, features animals from different, already accredited *ganaderías*, in a competition that offers a prize to the bull which excels in a particular quality (for example, bravery, in which case the number of pics is not limited; or *trapío*, his appearance in repose and in action). Such a corrida generally presents six bulls from as many *ganaderías*, fought in order of seniority (*antigüedad*), usually by three bullfighters. The winner emerges with a large money prize or a gold cup or silver tray; sometimes a commemorative plaque is affixed to a wall of the bullring. A particularly fine bull may be granted an *indulto* (pardon), in which case he is not killed in the ring.

For other types of corridas, in which the bullfighter shares the limelight with the bull, see the section entitled "The Corrida" in this introduction.

Hemingway's Experience of the Pedigreed Bull

For two reasons, the bulls Hemingway saw when he attended his first corridas were larger than those he saw later. First, the plazas of Madrid and Pamplona, which Hemingway visited in May, June, and July 1923, have always been partial to large bulls. And second, the *Reglamento* then in force required older and heavier bulls for *corridas de toros*. Hemingway's tastes, formed by the first bulls he saw, led him to object to the smaller bulls he saw in later years.

Change: Reduction in Age and Weight

It is important to note that the bulls Hemingway saw in the early 1920s were almost one hundred kilograms heavier than they would be in the bullfights he saw later that decade or in the 1930s and 1950s. *Artículo* 9 of Melchor Ordóñez's 1847 ruling defined the bull as being between five and eight years old. Spain's first national taurine *Reglamento* (1917), which unified and codified the rules governing various aspects of the bullfight, confirmed the *toro*'s minimum age as five years and defined minimum weights that were considerably higher than they are today. In a first-class bullring (at that time: Madrid, Barcelona, Sevilla, Bilbao, Valencia, Zaragoza, and San Sebastián), the bull had to weigh a minimum of 525 kilograms during the months from October to April, and 550 kilograms in the months that presented the most corridas, that is, May through September. In 1919, an amendment reduced the minimum age of the bull from five to four years; the *Reglamento* of 1923 (and the revision of 1924) maintained a minimum of four years and a maximum of seven, and *increased* the minimum weights to 545 kilograms in the months from October to April and to 570 kilograms for the rest of the year.[14] These are the bulls prescribed for the bullrings Hemingway visited in the 1920s, though in practice, the bulls were frequently smaller, lighter, and younger.

The revolutionary stylistic innovations introduced by Juan Belmonte required a smaller, faster, more responsive bull.[15] To satisfy artistic requirements and matadors' demands, bull breeders in the 1920s and early 1930s sometimes sent underage bulls into the bullring. *Toros y toreros en* . . . , a tolerant publication recognizing that Belmontistic maneuvers required these smaller, more agile bulls, remarked upon but accepted as necessary the occasional infractions of the law in terms of the age and weight of bulls. Tolerated infractions quickly led to intolerable abuses. In 1926, the same publication accused a particular breeder, Francisco Villar, of having crossed all permissible boundaries. The editors harshly remarked that the animals that Villar had sent to the Vitoria *corrida de toros* of 5 August looked as if they were two to three years old, far short of the requisite minimum of four years for *toros de lidia*.[16] In 1930, the new *Reglamento* reduced the minimal weight drastically, to 470 kilograms for those bulls fought in *plazas de primera categoría*, 445 kilograms for second-rank plazas, and 420 kilograms for third-rank plazas.[17] In 1959 minimum weights were again lowered slightly (ten kilograms per category), and these rulings about weight govern the bulls we see today.

Change: Reduced Importance of the Seniority of Bulls (*Antigüedad*)

The seniority of the *ganadería* was an important concept in the eighteenth and early nineteenth centuries, when the *antigüedad* of the herd determined the order of the bulls to be fought in the ring, just as the seniority of the bullfighters determined the order of their appearance. In the mid-nineteenth century, however, the bullfighter Francisco Arjona (Cúchares, 1818–68) daringly suggested that the bullfighters who fight them, and not the bull breeder who nurtured them, should determine the allocation of the bulls, or the order in which they are fought.[18] This challenge to the bull breeders' power went unheeded, but a generation later Luis Mazzantini (1856–1926) insisted on this privilege, and other bullfighters united behind him to demand a *sorteo* (the grouping of bulls into lots, with the bullfighters defining the lots) to guarantee a more equitable distribution of bulls. Bull breeders naturally objected to this procedure, and so did those bullfighters whose alliances with bull breeders assured them of precisely the bulls that best suited them, often to the detriment of fellow *toreros*. But matadors as a group were growing in prestige, the power shift was unstoppable, and by the end of the nineteenth century the *sorteo* was opposed only by Emilio Torres (Bombita) and Rafael Guerra (Guerrita). When Hemingway came to his first bullfights, the practice was already normalized in the *Reglamento*.[19]

This decline in the power of the bull breeder brought with it a lessening of the importance of the concept of *antigüedad*, or the seniority of the bulls. *Antigüedad* is difficult to define, because it involves both the breed and the breeder and because the method of its acquisition has changed over the years. The best definition I have found reads as follows:

> Antigüedad de la ganadería. Independientemente del año de su fundación, se considera la del día que por primera vez han lidiado sus toros, con su hierro y divisa actual, en la plaza de toros de Madrid. La ganadería más antigua que figura en la relación de la U.C.T.L. es la de don José Vázquez Fernández, antigua de Aleas, cuya antigüedad es de 5 de mayo de 1788 (Independent of the year in which the bull breeding ranch was established, its seniority dates from the day on which its bulls were fought, with their *current* brand and colors, in the Madrid bullring. The oldest bull breeding ranch in the records of the U.C.T.L. is that of don José Vázquez Fernández, formerly the property of Aleas, whose seniority dates from 5 May 1788).[20]

Ironically, in the days when *antigüedad* was more important, it was easier to acquire: it dated from the first time that the bull breeder presented a minimum of two bulls to be fought in a Madrid corrida. But in the twentieth century, six bulls—the full complement required for a corrida—needed to be fought in Madrid, displaying their breeder's brand and colors. If any one of these bulls is disabled or discarded, the corrida does not establish the *antigüedad*, and the bull breeder must present another six bulls on a different afternoon.

Although the brand and colors are usually spoken of in terms of the bulls that display them, they really belong to the owner of the herd, who may or may not sell these markers to whoever buys part or most or even all of the herd. Thus, a bull breeder could sell some or all of his animals and still retain the seniority, brand, and colors, which he might then attach to another herd, even if it has a different pedigree and different characteristics. This could be done for ethical reasons: if, for example, the herd had deteriorated, the breeder might decide to take drastic measures, like discarding all the lesser animals in order to ensure the production of good bulls. It could also be done for profit: if, for example, a bull breeder had a fine herd, he could sell most of it, keep the *antigüedad*, and apply it to other animals, whether good or bad, which had been retained or recently acquired. Francisco Villar was criticized for just such sharp dealings. Having sold his stock and its *antigüedad* at a good price to Arturo Sánchez Cobaleda in 1928, Villar continued to charge high prices for lesser stock, with a different *divisa* (colors), to bullring impresarios who did not keep careful track of changes in ownership. Thus Villar destroyed the reputation and value of the *ganado bravo* he had sold to Sánchez Cobaleda.[21]

In the 1920s, when Hemingway began to study the bulls, transmission of *antigüedad* was still largely a matter of inheritance rather than sale. When a bull breeder died, the heirs could decide to own the herd jointly, keeping its *antigüedad*, or they could divide the property. In the latter case, the older son, assumed to be wiser in the ways of breeding, normally inherited a larger share of the herd, and the younger inherited the brand and colors, in the expectation that he would outlive his siblings and therefore the *antigüedad* would be less exposed to change. If they wished to continue breeding their share of the herd, the other heirs could choose new colors or design a new brand. They sometimes also kept the old date or *antigüedad*, a factor that caused much blurring of the concept.

Further blurring of *antigüedad* was caused by the emergence of the *tratante*, a middleman who acquired bulls and horses from a variety of ranches and supplied them as needed to impresarios or plazas. When the bullring impresario, who is in charge of acquiring the *ganado bravo* to be fought in the plaza he runs, bought directly from the bull breeder, the latter often imposed conditions for the presentation of his bulls and the safeguarding of his reputation. But when he sold to the *tratante*, the bull breeder lost control of his animals as soon as they left the ranch. Often, the bull breeder did not know when or where his bulls would be fought, or under what conditions they would be kept until the day of the fight.[22]

Even though the bull-breeding world still has a long memory, keeping track of the genealogical and historical details involved in the tracing of *antigüedad* is difficult. The rules remain more or less the same: the brand and colors are usually transmitted with at least a fraction of the herd, and the new owners of the brand and colors, whether they inherited or bought them, can keep this *antigüedad*, presenting the bulls under the old name or their own name, but using the previous owner's brand and colors. But there are many variations: the new owners might decide to incorporate their new animals into their own herds and use their own *antigüedad*, especially if it is more ancient. Or they might keep the newly acquired herd separate but design a new brand and choose new colors. In this case, their seniority will date from the first time a full complement of these bulls is fought in Madrid, and the old *antigüedad* will be lost, though the brand or a variant of it could emerge elsewhere.

Other factors that also contributed to the gradual weakening of the bull breeders' clout, the blurring of the breeds, and the confusions attending *antigüedad* include the increase in the number of herds, the more frequent changes of ownership, the increased cross-breeding, and the foregrounding of commercial concerns over history and tradition. As a result of all this, extinct brands or variants of old brands sometimes show up, quite legally but rather jarringly, on the flanks of a herd that is only very faintly, if at all, related to the herd originally marked with it or to the family that owned its *antigüedad* (*see*, for example, the entries for Villar in *DIA* and for Gamero Cívico in *DS*).

To solidify their deteriorating position, bull breeders organized the *Unión de Criadores de Toros de Lidia* in 1905. The U.C.T.L. deals with matters like brands, seniority, and registration of herds; collectively, they can prohibit a matador or impresario from banning or boycotting any individual ranch. Their frequent publications—a quarterly journal, *Toro bravo*; and an annual book-sized compendium that lists all its member herds, their brands, colors, *antigüedades*, histories, current owners, addresses, and telephone numbers—communicate changes to all interested parties.[23]

By the time Hemingway came to see bullfights, the bullfighter was required to heed the bulls' *antigüedad* only on those occasions when the *sorteo* gave him bulls from two different ranches: in this case, he was required to fight the one with the greater seniority first. And the *antigüedad* of the ranches is still the determining factor in *corridas de concurso*, when several ranches are represented and the bulls are fought in order of their seniority: there is no *sorteo*.

THE BULLFIGHTER

The term *torero*, or *bullfighter*, includes the picador, the *rejoneador* (mounted bullfighter), and the banderillero as well as the matador. Each of these figures has its own history. By the time Hemingway came to the bullfight, the matador was the cynosure of all eyes, and so his career will be described in most detail.

The *rejoneador* or *caballero en plaza* is the original bullfighter. Early bullfighters were aristocratic warriors who, to sharpen and display their skills in peacetime, rode, hunted, jousted, and performed with bulls. As the word *caballero* indicates, these aristocrats were mounted (*caballo* is Spanish for horse), and the *rejoneador* is, by definition, a mounted bullfighter. One of the attractions of *rejoneo* is the delicate coordination between the rider and his well-bred and -trained horses. Together, they play and kill the bull.

In the nineteenth century, *rejoneadores* were seconded by unmounted attendants (*chulos*) who had little prestige: they merely positioned the bull and, if the fighter could not kill the bull from horseback (as often happened), they finished his work. These unmounted bullfighters are the ancestors of today's banderilleros and matadores. But even today, when the *torero de a pie* (bullfighter on foot) is the undisputed star of the show, the *rejoneador* will be named first in the *cartel*, to indicate that the mounted bullfighter takes precedence. And he is usually given the title of *don* (*de origen noble*, of noble or aristocratic descent), because he occupies the position of an aristocrat, even if he is not one himself.

The picador or *varilarguero* (person who wields a pic or long staff) has a complicated history. The tools he uses indicate his descent from the *vaquero* (cowboy) or *mayoral* (ranch foreman) who manages and tests animals by means of a staff or goad. In the *tienta* (testing of the calves), the animal's bravery is measured by his willingness to charge a mounted man armed with a pic. In the bullring, this important characteristic is revealed by his behavior vis-à-vis the picadors. As a mounted bullfighter, the picador is also related to the *caballeros* of old and to their descendants, the aristocratic *rejoneadores*. This distinguished lineage was reflected in the *carteles* which, until about the middle of the nineteenth century, gave the picador precedence over matadors who fought on foot.

In the eighteenth century, three mounted picadors awaited the entrance of the bull into the ring, remained on duty and ready to act for the rest of the bullfight, and left the ring only when the dead bull was removed. The *suerte de varas* was thus synchronous with the whole fight. In the early nineteenth century, the picadors' stay in the ring was drastically shortened: they left the bullring as the banderilleros began their work. This clarified the difference between the acts and between the functions of the professionals who intervened in the bullfight.[24] Late in the nineteenth century, the number of picadors was reduced from three to two.

As the picador's role was changed and reduced, his name moved down on the *carteles*. Early *carteles* featured the picadors, but by the 1920s, their names, like those of the banderilleros, appeared in small print—if they were listed at all—and the matadors and bull breeders headed the *carteles*.

In spite of this descent in prestige, the picador is distinguished from other members of the matador's *cuadrilla* (team) by the fact that he is entitled to wear gold embroidery to indicate that, like the mounted matadors from whom he is descended, he was permitted to kill the bull.

Banderilleros, or *peones de brega*,[25] work at the orders of their matador. Many started their careers with the hope of becoming matadors: the connection to the matador is that of apprentice to master. But the road is difficult, and most young men fail to achieve the rank of *matador de novillos* or, if they do manage to become *novilleros*, to maintain that rank; they swell the ranks of professional banderilleros. Some *matadores de toros*, including such famous ones as Cayetano Ordóñez (Niño de la Palma), are so bedeviled by the problems and stresses of their profession that they resign their *alternativas* and become banderilleros.

Many banderilleros have gained fame and enjoyed long careers, their experience making them invaluable to the matador who employs them. Because they are not permitted to kill the bull, banderilleros wear silver trim (matadors wear gold) and are therefore known as *hombres de plata* (men of silver).

The bullfighters Hemingway looks at most closely are the *matadores* (literally, killers). They are generally young men in their twenties and thirties, and for many, these years, when body and reflexes are finely tuned, mark the peak of their careers. By focusing on the active years

of the career itself, Hemingway necessarily neglects the long apprenticeship that precedes it and the long retirement that usually follows it.
The following chronological summary attempts to provide a more complete picture of the stages of a bullfighter's life. Like any generic composite, it is necessarily rough.

Childhood, Youth, and Education

The entry into the profession is forbiddingly difficult. Some *aspiran-
tes* have the way smoothed for them by family connections or by wealth,
but in general the young aspirant must overcome familial and financial
obstacles as he attempts to become educated in his craft and to master
the politics of the taurine world. In Hemingway's day, most aspiring
bullfighters dropped out of school to follow the bulls. Families with a
strong taurine tradition accepted and even expected such behavior; in
other families, it was often the source of great friction, and not a few
bullfighters, like Ignacio Sánchez Mejías, ran away from home. In poor
families, where education is a luxury, the conflict is between the benefits of a job and the unprofitability of bull fever. Whatever their family
situation, most bullfighters begin their training while they are still children.

The aspirant may or may not attend a bullfighting academy, but even
if he does, he will probably profit most from the instruction offered by
other bullfighters. Such instruction, while valuable, is usually haphaz-
ard, consisting of a pointer here or there. He will probably practice
toreo de salón with a fellow enthusiast, who will run at him with a set
of horns or with a *carretilla* (a mechanical contraption resembling a
bicycle wheel with handles, to which horns have been attached): the
handheld horns are used for training in cape and muleta work, the *carretilla* for practice in placing the banderillas and the sword. Most desir-
able, of course, is work with live animals, in *tientas* (where two-year-
olds are tested), *becerradas* (in which animals less than three years old
are fought), *capeas* (improvised village bullfights), or, more daring and
illegal, in the fields where the bulls graze. Here the aspirant is in danger
from the herd keeper and the police, as well as the animals.

During these years, the aspirant, usually still in his teens, may have
acquired a patron (an older bullfighter, a bull breeder, sometimes a relative, neighbor, or family friend) who will provide instruction, introduc-

tions, or financial aid. Or he might have attracted a professional *apoderado* (manager) who will offer to negotiate the profession's treacherous politics in exchange for high fees and a large percentage of the aspirant's potential profits.[26]

In the late nineteenth and early twentieth centuries, *cuadrillas* of child performers were popular (*see* Niños Cordobeses and Niños Sevillanos), and in some families boys as young as ten or twelve performed with their older brothers. Child labor laws, instituted around 1915, barred children younger than sixteen from working. The ban was inscribed into the 1917 and 1923 *Reglamentos*,[27] and some very young bullfighters, most famously the Bienvenida brothers, were taken by their families to Latin America, where no such ban forbade them the bullring. The ban seems to have been temporarily lifted late in 1928, which enabled José Mejías (Pepe Bienvenida) to perform in Spain in 1929, when he was fifteen. But the taurine code of 1930 again specified sixteen as the minimum age (*Artículo* 124); this was still in effect in 1940, when Luis Miguel Dominguín performed outside of Spain until attaining minimum age.[28] The requirement was dropped in the 1962 and subsequent *Reglamentos*.

The *Novillero*

If he is talented, persistent, clever, successful, uninjured, lucky, and can afford it, the aspirant bullfighter graduates to the rank of *matador de novillos* or *novillero*, fighting first in *novilladas* (bullfights in which he kills a bull that is at least three years old) without picadors and then in the more expensive ones, with picadors. He may also perform in *corridas mixtas*, which also feature *matadores de toros*, or in informal *festivales*, which might also feature graduated *matadores de toros* as well as *aficionados prácticos* (enthusiasts with training but no formal rank). In these *festivales*, all the participants, regardless of rank, fight *novillos* (often though not always with picadors) and wear the *traje corto* (high-waisted country suit) instead of the *traje de luces* (suit of lights).

Sometimes an unemployed bullfighter leaps into the bullring illegally, to draw attention to himself and thus, hopefully, launch a career. Most *espontáneos* are quickly removed, as the law requires, but occasionally the move succeeds, as it did for the impoverished Manuel Benítez (el Cordobés), who began his spectacular and highly profitable career by leaping into the arena of Las Ventas, on 28 April 1957. Today, with the proliferation of taurine schools and *novilladas*, aspiring bull-fighters have more possibilities, and it seems that the improved economic situation has curbed the *espontáneo* more efficiently than the earlier rulings, fines, and arrests.[29]

Presentation in Madrid

A *novillero*'s Madrid debut was and is an important but not necessary milestone in his career. In Hemingway's day, as today, it usually takes place after the *novillero* has obtained a good reputation in lesser rings. Because of the cachet attached to a Madrid debut, almost all important *novilleros* appear in Madrid on their way to their *alternativas*. Of course, an unfortunate Madrid performance can derail or even destroy a career, but a sparkling afternoon may generate large audiences and lucrative contracts. Important as it is, the Madrid debut does not guarantee promotion to the final rank, *matador de toros*.

The Doctorate

The *alternativa*, or promotion to *matador de toros*, is a solemn event in the life of a bullfighter. It can be conferred only by an accredited *matador de alternativa*, and he grants the *doctorado* by ceding his own turn in the bullfight to the candidate. The ceremony is short: the senior *matador* hands the candidate the sword and muleta he will use with the bull and welcomes him into the rank with a few words of advice and encouragement.

All the details surrounding the ceremony are significant: the date, the bullring, the bulls, the officiating matadors, and their performances. An *alternativa* taken during an important fiesta in a first-class bullring, attended by top-ranked matadors and involving bulls of good breeding, weight, and repute, carries the same cachet as a doctorate granted by a first-class department in a venerable university. An *alternativa* granted in an ordinary corrida in a lesser bullring draws much less attention, although the bullfighter may subsequently, by his own merits, ensure himself a place in the annals of the bullfight.

Although a *matador de toros*'s seniority dates from his promotion to that rank in whatever bullring the ceremony occurred, all *alternativas* granted outside of Madrid must be confirmed (i.e., repeated) in Madrid within a reasonable amount of time.[30]

In Hemingway's day, the *alternativa* was granted whenever the conditions could be arranged for it. That is, the *novillero* must feel himself ready for it, a senior matador must agree to grant it, a second matador to witness it, an impresario to host it, and financial arrangements satisfactory to all parties must be negotiated.[31] Today, the *matador de novillos* becomes eligible for promotion to *matador de toros* by performing in a minimum of twenty-five *novilladas picadas* (with picadors) within the preceding two years. At least twelve of them must have taken place in first- and second-rank plazas, though not necessarily in Madrid. Having satisfied these conditions, the *matador de novillos* or his representative must then settle all the other details concerning the sponsoring matadors, the plaza, the finances, and so on.[32]

Because the granting of the *alternativa* permanently links the *padrino* (the godfather who grants it) and the *ahijado* (the godson who receives it) in both their curricula vitae, such pairings are not lightly undertaken. The individuals involved are usually connected to each other in some significant way: they might be relatives, compatriots (from the same region of Spain), or subscribers to the same taurine style or philosophy. Often they are linked by several of these affinities.

Premature Promotion

Hemingway argues against what he calls premature promotions. He finds that these were popular in the mid-1920s when audiences, desperate for an heir to José Gómez Ortega (Joselito, 1895–1920) idolized promising young bullfighters. Hemingway writes that Antonio de la Haba (Zurito), Martín Agüero, Manolo Martínez, and Victoriano de la Serna were all promoted prematurely. If Hemingway is speaking of age, the word *premature* is difficult to justify in these cases: Martínez was twenty-seven years old when he was promoted, and the other three were twenty-one or twenty-two years old. And Hemingway doesn't complain about the promotions of other very young men, like Luis Miguel González (Dominguín), promoted at age fifteen; or Manuel Mejías (Manolo Bienvenida) and Fermín Espinosa (Armillita Chico), both promoted at age sixteen; or José Mejías (Pepe Bienvenida), Manuel Jiménez (Chicuelo), Pepe Amorós, and David Liceaga, all promoted at age seventeen; or Vicente Barrera, promoted at eighteen; or Manuel Granero, Enrique Torres, and Manuel Báez (Litri), promoted at nineteen. Some but not all of these bullfighters were frequently gored; many had long, successful careers.

Age is, of course, an inaccurate marker for knowledge: a boy who grows up in a bullfighting environment, like the Bienvenidas or Antonio de la Haba (Zurito), acquires solid experience of bulls well before his twentieth birthday—and yet Hemingway considers Zurito's promotion at age twenty-three premature.

Hemingway writes that "an apprenticeship should continue until the craft has been mastered" (*DIA*, 254), but it is difficult to know what this means.[33] If Hemingway means "until the bullfighter has acquired a sufficient repertoire," he disregards the many professional bullfighters who enjoyed long and even memorable careers with limited repertoires. Besides, other factors, like personality, grace, and talent, might warrant a promotion. In any case, the promotion to *matador de toros* does not mean that education ceases at this point. Most bullfighters continue to expand their repertoires and improve their styles for the first decade after their promotions: Belmonte is perhaps the most outstanding example. And external factors affect a matador's development as well, both before and after promotion: the competition he faces, the skill of his manager, his health, his family, his relationships with other bullfighters, the country's economic and even its political situation, and, of course, luck: the bulls he draws, the weather at the corrida, and so on.

Length of Career

Because matadors' careers are interrupted by injuries, political problems, personal issues, and other external factors, defining a "long" career is problematic. A career can be described as long if the bullfighter has performed in many corridas or has spent many years in the ring. The two are not necessarily related.

A skilled bullfighter who escapes injury and is popular with the crowds and the impresarios can achieve an impressive number of corridas in a relatively short time, whereas a frequently injured or less popular bullfighter might require twice or three times as many *temporadas* (seasons) to achieve a similar number of corridas. In terms of years, a bullfighter who started his professional life in his late teens or early twenties and is still performing in his forties is said to have had a long career, even if his career was interrupted by retirements or if there were years during which, for whatever reasons, he seldom performed. Among the many bullfighters who have enjoyed or, sometimes, suffered through long careers, in terms of years, we can list Pedro Romero, Salvador Sánchez (Frascuelo), Fermín Espinosa (Armillita Chico), Luis Freg, Rafael Gómez Ortega (el Gallo), Nicanor Villalta, Manuel Jiménez (Chicuelo), José Mejías (Pepe Bienvenida), and Domingo Ortega. One of the longest and most successful careers in the history of bullfighting is that of Rafael Molina (Lagartijo): he was nine years old when he first performed, twenty-three when he was promoted to *matador de toros*, and over fifty when he retired.[34] He is said to have performed in 1,645 corridas, although the number cannot be verified.

It is important to distinguish between a bullfighter with a long career and one who has become a *figura*, an enduring presence or personality of *toreo*, because of his individual contribution to the art. Pedro Romero, Rafael Molina (Lagartijo), Salvador Sánchez (Frascuelo), Rafael Gómez Ortega (el Gallo), and Domingo Ortega, all masters who enjoyed long careers, are indisputably *figuras del toreo*, while someone like the Peruvian Angel Valdés (el Maestro, 1838–1911), who began fighting at twenty and fought his last bull in his early seventies, is cherished in his own country but is little more than an esoteric footnote in the history of Spanish bullfighting. Length of career, in terms of numbers of corridas or years of service, is not necessarily the equivalent of fame or influence. One of the greatest *figuras* of all times is José Gómez Ortega (Joselito), who was killed in his mid-twenties. Another twentieth-century *figura*, Manuel Rodríguez Sánchez (Manolete, 1917–47), had a similarly "short" career.

Injury

Injuries require a bullfighter to absent himself from the ring, but these enforced absences are surprisingly short: bullfighters seem to heal more quickly than other people. Not infrequently a bullfighter attempts to fight before he is fully healed: the phrase *se resintió* means that the injury prevented him from performing as he wished to, or that because of his premature reappearance he aggravated the original injury and had to cancel subsequent contracts. In reading the statistics on the numbers of corridas or performances, we must take injuries into account: a serious injury can depress the statistics considerably, especially if it occurs early in the season, and an active but convalescing bullfighter will perform less well, which makes him a less attractive commodity for impresarios who are casting bullfighters for fights later in the season. Occasionally, injuries are so crippling that they spell the end of a career.[35]

Retirement

Injuries aside, bullfighting is a physically and psychologically exhausting profession. The successful bullfighter is exhausted by his schedule and made anxious by the fickle public, the competition edging up on him, and the aging of his own body. The less successful bullfighter lives with the constant, debilitating fear that his skills—probably the only skills he possesses—are insufficient to support him, his family, and his *cuadrilla*. Lacking the built-in relief of the sabbatical, that blessed institution that permits academics and other stressed-out professionals to recoup their energies and regain their balance, bullfighters resort to retirement.[36]

Retirements or *despedidas* are usually the occasion for a round of special bullfights, as the matador takes leave of his audiences in several cities. Like any other bullfight, these are sometimes triumphant, indicating that the matador is in full control of his powers and might return to the ring; and occasionally they are an embarrassment, which indicates that retirement is overdue. For most matadors, retirement is an impermanent condition, soon rescinded. Except for those killed within a few years of their *alternativas* (e.g., Manuel Granero, José Gómez Ortega [Joselito], Manuel Rodríguez [Manolete]), almost all of the major bullfighters named in *Death in the Afternoon* and *The Dangerous Summer* retired and then returned to the ring, sometimes only to fight *novillos* in the occasional festival, more often to perform in *corridas de toros*.[37] Notable exceptions to this pattern were Rafael González (Machaquito), Rafael Guerra (Guerrita), and Ricardo Torres Reina (Bombita), whom Hemingway never saw; and Rodolfo Gaona, Marcial Lalanda, and Joaquín Rodríguez (Cagancho), whose first retirements were also their last.

Matadors whose careers are faltering sometimes resign their *alternativas* and return to the ring in another capacity, as *matadores de novillos* or as banderilleros. Some, but not many, regain their standing as *matador de toros*. The move to a lesser rank is controversial, admired in some quarters as an expression of an *afición* so strong that the bullfighter finds himself unable to abandon the ring, derided in others as a lack of respect for the rank of *matador de toros*, or as a lack of *amor propio* (self-respect).

Other Careers

Matadors being a highly individual lot, the post-retirement careers they pursue are varied. Some, like Ignacio Sánchez Mejías, turned to literature; others, like Antonio Calvache, Pepito Fernández Aguayo, and John Fulton, became photographers or painters; and not a few appeared in movies. Most of these post-bullring careers have a strong taurine flavor, since in the great majority of cases, the passion for the bulls endures.

Many retired bullfighters, if they are wealthy enough, become bull breeders. Others maintain their connection to the profession by becoming impresarios of bullrings, managers of other bullfighters' careers (*apoderados*), advisers to the president in a bullring (*asesores*), or mentors to relatives or to promising bullfighters.

Death

One of the basic assumptions of the bullfight is that the matador will emerge alive. Hemingway's definition of the bullfight indicates that he understood this very clearly: "The formal bullfight is a commercial spectacle built on the planned and ordered *death of the bull* and that is its end. Horses are killed incidentally. Men are killed accidentally . . . in a perfect bullfight no men are wounded nor killed and six bulls are put to death in a formal and ordered manner by men who expose themselves to the maximum of danger. . . . It is the lack of understanding of this view-point in the public which has made the bullfight unexplainable to non-Spaniards" (*DIA h:* 404, my italics).

The fact that a bullfighter is supposed to survive the corrida is so basic that a fatal goring produces a whole library of professional worry and study. The bullfighter who dies while in the exercise of his profession is not forgotten by the taurine public and press: he is memorialized on the anniversary of his death, he becomes part of the history of the breed of the bull that killed him and, often, his death casts a pall over the bullring where he was killed. Some of the minor bullrings that have achieved such unwelcome prominence are Talavera de la Reina, where José Gómez Ortega (Joselito) was killed on 16 May 1920; Manzanares, where Ignacio Sánchez Mejías was fatally gored on 11 August 1934 (he died two days later, in Madrid); Linares, where Manuel Rodríguez Sánchez (Manolete) was gored on 28 August 1947 (he died in the early hours of the next morning); and Pozoblanco, where Francisco Rivera (Paquirri) was fatally gored on 26 September 1984 (he died en route to the hospital in Córdoba). The dates, the places, and the breed resonate somberly in the bullfighting world, which is very conscious of its history and rather prone to superstition.

More matadors have been killed in accidents outside than inside the ring. In 1927, Francisco Ferrer was killed in a car crash, the first bull-fighter to fall victim to this new mode of transportation. Fausto Barajas died in a car crash in 1934, and in 1953 Ricardo Torres became the first Mexican matador killed on the road: he died in a bus crash. As more bullfighters took to the roads the statistics became grimmer: the decade 1963–73 saw nine *matadores de toros* killed in car crashes, and by 1983 the total had grown to eighteen. In those same two decades, 1963–83, three bullfighters of that rank died as a result of being gored or otherwise injured while working with a bull. Héctor Saucedo was the first Mexican matador to die in an airplane crash, in 1954; the Spaniard Manuel Jiménez (Chicuelo II) died similarly in 1960. Between these two dates, no *matadores de toros* were killed in the ring. Between 1837 and 1983, almost 150 years, at least eight matadors were shot to death (not counting the huge number of those who fell in the Spanish Civil War) and seven committed suicide. Like all statistics, these are limited: they refer only to one of several ranks of bullfighters.

A surprising number of bullfighters of various ranks have died of heart attacks during or shortly after an encounter with *ganado bravo*. To mention just a few: in 1926, the famous banderillero Enrique Beren-guet (Blanquet) suffered a fatal heart attack soon after a corrida; he was still wearing his *traje de luces*. The *matador de novillos* Cándido Tiebas died suddenly of a heart attack in the *callejón*, on 9 March 1930; and the *rejoneador* Simâo da Veiga also suffered a fatal heart attack just after a corrida, in 1959. On 3 March 1968, the matador Pepe Bienvenida died of a heart attack after placing the banderillas, in Lima; the picador Agustín Alonson Sanjosé suffered a fatal heart attack in a *tienta*, in February 1973; Luis Segura died of a heart attack during a festival on 16 February 1975; he was thirty-seven years old. On 27 January 1981 Jorge Aguilar (el Ranchero) died while working with the muleta in a *tienta*, and the banderillero Mariano Martín Aguilar (Carriles) died of a heart attack during a corrida on 29 July 1982.[38]

All the bullfighters mentioned in *Death in the Afternoon* are now dead. A few committed suicide: Juan Belmonte in 1962, Antonio García in 1968, and Victoriano de la Serna in 1981; they were all in their seventies. Many lived well into their eighties and nineties: Nicanor Villalta and Enrique Torres died in 1980, Jesús Solórzano in 1983, Joaquín Rodríguez (Cagancho) in 1984, Antonio Márquez and Domingo Ortega in 1988, Marcial Lalanda in 1990, Luis Gómez (el Estudiante) in 1995, David Liceaga in 1996, José Amorós in 1997, Luis Fuentes Bejarano in 1999, and Alfredo Corrochano, the last to go, died in 2000. *Que en paz descansen.*

THE BULLRING

Classification of Spanish Bullrings

In the hierarchical world of bullfighting, even bullrings are ranked, their status defined by politics, law, and tradition. The *Reglamento* of 1917 established the first-class bullrings (*plazas de primera categoría*) as those of Barcelona (both the Monumental and Las Arenas), Bilbao, Madrid (the one on the Aragón Road), San Sebastián, Sevilla, Valencia, and Zaragoza. The next taurine code, published in 1923 and revised in 1924, added La Barceloneta (in the port area of Barcelona) and Vista Alegre (in Madrid) to the list of first-class bullrings.[39]

This listing was perpetuated almost intact in the next *Reglamento* (1930), which kept La Barceloneta (Barcelona), even though it was no longer in use; reduced Vista Alegre to second-rank; and added Las Ventas, which, although not yet inaugurated, would be Madrid's ranking bullring. This was the first taurine code to define the second-rank plazas (*de segunda categoría*): Madrid's smaller bullrings (Vista Alegre and Tetuán de las Victorias), the bullrings located in all the remaining provincial capitals (i.e., those capitals whose bullrings were not *de primera categoría*), and the plazas of Algeciras, Aranjuez, Calatayud, Cartagena, Gijón, Jerez de la Frontera, Linares, Mérida, and El Puerto de Santa María. All other bullrings were considered third-rank (*de tercera categoría*).

In the 1962 *Reglamento*, Barcelona had two *plazas de primera categoría* (Las Arenas and La Monumental) and Madrid one, the Plaza Monumental de Las Ventas. Calatayud was removed from the list of *plazas de segunda categoría*, all the others retaining the rankings they had been awarded in the 1930 *Reglamento*.

In the next major revision, the *Reglamento* of 1992, the plazas were not listed by name. Instead, the bullrings of provincial capitals that were traditionally classified as first-rank retain that ranking, and any bullrings that celebrate a minimum of fifteen taurine events, at least ten of which are *corridas de toros*, are also considered *plazas de primera categoría*. The bullrings of all other provincial capitals are ranked *de segunda categoría*, and all of Spain's remaining bullrings are *de tercera categoría*.[40] The rankings' most visible effect is the ruling about the size of the bulls, with heavier bulls mandated for first-class rings. Other requirements (e.g., the minimum number of pics, the kind and number of supplies in the infirmaries) are also more stringent for the first-class rings.

Size of Bullrings

Because Hemingway's tastes were formed in the Madrid bullrings he had known in the 1920s, he complained that Las Ventas "is too big to give real emotion. Even at ringside you are too far away from everything unless it is happening close in front of you. . . . [In] the old ring . . . you could see everything so well that even a bad fight was interesting because you saw the details so closely."[41] As a practical aficionado pointed out, the ideal size of the arena depends on whether one is working in it, in which case the larger area is preferable, or whether one is sitting safely outside it, in which case the smaller area affords the better view.

The Bullrings of Madrid

Traditionally, Madrid's is the premier bullring of Spain and, therefore, of the taurine world. In the years Hemingway went to the bullfights, from 1923 to 1959, he visited several bullrings in the province of Madrid (*see* Aranjuez) and in the city of Madrid proper: the small ones at Tetuán de las Victorias and Vista Alegre (Carabanchel) and the larger ones on the Aragón Road and at Las Ventas. Since this last one hosted only one corrida before the publication of *Death in the Afternoon*, the narrator's references to Madrid's main plaza are to the bullring on the Aragón Road, which no longer exists.

Madrid's records indicate that bullfights were held at various points of the city as early as 1546. Portable wooden bullrings erected in the city's main squares housed these spectacles, the most important of them taking place in the Plaza Mayor.

Puerta de Alcalá

The first permanent bullring was built near the Palacio del Buen Retiro, where the Museo del Ejército, or Military Museum, now stands. It was a luxurious, roofed wooden structure, suitable for its audience of aristocrats and royalty. King Philip V (1683–1746) ordered the construction of another wooden bullring that would admit the general public and raise money to support the government's ministers. It was built just outside the city boundaries, demarcated by the Alcalá gate (Puerta de Alcalá), in the block where today's Serrano, Alcalá, and Claudio Coello Streets converge. This bullring was inaugurated in 1743.

Shortly after his accession, the next king, Ferdinand VI, generously decreed that the proceeds of the bullfights held at the Puerta de Alcalá bullring be used to support Madrid's general hospitals. A few years later, he ordered that this wooden structure be demolished and a larger, more imposing masonry bullring erected in its place. The construction took several years, but the bullring, which could seat twelve thousand spectators, was finally inaugurated in 1754. In the new bullring's charter, Ferdinand VI transferred ownership of the property from himself to Madrid's hospitals. Periodically remodeled and expanded, this bullring served Madrid for 120 years. The last corrida in this bullring was celebrated on 16 August 1874, and the building was torn down soon after.

Tetuán de las Victorias

In the 1870s Madrid acquired two *plazas de toros*. The smaller one, located at Tetuán de las Victorias, was built in 1870–72 and inaugurated with a festive corrida on 4 October 1874. It was a charming two-story, square building that could seat seven thousand spectators at the time Hemingway knew it. Although it had been remodeled and improved several times, its basic character remained unchanged and it reflected its nineteenth-century origins. During the Spanish Civil War it was used to store munitions, and an explosion so damaged the building that it had to be torn down.

Carretera de Aragón

The bullring on the Aragón Road was inaugurated on 4 September 1874, shortly after the closing of the bullring at the Puerta de Alcalá and one month before the inauguration of its smaller sister at Tetuán de las Victorias. With a seating capacity of 13,210, it was Madrid's main bullring until 1934. But even before Hemingway came to Spain for his first bullfight in 1923, Madrid had decided that this large bullring was insufficient for its growing population. The question of whether to enlarge it or replace it raged in taurine circles. The fifty-year-old ring on the Aragón Road was beautiful and rich in tradition, and it was only after long and bitter argument that a new site, at Las Ventas, was chosen. Today, the Sports Palace occupies the location where Hemingway saw so many bullfights.

Vista Alegre

The much-smaller bullring known as "Vista Alegre," in Carabanchel Bajo, falls within the city limits of Madrid. Construction began in 1906, and it was inaugurated on 15 July 1908, with a corrida featuring Ricardo Torres Reina (Bombita), Rafael González (Machaquito), and Rodolfo Gaona (at that time Bombita and Machaquito were boycotting Madrid's main plaza, on the Aragón Road, in the affair known as *el pleito de los Miura*).[42] In the 1920s, Vista Alegre seated eight thousand people. Damaged during the Spanish Civil War, it was repaired, remodeled, and enlarged in the 1940s, to seat fourteen thousand. By the 1970s it had fallen into disrepair and, after much discussion, it was shut down in 1982. Eventually it was torn down and replaced by a state-of-the-art covered bullring that was inaugurated on 15 April 2000 by Francisco Romero López (Curro Romero), José María Dols Abellán (José Mari

Manzanares), and Enrique Ponce. Although the Juan Pedro Domecq bulls were undistinguished, the bullfighters worked well: Romero was awarded the ear of his second bull, and Ponce cut an ear from each of his two bulls. This new bullring-cum-amphitheater, now called Palacio de Vistalegre, seats fourteen thousand.

Las Ventas

In the 1920s, when this site was first considered as a possible home for a new bullring, Las Ventas was a slum on the outskirts of the city, far from the center of Madrid. Today the bullring is surrounded by urban construction and easily reached by subway and other public transport.

Construction of the new bullring began in 1930, and it was inaugurated on 17 June 1931, in a special corrida to benefit the unemployed. Eight bull breeders contributed one bull each, and the eight bullfighters donated their fees.[43] The event took place under uncomfortable circumstances: the arena was rough and pockmarked, building materials had not been cleared away, and the lack of paving made access difficult. Hemingway, who was in and out of Spain from May to September 1931, probably witnessed this inaugural corrida, the only one that took place at Las Ventas before the publication of *Death in the Afternoon*.[44] No more bullfights were held at the new ring until it was reopened on 21 October 1934, when Juan Belmonte, Marcial Lalanda, and Joaquín Rodríguez (Cagancho) fought six bulls from the ranch of Carmen de Federico.

Called "La Plaza Monumental de Las Ventas," Madrid's main bullring seats about twenty-three thousand. It has been much improved: today the approach is impressive, with several sculptures in the surrounding courtyard. The complex includes eight large interconnected corrals for the bulls; an open patio for training, testing, and examining horses; facilities for treating injured horses; as well as business offices, a chapel, doctors' quarters, an infirmary with two operating rooms, and a handsome taurine museum. The buildings surrounding the *abattoir* have storage rooms and offices for the night watchman and other guards; for the carpenters, the cleaning staff, and other bullring servants and their equipment; and for a variety of other professionals involved in the running of the bullring and its bullfights. Since 1934 this has been

Spain's premier bullring and, by extension, the most important, though not the largest, bullring in the taurine world.[45] It is in Madrid that the bull's *antigüedad* is established and that the bullfighter's *alternativa* must be validated. Reputations are made and destroyed in Madrid.

Bullfights are celebrated in Las Ventas throughout the season. The traditional Madrid fiesta, honoring the city's patron saint, San Isidro Labrador, is held on his feast day, 15 May, but today's *sanisidros* can last three to four weeks. A secondary fiesta, recently instituted, is held at the end of September and early October as part of the *Festival de Otoño*, or Fall Festival.[46]

For information on the other bullrings that Hemingway mentions, see the entries for individual cities.

THE CORRIDA

Types of Corridas

The modern corrida, formally defined, is a public *espectáculo* usually featuring three bullfighters who fight six bulls, four or more years old, from one or two *ganaderías* (bull-breeding ranches). But the format varies: there are solo performances, in which one matador fights six bulls (and occasionally seven) from one or more *ganaderías* (frequently six or even seven); and there is the *mano a mano* (literally, hand-to-hand competition), when two bullfighters share the afternoon, each one fighting three bulls. Occasionally, an important corrida brings together a large number of fighters: eight matadors participated in the June 1931 inauguration of Madrid's new bullring, Las Ventas.[47]

Spain's major bullrings offer *corridas de abono* (subscription series) as well as *corridas extraordinarias*, some of which may also be regularly scheduled events, like the annual *Corrida de Beneficencia*, the *Corrida de Prensa*, and the *Corrida de la Cruz Roja*.[48] Additional *corridas extraordinarias* may also be offered, usually to raise funds for a particular cause (the unemployed or victims of a natural disaster), to benefit or honor an individual bullfighter (*homenajes*, *corridas de despedida*) or some taurine cause (repairing or remodeling a plaza), or to celebrate an important occasion (a military victory, a royal marriage, the centennial of an artist).

Some events, like *corridas de prueba* and *corridas de concurso*, focus specifically on the bull and the bull-breeding ranches. Young animals appear in events called *becerradas*, *novilladas* (without picadors), and *novilladas picadas* (with picadors). *Corridas mixtas* and *festivales* mix animals of varying ages and bullfighters of various ranks (these events are discussed more fully in the section of this introduction entitled "Bulls and Bull Breeding"). *Corridas nocturnas* and *toreo bufo*, more popular in the 1920s than today, are flexible genres as well (*see Mojigangas*).

My assumption is that Hemingway saw all types of bullfights except, perhaps, *becerradas*. He might even have seen the occasional *capea* (informal village bullfight, usually presented in the town square), *corrida nocturna*, or *toreo bufo*.[49]

All formal corridas follow more or less the same pattern. They begin with preliminary ceremonies such as the *paseíllo* (processional), the handing of the *capa de paseo* to a friend in the stands, and the testing of the *capote* (the working cape to be used in the performance). These activities are followed by the three formal acts of the fight itself, the quality of which determines the informal conclusion of the afternoon, sometimes capped by a triumphant *salida en hombros* (the bullfighter's exit from the ring on the shoulders of admirers). The preliminary ceremonies are the only part of the corrida that have remained more or less unchanged throughout the twentieth century.

Hemingway and the Evolving Corrida

Hemingway's powerful, vivid painting of the corrida notwithstanding, we must remember that the corrida, like any art form, changes in time. The corridas Hemingway saw in the 1920s differ from those he saw in the 1950s, just as those differ from the ones his readers see today. Although the following survey focuses on the changes Hemingway witnessed in the 1920s, it includes some background information and discusses subsequent developments in order to create a historical framework for the corridas Hemingway saw before and during the writing of *Death in the Afternoon*.

Changes in Traditions, Decorations, and the Public

The white outfits, red neckerchiefs, and red cummerbunds that are now de rigueur in Pamplona's *sanfermines*, were largely absent from

the fiestas Hemingway witnessed in the more formal 1920s, when cele-
brants at the riotous July fiesta generally wore dark suits and ties. In
contrast to this sobriety, the sand of the bullrings was frequently decorated with brightly colored confetti, sawdust, or other lightweight materials which, kicked up by running feet and hooves, could choke and
blind the performers. These extraneous materials were banned from the
arena in the 1930 *Reglamento*, but they continued to appear, albeit with
decreased frequency, as late as 1948.[50] We seldom see them today.

Before the bullfight, Hemingway and the other members of the public
could walk about in the arena. The 1917 *Reglamento* required them to
take their seats fifteen minutes before the beginning of the bullfight; the
one of 1923 permitted them to stay until just five minutes before the
start.[51] The public's presence in the *redondel* (arena) was undesirable
on several counts: their feet disturbed the sand, which had been
smoothed and watered to settle the dust, and blurred the picadors' circle, which had been painted on the sand earlier in the day.[52] Papers,
wrappers, food, and other detritus further messed up the ring, and occasionally, members of the public got into fights, delayed the beginning
of the performance, and in other ways threatened public order. Accordingly, the 1930 *Reglamento* forbade the public access to the arena after
it had been prepared for the fight.[53]

Changes in the Three Acts of the Bullfight

Although all three acts of the bullfight changed during the 1920s, the
most significant changes occurred in the first and third acts. The first
act, which was dominated by the picador when Hemingway first came
to Spain, was slowly divided into two parts, the first emphasizing cape
work and the second the pic-ing. The third act, which begins with muleta work and ends with the sword thrust, saw a striking change of emphasis, as the muleta work lasted longer and became more artistic. In
short, the corrida Hemingway described in 1931 was quite different
from the corrida he fell in love with in 1923. To contextualize the
changes, some historical background is necessary.

Act I: *Suerte de varas,* or Pic-ing

The picador's work is the least picturesque and probably the most
difficult to understand: he holds off the bull's charge by inserting the

pic in the *morrillo* (the mound of muscle on the back of the bull's neck) in order to bleed the bull and weaken this muscle, thus making the animal playable for the *faena* that follows.

Of the bullfight's three *tercios* (thirds), the *tercio de varas* underwent the most drastic change.

The Pic-ing in Hemingway's Day

In the early 1920s, when Hemingway began to attend bullfights, two picadors greeted the bull as he entered the ring.[54] They were stationed five and twelve meters to the right of the president's box, which is located opposite the *toril* (the gate that admits the bull into the ring), and so were among the first objects that the bull saw. In fact, the 1917 *Reglamento* forbade the use of capes until after the bull had been properly pic-ed. In his first wild, undisciplined attacks, the bull rushed around the ring, injuring and killing horses but remaining largely un-pic-ed, because the picadors could not fully engage the easily distracted bull and because their instrument, the *puya* (goad or point; the business end of the lance) could not penetrate deeply enough.[55] The horses and picadors remained in the ring for the entire *suerte de varas*, and many horses—sometimes as many as forty—were killed at each corrida.

To reduce the equine slaughter, the bullring personnel attempted to distract the still unfocused bull away from the horses. Some maneuvers were illegal (e.g., having a carpenter or other bullring employee surreptitiously make a movement that would draw the bull's attention away from the horse, or having a *peón* cape him) and some experimental (changing the position of the picadors so that the bull would not see their horses immediately upon bursting into the ring).[56]

Changes in Hemingway's Day: The Pic-ing Delayed and Shortened

It was not until the *Reglamento* of 1930 that the order of the first act was formally changed, so that the bull was engaged first by the banderilleros, who exposed it to the cape and thus transformed it into the condition of *fijado* (focused on the cape, and therefore more susceptible to the bullfighters' manipulations). The picadors' entrance into the ring was delayed until *after* the bull had been run by the banderilleros. During Hemingway's first years as spectator, then, Hemingway saw the *suerte de varas* divided into two separate parts, the caping and the pic-ing.

In describing his first bullfight, seen on 27 May 1923, Hemingway accurately noted that the picadors were present in the ring *before* the bull entered.[57] But the bullfight Hemingway describes in Chapters Six and Seven of *Death in the Afternoon* reflects the new organization of the bullfight's first *tercio*, which by 1930 had become a more shapely, orderly, focused, and efficient affair.

The importance of the *suerte de varas* is reflected in the amount of attention devoted to it by the taurine codes. Melchor Ordóñez's 1847 code devoted the first eight articles directly to the *suerte de varas*. Articles 12, 13, and 14, which discussed the horses and the additional measures to supplement insufficient pic-ing, dealt indirectly with the same topic, so that in all, eleven of the fifteen articles, or almost 75 percent of the document, were devoted to pic-ing. By 1930, the *Reglamento* was composed of 137 articles, of which twenty-three dealt with the various issues related to pic-ing (16.8 percent).[58] And in the next *Reglamento*, dated 1962, only sixteen of the 138 articles (11.6 percent) addressed the pic-ing.[59]

Change: Introduction of the Peto

Perhaps the most basic and striking change in the pic-ing was the introduction of the *peto*, the protective carapace worn by the horse. The *peto* was proposed as early as 1906, designs for it began to appear in 1916, it was first used at a Madrid *novillada* on 6 March 1927, and it was mandated by law on 18 June 1928. Obviously, the *peto* was much discussed in the years Hemingway visited Spain, and he saw bullfights both before and after its adoption.

Although purists resisted such a drastic change in the *suerte de varas*, the public was becoming increasingly intolerant of the sight of injured horses. The fear was that, in order to protect the horses, the basic values of the *suerte de varas* would be distorted. The bull's charge is necessary because it reveals its character and temperament; the pic-ing is necessary because it weakens the bull so that the third act can be properly concluded. The horses, formerly deemed a necessary casualty, were now moving into the center of the debate. The *peto* was proposed as protection, but it was resisted: some worried that it would distort or diminish the bullfight, others argued that it offered insufficient protection for the horse, and still others felt that it would endanger the picador by limiting the horse's movements. Many alternative proposals were suggested, such as reducing the number of pics inflicted, changing the position of the horse or the length of its stay in the plaza, providing a horse clinic in the plaza itself, and writing (and enforcing) stricter rules for the *suerte de varas*. The controversy raged in the taurine publications of the day, and even after the *peto* was defined and incorporated into the bullfight code, its design and the rules governing its use continued to be modified for several years. For a fuller discussion of the issues raised by the *peto*, see the entry entitled *Peto* in the annotations.

Change: Reduction in Number of Horses Killed

The *peto* drastically reduced the number of horses killed in the ring. In 1847, a local ruling required that forty horses, inspected and approved by the authorities, stand ready for use in each bullfight. The 1917 and 1923 *Reglamentos* called for six horses per bull to be fought, with the added proviso that the management was required to provide as many horses as were necessary. Sometimes all the horses would be killed, and replacements would be hastily bought off local cabbies and rushed into the ring. But after the introduction of the *peto*, the 1930 *Reglamento* specified only four horses per bull, and the 1962 *Reglamento* lowered the number again, to a minimum of eight horses for the whole corrida. And that number was lowered in the 1992 *Reglamento*, which requires six horses per corrida in first-rank plazas and four in all others—that is, one or fewer horses per bull.[60] The spectators' attitude had changed from approving the death of many horses, because this meant that they were in the presence of a strong, brave bull, to the post-*peto* situation, when the expectation is that no horses will be killed. Occasionally one hears reactionary calls for the abolishment of the *peto*, but modern sensibilities would not allow a return to the pre-*peto* bullfight that Hemingway encountered when he first went to Spain.

Change: The Picador's Tools

While the total length of the pics (including both the *vara*, or pole, and the *puya*, or steel point) has remained constant at between 255 and

270 centimeters (8'3" to 8'9"), the *puya* itself was frequently redesigned. Before 1917 it consisted of the triangular point followed by a large, wooden ball covered with cord or rope, which was too large to permit any more of the instrument to pierce the bull's *morrillo* (neck muscle). In 1917, this corded section was narrowed into a cylinder that could and did enter the bull's flesh, making a greater wound than had previously been possible. That taurine code also introduced the *arandela* (a circular disk separating the *puya* from the shaft) whose diameter was much larger than that of the corded cylinder. This *arandela* effectively marked the end of the section of the pic that could enter the body of the bull, and thus frankly admitted that the corded area could be inserted, although such a maneuver was illegal. In 1923, when Hemingway started seeing corridas, excessively large wounds were already being inflicted on the bull.

Because the *arandela* offered insufficient protection for the bull, it was replaced in 1960 by the *cruceta* (a metal arm extending perpendicularly from the pole at the point where the corded cylinder and the pole meet).[61] This proved to be as unsatisfactory as the *arandela*, and abuses of excessive pic-ing continued: hence the reduction of the required number of pics (from four to three) before the bullfight moved on to the *tercio de banderillas*.

The design of the *puya* was controversial in Hemingway's day and it remains so today, with matadors generally opting for more damage during the *suerte de varas*, and bull breeders objecting to the weakening of their bulls, which prevents them from showing what they are capable of in the second and third acts of the bullfight.

Preparing the Bullring for the Picadors

Today we see two white circles drawn upon the arena, the first, or large one, delimiting the area in which the picador acts, and the second, or smaller one, enclosing the bull. But when Hemingway saw his first bullfights, only one circle separated the picador and the bull, and it was still a new item, not clearly fixed or defined.

Change: The Picador's Work Area Is Variously Defined

The territory in which the picador acts is so problematic that each new code defines it differently. Melchor Ordóñez's 1847 document, the model for later codes, enjoined the picador to "salir al menos hasta seis varas distante de la barrera en busca del toro" (go out at least six *varas* from the *barrera* [about five meters, as measured from the fence to the center of the ring] to cite the bull). It was up to the picador to judge this distance; there was no indication on the arena itself. The first national *Reglamento* (1917) did not specify distance, but simply allowed the picadors to advance as far as the *tercios* (the space between the *tablas*, which is the area closest to the ring's outer circumference, and the *medios*, or central area) to induce the bull to charge. This changed the picador's workspace from a specific distance, which would be the same in all bullrings, to a proportional space, which would vary according to the radius of the bullring. It also gave the picador a larger area in which to work, since most bullrings have a radius much larger than fifteen meters (diameter of thirty meters).

The three *tercios*, or thirds, of the ring (*tablas*, *tercios*, and *medios*) continued to be unmarked until the 1923 *Reglamento* mandated a visible circle.[62] This small circle marked the area (in the center of the ring) where the bull would be placed, allowing the picador to place himself anywhere within the remaining two-thirds of the ring. Since the picador could advance so far towards the center of the ring, the bull's charge was often quite short.

In 1930, the circle drawn on the sand was enlarged, its radius redefined as two-thirds that of the arena itself.[63] The bull would still be placed somewhere near the center of the ring, but the circle restrained the picador to the outer, or circumferential, third of the ring. This meant that the bull's charge was now considerably longer, unless, of course, he was placed closer to the painted line than to the center of the arena or, as often happened, the picador crossed the line.

During the 1920s, then, the space allowed for the picador expanded from six *varas* (five meters) from the *barrera*, as it had been earlier in the century, to between fifteen and twenty meters in 1923 (from the *barrera* to the white circle, in arenas measuring between forty-five and sixty meters in diameter, the usual size range). In 1930 it shrank by half, to a space anywhere from seven and a half to ten meters, again depending on the diameter of the ring.

In 1959, a second circle was mandated. This circle must be drawn seven meters from the *barrera*, regardless of the size of the ring, and thus further diminished the picador's workspace. It serves to demarcate the bull's and the picador's territories more clearly, to separate the one from the other, and thus to ensure a longer charge: the bull is positioned within the smaller circle, in the *medios*, and the picador must stay within the demarcated seven meters in the *tablas* (between the *barrera* and the first circle).

The reduction in the picador's territory is significant: if the picador works more closely to the center of the ring, the bull's charge is shortened and the bravery of the bull, measured by the alacrity with which he charges, becomes difficult for both the matador and the public to read. On the other hand, the picador who works far from the *barrera* will be more likely to use the pic properly to keep the bull from knocking over his mount, and himself with it. If the picador works closer to the *barrera*, he may permit the bull to exhaust himself first by smashing against the horse, then by shoving it up against the *barrera*, and finally by pushing against a horse that is propped up by the *barrera*, while the picador inflicts additional punishment with the pic. Such improper picing, writes Gregorio Corrochano, was rampant: picadors were merely placing their horses in the protective proximity of the *barrera* and from there, protected by the *peto* (i.e., the horse was not likely to die on the spot), the picadors were free to do what they liked with the pic, "sin riesgo ni arte . . . lo mismo podía hacerse detrás de la barrera" (without risk or art . . . they could have done the same from behind the *barrera*).[64]

Since 1923, then, the general tendency has been to allow the picador to work more closely to the *barrera*, an area that permits more abuses of the *suerte de picar*.

All these changes—the early intervention of the capes, the introduction of the *peto*, the increased punishment afforded by the modern *puya*, and the reduced age and weight of the bull (see the section entitled "Bulls and Bull Breeding" in this introduction)—allowed the picador to inflict fewer pics on the bull to achieve the same purpose: diminishing the bull's force and lowering its head so it could be killed by the matador. As the decade of the 1920s progressed and the artistic *faena* became the focal point of the third act, picadors had to achieve a delicate balance: weakening the bull sufficiently so it could be played, but not so much that it would run out of steam and fail to respond to the matador's muleta.

Change in the 1920s: Reduction in Number of Pics

The reduction in the number of pics was an unstoppable trend. The 1917 *Reglamento* required a minimum of four pics. By 1923, the president was empowered to close the *tercio de varas* even if fewer than the required four pics had been inflicted; no new minimum number was specified, but in practice two pics were often deemed sufficient.[65] The ruling remained unchanged in the 1930 *Reglamento*, but in point of fact, by this time four pics were the exception rather than the norm.

Adjusting law to fact, the 1962 *Reglamento* lowered the required minimum to three pics, with the face-saving proviso that black *banderillas de castigo* be used to announce that the bull had been insufficiently pic-ed. The more realistic 1992 *Reglamento* requires a minimum of two pics in first-ranked plazas, and a minimum of one in all others, with the option of double-barbed *banderillas de castigo*.[66]

Act II: The *suerte de banderillas*

Banderillas are sometimes called *alegradores*, *garapullos*, *palitroques*, *palos*, or *rehiletes*.[67] Variants of the *banderillas comunes* (standard) or *frías* (cold, as opposed to those tipped with explosives) are the *banderillas cortas* (short sticks, created by snapping a regular banderilla in half; these require closer work with the bull) and the *banderillas de adorno* or *de lujo* (heavily decorated sticks used for gala occasions).

Most of the changes in the development of the *suerte de banderillas* occurred in the eighteenth and nineteenth centuries. Hemingway witnessed few changes, and the *tercio* has undergone few changes from Hemingway's day to our own.

Early History

Banderillas seem to have been designed to awaken or prick the bull into action, specifically, the necessary action of charging. *Banderillas de fuego* (with explosives at the tip, which goad the bull into action by making noise and burning his hide) were also prescribed to enliven the *manso* (a bull who is unwilling to charge the mounted picador and who therefore cannot be sufficiently pic-ed).[68]

Banderillas used to be placed singly, but by the middle of the eighteenth century they were already placed in pairs, an innovation introduced by Bernardo Alcalde y Merino (Licenciado de Falces, 1709-c. 1780). As the *tercio de banderillas* achieved greater definition, the norm became four pairs. The *tercio* achieved luster at the hands of Antonio Carmona (el Gordito, c. 1838–1920), an agile gymnast whose major contribution was to introduce the placing of banderillas *al quiebro*: the stationary banderillero changes the trajectory of the charging bull by feinting. In addition, Carmona offered showy maneuvers, such as encasing his feet in a metal ring while placing the banderillas, or performing the maneuver while seated on a chair. He was the first to achieve fame and wealth through the banderillas. Hemingway's failure to mention either Bernardo Alcalde or Antonio Carmona reflects the paucity of discussion on this *tercio* in general histories, contemporary journals, and the *Reglamentos*. Only two of the fifteen articles of Melchor Ordóñez's 1847 ruling discuss the banderillas, with emphasis on the *banderillas de fuego*.[69] The 1917 and 1923 *Reglamentos* similarly prescribe these banderillas for the insufficiently pic-ed bull.[70] Altogether, they devote one and two articles to the banderillas and two and four articles, respectively, to the banderilleros. Subsequent *Reglamentos* pay similarly scant attention to the bullfight's second *tercio*, which is short and less weighty than those that precede and follow it.

Banderillas are intended to enliven the bull after its experiences with the pic, but some taurine critics feel that they serve no useful purpose and should be abandoned. Banderillas discompose the bull, they argue, and the caping performed in this *tercio* (for positioning the bull or rescuing a banderillero) weakens the animal unnecessarily and makes him less responsive to the muleta. Ignacio Sánchez Mejías, himself a master banderillero, described the placing of banderillas as inessential to the conduct of the bullfight, but nonetheless attractive, as "la manifestación poética del lidiador" (an expression of the bullfighter's poetic bent) and "un derroche de alegría infantil" (an outpouring of innocent or childish joy).[71] In the hands of a master, the placing of the banderillas can be a graceful, lively, and enlivening interlude.

Change: Disappearance of Banderillas de Fuego

In the bullfights Hemingway saw in the 1920s, *banderillas de fuego* were still legal, though used sparingly. Changes in the legal code reflect the diminishing interest in these instruments. They were outlawed from 1928 to 1930, but were legal again during Hemingway's last visits to Spain, before and during the writing of *Death in the Afternoon*.[72] Hemingway does not mention the *banderillas de fuego*, which suggests that he seldom or never saw them used.[73]

In 1950 the *banderillas de fuego* were replaced by *banderillas de castigo* (for punishment), also called *banderillas negras* (because they are decorated with black frilly paper), or *viudas* (widows, because mourning apparel is black). These double-barbed banderillas cause more discomfort than regular banderillas, which have a single barb, but they are less effective than the old *banderillas de fuego* which, with their noise and fire, stimulated the bull to jump about and toss his head (and thus perhaps weaken the *morrillo* slightly). *Banderillas negras*, however, are not likely to stir or enliven the sodden bull for whom they have been prescribed. They probably cause more discomfort to the bull breeder, whose bull is thus insulted, than to the bull itself. Although bullrings are still required to stock *banderillas negras*, they are almost never mandated by the president of the corrida.[74]

It must be emphasized that the *banderillas de fuego* and the *banderillas de castigo* do not in any meaningful way "punish" or weaken the bull; they do not continue or complete the work of pic-ing. They merely publicize the fact the pic-ing did not satisfy the *Reglamento*, perhaps because the bull was *manso* and refused to charge the picador, or because he was too weak to take more punishment, or because the first or second pic had inflicted sufficient punishment, or because the president, for whatever reason, decided to end this section of the bullfight. The main function of the *banderillas de castigo* or *de fuego* was to publicize the incompleteness of the *suerte de varas*.

Change: Matadors Delegate Banderillas to Banderilleros

In the years preceding Hemingway's first encounters with the bullfight, the placing of the banderillas was a showy, much appreciated part of the bullfight, frequently performed by the matadors themselves. Matadors often invited their colleagues to join them, and each tried to outdo the other, much as is done today with the *quite* (cape work to distract the bull away from the picador). Two of the leading matadors of the 1910s, José Gómez Ortega (Joselito) and Rodolfo Gaona, were superb banderilleros. Juan Belmonte, whose weak legs kept him away from the banderillas, had two notable banderilleros in his *cuadrilla*: Manuel García (Maera) and Luis Suárez (Magritas, qq.v.). In this *tercio*, as in so much else, Belmonte pointed the way to the future, when he granted his *peones de brega* the responsibility for the banderillas (in addition to their many other duties).

If the *edad de oro* of the 1910s was the high point of the *suerte de banderillas*, the 1920s enjoyed the spillover, so that Hemingway saw many matadors place the banderillas themselves. But the *suerte* was moving away from the matadors and to their banderilleros. In the 1940s and 1950s, Luis Miguel Dominguín and the Mexican Carlos Arruza, whose strong, long legs and great agility made them fine banderilleros, often placed their own banderillas, but most *maestros*, including Manuel Rodríguez (Manolete) and Antonio Ordóñez, took the sticks only on exceedingly rare occasions.

The shift in emphasis was duly reflected in the *Reglamentos*. The *Reglamento* of 1917 entrusts the placing of the banderillas to the *lidiadores*, which includes the matadors as well as the banderilleros. But the *Reglamento* of 1923 specified that the matador's role during this part of the bullfight is to rest and prepare himself for the coming *faena*.[75] The 1930, 1962, and 1992 *Reglamentos* similarly assume that the banderillas will be placed by the banderilleros, but recognize that the matador might decide to place them himself.[76]

Change: Number of Banderillas

José Gómez Ortega, like his predecessors, liked to place four pairs of banderillas, but by the time Hemingway came to the bullfight the trend towards three pairs was already well established.[77] The *Reglamentos* of 1917, 1923, 1930, and 1962 do not specify any minimum or maximum number of pairs. The 1992 *Reglamento* is the first to specify numbers: two or three.[78] Today three pairs are normally placed or, at least, attempted. Occasionally, one sees four.

Act III: The *Faena* and the *Suerte Suprema*

Tools: Muleta and Sword

Over the centuries, muletas have retained more or less the same shape but have changed in color, from the earliest, which were white, to later ones in red, yellow, and blue. Changing the color of the muleta, like changing horses in the *suerte de picar*, often does have good results (i.e., encourage the bull to charge the picador) because the bull, although color-blind, does distinguish between light and dark. The argument, however, is that the bull is attracted to the muleta's movement, not its color. Be that as it may, by the time Hemingway came to the bullfight, muletas were red, and red they remain to this day. Then as now, the size of the muleta varies according to the bullfighter's preference.[79]

The matador's sword has, similarly, undergone only minor changes in the twentieth century. The basic shape has remained the same, but improvements in the steel and in the art of tempering the steel have resulted in lighter, thinner, more flexible, and less brittle blades. Matadors normally own three to five swords and match the sword to the requirements of the situation in which it is to be used.

While the tools used in the last *tercio* have maintained more or less the same shape and design, the *tercio* itself has undergone significant changes.

Change: Increased Emphasis on the Muleta

The most important change has been the shift in emphasis, away from sword work to a display of artistry with the muleta. The changes in the first two *tercios*—the more intense pic-ing, and the matador's withdrawal from the *tercio de banderillas* in order to rest before the most important part of his performance—paved the road for this shift. The increased complexity and length of the *faena* with the muleta derives from Belmonte, who relied on long, sweeping arm movements to compensate for his weak legs. Working the bull close to his body, Belmonte wrought emotional *faenas* that entranced the public. Joselito, who mastered every innovation Belmonte introduced, had already established artistic muleta work as a requisite part of the *faena*.[80] Mere prowess with the sword could no longer sustain a career. As one taurine writer aptly put it, the modern matador "lives by the cloth, not by the sword."[81]

In the early 1920s, with Joselito gone and Belmonte in retirement, many of the new crop of matadors saw the final *tercio* in general, and the muleta in particular, as the key to fame. Among them was Manuel

Jiménez (Chicuelo), whose graceful and extended *toreo en re-dondo*—he could link together as many as eighteen *naturales*—helped the *faena* achieve the prominence it enjoys today (*see* Jiminiz, Manuel).

Although Hemingway complained of specialization during this period (*DIA*, 85–86), critics such as Uno al Sesgo rejoiced in the artistic inventiveness and variety of these performers, many of whom vied with each other in muleta and cape work. Gregorio Corrochano called this period the *edad de plata* (the silver age), a worthy successor to the *edad de oro* (golden age) of Joselito and Belmonte. This was the period that Hemingway was privileged to witness.

Change: Crowding the Faena

The third *tercio* is the longest one and the only one with a set time limit.[82] All *Reglamentos* define it as fifteen minutes, but this time period is broken up into smaller segments. After ten minutes, the matador who has not killed his bull hears an *aviso* (warning), with a second warning coming three minutes later and a final one when the fifteen minutes are up, at which point the bull is removed from the ring and killed offstage, indicating the bullfighter's failure.[83] In 1917 and 1923, the clock began to run when the bugle was blown to indicate the end of the second act and the beginning of the third.

This moment of transition was subtly but significantly modified in the 1930 *Reglamento*, which required the death of the bull "al cumplirse los quince minutos . . . de iniciada la faena de muleta" (fifteen minutes after the beginning of the *faena* with the muleta), that is, fifteen minutes from the moment the bullfighter, muleta and sword in hand, began his interaction with the bull. This created a break between the second and third acts, giving the matador free time to take up his tools, salute the president, offer a *brindis* (dedication), toss his *montera* (hat), evaluate the bull, allow it a short rest if he felt it necessary, and generally focus his mind on the coming *tercio*—all this before the clock started running. The bullfighter still had only fifteen minutes to kill the bulls, but he had the full fifteen minutes. The 1930 ruling reveals a consciousness that increased emphasis on muleta work tended to lengthen *faenas* and that the preparation and ceremonies preceding the actual *faena* should not come at the expense of the *faena* itself.

This intelligent modification was maintained in the 1962 taurine code, but the 1992 *Reglamento* reverted to counting time from the bugle call that marks the change of the *tercio*.[84] The result has been a more hurried and less graceful assumption of tools, a rushed *brindis* and *alternativa* ceremony, a general loss of composure, and a higher likelihood of an *aviso*. This unnecessary rushing of the third *tercio* saves perhaps two or three minutes, an inconsequential amount of time in absolute terms, but an important, even crucial, fraction of the matador's allotted fifteen minutes.

When Hemingway saw bullfights in the 1920s, there was no free time between the *tercios*, but at that time *faenas* were shorter than they are today, and matadors seldom heard *avisos*. In 1931 and again in the 1950s, Hemingway was fortunate to see bullfights which were timed according to the 1930 *Reglamento*.

Concluding Ceremonies

In the early 1920s, spectators often streamed into the bullring after the fight to carry a bullfighter out of the ring in triumph (sometimes all the way to his hotel), chase him out in disdain, or indulge in general rowdiness that sometimes required police intervention. The legislation and quantification which flourished during the Franco years curbed this energetic spontaneity. The 1962 *Reglamento* specified that the fighter who has been awarded two ears is to be carried out through the main portals of the ring and that his admirers—who are often paid admirers—may not carry him for more than three hundred meters beyond the ring.[85] An event which used to be unusual and spontaneous became a matter of legislation and money. Eventually, the intrusive media took over the concluding ceremonies: more often than not, the paid "enthusiasts" who orchestrate the *salida en hombros* act according to the television producer's instructions. The television audience gets a choreographed show; the live public's voice is preempted by that of the television announcer.

But even today, admiration sometimes moves the crowd to carry the matador out of the ring, sometimes even if he hasn't cut the requisite two ears,[86] or if the police or camera crew objects. The audience's response to art and gallantry cannot be legislated.

NAMES OF PLACES

The place names Hemingway mentions often carry a significance that the text does not spell out. Place names are important for two reasons: they give the flavor of the country in which the narrative is set, and they help define the knowledge and experience possessed by the narrator. Places bearing the names of saints, for example, remind us that Spain has traditionally been a Roman Catholic country, and that the church was a ubiquitous, intimate, and powerful factor in everyday life, not just in government and politics. References to coins bearing Alfonso XIII's likeness, or to hotels named Alfonso XIII and María Cristina, indicate the country's monarchical nature, just as glancing references to Primo de Rivera (e.g., in terms of the *peto*) remind us that dictators affected all aspects of Spanish life in the 1920s. Readers for whom secularism, democracy, or republicanism are the default positions tend to forget that for most of Hemingway's lifetime, Spain was ruled by a monarch or a dictator who was supported by the army, the church, and the landowners or landed gentry. Place names remind us.

Although Spain was unified in the late fifteenth century, the divisions created by history and geography still separate its several regions. The separatist sentiments of some of today's autonomies reflect the uneasy partnership that ties the parts to the whole. Place names situate the reader firmly in a particular region or autonomy whose history, geography, weather, and even language distinguish it from its neighbors.

Individuals are shaped by the culture of the place they come from, and bullfighters in particular carried regional significance. Even today, local pride and self-interest promote support for the local bullfighter. In the 1920s, this tendency was more strongly marked. It was traditional for a town, city, or province to support its aspiring bullfighters, and if one of them succeeded nationwide, he was expected to come home, build a large house, employ local help, improve public facilities, attract tourism, and inspire another generation of townsfolk to enter the profession. Spain's geography and history are, then, important factors in bullfighting, and when Hemingway says that a bullfighter is known as the Hayseed from Borox, or that his nickname is Trianero or Algabeño, or that he was popular in Seville, or that he was contracted for the Madrid feria, he is giving us important information. A bullfighter from Borox who is wildly popular in Borox (a small town near Toledo) is quite different from a bullfighter from Borox who triumphs in Madrid. The first has accomplished something, but the second has accomplished everything. And a bullfighter who succeeds in Borox, and in Madrid, and in Seville as well, has made a place for himself in history. Next we must see whether he buys property in Borox, in Madrid, or in Seville: this will reveal even more of his character. Place names are meaningful, then, not just because Hemingway said so in *A Farewell to Arms*, but because they are code words for Spanish history, culture, and character.

In addition to supplying the flavor of the country, place names also define the narrator's experience and knowledge, and thus help us read this important personage. In this area, specific place names become important signifiers. *Death in the Afternoon* carefully names the hotels, bars, restaurants, and cafés patronized by its narrator. These places are important not just in practical terms but as markers of acceptance and authority. The bullfighter and the bullfight crowd (bull breeders, managers, critics, followers, and so on) usually frequent the same establishments year after year, and they know that at these venues they will meet friends, hear gossip, obtain information, and meet important taurine personalities, as Jake Barnes does in the Hotel Montoya in *The Sun Also Rises*.[87] It is instructive to notice that the narrator of *Death in the Afternoon* stayed at the Pensión Aguilar, and that the text takes care to establish that it was taurine. Not only did it house bullfighters, but it was near establishments where one could discuss taurine matters, study the *carteles* (bills announcing performers, dates, bulls, and so on), buy tickets for bullfights, and generally partake of the taurine atmosphere. He did not stay at the nearby, equally inexpensive Hotel Inglés, which was a favorite of the Bloomsbury Group.

In Spain, as in France, people often gather regularly in public venues to discuss certain topics, be they literary, artistic, political, or taurine. Over the years, such an ongoing conversation, or *tertulia*, becomes associated with its host café or bar. Among these sites, there are, of course, styles and fashions, but they tend to change slowly. For more than a century, for example, Madrid's Café Gijón has catered to writers and journalists: it would seem a natural setting for the first-person, heavily autobiographical narrators of Hemingway's nonfiction books, who are obviously writers. Instead, the narrator of *Death in the Afternoon* frequents the Cervecería Alemana and the Café Fornos, both decidedly taurine, although with a strong literary and artistic flavor. Clearly, in telling us where he slept, drank, ate, and met his friends, Hemingway is communicating information about his narrator and his experiences in Spain.

Annotations to *Death in the Afternoon*

Note: Cross-references to entries in this volume are indicated by q.v. or the italicized *see* or *see also*. References to entries in the companion volume, *Hemingway's* The Dangerous Summer: *The Complete Annotations*, are introduced by a roman (nonitalic) see or see also: see Barcelona in *DS*; see also Ostos, Jaime in *DS*.

– A –

ABC. Founded as a weekly in 1903, *ABC* became a daily in 1905. It is Madrid's oldest daily. Its founder and owner, Torcuato Luca de Tena y Alvarez-Ossorio, maintained control of the paper until his death, after which the ownership and editorship passed to his son, Juan Ignacio Luca de Tena, who in 1928 added a separate Andalusian edition, published in Seville.

ABC has consistently supported the monarchy and the Church, and during the Spanish Civil War, when most nationalist papers were suppressed in Republican-held areas, the right-wing Madrid *ABC* was still allowed to appear, albeit under Republican censorship. The Seville *ABC* also continued to publish, without any Republican interference.[1]

> The narrator mentions that this influential Madrid daily was pro-monarchy (89, 229; *see also* Corrochano, Gregorio).

A. B., Mrs. *See* Bird, Sarah Costello.

Absinthe. Absinthe is an anise-flavored alcoholic drink whose main ingredient used to be wormwood, a substance so toxic that absinthe has been banned in Switzerland, France, and the United States (since

1912). In color it ranges from yellowish-green to greenish-blue; it turns milky when poured over ice.

Hemingway and Absinthe. In Hemingway's day absinthe was controversial but not illegal in Spain, where it is drunk in the 1920s by Hemingway's characters Bill Gorton, Jake Barnes, and Brett Ashley (*SAR*, 164, 166–67, 221–23); Georgette Hobin, who is often defined as Ashley's double, drinks "imitation absinthe" (*SAR*, 14–15). Catherine and David Bourne also drink absinthe in Spain (*GOE*, 38–39), as does Robert Jordan (*FWTBT*, 50–51, 56–57) and several characters in Hemingway's short stories, most famously in "Hills Like White Elephants."

Absinthe has the reputation of being an aphrodisiac and of being addictive. But excessive use may result in reduced fertility (which adds irony to "Hills Like White Elephants"), disorientation, insomnia, and even insanity. For a thorough discussion of this drink, see Doris Lanier, "The Bittersweet Taste of Absinthe." *See also* Drinks.

> The narrator gives the impression that he is not a stranger to absinthe: he finds it goes well with shellfish (*h:* 448, s.v. *Mariscos*) and conversation (154) but is detrimental to serious bullfighting (172).

Adjutant. An adjutant is a staff or executive officer who assists the commanding officer by distributing orders, handling correspondence, circulars, records, and so on. He connects the chief officer with the rest of the unit. The fact that the adjutant in "A Natural History of the Dead" (q.v.) is not at his post means that orders cannot be transmitted, an indication that chaos reigns.

> The adjutant at the dressing station works the cable railway that transports the wounded from the dressing station to the field hospital and is unavailable when the doctor calls for him (143).

Agrarian Reform. Spain's landless workers have suffered centuries of poverty. During the first Republic (1873–74), vague promises of improved conditions led them to make scattered and ineffectual attempts to occupy land and in other ways assert themselves. In 1931 and 1932, Spain's second Republic attempted to redistribute land and improve their situation. A variety of agrarian reform laws were passed in dizzying succession (on 29 April, 19 May, 11 July, and 6 August 1931), creating panic among landowners, heightened expectations for peasants, and a great deal of confusion and social unrest, particularly in Andalucía, where estates were large and the peasantry particularly poor. These laws banned hereditary land-ownership, confiscated the estates of the aristocracy, and attempted to limit the power of other large landowners, absentee landlords, and land speculators.

These laws gave insufficient definition to those factors (crops, water, quality of the land, profitability, number of employees, and so on) that qualified lands for nationalization.[2] The hastily formed peasants' juntas were not only unsure as to which lands came under their jurisdiction, they were also ill-equipped to redistribute and manage the lands, equipment, cattle, and structures that came to them or that they commandeered. As one historian put it, "during this period, rural Andalusia was in a state of constant, though usually nonviolent, turmoil."[3] The "exhaustive study" Hemingway mentions (268) led to the founding, in September 1932, of the *Instituto de Reforma Agraria*, which assumed ownership of expropriated lands and then distributed them to the peasants, whose unions decided if the land was to be held collectively or individually.

These policies, as well as the virulent anticlericalism and antimilitarism that characterized Manuel Azaña's government, energized the opposition. Azaña's successor, Alejandro Lerroux (1933–35), attempted to soothe the army, the church, and the landowners. In this phase of the second Republic's short life, the pendulum swung to the right, increasing discontent among the working classes. The aggressive agrarian reform, which had so distressed landowners like Manolo Mejías (q.v.) in 1931 and 1932, now faltered and faded. In 1936, after the Popular Front's electoral victory, agricultural workers simply moved in and occupied farmlands.

Hemingway writes that Madrid was unaffected by the troubles in the south (268), which is accurate in that Madrid, like most of the cities, remained prosperous. But the city's demographics were much affected by agrarian reform, as thousands of poor people moved from the countryside into urban centers. James Cortada writes that "In the 1930s, only one out of every two inhabitants was born in Madrid."[4] Bull breeding did suffer greatly: the Republic favored agriculture over cattle, and it had little use for the *toro de lidia* (the well-bred fighting bull). Many bull breeding ranches were wiped out during the

Spanish Civil War (see the section entitled "Bulls and Bull Breeding," in the introduction to this volume).

The narrator attributes Manolo Bienvenida's poor performances in Pamplona to his worries about his family's properties during this period of agrarian reform (251). He also remarks other negative effects of agrarian reform on bullfighting in Andalucía (267–69).

Agüero, Martín. Full name: Martín Agüero Ereño. Spanish bullfighter, 1902–77. Investiture as *matador de toros*, in Málaga, 31 August 1924; confirmed in Madrid, 7 June 1925.

As Hemingway reports, Agüero's first few seasons as a *matador de toros* were impressive (fifty corridas in 1926 and fifty-two in 1927), earning him the *oreja de oro* (golden ear) in the corrida for the Press Association for both those years. The fact that the same prize had been awarded to Manuel Báez (Litri, q.v.) in 1925 undermines Hemingway's claim that these two men had been promoted before they had mastered their craft (254).

For Agüero, 1928 was an unhappy year. In May and again in August he suffered serious gorings, which required so many operations that his 1929 season was reduced to only twenty-one appearances, although he had signed contracts for many more. The doctors were unable to repair the damage to his leg, and Agüero tried but was not able to regain his former agility and strength. He retired in 1930 or 1933 (accounts vary). Eventually both his legs were amputated, the left in 1949 and the right in 1973. He was considered to be one of the superior swordsmen of his time, but the two 1928 gorings forced him into early retirement.[5]

Hemingway and Agüero. Hemingway probably saw Agüero in Pamplona on 7, 8, and 9 July 1925. On the first of these afternoons Agüero shared the bill with Antonio Márquez and Cayetano Ordóñez (qq.v.). His two performances with the Villar bulls earned him a turn around the ring, but he was outperformed by his fellow matadors: Márquez was awarded an ear, and the applause for Ordóñez was deafening. On 8 July Agüero appeared with Antonio Márquez and Marcial Lalanda (q.v., *see also* Passchendaele); on 9 July, there was a *corrida de prueba* with four bulls from Cándido Díaz. Agüero performed with Márquez, Lalanda, and Ordóñez: he was not impressive with the muleta but "demonstró nuevamente que es un formidable estoqueador" (demonstrated anew that he is a powerful swordsman). One critic hailed him as "¡Agüero, Emperador de la espada!" (Agüero, emperor of the sword!).[6]

Hemingway was not in Spain in 1928, when Agüero was gored, but he read taurine journals published that year. He did visit Spain for the taurine seasons of 1929 and 1931. He knew at that time that Agüero's career was practically over, though he doesn't mention this.

Hemingway refers to but doesn't discuss Agüero's two younger brothers (259): José was born in 1913, and Manuel in 1910 (d. 1990). Both of them were, as Hemingway says, *matadores de novillos*, but they had short careers and never took the *alternativa* (q.v.).[7] *See also* Altrock, Nick, to whom Agüero is compared.

> The narrator correctly describes Martín Agüero as a leading matador in 1925, 1926, and 1927. He claims that Agüero's work with the cape and muleta is generally competent but undistinguished (223, 259), that Agüero is a skillful but unemotional swordsman (253, 258–59), that he was promoted prematurely (254), and that he looks like a baseball player, not a matador (258, 276).

Aguilar. Full name in the 1920s: Pensión Aguilar, Casa de Huéspedes. Manager and owner: Serapia Aguilar Camacho and her daughter, Josefa Aguilar (Pepita, died in the late 1980s). Address: 32 Carrera de San Jerónimo, Madrid 28014. The Aguilar family leased the space for the Pensión (later Hotel, now Hostal) Aguilar. The large building, which houses several other establishments, was originally owned by the Count of Villapadierna. In 1944 the Villapadierna family sold out to a commercial conglomerate. Several of the businesses in the building eventually bought the space they had formerly leased.

Throughout its history, the Aguilar has occupied part of the second floor. Directly above it was the Pensión Suiza, owned by José Hernández Coca. In the late 1950s or early 1960s, José Hernández Coca took over the management of the Pensión Aguilar, and in 1970 his son, Simón Hernández Hernández, bought the business outright from Josefa Aguilar, by then an old lady. Simón Hernández still runs the two-star Hostal Aguilar.

Hemingway's Room at the Aguilar. Room 107 (it was number 7 in Hemingway's day) is opposite the Aguilar's front desk; a large central hall, rather like a long lobby, separates them. In the 1920s, the room had a fireplace but no bathroom. Eighty years later, the room has a bathroom, central heat, and air-conditioning, but the fireplace disappeared and the elegant double doors, still in place in other parts of the hotel, were replaced by a small, single door. The room overlooks the Carrera San Jerónimo.

Simón Hernández confirms Baker's report that Hemingway stayed at the Aguilar in 1923, 1925, 1926, and 1927, although he cannot produce records for those years. The Aguilar was popular with bullfighters, who appreciated the inexpensive meals. (The Aguilar still has a dining room, but serves meals only to tour groups that book several rooms.)

Although it remained under the same management, the Pensión Aguilar became the Hotel Aguilar c. 1930. Hemingway's reference to Félix Merino (q.v.), who died in 1927, makes it clear that he is referring to the time when the Aguilar was still a pensión ("the old Aguilar").[8] *See also* Luis and the Unsuccessful Matadors.

> The narrator would have liked to describe the bullfighter Merino at the "old" Aguilar (272). The unnamed bullfighters' boarding house in Madrid (33) is probably the Aguilar.

Aguilar Beer. Correct spelling: Aguila. Address of the brewery in the 1920s and 1930s: 33 Calle General Lacy, Madrid.

In 1923, Madrid produced seven beers: El Aguila, La Corona, La Covadonga, La Espuma, El Laurel de Baco, Mahou, and Santa Bárbara. Bars called Aguila or El Aguila stood at 38 Carmen Street, at 32 Serrano, and 1 Hermosilla. By 1930, three of these beers—Corona, Espuma, and Laurel de Baco—had disappeared, and the Aguila bar at Hermosilla Street had closed.[9] At the end of the twentieth century, El Aguila beer is a subsidiary of Amstel. *See also* Drinks.

> The narrator considers Aguilar (*sic*) to be Madrid's best beer (*h:* 424, s.v. *Cerveza*).

Aguilar, Manuel (Rerre). Full name: Manuel Aguilar González. Spanish bullfighter, b. 1894.

As a child Aguilar performed in *cuadrillas de niños sevillanos* (q.v.). After three years of military service, he returned to the bullfight world where his skill with the banderillas brought him into the *cuadrillas* of the most important fighters of his day: Juan Luis de la

Rosa (1920), Varelito (1921–22), Maera (1922–24), Algabeño (1925), Chicuelo (1926), Cagancho and Belmonte (1927), Cayetano Ordóñez (1928–30), and Solórzano (1929–31, qq.v.). He was seldom wounded by the bulls, but after a bad motorcycle accident in 1924 he had to wear an orthopedic boot. Even with this impediment, he continued to excel as a banderillero, a profession that requires agility and strong legs.[10]

> The narrative identifies Aguilar correctly as an excellent banderillero, also noted for his work with the cape (201).

Alamendro. Correct spelling: Almendro. *See* Ortega Monge, Enrique.

Albayda, Marqués de. Full name: Antonio Pérez de Herrasti, the Marquis of Albayda. Spanish bull breeder, d. 1974. In 1928, when he acquired a carefully pedigreed herd, the Marquis of Albayda became an important bull breeder, a position he and his family maintained throughout the twentieth century.

The Albayda herd's pedigree can be traced to the Marquis of Villasequilla, who established a bull-breeding ranch at the end of the eighteenth century with *jijona* stock. Enriched by Miura and Murube blood, the herds passed through several hands before being acquired in 1909 by Eloy Sánchez Hidalgo, of Salamanca, and in April 1928 by don Antonio Pérez de Herrasti, the Marquis of Albayda. By this time they were almost pure Vistahermosa, the less popular *jijona* strain having been bred out. On 27 June 1929, soon after acquiring them, Albayda presented a corrida of his bulls at the Madrid plaza under his brand and colors (crimson and yellow), thus establishing their seniority, or *antigüedad*.

In July 1936, the Albayda ranch boasted two hundred cows and one hundred twenty bulls. Most of them were slaughtered during the Spanish Civil War, but in 1939 the Marquis began to breed the fifty or so cows he had left. The herd flourished, and in 1968 he sold a large fraction of it to Clemente Tassara. But the Marquis of Albayda retained the rights to his brand, colors, and *antigüedad* (27 June 1929), as well as a fraction of the original herd, which he continued to breed carefully: in 1973 he was able to acquire

Domecq seed bulls for his cows. Upon his death in 1974, the herd passed to his heirs, who still own it. The Albayda family's ranches are in Salamanca.[11] For a discussion of *antigüedad* and other important concepts relevant to the *toro de lidia*, see "Bulls and Bull Breeding," in the introduction to this volume.

> The narrator correctly identifies the Marquis of Albayda as an important breeder of *toros de lidia* (132).

Alcalareño II. Most bullfighters with this nickname are from Alcalá de Guadaira (Seville), but the one Hemingway discusses is from Alcalá de Henares, near Madrid. *See* Todó, Isidoro.

Aldeano (the Villager). *See* Gómez, Francisco.

Alfonso XIII. Full name: León Fernando María Isidro Pascual Antonio de Borbón y de Habsburgo, 1886–1941; king of Spain, 1902–31.

As the posthumous son of Alfonso XII, Alfonso XIII became king of Spain at his birth. His mother, María Cristina (see in *DS*), served as regent until he assumed the throne in 1902. He married Victoria Eugenia (q.v.) in May 1906. He was deposed when the Republicans won the election of 1931, at which point he and his family went into exile.

For most of the years that Hemingway followed the bulls, Spain had been a monarchy, and the king and queen's faces were to be seen everywhere. When Hemingway's first son, John Hadley (Bumby), was born in 1923, Hemingway remarked that his newborn son "looks . . . like the Roi d'Espagne" and that his "Hemingway nose made the child resemble the King of Spain." He also commented upon Alfonso's "familiarly photographed under-jaw on the five-peseta pieces. . . . He was much handsomer as a baby, if the peseta pieces are accurate, but then we all were."[12]

When Hemingway was writing the Glossary, Alfonso XIII had already fled Spain and the coins bearing his likeness were unpopular among anti-royalists. *See also* Garibaldi, Guiseppe; Primo de Rivera, Miguel.

> Alfredo Corrochano (q.v.), the son of a monarchist newspaperman, is said to resemble the Bourbon king (229) whose profile appears on five-peseta coins (*h:* 480, s.v. *Sevillano*).

Algabeño I, Algabeño II. The nickname identifies two matadors, father and son, as being from La Algaba, near Seville, Andalucía. *See* García Carranza, José; and García Rodríguez, José.

Almendro. *See* Ortega Monge, Enrique.

Alonso Bertolí, Rafael (el Chato). Spanish bullfighter, 1862–1910.
A consistently effective picador who worked with the great matadors of his time, el Chato suffered three horn wounds in 1884 when the bull Oficial (q.v.) threw him against the *barrera*. Alonso retired in 1906 and died four years later, demented and forgotten.[13] *See also* Arribas Brothers.

> The narrator correctly identifies Alonso (el Chato) as the picador who, in October 1884, was gored three times by Oficial (111).

***Alternativa*, Doctorate in Tauromachy.** The promotion of a bullfighter from the rank of *matador de novillos*, or *novillero*, to *matador de toros* is a decisive event. The matador's seniority dates from the event that, among other things, empowers him to grant the *alternativa* to other bullfighters. For more detail, see the discussion of "The Doctorate" in the section entitled "The Bullfighter," in the introduction to this volume.

Altrock, Nick. Full name: Nicholas Altrock. American baseball player, 1876–1965. Altrock pitched for three teams in the American League: briefly for Boston (1902–03), very successfully for Chicago (1904–09), and longest for the Washington Senators (1910–33), with whom he continued his association after he stopped playing.
Called in as a pinch hitter on the last day of the 1933 season, Altrock became the second oldest man (after Satchel Paige) to play in a big league game: he was fifty-seven. He retired as a player immediately after that game, with a lifetime record of 84 wins and 74 losses, for a .532 average, but he remained with the Senators "in various capacities" for another twenty years.
Altrock began clowning in 1912, by shadowboxing on the playing field. He and his partner "worked up nearly 150 pantomime acts covering almost every sport . . . Altrock was probably the first man to make a career of baseball comedy."[14] With a series of partners, he

performed many years before regular games, at World Series games, and in vaudeville. When Hemingway was a teenager, Altrock was still playing baseball and had already begun to make his mark as a clown.

Hemingway, Clowns, and Baseball. In both his fiction and nonfiction, Hemingway displayed his sense of humor and his interest in professional clowns. In addition to Altrock, *Death in the Afternoon* makes reference to Rafael Dutrús, El Empastre, the Fratellini brothers, and *Mojigangas* (qq.v.). Clowns are mentioned in several of Hemingway's novels, from the earliest, *The Torrents of Spring*, which mentions Grock (41) and Lauder (37), to *For Whom the Bell Tolls* (Marx Brothers, 231) to the posthumous *The Garden of Eden* (155).

Baseball is another recurring interest, used as a means of discussing moral values in early works like the short story "The Three Day Blow" (1925) and in later works like *The Old Man and the Sea* (1952). Hemingway connected baseball and bullfighting in his first report on bullfighting, when he described the bullfighters entering the arena for their ceremonial *paseo*: "From their faces they might be major league ball players."[15] The link reappears in expanded form more than a quarter of a century later: see Baseball in *DS*.

Hemingway's seemingly irrelevant remarks—like the short, easily overlooked references that link Martín Agüero to Altrock, or Corrochano to Alfonso XIII, or the longer, emotional digressions on Goya and el Greco (qq.v.)—should be examined carefully: with Hemingway, much of the meaning resides in the detail.

The narrator remarks that Agüero looks like Nick Altrock (258; *see also* 276).

Amorós, José. Full name: José Amorós Cervigón (Pepe Amorós). Spanish bullfighter, 1911–97. Investiture as *matador de toros*, San Sebastián, 1930; confirmed in Madrid, 30 April 1931.

As a *novillero*, Amorós did quite well (twenty-five *novilladas* in 1929), being contracted for 1930 by all the plazas where he performed in 1929. After twenty-three *novilladas* in 1930, he was promoted to *matador de toros* in August: he was only seventeen years old. His weak performance on the day of his investiture prompted an editorial castigating those of Amorós's "friends" who had flattered him into an early promotion and had thus compromised a promising career.[16] (For other "premature" promotions, see the section entitled "The Bullfighter," in the introduction to this volume.) After eight corridas he twisted his ankle and was unable to fulfill the ten remaining contracts he had signed for that season.

In 1931 Amorós performed in twenty-six corridas. He was generally given good marks, but his standing fell after that good year. In 1932 Amorós performed in twelve corridas; the number rose to fifteen in 1933, fell to three in 1934 (illness was blamed for the low number) and rose again to thirteen in 1935 (these were generally good performances). He was invited to perform in Madrid in the first bullfight held after the Spanish Civil War (the so-called *Corrida de la Victoria*, 24 May 1939) and returned occasionally to the Spanish ring in the following years. He retired from the Spanish bullring in 1943, but continued to perform as banderillero in Portugal and America for a few more years. Amorós's promising beginning did not lead to a great career.

After his retirement he managed the career of his daughter, Tere, a dancer. In the 1990s he was still connected to taurine matters, serving as *asesor de la presidencia* (technical advisor to the president) of the plaza of Madrid.[17]

Hemingway and Amorós. Hemingway, who was in Spain from May to September 1931, probably saw Amorós in Madrid, where he appeared on 10 May; and in Pamplona, where he performed on 9 and 11 July 1931. His assessment of Amorós, who was then at the height of his powers, is accurate.

The narrator finds that the highly touted Amorós is overrated and disparages his style as "rubbery" (224).

Androgyny. Mark Spilka's work, most particularly *Hemingway's Quarrel with Androgyny* (1990), alerted us to the presence of androgyny and the blurring of gender in Hemingway's work. *See also* Homosexuals; Jiminiz, Manuel (Chicuelo); Sebastian, Saint.

The narrator finds that both the faces and bodies in Greco's religious paintings are androgynous (204). He insists that Chicuelo and Chiquito look like girls (74, 228, 276) and mentions that Villalta has a high voice (70).

Anlló, Juan (Nacional II). Full name: Juan Anlló Orrío. Alternate spelling: Orríos. Spanish bullfighter, 1898–1925. Investiture as *matador de toros*, in Oviedo, 21 September 1921; granted by Alcalareño (q.v.) and witnessed by Emilio Méndez (see the account of Nacional II's death, below); confirmed in Madrid four days later by Luis Freg (q.v.).

Nacional II had four moderately successful seasons before he died. He was an eager but unreliable matador, good enough to be contracted in Madrid but not consistently successful. Cossío writes that Nacional II was not an artistic performer and that his reputation and popularity were due more to his forceful personality than to his skill. But other critics disagree, seeing the makings of a real artist in his marked improvement from season to season. When a performer dies young, as Nacional II did, his reputation is difficult to assess, but we can safely say that he was not a major star in the taurine firmament of his day. Still, he was "a major stylist and influential within his peculiar style . . . [he had a] tremendous personality and [was] very aggressive."[18]

Intent on success, Nacional II focused all his energies on every bull he fought, and in the process he expanded his repertoire and became more graceful. He had an impressive season in 1922, his first full season as a *matador de toros*, with fifty corridas. In 1923 and 1924, the numbers were again fairly high, thirty or thirty-six corridas in 1923 (reports vary) and thirty-nine in 1924. His frequent triumphs in 1924 led Tomás Orts Ramos (Uno al Sesgo) to predict that 1925 would be a fine season for him. In 1925, Nacional II had twenty-three corridas, most of them in first-class plazas (including seven in Madrid), before being fatally injured in a ringside brawl.[19]

Nacional II's Death. Hemingway's detailed account of Nacional II's death agrees in most details with a contemporary account quoted by both Cossío and Tapia: Nacional II was hit on the head with a bottle on 4 October 1925, taken to jail that night, and died on the sixth. The injury occurred in Soria (q.v.), as Hemingway reports, and "the fighter in the ring who was dealing with a difficult animal" (*DIA*, 77), whom Hemingway does not identify, was Emilio Méndez (1895–1974). Méndez had served as witness at Nacional II's *alternativa* and was a friend as well as a colleague.

Méndez had been a successful *novillero*, with forty *novilladas* in

1918 and forty-nine in 1919, many of them earning flattering reviews. He was promoted to *matador de toros* on 19 September 1920. Although brave and anxious to please, he was awkward and suffered frequent injuries, which decreased both his strength and his popularity. He fought twenty-two corridas in 1921 and twenty-eight in 1922, but the numbers fell to about ten corridas in 1924 and 1925, twelve in 1927 (but half of them in Portugal), and only two or three corridas a year for the next few years. By 1931 he had disappeared from the lists.[20]

When he came to Soria for the October *feria* of 1925, Méndez faced a hostile audience: he had fought in Soria before, giving one of his typically ugly performances, and was consequently unpopular there. Unable to deal with a "difficult animal" that was beyond his powers, he was showered with insults. Nacional II's defense of the hapless matador included his hitting a spectator (the doctor whom Hemingway mentions). As Hemingway reports, Nacional II was fatally injured in the ensuing brouhaha. Both the doctor and Nacional II were treated in the bullring's infirmary, after which the doctor was sent home and the bullfighter taken to jail. Nacional II's relatives recognized the seriousness of his condition and obtained medical attention: he underwent trepanning to relieve pressure on the brain but died within forty-eight hours.

The shocking event was much commented in the press, both at the time of its occurrence and during the two years of legal wrangling that followed it. Some facts are undisputed: the doctor's name was Antonio Cabrerizo, and all reports agree that Nacional II hit him on the head with his cane. It remains unclear, however, whether Anlló's fatal injury was inflicted by this young doctor or by another irate spectator. Eighty-eight witnesses were called at the hearing: they not only reported the event differently, but some even changed their stories as the investigation proceeded.

In August 1926, almost a year after the event, the Union of Bullfighters passed a resolution protesting the slowness of the judicial process and boycotting Soria's bullring. Dr. Cabrerizo was finally convicted of homicide and sentenced to six years and one day in jail. He appealed the sentence, arguing self-defense, and in October 1927, a full two years after the original event, he was acquitted and released. The event gave Soria a bad name.[21]

Hemingway and Nacional II. Hemingway saw Nacional II in Pamplona, where he performed on 9, 10, 11, and 13 July 1924; most of these were unsuccessful performances. On the ninth, a *corrida de prueba* in which four bulls, all from the same ranch, was fought by four bullfighters: Chicuelo was booed, Maera and Nacional II did well, and Fuentes Bejarano was boring. The corrida of 10 July was a disappointment, and Nacional II, his brother Nacional, and Chicuelo were all booed. The next day Nacional II tried to win the audience's approval with showy maneuvers such as touching the bull's horn and performing on his knees; he was applauded on his first bull, but with his second he was loudly booed. Maera was the star of the afternoon. On 13 July, Nacional II's last performance in that fiesta, the corrida started badly: both Chicuelo and Nacional II were whistled at, a mark of extreme disapproval. But with the third bull, the tide turned: Algabeño got a great ovation and a turn around the ring, Chicuelo enjoyed a similar success with the fourth bull, but Nacional II was so boring with the fifth that the audience whistled again. The last bull, fought by Algabeño, provided the high point of the afternoon, and Algabeño cut an ear.[22]

Hemingway seems to have formed his negative opinion of Nacional II in that 1924 Pamplona fiesta, when his performances were so weak that neither he nor his brother Nacional was contracted for the next year's fiesta. Hemingway missed Nacional II's 1924 successes in Barcelona and was not in Madrid when Nacional II performed there in 1925.[23] In October, when Nacional II died, Hemingway was in Paris, working on *The Sun Also Rises*, but he obviously kept up with the bullfighting news from Spain.

> The narrator discusses Nacional II's short and mediocre career during the "decadence" that followed Joselito's death in 1920 and Belmonte's retirement in 1921 (75). Fatally injured in a ringside argument, Nacional II was assumed to be drunk and died in jail (77, *h:* 497).

Anlló, Ricardo (Nacional, Nacional I). Full name: Ricardo Anlló Orrío. Spanish bullfighter, 1891–1977. Investiture as *matador de toros*, Madrid, 19 May 1918, granted by Rodolfo Gaona (q.v.).

After five or six years of apprenticeship, Nacional made his Madrid debut as *novillero* in 1916. His fine performance in Spain's premier ring brought him many contracts: in 1917 he performed in forty-three *novilladas*, becoming the year's top-ranked *novillero* and making his *alternativa* (q.v.), early in the next season, an occasion of general interest. Nacional performed in twenty-two corridas that year.

For a few years, Nacional enjoyed a respectable but not great following. He had to cancel several corridas each season because of injuries but even so he maintained a respectable standing, with between twenty and twenty-seven corridas a year. In 1923 the number fell to eight; in 1924 it rose to seventeen; and in 1925 it fell to ten. Although most of these performances were well-received by the critics, the numbers of contracts continued to descend, and Nacional began to fade out of the Spanish bullring. His occasional triumphs, many of them before the important and traditionally hard-to-please public of Madrid, failed to stem the tide. He had only a few engagements in 1926 and retired in 1927, at age thirty-five. He worked many years as a bullfight manager and then as an administrator in a Madrid hospital, the *Sanatorio de Toreros* (Bullfighters' Clinic).

Nacional was a brave, serious, and knowledgeable matador whose impressive performances could have made him one of the decade's top-ranking matadors. But his sober, spare style and his reserved personality did not endear him to the general taurine public, who flocked to see the younger, more dashing performers who emerged to fill the void left by Joselito's death and Belmonte's retirement (e.g., Antonio Márquez, Marcial Lalanda, Nicanor Villalta, and Cayetano Ordóñez [qq.v.], to name just a very few of the young men promoted to *matador de toros* in the 1920s).

Hemingway and Nacional. Hemingway saw Nacional in Pamplona on 8 and 10 July 1924. In the first of these corridas, all three matadors—Algabeño, Fuentes Bejarano, and Nacional—were lackluster. On 10 July, Nacional, Chicuelo, and Nacional II were similarly disappointing. The crowd whistled derisively and threw pillows at them. Hemingway may have seen Nacional on other occasions as well.[24]

> The narrator describes the eldest of the brave but uninspiring Anlló brothers as "a monument of probity, courage, undistinguished but classic style and bad luck." After the brilliance of Joselito and Belmonte, this "classic style" no longer pleased the audiences (75).

Antigüedad **(Seniority of a Herd).** A herd's seniority dates from the time when its bulls were first fought in the Madrid bullring, showing their breeder's brand (*hierro*) and colors (*divisa*). For more detail on this important and complicated concept, see the section on "Bulls and Bull Breeding," in the introduction to this volume.

Aranjuez. This city has been a royal property since the reign of Ferdinand and Isabella; the existing palace was built by Philip II (qq.v.) and expanded by subsequent monarchs. Its pleasant weather made it a popular summer resort, with horseraces and bullfights offered for the entertainment of the aristocracy seeking relief from the Madrid heat. Fountains, statues, and gardens attract many tourists, who feast on Aranjuez's famous strawberries and asparagus.

The Aranjuez Bullring. Aranjuez's plaza de toros was built in 1761 or 1796 (reports vary), rebuilt in 1829, and renovated in 1851 and 1881. The most recent renovation and modernization occurred in 1976. Aranjuez's important corridas are the fiesta of San Agustín, 28 August, and the fiesta of San Fernando, on 30 May.

Hemingway and Aranjuez. Hemingway visited Aranjuez for the San Fernando *feria* on 30 May 1923, one of the first corridas he ever saw. The corrida was not a good one: the performances of Marcial Lalanda, Pablo Lalanda, and Braulio Lausín (Gitanillo de Ricla) ranged from perfunctory to miserable. One reviewer summarized, "Marcial, regular en su faena de muleta, desacertado Pablo y mediano Gitanillo" (Marcial [was] average in his muleta work, Pablo off the mark, and Gitanillo so-so). Another wrote, "La corrida, en conjunto, pesada y aburrida" (On the whole, the corrida was tedious and boring). The *Zig Zag* reviewer was apoplectic: "los toreros, con una desfachatez, una desgana, una tan poca consideración al buen público que llenó la plaza pagando precios fabulosos, hicieron todo lo malo y poco que les vino en gana" (the shameless, reluctant bullfighters, completely disregarding the good public which had paid enormous entrance fees and filled the plaza, did very little and did it badly).[25] Little wonder that in describing Aranjuez in *Death in the Afternoon*, Hemingway focused on the picturesque and not on the bulls, the bullfighters, or his response to them. Hemingway saw other bullfights in that city as well.[26]

The narrator describes Aranjuez (39–42) and mentions it frequently (168, 169, 226, *h:* 376, 509, 512).

Armillita. Professional nickname of the Espinosa family (which *Death in the Afternoon* misspells as Espinoza), a Mexican bullfighting dynasty established by Fermín Espinosa Orozco and including his four sons, all of them fine banderilleros. *Death in the Afternoon* mentions the two brothers who became *matadores de toros*: Juan (Armillita) and Fermín (Armillita Chico), who became a superb matador. The other two brothers, José and Zenaido, worked as banderilleros for Fermín.[27] In addition to producing several generations of bullfighters, the family established a bull-breeding ranch, "Armillita Hermanos," in Mexico.

The family's nickname derives from the father, who supposedly got the name because his fighting style, particularly in the placing of the banderillas, resembled that of Matías Aznar y Ros, a Spanish banderillero (1883–1931) who used that nickname and was seen in Mexico during several seasons in the early twentieth century, when he worked in the *cuadrillas* of such stars as Vicente Pastor and Rafael and José Gómez Ortega (qq.v.).[28]

Arribas Brothers. Francisco and Basilio Arribas were Spanish bull breeders, active 1855–1912.

The Arribas brothers were important bull breeders from the middle of the nineteenth century until they sold their holdings in 1912. The herd which they owned during that time had a fine pedigree, traceable back to the 1750s, when don Pedro Luis de Ulloa y Calis, the first Count of Vistahermosa (q.v.), established his famous herd. The Vistahermosa herd was inherited and enlarged by the second and then the third Counts of Vistahermosa. When the latter worthy died

in 1821, his sister Luisa took possession of the herd. Over the next few years, she sold different portions of it.

The share bought by Joaquín Giráldez went through three owners until it was bought by the Arribas brothers in 1855 or 1856.[29] The Arribas *antigüedad* dates to 24 June 1882 (according to *Toros y toreros en 1931*, 102) or 24 June 1883 (the more likely date, reported by various sources). The bull Hemingway mentions misbehaved in the early years of the Arribas brothers' ownership of the herd.

The Arribas herd was managed by Felipe de Pablo Romero (q.v.), who may have crossbred it with some of his own bulls. In 1912 the Arribas brothers sold their herd, having owned it for a little more than half a century. Half of it was sold in two equal lots to Andrés Sánchez Sánchez and José M. García; the other half, which included the rights to the brand and colors (crimson and black), was bought by the Duke of Tovar (q.v.). In 1927 the Duke of Tovar, who owned the largest fraction of the herd, sold it to Luis Bernaldo de Quirós. Quirós kept the herd until his death in 1957; his heirs kept it in his name as "señores herederos de don Luis." (For a discussion of *antigüedad* and other important concepts relevant to the *toro de lidia*, see "Bulls and Bull Breeding," in the introduction to this volume.)

The Arribas brothers were from Guillena, in Seville (Andalucía); the herd's subsequent owners are based in Salamanca.[30] The Arribas brothers seem to have owned no other herds. *See also* Alonso Bertolí, Rafael; Oficial.

The narrator reports that Oficial, a specimen from the Arribas brothers' herd, injured five people in October 1884 (111–12).

Asch, Sholem (S. A.). Polish-born Yiddish playwright and novelist, 1880–1957.

Born in Poland to a poor Orthodox family, Asch's first languages were Hebrew, Polish, Yiddish, Russian, and German. During his extensive travels (to Switzerland, Germany, France, the United States, and Palestine), he acquired French and English and studied Aramaic. He claimed, however, that "I am not one of those Jews with many languages at my command. . . . All my thoughts are in Yiddish and I write in Yiddish." He immigrated to the United States at the beginning of World War I and became an American citizen in 1920.

Asch's interest in German and Polish secular literature caused his parents to suspect him of heresy, a charge that was repeatedly lodged against him as he turned away from the confines of the *shtetl* to address worldwide Jewish problems and even to explore the connections between Judaism and Christianity. His works include short stories, plays, novels, and two trilogies. *Three Cities, A Trilogy* (1929–31; first published in English, 1933) recounts the history of St. Petersburg, Warsaw, and Moscow during the Russian revolution of 1917; his three-volume study of the Jewish roots of Christianity—

The Nazarene (1939), *The Apostle* (1943), and *Mary* (1949)—treats Jesus as the greatest of Jewish prophets. These books brought him so much adverse criticism from the American Jewish community that in 1953 he left the United States for England. Three years later he moved to Israel.

In 1932 Asch was elected honorary president of the Yiddish PEN Club, and in 1933 he was nominated for the Nobel Prize. He was a famous, prolific, and controversial writer who brought Yiddish literature onto the world stage.

Hemingway and Asch. By the time Asch and Hemingway met, in the 1920s, Asch had already written one of his best stories, "Reb Shloyme Nogid," and several novels, including *The Way to Oneself*, *Kiddush haShem* (Sanctification of God), *The Witch of Castile*, and *Death Sentence*. In 1920, Asch's collected works were published in twelve volumes. In 1926, the Kultur-Liga of Warsaw again published the collected works (in Yiddish), in twenty volumes. This second collection includes *Mein Reize über Spanien* (in Yiddish, not translated), which records Asch's experiences in Spain, including a description of the bullfight, with long sections on the picador, the banderillero, the matador, and Asch's own, very positive reactions: he was surprised to find that he was deeply stirred by a spectacle he had been prepared to dismiss as inconsequential and pointlessly cruel.

Asch and Hemingway admired each other's work. Hemingway owned several of Asch's books, and Asch's daughter, who inherited his library, still has the autographed first editions that Hemingway gave her father. She remembers several meetings between the two writers. In 1956, identifying "the only writers I ever liked, really," Hemingway included Sholem Asch in the list.[31] Both writers left their closely knit families and the villages in which they had grown up in order to define and practice their craft. Both became knowledgeable about cultures, languages, and religions different from those which had shaped them. Their openness to new experiences enabled them to appreciate a spectacle as foreign to their backgrounds as the bullfight.

The narrator describes S. A.'s response to the bullfight (*h:* 500).

A. U. *See* MacLeish, Archibald.

Author. *See* Narrator.

Authors: Americans, British, French, Spanish, German. Hemingway's education, supervised by his parents and his high school English teachers, concentrated on British rather than American writers, and *Death in the Afternoon* reflects the range of Hemingway's reading of British authors. The narrator mentions Marlowe, Marvell, and Shakespeare, as well as English naturalists and travel writers like Ford, Hudson, Park, Stanley, and White. Of the dozen or so British writers he mentions, only four are his contemporaries: Eliot, Firbank, Huxley, and Woolf.

Among the American authors, however, the proportions are reversed: four belong to earlier generations (James, Longfellow, Whitman, Whittier) and would have been obligatory reading in school. But most of the American writers Hemingway names in *Death in the Afternoon* are his contemporaries: Bird, Faulkner, Frank, Hammett, Harrison, MacLeish, Shipman, Stein, and Stewart. Interestingly absent from *Death in the Afternoon* are Sherwood Anderson, F. Scott Fitzgerald, and John Dos Passos, who were much in evidence in Hemingway's first novel, *The Torrents of Spring* (1926), as well as in *A Moveable Feast* (1964).

Of the few French authors Hemingway mentions, Dumas and Stendhal are admired, while contemporaries (Cocteau, Gide, and Radiguet) are derided. Among the Spanish, Hemingway mentions that bullfighters ocassionally produced *tauromaquias* (mostly ghostwritten; *see* Guerra Bejarano, Rafael) and he mentions two taurine critics (Gregorio Corrochano and Rafael Hernández). He names only three creative writers: Cervantes, Lope de Vega, and Sánchez Mejías. Hemingway does not give the titles of Sánchez Mejías's plays, and he attacks both his character and his performances in the bullring. Hemingway does not admire the two Germans he mentions, Baedeker and Meier-Graefe.

Consistently, Hemingway focuses on his contemporaries, and just as consistently, he insults and dismisses them. He was clearly keeping track of the competition. He makes the point that he is not only a taurine expert but a writer and a published author: he talks about his literary apprenticeship (*DIA*, 2–4), refers to his published work (*see* the entries for Smyrna and *The Sun Also Rises*) and to his work-in-progress (*DIA*'s Chapter Twenty), creates a story ("A Natural History of the Dead"), and pointedly dramatizes himself under the rubric Author (133, 139–41, 144). *See* Boxing; Critics; Homosexuals; see also Authors in *DS*.

– B –

Baedeker, Karl. German publisher of guidebooks, 1801–59. Baedeker's purpose was to enable tourists to conduct their own tours. His guidebooks described important sights and hotels and ranked them by a system of stars. Baedeker himself would make incognito journeys to check how tourists were received at various places. His name became synonymous with the guidebooks. In *Across the River and Into the Trees*, a nameless writer is mocked for being so excessively dependent on his Baedeker (*ARIT*, 270; *see also ARIT*, 124, 126, 130).

The narrator refers the reader to Baedeker (40) and to other superficial travel guides written by Germans (52).

Báez, Manuel (Litri). Spanish bullfighter, 1905–26. Investiture as *matador de toros*, Seville, 28 September 1924, at age 19 (for Hemingway's treatment of "premature promotions," see the section entitled "The Bullfighter," in the introduction to this volume). His *alternativa* was confirmed in Madrid, October 1924.

The son of the matador Miguel Báez Quintero (Litri, 1869–1932) and the grandson of Miguel Báez (el Mequi, also a matador), he showed a strong aptitude for the bulls early in his life and quickly attracted attention for his bravery and style. His performances at his investiture and at its confirmation in Madrid were not outstanding, but his 1925 season was spectacular, and he was awarded the "golden ear" trophy by the Press Association, quite an achievement for a newly promoted matador.

Litri fought very close to the bull, with a cool, almost detached air that was very impressive. He was gored so frequently in 1925 that he was able to perform in only forty-three corridas, although he had been contracted for many more. Early the next year, on 11 February 1926, at a benefit performance in Málaga attended by King Alfonso XIII and Queen Victoria Eugenia (qq.v.), he was gored in the right leg. The wound became gangrenous and the leg was amputated on 17 February, but Litri died the next day, at age twenty-one.

Litri's Reputation. Cossío remarks that Litri's style reflected the fashion of his period: both for passes and for the kill, he tended to wait for the bull, standing very still rather than moving forward to meet him or to encourage him to move, a dramatic attitude used by

Joselito to great effect and therefore much admired in the 1920s. Cossío adds that Litri had an absent, abstracted air while in the ring, and that he brought nothing new to *toreo*. He also mentions the tic "que le hacía cerrar los ojos en el momento de embestirle la res" (which made him close his eyes when the bull charged), and which may account for the "abstracted air."[32] Summarizing Litri's 1925 season, Tomás Orts Ramos (Uno al Sesgo) was more flattering: although the matador still has much to learn, his personality and record thus far suggest he is well on his way to becoming an important bullfighter. That year, Hemingway saw Litri in Valencia, on 25, 26, and 31 July.[33] *See also* the entry for Berenguet, Enrique, a banderillero who was present when Litri was gored.

Litri's girlfriend married his father, and their son, Miguel Báez Espuny (Litri, b. 1930), was one of the most popular matadors of the 1950s. This Litri's son, named Miguel Báez Spínola (Litri, b. 1969), also became a popular *matador de toros*.[34]

> The narrator argues that the "sensational" Litri was promoted to matador before he had acquired sufficient repertoire and technique. He was so brave and took so many risks that his early death was inevitable. The narrator accurately summarizes Litri's dramatic career and death (254–56).

Barajas, Fausto. Full name: Fausto Barajas Sánchez. Spanish bullfighter, 1902–34. Investiture as *matador de toros*, in Linares, 30 August 1922. The investiture was to be confirmed in Madrid in October of that year, but Barajas was gored badly while placing the banderillas in the first bull and the ceremony could not be completed.

Although he was a brave fighter, had the requisite strong legs, and was skillful with the banderillas, Barajas achieved only a modest reputation because he was not aesthetic with the cape or muleta and merely competent with the sword. His best seasons were 1923 and 1924, with about twenty appearances each year. In 1925 he performed in fifteen corridas, and in April 1926 he was gored so badly that he lost a month of work, finishing that season with twelve corridas. Although he continued to reap praise for his work with the banderillas, for his courage and his desire to please, he had no notable afternoons and his reputation declined rapidly: he appeared four times in 1929, and hardly at all in the following two years. He turned to the business end of the bullfight, equipping and supplying horses for the ring. Badly hurt in a car crash on 18 September 1934, he died a month later.

Hemingway and Barajas. On 27 May 1923, Hemingway saw Barajas in Madrid: this was Hemingway's first bullfight. He also saw him on 23 May 1926. In 1931, Hemingway was in and out of Spain from May to September; he probably saw Barajas on 17 June, at the gala opening of Madrid's new Plaza Monumental de las Ventas: Barajas was one of eight performers that afternoon. But, as the narrator notes, in 1931 Barajas was at the end of his bullfighting career. He fought only five corridas that year.[35]

The narrator describes Barajas as "excellent" with the banderillas but "on the decline" (201).

Barcelona. Barcelona's important fiestas honor St. Joseph (San José, q.v.), whose feast day is 19 March, and the city's patron saint, Nuestra Señora de la Merced (Our Lady of Mercy), whose feast day is 24 September. Bullfights are held throughout the taurine season. For details about Barcelona's bullring, see *DS*.

The narrator seldom mentions Barcelona (79, 111, 168, 264).

Barrera, Vicente. Full name: Vicente Barrera Cambra. Spanish bullfighter, 1908–56. Investiture as *matador de toros*, in Valencia, 17 September 1927, granted by Juan Belmonte; confirmed in Madrid, 1928.

Like many bullfighters, Barrera committed himself to the bulls at an early age and endured a long and bitter struggle with his mother and uncles (his father had died when Vicente was eight) who opposed his entering such a dangerous profession. He often ran away from home to work with bulls or see a fight, and was as often punished when he returned. Eventually he had his way and, with his family's reluctant help, began his apprenticeship at age fifteen. He quickly became one of Spain's leading *novilleros*, competing often with another rising star and fellow Valencian, Enrique Torres (q.v.).

Barrera promoted himself in various spectacular ways. In 1927, for example, he fought in three *novilladas* within twenty-four hours, cutting ears in the afternoon and evening of July 25 and at a dawn corrida on July 26.[36] All told, in 1927 Barrera fought forty-three *novilladas* and sixteen *corridas de toros*, all this in spite of a wound on 31 July that kept him out of the ring for six weeks and postponed the *alternativa*, originally scheduled for 1 September, to 17 September.[37]

From 1928 until he retired in 1935 Barrera was among Spain's most sought-after fighters, appearing in about sixty corridas a season and usually fighting the lucrative circuit in Mexico and South America after the Spanish season was over. He often cut ears; in 1932 he was awarded the ears of 104 of the 131 bulls he killed. He was seldom gored and his retirement, in 1935, surprised the public and the critics. Vicente Barrera returned to the ring in 1939 (after the Spanish Civil War), retired in 1942, came out of retirement in 1944, and retired for the last time in 1945, a wealthy man.

Popular as he was, Barrera's career was controversial: his style was said to be unaesthetic and his sword work deficient. Bagüés reports that he would stick in his sword any which way and then resort prematurely to the *descabello* (coup de grâce): "Se fué de los toro sin haber estoqueado ninguno a ley" (he retired from the bulls without ever having killed one legally). Silva Aramburu calls him a "torero sin afición," and in an insulting poem, Gregorio Corrochano (q.v.) wrote that Barrera hopped around the bullring like a sparrow. Tomás Orts Ramos (Uno al Sesgo), however, finds him an "extraordinaria figura del toreo actual," who has turned his so-called defects (nervousness and darting movements) into useful tools, part of his very individual style. He concludes admiringly, "¡Es mucho torero, ese gran torero valenciano!"[38] And Cossío praises his strong personality, his bravery, his intelligence, his thorough understanding of the bull, and his consistently excellent work with the muleta.[39]

Hemingway and Barrera. Hemingway may have seen Barrera while he was still a *novillero*: Barrera was all the rage in 1926 (thirty-two *novilladas*), and 1927 (forty-four *novilladas* before the *alternativa*), years when Hemingway spent several months in the bullrings of Spain. Hemingway did not go to Spain in 1928, but the next year he saw Barrera in Palencia on 2 September 1929 and probably several other times as well: the young Barrera appeared in sixty-six corridas in 1929 and Hemingway was in Spain from July through most of September.

Hemingway did not go to Spain in 1930, but in 1931 he saw Barrera in Madrid on 24 May, as well as in Pamplona, where Barrera performed on 7, 9, and 11 July of that year, and probably at the *feria* of Valencia, where Barrera was injured on 26 July 1931.[40] Hemingway may have seen Barrera at other times that year as well, as he was in Spain from May to September and Barrera performed in seventy corridas.[41] Hemingway's remarks echo some of the contemporary critical positions about Barrera.

Both Barrera and Torres were born in 1908 and took their *alternativas* in 1927. Although Barrera was eighteen and Torres was barely nineteen years old when promoted, Hemingway does not call these "premature" *alternativas* (see "The Bullfighter," in the introduction to this volume).

The narrator refers to Barrera's "eagle nose" twice (177, *h:* 459, s.v. *Oreja*).

> The narrator reports he saw Barrera perform in 1931, and found that this "steel-sinewed, leg-jittering eagle nosed" bullfighter (177) from Valencia (267) was more impressive than Ortega, the current favorite (169). Although the narrator dislikes Barrera's "nervous" style and method of killing (248–49), he grants that the bullfighter is talented, controls a large repertoire, is maturing and may yet become "great" (214, 216; photographs, *h:* 306–07).

Baseball. *See* Altrock, Nick; Sports. See also Baseball in *DS*.

Beer. *See* Drinks.

Behr, General von. Correct spelling: von Berrer. On 27 August 1917, Lt. General Albert von Berrer, then Commander of the 51st General Command, was awarded the Prussian Order of Merit "for outstanding leadership and distinguished military planning" in several campaigns on the eastern front. The general was shot dead in Gottardo, on 28 October 1917, one week after the German breakthrough at Caporetto (q.v.). He was buried in Cividale, near Caporetto and Udine.

When he was shot, von Berrer had been "the commander of the 200th Division, which was an Alpenkorps formation. The [Italian] Commando Supremo and Second Army HQ had departed from Udine only two or three hours before von Berrer's advance guard entered the town, with the General himself immediately on their heels. A Carabinieri recognized that he was a senior officer and shot him. While their role is that of police and Gendarmerie in peacetime, the Carabinieri are part of the military and serve as military police or combat troops in time of war."[42] This historical figure appears as a character in the story "A Natural History of the Dead" (q.v.). For another general killed in action, *see* General.

> In the interests of accuracy, the narrator would amend the title of the 1930 war novel *Generals Die in Bed* (q.v.), to *Generals Usually Die in Bed*. In support of this correction he cites military leaders killed in action, like General von Behr (*sic*; 140).

Bejarano. *See* Fuentes Bejarano, Luis.

Belmonte. Full name: Juan Belmonte García. Spanish bullfighter, 1892–1962 (died by his own hand). Investiture as *matador de toros*, in Madrid, October 1913.

Belmonte was born in Seville's Calle Feria, and he did not go to live in Triana (q.v.) until after his mother died. But it was in Triana that his career began, hence his nickname "El Pasmo de Triana" (the Wonder of Triana). Belmonte's poor health, like Manolete's, could have been due to the poverty of his childhood. His father mismanaged his small business, and the boy was malnourished.

Belmonte's career was unusual in several ways. Unlike most great bullfighters (e.g., the Gómez Ortega brothers, Machaquito, Guerrita, Chicuelo, Cayetano Sanz, the Bienvenida brothers, Lalanda, qq.v.), Belmonte was not a child prodigy and his beginnings were inauspicious. He did not come from a bullfighting family and seems to have drifted into it simply because Triana was full of aspiring bullfighters. The romantic picture of young Belmonte fighting bulls in the moonlight is probably true, says Cossío, but commonplace: many teenagers did the same (see *DIA*, 77). At any rate, when he was about sixteen (an age when young men are already famous *novilleros*), Belmonte was only beginning to teach himself the rudiments of his craft.

Belmonte's early fame was due to his reckless, aggressive style. He took unbelievable risks and was injured in almost every fight. Purists decried his lack of polish and complained that his injuries were unnecessary and the sort of thing that gave bullfighting a bad name.

But his apologists lauded his strong personality, and the crowds rushed to see the passionate daredevil.

In 1914, Belmonte and Joselito met for the first time in the ring. Belmonte acknowledged in his autobiography that Joselito, a natural master who grew up in the profession, was his superior, but it was widely acknowledged that, inspired or perhaps goaded by Belmonte's unconventional maneuvers, Joselito's style changed: he quickly mastered Belmonte's moves, polished and improved them, and retaught them to Belmonte, who in turn challenged him with increasingly dangerous innovations, while becoming a more sober and artistic performer himself. As he achieved polish, Belmonte suffered fewer gorings. But he always maintained his revolutionary closeness to the bull.

The season of 1917, in which Belmonte appeared in ninety-seven corridas, is sometimes considered his most important, although in 1919 he fought 109 corridas, a remarkable record that stood for almost half a century.[43] That year Belmonte killed 234 bulls and suffered very few injuries. But the public that had once rushed to see him risk his neck objected to his newly acquired control and authority, which they read as coldness, self-interest and, most damning, lack of *afición*—a remarkable charge to levy against a *figura* who spent almost all of his long life with the bulls, as matador and as bull breeder. These criticisms were fueled by Belmonte's absence from the Spanish rings for two entire seasons (1918 and 1922), which he spent in South America; and by his sudden retirement early in 1923. Fortunately, the retirement was temporary. The enormous fees he could command and his love of the art, which had grown as his understanding of its subtlety developed, lured him back to the ring, where his performances, though few (he accepted only nineteen contracts in 1925), were increasingly masterful. As one taurine critic wrote, "Juan cuando se fué de los toros era el mejor, y cuando ha vuelto ha sido el mejor" (when Juan retired he was the best, and now he's come back he's still [or again] the best).[44]

Belmonte enlarged bullfighting by diminishing the distance between himself and the bull, by depending on his strong wrists and arms rather than his weak legs, and by drawing attention away from the *suerte suprema* (the killing) to the *faena* (the work with the muleta) that precedes it. The revolutionary closeness with which he fought the bull transformed the art, but one can also say that it diminished it. Cossío explains that Belmonte "ha mejorado, aunque en una sola dirección, el estilo de torear; pero ha sido a expensas de principios fundamentales de la lidia y aun más de la variedad que hacía posible el ideal de arte del propio diestro" (he improved, although in only one direction, the style of bullfighting; but this has come at the expense of fundamental principles of the fight and, more damagingly, of the variety which made possible the ideal of the fighter's art).[45] A strong personality himself, his stylistic innovations forced others to copy him (in the period that Hemingway calls the "decadence of bullfighting" but which other critics call *la edad de plata*, the silver age) and deprived the art of more than a few talented young men: some gave up and retired prematurely, others were killed trying to imitate him.

Hemingway saw Belmonte in Pamplona on 11 July 1925, when he came out of retirement. Belmonte performed in a *gran corrida extraordinaria* with Marcial Lalanda and Cayetano Ordóñez; the bulls were Gamero Cívicos. Belmonte was serenaded at the Hotel Quintana the evening before his performance and greeted with a standing ovation when he entered the packed bullring. Everyone had come to see if "¿Renovará el célebre trianero, el que revolucionó el arte taurino, sus famosísimas escalofriantes faenas de antaño?" (if the famous man from Triana, who revolutionized taurine art, would again perform the famous, thrilling *faenas* of the past). The public was disappointed: the older Belmonte was not the daredevil of yesteryear. Belmonte's performance with his first bull was not distinguished (he complained that the bull had problems with his vision, but his request for another bull was denied), but he was politely applauded. During his second performance, Belmonte was smacked by the bull, which knocked the sword out of his hand. He killed the bull only after several tries, and the audience responded with a mixture of applause and derisive whistles. One reviewer wrote that although Belmonte showed himself to be a skillful artist, a master of the cape and the muleta, he certainly could have fought more closely to the bull. He also indicated that "one can see in Belmonte's face that the matador is in poor health."[46] As a matter of fact, Belmonte was in poor health all his life: he grew up motherless, in poverty, his legs were weak and, according to some experts, they were covered with sores that would not heal. Lacking stamina and unable to run, Belmonte tended to stand still and control the bull with long, sweeping arm movements.

In 1926 Belmonte fought a full season (forty-five corridas, his season shortened by a bad goring on 26 August) and revealed himself a master swordsman, correcting a weakness that had previously drawn much criticism. In 1927 (forty-two corridas) he drew high praise from aficionados,[47] although some of the public, their minds still on the younger, reckless Belmonte, continued to accuse him of coldness. Belmonte's second retirement came at the end of the 1927 season, after a severe goring at the end of October.

When Belmonte returned to the ring in 1934 (at age forty-two), he was unable to achieve his former successes. But he continued to fight, albeit in Portugal, as late as 1937. He was by this time a major bull breeder. Here too, he was imperious and often at odds with the establishment (Unión General de Criadores), who for several years vetoed his bulls.[48]

The literature on Juan Belmonte is rich. Book-length studies include Francisco Gómez Hidalgo's *Juan Belmonte: Su vida y su arte* (Barcelona, 1914), Abraham Valdelomar's *Belmonte, el trágico* (Lima, 1918), Enrique Vila's *Juan Belmonte* (Madrid, 1946); Manuel García Santos's *Juan Belmonte: Una vida drámatica* (Mexico, D.F.: La Prensa, 1962), and Francisco Narbona's *Juan Belmonte: Cumbre y soledades del Pasmo de Triana* (Madrid: Alianza Editorial, 1995). Belmonte's autobiography, *Juan Belmonte, Matador* (Garden City, N.Y.: Doubleday, Doran & Co., 1937), was ghostwritten by Manuel Chaves Nogales and translated into English by Leslie Charteris, who wrote an excellent introduction for it.

Hemingway and Belmonte. Since Hemingway first came to Spain in 1923, he did not see the younger, more shocking Belmonte. Belmonte did not perform in Spain in 1923 and 1924, so Hemingway could have seen him only in 1925, 1926, and 1927 (when Belmonte retired again).

In *The Sun Also Rises* Hemingway attacks Belmonte for his looks, especially his "wolf jaw" and "wolf smile," and denigrates his performance in order to exalt Romero (212–15, 221). Although in *Death in the Afternoon* he treats Belmonte more fairly, he repeats the wolf image (178, 212, 213), focuses on his greed (82, 243), and connects his style to what he considers Belmonte's physical defects (69, 212), perhaps to exalt Maera and Joselito.

However, in evaluating Belmonte's performances in 1925–1927 seasons, Hemingway agrees with most taurine critics that the later Belmonte was the finer artist: "I swear this [1926 or 1927] was the best [season] he ever had" (243). Elsewhere, Hemingway wrote that Belmonte is "The only living bull fighter that I unreservedly admire."[49] Hemingway also mentioned Belmonte in *The Dangerous Summer* (54, 189).

> The narrator identifies Belmonte as a revolutionary bullfighter, the contemporary and competitor of the great Joselito. His understanding is that Belmonte developed the showy and dangerous cape work that became obligatory for all bullfighters after him in order to compensate for "his lack of stature, his lack of strength, [and] his feeble legs" (69, 78–79). But he had great wrists (14), and his extraordinary work with the cape and muleta did much to shift the emphasis away from the sword to the cloth (174–75). The narrator blames him for the "decadent" style of modern bullfighting, which requires smaller bulls "made to order" to enable less able bullfighters to perform Belmonte's techniques (161). The narrator mentions Belmonte often: 14, 59, 68–70, 73–74, 77–78, 82, 84, 88–89, 100, 158–59, 161–62, 168, 175–76, 178, 198–99, 211–13, 218, 226, 239, 243–44, 262, 267, *h:* 450, s.v. *Media verónica*; 474, s.v. *Renovador*; 476, s.v. *Rondeño*; 504; photographs, *h:* 294–95, 298–99, 346–47, 350–53.

Berenguet, Enrique (Blanquet). Alternate spelling: Belenguer. Full name: Enrique Belenguer Soler. Spanish bullfighter, 1881–1926.

An excellent banderillero, Blanquet worked with the outstanding matadors of his time, *figuras* like Rafael González Madrid (Machaquito), José Gómez Ortega (Joselito), his brother Rafael (el Gallo), Manuel Granero, and Ignacio Sánchez Mejías. The deaths of Joselito (in 1920) and of Granero (in 1922) affected him so deeply that he retired in 1922. Sánchez Mejías, in whose *cuadrilla* Blanquet had worked in 1920 and 1921, coaxed him out of retirement. He was working for Sánchez Mejías when he died.

In *For Whom the Bell Tolls*, the character Pilar says that that although Blanquet was not a gypsy, he had the gypsies' ability to smell death on a person about to die (*FWTBT*, 252–53). Barnaby Conrad writes that Blanquet had smelled it—it was the smell of the candles that had burned at his father's funeral—at the beginnings of the corridas in which Joselito and Granero were killed. He smelled it again on 15 August 1926, when Sánchez Mejías and his *cuadrilla* performed in Seville. This of course made all the bullfighters very nervous. They kept a careful distance from the bull, finished the corrida safely, and then rushed to the train station, because they were fighting in Ciudad Real the next day. At the station, still wearing his bullfight uniform, Blanquet had a heart attack. He was taken off the train and entrusted to Sánchez Mejías's brother, a physician, but he died that day: he had smelled his own death. He was buried in his native Valencia.[50]

> The narrator praises Blanquet's intelligence and cape work and correctly reports that even so he was unable to rescue the matadors José Gómez Ortega (Joselito), Manuel Granero or Miguel Báez (Litri), all of whom were killed in corridas at which this banderillero officiated. Always gray-faced, he died of a heart attack (201–03; photograph, *h:* 330–31, 338–39).

Bibliographical Note. *See* Díaz Arquer, Graciano.

Bienvenida. Professional name of the Mejías family, natives of the town of Bienvenida, in Badajoz (in Extremadura, and not in Andalucía, as Hemingway claims, *DIA*, 267). The founder of this bullfighting dynasty was Manuel Mejías Luján (1844–1908), an excellent banderillero. His sons were also bullfighters: the elder, José Mejías Rapela (Pepe Bienvenida, 1880–1959), was a banderillero, and the younger, Manuel Mejías Rapela (q.v.) was an inspired and talented matador whose career was derailed by a serious goring that permanently weakened his left leg. This Mejías had nine children, two of whom died in infancy: Antonio lived only five months, 1915; and Carmen (Carmelita) fourteen months, 1919–20. The other children, who survived to see the family prosper, were the daughter, Carmen Pilar, and the six bullfighting sons: Manuel Mejías Jiménez (1912–38), José (1914–68), Rafael (1917–33), Antonio (1922–75, see in *DS*), Angel Luis (b. 1924), and Juan (1929–99). Because the family traveled all over Spain and to Central and South America, several of the Bienvenidas were not born in the town which provides their nickname: Manuel was born in Dos Hermanas, Seville (not in South America, as Hemingway claims, *DIA*, 267); José was born in Madrid; and Antonio in Caracas. All but Rafael, who was murdered at age sixteen by an employee of the family, attained the rank of *matador de toros*.[51]

The remarkable family is the subject of several books, such as Antonio Santainés Cirés's *La dinastía de los Bienvenida: Un siglo de gloria y tragedia* (Zaragoza: Mira, D.L., 1988), and María de la Hiz Flores's *Bievenida: Dinastía torera* (Madrid: Espasa-Calpe, 1993).

Hemingway's book mentions the three older sons (165) and discusses Manuel (Manolo) and José (Pepe), who were nineteen and seventeen in 1931, when Hemingway was finishing *Death in the Afternoon*. Both were promoted to the rank of *matador de toros* while still in their teens: Manolo at age sixteen, Pepe at seventeen. In 1931 the three younger Bienvenida boys were still children, aged nine, seven, and two. Like their older brothers, they were educated by their father. *See* Mejías, Manuel, in this volume; and Mejías Jiménez, Antonio in *DS*.

Bird, Sarah Costello (Sally). Sally married William A. Bird (q.v. below) shortly after his graduation from Trinity College, Hartford, Connecticut, in 1912; hence Hemingway's reference to her as Mrs. A. B. The newlyweds sailed to Paris so that Bill, as a Russell Fellow, could study Romance languages at the Sorbonne. In 1916, when their daughter, Ann, was born, the Birds were in Washington, D.C.; by 1921 they were back in Paris, where their son, William, was born.

With her husband and several other friends, Sally accompanied the Hemingways to the Pamplona fiesta of 1924.[52] Although they were living in France, where Bill Bird was Paris correspondent for the *Baltimore Sun*, they did not accompany Hemingway on his later trips to Pamplona. Hemingway reports that "Sally did not like" the bullfights,[53] and her opinions were not easily disregarded: "The quiet Bill, married to that dynamo, was something to observe." Sally had a "superb voice . . . a much praised voice . . . she sings beautifully"; her voice "had conditioned all their lives."[54]

> The narrator reports that Mrs. A. B. [Mrs. William Augustus Bird] was a trained opera singer who did not enjoy the bullfights and so "Did not go again" (*h:* 497). In the entry for W. A., the narrator reports that because W. A.'s wife "disliked" the bullfights, W. A. stopped going (*h:* 500).

Bird, William Augustus, IV (Bill, W. A.). American publisher and newspaper correspondent, 1889–1963.

   Bill and his wife, Sally (q.v. previous entry), first came to Paris
soon after Bill's 1912 graduation from Trinity College, Hartford,
Connecticut. Bill served in the American ambulance service in World
War I and returned to Paris after the war as the European manager of
the Consolidated Press. He and Bob McAlmon owned and operated
the Three Mountains Press, which published Hemingway's *in our
time* (1924) as well as books by Ezra Pound, William Carlos Williams, Gertrude Stein and Ford Madox Ford. During his years in
Paris, Bird worked as part-time correspondent for several American
newspapers, and in the late 1920s he was president of the Anglo-
American Press Association.

   When France fell to the Germans in 1940, the Birds went to Spain.
After the war, they moved to Tangiers, where Bird edited *The Tangier
Gazette*, an English-language weekly, until the Moroccan government closed it in 1960. They then returned to France, where they had
an apartment in Paris and a country home near Chartres.[55]

   Bird's Palate. Like Hemingway, William Carlos Williams also refers to Bill's expertise in matters of food and wine, noting that Bill
often treated his friends to fine meals during which he had learned
discussions with the wine steward and delivered "long lecture[s] on
the wines of France, north and south." Once he obtained "a special
permit . . . to visit the famous Veuve Cliquot champagne cellars"
where "a big fellow with a full beard . . . opened several bottles of
their best" for him.[56] Bird wrote *A Practical Guide to French Wines*
(Paris: Three Mountains Press, 1922, 1938, 1948).

   Hemingway and Bird. Hemingway met Bill Bird in Paris, early in
1922. In August 1922, the Birds and the Hemingways went on a
walking tour in the Black Forest. Ernest, Bill, and Bob McAlmon
went to Spain in the spring of 1923 (Hemingway's first trip to Spain),
and Bill and Sally accompanied the Hemingways to Pamplona in
1924.[57] They did not go to Pamplona again.

> The narrator mentions that W. A. [William Augustus] is a successful jour-
> nalist who likes food and drink. W. A. liked the bullfights but stopped
> going because his wife (Mrs. A. B.) didn't (*h:* 500).

Blanquet. *See* Berenguet, Enrique.

Bombilla. Full name: Restaurante La Bombilla, also known as Dancing-Madrid. Address: 1–3 Camino del Pardo, Madrid, near the Esta-
   ción del Norte (train station).

La Bombilla was near the Reina Victoria Bridge, which crosses the Manzanares River, and close to the two-hundred-year-old Chapel of San Antonio de la Florida, with its well-preserved Goya frescoes that depict one of St. Anthony's miracles.[58] The area was a center for the celebrations honoring St. Anthony on his saint day, 13 June.

La Bombilla and the Café Mingo. In the 1920s, La Bombilla shared a block with several other establishments which supplied wines, drinks, snacks, and meals. La Bombilla seems not to have had a kitchen of its own, but was supplied by the Café Mingo, named after its founder, Domingo (Mingo) García. The café-bar has been in the same family for four generations and, still faithful to its Asturian origins, dispenses cheese, roast chickens, Asturian cider, and Galician-style snacks: probably the same type of cider and foods that Hemingway enjoyed at the Bombilla and on some of the picnics by the Manzanares River (*see* Luis and the Unsuccessful Matadors).

In the Madrid directory of 1923, La Bombilla was identified as a restaurant owned by Melitón Pérez. In the 1927 and 1930 Madrid directories, it was identified as "Dancing-Madrid, restaurant," owned by the widow and sons of Melitón Pérez. By 1959 it was listed as "Dancing Bombilla" and its address had changed to 19 Camino del Pardo, probably because the buildings on that road, now called Avenida de Valladolid, had been renumbered.[59] The area itself is called Parque de la Bombilla; it is on the Madrid side of the Manzanares River.

Although La Bombilla is gone, the Café Mingo still stands, obviously renovated and modernized (address: Paseo de la Florida, 34, Madrid).

The narrator mentions the cider drinking and the dancing at the Bombilla restaurant (48, 271).

Bombita. Professional nickname of the three Torres Reina brothers, all of them bullfighters: Emilio (Bombita, 1874–1947), Ricardo (Bombita Chico, 1879–1936) and Manolo (Bombita III, 1884–1936). *See* Torres Reina, Ricardo. For Bombita IV, *see* García, Antonio. Although not related to the Torres Reina brothers, García adopted their nickname on the excuse that he was also a native of Tomares (Seville), their hometown.

Boni. *See* Perea, Bonifacio.

Borox. *See* Ortega, Daniel (The Hayseed of Borox).

Botín's. The restaurant, named "Antigua casa sobrino de Botín" (Ancient House [of the] Nephew of Botín)," occupies the site of an ancient inn at 17, Calle de los Cuchilleros, off the Plaza Mayor of Madrid. In 1725 the large, handsomely tiled oven was built, presumably by the Botín family, and over the years the guest rooms were converted into small, well-appointed dining rooms. Botín's is in the *Guinness Book of World Records* as the oldest restaurant continuously under the ownership and management of the same family. Botín's menu still features the roast suckling pig enjoyed by Jake Barnes and Brett Ashley in *The Sun Also Rises* (*SAR*, 245–46).[60]

> The narrator would rather eat suckling pig in Botín's than discuss illness and other misfortunes (104).

Boxing. Hemingway, who was knowledgeable about boxing and proud of his own boxing skills, used a pugilistic image to define his place in literature: "I started out very quiet and I beat Mr. Turgenev. Then I trained hard and I beat Mr. de Maupassant. I've fought two draws with Mr. Stendhal, and I think I had the edge in the last one. But nobody's going to get me in any ring with Mr. Tolstoy unless I'm crazy or I keep getting better."[61]

Hemingway's boxing stories include "Fifty Grand" and "The Battler," and several characters in his novels are boxers: Robert Cohn in *The Sun Also Rises* learned to box in college; Joey and Benny Sampson are broken-down fighters in *To Have and Have Not*. In addition to these fictional pugilists, historical boxers like Carpentier, Dempsey, Firpo, Greb, Tunney, and several others are mentioned in Hemingway's fiction. A concentrated boxing passage appears in *Green Hills of Africa* (166). *See also* Sports.

> The narrator mentions various aspects of boxing (29, 35, 49, 100, 101, 104, 112, 150–51, 178 et passim) and several heavyweight champions: Carnera, Fitzsimmons, Jeffries, Johnson, and Tunney (qq.v.).

Brancusi, Constantin. Rumanian sculptor, 1876–1957. Brancusi went to Paris in 1904 and studied at the Ecole des Beaux-Arts until Rodin encouraged him to come work with him instead. Brancusi's 1908 *The Kiss* presents primitive, block-like figures, but he evolved toward smoother, more polished curves and became known for his symbolic, elegant, hand-polished work, including the sensuous bird of *Maiastra* (1912) and the more elongated *Bird in Space* (1940).

Emily Stipes Watts writes perceptively that "Hemingway's reference to Brancusi suggests that Brancusi's sculpture was able to capture some elemental and primordial qualities which a bullfight also made evident. . . . Both the bullfight and Brancusi express a sense of life in its most reduced and thus most real sense . . . the clean lines of Brancusi's geometrical forms are an expression of order in the world. . . . For Hemingway, too, the bullfight represented a kind of order [and Brancusi's] geometrical shapes . . . would surely have appealed to Hemingway, who also saw nature and mountains manifesting the same forms."[62]

Using phrases similar to those Hemingway used to describe bullfighting, another art critic wrote about the "courage and simplicity" in Brancusi's works, and about "the honesty of his patient, subtle craftsmanship. . . . Although his [Brancusi's] forms sometimes suggest the purity of geometry they are never actually geometric but usually organic both in name and shape."[63] Hemingway admired the slow, measured sweep of the cape or muleta, the flowing movement which shows that the bullfighter is in perfect control of himself, his art, and his subject. He may have felt that the smooth, attenuated arcs of Brancusi's sculpture expressed the same confident mastery.

> The narrator compares the impermanent art of bullfighting to sculpture, although only Brancusi's art warrants the comparison to modern bullfighting (99).

Bueno, don José. Spanish bull breeder, d. 1928.

Don José Bueno owned a herd of Veragua bulls (q.v.: Veragua bulls were predominantly but not exclusively of Vistahermosa blood) which he presented in Madrid on 13 February 1904 (the date of their seniority, or *antigüedad*, q.v.). Víbora, the bull Hemingway mentions, was fought in 1908 and obviously came from this herd.

In 1920, José Bueno acquired another herd, which had been established in 1912 by the Marquis of Albaserrada with Santa Coloma stock;[64] this herd's *antigüedad* dates from 29 May 1919, when the

bulls were still the property of Albaserrada and displayed the Albaserrada brand and colors (blue and crimson). Bueno acquired the rights

to this herd's *antigüedad*, and added his Veragua
herd to this Albaserrada stock.

When José Bueno died in 1928, his widow,
doña Juliana Calvo vda. de Bueno, and his
nephew, don Bernardo Escudero Bueno, inherited his holdings equally. Juliana added more
Santa Coloma stock to the herd. Both heirs
earned high marks for their Vistahermosa bulls.
When Juliana died in 1941, her nieces and nephews ("Escudero
Calvo Hermanos") inherited her famous herd. In 1965, the herd was
sold to Victorino Martín Andrés, its current owner, who also acquired the rights to the original (i.e., Albaserrada) colors (blue and
crimson) and brand (an A topped by a stylized curved crown), which
means that the bulls' *antigüedad* (seniority) dates back to 29 May
1919, even though ownership has changed. The bulls continue to win
prizes to this day.[65] *See also* Víbora; Vistahermosa.

> Don José Bueno's ranch produced the bull Víbora, whose exploits are re-
> corded in *Toros célebres* (110).

Bullrings. See "The Bullring," in the introduction to this volume; and
under individual cities, in this volume and in *DS*.

– C –

Cabrera, José Rafael. Spanish bull breeder, 1738–1823.

The caste or race of bulls known as Cabrera is generally traced
back to José Rafael Cabrera, but taurine scholar José María Sotomayor asserts that Luis Antonio Cabrera (d. 1768) was the first Cabrera to become a *ganadero*. Records indicate that in 1745 Luis
Antonio acquired three bulls from the Carthusian monks of Jerez (the
monks, accomplished bull and horse breeders of the seventeenth century, accepted cattle as part of the tithe levied upon the neighboring
ranchers). Luis Antonio's nephew, José Rafael Cabrera, became his
son-in-law in 1761, eventually took over the management of the herd,
and finally inherited it. He was an excellent breeder, and in the sixty

years that he had it, he developed the famous Cabrera bull. He registered his bulls under his own name, colors, and brand for the Madrid corrida of 16 June 1800.

Cabrera's Widow, her Sister, and her Nephew. José Rafael, who was childless, was survived by his much younger third wife, María Soledad Núñez del Prado (1772–1835). She registered the herd in her own name, thus changing the *antigüedad* (seniority) from 1800 to 1829. She left the herd to her long-lived sister, Jerónima Núñez del Prado (1760–1852), who is often mistakenly identified as Cabrera's widow but was, of course, his sister-in-law. As happens surprisingly often in bull-breeding families, the herd then went to a nephew, in this case Ildefonso, who had his own herds and seems to have been uninterested in the Cabreras (*see* Saavedra).[66]

According to Vera, doña Jerónima sold one hundred head to Juan Miura (q.v.) in 1850; she may have sold him some Cabrera stock in the 1840s as well (*see* Pablo Romero; Vasquez). Either she or her heir, Ildefonso Núñez del Prado (1814–80), sold the rest of the Cabrera holdings to Juan Miura and to Ramón Romero Balmaseda. The Romero portion was so thoroughly crossbred by its several succeeding owners that very little Cabrera blood remains, but the Miura family crossbred selectively. They also kept a herd of pure Cabrera stock, now the only such stock in existence. Its *antigüedad* goes back to 1842, when they were probably still in the possession of the widow Cabrera. These are not what we know as the famous Miura bulls which, although based on Cabrera stock, also carry Vistahermosa and Vázquez blood.[67] For a discussion of *antigüedad* and other important concepts relevant to the *toro de lidia*, see "Bulls and Bull Breeding," in the introduction to this volume.

The narrator includes the Cabrera among the main strains from which the modern *toros de lidia* are descended (132).

Café Fornos. *See* Fornos, Café.

Cafés. Bullfighters, their managers, friends, and followers often conduct business, exchange gossip, and discuss professional matters in cafés and restaurants (226, 277; see, for example, bullfighting stories like "The Undefeated"). Literary and political figures may also adopt a particular café for such *tertulias* (*see* Cervecería Alemana; Fornos; Rotonde).

The narrator evaluates the drinks served in various places in Madrid (the Bombilla, q.v.), in San Sebastián (the Café de Madrid, the Café de la Marina, and the Café Kutz), and in Pamplona (the Café Kutz [q.v.] and the Café Iruña)—all these are praised for their cider and beer (48, *h:* 424–25, s.v. *Cerveza*). The narrator also reports on the private or political lives of the customers at three Parisian cafés, all of which still flourish today (beginning of twenty-first century): the Café de la Paix, at 12, Boulevard des Capucines; the Café des Deux Magots, at 170, Boulevard St. Germain; and the Café de la Rotonde, at 103, Boulevard du Montparnasse (181–82, 274; *see also* Deva).

> Bullfighters are mentioned in connection with two cafés: they congregate at the Fornos in Madrid (64) and they fight at the Kutz in Pamplona, where the narrator himself once pontificated on taurine matters (154).

Cagancho. *See* Rodríguez, Joaquín.

Cano Iriborne, Enrique (Gavira). Spanish bullfighter, 1890–1927. Investiture as *matador de toros*, in Cartagena, April 1923; confirmed in Madrid, June that same season.

Gavira was a stonecutter who became interested in bullfighting comparatively late. He was a *novillero* for eight years before advancing to the final rank of *matador de toros* in his mid-thirties. He was very talented but, in spite of the long apprenticeship, not well educated. After his promotion he was engaged for only a few fights in 1924 (thirteen corridas), seven in 1925, and six in 1926. On his first performance in 1927, on 3 July, he was fatally gored while killing his third bull, Saltador, and died on the way to the infirmary. The bull, killed by one of Gavira's colleagues, died in the ring at about the same time. During the next day's *novillada*, the public was asked to contribute money for the widow: 3,800 pesetas were gathered.[68]

> The narrator correctly identifies Gavira as a bullfighter who was gored as he killed so that both matador and bull died at the same moment (272).

Caporetto, Italy. The Italians were forced to retreat when the Austro-Hungarian army broke through their lines at Caporetto, in northeastern Italy, on 23 October 1917. Many soldiers and officers of the Second Army defected during the disordered retreat, and many more were shot by fellow Italians as defectors or on suspicion of being defectors. King Vittorio Emmanuele III commanded the tattered remains of the Italian Second Army to hold at the Piave River. Some military historians argue that the defeat at Caporetto and the ineffective holding action at the Piave were instrumental in convincing Britain and France to transfer support troops from the western front to the depleted Italian lines.

Hemingway was not present at the Battle of Caporetto, but he wrote movingly about its aftermath in *A Farewell to Arms*, whose protagonist, Frederic Henry, defected during the confusion and misery of the retreat. Hemingway reprinted this section of the novel as "The Retreat from Caporetto," in *Men at War*. *See also* Behr; Victor Emanuel.

The narrator mentions that General von Behr was killed at Caporetto (140).

Captain General of Burgos. Burgos housed the headquarters of the Civil Guard in the Sixth Military Region, which encompassed North Eastern Castille and the Basque Country, including Navarre and thus Vera and Pamplona. In 1924, that region's *capitán general* was Ricardo Burguete y Lana (1871–1937), who had been promoted to Lieutenant General (five star general) in 1922 and given the command of the First (Madrid) as well as the Sixth Military Regions. He later became Director-General of the Civil Guard and President of the Supreme Court of the Army and Navy (*Consejo Supremo del Ejército y Marina*). Burguete wrote several books on military science and theory: *Teoría y práctica de la guerra, Rectificaciones históricas, La ciencia militar ante la guerra europea*, and others.[69]

In November 1924 Burguete authorized the summary court martial of four men accused of killing two civil guards and then, when they were acquitted, he rejected the verdict and insisted that they be executed. A higher court reviewed the case and upheld Burguete, for political rather than judicial reasons. *See* Deva; Guardia Civil.

The narrator accurately reports that the (unnamed) captain general of Burgos "reversed" the decision of the military court (274).

Capt. D. S. *See* Dorman-Smith.

Carnera, Primo (Da Preem, the Ambling Alp). Italian prizefighter, 1906–1967; heavyweight champion of the world, June 1933-June 1934.

Carnera obtained the heavyweight title when he defeated Jack Sharkey; he lost it to Max Baer. A large man, 6'6" tall and 260 pounds in his prime, Carnera had been a circus strongman before he entered the world of American boxing where, untrained, uneducated, and speaking almost no English, he was an easy prey for criminal elements. His strength and stamina enabled him to win eighty-seven of the one hundred bouts of his fighting years (1928 to 1945), but many of these victories, including the 1933 victory over Sharkey which won him the heavyweight crown, were rumored to be "prearranged." The narrator of *Green Hills of Africa* comments on this fight: "Carnera knocked him out. What if nobody saw the punch?" (*GHOA*, 166).

Carnera earned more than a million dollars between 1930 and 1934, but the profits went to his managers and Carnera was legally bankrupt at the time he lost the title. He suffered two successive knockouts by Leroy Haynes in 1936 and was suspended from boxing by the New York State Athletic Commission later that year. Penniless, he left the United States, worked in vaudeville in Italy, and held other low-paying jobs during the war years. When he returned to the United States in 1946, he took up wrestling, became a referee, opened a business, and appeared in a few films, including the role of a dockside hoodlum in *On the Waterfront* (1954). Sports commentator Arthur Daley described Carnera as "a pathetic figure . . . [who] wore a tarnished crown . . . made from the brass left over from the hoods who controlled his destinies."[70]

Budd Schulberg's book *The Harder They Fall* tells the story of an innocent, ignorant Argentinian villager, El Toro Molina, "the biggest son-of-a-bitch who ever climbed into a ring. Six feet seven and three-quarters inches tall. Two hundred and eighty-five pounds" (33). The boxing novel relies on the taurine image: el Toro's final bout "had ceased to be a contest; it was a bull-fight, a thrilling demonstration of man's superiority over the beast, the giant, the great shapeless fear" (329). After he is destroyed in his final fight, Molina discovers that his entire career has yielded him less than $50. The man who discovered and exploited el Toro is called Nick Latka. Hemingway found much to dislike in the book, which he described as "a novelized life of Primo Carnera full of strange distortion due to the fear of libel."[71]

The heaviest bulls are in the "Primo Carnera class" (*h:* 443, s.v. *Kilos*).

Carnicerito (the Little Butcher). *See* Muñoz, Bernardo.

Carnicerito de México. *See* González, José.

Caro, Juan Martín. *See* Martín-Caro, Juanito.

Carrato, Mariano. Full name: Mariano Carrato Baquedano. Spanish bullfighter, 1893–1969.

An excellent banderillero, Carrato worked in the *cuadrillas* of the most renowned matadors of his time, including Valencia II (1919), Fortuna (1920), Chicuelo (1921, 1922), Nicanor Villalta (1924–27), Gitanillo de Triana (1928–31), and Manuel Bienvenida (1932–36). In 1920 he began training to become a matador himself, but he was badly gored in 1923 and abandoned the effort by 1924. He returned to his original profession as banderillero, from which he retired in 1936. He had a leg amputated in 1953.[72]

The narrator accurately describes Carrato as one of the best banderilleros of his day (201).

Carreño, Pedro. Full name: Pedro Carreño Martínez. Spanish bullfighter, 1908–30.

In 1928 Carreño, a promising *matador de novillos*, appeared in eight *novilladas*. In 1929 he performed in fifteen *novilladas*, five of them in Seville. But on his second appearance in 1930, in Ecija (Seville) on 21 May, he was violently tossed and gored by a Miura *novillo*. Realizing that his wounds were serious, perhaps fatal, Carreño asked to be taken home to Huelva (Andalucía).

There are conflicting reports about his death: one is that he died the next day in the clinic to which he had been transferred, but a more dramatic report indicates that he died en route to Huelva, where he was much loved. In that case, it is not unlikely that his body, divested of his *traje de luces* and wrapped, or partially wrapped, in a sheet from the bullring's infirmary, was carried through the town and straight into the church. This may be the basis for Hemingway's account, although I cannot confirm it.

Hemingway and Pauline were in Spain in 1929 and 1931, but not in 1930. However, the death of Carreño, like all taurine-related deaths, was widely reported in the taurine press, and Hemingway subscribed to several journals. He also owned the annual *Toros y toreros en 1930*.[73]

The narrator offers a short but vivid account of Carreño's dramatic funeral (272).

Casanova. Full name: Giovanni Giacomo Casanova de Seingalt. Italian adventurer and writer, 1725–98.

Casanova was descended from an old, well-connected family but grew up in poverty, his father having alienated the family by becoming an actor and marrying a shoemaker's daughter. Their son was intelligent, well educated, inventive, dashing, and constantly in and out of trouble. At one point he was imprisoned in Venice for spying; he made a daring escape. When his family managed to have him appointed director of the French lottery, he quickly made a fortune and then spent it all on food, clothes, travel, and glamorous love affairs which were followed by scandals, duels, and deportation. He was repeatedly rescued by an aristocratic patron. His posthumous *Mémoires* (Leipzig, 1826–38, 12 vols.) detail his "rogueries, adventures, and amours" and in the process supply interesting details about the various European societies in which he lived.[74]

Casanova captured the public imagination to such an extent that his name has become a generic term for a high-living, womanizing rogue. A similar character is Zorrilla's Don Juan Tenorio (based on the Tenorio family of Seville), who is mentioned by Pilar in *For Whom the Bell Tolls*, 92). See also Don Juan in *DS*.

The narrator credits venereal disease with keeping the populations of Casanovas and bullfighters in check (102).

Casielles, Miguel. Full name: Miguel Casielles Puerta. Spanish bullfighter, d. 1934.

Casielles's older brother, Bernardo (1895–1983), horrified his family by announcing he wanted to become a bullfighter. Overcoming stiff parental opposition, Bernardo achieved an excellent reputation as a *novillero* and was promoted to *matador de toros* at the end of the 1920 season. His descent from fame was even more spectacular than his early success: he performed in only five corridas in 1922 and wisely retired in 1924.

Probably impressed by Bernardo, his younger brother Miguel became a *matador de novillos*. He progressed well enough to reach the Madrid bullring on 28 August 1924. Less gifted than Bernardo, he was unable to maintain a career as *novillero*, let alone achieve the promotion to *matador de toros*.

Hemingway and Casielles. The afternoon that Hemingway mentions, on which Isidoro Todó (q.v.) was killed, was the *novillada* of 23 August 1931. Casielles was the youngest of the afternoon's *novilleros*, in terms of the Madrid debut which determines their seniority; hence Hemingway correctly refers to him as "The third fighter." All three *novilleros* had served at that rank for years: Alfonso Gómez since 1921, Todó since 1923, and Casielles since 1924. They were clearly unsuccessful bullfighters, and the afternoon went badly. *El Clarín* describes Casielles that afternoon: "está mal, muy mal" (bad, very bad).

Unable to succeed but unwilling to abandon bullfighting altogether, Miguel Casielles renounced his standing as *novillero* in order to become a banderillero. Acting in this capacity, he was fatally gored on 19 August 1934, in a *novillada* in the Madrid plaza of Tetuán de las Victorias.[75] He seems to have been as inept a banderillero as he was a *novillero*.

> The narrator reports that he saw Casielles perform in 1931 when he was a *matador de novillos*: he was "a complete coward" (227).

Cervantes. Full name: Miguel de Cervantes Saavedra. Spanish writer, 1547–1616. The author of *Don Quijote de la Mancha* is generally regarded as one of the most important figures of Spanish literature. For Waldo Frank's use of *Don Quijote*, see *Virgin Spain*.

> Joselito and Belmonte are to bullfighting what Cervantes and Lope de Vega are to Spanish literature (73).

Cervecería Alemana (German brewery, or bar). Address in 1920s and 1930s: Príncipe Alfonso, 6, not far from the Hotel Aguilar (q.v.) and the Hotel Victoria, perennially popular with bullfighters. The Plaza Príncipe Alfonso has since been renamed Plaza de Santa Ana, and the Cervecería Alemana, although still in its original building, now has the address Plaza Santa Ana, 6, Madrid 28012.[76]

The bar-café was established as a private club by Germans (Bavarians) at the beginning of the twentieth century. In the early 1920s it came into Spanish hands and was opened to the general public. The Plaza Santa Ana having many literary connections, the establishment was the site of literary as well as taurine *tertulias* (discussions; see "Names of Places," in the introduction to this volume). Ramón del Valle Inclán, Jacinto Benavente, the Bienvenidas, and the Dominguíns were regular patrons. In the 1950s the *cervecería* was acquired by Ramón González Peláez, and in the year 2000 it was still in the family, under the management of his son and daughter. *See also* Fornos, Café.

Hemingway and the Cervecería Alemana. In the 1960 *Life* serialization of *The Dangerous Summer*, Hemingway mentions that Domingo González Mateos, the father of Luis Miguel Dominguín, "did his business in the Cervezeria (*sic*) Alemana, a good café and beer place on the Plaza Santa Ana in Madrid which I had frequented for many years. The family lived just around the corner."[77] Mary Hemingway mentions that in 1953 "the Cervecería Alemana, the bullfighters' bar in the Plaza Santa Ana, became our rendezvous place before lunch . . . and we made friends there," including Domingo Ortega and the elder Dominguín.[78] *See also* Cafés.

The narrator praises German beer made in Madrid (*h*: 424, s.v. *Cerveza*).

Cervecería Alvarez (Madrid). Full name: Cervecería Alvarez y Alvarez, also known as Casa Alvarez. Owner in 1923: Joaquín Alvarez. Owner in 1930: Antonio Alvarez. Address: corner of Calle del Príncipe, 33 (later renumbered 27), and Calle Prado, 1. In the 1970s, the business was sold out of the Alvarez family and its name was changed to Cervecería Punto y Coma, the name under which it still operated at the end of the twentieth century. Like the Cervecería Alemana (q.v.), it faces the Plaza Santa Ana (formerly the Plaza Príncipe Alfonso).[79] The Cervecería Alvarez is near but not on the Calle Victoria (q.v.); *see also* Pasaje Alvarez.

The narrator praises the beer at the Cervecería Alvarez, which he identifies as being on Victoria Street (*h*: 424, s.v. *Cerveza*).

Cézanne, Paul. French postimpressionist painter, 1839–1906. Cézanne's landscapes depict the scenery around Bouffan, Auvers, and the gulf of Marseilles at l'Estaque, as well as the fine gardens of his father's country house, near Aix, and the surrounding countryside—his native countryside, where he spent most of his life. His innovative work influenced generations of artists, including writers like Hemingway, who mentions Cézanne often (*Torrents of Spring*, 23; *Islands in the Stream*, 382; *Garden of Eden*, 71; and most notably, *A Moveable Feast*, 13, 69, where he claims that Cézanne taught him a great deal about writing).[80] Although he acknowledges influence, Hemingway insists that each artist must create his own forms, that his work must be independent and original. Even if he is admired and imitated by others, as Cézanne most certainly has been, his reputation must be defined solely by his own work, and not by his influence on others. Thus Hemingway rejects both imitative and derivative art, and argues against the concept of "schools" or "styles." He writes, "All art is only done by the individual" (*DIA*, 99).

If art resides only in the individual artist's work, then the bullfighter's art is all the more tragic, for it ceases to exist the moment the artist ceases to perform. The performance leaves no record of itself: no canvas or script or score (*see also* Leonardo da Vinci).

Hemingway's own work disappeared when Hadley's suitcase, containing most of his early fiction, was stolen from her in 1922—a painful experience which may have made him more sensitive to the impermanence of the bullfighter's art. The loss of the manuscripts is related in *A Moveable Feast* (73–75) and is replayed in Catherine Bourne's burning of her husband's manuscripts in *The Garden of Eden*.

The narrator uses Cézanne as an example to rebut the argument that art is cumulative. He does not believe that ideas and innovations survive in the work of imitators, a position taken by those who argue that the loss of individual production is inconsequential (99).

El Chato. *See* Alonso Bertolí, Rafael. Victoriano Roger (q.v.) was known as Chato, but not El Chato.

Chaves. *See* Tamarit, Francisco.

Chicuelo. Father and son shared the same professional nickname. *See* Jiminiz (*sic*), Manuel. The bullfighter Manuel Jiménez Díaz (Chicuelo II, 1929–60, see in *DS*) is no relation.

Chiquito de la Audiencia. Because his father was an official in the Sala de la Audiencia (official Courtroom and Reception Hall) in Madrid, his bullfighting son Juanito was given this nickname. *See* Martín-Caro, Juanito.

Christian Endeavor. Full name: Christian Endeavor Societies. Original name: Young People's Society of Christian Endeavor. It was founded by Francis E. Clark in 1881, in Portland, Maine, "for the purpose of promoting spiritual life among young people." Clark began the society as a small group in his Congregational church, but the idea spread to other churches in the United States. It was soon an interdenominational and international phenomenon, requiring the formation of the World's Christian Endeavor Union in 1895. Clark was tireless in promoting the organization, about which he wrote several books whose titles chronicle its espansion: *The Children and the Church* (1882), *Looking out on Life* (1883), *Young People's Prayer Meetings* (1884), *Some Christian Endeavor Saints* (1889), *Christian Endeavor Manual* (1903), *The Young People's Christian Endeavor, Where It Began* (1903), *World Wide Endeavor* (1895), *A New Way Round an Old World* (1900), and *Christian Endeavor in All Lands: Record of Twenty-five Years of Progress* (1907).

The organization's motto is "For Christ and the Church," and the societies "have done much, especially in the non-episcopal churches, to prepare young men and women for active services in the Church."[81]

Hemingway and the Christian Endeavor Society. Ernest Hemingway came from a religious family: one uncle was a missionary and his parents were committed Christians. As a schoolboy, he was a member of the Christian Endeavor Society in the Third Congregational Church of Oak Park. Their activities included a Bible reading contest. Ernest did not finish first, but he did read "every word" of the King James Bible. A few years later, as a high school senior, he was active in the Plymouth League, another church group.[82] *See also* Yale; YMCA.

> The narrator fears that his outline for proper behavior at a bullfight sounds like a Christian Endeavor manifesto. To counter this, he advocates illegal behavior as well (163).

Chucho. Diminutive for the popular first name Jesús (224). *See* Solórzano, Jesús.

Circus. The text mentions circuses which, like bullfights, fall under the generic name *espectáculos* but which the narrator obviously considers a far inferior production (7, 151, 265, *h:* 421, s.v. *Caballero en Plaza*).

Citroën. *See* Palace Hotel.

Civil Guard. *See* Guardia Civil.

El Clarín (The Bugle). A taurine weekly that pledged itself "to transmit to posterity all which is good and bad" in tauromachy. Founded in Madrid in 1850 by don Joaquín Simán, it was one of the earliest taurine journals. Periodicals by this name were also established in Cádiz in 1885 and in nearby Puerto de Santa María in 1888.[83]

The journal Hemingway refers to was the more modern weekly *El Clarín*, established in Valencia in 1922. Its subtitle described it as a *Semanario taurino defensor de la verdad* (weekly taurine journal, defender of the truth). The journal was lavishly illustrated, with frequent two-page picture spreads of individual bullfighters. Its photojournalism, which Hemingway singles out for praise, was far better than its prose, which was informal and colloquial. Readers are often addressed directly; silly, rhymed headlines appear frequently; and the general tone is one of breathless admiration for all bulls, bull breeders, and bullfighters, with the notable exception of Domingo Ortega.

Hemingway and El Clarín. Hemingway read *El Clarín* in Spain and liked it sufficiently to maintain a subscription when he returned home to Key West.[84]

Almost every year, the journal published an almanac summarizing the season and featuring important personalities; it also published several supplements each year. Hemingway saved one such undated *número extraordinario* (probably from spring 1924) that profiles Luis Fuentes Bejarano, Nicanor Villalta (centerfold), Martín Agüero, Gavira, and others. The statistics and the photographs that dominated these special issues gave them a weight and seriousness lacking in the regular issues.[85]

In 1931 *El Clarín* was openly hostile to that season's star, Domingo Ortega, and to his manager, Domingo González (qq.v.); this may account for Hemingway's own hostile attitude toward them. Hemingway's claim that the journal was "only a propaganda sheet" (*h:* 475) whose contents were determined by financial interests contradicts his insistence that Ortega's success was due to "many thousand columns of paid publicity" (171) in an "elaborate press campaign" for which his manager "was spending much money" (168).

The Biblioteca Nacional, Madrid, has a fairly complete collection of the Valencia *El Clarín*, 1923–36, although some pages and even whole issues seem to be missing. The journal's pages carry no dates, page numbers, or other headings or footers, so that it is difficult to determine dates and sequences and to prepare precise documentation.

The narrator identifies *El Clarín* as a periodical published in Valencia: he admires its photographs but dismisses it as "a propaganda sheet" (*h:* 475, s.v. *Revistas*).

Clowns. *See* Altrock, Nick; Circus; Fratellini; *Mojigangas.*

Cocteau, Jean. French poet, novelist, dramatist, critic, filmmaker, and artist, 1889–1963. Among the best-known works of this versatile genius are the plays *Orphée* (1926), *La machine infernale* (1934), *Les parents terribles* (1938); the novel *Les enfants terribles* (1929); the long poem *L'Ange Heurtebise* (1925); and the films *Le sang d'un poète* (1932), *La belle et la bete* (1945), and *Orphée* (1950). Cocteau also wrote several ballets and an opera-oratorio, *Oedipus Rex* (1927), with music by Igor Stravinsky. In the 1950s he painted frescoes in various public buildings and chapels. During the last decade or so of his life, his drawings often featured bullfighters.

Cocteau was interested in classical myths, fantasy, religion, and the nature of poetry, of human relationships, and of death. He was an opium addict and a homosexual.

> Discussing the meaning of the word *decadent*, the narrator cites an incident in which Cocteau denounced as "decadent" a man who slept with women (71; see also Radiguet, Raymond).

Comisario. There were two famous bulls by this name, both very strong. One was pic-ed eight times and killed four horses in the process, on 19 September 1887, in Madrid. Hemingway's anecdote is not about this Comisario, but about the one that jumped into the stands of the Barcelona bullring on 14 April 1895. Cossío claims that this bull was shot to death by the Civil Guard, a detail repeated by Silva Aramburu. Carralero and Borge, however, write that the bull suffered repeated injuries: first a saber wound, inflicted by Isidro Silva, a municipal guard; then a gunshot wound, inflicted by Ubaldo Vigueres: the bullet passed through the bull's neck muscle (*morrillo*) and lodged in the chest of Juan Recasens, killing him. And finally, death by sword stroke, while the bull was held down by Vicente Ferrer. In Carralero and Borge's words: "un tiro . . . traspasó el morrillo . . . Comisario . . . fué muerto á cachetazos" (a shot passed through the neck muscle . . . Comisario . . . was killed by dagger strokes; *Toros célebres*, 92). Hemingway follows Carralero and Borge's account closely on this point.

But Hemingway's text differs from Carralero and Borge's on several points. Their Juan Recasens appears as Recaseus in *DIA*, probably a typographical error. Hemingway gives Juan a sudden, dramatic death ("died on the spot"), although Carralero and Borge merely say that the bullet lodged in Juan's left chest. While Hemingway's deduction as to the likely outcome of such a wound is probably accurate, it is his own contribution to the story, and not a fact which Carralero and Borge or any other taurine historian reports.

The biggest difference between *Death in the Afternoon* and *Toros célebres* is the absence of Vicente Ferrer, mentioned by Carralero and Borge but not by Hemingway. Hemingway missed a good story here, as Ferrer was a daredevil *matador de novillos*, given to "toda clase de suertes" (all sorts of techniques), such as pole-vaulting over the bull (*salto a la garrocha*) and engaging him in direct physical battle, with kicks and punches. He was a great favorite in Barcelona, where he performed often and where his unorthodox maneuvers drew much applause. Holding down the bull by the horns was one of his specialties, and this seems to be what he did to Comisario, undoubtedly delighting the crowd.

Not surprisingly, Ferrer was frequently gored. In 1897, he was described as "el torero más castigado de los toros que se ha conocido, que se conoce y que se conocerá. Así y todo aun no sabe lo que es tener miedo" (the most frequently injured bullfighter ever known, in the past, the present, or the future. And even so, he does not know fear).

Missing from Carralero and Borge's report is the fact that when Comisario escaped, he was being fought by Antonio Fuentes (q.v.) who, with his customary presence of mind, followed his bull into the stands, where he was subdued. Ferrer, who was never promoted to *matador de toros*, would not have appeared on the same bill with Fuentes. He was in the plaza as an unarmed spectator, and attacked the bull with his bare hands. The sword that finally finished off Comisario was wielded by Fuentes, who then returned to the arena to continue the serious business of the afternoon's bullfight.[86] Nancy Bredendick argues that "The scenes from *Toros célebres* give us images of a bullfight gone crazily awry. . . . We have excitement but no art."[87]

Beige and red bulls sometimes have what is called "ojo de perdiz" (eye of partridge), a ring around the eye that is lighter in color than the rest of the animal's pelt).

The narrator describes Comisario and his exploits (111).

Concha y Sierra, doña Concepción de la. Spanish bull breeder, d. 1966.

The Concha y Sierra family have been bull breeders since the nineteenth century, when two brothers, Joaquín and Fernando, established their herds, each working with a different strain.

Joaquín: Vistahermosa. Don Joaquín, who favored Vistahermosa stock, began breeding bulls in 1823. His bulls were fought in Madrid

under his brand and colors (sky blue and pink) for the first time on 9
September 1850. He died in 1861, but subsequent owners—his
nephew Joaquín Pérez de la Concha (d. 1899) and his nephew's descendants—have kept the breed and the rights to the brand and colors
in the family. In Hemingway's day, like today (beginning of twenty-
first century), the bulls were registered under the name Pérez de la
Concha, though their seniority dates back to 1850. Their Vistahermosa blood has been strengthened by the addition of several Santa
Coloma cows and a Santa Coloma bull in 1925. *See also* Hechicero.

Fernando: Vazqueño Stock. The two women
Hemingway identifies as famous bull breeders
are the wife and daughter of Joaquín's brother,
Fernando, who established his herd in 1873, basing it on *vazqueño* stock (i.e., from the herd established in 1757 by Gregorio Vázquez and
developed by his son Vicente José Vázquez),
which he had acquired from Vicente Taviel de
Andrade. Don Fernando's bulls were fought in the Madrid bullring
for the first time on 10 April 1882 (the herd's *antigüedad*). When
Fernando died in 1887, the herd was divided into two parts: one was
acquired by the Marqués de Villamarta (q.v.), and the other, which
included the rights to his brand (a large C with an S inside it), colors
(white, lead gray, and black), and therefore the *antigüedad* or seniority (10 April 1882), was inherited by his widow, doña Celsa Fontfrede, the famous "widow of Concha y Sierra." She managed the
breed for forty-two years, from 1887 until her death in 1929. The fine
herd was inherited by her daughter, doña Concepción de Concha y
Sierra y Fontfrede, who owned it from 1929 until 1966.

Such was the renown of the Concha y Sierra ranch that they were
invited to supply a bull for the inaugural corrida of the new Madrid
plaza, Las Ventas, on 17 June 1931. This marked the first occasion
that the daughter's name appeared on the bullring posters. After doña
Concepción died in 1966, the herd was sold several times. Because
these subsequent owners also acquired rights to the original brand
and colors, the current herd's seniority remains the same, 1882. And
because the bulls had been in the same family for so long, they are
still known as Concha y Sierra bulls.[88] For a discussion of the rela-

tionship between ownership and *antigüedad*, see "Bulls and Bull Breeding," in the introduction to this volume.

A Concha y Sierra bull named *Carbonero* entered the history books on 2 October 1910 by losing an ear to Vicente Pastor (q.v.). This was the first "serious" ear awarded in the Madrid bullring (see Trophies in *DS*).

The narrator correctly includes both doña Concepción and her famous mother among the leading bull breeders of his day (132; *see also* 158). He mentions Hechicero, a bull from this ranch (110).

Corrochano, Alfredo. Full name: Alfredo Corrochano Miranda. Spanish bullfighter, 1912–2000. Investiture as *matador de toros*, 28 February 1932, in Castellón de la Plana, granted by Marcial Lalanda and witnessed by Domingo Ortega; confirmed in Madrid, May that same year.

Because he was the son of *ABC*'s taurine critic, Gregorio Corrochano (q.v. following entry), Alfredo entered the profession with ready-made friends and enemies. Very early on, his thorough education evidenced itself and his elegant work won him contracts in important plazas. He fought in twenty-two *novilladas* in 1929, sixteen in 1930, and thirty-two in 1931, his last season as *novillero*. His Madrid debut as *novillero* took place on 19 July of that year. The Madrid public was loudly hostile to him or, more precisely, to his relationship to the critic of Madrid's *ABC*. Although this antagonism added stress to an already stressful event, the young man produced a cool, professional performance, excelling with the cape and the muleta and earning good critical marks. When he appeared in Madrid one week later, the public was kinder and Alfredo was again praiseworthy, leaving no doubt that he was ready for his promotion, which duly occurred at the beginning of the next season.

After his promotion, Alfredo fought seventeen corridas in 1932 and twenty in 1933, but he was badly gored early in the 1934 season and had to cancel most of his performances: he appeared in only fifteen corridas that season (including one magnificent success in Madrid, when he shared the bill with Belmonte) and in thirteen in 1935. He did not perform in bullrings during or after the Spanish Civil War, which suggests that he shared his father's Republican orientation; an attempted comeback in 1949 was abandoned after two lackluster corridas.

Alfredo was not always able to control the bull or win over his audiences. Cossío attributes the first drawback to Corrochano's short stature and the second to his father's reputation. Cossío focuses on strengths: Alfredo is "desigual en su estilo . . . Es muy buen banderillero . . . [y] un formidable muletero . . . es el que más y mejor usa de la mano izquierda en estos tiempos. En el pase natural . . . es la perfección misma" (he is an uneven stylist . . . a very good banderillero . . . and formidable with the muleta . . . excels with the left hand and embodies perfection in the *pase natural* [a muleta pass]). Cossío is ominously silent about Alfredo's cape and sword work.[89]

Hemingway and Corrochano. In 1931, Hemingway's last season in Spain before publishing *Death in the Afternoon*, Alfredo was still a *novillero*. Hemingway was in Madrid when Alfredo first performed there, on 19 and 26 July 1931.

> The narrator explains that as the son of Gregorio Corrochano, Alfredo attracted much interest when he first appeared in Madrid in 1931. He reports that Corrochano worked well with the banderillas and muleta but not with the cape or sword, and predicts that he will soon lose his popularity (229–30).

Corrochano, Gregorio. Full name: Gregorio Corrochano Ortega (Arévalo). Spanish newspaper critic, editor, author, 1882–1961.

After a stint at the newspaper *La mañana*, 1905–12, Corrochano wrote taurine criticism for the Madrid daily *ABC* (q.v.) for almost a quarter of a century, 1912–36. When his own son, Alfredo Corrochano (q.v. above), started performing, Gregorio Corrochano gradually withdrew from taurine criticism.[90] In the late 1930s he moved to Tangier, where he founded and directed the daily paper *España*, 1938–45. Like Hemingway and other Republican sympathizers, he returned to Spain in the 1950s. He wrote taurine criticism for *ABC*'s magazine, *Blanco y negro*, including reports on many of the corridas that Hemingway saw in the last decade of his life.

Corrochano was a literate, perceptive, and philosophical critic. His reviews are carefully constructed and reasoned, larded with relevant historical and literary references, and always interesting (see, for example, the entries for Rivalry and Trophies, in *DS*). Corrochano was not committed to any particular torero or any particular style. Instead, he reported, analyzed and discussed without partisanship.[91] *¿Qué es torear?* (Madrid, 1953), collects his more theoretical essays as well as his overview of the art of José Gómez Ortega and Domingo Ortega. His last comments on the art were published posthumously as *Teoría de las corridas de toros* (Madrid, 1962).[92]

Hemingway and Corrochano. Like Hemingway, Corrochano saw two generations of Ordóñezes. When Cayetano Ordóñez first appeared, Corrochano coined the famous phrase, "Se llama Cayetano y es de Ronda" (His name is Cayetano [like Cayetano Sanz] and he hails from Ronda [the home of Pedro Romero]). Corrochano praised Cayetano's son Antonio when he did well and, unlike Hemingway, chided him when he did not (for Corrochano's praise of Antonio, see the entries for Madrid and Málaga; for his criticism, see Jerez de la Frontera, all in *DS*; see also the entry for Ordóñez, Antonio, especially endnote 214, in *DS*).

In *Cuando suena el clarín* (Madrid, 1961), Corrochano took Hemingway to task for some of his remarks in *The Dangerous Summer*, such as his attacks on Manolete and Dominguín, his emphasis on money, his misrepresentation of the Ordóñez-Dominguín rivalry, and his lack of understanding of the finer points of the bullfight as it was practiced in 1959. Hemingway apologists like Angel Capellán believe that Corrochano's negative remarks about Hemingway were politically motivated, but I find most of Corrochano's objections to be quite reasonable.

Hemingway owned only one of Corrochano books, *¿Qué es torear?* (Madrid, 1953).[93]

The narrator correctly identifies Gregorio Corrochano as a taurine critic for *ABC* and the father of Alfredo Corrochano (89, 229–30).

Corte, Conde de la. Full name: Agustín Mendoza y Montero, the Conde (count) de la Corte. Spanish bull breeder, d. 1964.

In 1920, the Count de la Corte acquired the Marquesa of Tamarón's ranch in Zafra, Badajoz, which was stocked with Parladé animals. These highly regarded Vistahermosa bulls were much in demand in Spain's plazas.

The Count de la Corte replaced the Tamarón brand and colors with his own (green, scarlet, and gold) as soon as he acquired the herd, and his bulls appeared in important Spanish bullrings all through the 1920s. But he did not establish a new *antigüedad* for them until the fiesta of San Isidro, on 17 May 1928, when he presented his first full corrida in Madrid. For bulls, as for bullfighters, Madrid establishes seniority.

In 1931 the Conde de la Corte supplied forty-eight *toros de lidia* and five *novillos* to important plazas. Their performance "No ha podido ser más brillante" (could not have been better). The bulls are still (1995) registered as belonging to the "Herederos" (heirs) of the Count.[94]

The narrator identifies this aristocrat as a leading bull breeder (132).

Costillares. *See* Rodríguez, Joachín.

Cova, Enriqueta de la. Twentieth-century Spanish bull breeder.

In 1921, doña Enriqueta's husband, the respected bull breeder Félix Moreno Ardanuy (q.v.), acquired an important herd which he registered in his wife's name. This herd traces its pedigree to the herds of Joaquín de la Serna and Rafael Lafitte Castro, bull breeders of the early 1800s whose bulls were fought in important bullrings throughout the nineteenth century. In 1878, Valentín Collantes bought stock descended from both these ranches to begin his own herd. He increased the herd considerably, adding Murube and Vista-hermosa (qq.v.) stock. Collantes's son sold the herd, which passed

through several more owners before being registered to doña Enriqueta in 1921.[95] Her husband strengthened it with Lesaca-Saltillo blood, and the fine bulls earned accolades throughout the 1920s and 1930s. The herd's inaugural Madrid corrida took place on 7 July 1926; the colors are black and white.

In 1931, Hemingway's last taurine season before the publication of *Death in the Afternoon*, fourteen de la Cova bulls and three *novillos* were fought, all in prestigious *plazas de toros*: "Poco, pero bueno" (Not many, but good ones).[96]

The narrator correctly identifies doña Enriqueta de la Cova as the owner of an important herd (132).

Critics. From the beginning of his career Hemingway was intensely aware of the power of critics. As a young author he cultivated Edmund (Bunny) Wilson, who had praised his early work,[97] but from the beginning of his career his tendency was to attack, disparage, and discount critics. He lashed out quickly and fiercely at negative criticism and did not, at least publicly, express pleasure when his work was lauded: praise makes American writers "impotent" (*GHOA*, 24). In the 1920s and 1930s, when the critical establishment was a generation older than he, his rejection of critics was visceral—particularly when they echoed his parents' objections to his work.

Hemingway had no tolerance at all for contemporary authors (the competition) and for compliments paid to writers other than himself. His competitive jealousy is a strong motif in *Death in the Afternoon*. It appears most clearly in his contempt for travel writers, to whom he fears he will be compared, and for taurine critics, whom he accuses of accepting bribes, exalting dead matadors, and devaluing living artists. For more detail on Hemingway's response to his critics, *see* Humanism, Naturalism; Huxley, Aldous; Meier-Graefe, Julius; Narratee; Narrator; and Woolf, Virginia. For his attacks on writers who have achieved popularity or critical esteem, *see* Frank, Waldo David; Longfellow, Henry Wadsworth; and Whittier, John Greenleaf; *see also* Authors; Boxing. For taurine critics, *see* Corrochano, Gregorio; and Hernández Ramírez, Rafael.

Hemingway continued his quarrel with the literary and critical establishment in *Green Hills of Africa* (1935), where he attacks the American literary canon—"Emerson, Hawthorne, Whittier, and Company"—with the glowing exception of Mark Twain, and dismisses critics as "the lice who crawl on literature" (*GHOA*, 21, 109).[98] The attacks continued in *A Moveable Feast*, where F. Scott Fitzgerald, John Dos Passos, Gertrude Stein, and other acclaimed writers are mauled. Minor writers, like Evan Shipman, managed to hold on to Hemingway's affection.

Hemingway's fiction is equally belligerent. In *The Torrents of Spring*, the attack focuses on Sherwood Anderson, with several swipes at critics, editors, and other writers. In *The Sun Also Rises*, his ire falls on H. L. Mencken, who had rejected his submissions. In *The Garden of Eden*, Catherine Bourne repeats the argument presented in *Green Hills of Africa* when she argues that critics are destructive even, or especially, when their evaluations are complimentary (*GOE*, 23–25); she burns their reviews of her husband's work. The hateful, bloodthirsty sharks in *The Old Man and the Sea* have been said to represent the critics, a reading that Hemingway rejected, as he rejected almost all attempts to interpret or evaluate his work.

Hemingway was expecting unfavorable reviews for *Death in the Afternoon*, including comparisons with Waldo Frank's *Virgin Spain* (q.v.). He was pleasantly surprised that the book was, on the whole, well received. It sold well, though not as spectacularly as he would have liked.

> The narrator attacks taurine critics as corrupt, susceptible to bribery, and unfair to living artists (163–64, 240–44, et passim).

Cruz Blanca (beer). *Cervecerías* were often named after the popular beers they served: *see*, for example, the entry on Aguilar Beer. Madrid's city guides for 1923 and 1959 list a bar called Cruz Blanca, at 142 Alcalá.[99] *See also* Drinks.

> The narrator admires the beer Cruz Blanca, brewed in Santander (*h:* 424, s.v. *Cerveza*).

– D –

da Veiga, Simão. *See* Veiga, Simão da.

da Vinci, Leonardo. *See* Leonardo da Vinci.

The Dain Curse. Novel by Dashiell Hammett (q.v.), published in 1929.
The word *killed*, which upsets the narrator's son (228) appears often in *The Dain Curse*. Chapters Six and Seven are particularly full of killing. The novel presents the body of Edgar Leggett, an apparent suicide who has left a letter in which he confesses to murdering his first wife and describes three other murders of which he has been, so

he says, wrongly accused. The first victim died "of starvation and exposure . . . on a flimsy raft"; his death enabled Leggett, his fellow traveler, to survive. The second man was killed by John Edge; and the third victim was Edge himself, who was blackmailing Leggett and whom Leggett killed "in self-defense: he struck me first." Leggett also confesses that he intended to kill a private investigator, Upton, but that another investigator, Ruppert, who also intended to blackmail Leggett, had "saved me from killing Upton by himself killing him"—whereupon Leggett killed Ruppert. It all sounds rather like an opera.

The problem of who killed Ruppert and Lily Dain (the first Mrs. Leggett) dominates the next chapter. Several people might have done it: Lily's sister Alice, who became the second Mrs. Leggett; Lily's daughter Gabrielle, who happens to be a drug addict; and Leggett himself. The chapter offers vivid details of a small family seething with sibling rivalry, sexual jealousy, duplicity, deceit, and psychological abuse. At the end of the chapter, Alice Dain Leggett is killed and Gabrielle Leggett slumps to the floor in a faint.

Even with the substitution of *umpty-umped* for the word *killed*, this seems a peculiar text for parents to read out loud to a little boy, pointing us to the question of censorship, both of subject matter and of language—a question that plagued Hemingway throughout his career. Hemingway chafed under critical objections to his "rough" characters (hunters, killers, bullfighters, drunks, boxers, prostitutes), subject matter (war, bullfighting, sex, pain, violence, death), and language. He acquiesced with ill grace to Scribner's restrictions of his "words" (e.g., "shit," "cocksucker," and "balls") in *A Farewell to Arms,* and his resentment boiled over years later when James Jones's *From Here to Eternity* (1951) was praised for its forthright language. He angrily wrote to Charles Scribner, "Boy I can remember when Scribners cut Go Fuck yourself out of A Farewell to Arms and all the different times when blanks were left in soldier talk . . . Then along comes this boy and he is allowed to use them all and the critics say, 'This is the first man with the courage to write as soldiers talk, etc.' They should say this is the first man Scribner's allowed to say 'Go fuck yourself.' "[100]

Hemingway and his publishers had similar arguments over "words" in *Death in the Afternoon.* When the book was published,

Hemingway provided his publishers with a form letter to be sent to readers who complained about its language. Addressed to "Dear Mr. —," the letter justified his use of "certain words no longer a part of the usual written language" because they "are very much a part of the vocabulary of the people I was writing about."[101]

In view of all this, it seems that Hemingway uses *The Dain Curse* to debate the issue of censorship, and he does so on a variety of (contradictory) levels. The narrator speaks freely about a real death in front of his young son but soon regrets his lack of self-censorship: this suggests a justification of censorship, or at least of parental censorship. However, the narrator rejects even parental censorship by applauding his wife's continued reading of a violent, death-filled text to the boy.

The passage suggests that Hemingway distinguishes between death in books (which even children can deal with) and in the real world (which they can't). This is an uncharacteristic distinction for Hemingway, who considered literature a powerful force. And the passage also contradicts Hemingway's continued battle against linguistic censorship by endorsing the repeated, formulaic substitution of a nonsense word, *umpty-ump*, for *death* or *killed*.

The effectiveness of literature (the novel, the essay) and literary techniques (repetition, familiarization) in inuring an audience to painful truth may itself be a justification for *Death in the Afternoon*. Neither the child nor the reader of *Death in the Afternoon* sees death; it is mediated by a friendly, authoritative voice—that of the narrator or the (step)mother—which substitutes foreign or nonsense words for the violent actions themselves. Thus the subject matter itself remains uncensored; the language is transparently modified; and the combination soothes and strengthens the audience, enabling it to accept what it fears. This seems a justification of the compromises, mostly linguistic, that Hemingway worked out with Max Perkins and Charles Scribner. But Hemingway also attacks these compromises, by showing them at work with a very young audience, a child seven years old. He may be suggesting that, by censoring their author's language, Perkins and Scribner were assuming the parental role and thus pandering to, and perpetuating the immaturity of the reading audience. *See also* Hemingway, John Hadley Nicanor.

The narrator claims that by substituting *umpty-umped* for *killed* while she read *The Dain Curse* out loud, Pauline Hemingway helped Hemingway's son overcome his upset over the death of Isidoro Todó (228).

D'Artagnan. In Dumas's *The Three Musketeers*, D'Artagnan is the young, self-confident hero who was accepted as the fourth musketeer by Athos, Porthos, and Aramis. He emerges unscathed from a variety of duels and other dangerous adventures.

The comparison of D'Artagnan with Joselito is not far-fetched. Joselito triumphed so consistently that he seemed immune to the dangers offered by the bulls. His work seemed so easy and effortless that the public was angered that such high prices were charged for a performance that, as far as they could see, involved no risk, difficulty, or danger.

That such a bullfighter should be killed by a bull was incomprehensible: Belmonte himself rejected the news as "nonsense." When he finally understood that Joselito had been killed, he "broke into sobs and wept as I had never wept before in my life." Bullfighters, taurine critics, and the general public responded with "terror . . . a strange reaction of collective remorse . . . exaggerated nervousness . . . fanatical anxiety for the lives of bullfighters." Corrochano, a fine observer and theorist of the evanescent art, describes the despair that gripped Joselito's fellow matadors: "Si a Joselito, el maestro, le ha matado un toro, a ellos ¿qué va a sucederles?" (If Joselito, the master, has been killed by a bull, what will happen to them?).[102] Joselito had dominated bulls so expertly, consistently, and gracefully throughout his career, that it was unimaginable that a bull would ever get the better of him. *See also* Gómez Ortega, José.

Although the comparison with D'Artagnan suggests that Hemingway had seen Joselito perform, he obviously had not: Joselito was killed on 16 May 1920. But three years later, when Hemingway went to Spain to see his first bullfights, the newspapers were full of Joselito.

To give a sense of Joselito's mastery of all aspects of bullfighting, the narrator refers to D'Artagnan: "You did not worry about him" (212–13; *see also* Dumas, Alexandre).

David, Alfredo. Full name: Alfredo David Puchades. Spanish bullfighter, 1895–1978.

The son of a butcher, David opted for the bullring when he was a child. His original ambition was to be a matador but he realized he was unsuited for that rank and decided to be a *peón*, a member of a matador's *cuadrilla*. In this capacity he was an enormous success.

For more than thirty years David worked for the most famous matadors of his time, including Varelito (1918–20), Granero (1921), Fortuna (1922), Algabeño (1923), Marcial Lalanda (1924–27), Vicente Barrera (1928–35), Domingo Ortega (1935–40), Manolete (1941–47), and Luis Miguel González (Dominguín) (1948–51). He retired in 1965, at age seventy-one. In his long career he was gored only three times.

Critics describe David as brave, intelligent, strong (particularly in the legs), and thoroughly knowledgeable about bulls. Cossío heaps praise on him: he was "excelente, extraordinario . . . uno de los mejores de . . . todas las épocas" (excellent, extraordinary . . . one of the best of all times). Like Blanquet and Carrato (qq.v.), he was an accomplished banderillero.[103]

Hemingway and the Fight at the Café Kutz (between Maera and David). Since Hemingway first came to Pamplona in 1923 and Maera died at the end of 1924, the fight Hemingway mentions could only have occurred during the *sanfermines* of those two years. Maera performed in Pamplona's *sanfermines* both those years, and David, who was a member of Algabeño's *cuadrilla*, was also in town for both those *sanfermines*.

In 1923, Maera and Algabeño coincided in Pamplona from at least 10 to 13 July. The fight may well have occurred a day or two later, at the end of the fiesta.

It is more likely that the fight occurred in 1924, when Maera and Algabeño again coincided in Pamplona. David was still in Algabeño's *cuadrilla* that July, and Maera had recently hired Antonio García (Bombita IV, q.v.), the notorious strikebreaker during the previous year's banderilleros' strike. The galley proofs of *Death in the Afternoon* mention that Maera fought David and Juan de Lucas; this last name was deleted when the book was published, but it is important: Juan de Lucas (b. 1893) was a banderillero in the *cuadrilla* of Ricardo Anlló (Nacional, q.v.), who also performed in the *sanfermines* of 1924 (he did not come to Pamplona in 1923).

Lucas had been and probably still was the president of the Picadors' and Banderilleros' Union, from which Antonio García (who was now in Maera's *cuadrilla*) had been expelled. The strike had been settled by 1924, but feelings were still strong: it seems certain that the fight between Maera, David, and Juan de Lucas was about the strike. Antonio García was probably involved, and other banderilleros, picadors, and perhaps even matadors and aficionados were drawn into the fray. A local paper, *El Diario de Navarra* (July 1924), remarked that the fight turned into a free-for-all, an "espectáculo lamentable."[104]

Hemingway, who read taurine journals and attended the *sanfermines* of 1923 and 1924, must have been aware of the banderilleros' strike. For other allusions to the labor unrest of the early 1920s, *see* Noy de Sucre.

The narrator would have liked to include more material on the fight between Maera and Alfredo David (272–73).

de Vega, Lope. *See* Lope de Vega.

Death in the Afternoon. The present book is a taurine manual for English-speaking peoples, perhaps the best one ever written. But it discusses a wide range of other subjects as well: critics and criticism, history and the writing of history, luck, skill, character, and, above all, death and art. It is, in every way, the "very big book" Hemingway promised Perkins.

Hemingway mentioned this book early in his career, in his very first letter to Max Perkins, while he was still under contract to Boni & Liveright. Not having yet written *The Torrents of Spring* or *The Sun Also Rises*, he attempted to interest Perkins is the as-yet-unbegun *Death in the Afternoon*: "I hope some day to have a sort of Doughty's Arabia Deserta of the Bull Ring, a very big book with some wonderful pictures." In December 1926 he seemed more eager to work on this project than on the collection of short stories that Perkins wanted. He described the organization and audience of "the bull fight book" but recognized that "it won't be ready for a long time."[105] *Men without Women* (1927) and *A Farewell to Arms* (1929) preceded *Death in the Afternoon* into print.

Published in 1932, *Death in the Afternoon* is the first and longest of Hemingway's nonfiction works. It is written in the first person and presents a narrator who is named Hemingway, shares most of Hemingway's family ties and life experiences, and contributes not a little to the persona Hemingway constructed for his contemporary American audience. *See also* Narratee; Narrator.

The book surprised Hemingway by selling well in the United States. It was also well received in Spain: Tomás Orts Ramos (Uno al Sesgo) gave it a long and glowing review in *La fiesta brava* (7 April 1933) and repeated the praise in his annotated "Bibliografía taurina" (1933).[106]

The narrator, himself a writer, refers frequently to his current narrative (4, 7–8, 179, 270–78, *h:* 517).

Delgado, José (Pepe Hillo). Full name: José Delgado Guerra. Spanish bullfighter, 1754–1801. The nickname is a variant of the diminutive for his first name, Josefillo or Josep-hillo. Pepe being the common nickname for José, Josefillo became Pepe-Hillo.

Unlike Costillares and Romero, the other two great matadors of the eighteenth century, Pepe-Hillo was not born into a taurine family. Even so, his *afición* manifested itself very early, and Costillares, who saw him as a child, recognized his talent and undertook his education. In 1770, when he was just sixteen years old, Pepe-Hillo performed with Costillares in the Córdoba bullring, thus achieving the status of *matador de toros*. A few years later, when the dispute between Pedro Romero (q.v.) and Costillares resulted in Pedro Romero's absence from Madrid, Pepe-Hillo performed with his master at the court.

Graceful, talented, and courageous, Pepe-Hillo quickly became as popular as Pedro Romero, with whom he performed frequently. He was a southerner, from the outskirts of Seville, and displayed all the grace and superstition traditionally associated with Sevillian bullfighters. The contrast to the more sober Ronda school or style of bullfighting represented by Pedro Romero guaranteed an interesting bullfight.

By 1799, Pepe-Hillo was the undisputed star of the ring: Costillares was in ill health, Romero had retired, and no younger man had the talent, skill, or popularity to challenge him. On 11 May 1801 he was terribly gored in the chest and abdomen. He died within minutes.

The important book, *La tauromaquia o Arte de torear de Pepe-Hillo* (1796), was written by Pepe-Hillo's admirer and friend, José de la Tixera. Its definition of the rules and theory of the bullfight are based on Pepe-Hillo's performances and pronouncements but, writes Cossío, "es seguro que Pepe-Hillo no la escribió, ya que apenas si sabía dibujar toscamente su firma" (Pepe-Hillo certainly did not write it, as he could barely sign his own name).[107] For other ghost-written *Tauromaquias*, *see* Guerra Bejarano, Rafael.

The narrator mentions that Pepe-Hillo's book on the bullfight was written by someone else (*h:* 483, s.v. *Tauromachia, sic*).

Desperdicios. The bullfighter Manuel Domínguez (1816–86) was known by this nickname, but Hemingway's reference is to Aureliano López Becerra (Desperdicios), Spanish journalist and lawyer, b. 1882.

Aurelio López began writing for the Bilbao paper *La Gaceta del Norte* at the turn of the century and became its director in 1910, a position he held into the 1940s and perhaps even longer. Because of its Catholic, right wing orientation, the newspaper was ransacked by the Republicans during the Spanish Civil War. For the same reason, it flourished under the Franco regime.

Under the byline "Desperdicios," López also wrote humorous, witty taurine articles, reviews, and occasional pieces for *La Gaceta del Norte* and other papers. He also wrote several humorous books: *De compras con mi mujer* (Going Shopping with My Wife), *Ha llegado el Sr. López* (Mr. López is Here), *Los ingleses y los toros* (The English and the Bulls), *Los italianos y los toros* (The Italians and the Bulls, Bilbao, 1935), and *El arte de torear de "Botines"* ("Botines" and the Art of Bullfighting, Bilbao, 1913; 2nd ed. 1943).[108]

The narrator praises Desperdicios as the "wittiest" of the taurine critics (276).

Deva. Modern spelling: Deba. Correct setting for the events Hemingway locates at Deva: Vera de Bidasoa, a town in the province of Navarra, on the Bidasoa River and near the French border. The events that Hemingway incorrectly locates in Deva (*DIA*, 274) actually occurred in Vera, on the night of 6–7 November 1924. The events are complicated and must be seen in the context of the social unrest and political intrigue that characterized Primo de Rivera's dictatorship.

The *coup d'etat* of September 1923 which brought Primo de Rivera to power was followed by revolutionary plots, several of them hatched in neighboring France: hence Hemingway's reference to the Parisian Café Rotonde (q.v.), where Miguel de Unamuno, Vicente Blasco Ibáñez, Eduardo Ortega y Gasset, and other intellectuals concocted pamphlets and manifestos calling for strikes, marches, armed uprisings, and sedition in general. Border police, Civil Guards, and other branches of the military were alert to traffic from France into Spain. At about 1:00 A.M. on 7 November 1924, a constable at Vera de Bidasoa noticed a group of people making their way through the town. He reported the presence of these suspicious characters to the Civil Guard, two of whom went with him to find them. But the men had by now reached the outskirts of Vera and were on the road to the next town, Lesaca. The constable turned back, towards Vera, and the two civil guards, Julio de la Fuente Sáinz and Aureliano Ortiz Madrazo, kept going.

Minutes later, hearing shots, the constable rushed into Vera, recruited another two civil guards—they always patrol or "hunt in pairs," as Hemingway notes (*DIA*, 274)—and led them to the spot where he had turned back: they found Fuente's corpse nearby. This second pair of guards returned to Vera for reinforcements, and a thorough search was launched, by car and on foot. Two more bodies were found, one a civilian and the other that of Fuente's partner, Aureliano Ortiz, as well as a good number of spent cartridges, maps, a compass, a first-aid kit, and subversive pamphlets: clear evidence that the Civil Guard had engaged armed revolutionaries. Several men were arrested within a few hours.

The shooting had also been heard by carbineers on night duty at a nearby village. Going out to investigate, they arrested a man trying to make his way back into France. Within minutes they came upon another three men and ordered them to halt: two of them sprinted off toward France and successfully evaded their pursuers, but the third started shooting, whereupon the carbineers returned fire and killed him. In two other incidents that night, a carbineer was wounded, another suspected revolutionary was killed, several others were wounded, and many of them managed to cross the border back into

France. During the nightlong search, fourteen men were captured on the Spanish side and turned over to the commandant at Vera. Seventeen more were arrested on the French side, at St. Jean de Luz. The revolutionary cadre was later estimated to number as many as seventy men.

The military authorities acted quickly, subjecting four of the captured men—Pablo Martín Sánchez, Enrique Gil Galar, Julián Santillán Rodríguez, and José Antonio Vázquez Bouzas—to a *juicio militar sumarísimo* (summary court martial) on 14 November, just one week after the events. Because such a trial admits only one charge, the men were accused only of firing on civil guards and killing two of them. The charge of sedition, which was leveled at all the other captured conspirators, was relegated to a more thorough and leisurely *juicio militar ordinario* (regular military trial).

Spanish military law requires that, in order for a suspect to be found guilty in a summary military trial, he must be caught in the act (*en flagrante delicto*) or after short and uninterrupted pursuit by eyewitnesses, so that there is no doubt that he is the perpetrator. The shootout at Vera had occurred shortly after 1:00 A.M.; the accused were not apprehended until morning, between 6:00 and 11:00 A.M. Furthermore, the pursuing constable had returned to Vera to report the sound of shooting, and the pursuing civil guards who had found the first body had turned back to seek reinforcements. The court decided, therefore, that there was no necessary connection between the men who were captured and charged, and those who had actually shot Fuente and Ortiz. This point was made more obvious in that four men were charged collectively for the murder of both civil guards.

Reversing the Verdict. Hemingway's report that the men had been "acquitted once and held until the Captain General of Burgos [q.v.] reversed the finding of the court" is accurate. Burgos housed the headquarters of the army's Sixth Military Region, with jurisdiction over parts of Castile and Navarre (and thus Vera and Pamplona). The supreme military authority over the region, the Captain General, demanded speedy and showy reprisal. When the verdict given at the court martial was forwarded to him, he refused to sign it. Instead, he demanded the death sentences for three of the accused and six years in prison for the fourth.

The conflicting positions—the acquittal and the call for death sentences—were forwarded to the *Consejo Supremo del Ejército y Marina* (Supreme Court, or Tribunal, of the Army and Navy) for review and resolution. At this level, the ranking legal authority is the *fiscal togado* (prosecutor with a law degree, as opposed to a military officer who can act as prosecutor or defender in a military trial). He recognized that the insufficiency of evidence justified the acquittal originally recommended at the court martial. He noted additional procedural errors, such as the impropriety of separating the charge of killing the civil guards from the charge of sedition (or conspiring to commit sedition), and quite properly recommended annulling the summary court martial, setting aside the Captain General's death sentences, and proceeding instead with a more leisurely and thorough *juicio militar ordinario* that would address all the issues. He repeatedly emphasized the need for strict adherence to all legal safeguards in such a complicated trial, with so many defendants.

As required by law, he submitted his findings and recommendations to the government, adding that if the court martial were not annulled, its call for acquittal should be confirmed, to enable the defendants to stand for a second trial, in a *juicio militar ordinario*. That is, he completely rejected the Captain General's death penalties and insisted on a new trial. But the president of the Supreme Court, intent on supporting the Civil Guard and, of course, the government which had appointed him, not only opposed this legal recommendation, he supported the called-for death sentences and further demanded that the *fiscal togado* be relieved of his position. He even threatened to resign if the prosecutor continued to confirm the acquittal or to call for a new trial. In the standoff, the government finally and shamefully sided with the president of the court, because the public execution of revolutionaries "convenía a los intereses políticos" (served political interests).[109]

The complicated legal situation resulted in the government's being forced to abandon all order and logic by emitting three contradictory statements: first, the prosecutor's properly filed legal opinion that a retrial was needed because it was legally impossible to either acquit or condemn; second, the Captain General's demand for three death sentences, backed by the president of the Supreme Court; and finally, the request for a pardon, put forward by the mayor of Pamplona, who was distressed by the unpleasant notoriety the trial had brought to his city.

Two Executions and One Suicide in Pamplona. The convicted men had been held and tried in Pamplona (*see* Loyola, Ignatius of), the next big town close to Vera, on 14 November 1924, and they remained there while their case was reviewed by the higher court. When the death sentence was announced to them, Pablo Martín Sánchez cried out that he would not permit himself to be garroted, a remark that led his parents to fear he would kill himself. At their request, the jail's chaplain and the other priests attending the jailed men exhorted him to die "cristianamente." He seems to have agreed: the newspapers report that the three condemned men went to confession, attended mass, and took communion. The two others wrote farewell letters to their families, but at the end Pablo Martín said he lacked the strength to write and asked a priest to write to his mother that he intended to die in a Christian fashion.

At 7:00 A.M. on 6 December, the handcuffed prisoners were led from the chapel to the two platforms erected at the northern end of the jail. The procession was led by armed soldiers, two civil guards, several jail officials, and the confessors who had attended the men during their last hours. The men themselves were flanked by monks who held their arms. At the foot of a staircase Martín suddenly broke away from his companions, dashed up the stairs, and leapt down onto the jail's courtyard. He died instantly. Hemingway's account of Pablo Martín's defiance when the judgment was pronounced, his family's worry that he would commit suicide, and his dramatic final moments are in full agreement with the newspaper reports of the day.

After Martín was pronounced dead, Enrique Gil Galar and Julián Santillán were garroted. Within the hour, their bodies were taken away for Christian burial; some time later, Martín was taken to the hospital to be autopsied.

Martín's Mother. The condemned men approached their deaths in the company of clerics and soldiers: relatives apparently were not permitted to see them. The families' farewell messages were reported in the press, as were the prisoners' responses to them. Hemingway's parenthetical reference to Martín's Roman Catholic mother—she "tried to make him promise not to take his life because she worried most about his soul" (275)—derives from her final telegram to him:

"Hijo mío, Perdida toda esperanza humana, tu madre, transido el corazón de dolor y postrada ante la Virgen de los Dolores, implora que te dispongas a morir cristianamente como cristianamente te enseñé a vivir. No le niegues este último consuelo a tu madre María Sánchez" (My son, Having lost all human hope, your heartbroken mother, prostrated before the Virgin of Sorrows, implores you to die in Christian fashion, in accordance with the Christian tenets I taught you. Do not deny this last comfort to your mother María Sánchez"). The newspaper's flowery account reports that Martín wept "copiously" and showered "a sea of kisses" on the telegram.[110]

Legal Irregularities. The legal proceedings that led to these executions were hopelessly flawed. The two basic charges, armed aggression against the Civil Guard and sedition against the government, were inseparable, the one an expression of the other. All legal action based on their separation was inevitably compromised. Moreover, as Carlos Blanco points out, civilians who are accused only of sedition should be tried in a civil, not a military court. In this case, however, where sedition was aggravated by armed assault on the Civil Guard, the correct charge was *rebelión militar* (military rebellion) for all the men, and they should all have been tried in a *juicio militar ordinario*.

The illogical separation of two charges (armed aggression and sedition), for the obvious purpose of enabling a summary trial and avenging the deaths of the civil guards, inevitably created judicial confusion and stalemate. Safeguards designed to prevent the miscarriage of justice in summary court martials were disregarded; judicial definitions and hierarchies were set aside; legal distinctions were muddied; the law was subordinated to military pride—and so three men died, victims of a deeply flawed procedure and the political imperative to appease military agencies like the Civil Guard, which shored up Primo de Rivera's dictatorship.

The officers who had voted to acquit the accused at the summary court martial of 14 November were jailed for two months, yet another patently illegal action. The five who had cast dissenting votes remained at liberty. Spain's leading intellectuals, among them Blasco Ibáñez, Unamuno, and Ortega Gasset, vehemently protested all aspects of the events at Vera and Pamplona.[111]

The Trap. Hemingway's reference to "the trap at Deva" admits several interpretations. The four conspirators chosen to be tried for shooting the two civil guards had been identified or "fingered" by some of their fellow revolutionaries, men who were themselves awaiting trial for sedition. In cases of conspiracy to commit sedition, Spanish law prescribes a more severe penalty for the leaders (usually death) than for the rest of the conspirators. By identifying some of their group as their leaders, and thus aligning themselves with the general membership, these informers clearly stood to gain a great deal. In addition, one of the informers, Julián Fernández, was only eighteen years old and obviously vulnerable to pressure. One possibility, then, is that the four defendants at the summary court martial were entrapped by some of their fellow revolutionaries. The government and the government-controlled press took this position, going so far as to accuse the more active planners, Unamuno and Blasco Ibáñez, of betraying the very men they were encouraging into seditious action.[112]

Another possibility is that the group included agents provocateurs, who could have infiltrated the revolutionary group at any stage or any place. In the aftermath of the events, theories and accusations of this ilk proliferated: it was widely thought that the code used in communications between the planners at the Café Rotonde and their informants back home had been broken or leaked, and that the government had sent false telegrams to trick large groups of plotters to return to Spain where they could be apprehended.[113] Although the ineptness of the police and guards at Vera would indicate a lack of foreknowledge, the fact remains that three revolutionaries were killed in that night's shootout, that several more were wounded (one man lost a leg), and that altogether twenty-seven men were tried. In the summary court martial, three were sentenced to death and one to jail, and in the trial for sedition, which lasted until 1927, thirteen were jailed for various lengths of time, and another ten were absolved. Rumors were rife, then, that one or more agents provocateurs—whether policemen, border guards, carbineers, or even civil guards intent on promotion and fame—had infiltrated the revolutionary group and delivered the conspirators to the authorities.

It is also possible to see the entire operation as "un *bluf* montado por el propio gobierno dictatorial para demostrar su poder contra posibles *sublevaciones de verdad*" (a *bluff* staged by the dictatorship itself, to display its power and thus frighten or discourage *actual re-*

bellion [emphasis in the original]).[114] The organizers could have been Primo de Rivera's henchmen, rather than Primo de Rivera himself, and the "conspirators" would have been his or their underlings. But the plot that brought the conspirators to Vera involved such a large number of men—estimates range from thirty to seventy—that it is difficult to see them all as mercenaries or undercover government agents working together.

Still, the "bluff" theory found its adherents. The fact is that Primo de Rivera's precarious dictatorship saw a rash of plots, some concocted by patriotic individuals and others by groups intent on securing their position. Police and border agents were known to have planted and then "discovered" caches of contraband, and even entire "revolutionary plots," in order to "uncover" or "discover" them and thus ingratiate themselves with their superiors. Thus many people who were innocent of seditious intent or action, were fined, jailed, exiled, and even executed.[115]

Although it was never proven, entrapment is a distinct possibility. Primo de Rivera's capricious dictatorship and Alfonso XIII's (q.v.) tottering monarchy invited action from a wide range of people. Fueled by idealism, greed, uncertainty, and the lust for power, revolutionary and counterrevolutionary plots proliferated at this time.

Hemingway's Mistake: Deva / Vera. Hemingway's details about Deva coincide precisely with the events at Vera de Bidasoa, 6–7 November 1924 and the subsequent trial in Pamplona. The events impressed him: a 1925 one-paragraph fragment indicates that he had intended a journalistic essay or short story based on this material. It begins, "In Paris there was a revolution being plotted," and then mentions the Café Rotonde and "a famous author," probably Blasco Ibáñez.[116] The fragment, which mentions neither Deva nor Vera de Bidasoa, was abandoned, and in 1932 Hemingway resuscitated the "Deva" material, adding it to the galley proofs of *Death in the Afternoon* as a handwritten insert.[117]

Situating the events in Deva is clearly a mistake, albeit an understandable one: the two place names are very similar, both places are riverside towns, and both are in the north, in neighboring provinces: Deva (today given the Basque spelling, Deba) in Guipúzcoa and Vera (today spelled Bera) in Navarra. In spite of his "rat trap memory" for places and place names, Hemingway seems not to have realized his mistake. Twenty-five years later, he traveled the same route as the unfortunate revolutionaries, going south from Paris and being stopped at "checkpoints along the Bidassoa (*sic*) river [where] I expected us to be detained or sent back to the frontier" (*TDS*, 45). But even retracing the same ground did not jog him into mentioning either the events of 1924 or his own published and unpublished writing about them. It seems Hemingway never noticed his Deva / Vera transposition. The only one to have noticed an irregularity is the translator of *Death in the Afternoon*, Lola Aguado, but her footnote to the name "Deva" merely notes "Sic, en el original." She may be referring to the fact that Hemingway used the Spanish rather than the Basque spelling, or she may have noticed that Hemingway names the wrong city. In any case, she does not offer a correction.[118]

The events at Vera, widely reported in the contemporary press, were transparently dramatized in Pío Baroja's *La selva oscura: La familia de Errotacho, Novela* (Madrid: Espasa-Calpe, 1932). Baroja justifies the subtitle *Novela* in a prologue in which he explains that although he uses historical names and reports the facts accurately, he adds fictional characters whose involvement with the historical event suggest its larger political and social significance. *See also* Guardia Civil; Primo de Rivera, Miguel.

> The narrator wishes he could describe the members of the Civil Guard who looked for the revolutionaries captured at Deva (274).

Diano. Also known as Indiano, this seed bull was the property of Eduardo Ibarra (q.v.) who, when he divested himself of his holdings, sold Diano to Vicente Martínez's heirs, namely his son-in-law Luis Gutiérrez Gómez, in 1904. Diano's first batch of sons, presented in Madrid on 10 June 1909, were magnificent, and the Martínez herd's subsequent generations were considerably enriched not just by Diano, who had an extraordinarily long and fruitful life, but also by his descendants, all carefully bred by Julián Fernández Martínez (q.v.). He produced graceful, pliant animals that readily followed the muleta (the quality known as *nobleza*): the sort of bull preferred by Joselito, Belmonte, and all who came after them.[119]

The Story about Diano's Story. The remarkable Diano is the subject of at least two books, Marcos Ricardo Barnatán's *Diano* (Madrid: Júcar, 1982) and Luis Fernández Salcedo's *Diano, o el libro que quedó sin escribir* (*Diano, or the Unwritten Book* (1959; reissued Madrid: Agrícola Española, D.L., 1988). Luis Fernández Salcedo is a descendant of Luis Gutiérrez Gómez, who was the son-in-law and heir of Vicente Martínez. Gutiérrez Gómez had bound the letters and other documents that detail the important transaction; he willed this "book" to his nephew, Julián Fernández Martínez. Don Julián, who managed the herd for about forty years, recognized the importance of the seed bull but never found time to sort out the papers which documented his acquisition. It was his son, Luis Fernández Salcedo, who eventually wrote the book about three generations of his family, their herd, their fortunes, and his relationship to the "unwritten book" he had inherited. His *Diano* is interesting not only because it depicts a family, an industry, and a way of life in the throes of change, but also because it is a book about the writing of a book about an "unwritten book" about that Spanish icon, the bull. *See also* Martínez, don Vicente.

Diano died in 1920, aged twenty; more than six hundred of his descendants achieved adulthood. According to Fernández Salcedo, the photograph that appears in *Death in the Afternoon* shows Diano's grandsons and not, as Hemingway's caption claims, his sons; they were photographed shortly before they were fought in San Sebastián in 1919. The picture captioned "The Seed Bull" was taken that same year by the same photographer, Juanito Vandel.[120]

Diano and his descendants appear in photographs (*h:* 280, 304).

Díaz, Porfirio. Mexican lawyer, military man, and politician, 1830–1915. President of Mexico, 1876-c. 1882, 1884–1911.

Born into a poor family and bereft of his father at an early age, Díaz struggled to achieve a law degree and then opted for the army, where he was frequently promoted. He was prominent in the fight against the French attempts at colonization (1862) and fought against the Austrian Archduke Maximilian (1832–67; emperor of Mexico, 1864–67). By 1863, Díaz had achieved the rank of general of a division.

After Maximilian was killed, Díaz retired to his native town of Oaxaca as a protest against the policies of Presidents Benito Juárez (1867–72) and Sebastián Lerdo (1872–76). In 1876, he assumed the presidency in a military coup, ruling for the maximum number of years permitted by Mexico's laws. He was followed in the presidency by General Manuel González, a former minister of war; Díaz was re-elected in 1884. This time, his government changed the laws, enabling Díaz to remain in the presidency for six consecutive "terms." He was removed from office in 1911 by Francisco Madero's revolutionary party, whose members included Francisco (Pancho) Villa and Emiliano Zapata. Their pointed slogan was, "Effective Suffrage, Not Re-election." The Porfirian reign was followed by six years of civil war, during which he lived abroad.

Porfirio Díaz's decades in power have been variously assessed. The 1911 edition of the *Encyclopaedia Britannica* reported approvingly that "His term of office marks a prominent change in the history of Mexico; from that date he at once forged ahead with financial and political reform, the scrupulous settlement of all national debts, the welding together of the peoples and tribes (there are 150 different Indian tribes) of his country, the establishment of railroads and telegraphs, and all this in a land which had been upheaved for a century with revolutions and bloodshed, and which had had fifty-two dictators, presidents and rulers in fifty-nine years."

Fifty years later, the *Encyclopedia Americana* tempered this evaluation. Granting that Díaz was "a good administrator," it pointed out "the dictatorship nullified political progress. . . . The work of progress did not reach the immense Indian population, living in poverty and debt peonage in the fields."[121] This discrimination, which finally unseated Díaz, was not corrected by the civil war. Financial, social, and educational inequality have plagued Mexico throughout the twentieth century.

Rodolfo Gaona (q.v.), born in 1888, grew up and rose to taurine fame in Díaz's Mexico. Díaz was still in power when Gaona went to Spain in 1908. As Hemingway points out, Gaona was successful in Spain during the years of Mexico's civil war. After 1920, he lived and worked mostly in Mexico.

The narrator notes that the great Mexican matador Rodolfo Gaona grew up and was educated during the dictatorship of Porfirio Díaz (198).

Díaz Arquer, Graciano. As Hemingway remarks and as Díaz Arquer's own title page announces, the annotated bibliography that Díaz Arquer compiled is based on the library of José Luis de Ybarra y López de Calle; the book's "Prólogo" also acknowledges earlier compilations prepared by Luis Carmena y Millán in 1883, 1888, and 1903.

Díaz Arquer's bibliography presents 2,077 numbered items, which include pamphlets, journals, volumes of poetry, and individual poems, plays, and novels; biographies of bullfighters, bull breeders, and other taurine personalities; reviews or summaries of individual bullfights, organized by city, by bullring, or by bullfighter, and often covering a period of several years; and public announcements, warnings, and other official proclamations. The bibliography includes items written in French, English, Portuguese, and Spanish; it also offers illustrations or facsimile reproductions of some of the items (e.g., half-page drawings, small posters, or printed announcements). Some of the listed items are quite substantial (multivolume reference works such as Item 1634: *El toreo: Gran diccionario taurómaco*, a two-volume dictionary compiled by J. Sánchez de Neira and published in 1879).

Sometimes several of Díaz Arquer's entries refer to the same book or kind of book: Items 513–19, for example, all refer to *La tauromaquia de Josef Delgado (Illo, Pepe Illo)*, including several illustrations; Items 1371–1436 list several *Reglamentos* (legal codes) that governed the bullfight in various places and at various times.

Items are variously presented by title, by author, and by nickname. Items 1915–20, for example, are under the heading Uno al Sesgo (the nickname used by Tomás Orts Ramos) and his co-compiler don Ventura (Ventura Bagüés), who produced the annual statistical summaries, *Toros y toreros en. . . .*

Díaz Arquer's book contains 390 pages, including the bibliography, the several indices one needs to find one's way, and the colophon. It was announced in the bibliography of *Toros y toreros en 1931* as having been published on 13 August 1931, in a limited edition of 410 numbered copies, the first ten in luxury edition; the announcement incorrectly describes it as listing over 2,100 titles, including some as recent as the first months of 1931. The publication of Díaz Arquer's compilation was an important event for taurine bibliophiles.

Hemingway, Díaz Arquer, and Other Sources. Although Díaz Arquer's book appeared just as Hemingway was about to leave Spain for Paris and his return to the United States, he managed to acquire a copy. He mentions it, as well as *Toros célebres* (q.v.) and the several other taurine newspapers and journals he consulted, but his reading was much wider than he indicates. Brasch and Sigman's comprehensive record of Hemingway's library lists about 125 books on Spanish and taurine subjects, many of them rare items. To give just a few examples: Hemingway owned José Velázquez y Sánchez's *Anales del toreo* (Sevilla: Juan Moyano, 1868), an important taurine reference book that offers a historical survey of the bullfight, with biographies of important bullfighters and bull breeders. He also had Juan Gualberto López Valdemoro y de Quesada (Conde de las Navas), *El espectáculo más nacional* (590 pp.; Madrid, 1899), a comprehensive, authoritative, well-indexed and -footnoted staple of any taurine library.[122] He also had several volumes of the annual *Toros y toreros en* . . . , which record practically every detail of the taurine season; and a similar series, entitled *Desde la grada: Anuario taurino.*[123]

Hemingway's "Bibliographical Note" is misleading in that it minimizes the extent of Hemingway's considerable research. We do not know exactly when Hemingway acquired his taurine library, but we do know that he saw his first bullfights in the spring of 1923 and that he was planning and researching *Death in the Afternoon* as early as 1925. For further discussion of concealed or unacknowledged sources, *see* Frank, Waldo David; Meier-Graefe, Julius; *Toreros y toros*; Vindel, Pedro.

In a "Bibliographical Note," the narrator recommends Graciano Díaz Arquer's bibliography to interested readers (*h:* 517).

Disease. The narrator discusses diseases in animals (glanders, 186; hoof-and-mouth disease, *h:* 464, s.v. *Pesuña* (*sic*); 478, s.v. *Sano*); and in humans: gangrene (255, 259, *h:* 505), mumps (94), pneumonia (82), Spanish influenza (139, q.v.), tetanus (*h:* 505), tuberculosis (79, 82, 83, 100–101, 157), typhoid (72), and various venereal diseases (93–94, 100–104, 133, 171, *h:* 488, s.v. *Uretritis*). *See also* Doctors.

Doctors. Paul Smith connects the doctor in "A Natural History of the Dead" to the "weary surgeon and often self-righteous [medical] officers" in *A Farewell to Arms* (1929), which Hemingway was revising as he attempted early drafts of this story. The doctor's loss of control and the image of a broken skull suggest Hemingway's father, Dr. Clarence Hemingway, who committed suicide in 1929 by shooting himself in the head. With its insistence on naturalistic detail and on the confusion, disorder, violence, and pain that accompany war, "A Natural History" is part of the attack against the Humanists who panned *A Farewell to Arms*, and against the Christian optimism of his parents' generation. *See also* "A Natural History of the Dead"; Humanism, Naturalism.

Doctors appear frequently in Hemingway's short fiction; see, for example, "Indian Camp," "The Doctor and the Doctor's Wife," "God Rest You Merry, Gentlemen," and "A Reader Writes." The narrator of *A Moveable Feast* derives some of his medical expertise from his father's books (163 ff). Civilian and army doctors appear in *A Farewell to Arms*, where good doctors and nurses are tolerant of drink, and bad doctors are abstemious.[124]

Although every bullring has its infirmary, not all are well equipped. The larger first-class rings, such as Madrid and Valencia, have better facilities and doctors. Taurine surgeons, as Hemingway notes, have a double aim: "to save the man, the aim of ordinary surgery; and to place the torero back in the ring as soon as possible" (255). Dr. Francisco (Paco) Serra (q.v.) served in the Valencia infirmary; Drs. Mascarell and Segovia were the Madrid taurine specialists in the 1920s and early 1930s. *See* Disease, in this volume; and Tamames, Dr. Manuel, in *DS*.

> Bullfighters are dependent on doctors, and particularly on surgeons, who are mentioned often (31, 77, 85, 219, 255–56, 261–62, *h:* 437, s.v. *Facultativo*; *h:* 457, s.v. *Novillada*; *h:* 505). Occasionally matadors honor a "quack doctor" (60). The Old Lady is encouraged to speak frankly, as one does to one's doctor (120). The narrator complains that bullfighters have become specialists, like doctors (85).
>
> In "A Natural History of the Dead," an exhausted and overworked Italian army doctor curtly refuses to move the wounded man out of the cave where he lies among the dead; he also refuses the demand for mercy killing. In the resulting argument, he throws iodine in the lieutenant's face;

kicks, disarms, and injures him; and then oversees medical treatment for him (141–44). Doctor speaks: 141–44.

Domecq Brandy. *See* Drinks. For the Domecq bulls, see *DS*.

Domingo, Roberto. Spanish painter, 1883–1956. The son of Francisco Domingo, who was also a painter, Roberto was born and educated in Paris. He came to Madrid in 1906 and by 1909 was installed in the home (Goya 44, Madrid) and studio (Alcalá 63, Madrid) where he lived, worked, and exhibited for the rest of his life. His paintings won medals and were exhibited at various galleries at home and abroad (London, Buenos Aires, and Rome), and his work gained high visibility because many of his paintings were reproduced as *carteles* (posters) to advertise bullfights throughout Spain. Domingo is one of the better-known taurine painters.

Hemingway and Domingo. Hemingway met Domingo and visited his studio to buy paintings and drawings to use as illustrations for *Death in the Afternoon.* Domingo provided signed photos of several of his works: *Esperando la hora* (also called *Patio de caballos*): it shows four picadors and a *monosabio* preparing to enter the ring for the paseo; *Mercado en Avila* (Market in Avila) shows massive city walls and a market scene in the foreground; *Víspera de corrida* (Eve of the Bullfight) shows two mounted men herding bulls across the country towards a bullring), *Cartel de toros* is the original painting for the poster advertising the Bilbao 1925 feria; it shows the bulls entering the corrals in the bullring; and *El pelele* (The Rag Doll) presents an action-filled village *capea*. We do not know which of these paintings Hemingway bought, although his correspondence with his publishers suggests that he owned two gouaches as well as the painting which was used for the dust jacket of *Death in the Afternoon.* That painting still hangs in Hemingway's Cuban home, the Finca Vigía.

When Hemingway first broached his bullfighting book to Scribners, he intended it to include many "wonderful pictures." To this end, he acquired hundreds of photographs and canvassed the work of painters like Goya, Carlos Ruano Llopis, and Roberto Domingo, in search of relevant materials. But by the time the book went to press, the Depression had hit. Worried about the cost of the book, Scribners cut the number of illustrations drastically, a decision that Hemingway bitterly contested. There was some talk of a more heavily illustrated deluxe edition, but it never materialized. In the end, only two paintings were used in *Death in the Afternoon*: the Juan Gris for the frontispiece, and the Roberto Domingo for the dustjacket.[125]

> The narrator would have liked to include more material about [and by] his good friend Roberto, whom he identifies only by first name (271).

Dominguín. The professional nickname of the famous González family (father and three sons) derives from the patriarch's first name, Domingo (Sunday), because he was born on that day.[126] *See* González, Domingo, in this volume; see also Dominguín in *DS*.

Dorman-Smith (D. S.). Full name: Eric Edward (Chink) Dorman-Smith, later Dorman O'Gowan. Irish soldier, 1895–1969. Dorman-Smith acquired the nickname "Chink" at age eighteen, when he graduated Sandhurst and joined the First Battalion, Northumberland Fusiliers. A fellow subaltern remarked that with "his narrow head and pointed ears," the young man resembled the Chinkara antelope, the regiment's mascot. For Dorman-Smith's education, *see* Sandhurst.

Dorman-Smith and World War I. Dorman-Smith first saw action on 22 August 1914, shortly after his nineteenth birthday. As platoon commander of B Company of the First Battalion, Northumberland Fusiliers, he was ordered to hold the sixty-foot double bridge at Mariette, at the Mons Canal. Outmanned and outgunned, the Northumberland Fusiliers suffered many casualties even as they withdrew. Chink was wounded in the retreat. He did not return to his frontline platoon until November, to face the horrifying fact that he was one of only four survivors of the original twenty-five officers of the First Battalion with whom he had sailed to France. Chink mourned the loss of his friends and of the thousands of troops who had been killed: "The catalogue of loss was almost too much to take in." He was wounded again on December 1914 and returned to the front in March 1915; a third wound, in June, kept him away from the front for only two weeks. For months he suffered through trench warfare at the battles of Messines, Armentières, and Ypres, as the slaughter continued unabated. He lost good friends and respected colleagues and daily saw men suffering and dying in a variety of horrible ways.

In August 1915 he was sent home to recuperate from "nervous exhaustion caused by stress of active service and previous wounds." Within six months he was back in the front lines. He was diagnosed as shellshocked in April 1916. Even so, the need for experienced officers was so pressing that, after a stint of teaching young recruits, Chink was returned to France in July 1917. Later that year, he was assigned to the Italian Piave Front, where he once again undertook to train recruits. As the war came to an end, he was recovering from a severe case of gastroenteritis.

Promotions and honors had come quickly during wartime years: Chink made lieutenant in March 1915, captain in February 1916, and acting major early in 1917; he was awarded a Military Cross with a star and was mentioned three times in dispatches. He was only twenty-three years old when the war ended, but he was a decorated warrior, accustomed to being in command.

Witty, sophisticated, well versed in military history, and heavily decorated, Chink obviously impressed Hemingway when they met in 1918. Hemingway was four years younger and had had less than one month's experience of war: he had served briefly with Ambulance Section 4 of the Red Cross and was operating a rolling canteen service when he was wounded and sent to Milan to convalesce. Chink dubbed him his a.d.c. (aide-de-camp), "a role that Hemingway was proud to accept" at the time.[127]

Dorman-Smith and Bullfighting. Hadley, Ernest, and Chink vacationed together in Switzerland, France, and Italy in 1922 and 1924. Dorman-Smith accompanied Hemingway to the bullfights in Pamplona, July 1924.[128]

Michael Reynolds has tracked down the two articles Hemingway mentions, both published in the *Royal Military College Magazine and Record*. The first, "A Bull Fight at Pamplona" (1924, pages 19–29), begins with a general discussion of the bullfight and of the foreigner's invariably negative response to it because of its "cruelty." Dorman-Smith remarks, however, that on their way to the "bloodless entertainments in London," the English are oblivious of their own "slums the foetid misery which would never be tolerated in the easy-going, laughter-loving land of Spain" (19). After the necessary disquisition on the horses, the author describes the bullring, the entry of the bullfighters, and the performance of the first bull, who manages to rip open the matador's sleeve before being killed and dragged out. The matador is not named, but at the end of the essay Maera, Algabeño, and Chiquelo (*sic*) are mentioned. The organization of this article foreshadows the organization of the early sections of *Death in the Afternoon.*

Dorman-Smith's second bullfighting essay, "Il (*sic*) Encierro," published soon after the first (January 1925, pages 87–92), is also set in Pamplona during the "Festa of St. Firmin" (*sic*). It begins with a mistranslation of *encierro* as "literally 'the barrier' " (87). The word really means "the enclosing" or "locking up": the bulls and their accompanying steers are driven through the streets to the bullring so that they can be enclosed in the bullring's large holding pens, where they will remain until the afternoon's bullfight. The article mentions Pamplona's famous giants, the fireworks, the music, and the other entertainments connected with the July fiesta. Its central section describes the amateur bullfighting that follows the *encierro*. This essay, which is less serious in tone than the earlier one, presents several paragraphs of slang-filled interior monologue and disjointed conversation. It mentions "our wives" (Dorman-Smith was then single), "Don" (Don Stewart), and "Hemingway," who is knocked over by a steer:

"Bump!! Hemingway swings under the impact of the horn on his ribs, and slides forward on to the steer's head. He grips the horns as the steer dashes on, pushing him over the sand.

"We rush to the rescue, and the steer, his head released, turns to some less strenuous fun." (91)

In the last paragraph, the essay describes Hemingway as "a veritable afficionada"—the feminine ending of the misspelled noun producing an unintended affront.[129] There is no evidence confirming that Hemingway entered the ring to fight steers, as Dorman-Smith reports. Both essays offer photographs and captions.

Hemingway and Dorman-Smith. Traces of Chink appear in several of Hemingway's works. Chink's stories about his experiences at Mons and Ypres went into the making of *in our time* (1924), which was dedicated to him, and Chink's biographer, Lavinia Greacen, also identifies him as the prototype for Harris (also called Wilson-Harris) in *The Sun Also Rises*.

In 1918, Chink, Ernest, and Ernest's girlfriend Agnes von Kurowsky had explored Milanese settings like San Siro, Biffi's, and the Cova café, settings that appear in *A Farewell to Arms* and are mentioned in *A Moveable Feast*. Greacen claims that Dorman-Smith's voice echoes in other Hemingway works: "one Shakespearean line that Chink recited whenever they discussed courage—as they frequently did—. . . became [Hemingway's] lucky charm, one that he would often quote in his books."[130] The line—"By my troth, I care not; a man can die but once; we owe God a death" (*Henry IV, Part Two*, 3, ii, 216–17)—is spoken by the white hunter Wilson in "The Short Happy Life of Francis Macomber"; Wilson "was very embarrassed, having brought out this thing he had lived by." It was also quoted in Hemingway's "Introduction" to *Men at War*, and paraphrased versions appear in *A Farewell to Arms* ("The coward dies a thousand deaths, the brave but one," *AFTA*, 139–40) and in *Across the River and Into the Trees* ("he who dies on Thursday does not have to die on Friday," *ARIT*, 59). Mark Spilka has pointed out, however, that Hemingway encountered the line long before he met Dorman-Smith; the line appears at least three times in Frederick Marryat's *Percival Keene*, which Hemingway read as a boy.[131]

Hemingway and Hadley invited Chink to be godfather to their son (Gertrude Stein [q.v.] was the godmother). Although the two men lost touch with each other, Hemingway recalls Dorman-Smith affectionately in *Green Hills of Africa* (280) and *A Moveable Feast* (55), and in two poems, "To Chink Whose Trade Is Soldiering" and "[Some day when you are picked up. . .]."[132]

Born on 24 July 1895, Dorman-Smith was four years older than Hemingway. He was almost twenty-nine, and not twenty-six, as the narrator claims, when he saw his first bullfight in early July 1924. Probably to increase his authority, Hemingway frequently presents himself as older, and most of his male friends as younger than their actual ages.

The narrator describes Dorman-Smith as receptive to and enthusiastic about bullfighting (*h:* 496–97). He also writes that the English say, "Never discuss casualties . . . and I have heard them say it very well" (265). "The English" who speak "very well" is probably Dorman-Smith.

Drinks. Although there is less drinking in *Death in the Afternoon* than in most of Hemingway's fictional works, the narrator does mention absinthe (154, 172, *h:* 448, s.v. *Mariscos*), brandy (47, 48, 181, *h:* 496), the refreshing, sweet, nonalcoholic drink called *horchata* (271), and some well-known brand names, like Domecq (47), Fundador (278), and the beers Aguila and Cruz Blanca (*h:* 424, s.v. *Cerveza*).

> The most frequently mentioned drinks are beer (33, 44, 234, 271, 272, *h:* 409, s.v. *Aburrimiento*; 424–25, s.v. *Cerveza*; 448, s.v. *Mariscos*; 512) and wine (*10–12*, 43, 44, 270, 273, 275, 276, *h:* 418, s.v. *Bota*; 447, s.v. *Manzanilla*; 483, s.v. *Tapas*; 491–92, s.v. *Vino*). The only wine identified by region and name is Valdepeñas (39, 40). Drunkenness is also mentioned (30, 74, 77, 82, 119, 271, 273, *h:* 418, s.v. *Botellazo*; 447, s.v. *Manzanilla*). *See* Doctors, in this volume; see also Drinks in *DS*.

D. S. *See* Dorman-Smith.

Duarte, Antonio. Full name: Antonio Duarte Acuña. Spanish bullfighter, b. 1900.

The son of a *novillero*, Duarte grew up with bulls and bullfighters. He was a member of Cayetano Ordóñez's *cuadrilla* through the 1920s, being his *peón de confianza* from 1925 until 1928, after which he also worked with Valencia II, Cagancho, Villalta, and other great matadors. Hemingway, who undoubtedly saw him in the ring, echoes Cossío's evaluation: "Como peón es valiente . . . como banderillero, muy bueno" (As a peon he is brave . . . as a banderillero, very good). He had a long career, being gored, as far as I can determine, only twice. His older brother José, a banderillero, was ineffective and unimpressive.[133]

> The narrative ranks Duarte among the best banderilleros (201).

Dumas, Alexandre (Dumas père). Prolific French dramatist and novelist, 1803–70; famous for his historical novels, such as *The Three Musketeers* and *The Count of Monte Cristo*. Hemingway, who admired Dumas, owned about a dozen of his books, several of them in the original French.[134]

Hemingway mentions the historically based characters Coconas and Salcede (*Green Hills of Africa*, 108), who appear in Dumas's trilogy about the turmoil which ended the reign of France's Valois kings, King Charles IX and Henri III (*Marguerite de Valois*, *La Dame de Monsoreau*, and *Les Quarante-cinq*). *See also* D'Artagnan.

The narrator compares the great Joselito to Dumas's D'Artagnan (212–13).

Dutrús, Rafael. Full name: Rafael Dutrús Zamora (Llapisera). Spanish bullfighter, d. 1960.

Llapisera was a *matador de novillos* who developed a successful variety of comic-musical taurine acts. His costume (long coattail and tall top hat) was designed to accentuate his height. He worked with several other comic bullfighters. In one popular act, they would present a musical performance that was interrupted by a young bull, a *becerro* or *novillo*, which would, of course, attack them. The group tried to finish their musical offering while fighting the bull. Although these animals are smaller than *toros de lidia*, they are still large creatures with fearsome horns. Like any other torero, the comic bullfighter was occasionally smacked, knocked over, stepped on, and gored.

Llapisera frequently teamed up with another *novillero*, Carmelo Tusquellas Forcén (1893–1967), who dressed up as Charlie Chaplin, hence his nickname, Charlot; and with Charlot's partner, the banderillero José Colomer (d. 1931), who dressed as a bellhop, or *botones*. Charlot and Botones first appeared in 1916, and their act, like that of Llapisera, became so popular that their manager, the well-known impresario Eduardo Pagés, was soon advertising them as the "Auténticos Charlots" to distinguish them from other *charlotadas*.

Llapisera and Charlot appeared so frequently that in 1924 the prestigious annual *Toros y toreros*, which reviewed and documented the taurine season, devoted a chapter to "Toreros cómicos" which included a list of all their performances: forty-seven for Llapisera and fifty-eight for Charlot and his group, including a special performance at a gala *corrida de toros* held in honor of the Italian monarchs. In 1929, these two comics established the successful taurine band *El Empastre* (q.v.), which Dutrús managed until 1931. Dutrús also worked as agent/manager for several bullfighters and as impresario, organizing bullfights in several plazas.[135] *See also Mojigangas.*

The narrator correctly identifies Dutrús as the founder of the bullfighting band *El Empastre*: some of its members would dispatch a bull while the others continued playing their musical instruments (*h:* 451, s.v. *Moji-ganga*).

Dynasties. *See* Taurine Dynasties.

– E –

El eco taurino. Taurine periodicals by this name were established in Córdoba in 1891; in Cádiz in 1893; and in Madrid in 1900, 1909 and 1910.[136] This last one was the most successful, publishing continuously until 1935; it began publishing again in 1946, but had only a short run.

El eco taurino reported on corridas in Madrid and, through cabled reports, in the Spanish provinces and the Americas. A sober weekly, it presented editorials and a few jokes but generally eschewed the gossip and rumors favored by the genre. The last page of each eight-page issue listed working *matadores de toros*, *matadores de novillos*, *becerristas*, juvenile *cuadrillas* (each entry included the name and address of the individual or group and of the manager or *apoderado* who handled them). Spanish and foreign readers could subscribe to the journal at a trimester rate. In the early 1930s, a single issue cost ten *céntimos*. The Biblioteca Nacional, Madrid, has a full run, 1910–35.

Hemingway and El eco taurino. Hemingway saved a 1927 eight-page issue of *El eco taurino* which reviewed several bullfights and discussed the founding of the charitable organization Montepío (*see* Torres Reina, Ricardo). He subscribed to the journal in 1931 and 1932 and was thus able to keep abreast of bullfighting news even while in the United States.[137]

> The narrator praises the Madrid-based *El eco taurino* for its thoroughness and accuracy (*h:* 475, s.v. *Revistas*; *see also* 466, s.v. *Periódicos*).

Eliot, T. S. Full name: Thomas Stearns Eliot. American-born poet, dramatist, and editor, 1888–1965; became a British subject and a member of the Church of England in 1927. He received the Nobel Prize in 1948.

Eliot is the author of *The Wasteland, Four Quartets, Murder in the Cathedral.* The influence of Eliot, particularly *The Wasteland*, on Hemingway was noted in many of the early reviews of Hemingway's work, most frequently in connection with *The Sun Also Rises*.[138] *See also* Marvell, Andrew.

The narrator claims he learned to do parody from Eliot (139).

El Empastre. A successful musical/taurine band founded in 1929 by the bullfighters Rafael Dutrús (Llapisera, q.v.), Carmelo Tusquellas Forcén (Charlot), and Rafael Ponce (Rafaelillo). El Empastre was so popular that by 1931 it had an imitator, El Empas ¿3?. *Toros y toreros en 1931* lists El Empastre and Charlot as two separate spectacles, but notes that they often perform together.[139] For a description of these taurine entertainments, *see Mojigangas.*

The narrator correctly identifies Rafael Dutrús with the bullfighting band El Empastre (421).

English-born Ex-Queen. *See* Victoria Eugenia.

Epinard. Foaled in France in 1920, Epinard was sired by Badajoz out of Epine Blanche by Rock Sand. He was bred by Pierre Wertheimer, trained by Eugene Leigh, and ridden by Everett Haynes. He had an "amiable disposition" and was a handsome creature, "a brilliant golden chestnut, his coat being rich and glowing in hue."[140]

In August 1922, Epinard "broke his maiden at first asking": that is, he won his first, or maiden, race (the 100-meter, 6-furlong Prix Yacoulef, run at Deauville). He ran six more races in that year, winning five and attracting a great deal of attention. The next year, as a three-year-old, he raced in England as well as in France. His English performances included a "brilliant exploit at Goodwood" and an even better performance in Cambridgeshire, which "stamped him as probably the best racehorse in Europe."

In 1924, Epinard was France's champion handicap horse. He was brought to America in July 1924, to begin training for three major races: at Belmont Park, New York (September 1); at Aqueduct, Long Island, New York (September 27); and at Latonia, Kentucky (October 11).

To the surprise of his fans, Epinard came in second in all three of these races, losing to Wise Counsellor in Belmont (by half a length), to Ladkin at Aqueduct (the blame fell on Epinard's jockey), and to Sarazen in Latonia (Epinard was said to be suffering from a quarter crack). However, Epinard "suffered no loss of prestige by [these] performances . . . for in his races in New York he defeated each of the colts . . . that had defeated him—and by more ground than they did him. . . . That Epinard is a horse of high class hardly admits of a doubt." He was also so popular that a fourth race, at Laurel Stakes, Maryland, was added to his schedule. This was run on 18 October, and Epinard came in fifth: "he was in trouble leaving the barrier, his foot gave way early in the running, and he finished unplaced."[141]

Epinard returned to France in November 1924 and was put to stud. In this capacity he also had an international career, returning twice to the United States.[142] Many of his offspring won races, but none achieved his fame or popularity.

After a sedate decade as stud, Epinard broke into the news again, a victim of German occupation. It seems that when the Germans occupied Paris, Epinard disappeared, apparently stolen or kidnapped in the confusion. Later that year he was found, thin and in poor condition, pulling a cart. He was returned to his owner but died at the end of 1942.

Hemingway and Epinard. According to Evan Shipman, Hemingway bet very profitably on Epinard in 1922. A friend (probably Shipman himself) had advised Ernest to bet on the Wertheimer two-year-old at his first race, and "Hemingway momentarily exhausted his credit—even obtaining a thousand francs from his barber—but he was 'on' Epinard, who started in the Prix Yacoulef at Deauville at 59 to 10 for his debut and won easily, paying enough to carry the family for a good six months. . . . Hemingway has been ready ever since to call Epinard, 'the horse of the century' " although he seems not to have seen the race himself.[143]

The narrator remembers Epinard (5).

E. R., Mrs. Full name: Elizabeth Hadley Richardson. She became Hemingway's first wife in September 1921. *See* Hemingway, Hadley.

El Escorial. Full name: El Real Monasterio de San Lorenzo del Escorial. The large, square, somber complex holds a monastery, church, palace, mausoleum, library, and many interior courtyards. It was built in 1563–84 by Philip II (q.v.) to fulfill a vow he had made at the battle of St. Quentin, in 1557, on St. Lawrence's feast day (10 August). Philip II lived monastically in El Escorial for the last fourteen years of his life, leaving to others the management of Spain's various military conflicts. El Escorial was a royal residence until about 1860, after which it housed an Augustinian monastery. *See* Mexican Feather Work; see also El Escorial in *DS*.

The narrator mentions El Escorial (51, 59).

El Espartero. *See* García Cuesta, Manuel.

Espinoza, Fermín (Armillita II, Armillita Chico). Correct spelling: Espinosa. Full name: Fermín Espinosa Saucedo. Mexican bullfighter, 1911–78. Investiture as *matador de toros*, 23 October 1927, in Mexico City; Spanish investiture on 25 March 1928, in Barcelona; confirmed in Madrid, 10 May 1928. The second promotion was necessary because Mexican promotions were not accredited in Spain. Fermín was sixteen when he was promoted in Barcelona and barely seventeen when this second promotion was confirmed in Madrid.

Like so many bullfighters, Fermín was a child prodigy, leaving school at an early age and killing his first *becerro* (very young bull, one year old or younger) at thirteen. By the age of fifteen he had a strong following in his native Mexico; as *matador de novillos* he was so outstanding that he was promoted to the rank of *matador de toros* in Mexico City in 1927. When he came to Spain for the 1928 season (the taurine legal code forbade sixteen-year-olds from performing), he was hailed as "the Mexican Joselito."

In his first few seasons in Spain (1928–32), Armillita appeared in about twenty-five corridas a year, his reputation growing steadily in spite of his "falta de alegría . . . una frialdad que restaba emoción a cuanto ejecutaba" (a lack of liveliness or joy . . . a coldness that diminished the emotion of his performance).[144] But as his work became more emotional and intense, the numbers more than doubled, to fifty-three corridas in 1933, sixty-three in 1934, and sixty-four in 1935, when he tied for first place nationwide with Manolo Bienvenida. Armillita was contracted for eighty corridas in 1936.

Armillita's success, and the general popularity of Mexicans in Spain, alarmed Spanish bullfighters. Individually and through their union, they did their best to keep Mexicans out of Spanish bullrings. In May 1936 Armillita and all the other Mexicans left Spain *en masse*; a retaliatory boycott against Spaniards was soon declared in Mexico. Armillita did not return to Spain until the boycotts were lifted in 1944.[145] Thereafter he maintained a busy transatlantic schedule until his retirement in 1949. (He came out of retirement briefly during the 1953 season.)

Critics agree that Espinosa was superb in all aspects of the art, controlling the bull so completely and so coolly that, like Joselito, he failed to give the sense of danger. In twenty-five years of fighting, he suffered only one serious goring, in 1944. After his retirement he and his brothers established a bull-breeding ranch in their native Mexico, where he died.[146]

Hemingway and Armillita Chico. Hemingway was not in Spain in 1928, when Fermín burst upon the Spanish scene, or in 1930. He did see Villalta, Barrera, and Fermín Espinosa on 24 May 1931, in Madrid, and may have seen Espinosa on other occasions that season. In an article published two years after the publication of *Death in the Afternoon*, Hemingway praised Armillita Chico wholeheartedly, mentioning his long legs, "wonderful wrists . . . cold intelligence, his classic perfection and his superlative skill" and noticing that he performed often, although the public seemed to prefer Domingo Ortega (q.v.), whom Hemingway disliked.[147]

> The narrator correctly describes Fermín Espinosa as excellent with the banderillas and the muleta, but does not indicate the extent of his artistry and reputation (200, 220–21; *see also* 267).

Espinoza, Juan (Armillita). Correct spelling: Espinosa. Full name: Juan Espinosa Saucedo. Mexican bullfighter, 1905–64. Investiture as *matador de toros* in Mexico City, 30 November 1924; again in Talavera de la Reina, 16 May 1925; confirmed in Madrid on 20 September 1925.

From the time of his Spanish investiture, Armillita performed regularly in Spain as well as in Central and South America. In 1925 the always perceptive critic Tomás Orts Ramos (Uno al Sesgo) applauded Armillita's work with the banderillas but found that, in spite of all the propaganda which had preceded him to Spain, he was deficient in the other areas of the bullfight ("un virtuoso de las banderillas . . . pero nada más"). Juan Armillita had successful seasons in 1926 (twenty-two corridas in Spain and thirteen in Mexico) and 1927 (twenty-two in Spain and ten in Mexico), but after this his career declined. He appeared in sixteen corridas in 1928, ten in 1929, eight in 1930, seven in 1931, and two in 1932. When he was first promoted, he was skillful in all aspects of the fight. But he soon became unsure with the sword and his work with the cape and muleta weakened; he maintained only his skill with the banderillas, always his strongest point.

As his *cartel* declined and his brother's fame soared, Juan resigned his *alternativa* (q.v.) in 1932 to become a member of Fermín's *cuadrilla*. After Fermín's retirement in 1949, Juan worked for other matadors. A severe goring in the early 1950s led to his retirement; he was about fifty years old then. He became a partner in the family's successful bullbreeding ranch "Armillita Hermanos." He died in Mexico City.

Since Juan Armillita was never contracted for Hemingway's favorite *ferias* (Madrid in May, Pamplona in early July, Valencia in late July), it is unlikely that Hemingway saw him perform. Although Hemingway spent several months in Spain in 1929 and 1931, Armillita did not perform as matador often in those years.[148] In that sense, he was "on the decline" (201), though as a banderillero he continued to be successful for another twenty years.

> The narrator correctly identifies Armillita as the older brother of Fermín and thinks him a fine banderillero, though already fading in the late 1920s (201).

El Estudiante (the Student). Nickname of Luis Gómez Calleja, who studied accounting and business administration in Madrid before turning to bullfighting.[149] Hemingway incorrectly describes him as "a young medical student" (*DIA*, 229). *See* Gómez, Luis. For a physician-bullfighter, *see* Serna, Victoriano de la.

Exterminator. Foaled in May 1915, Exterminator was sired by McGee out of Fair Empress. Breeder: the family of F. D. (Dixie) Knight. J.

Cal Milam bought the horse as a yearling, and Willis Sharpe Kilmer acquired him as a two-year-old.

Exterminator was a chestnut gelding, rather dull in hue, with a large triangular star between his eyes. He burst into prominence when he won the Kentucky Derby in 1918, to which he had been sent as a substitute for his stablemate, Sun Briar. The Kentucky Derby was only the fifth race of his life, and after the unexpected victory he had a summer-long string of defeats, followed by a streak of victories in the fall.

Exterminator had a long career, winning fifty of one hundred races over eight seasons and succeeding both in sprints and long-distance races. He became "America's top winner in cup races and, according to many experts, the greatest thoroughbred ever developed in this country." He seemed impervious to mud, rain, and heat, running well in all weathers. He traveled well and adjusted easily to different feed and to different tracks. He was also unaffected by the stress of having to adjust to nine different trainers, running well for all and making several of them famous. He continued to win trophies even when his many victories required him to carry as much as thirty pounds more than some of his competitors.

Exterminator's easy going ways, stamina, and enthusiasm for the track made him a folk hero in spite of his bony homeliness, which earned him the nicknames "Old Bones" and "Bones." But the ungainly horse became graceful when in action. He lived to be thirty years old and drew many fans to the Kilmer farm, near Binghamton, New York, where he was stabled and where he is buried.[150]

Hemingway and Exterminator. Exterminator ran all of his one hundred races in North America, eighty-six of them during the five-year period from 1918 to 1922, most of which Hemingway spent in Europe. It is unlikely that Hemingway ever saw him run or bet on him. And even if he had, he wouldn't have made much money, since Exterminator was a famous horse with a good record for winning. By betting on horses like Man o' War and Exterminator, the narrator was not taking much of a chance.

As a consistently best-selling author who felt himself entitled to higher royalties, Hemingway wrote his publisher that "I am an old horse like Exterminator that won for you every time but once. And I won't run for ten percent. . . . The only thing that makes horses like

Exterminator and me sore is when . . . the people that start you haven't got the guts to bet."[151]

The narrator remembers Exterminator with admiration and affection (5).

– F –

Familiar History of Birds. See Stanley, Edward.

Families. *See* the several entries under Hemingway; *see also* Nicknames; Taurine Dynasties.

A Farewell to Arms. Novel by Ernest Hemingway, set in Italy and Switzerland during World War I, published in 1929, and discussed in an essay by Aldous Huxley (q.v.).

The narrator comments upon Aldous Huxley's remarks about one of Mr. H's (unnamed) books (190–91).

Faulkner, William. Full name: William Harrison Faulkner. American novelist and short story writer, 1897–1962. His best-known novels include *The Sound and the Fury* (1929), *As I Lay Dying* (1930), *Sanctuary* (1931), *Light in August* (1932), and the trilogy composed of *The Town*, *The Hamlet*, and *The Mansion*. He was awarded the Nobel Prize in 1949 and the Pulitzer Prize twice: in 1955, for *A Fable*, and in 1963, for *The Reivers*.

Several critics have found parallels among the major writers of Hemingway's generation, comparisons that always irked Hemingway, who rejected all claims of influence.[152] Hemingway often mocked fellow authors who were successful or who had befriended and helped him: Sherwood Anderson was parodied in *The Torrents of Spring*, and Ford Madox Ford, Gertrude Stein, and F. Scott Fitzgerald were all attacked in *A Moveable Feast*.

Hemingway read Faulkner's work, mentioned him often in letters and essays, and jealously reviled him for being so prolific (Faulkner published a novel a year for several years, a rhythm Hemingway never achieved) and for writing shocking sex scenes like those in *Sanctuary*—the "kind of stories" the Old Lady (q.v.) would like to hear (*DIA*, 179) and which so strikingly increased Faulkner's sales.[153] Recognizing Faulkner as important literary competition, Hemingway emphasizes his own success by creating an intelligent Old Lady who recalls the details of his own work but has not read any of Faulkner's stories or novels.

Hemingway and Faulkner sniped at each other in public and private pronouncements and even in their Nobel Prize acceptance speeches. In his, Faulkner used precisely those words which Fredric Henry had proscribed in *A Farewell to Arms*: "love and honor and pity and pride and compassion and sacrifice." Hemingway, in turn, "has Faulkner as a subtext" in his own acceptance speech, in which he implicitly rejects Faulkner's commitment to "old verities and truths" by insisting that "For a true writer each book should be a new beginning. . . . He should always try for something that has never been done or that others have tried and failed."[154] *See also* Authors; Boxing; Critics.

> The narrator acidly recommends Faulkner both for his productivity and his subject matter (173, 179).

Feather Work. *See* Mexican Feather Work.

Federico, doña Carmen de. Full name: Carmen de Federico de Urquijo. Spanish bull breeder, d. 1946.

When Carmen de Federico's husband, don Juan Manuel de Urquijo y Usía (or Ussía), bought the Murube herd in 1917, he registered it in his wife's name. By the time Hemingway came to Spain and began to follow the bulls, she was a famous breeder with extensive holdings. In 1931, for example, she sent fifty-nine bulls and six *novillos*—an impressive number—to Spanish plazas; almost all of them got very high marks. *Toros y toreros en 1931* ranks her herd

among the nation's three or four best: "su nombre es obligado en los carteles de las principales ferias" (her name is indispensable for the important fairs).

When Carmen de Federico died in 1946, her sons Antonio and Carlos Urquijo de Federico inherited their parents' ranches and stock, including their mother's Murube herd. In 1980,

Carlos, who survived Antonio, sold this herd to Antonio Ordóñez (see in *DS*), and this famous bullfighter-*cum*-bull breeder sold the Urquijo-Federico-Suárez herd to José Murube, thus returning the herd to the family whose name it had carried even during the half-century when it belonged to Carmen de Federico and her sons.[155] For the earlier history of this herd, *see* Murube.

> The narrator correctly identifies doña Carmen de Federico as a leading contemporary bull breeder and current owner of the Murube breed (132).

Ferdinand. Ferdinand V (the Catholic), 1452–1516; king of Sicily (1468–1516); of Aragón (as Ferdinand II), 1479–1516); of Naples (1504–16).

Ferdinand and his wife Isabella (q.v.) ruled the large provinces of Castile, León, and Aragón jointly from 1474 until her death in 1504, when he became regent for their daughter Joanna (Juana la Loca). Ferdinand and Isabella, the Catholic Monarchs, unified Spain, tortured and expelled the Moors and Jews, and colonized the New World. They took Ronda on 12 May 1485.[156]

In the 1920s and early 1930s, when Hemingway visited Spain, Ronda (q.v.) held no *corridas de toros* and only the occasional formal *novillada*, such as the one on 20 May 1929. Informal, unrecorded bullfights might also have taken place.

> The narrator reports that Ronda's annual bullfight and fair begins on 20 May, to commemorate the date of its conquest by Ferdinand and Isabella (43).

Fermín, Saint. Spanish prelate, c. second century C.E. Since the seventeenth century, Sts. Fermín and Francisco Javier have been joint patron saints of the province of Navarre; the patron saint of the city of Pamplona is St. Saturnino.

Fermín was the son of Firmo, the president of the Senate of the then-Roman city of Pamplona and an early convert to Christianity. Firmo, who had been baptized by St. Saturnino, brought up his son in the Christian faith, and Fermín became a great evangelizer and the first bishop of Pamplona. He was martyred by beheading, in Amiens, shortly after baptizing more than three thousand converts there.

In 1591 the city of Pamplona, where St. Fermín had a great following, asked that his feast day be changed from the fall, the time of his martyrdom, to July 7, to coincide with the important midsummer fair and market. This date marks the beginning of the city's annual week-long revels, the *sanfermines*.[157]

Hemingway and Pamplona's Sanfermines. Much of the action of *The Sun Also Rises* (q.v.) is set during the July fiesta of San Fermín, which Hemingway attended in 1923–27, 1929, 1931, 1953, and 1959; see also Pamplona in *DS*.

At Pamplona's *sanfermines* of 1924 and 1925, Hemingway was very impressed with the matador Cayetano Ordóñez (q.v.), who became the prototype for the character of Pedro Romero in *The Sun Also Rises*. Hemingway refers to those Pamplona fiestas when he remarks that he "tried to describe" Ordóñez "in a book one time" (89).

> The narrator describes the San Fermín fiesta briefly (*h:* 510) and alludes to the *sanfermines* of 1923 (161), 1924 (*h:* 318), 1930 (224), and 1931 (251–52). He saw Miuras fought at one of these (154; probably in 1925) and fictionalized Ordóñez's peformance at the fiesta 1925 (89).

Fernández Martínez, don Julián. Spanish bull breeder, 1868–1938.

Don Julián registered his bulls in 1926 but retained his grand-

father's name so that in Hemingway's day the breed was officially listed as belonging to "don Vicente Martínez (hoy [today] don Julián Fernández Martínez)" or to "don Julián Fernández Martínez (antes [formerly] Vicente Martínez)."[158] For more detail, *see* Martínez, Vicente; *see also* Diano.

> The narrator reports accurately that Julián Fernández Martínez is the current owner of Vicente Martínez's herds (132).

La Fiesta Brava. Subtitle: *Semanario taurino* (taurine weekly). Several journals had this name, but Hemingway seems to be most familiar with the one from Barcelona, a weekly founded in April 1926. Its eight-page issues carried signed articles, some cartoons and drawings, and a few small advertisements. Most of the space was devoted to reviews of bullfights, biographical essays about bullfighters, interviews with important figures, editorials about current issues or problems (e.g., the debate about the *peto*, q.v.), and historically oriented discussions in regular features such as "Las suertes olvidadas" (forgotten techniques), "Retratos viejos" (old portraits, or biographies of long-dead bullfighters), and "Hoy hace años" (several years ago, today). The journal offered more text and fewer pictures than most such publications.

Hemingway saved the issue of 7 April 1933, which carried a glowing review of *Death in the Afternoun* (*sic*). He also kept the receipts which indicate that he ordered twenty-two back issues of *La fiesta brava* (published in Barcelona) as well as maintaining a current subscription to this journal.[159] The Biblioteca Nacional, Madrid, has *La fiesta brava* for the 1920s and 1930s.

> The narrator admires *La fiesta brava*, but warns that its taurine criticism is biased (*h:* 463, s.v. *Periódicos*; *h:* 475, s.v. *Revistas*).

Finito de Valladolid. *See* Gómez, Alfonzo.

Firbank, Ronald. Full name: Arthur Annesley Ronald Firbank. Prolific minor English novelist, 1886–1926. Among his books are *Odette* (1908), *Vainglory* (1915), *Inclinations* (1916), *Caprice* (1917), *The Princess Zoubraroff* (1920), *Santul* (1921), *Prancing Nigger* (1924), *Sorrows in Sunlight* (1924), and *Concerning the Eccentricities of Cardinal Pirelli* (1925).

Firbank was one of the better-known London bohemians. His style was "a witty blend of fantasy, elegance, and absurd understatement, occasionally descending to the sentimental. He was at his best in dialogue, odd, inconsequent, ludicrously irrational." His fiction is often classified as "frivolous" or "decadent."

Cyril Connolly classifies Firbank, Eliot, and Huxley (qq.v.) as "dandies in literature" whose defining characteristics were "wit and lyricism." Connolly defines Firbank as an intellectual who "took pains to conceal the fact . . . his object was to cast a sheen of wit over his writing . . . he was obsessed with the beauty of the moment . . . and the problem of recording that beauty . . . [Firbank's] method was to write in dialogue, and to omit what would not fit in . . . it is to Firbank that we owe the conception of dialogue—not as a set-piece in the texture of the novel . . . —but as the fabric itself." Firbank's methods and strengths, superficially similar to Hemingway's, may have prompted Hemingway's remark that Firbank "wrote very well."

Connolly says that Firbank's homosexuality expresses itself in "a naughtiness in his books, a sniggering about priests and choirboys, nuns and flagellation, highbrows and ostlers which . . . is meant to be a joke but . . . [which] actually betrays the author, his inhibitions and his longings." This judgment may account for the second half of Hemingway's remark, that Firbank "wrote very well about what he wrote about but was, let us say, a specialist" (*DIA*, 73).[160] In *A Moveable Feast*, Firbank is identified as one of only two writers Gertrude Stein disinterestedly praised, the other being Fitzgerald (27). *See also* Authors; Homosexuals.

> To explain the discrepancy between the golden age of Joselito and Belmonte and the "decadence" that followed them, the narrator refers to the difference between masters like Shakespeare and Marlowe, on the one hand, and Ronald Firbank on the other (73).

Fitzsimmons, Robert. British prizefighter, c. 1863–c. 1917; world middleweight champion (1891—); world heavyweight champion (1897–99).

Fitzsimmons began his boxing career in New Zealand and Australia, coming to the United States in 1890. He won the world middleweight crown from Jack Dempsey (The Nonpareil, not to be confused with the more famous Jack Dempsey, the Manassa Mauler, who was a heavyweight champion, 1919–26). Fitzsimmons successfully defended this title against all challengers. Although he only weighed about 170 pounds, Fitzsimmons also held the heavyweight title for two years. He won it by knocking out Gentleman Jim Corbett in 1897 and lost it to his first challenger, James J. Jeffries (q.v.), in 1899. He retired in 1914, after thirty-five years in the ring: he was fifty-two. His last fight lasted six rounds and was declared a draw. He never lost the middleweight title.

Hemingway's attack on Domingo Ortega (q.v.), which is one of the weak points of *Death in the Afternoon*, is partially redeemed by his carefully hedged prediction that Ortega may enjoy lasting success. As one of the outstanding performers of the twentieth century, Ortega's reputation as a *figura del toreo* (a major figure of bullfighting) is unshakable. Born in 1908, Ortega was still performing occasionally in the late 1950s.

> Discussing the currently [1931] top-ranked bullfighter Domingo Ortega, the narrator speculates that if he maintains his strength and improves his technique he will become a champion like Fitzsimmons (171).

Football. *See* Sports.

Ford, Richard. English lawyer, writer and art collector, 1796–1858.

Ford lived in Spain in the 1830s and wrote a pamphlet entitled *An Historical Inquiry into the Unchangeable Character of a War in Spain* (1837). After his return to England, he wrote his major work about Spain, *A Handbook for Travellers in Spain and Readers at Home* (2 vols., 1845), which he expanded and revised through several editions. Selections of this popular work were published under the titles *Gatherings from Spain* (1846) and *The Spaniards and Their Country* (1847). His books established him as an authority on all aspects of Spain.

Ford admired the painters Murillo and Velázquez, then largely unknown in Britain. His short biography of Velázquez was published in a limited edition of twenty-five copies. Ford's collection of rare books "and works illustrative of Spanish, classical and miscellaneous literature" was catalogued and auctioned by Sotheby's in 1861.[161]

Hemingway and Ford. Hemingway read Ford's *Gatherings from Spain*.[162] Robert Jordan, the main character of *For Whom the Bell Tolls*, also admires Ford's books about Spain (*FWTBT*, 248). *See also* Authors; Critics.

> In what seems a preemptive attack on the critics of *Death in the Afternoon*, the narrator expresses regret that facile, "mystical" travelogues like Waldo Frank's *Virgin Spain* (q.v.) receive more praise than serious studies like Ford's [and, implicitly, Hemingway's own] of that complicated country (53).

Fornos, Café. Full name: Café Fornos Palace. Address: Alcalá, 25, corner of Calle Peligros (Virgen de Peligros), Madrid. Founded 1880s, closed c. 1930. In spite of its name and its proximity to the Palace Hotel (q.v.), only three blocks away, the Café Fornos was not associated with the hotel, which had its own "café-cervecería restaurant y billares" at 5, Plaza de las Cortes.

By 1930, the well-appointed Fornos was gone, replaced by the "café y restaurant Riesgo" and later by the Vitalicio Bank.[163] In a 1934 essay, Hemingway mourned that "The old café Fornos is gone, torn down to put up an office building."[164] At the end of the 1990s, an insurance company, The Equitativa, occupied the site. *See also* Cafés.

The Spanish *tertulia* (regular, sometimes daily meetings of people with similar interests) usually takes place in a particular café or similar venue, which then becomes associated with it. Although the Café Fornos attracted a varied clientele—"políticos, periodistas, estudiantes, taurófilos, vagos, ricos y pobres" (politicians, journalists, students, lovers of the bulls, vagrants, the rich and the poor)[165]—it became known as the home of a *tertulia* whose regulars included literary figures like Ramón del Valle Inclán and Ramón Pérez de Ayala, the painter Julio Romero de Torres, and the sculptor Sebastián Miranda, all of them interested in tauromachy. They invited Juan Belmonte to join them and eventually hosted a banquet in his honor, at which they issued a manifesto declaring that bullfighting was "una manifestación estética de alto rango nada despreciable" (an important aesthetic activity that should not be underrated).[166] It is not unlikely that the photographers Antonio and José Calvache, both closely connected to the taurine world, occasionally dropped in at the Café Fornos (*see* Luis and the Unsuccessful Matadors) as, of course, did many bullfighters. Hemingway was clearly familiar with the taurine flavor of this café. *See also* "Names of Places," in the introduction to this volume; Cervecería Alemana, in this volume; and Hotel Keepers in *DS*.

The narrator and the Old Lady go to the Café Fornos (64–65).

Fortuna. *See* Mazquiarán, Diego.

Frank, Waldo David. American novelist and critic, 1889–1967.

Frank's novels, most of which explore social and political themes, include *The Unwelcome Man* (the story of a sensitive, unloved child, 1917), *Our America* (a survey which finds that the United States is materialistic, shallow, and morally feeble, 1919), *The Dark Mother* (a novel dealing with the old and the new generations of Americans, 1920), *Rahab* (a novel about a devout woman who descends to prostitution but saves her soul, 1922), *City Block* (1922), *Holiday* (about race problems in the American South, 1923), *Chalk Face* (a horror tale, 1924), and *Salvos* (1924). His fictionalized travelogues are "marked by mysticism, poetic style, and introspective analysis." The earliest, *Virgin Spain* (1926), was followed by *Down in Russia* (1932), two books about South America (1931, 1943), one about Israel (1957), and one about Cuba (1961).[167]

Hemingway and Frank. Hemingway owned several of Frank's books, including *The Rediscovery of America: An Introduction to a Philosophy of American Life* (New York: Scribner, 1929), *Tales from the Argentine* (edited by Frank, translated by Anita Brenner; New York: Farrar & Rinehart, 1930), and the maligned *Virgin Spain* (q.v.).[168]

In a long, openly anti-Semitic harangue, Hemingway insists that Frank is unqualified to write about America because his family of Jewish immigrants had not lived long enough in the country: they may be citizens, Hemingway wrote, but they are not yet Americans. Hemingway seems particularly offended by Frank's *Our America.* In galleys, Hemingway modified his attack on Frank, removing the anti-immigrant strain, focusing his attack on Frank's "solemn journalistic conceit," and comparing him to an owl. That comparison, detached from Frank's name, appeared in print: "a solemn writer is always a bloody owl" (*DIA*, 192).

Accepting Dos Passos's advice, Hemingway finally cut most of his anti-Frank remarks from the published version of *Death in the Afternoon.* What remains, however, is sufficient for an accurate identification of an author whose success obviously grated on Hemingway, especially since he defined himself as a pioneer spokesman for the Spanish bullfight.[169]

Hemingway clearly considered Frank incompetent to write about Spain or bullfighting: "The silliest thing I ever read about bullfighting was written by a man named Waldo Frank." Hemingway was probably objecting to Frank's sexual reading of the bullfight, expressed in his reading of the last act of the drama: "The man becomes the woman. This dance of human will and brutish power is the dance of death no longer. It is the dance of life. . . . The bull is male; the exquisite torero, stirring and unstirred, with hidden ecstasy controlling the plunges of the bull, is female" (*Virgin Spain*, 235).

It is interesting, however, that Hemingway repeats several of Frank's opinions, such as his claims that the third act of the bullfight is "the ultimate tragic scene" and "The horse is the comedian of the drama" (*Virgin Spain*, 232–33; cf. Hemingway's claims that "The tragedy is all centred in the bull and in the man" and that "the horse is the comic character" [*DIA*, 6]). Frank saw the bullfight as an artistic creation, and a fine performance by Belmonte as "a masterpiece. And in an art so profound and dangerous, the masterwork is rare, even as in other aesthetic fields" (*Virgin Spain*, 236), an evaluation that surfaces time and again in *Death in the Afternoon*. For other concealed or unacknowledged sources, *see* Díaz Arquer, Graciano; Meier-Graefe, Julius; and *Toreros y toros*; for further discussion of Hemingway's antipathy for Frank, *see S 4 N*; for Hemingway's attitude to other contemporary writers, *see* Authors.

Frank canvassed all of Spain and limited his discussion of the bullfight to one short chapter (*Virgin Spain*, 229–38). Hemingway's book-length study of the bullfight is more detailed, accurate, and thorough.

The narrator rails against but does not name this writer (53–54).

Franklin, Sidney (né Frumpkin). American bullfighter, c. 1903–76. Investiture as *matador de toros*, 18 July 1945, in Madrid, granted by Luis Gómez (el Estudiante, q.v.).

Franklin is the first North American to have a confirmed *alternativa* (i.e., an *alternativa* given or confirmed in Madrid), but not the first to have an *alternativa* (q.v.). On 20 February 1910, Harper B. Lee was promoted to *matador de toros* in Monterrey, Mexico. At that time, Mexican *alternativas* were not valid in Spain; even today (the year 2001), they have to be confirmed in Madrid.[170] Franklin's Spanish *alternativa* was also his last corrida, which enables the admirers of John Fulton (1932–98) to claim that he is actually the first North American bullfighter to have a real career as a recognized, confirmed *matador de alternativa*. But, as Lee's biographer points out, "To call anyone the first anything is to invite controversy."[171]

Franklin was the son of a middle-class, Russian-Jewish family from Brooklyn. He dropped out of school and went to Mexico in 1922 to establish himself as a commercial artist. His first visit to the bullring inspired him to commit himself to the art. He began training and fighting in Mexico, returned to the United States briefly early in 1929, and went to Spain as a *matador de novillos* (*novillero*) later that year. His blonde good looks and the fact that he was an American attracted the Spanish public, and his successful debut as *novillero* at Seville's prestigious Maestranza Plaza solidified his reputation. He was in demand and he fought, but his inordinately high fees limited the number of bullrings who could hire him. Cossío reports that Franklin appeared fourteen times in 1929 but that a serious goring in March 1930 reduced that season's appearances to nine (Franklin's own count is much higher); he adds that Franklin is skillful with the cape and muleta, elegant with the banderillas, and accurate with the sword. In his own book, Franklin emphasizes his work with the cape, muleta, and sword, which suggests that, as Hemingway says (473), he delegated the placing of banderillas.

After his two Spanish seasons as *novillero*, Franklin returned to the United States in October 1930. Later that year he fought in Mexico, returning to Spain in April 1931 but too sick to fight: "I spent most of that year in Spain with Ernest Hemingway hunting or fishing or just lying around and taking it easy."[172] In 1932 he appeared in the Hollywood musical, *The Kid from Spain*. He returned to Spain briefly during the Spanish Civil War. And then, in 1945, at an age when most bullfighters have long since retired, he resumed his bullfighting career and was promoted to the rank of *matador de toros* in a Madrid corrida which marked his last appearance in the Spanish ring. After that he fought occasionally and without much success in Portugal, Mexico, and Tangier and, after several years of inactivity, fought again in 1959 and in the early 1960s, thus ending a most peculiar taurine career.

Franklin's self-congratulatory autobiography, *The Bullfighter from Brooklyn* (1952), focuses on his many adventures from 1922 to 1937, claiming stupendous success as a businessman and apprentice bullfighter and detailing his adventures: an incredible drunken rampage, a week of being feted by a Mexican tribe (complete with many maidens wishing to be ravished by him), a shipwreck, and his meeting with Hemingway (probably the only accurate part of his story). In an impromptu interview granted to *La fiesta brava* in October 1929, Franklin displays the same penchant for self-aggrandizement. Asked what he did before he took up bullfighting, the twenty-five-year-old answered inaccurately: "I am a painter. I've always been attracted to the visual arts, and believe me, I earn more as a painter than I do as a bullfighter. I also have a B.A. from Columbia University, I am an architect, and I speak French, English, and German."[173]

In his middle age, Franklin ran a bullfighting school, a café, and a variety of other enterprises that capitalized on his early success in the ring. Sadly enough, he became a figure of ridicule in his adopted hometown of Seville. He appears, only slightly disguised, as Stanley Philips, the protagonist of Patrick Cunningham's novel *A River of Lions*: Stanley is an American living in Seville, a former bullfighter, a homosexual, and an embarrassment to his students, who quickly get the better of this unattractive, stingy, dishonest, vain, cowardly, and vulgar man.

Hemingway and Franklin. There is no doubt that Hemingway admired the young Franklin who had done so well in 1929. But in *The Dangerous Summer*, there is a suggestion that the admiration had turned to dislike. Bill Davis reads "a rather silly and confused book about bullfighters" whose unnamed author he and the narrator have come to dislike "intensely" and who is identified in the manuscript as "an ex-," that is, an ex-bullfighter.[174] As Davis drove through Spain in the summer of 1959, he would have noticed that Franklin, in his book about his taurine season, mentions his arrival and departure from several train stations. This may explain Hemingway's remark that "we had all assumed, *mistakenly*, that he had driven these barbarous distances himself" (124, my italics). *See also* Luis and the Unsuccessful Matadors; Mercedes.

The narrator devotes an admiring appendix to Franklin (*h:* 503–506) and mentions him often (169, 199, 228, 253, 276–77, *h:* 496; photographs, *h:* 388–89). The unnamed "son of a Brooklyn policeman" is, of course, Franklin (196). Franklin speaks: 228.

Frascuelo. *See* Sánchez, Salvador.

The Fratellinis. An Italian family of clowns. The father, Gustavo Fratellini (1842–1905) was an acrobat, clown, and horseback performer. Three of his sons also became circus clowns: after ten years touring Russia and Europe with the Salamonsky Circus, they joined the Medrano Circus of Paris during World War I. They were the most famous clowns in the period between the world wars. Pablo (1877–1940) played the placid, self-satisfied bourgeois; Francisco

(1879–1951) was the chubby dreamer, stuffed into a sparkling sequined and spangled outfit; and Alberto (c. 1886–1961) played the hirsute buffoon whose make up (heavy eyebrows, big red nose and mouth) is now standard for clowns. In 1956 Alberto came out of retirement for a final performance to celebrate his fiftieth anniversary in the profession. He had outlived his two brothers but was joined by his nephews Max, Louis, and Nino, the next generation of Fratellini clowns.[175]

Jean Cocteau and Raymond Radiguet (qq.v.) based some of their fictional characters on the three Fratellini brothers.

Hemingway, Clowns, and the Fratellinis. Hemingway mentioned clowns often; *see* Altrock, Nick. References to the Fratellinis appear in his first two novels, *The Torrents of Spring* (41) and *The Sun Also Rises* (114).

> The narrator mentions that the Fratellinis perform a burlesque of a gored horse trailing its entrails (7).

Freg, Luis. Full name: Luis Freg Castro. Mexican bullfighter, c. 1890–1934. Investiture as *matador de toros* in Mexico City, 23 October 1910; in Alcalá de Henares, 25 August 1911; confirmed in Madrid a month later.

Freg was a brave matador, excelling in sword work but weaker with the cape and the muleta. Because of his desire to provide the public with an impressive *faena* in spite of his problems with the muleta, he was often injured during this phase of the bullfight. He pursued his career in Spain and in Mexico; the frequent gorings curtailed his performances every year, and he never achieved the large following that most critics feel he deserved. While the critics dubbed him *don Valor* and *don Voluntad* (Mr. Bravery, Mr. Eager Beaver), the Spanish public remained cool to a foreign bullfighter, especially one who was frequently gored and consequently unable to fulfill his contracts. All too often, he appeared in the ring before his wounds had healed completely and was therefore more likely to be injured again. Even so, in 1914 Freg appeared in twenty-three corridas; twenty in 1915; and thirty in 1921. Freg often returned to Mexico after the Spanish season was over in late fall; it was there that he suffered the worst goring of his career (March 1922; it took months to heal and delayed his return to Spain). Back in Spain, Freg managed only eighteen corridas in 1922.

Freg ended the 1923 season with a horrific goring on 23 September 1923. The taurine public was convinced that his career was over, but the indomitable Freg fought ten corridas in 1924 (he was the fourth oldest performer that year, in terms of years since the *alternativa*, q.v.); sixteen in 1925; nine in 1926; and eleven in 1927. From then on, he performed only occasionally in Spain. In 1931 he was the dean of active bullfighters. He retired from the Spanish bullrings at the end of the season but continued performing quite successfully in Central and South America. When he drowned in a boating accident, he was the most highly regarded bullfighter in his country.

Luis Freg's three brothers (Miguel, Salvador, and Alfredo) were also bullfighters, as was his nephew, Ricardo Romero Freg, but none of these relatives attained his stature and fame. Hemingway focuses on Freg's current performances and disregards the critical acclaim accorded Freg in Mexico and Spain in the years before Hemingway saw him perform.[176]

Hemingway and Freg. Hemingway probably didn't see Freg very often because in 1923, when he first came to Spain's bullrings, Freg was in his mid-thirties and already on the decline. Hemingway saw Freg perform at the first corrida he ever saw in Pamplona, on Friday, 6 July 1923: Freg headed the bill, which included Antonio Márquez and Nicanor Villalta (qq.v.). He may have seen Freg in Madrid once or twice in subsequent years. Freg was not contracted in Pamplona or Valencia, Hemingway's favorite *ferias*, after 1923.

The reference to the Jeffries-Johnson boxing match (*DIA*, 263) is apt, because the popularity of a Mexican-Indian matador caused racial issues to surface both in Mexico (because Freg was Indian) and in Spain (because Freg was Mexican). *See also* Jeffries, James Jackson.

In the Glossary, Hemingway writes that two bullfighters are homosexuals. One of them, not named but recognizable from the description, is Freg: he "has a reputation for great valor" (*h:* 448, s.v. *Maricón*). For the second one, Hemingway may have had José Ortiz Puga (Pepe Ortiz) in mind. He is not discussed in *Death in the Afternoon* but he is recognizably the historical prototype for the homosexual bullfighter in Hemingway's short story, "Mother of a Queen";

but the reference may be to Manuel Jiménez (Chicuelo, q.v.): he "is very skillful and delicate with the cape" (*h:* 448, s.v. *Maricón*). The "strange-enough story" (264) that Hemingway does not tell us about Freg, is that he was a "pansy."[177] A more accurate story, which was an open secret in Mexican taurine circles, is that he was a transvestite.

> The narrator describes Luis Freg as a slow, awkward Mexican-Indian bullfighter with a long career interrupted by frequent gorings, a brave killer and accomplished swordsman, one of the few contemporary matadors who can kill *recibiendo* (standing still and waiting for the bull). He fought in the classical style made obsolete by Belmonte (75–76, 238, 253, 262–64, 272; photographs, *h:* 326–29, 392–93; described but not named, *h:* 448, s.v. *Maricón*). Freg speaks: 264.

French. *See* Authors, in this volume; and Frenchman, in *DS*.

Fuentes, Antonio. Full name: Antonio Fuentes Zurita. Spanish bullfighter, 1869–1938. Investiture as *matador de toros*, Madrid, 17 September 1893.

Entering the profession against his parents' wishes, Fuentes rose steadily and unspectacularly through the ranks, performing competently and fairly frequently. He was a banderillero for such luminaries of the day as Emilio Torres Reina (Bombita), Francisco Arjona Reyes (Currito), and José Sánchez del Campo (Cara-Ancha). In May 1894, he was in the ring when the controversial twenty-nine-year-old Manuel García Cuesta (el Espartero, q.v.) was killed. Fuentes did not lose his nerve, and his fine performances on that dreadful afternoon catapulted him into the limelight early in his first full season as a *matador de toros.*[178]

Like el Espartero before him, Fuentes aimed to dethrone the fading hero, Luis Mazzantini, and the current strongman, Rafael Guerra Bejarano (Guerrita, qq.v.). Perhaps because so much was expected of him, he was disappointing for much of the 1894 season, and he was not contracted to perform in the important San Isidro fiestas of 1895 or 1896. But he performed frequently and well elsewhere (*see,* for example, Comisario), and Madrid soon invited him back. From 1897 to 1908, when he retired, he was a permanent fixture of the Madrid fiesta. In these years, Fuentes's *afición* seems to have wavered: his lack of commitment showed in the ring, and his uneven performances alienated the public. His sword work was particularly erratic, but his power and talent were indisputable.

In 1899, when Guerrita, the reigning matador of his day, retired, he reputedly bragged, "Después de mí, naide [nadie]. Y después de naide, Fuentes" (After me, no one. And after no one, Fuentes).[179] Fuentes blossomed after Guerrita's retirement, and although he still produced lackluster performances, he was frequently so brilliant that the public complained loudly on afternoons when he was merely competent. In 1901 he performed in more corridas than any other bullfighter, charged high prices, frequently behaved like a prima donna, and garnered complaints as often as praise. In 1902, probably his best year, he refused to perform in the Madrid fiesta but was impressively elegant throughout the rest of Spain. But in 1903 he was disappointing, and the weak season ended badly, with a gored knee that required months of operations and therapy and affected his work for the next two years, although he was still capable of electrifying the public.

By 1906 his body and spirit were completely healed, and Fuentes produced two memorable seasons, 1906 and 1907, before deciding to retire in 1908. His round of farewell performances was cut short by a goring in Valencia and an automobile accident. He came out of retirement within a year or two, but his performances were few, disappointing, and, eventually, embarrassing.[180]

Cossío describes Fuentes as uneven and even unambitious and it is true, as Hemingway remarks, that Fuentes was much criticized during his career. But the glowing reviews, which Cossío also quotes, undermine Hemingway's claim that fine bullfighters are not appreciated until after they retire.[181]

> The narrator correctly identifies Fuentes as a fine matador who worked in the early years of the twentieth century. To support his theory that historians and critics disdain even the best of contemporary artists, the narrator reports that only when he retired was Fuentes praised as "incomparable" (241–42).

Fuentes Bejarano, Luis (Bejarano). Full name: Luis Moragas Fuertes Fuentes Bejarano. Spanish bullfighter, 1902–99. Investiture as *matador de toros*, in Vitoria, 5 August 1923; confirmed in Madrid, 1924.

As a *novillero* Fuentes Bejarano attracted admiration for his skill and determination, clearly evidenced the afternoon that he insisted on finishing a fight though wounded. On 20 April 1924, early in the season, he was badly gored and he returned to the ring before he was properly healed; consequently the twenty-one performances he managed that season were not impressive and he was offered few contracts for the next two years (ten in 1925, twelve in 1926).

Determined to improve his standing, Fuentes Bejarano went to Mexico, established a great reputation there, and then resumed his career more successfully in Spain. He performed in twenty-eight corridas in both 1928 and 1929, forty in 1930, thirty-one in 1931 (his last good year: he was one of the eight matadors invited to perform at the inaugural corrida of Las Ventas), sixteen in 1932, nine in 1933, two in 1934, and one in 1935. He retired in 1940 but celebrated each passing decade of his life by killing a bull, the last such event occurring on his eightieth birthday.

Cossío remarks that Fuentes Bejarano was a highly competent and generally popular performer, with a penchant for elegant uniforms. Tapia writes that he was one of the best bullfighters of his time, whose expertise with the sword made up for some deficiencies in style. Abella concurs that he was a great swordsman, and another critic generously writes that "Fuentes Bejarano podía con todo" (he was expert in all areas and could handle all kinds of bulls). Bagüés opines that he had more character than art.

Although born in Madrid, he lived in Seville most of his life, and was feted as Spain's oldest living matador for the last decade or so of his long life.[182]

Hemingway and Fuentes Bejarano. Hemingway saw Fuentes Bejarano in Pamplona, 7, 8, and 9 July 1924: according to the reviews, Fuentes Bejarano did not shine on any of those afternoons. On 7 July 1924, the matadors were Chicuelo, Maera, and Fuentes Bejarano. Maera cut both ears and the tail of his second bull, and Fuentes Bejarano was not applauded, though he should have been, the critic says, for his work with the last bull of the afternoon. On 8 July, Algabeño, Fuentes Bejarano, and Nacional performed, and no one did anything interesting. On 9 July there was a *corrida de prueba*, with four bullfighters: Chicuelo (poor performance), Maera (fine), Nacional II (a turn around the ring), and Fuentes Bejarano (boring).[183]

Hemingway may also have seen Fuentes Bejarano in Madrid (e.g., 20 and 22 June 1926; or 17 and 19 June 1931).

The narrator's description of Fuentes Bejarano is contradictory: he is a "valorous and worthy workman" but his "style is simply bad modern tricks" (70, 222–23).

Fulano. So-and-so or such-and-such; a generic noun used to refer to a man whose name is not known or mentioned. Sometimes the phrase *fulano de tal* or, for a woman, *fulana de tal*, is used.

Obviously Hemingway did not attend any of Rafael Gómez Ortega's farewell performances of 1918, the year of the infamously unkilled farewell bull.[184] But the people to whom Rafael dedicated the farewell bulls of his last two corridas can be identified.

Rafael bid farewell to his Seville public on 30 September 1918. After killing his first bull of the afternooon, he dedicated his second to three bullfighters—Antonio Fuentes, Emilio Torres Reina (Bombita), and José García Rodríguez (el Algabeño, qq.v.)—and not to his patron or his friend the composer, as Hemingway says (157–58). But after the triple dedication, he refused to kill the Concha y Sierra bull, giving it to his brother Joselito who, he felt, had forced him into retirement. Rafael made his protest clear: after refusing to kill his farewell bull, he called for the *sobrero* (a Martínez bull), fought it, and killed it.[185]

Rafael bid farewell to his Madrid public on 10 October 1918. That farewell bull, the only one Rafael fought that day, was also triply dedicated: to the President of the bullfight, to the Duke of Tovar, and finally to the public of Madrid. Rafael killed his bull on that afternoon, on which he shared the *cartel* with his brother (who outdid himself) and with José Gárate Hernández (Limeño) and José Flores González (Camará). Seven bulls were fought: the first one was a Contreras, the remainder were Guadalest. Another farewell corrida, scheduled for Zaragoza later that September, was canceled because of the epidemic of Spanish influenza (q.v.).[186]

The photograph (*h:* 400–401) shows Rafael el Gallo in the Seville ring, at the farewell corrida described in the text, although the text of the caption suggests the Madrid farewell.[187]

The 1918 retirement was short lived: Rafael performed in Ceuta on 13 April 1919 (very early in the taurine season) and fought twenty more corridas that year. But after the Madrid farewell, he and Joselito never again shared a *cartel*, a clear sign of their disagreement on the conduct of Rafael's career. In 1918, Joselito had appeared with his brother in eight of Rafael's ten performances.

Rafael's Other Unkilled Bulls. The bull of the Seville farewell was not the first or only one that Rafael el Gallo refused to kill. In 1899, very early in his career, Rafael suddenly took fright and refused to kill a *novillo*, even though he had just dedicated it to a high-ranking officer. Resisting the threats and fines imposed by the president of the bullfight, Rafael was arrested and taken to jail, still in his performance outfit. The story is that he had been so graceful in the ring that various impresarios showed up at the jail, eager to pay his fine and contract him for their bullrings. On 24 August 1924, at a gala benefit for the Press Association in Santander, Rafael again refused to kill his bull: he was arrested and the affair "produjo un monumental escándalo," a near-riot.[188]

> The narrator reports that Rafael Gómez Ortega dedicated a bull to an unnamed "Señor Fulano" and then refused to kill it (157).

– G –

Gabriel. Gabriel is an archangel, whose name means "man of God" or "power of God." He is considered the divine herald.

Gabriel appeared to Daniel, to interpret his visions of horned rams and goats (Dan. 8.16–26) and to prophesy the restoration and destruction of Jerusalem (Dan. 9.21–27). Gabriel also delivered special revelations, telling Zacharias that his wife, the old, barren Elizabeth, would bear John the Baptist (Luke 1.11–19). Most famously, he announced to the Virgin Mary that she would give birth to Jesus (Luke 1.26–38).

Gabriel figures largely in extracanonical literature. In the first book of Enoch he is portrayed as an archangel, close to the throne of God and able to mediate between the divine and the human (see 1 Enoch 9.1–11, 10.9, 20.7, and 40.3; 2 Enoch 21.3–6). Christian tradition makes him the messenger who brings revelations to human beings, including the miraculous births of sons to Zacharias (Luke 1.8–20) and to Mary (Luke 1.26–38). He is also the archangel trumpeter of the Last Judgment, who is mentioned in the passage in I Thessalonians 4.16: "the Lord himself shall descend from heaven with a shout, with the voice of the archangel, and with the trump of God: and the dead in Christ shall rise first."[189] As Hemingway correctly notes, the *torilero*'s opening of the *toril* (the heavy door through which the bull enters the bullring) is preceded by the blowing of the *clarín* (bugle), which makes Gabriel an appropriate name for a *torilero*.

Madrid's Torileros. Madrid's *torileros* have been quite long-lived, with the result that there have been only a few of them. Because they are minor functionaries, little is written about them. A *torilero* known only as Ramoncillo retired from this post in 1843. He was succeeded by the failed bullfighter Carlos Rufo Albarrán (el Buñolero, 1819–1910), who was *torilero* for sixty years (1843–1903). In 1903, Antonio Sierra (Morenito), a former banderillero, took over the octogenarian's duties, generously making sure that the meager income of the *torilero* should continue to accrue to El Buñolero until the latter's death in 1910.

For the next decade or so, Jerónimo Orejón (Jeromo), formerly a banderillero, served Madrid as *torilero*. He died in 1922, a year before Hemingway saw his first bullfights, and was succeeded by Germán Hidalgo (1879–1956), who was *torilero* for more than thirty years, until just two months before his death at age seventy-seven. This is the *torilero* Hemingway would have seen in Madrid in the 1920s. Photographs show a slight, trim, straight-legged man, not at all "wide" like the Gabriel whom Hemingway mentions.[190]

Was there a Gabriel? A brief note in a taurine journal describes Hidalgo as "the successor of El Buñolero and of Gabriel," which suggests that someone named Gabriel served as interim *torilero* until Hidalgo took over.[191] Details about this Gabriel are hard to come by, but we do know that he was "lento, gordo, fofo, robicundo de cara y estavado de piernas" (slow, fat, nondescript, round-faced, and bowlegged). His suit was shabby: "grana resudada y oro, que parecía plomo, por lo mohoso" (sweat-stained red and gold, which looked like lead, because it was so rusty).[192] In a manuscript account of his first corrida, Hemingway mentions an elderly bowlegged man who admits the bull into the bullring: this seems to be Gabriel.[193]

By virtue of their former professions, El Buñolero, Sierra, and Orejón already had *traje de luces* when they became *torileros*. But

Hidalgo, a bullring carpenter, and Gabriel, a bullring servant, had no such outfits, which accounts for Hemingway's remark that "a suit was bought for him [Gabriel] by popular subscription" (62).

> The narrator refers to the serious, ill-clad old man who opens the *toril* as Gabriel; his portentous action is preceded by the sound of trumpets (61–62).

La Gaceta del Norte. See Desperdicios.

Gallo, Gallito (Rooster, Little Rooster). Professional nickname of the extraordinary Gómez dynasty, a "great family of gypsy bullfighters" (21, *h:* 439). The first to be called "Gallo" was José Gómez, a banderillero who attracted the bull's attention with short, choppy hops, reminiscent of a cock's strutting. The nickname was subsequently applied to José's younger brother Fernando (q.v.) and to Fernando's three sons, all of whom were bullfighters: the colorful Rafael Gómez Ortega (q.v.), the undistinguished Fernando (Gallito, 1884–1921), and the great José (q.v.). Their four sisters—Eloisa (an illegitimate half-sister), Dolores (Lola), Gabriela, and Trinidad—all married bullfighters.[194]

Gaona, Rodolfo. Full name: Rodolfo Gaona Jiménez. Mexican bullfighter, 1888–1975. Investiture as *matador de toros*, Madrid's plaza of Tetuán de las Victorias, 31 May 1908; confirmed in Madrid's main plaza, 5 July that same season.

Hemingway, who has obviously read a good bit of taurine history, correctly reports that Gaona was trained by Frascuelo's banderillero (474), whose name was Saturnino Frutos (Ojitos, 1855–1913).[195] A talented pupil, Gaona soon established himself in Mexico and several neighboring countries, and came to Spain, in the company of the watchful Ojitos, in February or early March 1908. His early years in Spain were marred first by the opposition of the press to foreign bullfighters, and then by the clannishness of powerful managers and impresarios, whose veto ruined more than one career. Perhaps because of this, Gaona fought Miura bulls in 1908 and 1909, in defiance of the boycott organized by bullfighters who were demanding extra pay for facing these deadly bulls (*see* Miura, don Eduardo; Mosquera, don Indalecio, in this volume; and Manager in *DS*). Several Spanish bullfighters, like Rafael el Gallo and Vicente Pastor (qq.v.) also fought Miuras in those years; the boycott was strong but not universal.

In his next three seasons as *matador de alternativa* Gaona was consistently in top form: forty-two corridas in 1909, forty-six in 1910, and seventy-one in 1911 (these were the years that Bombita and Machaquito dominated the ring). A serious chest wound early in the 1912 season cut Gaona's performances to only nine corridas that year. Fully recovered by 1914, he fought in sixty-four corridas. The next year he was gored three times, but in 1916 he fought sixty-seven corridas, fifty-eight in 1917, and sixty in 1918 (he had been contracted for an even higher number, but the influenza epidemic closed the ring on several afternoons: *see* Spanish Influenza). On many of these afternoons he appeared with Joselito and Belmonte, the two stars who dominated that decade.

Later seasons saw an occasional uncertainty and lack of enthusiasm. Most critics agree, however, that Gaona was a master of all aspects of bullfighting. He fought on both sides of the ocean, with great critical and popular success, from 1908 to 1919. He was an elegant, accomplished bullfighter who was able to maintain his standing as a premier matador in times when Joselito and Belmonte controlled the bullring. Cossío writes that he was "la suprema elegancia, la elegancia personificada" (supreme elegance, elegance personified), excellent with the cape and banderillas, less artistic with the muleta and uneven with the sword.[196] Gaona entered the taurine lexicon with the *gaonera*, a complicated old cape pass known as *de frente por detrás* until he revived and popularized it.

In 1919, Gaona fought twenty-six corridas in Spain. From then on, he fought mostly in Mexico (the civil war there had ended in 1917; *see* Díaz, Porfirio), not returning to the Spanish bullring until 1923, when the politics of the Madrid bullring kept him from performing in that city. That season he fought only five corridas, all in Barcelona. He closed his career with thirty-two corridas in 1924 and eighteen in 1925, all in Mexico, and retired on 12 April 1925, sharing the *cartel* with Rafael Rubio Oltra (Rodalito, q.v.). Gaona was then only thirty-seven years old; he lived another fifty years.

Hemingway and Gaona. Hemingway's statement that 1916 was Gaona's last great season in Spain is moot, as the statistics above indicate.[197] It seems to me that Hemingway, whose first taurine visits to Spain (May-June 1923 and again in July of that year) did not include a visit to Barcelona, never saw Gaona perform. Still, he is remarkably well informed about him, even knowing about Gaona's "unfortunate marriage," to Carmen Ruiz Moragas, who turned out to be the favorite mistress of King Alfonso XIII (she bore him two children). Sidney Franklin (q.v.), who trained in Mexico under Gaona, is probably the source of much of Hemingway's information about this Mexican maestro.

> The narrator describes Rodolfo Gaona as comparable to José Gómez Ortega (Joselito) and Juan Belmonte (198, *h:* 504; *see also* 176, 225), but he feels that Gaona's work deteriorated after his two spectacular seasons of 1915 and 1916 (198–99; photograph, *h:* 300–01).

García, Antonio (Bombita IV). Full name: Antonio García Bermúdez. Spanish bullfighter, 1891–1968 (died by his own hand). He was not related to the famous Bombitas (q.v.) but took their nickname because he came from the same town, Tomares (Seville).

Growing up in a town enamored of its bullfighting sons, the Torres Reina brothers, García decided to become a matador. A few lackluster seasons as *matador de novillos* served to clarify his unsuitability for that rank. But he was talented with the banderillas, and this enabled him to make a living in the bullring. At first he worked in low-quality *cuadrillas*, but he slowly improved his standing and in 1920 joined the crew of the top-ranked Ignacio Sánchez Mejías (q.v.), for whom he worked until Ignacio's first retirement, in 1922.

The early years of the twentieth century were marked by social unrest (*see* Noy de Sucre) which spread to the bullfighting world. Picadors and banderilleros formed unions and lobbied to improve their salaries and working conditions. In 1923, they attempted a boycott against bullrings that offered *charlotadas* and other types of *toreo bufo*, then very popular (*see Mojigangas*). García did not support this strike: instead, he worked as a freelancer and, employing other strikebreakers, formed his own *cuadrilla* and appeared once again as *novillero*. He was expelled from the Society of Banderilleros, vilified in editorials, shouted at in the street and in the ring, and physically attacked by his unionized colleagues and their sympathizers. On 5 April 1923, the day after one such violent assault, he showed up with a bandaged hand and head for his belated Madrid debut as *novillero*. A few days later he was involved in a shoot-out in Zaragoza. He continued to perform as *novillero* until he was badly gored on 15 August.

By the start of the 1924 season, the strike was settled, García was reinstated in the Society of Banderilleros, and Manuel García (Maera, q.v.) hired him. Hemingway saw Antonio García in the 1924 *sanfermines*, at which Maera performed. García was probably a precipitating factor in the fight between Maera and David that Hemingway mentions (*see* David, Alfredo). For the next decade Bombita IV worked for all the leading matadors of Hemingway's day, including Ignacio Sánchez Mejías (when he came out of retirement), Rafael Gómez Ortega (el Gallo), Cayetano Ordóñez (Niño de la Palma), Francisco Vega de los Reyes (Gitanillo de Triana), and Manuel Mejías (Bienvenida) (qq.v.). He was badly gored in 1934 but recovered and worked for fifteen more years, retiring in 1949 at the age of fifty-eight.[198]

The narrator correctly ranks García among the top banderilleros of the late 1920s and early 1930s (201).

García, Heriberto. Full name: Heriberto García Espejel. Mexican bullfighter, b. 1907. Investiture as *matador de toros* in Mexico, 1928; in Barcelona, 31 March 1929; confirmed in Madrid, May 1929.

García was a highly successful *novillero* who, as soon as he was promoted to *matador de toros* in Mexico, attempted to establish himself in Spain. Probably because he was a foreigner, he obtained contracts for only nine corridas, in which he did not distinguish himself. After this inauspicious beginning, García returned to Mexico and had a successful season there (the winter of 1929–30). He returned to Spain and gave a magnificent performance in his first appearance of the 1930 season (20 April 1930, in Madrid: he was awarded both ears, the tail, and rave reviews) but was badly gored while killing his second bull. He recuperated sufficiently to perform in twenty additional corridas that year, but he never again achieved the heights of that Madrid afternoon. He did not come to Spain for the 1931 season and had only five corridas in Spain in 1932, after which he performed only in Mexico and Central and South America. In the 1934–35

Mexican season he fought more corridas than any other matador. He retired in 1940.[199]

Hemingway and García. The only year in which Hemingway and Heriberto García were both in Spain for the season was 1929. Hemingway saw him perform in Pontevedra on 11 August and may have seen another of his nine corridas as well. In summing up García's 1929 season, Tomás Orts Ramos (Uno al Sesgo) wrote, "es uno más y no de los mejores" (he's run of the mill).[200]

> The narrator explains that the Mexican matador García is noted for his excellent work with the banderillas and the muleta (200, 220; *see also* 267).

García, José (Maera II). Full name: José García López. Spanish bullfighter, 1907–40. Investiture as *matador de toros*, in La Coruña, 4 August 1929; confirmed in Madrid, 20 April 1930. As Hemingway notes, the younger brother of Manuel García (Maera) attracted a great deal of attention as a *novillero*. At his Madrid debut, on 11 September 1927, he cut both ears of his first *novillo*. In 1928 he fought twenty-one *novilladas*, and the following year he fought eighteen, to which he added fourteen *corridas de toros*. This was probably his best season.

In 1930, when Hemingway did not see bullfights in Spain, Maera II had only eight *corridas de toros*. In 1931, Hemingway's last season before publishing *Death in the Afternoon*, he fought only one: his career as a bullfighter was over. Maera II lacked the drive, bravery, and *afición* that brought such fame to his older brother.

In later years, Maera II worked occasionally as a banderillero, but he eventually gave up all taurine efforts and became a flamenco singer.[201]

> The narrator reports correctly that the younger Maera was a successful *novillero* but a failure as a *matador de toros* (83).

García, Julio (Palmeño). Full name: Julio García Fuillerat. Spanish bullfighter, 1900–71. Investiture as *matador de toros*, in Ecija, September 1928; confirmed in Madrid, March 1929; renounced, 1934.

As a successful *matador de novillos* Palmeño was hailed as brave but uncontrolled. His reputation as *novillero* and his performance at his investiture were impressive enough to earn him fifteen contracts for 1929, his first full season as *matador de toros*. But he would not or could not correct his faults and he appeared less and less over the next few years: fourteen corridas in 1930, thirteen in 1931, seven in 1932 (he lost much of this season to a serious wound), and three in 1933. In 1934 he renounced his rank, presenting himself as a *matador de novillos* in 1935 but giving only one (disastrous) performance. He hardly performed after this and retired officially in 1940. He was "muy valiente, siempre muy valiente, pero carente de cualidades y conocimientos que necesariamente han de acompañar el valor; por eso tuvo que desistir de ser torero" (he was always brave but he lacked the character and knowledge that should accompany valor; that's why he couldn't continue as a torero).[202]

The narrator considers Palmeño a brave young matador with a bright future, though his lack of height may work against him (224).

García, Manuel (Maera). Full name: Manuel García López. Spanish bullfighter, 1896–1924. Investiture as *matador de toros*, in El Puerto de Santa María, August 1921; confirmed in Madrid, 1922.

As a *becerrista* and *novillero*, Maera showed great talent and skill but was unable to attract a patron or to obtain a contract in the major bullrings. Rather than quit the profession, he joined the *cuadrilla* of Juan Belmonte as banderillero in 1915. From this master and from his competitor Joselito, Maera learned about bulls and about the new style of bullfighting. He soon rose to be chief of Belmonte's *cuadrilla*. In 1919 he again began to appear in *novilladas* where, in spite of his excessive height, he built a modest reputation, being promoted to *matador de toros* in 1921.

After this difficult beginning, Maera's career took off. By the end of his successful 1922 season (forty-five corridas), he was counted as one of the top-ranked matadors. The next two seasons he performed even more frequently, with sixty-four corridas in 1923, more than any other matador (these were followed by a successful Mexican tour), and fifty-seven in 1924, generally to great acclaim. In this last year he was awarded the Press Association's "golden ear" trophy. On 16 November 1924, the season having finished, he fought magnificently at a benefit performance, was awarded the ears of both bulls, and went from the ring to his hotel, feverish and too weak to attend the celebratory banquet that followed the fight. He was transferred to his home in Seville and died within a few days.[203]

The bullfight critics I've read, who generally don't comment on a bullfighter's height, report that Maera was very tall and that he adjusted his style accordingly.[204] Hemingway, who generally does comment on height (he reports that Barrera, Chicuelo, Gitanillo de Ricla, Palmeño, and Todó were too short and that Villalta was often awkward because he was too tall), doesn't mention height in relation to Maera, whom he admires enormously. (For Hemingway's attitude to lack of height, see the entry on Isidoro Todó.)

Hemingway and Maera. Maera and Algabeño were the stars of Pamplona's *sanfermines* in 1923 and 1924, the years of Hemingway's first visits to Spain. Maera performed in both those years: on two afternoons in 1923, 12 July (awarded the ears of both of his bulls) and 13 July; and on three afternoons in 1924, 7 July (he was poor with his first bull and great with his second one, being awarded both ears and the tail), 9 July (fine performance), and 11 July (satisfactory performance).[205] It is not unlikely that, as Hemingway says (271), he would have dressed in a priest's cassock: the exuberant Maera was given to all sorts of outlandish behavior.[206]

Maera appears in Interchapters XIII and XIV of *In Our Time*; the second of these, written in 1923 when Maera was still alive, describes Maera's death at the horns of a bull. More accurately, "A Banal Story," written in 1925, reports that Maera died of tuberculosis. For the fight between Maera and David, see David, Alfredo. For Maera's younger brother, see García, José (Maera II).

The narrator rhapsodizes over this brave bullfighter (77–83; mentioned, 94, 238, 243, 267, 271, 273; referred to but not named, 100, 171; photographs, *h:* 314–21). Maera speaks: 80, 81, 82.

García Carranza, José (Pepe, Algabeño II). Spanish bullfighter, 1902–36. Investiture as *matador de toros*, Valencia, June 1923; confirmed in Madrid, May 1924.

Although his father, José García Rodríguez (Algabeño, q.v.) had earned both fame and fortune as a matador, young José encountered a great deal of parental opposition when he declared he intended to become a bullfighter as well. He arranged his first performance behind his father's back, but his father found out and, as a rich ex-matador, possessed sufficient clout to have the performance canceled. The son threatened to run away and start his career in America, the dispute hit the newspapers, but in the end, as usually happens in these cases, the son prevailed. He was a success from the beginning, applauded for his style and obviously strong character.

In 1922, Algabeño II fought thirty *novilladas* in spite of two serious injuries. In 1923 he won over the Madrid public, and in 1924, his first full season after the promotion to *matador de toros*, he fought in all the important *ferias* and bullrings of Spain, chalking up fifty-nine corridas, more than any other matador that year. He was much admired for his cape and sword work and was judged to be "un torero grande," although on some important occasions he did not achieve the fine level of performance the critics had come to expect from him. In 1925 he fought fifty-two corridas even though a goring in Madrid in July caused him to lose the Pamplona *feria* for which he had been contracted.[207] Wounded again early in the 1926 season, he lost three weeks of April, including the Seville fiesta; his thirty-three corridas that year were, on the whole, weaker than his performances in earlier seasons. The number descended to twenty-five in 1927, rose to thirty-eight in 1928, and descended again to twenty-five in 1929 (he was wounded early in the season), the year that marked his retirement.[208]

It is clear that Pepe Algabeño's auspicious beginnings did not lead to a long, successful career. Although strong enough to defy his parents, he seems to have been discouraged by his injuries and by the enormous competition. He lacked the stamina, determination, and elegance which had made his father famous, and he rapidly lost his early desire to please his audiences. His growing unpopularity and critics' coolness made contracts difficult to obtain, and Algabeño made no attempt to recoup his lost position of leadership, preferring the luxurious lifestyle he could easily afford. Several critics mention his womanizing; Cossío reports that Algabeño was "legendario con las mujeres" (legendary with women) and he particularly enjoyed the attentions of aristocratic ladies.[209]

In 1933 Algabeño returned to the bullring as a *rejoneador* (fighting bulls on horseback). In 1934 he was shot by unknown assailants, probably because of his support for the Nationalist movement. He sustained a shoulder wound that required repeated operations. In 1936 he was gunned down by Loyalist forces.

Hemingway and Algabeño. Hemingway saw Algabeño on his first two trips to Pamplona, in 1923 and 1924, and must have been impressed by his fine performances. In 1923, the recently promoted Algabeño performed on 12 and 13 July. On the first of these afternoons, he was awarded an ear, the tail, and two triumphant turns around the bullring for his performance with his first bull, but had great trouble killing his second one. On the next day, the Villar bulls generally outperformed the bullfighters, but Algabeño was fine, killing an extra bull when one of his colleagues was injured and removed to the infirmary.

In 1924, Algabeño performed in Pamplona on three afternoons. On 8 July he was "regular nada más en sus dos toros" (OK, nothing special with his two bulls) and he was similarly unimpressive on 11 July. But he was spectacular with both his bulls on 13 July: he cut ears, was much applauded, and was carried out of the ring on his admirers' shoulders.

In 1925 an injury forced Algabeño to cancel his Pamplona contracts, a fact mentioned in *The Sun Also Rises* (*SAR*, 185; *see also SAR*, 172), but Hemingway, who was in Spain for several months that year, may have seen him on other occasions, perhaps the Madrid performances of 8 and 15 May. In 1926, Hemingway saw Algabeño on 23 May, in Madrid; he may have seen him perform on the 16th as well. In 1927, 1929, and 1931 Algabeño was not contracted for the important *ferias* of Madrid, Pamplona, and Valencia, which were Hemingway's favorites.[210]

> The narrator reports that Algabeño II was more famous than his father, but whereas the father was honest, the son was "the worst faker of them all" (271).

García Cuesta, Manuel (el Espartero). Spanish bullfighter, 1865–94. Investiture as *matador de toros*, in his native Seville, 1885; confirmed in Madrid that same season.

Espartero was a highly newsworthy bullfighter. Spectacular performances alternated with disasters, and he was often the center of a controversy or scandal. He was graceful, very brave, and he worked closer to the bull's head than anyone before him; when he was good, he was superb. But his sword work was weak, he was sometimes awkward or even incompetent in killing, and he was often cited for infractions of the bullfighting regulations. His frequent gorings were variously attributed to bravery, carelessness, or lack of skill; his infractions and citations were hotly debated in the ring and in the press. His investiture, for example, was highly praised; he had fought well. But four days later he fought in a *novillada* and was gored; the ensuing argument over whether he was a *novillero* (*matador de novillos*) or a graduated *matador de toros* was so tempestuous that he did a second *alternativa* in Seville the next month—and performed badly, perhaps because of the recent goring.

Espartero was Seville's first taurine folk hero, and his region's enthusiasm for him amounted to mania. As a *novillero* he was lionized by the city's press, in popular verse and in song, to such excess that the Madrid aficionados developed a cynical attitude toward him even before they saw him. His first appearance in Madrid (1885) was a disaster, and the Madrid press was merciless. In 1886 el Espartero fought all over Spain, sometimes well, sometimes not; he was often gored, though not seriously. On one occasion, the argument between doctors and fans as to the severity of the wound delayed treatment for so long that he lost a dangerous amount of blood. The case eventually landed in court, and when Espartero was called in to testify his disrespectful jokes earned him a month in jail.

The frequent gorings of 1887 intensified Seville's attachment to its native son, but when he was bested in the Seville plaza by his contemporary, Rafael Guerra (Guerrita), the top-ranked matador of his time, his city turned against him. This, as well as his unsatisfactory performances in Madrid that year, led to his fighting most of 1889 and 1890 in the provinces. Having rebuilt a strong reputation, he reconquered his Seville public and returned to Madrid in 1891, probably his best season. Even at the height of his powers, he was gored often, but his courage was unaffected. On one notable occasion, he insisted on continuing to fight the bull that had wounded him; he even disregarded the president's order to quit and finally had to be forcibly removed from the ring by the police. He maintained his reputation through most of 1892 and 1893 and was killed in the Madrid ring in 1894, by a Miura bull named Perdigón. El Espartero was then only twenty-eight years old.

Throughout his tumultuous career, el Espartero was both praised (for his courage, his muleta work, and his closeness to the bull) and damned (for his disregard of rules and his awkwardness in killing) by his public. Cossío remarks that the controversy that accompanied el Espartero during his lifetime continued after his death and describes him as "el más discutido de los diestros" (the most controversial of the matadors).[211]

> The narrator employs the taurine metaphor to express his own dissatisfaction with critics (and the general public) who withhold their admiration for the living artist and admire him after his death. He [inappropriately] cites el Espartero to prove his point (240–41; *see also* 272; photographs, *h:* 392–93).

García Rodríguez, José (el Algabeño). Spanish bullfighter, 1875–1947. Investiture as *matador de toros*, in Madrid, 1895.

Algabeño was studying veterinary medicine in Córdoba when the family's financial reverses brought his studies to an end and he had to return to La Algaba (Seville) to help out on the family farm. In Seville he saw Mazzantini fight and, impressed by this matador's style, fame, and fortune, he decided to try bullfighting himself. He was a popular and successful *novillero*, was quickly promoted to *matador de toros*, and appeared in thirty to forty corridas a year during the seasons 1896–1904, increasing the number to fifty-two in 1899 and sixty-one in 1900—very impressive numbers indeed, when one considers that transportation was slow and difficult then.

Algabeño was one of Spain's top-ranked matadors for more than fifteen years, maintaining this position in spite of the frequent injuries, especially in the wrists and hands,[212] which caused him to cancel several performances almost every year. In June 1901 he suffered such a serious neck wound that his death was reported in the Madrid press. Cossío mentions a spectacular episode in Algabeño's career: at the end of the 1900 season he was fighting *mano a mano* with Domingo del Campo: the two matadors had contracted to kill six Miura bulls, but Campo was fatally injured by the first bull and Algabeño fought and killed all six Miuras by himself. He was, as Hemingway points out, particularly skillful with the sword. Algabeño retired in 1912 and died in 1947.[213]

For the incident in which Rafael el Gallo refused to kill his retirement bull, which he had dedicated to Algabeño (*DIA*, 158), *see* Fulano.

The narrator describes the older Algabeño as one of Andalucía's foremost killers (158).

Garibaldi, Guiseppe. Italian patriot and soldier, 1807–82. Guiseppe Garibaldi fought against Austrian and French intervention in Italian affairs. With his volunteer militia, the Red Shirts, he wrested Sicily and Naples from the Bourbon king Francis II, thus liberating southern Italy from foreign rule. Garibaldi opposed the constitutional monarchy advocated by Cavour; he favored the republican form of government for the newly united Italy. Ultimately, Cavour's plan was adopted.

Garibaldi was much admired in Spain during those periods when that country tried to overcome its own regional differences, get rid of the monarchy, and establish a unified Republic—that is, during Spain's short-lived first Republic (1873–74). In 1931, when Spain ousted Alfonso XIII (q.v.) and established its second Republic (1931–39), mementos from the days of the first Republic were happily displayed. Hemingway mentioned this phenomenon in a letter to John Dos Passos, written from Madrid on 26 June 1931: "Barco de Avila is wonderful town . . . —all people nice—old banner of Garibaldi from 1st Republic at Verbena of San Juan—all for 8 pesetas a day."

In preparing Chapter Twenty for publication, Hemingway cut the derogatory references to Garibaldi's son, who betrayed his father's republican principles by offering his support to Mussolini.[214]

The narrator mentions having seen a portrait of [Guiseppe] Garibaldi (271).

Gaskell, Mrs. Full name: Elizabeth Cleghorn (Mrs. William Gaskell). English novelist, 1810–65. Among her novels are *Mary Barton, a Tale of Manchester Life* (1848), *Ruth* (1853), *Cranford* (1853), *North and South* (1854–55), and the unfinished *Wives and Daughters* (1864–66). The novels deal with social, economic, and ethical issues, as these affect well-bred single women in straitened circumstances (though most can afford at least one servant). For contemporary attitudes on good taste and self-censorship, *see* Humanism, Naturalism.

The narrator quotes Aldous Huxley's remarks about Mrs. Gaskell's reticence about bodily functions (190).

Gavira. *See* Cano Iriborne, Enrique.

Gayarre. Full name: Sebastián Julián Gayarre Garjón. Spanish tenor, c. 1843–90.

Gayarre, who achieved international fame as an operatic tenor, was much loved and honored throughout Spain. Bagüés remarks that the huge Madrid crowds which accompanied José Gómez Ortega's body to the train that would take him home for his funeral (in 1920) reminded him of the crowds that had gathered when Gayarre died thirty years earlier (*Historia de los matadores de toros*, 147).

Pamplona honored this famous Navarrese singer by naming one of its two theaters after him. The theater was torn down in 1931, but its replacement, on the Avenida de Carlos III, is also called the Gayarre.[215]

> The narrator mentions the changes in Pamplona (the *ensanche*, or expansion), among them the destruction of the old Gayarre Theater (273).

The General. The general whom Hemingway doesn't name is Antonio Tommaso Cantore, Italian military man, 1860–1915. He was graduated from the Military College of Modena in July 1880 and advanced steadily through the ranks until he became *maggior generale* in February 1914. He was twice awarded the Military Cross of Savoia.

Cantore commanded the Italian IV Armata when he was killed in battle on the Tofana at Forcella Fontana Negra (Black Fountain Saddle) near Cortina d'Ampezzo, province of Belluno, Italy, 20 July 1915. The isolated pass at the Fontana Negra was held by the well-fortified Austrian Landsturmerbataillon 165, who, aided by the craggy mountainous territory and frequent snows and fog, caused many casualties to the Italian forces which, in late June and early July, repeatedly tried to capture it. Antonio Cantore probably led the attack of 17 July, during which a well-placed Italian mine reduced the stronghold to a pile of rubble. Even so, successive attacks failed to dislodge the enemy, and the Italians suffered losses at each attempt.

Cantore was blamed for the enormous loss of Italian lives, and rumor has it that the bullet which killed him that day came from the gun of an Italian soldier, although the official version is that he was killed by an Austrian sniper. He is honored as the first Italian general to die on the battlefield. Although killed in July, he died "in the snow," because the fighting was "high in the mountains" (140).

Cantore's Alpini Hat. Cantore commanded Alpini troops from 1898 to 1912, when he was transferred to Lybia. Upon his return to Italy in 1914, he became the Commander of the Third Alpini Brigade. At the time of his death, his command again included Alpine troops, for whom he felt respect and affection.

The feathered Alpine cap, pierced by the projectile that killed Cantore, supposedly lay on his bier in the Chapel of San Francesco in Cortina and was then displayed at the nearby Hotel Posta, which was frequented by Italian officers. Cantore wears this cap, which has been called "il berretto più famoso d'Italia," in the commemorative sculpture that honors him in Cortina. His nephew, however, insists that Cantore always wore the regulation headgear appropriate to his rank, and not the cap that distinguished his beloved Alpini troops.

The fact that Cantore is buried at Pocol (q.v.) completes the identification of the unnamed "damned fine general" whom Hemingway mentions.[216] For another general killed on duty, *see* Behr, General von; and *Generals Die in Bed.*

> The narrator mentions a general who was shot through the head during fighting in the mountains, and was buried in Pocol (140).

Generals Die in Bed. War novel by Charles Yale Harrison, American author (1898–1954). Harrison spent several years in Canada, enlisted in the Royal Montreal Regiment, and served as a machine gunner in France and Belgium until he was wounded in 1918. *Generals Die in Bed* (1930), his first and perhaps best book, is a realistic depiction of the trench warfare of World War I as experienced by Canadian soldiers. The title comes from a scene set in Bethune, a French town "blackened with the smoke of war" (135), where the battle-weary recruits discuss the Chief of Staff who has swept in and out of town to inspect them:

> "A little runt, ain't he?"
> "Got a cushy job, too."
> "Bet he's•got a hundred batmen to shine his leather."
> "He's got fifty medals . . ."
> "Yeah, but he'll never die in a lousy trench like Brownie [one of the

characters, shot in the head when he stood up in the trench to reach for a spoon (62)] and them did."
"God, no. Generals die in bed."
"Well, that's a pretty good place to die." (141)

Harrison's successful war novel was followed by several other books: *Clarence Darrow* (1931), *A Child Is Born* (1931), *There Are Victories* (1933), *Meet Me in the Barricades* (1938), *Nobody's Fool* (1948), and *Thank God for My Heart Attack* (1949). For two other generals who died in the field, *see* Behr, General von; and The General.

> In his persona as scientist or natural historian, the narrator objects to the title of Harrison's book, citing two generals who were killed in the field. In the interest of accuracy, he would amend the book's title to *Generals Usually Die in Bed* (140).

Germans. *See* Authors.

Gide, André. French novelist, essayist, playwright and translator, 1869–1951. His novels include *The Immoralist* (1902) and *The Counterfeiters* (1925). In 1909 he founded the *Nouvelle Revue Français*. He published his autobiography, 1920–24. He was very open about his homosexuality. *See also* Homosexuals.

> The narrator attacks Gide for his homosexuality and for his "prissy, exhibitionist . . . arrogance" (205).

Gitanillo. So called not because he was a gypsy but because he worked for a horse dealer, a job traditionally held by gypsies. He was also called Gitano de Ricla because he was born in Ricla (Zaragoza). *See* Lausín López, Braulio.

Gitanillo de Triana. Professional nickname used by all three Vega de los Reyes brothers, who were natives of Triana (q.v.): the famous Francisco (q.v.), the younger José (a *novillero* with a short career), and Rafael (also a *matador de toros*, 1915–69).[217]

Golf. *See* Jones, Bobby; Sports.

Gómez, Alfonzo (Finito de Valladolid). Correct spelling: Alfonso. Full name: Alfonso Gómez Moro. Spanish bullfighter, 1897–1959.

Finito de Valladolid was a *matador de novillos* who was never promoted to *matador de toros*. He made his Madrid debut as *novillero* on 11 August 1921. In 1924 and 1925 he performed in fifteen *novilladas*, including one Madrid appearance each year. In 1926 the number remained the same, but without a Madrid appearance; in 1927 he had a successful afternoon in Madrid, and in 1929 he had thirteen *novilladas*. Each year the dream of the *alternativa* (q.v.) receded further.

In 1931, the year Hemingway claims to have seen him, he was contracted for only five afternoons: 17 May (Valladolid), 3 and 4 June (Monbeltrán), 23 August (Madrid; this is when Hemingway saw him; *see* Todó, Isidoro); and 4 October (Cáceres). He had a better year in 1932 (seventeen *novilladas*) but in 1933 the number was down to three. Finito persisted as a *matador de novillos* until the Spanish Civil War, after which he worked mostly as a *banderillero* in various *cuadrillas* and as a manager for other bullfighters, among them Cayetano Ordóñez Araujo (see in *DS*).[218]

Born on 1 January 1897, Finito was thirty-four years old on 23 August 1931 when he appeared with Isidoro Todó. Hemingway, frequently inaccurate with ages, makes him older, "well over thirty-five" (227), to emphasize his failure.

Taurine scholar Anthony Brand finds sufficient similarities between Finito de Valladolid and Hemingway's character Finito de Palencia (Pilar's lover in *For Whom the Bell Tolls*) to suggest that the one was the historical prototype for the other. Although the Spanish word *fino* and its diminutive, *finito*, suggest delicacy and elegance, the Italian meaning—"finished"—is appropriate for a failed professional. And Palencia completes the gloomy atmosphere: it is a somewhat characterless provincial capital with a history of loss. It was conquered first by the Goths and then by the Moors, it became a royal seat but was abandoned, it housed Spain's first university but then lost it to Salamanca. It is not far from the much more important city of Valladolid, the home of Alfonso Gómez, thus strengthening the identification of that failed *novillero* with Pilar's lover.[219]

> The narrator admires Gómez as "dignified, intelligent and brave," although not successful: ten years after his Madrid debut as *novillero*, he had not yet been promoted to *matador de toros* when the narrator last saw him perform in 1931 (227).

Gómez, don Félix, widow of. Full name: Mercedes Ugalde Bañuelos viuda de Gómez Pombo. Spanish bull breeder, 1860–1959.

The Gómez herd was founded in the 1820s in Colmenar Viejo, Madrid, by don Elías Gómez, with *jijona* stock acquired from the López Briceño ranch. Two of don Elías's inaugural bulls made such a good impression in Madrid (on 3 October 1831, the date which defines the herd's *antigüedad*), that Gómez stock was soon as expensive as that of Veragua (q.v.).

Don Elías's ranch remained in the family, being inherited by his son Félix and his daughter Alfonsa, with the rights to the brand, colors, and seniority going, as custom dictated, to the male heir. When Alfonsa died in 1866, the herd was registered to "don Félix Gómez y sobrinos" (don Félix and his nieces and nephews), but in 1866 their partnership was dissolved. Félix retained half of the holdings and the seniority, and under his management the herd maintained its fine reputation.

When Félix died in 1894, the herd was inherited by his three children, with all the rights going to his son, don Félix Gómez Pombo (grandson of don Elías, the founder). This grandson died in 1904, but his widow and sons kept the stock and the ranch in his name, a not uncommon practice, as the "viuda e hijos de don Félix Gómez" (widow and children of Félix Gómez).

In 1916 the stock was crossbred with a Gamero Cívico (formerly Parladé) seed bull, and in 1923 and in 1931 the fine old herd was exposed to more Vistahermosa blood, which further improved it. The grandson's widow, doña Mercedes Ugalde Bañuelos, died in 1959, aged ninety-nine; thus, for more than half a century (1904–59), the famous herd was officially registered as belonging to the "Viuda e hijos de don Félix Gómez."

In 1962 doña Mercedes's heirs sold the herd to its present owner, Mariano Sanz Jiménez, who also acquired its famous brand, colors (turquoise blue and white) and venerable *antigüedad* (3 October 1831).[220] For a discussion of *antigüedad* and its relationship to ownership, see "Bulls and Bull Breeding," in the introduction to this volume.

The narrator correctly identifies the widow of Félix Gómez as the current (in 1932) owner of this important ranch (132).

Gómez, Fernando (el Gallo). Spanish bullfighter, 1847–97. Investiture as *matador de toros*, 1877, in Seville; confirmed in Madrid in 1880.

Originally a shoemaker, Fernando quit this trade when he saw that his brother José was doing well as a banderillero. Fernando became a banderillero and then a *matador de novillos* for many years, not taking the *alternativa* (q.v.) until 1876, at age twenty-nine. His performance on that day was so poor that he resigned the *alternativa* and then attempted it again, more successfully, in 1877. This shows a great deal of respect for the rank.

Although an uncertain swordsman and in general an uneven performer, Fernando was graceful and artistic with the cape, banderillas and muleta. He invented the "cambio de rodillas" (changing the bull's direction while kneeling). His artistry enabled him to maintain his popularity in spite of his usually undistinguished sword work. He was also very knowledgeable about the history and theory of bullfighting.

Fernando's friendship with Menéndez de la Vega, the manager of the Madrid bullring,[221] as well as the presence of the popular Rafael Guerra (q.v.) in his *cuadrilla* helped him obtain a good number of contracts in the early 1880s, but success alternated with failure. The seasons of 1884 and 1885 were, in Cossío's estimation, a disaster. Guerra left his *cuadrilla*, Fernando suffered several gorings, developed cardiac disease, and saw the competition get increasingly younger. Fernando el Gallo persisted, and his uneven career was actually quite long: he did not retire until 1896, and died the next year.[222]

Fernando's wife, Gabriela Ortega, was a *bailaora de tablao* (flamenco dancer, d. 1919). She was also from Seville, from a family that had produced many bullfighters. All three of their sons were bullfighters. Hemingway mentions the two famous ones often: *see* Gómez Ortega, José; and Gómez Ortega, Rafael. Fernando did not live to see their success.

The narrator mentions Fernando Gómez in the context of his family (*h:* 429, s.v. *Cruz*; *see also h:* 439, s.v. *Gallo*).

Gómez, Francisco (el Aldeano). Full name: Francisco Gómez Tarazona. Spanish bullfighter, 1903—. Investiture as *matador de toros*, in Bogotá, Colombia, December 1931; never confirmed in Madrid.

As a *matador de novillos*, Gómez achieved a modest reputation in the seasons of 1926–29, his sword work being his strongest point. He was seriously gored in April 1929 and again in August of that year, and had to cancel much of that season, ending up with a total of thirteen *novilladas*. In 1930 he was again gored, lightly on 15 June but quite badly on 20 July. This second incident left terrible scars on his face.

In 1931, Aldeano fought thirteen *novilladas*, some of them in important plazas, including three in Madrid. He was promoted to *matador de toros* late in 1931 in Bogotá. But Gómez did not confirm this *alternativa* (q.v.) upon his return to Spain, where, having lost most of his energy and reputation, he continued to fight as a *novillero* until 1935.

Hemingway and Aldeano. Comparing Hemingway's schedule with Aldeano's, it does not seem likely that Ernest saw this bullfighter perform in 1929 or after his face was disfigured in 1930. However, the records are scanty, and Hemingway may have met him outside the ring, perhaps through Sidney Franklin (q.v.).[223] *See also* Luis and the Unsuccessful Matadors.

The narrator accurately reports that el Aldeano's face is heavily scarred and regrets that he can't discuss him at any length (272).

Gómez, José. *See* Gómez Ortega, José.

Gómez, Luis (el Estudiante). Full name: Luis Gómez Calleja. Spanish bullfighter, 1911–95. Investiture as *matador de toros*, in Valencia, 20 March 1932, granted by Marcial Lalanda; confirmed in Madrid, 21 April 1932.

As a *novillero*, Gómez did not excite much interest. He managed to appear a couple of times in Madrid, late in the 1928 season, but these performances went largely unremarked. The next year he fought only eight *novilladas* and none in 1930. In 1931, however, he had nineteen fights, and several got favorable reviews. Promoted to *matador de toros* quite early in the 1932 season (*see* José, San), he performed in forty-eight corridas (ranked fifth nationwide), finally earning the praise his cape and muleta work deserved. At this stage of his career he was, however, awkward with the sword.

Gómez lost much of the 1933 season because of a serious goring and consequently was engaged for only fourteen appearances for the next year. In 1935 he appeared twenty-seven times, performing creditably but unable to recapture the public's attention. All too often, his poor sword work lost him the ears his elegant *faenas* promised.

During the Civil War (1936–39) El Estudiante served with the Nationalist forces. He was therefore allowed to perform in Franco-controlled areas, although there was not much bullfighting in those years. After the war, he fought more frequently and reestablished himself as a creditable bullfighter. His cape and muleta were his strong points, and he had finally corrected his technique with the sword.

Overcoming a serious goring late in the 1941 season, he appeared in thirty corridas in 1942 and had several important triumphs in Madrid. In spite of the competition offered by younger matadors (including the remarkable Manuel Rodríguez [Manolete, 1917–47] with whom he often appeared), he fought forty-five corridas in 1943, many of them excellent. In 1944 he was fully in control of his art and his public. Although he suffered a serious neck wound on July 7, in Pamplona, he managed sixty-one corridas, most of which were highly acclaimed. He slowed down after this high point (although he did a couple of very lucrative South American tours), and retired in 1947.

Unlike most bullfighters, who reach their peak in their last year as *novillero* or in their first years after the *alternativa* (q.v.), Luis Gómez matured and developed slowly, was able to incorporate innovations introduced by younger bullfighters, and could therefore recapture the public he had lost. He reached the top of his profession when he was in his mid-thirties. The general concensus is favorable: most critics agree that he was skillful, intelligent, and brave.

After his retirement from active fighting El Estudiante served on juries, panels, and ceremonies connected to bullfighting.[224]

Hemingway and el Estudiante. Hemingway, who was not in Spain for the 1932 season, did not see el Estudiante perform as a *matador de toros*, though he could have seen him as a *novillero*.

Gómez studied business administration, not medicine; he did not finish his academic degree. And he was, at the time of his *alternativa*, still uncertain with the sword. But he was certainly a promising *matador de toros* at the time Hemingway was writing.

The narrator identifies Luis Gómez as one of the two most promising newly promoted matadors of the 1932 season. He has heard that Gómez works elegantly with the cape and muleta and is an efficient killer, but that he sometimes gets into tight spots (228–29).

Gómez, Rafael. *See* Gómez Ortega, Rafael.

Gómez Ortega, José (Joselito, Gallito, Pasos Largos). Hemingway translates the rarely used nickname Pasos Largos as "big jumps" (242) but "long steps" or "long strides" would be more accurate. Spanish bullfighter, 1895–1920. Investiture as *matador de toros*, in Seville, September 1912; confirmed in Madrid, October 1912.

Joselito is in a class by himself. Any account of his life and work must necessarily overflow with extravagant praise.

Descended from bullfighters on both his mother's and father's sides,[225] Joselito showed great talent as a little boy—there is a photograph of the three-year-old preparing to "kill" with a stick—and had a large following long before his investiture, in 1912, at age seventeen. After the *alternativa* (q.v.) his reputation continued to soar: by 1913, his first full season as *matador de toros*, he was ranked first nationwide, a position he maintained for six years running. In 1913, he appeared eighty times; it was an extraordinary season, in terms of the number and the quality of his performances. He had to cancel some contracts in 1914, because of illnesses and gorings, but even so fought seventy-five corridas, sharing the ring with Belmonte (q.v.) for the first time. Cossío writes that Belmonte's stylistic innovations spurred Joselito to new heights.

In 1915, 1916, and 1917 Joselito continued to dominate the ring, being the first matador in history to appear in more than one hundred corridas a year: 102 in 1915, 105 in 1916, and 103 in 1917. Some of these were *mano a mano* with Belmonte (the six bulls being fought by two instead of three matadors) and not a few were solo performances.[226] Minor illnesses and wounds cut the 1918 season to eighty-one appearances (he had contracted for 105) and the 1919 season to ninety-one (one serious wound early in the season caused him to miss eighteen fights, and Belmonte was that year's first-ranked bullfighter, with a breathtaking 109 corridas).

Joselito's performances in the bullring were almost consistently magnificent. He was perfectly built for a bullfighter; had superb health, reflexes, and timing; was well-educated in all aspects of bullfighting; and fought with grace, gallantry, and courage. Joselito and Belmonte dominated the bullring, defining the 1910s as a golden age of bullfighting.

The Death of Joselito. Joselito's death at the horns of the bull Bailaor (16 May 1920; see Talavera de la Reina, in *DS*) shocked the public. He and Belmonte had been so spectacular for so long that the public thought of them as immune to danger in the bullring. Belmonte explains that "we had reached a state of mastery in our craft which permitted us to give an impression of confidence that made it seem as if the risk of bullfighting had ceased to exist . . . this was the very reason why the public was tiring of us; and . . . it was even more serious for Joselito than for me, because he gave, even more than I did, the impression that he fought without danger . . . the spectators were becoming convinced that we had eliminated all the risk of the fight and were enriching ourselves with impunity at their expense. The aficionados . . . began to think they were being cheated" (*Killer of Bulls: The Autobiography of a Matador*, 288–90).

Belmonte adds that on 15 May 1920, in what turned out to be Joselito's last corrida in Madrid, "The bulls were small, and the aficionados were protesting noisily even before the fight had started." The public jeered so violently that Joselito, "deeply affected by this savage attack," canceled the next day's performance, which was to have been in Madrid, and went to Talavera de la Reina instead (a minor bullring), to fight bulls from the unaccredited *ganadería* of the widow of Ortega (*Killer of Bulls*, 289–90).

Filiberto Mira reports that Joselito was also encouraged to go to Talavera de la Reina by Gregorio Corrochano, a relative of the widow of Ortega (q.v.), who wanted to heal the breach between Joselito and his brother Rafael el Gallo. Rafael and Ignacio Sánchez Mejías were scheduled to perform at Talavera de la Reina on 16 May, and Corrochano wanted Joselito to join them as a public expression of fraternal reconciliation. At the last moment, after his unhappy experience in Madrid on 15 May, Joselito agreed. Rafael decided to absent himself, and thus Joselito and Ignacio were the only two performers on the fatal afternoon.[227] As a result of all these changes and last-minute arrangements, small posters were hastily printed both in Madrid and in Talavera de la Reina. After the bullfight, these became collectors' items, and other posters, far too elaborate to have been produced before the corrida itself, began to appear.

Joselito's death evoked an enormous outpouring of grief, formalized by a week of national mourning, with flags at half-mast. Decades later, his death is still commemorated every year with lectures, exhibitions, publications, and bullfights. His family, life, art, and death are discussed in an always-expanding number of books, articles, paintings, songs, and films. He is one of the major figures of bullfighting in the twentieth century and a cultural icon in the Spanish world.[228] His mausoleum, in the San Fernando cemetery of Seville, is the work of the famous sculptor Mariano Benlliure (1866–1947). *See also* D'Artagnan.

Hemingway and Joselito. Hemingway, who saw his first bullfights in 1923, never saw Joselito perform, but he repeats all the superlatives and clichés that inevitably attach to Joselito; they were and are common currency among aficionados.[229] Hemingway mentions Joselito in *The Sun Also Rises* (168), *For Whom the Bell Tolls* (251, 252, 253), and *The Dangerous Summer* (107, 171, 189) as well as in *Death in the Afternoon.*

> The narrator recognizes Joselito as the premier matador of all times, for whom "all bulls were easy" (69, 70). Although he abhors the "disastrous" practice of early promotion to full *matador de toros* because it deprives promising *novilleros* the time to mature and perfect their art, he finds that such promotion was justified in two cases: Costillares (q.v.) and Joselito, who were fully developed matadors at age sixteen (88). The narrator reports that Joselito was gored seriously only three times (167),[230] that he was booed on his last appearance in Madrid, and that his later style was influenced by Belmonte. He mentions Joselito often: 1–2, 21, 39, *69–70*, 73–74, 75, 77–78, 84, 88, 94, 158–59, 161, 167–68, 171, 198–99, 202, *212–14*, 216, 229, *242–44*, 267, *h:* 476, s.v. *Rondeño*; *h:* 504; and shows him in photographs, *h:* 330–48.

Gómez Ortega, Rafael (el Gallo). Spanish bullfighter, 1882–1960. Investiture as *matador de toros*, in Seville, 28 September 1902; confirmed in Madrid, 20 March 1904.

Rafael el Gallo was a child prodigy. At age thirteen, he helped found the *cuadrilla de niños sevillanos*, following the model of the *cuadrilla de niños cordobeses* (qq.v.), of which Rafael Guerra Bejarano was a member. The *cordobeses* and *sevillanos* were soon in competition, all their teenaged bullfighters achieving fame. The group disbanded in 1899, as its members set out on independent careers as *novilleros*. Rafael's career was surely the most interesting.

Even as a young *novillero* anxious for reputation, Rafael succumbed to his *espantás* (frights) and superstitions, which caused him, among other contretemps, to be jailed in Seville for refusing to kill the bull that he had dedicated to Agustín Luque, the Captain General of Andalucía (who was probably acting as president of the bullfight). But the rest of his work at that fight had been so graceful and artistic that two competing bullring impresarios rushed to see him in jail, anxious to bail him out and outbidding each other for his services. Rafael was often taken from the bullring to the jail, and not infrequently rescued by admirers, sometimes within minutes. Such incidents embarrassed some bullfighters (among them his brother Joselito) and repelled some critics, but Rafael Ortega was a law unto himself.

A rash of weak performances caused Rafael's popularity to decline after his *alternativa* (q.v.), and in 1907, five years after the promotion, he had contracts for only six corridas. But he did so well in these that in 1908 he was engaged for forty-one, an increase of practically 700 percent. He was sick for much of 1909, but was again able to recoup his popularity quite quickly. In 1911 he married Pastora Rojas Monje (Pastora Imperio, 1889–1979) who, like his mother, was a flamenco artist. Gossip columns faithfully reported the ups and downs of their stormy marriage.

Rafael's peak years were probably 1910–14. In 1912 he fought seventy-four corridas, sixty-six in 1913, and seventy-one in 1914, in spite of a serious goring early in the season, which caused him to cancel many appearances. By 1917 his erratic behavior had become so extreme that the leading taurine critic, Gregorio Corrochano, demanded that the thirty-five-year-old Rafael absent himself from the ring, "por decoro, por dignidad de la persona y de la profesión. No se puede ir en constante humillación, arrastrándose por todas las plazas huyendo de los toros" (for the sake of decorum, of the dignity of the human being and of the profession. One cannot face constant humiliation, one cannot drag one's self from plaza to plaza, evading bulls).[231] Rafael retired in 1918, possibly under pressure from his family (*see* Fulano; Patti, Adelina Juana María).

Predictably enough, the retirement lasted only a few months and Rafael fought off and on, here and there, throughout the 1920s. Some years he performed frequently, some hardly at all; some corridas were spectacularly fine, others were disgraceful. Sometimes excellence alternated with shoddy work in a single fight. In 1924 and 1925, he fought in America but not in Spain. When he returned to Spain in 1926, he was contracted for thirty-four performances, even after such a long absence. In 1927, after he performed in thirty-one corridas in Spain, the critic Uno as Sesgo urged him to retire, claiming that it was "intolerable" that he should still be fighting (he was forty-five years old, bald, and fat).[232]

Rafael el Gallo had an extraordinarily long career, longer even than his father's. In September 1924, when Antonio Guerrero (Guerrerito) retired—he had been promoted to *matador de toros* in 1897—Rafael became the dean of matadors. He celebrated his silver anniversary (twenty-five years since the *alternativa*) in 1927 and was still fighting occasionally in the late 1930s, when he was more than fifty years old.

Rafael was capable of excellence in all aspects of the bullfight: with the cape, the banderillas, the muleta, and the sword. Occasionally all his powers came together for a consistently electrifying performance; more often he gave his audience moments of brilliance. Sometimes called "el divino Rafael" (the divine Rafael) or "el divino calvo" (the divine bald-headed one), he was an extraordinary personality, with enormous talent, inimitable style, and bursts of erratic behavior, both in and out of the ring.[233] Many poems, essays, and books have been written about him, and an anecdote about Rafael colors almost every taurine publication and conversation. *See also* Mexican Feather Work; Miura, don Eduardo.

Hemingway and Rafael el Gallo. Hemingway probably did not see Rafael often, but he could not have avoided reading and hearing about him. In 1924 and 1925, el Gallo did not perform in Spain. In 1926, when Hemingway spent more than four months in Spain, he probably saw Rafael in the Valencia fiesta, where el Gallo performed

on 26 and 30 July. I cannot determine if Hemingway saw him in
1927, but I doubt it. Hemingway did not come to Spain in 1928 or
1930, and Rafael was absent from Spanish bullrings in 1929 and
1931.[234]

Hemingway mentions Rafael in two of his novels: unflatteringly in
The Sun Also Rises (172), and amusingly in *For Whom the Bell Tolls*
(187).

> The narrator reports that Rafael was handsome, graceful, and innovative
> with the cape (212–14) but not an accomplished swordsman, explaining
> that the skills are incompatible (232). Temperamental and showy, he would
> sometimes jump out of the ring or refuse to kill a bull; he retired ceremoni-
> ously from the profession several times. The narrator counts him among
> those who corrupted the bullfight but still admires him greatly: he was
> "lacking in courage and a little simple minded," but he was a great artist, a
> real showman, a superb bullfighter. The narrator mentions Rafael el Gallo
> often: 2, 21, 157–59, 177–78, 203, 212–14, 216, 223, 241, 243, *h:* 411,
> s.v. *Adorno*; photographs, *h:* 292–93, 330–31, 400–03. Rafael el Gallo
> speaks: 21, 157, 158.

González, Domingo (Dominguín). Full name: Domingo González
Mateos. Spanish bullfighter, manager, and impresario, 1895–1958.
Investiture as *matador de toros* in Madrid, 26 September 1918.

Born to poor and uneducated parents in Quismondo, near Toledo,
Domingo (so named because he was born on a Sunday) determined
to conquer poverty through bullfighting. As an adolescent he ran
away from home in search of taurine fame. Twice he was found and
returned to his parents, but eventually he managed to stay in Madrid,
working in a tavern and lodging in a nearby whorehouse while studying the bullfighter's craft—a suitably dramatic beginning for the
founder of a taurine dynasty. Dominguín's first patron, Ramón Mer-
chán, bought him the *traje de luces* in which he first performed, in
1916, as substitute banderillero. His apprenticeship took him, as is
usually the case, to a variety of minor plazas, until he was contracted
to appear in Madrid, where he did not perform well. He persevered,
however, and enjoyed his first success in Barcelona, at the end of the
1917 season. Several good performances, particularly in Barcelona,
early in the 1918 season, resulted in a return visit to Madrid, where
he distinguished himself in May and again in June. Then his career
took off: he became one of the top-ranked *novilleros* of that year, and

was promoted to full *matador de toros* late in September 1918. By then his standing was such that the promotion was awarded by José Gómez Ortega (Joselito, q.v.), in Madrid.

Dominguín's first few seasons as *matador de alternativa* were uneven but, on the whole, quite successful: numbers are not available for 1919, but he performed in thirty-two corridas in 1920, thirty-five in 1921, and twenty in 1922 (although mediocre and even poor performances were unfortunately frequent). By 1923 he was able to afford a home in Madrid and a ranch, "La Companza," in the neighborhood where he had been born.[235] But in those years Joselito and Belmonte were insuperable competition, and Dominguín recognized that his skills and talents were not of the first rank. He was graceful with the muleta, generally competent with the cape and banderillas, and too often inept with the sword. Although he continued to fight as often as possible (including several profitable South American tours), he became increasingly involved in the administrative aspects of the bullfight, working as impresario and manager (for several years he managed his own career as well, instead of hiring an *apoderado*). In 1924, he performed in seventeen corridas, a respectable number, but in 1925 he only had three, and all of these were in fiestas that he himself had organized. He retired as *matador de toros* at the end of this season.

Domingo as Apoderado (Manager). Domingo González recognized the talent of two major matadors while they were still unknown *novilleros*, and made his fortune and reputation as their manager: they were Joaquín Rodríguez (Cagancho) and Domingo Ortega (qq.v.).[236] He also educated and managed his three bullfighter sons: Domingo González Lucas (1920–75), José (1921—), and the superstar Luis Miguel (Dominguín, 1926–96; see in *DS*). For a fuller account of his career as impresario, see González Mateos, Domingo, in *DS*. *See also* Manager, in this volume and in *DS*.

Hemingway and Domingo González. In one way, the antipathy to Domingo that Hemingway displays in *Death in the Afternoon* carried over into *The Dangerous Summer*, where he attempts to discredit Domingo's son Luis Miguel. In that later book, however, Domingo gets posthumous praise as a "very able and astute businessman" who was "wise and cynical and knew the odds." This is an interesting turnaround, in view of Hemingway's attack on critics and historians who attack taurine personalities while they are alive and then praise them after they are dead (*DIA*, 240–44).

I doubt that Hemingway ever saw Domingo González in the bullring. In 1923 or 1924, Domingo did not perform in Pamplona, the only fiesta Hemingway attended those years. Domingo fought only three corridas in 1925, and none after that.

The narrator correctly identifies Domingo González as a retired bullfighter who in 1931 was acting as manager of Domingo Ortega (93, 168; alluded to but not named, 170).

González, José (Carnicerito de México). Full name: José González López. Mexican bullfighter, 1905–47. Investiture as *matador de toros*, in Murcia, 13 September 1931; confirmed in Madrid on 18 September.

González first came to Spain in 1930, as a banderillero. In 1931, in spite of an injury suffered in March and a more serious one late in July, he performed in thirty-one or thirty-five *novilladas* (reports vary), being promoted to *matador de toros* late that season.

In 1932 he fought eighteen corridas, twenty-nine in 1933, and twenty-one in 1934. An unusually large proportion of these took place in France and Morocco; he was also popular in Barcelona but not in the rest of Spain. During the next decade, from 1934 to 1944, he was not contracted to fight in Spain, but pursued a successful career in France and Latin America. In 1945 he fought twelve corridas in Spain, being seriously gored twice; in 1946 he fought once in Spain and nine times in France. He died the next year in Villa Viçosa, Portugal, one day after being severely gored in the right thigh.

Although González was brave and an expert with the banderillas and the sword, he liked to exaggerate and was considered something of a faker, pretending to do dangerous maneuvers *a la* Belmonte while actually taking care to keep himself safe. The combination of bravery, showmanship, and ignorance resulted in thirty-six dangerous gorings during his career.[237] For other "toreros cortos" (bullfighters with limited repertoire), *see* Vicente Barrera, Luis Freg, Mariano Montes, and the early Belmonte.

Hemingway and José González. Hemingway was in Madrid when Carnicerito de México gave his last performance as a *novillero*, on 4

September 1931, and when he confirmed his *alternativa* two weeks later. He may have seen him perform.

> The narrator describes González as "a very capable and very emotional" young Mexican-Indian matador making a good name for himself in Spain in the early 1930s, but fears he will not last long because he takes great chances with the bull (224). The narrator praises his work with the banderillas (200; *see also* 168, 198).

González, Luis. Carralero and Borge give his first name as Lucio and indicate that he was wounded on the *left* thigh (*Toros célebres*, 310). *See also* Víbora.

> The narrator mentions this carpenter, inaccurately reporting his first name and the site of the wound inflicted by the bull Víbora (110).

González Madrid, Rafael (Machaquito). Spanish bullfighter, 1880–1955. Investiture as *matador de toros*, September 1900, in Madrid. Machaquito was attracted to bullfighting at a very early age, performing with Rafael Molina (Lagartijo chico, also a child star), in a juvenile *cuadrilla* (modeled on the one from which Rafael Gómez el Gallo launched his career). Machaquito and Molina, both brilliant *novilleros*, were promoted to *matadores de toros* in the same corrida in Madrid, September 1900.

Machaquito's 1901 season was very full (sixty corridas) but generally undistinguished. From 1902 to 1907, however, he was consistently spectacular. In sharp contrast to his great contemporary and rival, Ricardo Torres Reina (Bombita), who was frequently inept with the sword, Machaquito was an accurate swordsman. Although short, he was able to kill most of his bulls on the first sword thrust, often being bumped but seldom hurt.[238] The moment of Machaquito's sword thrust, taurine critics claimed, was so beautiful that it should be preserved. This demand was soon satisfied: Mariano Benlliure (1867–1947), the foremost taurine sculptor of his day, was commissioned to do this. His famous sculpture *La estocada de la tarde* (The Sword Thrust) shows Machaquito with his sword completely buried in the dying bull, from whose right horn hangs a piece of Machaquito's shirt front.[239]

For the first decade of the twentieth century, Machaquito and Bombita were Spain's two top-ranked matadors (a position Joselito and Belmonte would occupy in the 1910s). They fought between fifty and sixty-five or sixty-six corridas almost each season, often appearing together. In 1908 Machaquito fought sixty corridas (he had been contracted for eighty-one), but his performances were not up to his usual standard. In 1909 he performed only twenty-nine times because he suffered a serious goring, which almost cost him his leg, and because he was at odds with the management of the Madrid bullring (the great Miura controversy; *see* Miura, don Eduardo; Mosquera, don Indalecio; *and* Torres Reina, Ricardo [Bombita]). All told, in 1909 Machaquito fought only twenty-nine of the sixty-five corridas he had been contracted for.

In spite of these two difficult years, Machaquito's 1910 season was brilliant: he fought sixty-two corridas, many of them with Vicente Pastor (q.v.), then at his peak. In 1911 (at age thirty-one) he fought seventy-three corridas in spite of a serious wound that caused him to cancel a number of contracts.[240] That year he was awarded the ear of a bull; this marked only the second time such a trophy was granted in the Madrid bullring (the first "serious" ear had been given to Vicente Pastor; see Trophies in *DS*).[241] In 1912 and 1913 Machaquito again fought a full schedule, but some of his performances were lackluster, although there were many triumphs and his ability to kill on the first try was still impressive. Two days after the season ended, he unexpectedly announced his retirement: he was thirty-three years old, still a powerful and popular fighter, but aware that he could not compete with Joselito (promoted in 1912) and Belmonte, whom Machaquito promoted to *matador de toros* on the afternoon of his last performance.

The coincidence of Machaquito's retirement and Belmonte's promotion emphasizes the revolutionary shift in bullfighting styles. Machaquito and his contemporaries Ricardo Torres Reina (Bombita, 1879–1936), Vicente Pastor (1879–1966), and the somewhat older Antonio Fuentes (1869–1938) were fine but very different matadors[242] whose careers were adversely affected by the innovative techniques of Joselito and Belmonte. In fact, the first two decades of the twentieth century were dominated by a few superstars which, as several taurine commentators have pointed out, was detrimental to the profession as a whole. The death of Joselito (1920) opened up the field, and the years between that event and the outbreak of the Spanish Civil War (1936) were characterized by a great increase in the numbers of *novilleros* and *matadores de toros*. In this sense, *la edad de oro* (the golden age) of the bullfight was followed by a flowering of talent, sometimes called *la edad de plata* (the silver age).

Although his technique was sometimes flawed Machaquito impressed his audiences with his bravery and original style; as a killer he was accurate and impressive.[243] He was criticized, as Hemingway reports, but he was also the recipient of a great deal of praise, even adulation, while he was still alive.

> The narrator claims that this early twentieth century matador, like all Spanish bullfighters, was severely criticized while alive but "became incomparable" when he retired (241–42, 243).

Goya. Full name: Francisco José Goya y Lucientes (known among taurine aficionados as don Francisco de los toros). Great Spanish painter, 1746–1828.

The young Goya prepared gay, bright tapestry cartoons and painted portraits of the aristocracy, including the sovereigns Charles III, Charles IV, and Ferdinand VII. As he grew older and more critical, the vices of the Court, the Church, and society as a whole dominated his canvases. Illness caused him to lose his hearing in 1792; the consequent depression and isolation affected his style. The two large canvases depicting events in the Peninsular War, *The Second of May 1808* and *The Third of May 1808*, reflect his growing pessimism. The horrific series *Los Desastres de la Guerra* is also powerful condemnation of war. His paintings and etchings (*Los Caprichos*, *Los Proverbios*) became increasingly bitter, distorted, tortured, and even surrealistic.

As a young man Goya had belonged briefly to a *cuadrilla* of bullfighters; his series of etchings, *La Tauromaquia*, record the bullfight with great force and accuracy. Edward Stanton argues that Hemingway "perceived the parallels between his own life and the painter's: both were born in the provinces and gravitated to metropolitan centers of artistic activity . . . both were self-educated. . . . Each was a revolutionary in his art, defying the accepted rules and working against the grand manner of his predecessors. Both . . . were anticlerical and liberal in politics, and supreme lovers of the bullfight. . . . [Goya] was the first man to consider the corrida worthy of treatment by a serious artist. . . . Both . . . lived in periods of crisis and were profoundly marked by the great wars of their times . . . [and each took his subjects] not from classical or Christian tradition but from the life and events of his time." Stanton concludes that while "Veláz-quez painted from the head and Greco from the spirit," Hemingway preferred Goya who worked "from all the senses, his body, heart, head, spirit, and cojones." Stanton finds that when Hemingway speaks of Goya (*DIA*, 205), he is actually giving us the "most force-ful expression of his own artistic convictions and methods in *Death in the Afternoon*."[244]

There is no doubt that Hemingway was familiar with Goya's work, which he saw in Spanish, French, and U.S. museums.

The narrator knows and admires Goya's work, which he mentions often (3, 40, 73, 135, 141, 203–205).

Granados, José (Veneno). Spanish bullfighter, d. 1921. *Veneno* (poi-son) seems to have been a popular nickname for picadors, used most notably by José Pacheco in the nineteenth century and by José Gra-nados and his contemporary Anastasio Oliete Casquero (Veneno chico) in the early twentieth century. In 1926, the *cuadrilla* of Rafael Gómez Ortega (Gallo) included the picador Francisco López, known as Curro Veneno. Less notable picadors who used this nickname were José García, from El Puerto de Santa María (Cádiz), born in 1844; Francisco Cano Rodríguez, from Osuna (Seville), born in 1889; and the Mexican Agustín Espejel. One banderillero, José Romero, also used this nickname. A lot of Venenos indeed, but the one Hemingway refers to is José Granados, born in Málaga.

Little is known of this Veneno's background and early education. As a young man he worked for a horse contractor, and began his ca-reer as a freelance picador in the early 1900s. By 1911 he had ob-tained permanent employment in the *cuadrilla* of Isidoro Martí Flores, and the next year in that of Paco Madrid. A brave, energetic, and aggressive picador, he became a member of Belmonte's *cua-drilla* in 1915. On 13 March 1921, he was gored in the face while working in the Madrid ring; he died a few days later.[245] Hemingway, who saw his first bullfights in 1923, never saw Veneno perform.

Hemingway includes a photograph of Veneno at work (*h:* 288–89).

Granero, Manuel. Full name: Manuel Granero Valls. Spanish bull-fighter, 1902–22. Investiture as *matador de toros*, in Seville, September 1920; confirmed in Madrid in 1921. Hemingway cites Granero's death date correctly on page 45, but erred by one year on page 73: Granero died two years after Jose Gómez Ortega (Joselito) was killed.

Granero was a promising violinist, well on his way to a professional career in music, when he suddenly, in his mid-teens, fell in love with bullfighting. He learned this new art quickly, was a popular *novillero*, and in 1920 was hailed as a successor to Joselito, who had been killed in May of that year. In 1921 Granero was lightly gored four times but still managed a stunning ninety-four appearances (as Hemingway correctly says, *DIA*, 45). Critics and public agreed that he was a fine, elegant fighter.

Granero's 1922 season began triumphantly but ended suddenly, after only thirteen corridas, when he was fatally gored by the Veragua bull Pocapena, the second bull he faced on 7 May 1922. Pocapena gored him first in the thigh and then through his right eye: it was a horrific sight. The event was and still is much discussed.[246] Although Hemingway didn't see Granero perform or die, he describes Granero's death in *For Whom the Bell Tolls* (251–52); *see also* Lalanda, Marcial, who performed with Granero at his last corrida.

Vicente Barrera (q.v.), also from Valencia, was much in vogue in the years when Hemingway followed the bullfight; critics inevitably compared him with Granero.

> The narrator sketches Granero's short career, describing him as handsome, talented, the master of the new "Belmonistic" style, and Valencia's finest bullfighter (45, 73; *see also* 202; photographs, *h:* 366–69).

La Granja. The oldest parts of the royal estate at La Granja are the hunting lodge and the chapel dedicated to San Ildefonso, both built c. 1450. Ferdinand and Isabella (qq.v.) gave the property to monks, to use as farm or *granja* to supply their needs. Philip V, who acquired the property in 1719, built a summer palace with extensive gardens like those of Versailles.

Located in the Sierra de Guadarrama, near Segovia, La Granja is still, or again, a cool summer palace for the kings of Spain. It looks like "a theatrical French chateau, the antithesis of the proud, gloomy Escorial [q.v.], on which it turns its back."²⁴⁷ It has fountains which, as Hemingway mentions, sometimes play and sometimes don't.

The narrator recalls La Granja (51, 278).

El Greco. Full name: Domenikos Theotokopoulos. Painter and sculptor, c. 1548-c. 1614. He was born in Crete but was active in Italy, where he was known simply as "the Greek."

El Greco studied in Venice, probably with Titian, and came to Spain c. 1576. Unable to get the desired court appointment, he settled in Toledo.

El Greco's highly individual style is noted for its exaggerated vertical lines, particularly in the elongated human figures, and, in the religious pictures, the almost mystical fervor.

Hemingway and El Greco. Hemingway greatly admired El Greco's *View of Toledo*, which he saw in New York's Metropolitan Museum, and various other paintings that he saw in Madrid's Prado Museum: the famous *Crucifixion*, *The Adoration of the Shepherds*, and *The Pentecost*. The Prado also has many of El Greco's portraits of aristocrats.

El Greco never married, but in 1578 he had a son by Doña Jerónima de las Cuevas.²⁴⁸ *See also* Homosexuals.

The narrator, who scorns homosexuals, suspects El Greco of being one. He adds that El Greco was so great that if he really was a homosexual, he would "redeem" all the others (203, 205).

Greeks. *See* Smyrna.

Gris, Juan. Full name: José Victoriano González. Spanish cubist painter, 1887–1927.

In 1906, when Gris came to Paris to work and study, he quickly became part of the group of intellectuals and artists who gathered in Picasso's studio. Gris was also advised and helped by Gertrude Stein, who bought a number of his paintings, including *The Table in Front of the Window*, *Seated Woman*, and *Dish of Pears*. She also contributed an admiring essay, "Pictures of Juan Gris," to the Juan Gris number of the *Little Review* (1924), and wrote her only elegy, "The Life and Death of Juan Gris," when he died in 1927. In *The Autobiography Alice B. Toklas* (1933), Stein reiterated her admiration for him, writing that "the only real cubism is that of Picasso and Juan Gris."[249]

Gris is known mainly for his still-lifes, often done in blues and grays: *Gray Still Life* (1912), *Still Life with Oil Lamp* (1912), *Three Cards* (1913), *Still Life with Fruit Dish and Carafe* (1914). He also painted a *Portrait of Picasso* (1912).

Hemingway and Gris. Perhaps influenced by Stein, Hemingway acquired two Gris paintings: *The Guitar Player* and *The Torero.* Gris appears in three of Hemingway's posthumous works. In *A Moveable Feast*, Hemingway refers to the friendship between Stein and Gris (119). Thomas Hudson, a painter who is the main character of *Islands in the Stream*, has Gris's *The Guitar Player* in his bedroom: he loves it because it succeeds in representing nostalgia, something which Hudson feels he cannot achieve (237–38). And Gris's *Woman with a Basket* decorates the dust jacket of Hemingway's *The Garden of Eden.*]

Hemingway chose Gris's *El Torero*, which he owned, as the frontispiece for *Death in the Afternoon.*

Guardia Civil. The Guardia Civil, established by a series of royal decrees (28 March, 12 April, and 13 May 1844), was designed to replace independent provincial law-enforcement agencies working under separate, uncoordinated sets of regulations. It was an expression of the movement towards unification and uniformity among Spain's various regions. Its members receive military training, its director general carries the rank of major general, and like the army, it is organized into *tercios*, one *tercio* for each of the military regions (*tercios*, thirds, was "the name used in the sixteenth century for regiments in the Army of Flanders which had been composed of three groups, pikemen, crossbowmen and arquebusiers").[250] In Hemingway's day, the Civil Guard divided Spain into eight regions, named after the cities where their captains general had their headquarters: Madrid, Seville, Valencia, Barcelona, Zaragoza, Burgos/Navarra, Valladolid, and La Coruña.

By virtue of their training and organization, the Guardia Civil are aligned with the Army and, therefore, with the Church, the aristocracy, and the landowners. They were more visible and active during Primo de Rivera's dictatorship, the Spanish Civil War, and the Franco years, than they are now: Hemingway was certainly aware of them and their weapons. They still wear their distinctive black patent leather hats; their "yellow patent leather belts" (274) appear as "yellow leather cross-straps" in *The Sun Also Rises* (109). The police, who maintain a lower profile, are not associated with the military.

The Civil Guard and the Government. The Civil Guard patrol in pairs (270), and one such pair was killed in a 1924 shootout with revolutionaries intent on overthrowing Primo de Rivera. For the ensuing trial and miscarriage of justice, *see* Deva and related entries: Captain General of Burgos; Host; Primo de Rivera, Miguel; and Rotonde.

> The narrative focuses on the Civil Guards's weapons and their authority (111, 270, 274, *h:* 440, s.v. *Guardia*) and also mentions the police, who jail bullfighters, often to protect them from unruly spectators (60, 77, 157; *see also* 251–52).

Guerra Bejarano, Rafael (Guerrita). Spanish bullfighter, 1862–1941. Investiture as *matador de toros*, in Madrid, September 1887. A child prodigy, Guerrita was first known as "el niño del llavero" and "Llaverito," because his father, in charge of the local slaughterhouse, held its keys (*llaves*). His vocation was so obvious that he overcame his family's strong objections[251] and began his career as banderillero in a youthful *cuadrilla* known as *los niños cordobeses* (q.v.). At his first Madrid appearance, as banderillero in the *cuadrilla* of the matador Fernando Gómez (el Gallo) (q.v.), he was singled out for a triumphant tour of the ring. In spite of his enormous popularity, he did not become an independent *matador de toros*, but continued to work in *cuadrillas*, most notably those of Gómez and Lagartijo, until his promotion to full *matador de toros* at age twenty-five. Even in those days, when long training was the rule, Guerra was overdue for his *alternativa* (q.v.): he had been fighting since age fourteen and famous since age twenty.

Guerrita was a *torero muy largo* (possessed of a large repertoire). He killed 2,399 bulls, many of them the fierce Miuras and Pablo Romeros; he was gored seriously ten times. During his triumphant 1889 season, he became the first matador to hear music in Madrid (a clear sign of the spectators' approval; see Trophies in *DS*). But in spite of his obvious talent and extravagant successes, Guerrita suffered at the hands of the Madrid critics. Although Madrid seemed to prefer Guerra to his contemporary, Manuel García (el Espartero, q.v.), the old rivalry, between supporters of Frascuelo and those of Lagartijo, undermined Madrid's affection for him. Guerra had received his *alternativa* from Lagartijo, who had been a great favorite in Madrid. But his participation in Frascuelo's farewell performance in 1889 marked a serious deterioration in Madrid's relationship with Guerra: the fervently pro-Lagartijo Madrid audience took offence at Guerra's compliment to Frascuelo. Hoping that critics would forget the previous generation's rivalries, Guerra avoided the Madrid bullring as much as possible during the next two years. But his refusal to perform in Lagartijo's farewell performance (1893) reinforced Madrid's aversion to him.

After el Espartero's death in May 1894, Guerra reigned as the undisputed star of the taurine world, fighting eighty corridas and killing 224 bulls that year. He occasionally gave solo performances, killing six bulls in a single afternoon. And on one memorable day, 19 May 1895, he fought three separate corridas in three different towns (San Fernando, Jerez, and Seville); special trains were provided for aficionados.[252] But his problems with Madrid continued, no doubt exacerbated by the high fees he demanded and his defiant refusal to pay the usual bribes to taurine critics (*see also* Spanish-American War). Angered by taurine politics and the hostility of the Madrid public, Guerra decided to retire in 1899. After killing his last bull, he is reputed to have wept, claiming repeatedly that "Yo no me voy de los toros. Me echan" (I am not leaving the bulls; I am being expelled). In spite of his problems with the Madrid public, however, Guerra did not lack for praise during his lifetime. Hemingway exaggerates the situation.

Guerra's Tauromaquia. Even though they carry a particular bullfighter's name, most *tauromaquias* (books describing and analyzing that matador's art, theories, and opinions) are ghostwritten by critics, friends, historians, or other professional writers. The influential *Tauromaquia completa* of Francisco Montes (Paquiro, q.v.) was penned by the taurine critic Santos López Pelegrín (Abenamar), and that of José Delgado (Pepe-Hillo) by José de la Tixera. The *Tauromaquia* that describes Guerra's style and ideas was written by Leopoldo Vázquez, Luis Gandullo, and Leopoldo López; Hemingway owned both volumes. The practice of ghostwriting continues to this day; for jokes on this subject, see Davis, Bill, in *DS*.

Hemingway used the historical names of Rafael Guerra (Guerrita) and Cayetano Ordóñez (Niño de la Palma, q.v.) before settling on Pedro Romero (q.v.) as the most appropriate name for the fictional bullfighter in *The Sun Also Rises*.[253]

> The narrator explains that in typical Spanish fashion the critics and public of his day compared Guerra unfavorably to his predecessors but declared him "the master of masters" after his retirement (240–43). He mentions that Guerra did not write the *Tauromaquia* that carries his name (*h:* 483, s.v. *Tauromachia*; *see also* 159).

Guerrita. *See* Guerra Bejarano, Rafael.

Gypsies. Spain's gypsies generally live in the south of the country and are said to be instinctive, graceful, possessed of supernatural powers, careless with money, and disdainful of rules. Over the centuries they have exerted a strong influence on the spirit, language, dress, and folklore of Spain, their contribution being most easily recognized in the bullfight and in flamenco music and dance. Even so, they remain foreign to mainstream Spanish society.

Marriages between bullfighters and flamenco singers and dancers were not unusual (e.g., Fernando Gómez and Gabriela Ortega; their son Rafael and Pastora Imperio; Cayetano Ordóñez and Consuelo Araujo), and such unions often produced remarkable bullfighters. Just as the typical Cordoban bullfighter is unbending, dry, hardworking, and reliable, the stereotypical gypsy bullfighter is joyful, lively, graceful, and capable of sudden outbursts of surprising ingenuity or embarrassing cowardice. In 1930 the popularity of the gypsy bullfighters Joaquín Rodríguez (Cagancho) and Francisco Vega de los Reyes (Gitanillo de Triana; qq.v.) inspired a historical review of the gypsy tradition in bullfighting, "Los faraones del toreo" (The Pharaohs of the Bullfight); the title reflects the frequent but inaccurate linking of Egypt with gypsy. The essay identifies Manuel Díaz (el

Lavi, 1811–58) as "el primer espada 'flamenco' " (the first gypsy matador) and then reviews the careers of José Lara (Chicorro, 1839–1911), Francisco Díaz (Paco de Oro, 1840–1910), Manuel Hermosilla (1847–1918), Antonio Ortega (el Marinero, 1857–1910), Manuel Lara (Jerezano, 1864–1912), and the famous brothers Rafael (el Gallo) and José Gómez Ortega (qq.v.). All were individualistic and capable of breathtaking performances.[254]

Note: Gypsies often refer to each other as "cousin," even if no blood relationship exists. Hemingway's remark that Gitanillo de Triana was a cousin of Cagancho (*DIA*, 217) reflects this usage and is not to be taken literally.

The narrator mentions gypsies often, telling the story of the gypsy boy and girl who avenge their brother's death by eating the testicles of the bull that killed him (24–25). Some gypsy bullfighters openly reveal their fear (157, 223) and their grief (243); most are graceful (13–14, 216–17, 223). He identifies several bullfighters as gypsies: the Gómez Ortega brothers, Andrés Mérida, Joaquín Rodríguez (Cagancho), and Francisco Vega de los Reyes (Gitanillo de Triana, qq.v.).

– H –

Haba, Antonio de la (Zurito). Full name: Antonio de la Haba Torreras. Spanish bullfighter, 1901–65. Investiture as *matador de toros*, in Gandía, September 1924; confirmed in Madrid, July 1925; resigned in 1930. His father, a famous picador, was the original Zurito (q.v.).

Antonio de la Haba had been a promising though not a spectacular *novillero*, whose reputation shone most brightly in the provinces. His Madrid debut as a *novillero* (25 August 1922) was disappointing. Altogether, he was seen in twenty-four *novilladas* that year. He had a similarly respectable record in 1923 and 1924, the promotion coming at the very end of his 1924 season.

As a new *matador de toros* Haba enjoyed two consecutive strong seasons, performing in twenty-three corridas in 1925 and twenty-seven the next year, even though a goring on 7 March forced him to cancel the next two months' contracts. In both these years he had good reviews. But illness forced him to cancel many of the contracts he had signed for the 1927 season, and for almost two months, from

1 July until 21 August, he did not fight at all. On several of the afternoons when he did fight, he fainted and had to be removed from the ring. All told, he performed in twenty-one corridas that year, although he had signed contracts for many more. At this point, after three years of limited exposure and without major triumphs, Zurito began to lose his standing. He had fourteen corridas in 1928, five in 1929, two in 1930, and six in 1931, at which point he resigned his rank and became a *matador de novillos* again.

Cossío reports that Zurito was spectacular with the sword but unimpressive with the cape and muleta. Bagüés writes that he was "un matador fácil y un torero vulgar" (a gifted killer and a vulgar bullfighter). By 1930 his career as matador was essentially over, although for the rest of the decade he occasionally freelanced as a banderillero. After he retired from active bullfighting, he was appointed technical adviser (*asesor*) to the president of the bullring in his native Córdoba.[255]

Hemingway and Zurito. Hemingway's remarks about Zurito's premature promotion to *matador de toros* echo Tomás Orts Ramos (Uno al Sesgo)'s remarks in 1924: that as a "novillero de primera fila" (of the first rank) Zurito could and should have waited until the next season, in order to take the *alternativa* (q.v.) at an important plaza instead of in Gandía, and at the hands of an established, stellar figure, instead of from Manuel Martínez, himself promoted to *matador de toros* only a month earlier. Both these circumstances diminished this event, so important in a taurine career.[256] But this is not the same as a premature promotion of a person who lacks the necessary maturity or education. Not only was Zurito twenty-three years old, he had had the advantage of growing up in a family of bullfighters, in the bullfighting circles of Córdoba. His short repertoire can only be blamed on his unwillingness or, more probably, his inability to learn, not on a "premature" promotion. Throughout his career, his strong point was his accurate, effective sword work. He was, in a sense, one of the "specialists" typical of his period, and not a well-rounded maestro. *See also* Luck.

Hemingway and Zurito. Hemingway saw Zurito in Pamplona, where he performed on 8, 9, 10, and 11 July 1926. Zurito had been contracted for three corridas in the 1927 Pamplona *feria*, but his ill-

ness forced him to cancel these and other appearances. Hemingway
may have seen him on one or two other occasions.

> The narrator reports that Zurito was a sensational *novillero* who "killed
> classically, slowly, and beautifully" (254) but was harmed by his prema-
> ture promotion to *matador de toros*. Failing to develop sufficient technique
> and a large enough repertoire, and devoid of "artistic ability" with the
> cape and muleta (223–24), he was often injured and occasionally shocked
> his audiences by fainting in the bullring from the pain and weakness of
> internal injuries. He "had two good seasons" after which he could obtain
> only a few engagements a year. The narrator seems very interested in Zur-
> ito and discusses him at length (223–24, 253–54, 256–59, 262).

Hadley. *See* Hemingway, Hadley.

Hammett, Dashiell. American writer of detective fiction, 1894–1937.
Author of *Red Harvest* (1929), *The Dain Curse* (1929), *The Maltese
Faction* (1930), *The Thin Man* (1931), *The Glass Key* (1931), *Blood
Money* (1942), *Adventures of Sam Spade* (1944), *Continental Opera-
tor* (1945), *Hammett Homicides* (1946). Hammett's eight years as a
detective for the Pinkerton Agency provided the material for his novels, several of which were made into popular films. His hard-boiled
characters, tough language, and violent action made his books very
popular. After his death, his companion, Lillian Hellman, published
several of his works. *See The Dain Curse.*

> The narrator mentions that his wife was reading Dashiell Hammett's *The
> Dain Curse* out loud to his son (228).

Harrison, Charles Yale. *See Generals Die in Bed.*

The Hayseed of Borox (el paleto de Borox, el pardillo de Borox).
Nickname of Domingo López Ortega, generally known as Domingo
Ortega, who was born in in the small town of Borox, Toledo. *See*
Ortega, Domingo.

Hechicero. Like Carralero and Borge, who were Hemingway's source,
Cossío reports that this bull, who was from the ranch of Joaquín de
la Concha y Sierra (*see* Concha y Sierra, doña Concepción de la; don
Joaquín died in the early 1860s), was fought in Cádiz in 1844. But

Carralero and Borge give more details than Hemingway does. They write that Hechicero was "cárdeno" (having evenly distributed black and white hair, without solid patches of either color, giving the appearance of gray); that he was bred in the ranch of Concha y Sierra; and, as Hemingway reports, that he earned his place as a "toro célebre" by disabling seven horses and injuring all the picadors present at the corrida. Vera mentions this same bull, the seven disabled picadors, and the seven dead horses.

Carralero and Borge also mention another bull with this same name: he was black, came from the Vázquez ranch, and killed five horses when he was fought in Madrid on 29 September 1887.[257]

The narrator reports the exploits of a bull named Hechicero (110, 112).

Hemingstein. For a discussion of Hemingway's nicknames, *see* Smith, William Benjamin in this volume, and Papa in *DS*. Hemingway often called himself Hemingstein or the Stein.

The narrator and Ernest Hemingway share the nickname Hemingstein (53–54). The narrator also refers to himself as Mr. H. (190).

Hemingway, Ernest Miller. American author, 1899–1961. Among his books are *The Sun Also Rises*, *A Farewell to Arms*, and *Death in the Afternoon*. For good biographies, see Carlos Baker's *Ernest Hemingway: A Life Story* and Michael Reynolds's five-volume biography.

The narrator of *Death in the Afternoon* shares many life experiences with his creator, Ernest Hemingway, though there are some omissions, most notably the divorce from his first wife, Hadley, and the affair and marriage with the second wife, Pauline (qq.v.). The narrator seems to have a more active involvement with bullfighting than Hemingway did (171–72).

Hemingway, Hadley (Mrs. E. R.). Full name: Elizabeth Hadley Richardson, 1891–1979; married to Ernest Hemingway, 1921–26.

Like Hemingway, Hadley grew up in a large, comfortable home, with a strong-willed mother and a father who committed suicide. When Hadley was six, she injured her back so badly that it required several months to heal. Thereafter her mother insisted that "Hadley was physically and psychologically weak and treated her as an invalid," keeping her home from school and restricting her activities.[258]

Hadley studied a year or two at Bryn Mawr College, worked part time in the St. Louis Public Library during World War I, cared for her sister's children, and resisted her family's definition of her as an invalid. Once married to Ernest, she was able to keep up with his strenuous lifestyle, which included hiking, skiing, frequent journeys, late nights, and heavy drinking. She led a more sedate life with her second husband, Paul Scott Mowrer (journalist, author, Pulitzer Prize winner), whom she married in 1933.[259]

Hadley is the subject of two biographies, Alice Hunt Sokoloff's *Hadley: The First Mrs. Hemingway* and Gioia Diliberto's *Hadley*. She figures largely in the memoir written by her son, Jack Hemingway, *Misadventures of a Fly Fisherman: My Life with and without Papa*, in Hemingway's *A Moveable Feast*, and in all the biographies about Hemingway.

Hadley accompanied Ernest to the bullfights in the summers of 1923, 1924, 1925, and 1926. The boy with the wine, the drunk Civil Guards, the lost tickets, and the detail of Hadley and the bull's ear are all biographically accurate. Unlike Brett Ashley in *The Sun Also Rises*, Hadley kept the bull's ear that was given to her by Cayetano Ordóñez (q.v.) in 1925.[260]

Hemingway's portrait of Hadley acknowledges her passion for literature and music. Although Hemingway was married to Pauline at the time he published *Death in the Afternoon*, the description of Hadley is affectionate and admiring. He makes her younger than she was: born in 1891, Hadley was actually more than thirty years old when she saw her first bullfight in Pamplona, July 1923.

> The narrator accurately describes Mrs. E[lizabeth] R[ichardson] and her response to the bullfight. He suggests that Hadley and Cayetano Ordóñez (unnamed but clearly identifiable) admired each other (270, *h:* 497–98).

Hemingway, John Hadley Nicanor (Bumby, J. H., Jack). Hemingway's son by Hadley, his first wife; 1923–2000.

Several anecdotes involving his oldest son appear in Hemingway's *Islands in the Stream* and in *A Moveable Feast*. Jack's memoir, *Misadventures of a Fly Fisherman: My Life with and without Papa*, appeared in 1986.

When Hemingway and Pauline were in Spain in the summer of 1931, Bumby was living with Hadley in Paris but spent time with Ernest in Pamplona and with Ernest, Pauline, and Patrick in Hendaye. Since Patrick (Hemingway's second son, b. 1928) remained in Hendaye with his nurse for the whole summer, the boy who is with the Hemingways in Madrid ("my son," *DIA*, 227–28) is based on Bumby, not Patrick. Bumby, Pauline, and Hemingway were together in Madrid on 23 August 1931, when Isidoro Todó (q.v.) was fatally gored.[261]

Hemingway took Bumby to the Pamplona bullfights in July 1931. A photograph in Fernando Hualde's *Hemingway: Cien años y una huella* clearly shows them together in the bullring (page 32). Born in October 1923, Bumby was then still seven years old, and not nine as the narrator claims (*DIA, h:* 495). For other references to this Hemingway son, *see* Alfonso XIII.

Hemingway may be playing with the two translations of "torero corto": a short bullfighter (as opposed to a tall one), or a bullfighter with a short or "limited repertoire" (*DIA, h:* 428, s.v. *Corto*; for a longer discussion of Hemingway's concern with a bullfighter's height, *see* the entries for Manuel García [Maera], who was tall, and for Todó, Isidoro, who was short). In Hemingway's short story "A Day's Wait," the narrator's son similarly fears death because of a mistranslation. In that story, however, the father clears up the misunderstanding and thus calms the boy.

> When the narrator's son heard that Isidoro Todó had died, he feared that the bullfighter "was killed because he was so small," as of course he himself was. The narrator and his wife attempted to allay the boy's fears (*see The Dain Curse*); the boy eventually stopped brooding about it (228). The narrator reports that J[ohn] H[adley] had strong opinions on bullfights and bullfighters (*h:* 495–96). John Hemingway speaks: 228, *h:* 495–96.

Hemingway, Patrick. Hemingway's second-born son, his first son by his second wife, Pauline; b. 28 June 1928. Patrick, also called P. H., is the younger brother of J. H. (*see* Hemingway, John Hadley Nicanor). When Hemingway made his last visit to Spain before the publication of *Death in the Afternoon*, Pauline was pregnant with his third son, Gregory, born November 1931.

In 1931, when Ernest, Pauline, and Patrick were in France and Patrick saw his first bullfights, the boy was three years old, and not four, as the narrator claims (*DIA, h:* 495), though he would have been four when *Death in the Afternoon* was published in September 1932. While his parents traveled in France and Spain, Patrick remained in and around Hendaye with his French nanny, Henrietta Lechuer, with whom he probably spoke French.[262]

I have not been able to verify that Patrick went to a bullfight in Bordeaux that summer, but the precise detail Hemingway gives—that three months after the Bordeaux bullfight Patrick was taken to a bull-fight in Bayonne—enables us to date the events. In the months the Hemingways were in Europe, Bayonne celebrated only one bullfight, on 6 September. Precisely three months earlier, on 7 June 1931, there had been a *novillada picada* (with mounted picadors) at Bordeaux, hence Patrick's remark about "le horsy."[263]

> Apparently as reported by his nurse, Patrick's reactions to his first bullfight are recorded in *Death in the Afternoon* (*h:* 495). Patrick Hemingway speaks: *h:* 495.

Hemingway, Pauline. Full name: Pauline Marie Pfeiffer Hemingway (P. M.). American newspaperwoman, 1895–1951; and Hemingway's second wife, 1927–40; mother of Patrick (q.v.) and Gregory Hancock Hemingway (b. November 1931).

The daughter of wealthy, Catholic parents, Pauline (P. M.) was educated at the Visitation Convent in St. Louis and at the University of Missouri, where she earned a degree in journalism. Her first job was with the *Cleveland Star*, after which she worked for the *Daily Telegraph* and *Vanity Fair*. Her work with *Vogue* magazine and the fashion house of Mainbocher took her to Paris, where she met Hemingway and Hadley in the spring of 1925. She skiied with them in Austria in the winter of 1925, accompanied them to the Pamplona fiesta in 1926, and married Hemingway in May 1927. With Ernest, she returned to Spain in the summers of 1927, 1929 and 1931. She was older than twenty-eight when she saw her first bullfight.[264] *See also* Horses, Horse Racing.

> The narrator writes that in the summer of 1931, when Isidoro Todó (Alcalareño II) was killed in the bullring (228), his wife was reading Dashiell Hammett's 1929 novel, *The Dain Curse* (q.v.), out loud to his son. Hemingway dedicated *Death in the Afternoon* "To Pauline" and described her reaction to the bullfights (*h:* 499).

Hemingway's Son. *See* Hemingway, John Hadley Nicanor.

Hemingway's Wife. *See* Hemingway, Pauline.

El Heraldo de Madrid. Subtitle: *Diario Independiente.* Newspaper published from 1890 to 1938. It was a daily until 1920, when it ceased Sunday publication. The paper's bullfight critic was Angel Caamaño (el Barquero, 1861–1927), a sometime actor and bull-fighter, author of about thirty plays and three bullfight books: *Agraz en polvo*, *Cabezas, cabecillas y cabezotas* (1888), and *De la torería* (1914). He wrote for the paper from its founding until his death, en-livening his taurine reports with amusing and relevant verses. In the last year of his life he founded a taurine publication called *Estafeta taurina*, which did not survive him.[265] Another taurine critic who wrote for *El Heraldo de Madrid* was Celedonio José de Arpe (Pepe el de las Traineras; d. January 1927).[266]

The Biblioteca Nacional, Madrid, has an almost complete run of this newspaper, 29 October 1890–3 October 1938. Over the years the format varied. *See also* Ortega, Domingo.

> The narrator claims that the *Heraldo* praised Ortega's performance at a 1931 bullfight in Aranjuez at which Ortega had actually been "lousy." Or-tega's promoter "was spending much money on his publicity" and the *Heraldo*, like many papers, accepted subsidies (168–69).

Hernández, Esteban. Spanish bull breeder, d. 1913.

Esteban Hernández established an impressive bull-breeding estab-lishment by buying a great deal of stock over a short period of time. In about 1890, he bought breeding cattle from Alejandro Arroyo; this consisted mainly of Mazpule stock. In 1892 he acquired the rest of the Mazpule holdings; and in 1893 he bought 824 head of the Count of Patilla's herd (established in the 1800s), as well as the rights to its brand, colors (sky blue, white, and crimson) and its *antigüedad*, or seniority (12 November 1882). He kept these three herds separate for a few years, bred and studied them, and then sold the Arroyo and Mazpule stock in order to focus on the Patilla herd, to which he added some *vazqueño* stock acquired from Jacinto Trespalacios. The excellent results were much sought after, "no sólo por su irreprocha-ble crianza y trapío, sino por la bravura y el poder que desarrollaban a lo largo de la lidia" (not only because of their impeccable breeding and their good looks and bearing, but also for their bravery and the power they developed during the course of the bullfight).

After don Esteban died in 1913, his heirs experimented by crossing the herd with Saltillo stock (*see* Santa Coloma, Conde de; Saltillo cattle are descended from Vistahermosa) but according to the review in *Toros y toreros en 1931*, the results were disappointing and the herd deteriorated rapidly. It was already in decline when Hemingway began to follow the bulls.

The Spanish Civil War decimated the herd. In 1948, Esteban Hernández Plá began to rebuild it with Pinohermoso and Albaserrada stock. Today (2000), the herd is still owned by the family, who have kept its seniority.

Hemingway and the Esteban Hernández Bull. The strong, impressively horned bull Hemingway mentions probably belonged to the founder himself, don Esteban Hernández, and not to his heirs.[267]

> The narrator mentions that a bull from this ranch drove his horn through an iron stirrup without, fortunately, wounding the picador (109–10).

Hernández Ramírez, Rafael (Rafael). Spanish journalist, 1889–1971. Before the Spanish Civil War, he wrote taurine criticism and other reports for several newspapers, including *ABC* (q.v.) and *El Debate*, and became the editor of *La Libertad* (1919–34; q.v.). After the war, he edited *Informaciones* (1939–71) and also wrote for and other papers. He signed his work only with his first name.

Hemingway and Rafael. Iribarren claims that Hemingway met Rafael in 1924 and that it was Rafael who told Hemingway about Juan Quintana and encouraged him to stay in the Hotel Quintana in Pamplona. In the early 1930s Hernández helped Hemingway subscribe to several of the Spanish taurine journals Hemingway wished to receive in Key West. Hernández reviewed Hemingway's career generally, and *Death in the Afternoon* in particular, very favorably in "Míster Ernest Hemingway, el amigo de España" (*La Libertad*, 23 September 1933). Hemingway referred to this essay in his own, "A Friend of Spain: A Spanish Letter" (*Esquire*, January 1934).

Mary Hemingway recalls that in 1953, she and Hemingway had met "Rafael Hernández, the bullfight critic and his old friend" in Pamplona.[268]

Hernández's major work is *Historia de la plaza de toros de Madrid* (1955). He appears as the critic Rafael in Hemingway's *The Sun Also Rises* (173–77).

Among the many people the narrator wishes he could have discussed in his book is Rafael (271, 272, 277–78).

Hernandorena, Domingo. Spanish bullfighter, d. 1944.

Hernandorena made his debut as *matador de novillos* in his native Bilbao in 1922, and his Madrid debut in 1923, although in the latter he was "sin fortuna" (without luck). His was a very minor career: he never fought more than a few *novilladas* a year until he retired from the ring, without achieving the rank of *matador de toros*. Adept at drawing, he worked as an illustrator of bullfight posters.[269]

Hemingway and Hernandorena. The goring Hemingway mentions occurred on 19 July 1925. This was probably Hernandorena's first opportunity to redeem himself in Madrid after his miserable performance there in 1923, and so it was a particularly important afternoon for him. But he was not up to the challenge: he was gravely injured in the right thigh by a Tovar *novillo* called Morito.[270] Hemingway was in Madrid on that day. *See also* Tovar.

The narrator correctly identifies Hernandorena as a *novillero* from the Basque provinces who never succeeded in the profession and was gored in Madrid on a hot summer afternoon (17–20).

Héros XII. The breeding of this bay gelding, foaled in 1915, is Ex Voto and Historienne. He was owned by M. Henri Coulon and trained by Roch Filippi. In 1921 and again in 1922, he won the Prix du Président de la République, a famous classic handicap hurdle race run in the spring at Auteuil.

In 1922, Héros XII was the top money earner, followed by L'Yser. That year he ran in eight races, of which he won three, all at Auteuil: on 19 March (Prix Adolphe-Abeille), 16 April (Prix du Président de la République), and 18 June (Grand Steeplechase de Paris); the last two have large stakes. Hemingway was in Paris for the first of these, when the betting was 14 to 10. Hemingway also saw Héros XII in the fall: he saved the program for the *Courses a Auteuil, Réunion d'Automne*, 19 November 1922, at which Héros XII and Master Bob (q.v.) ran in the third race (the Prix Montgomery Steeplechase—Handicap). Héros XII finished seventh, Master Bob third, L'Yser second, and Odoacre first.

In 1923, his last racing season, Héros XII ran eight races, won two, and placed in one. Hemingway saw him run on 18 June 1923, at the Grand Steeplechase de Paris, at Auteuil, won by L'Yser; he and Hadley made money on Master Bob, who came in second; Héros XII came in third.[271] Hemingway may have seen the same two horses at the same track a few days later: Héros XII won the race of 22 June (the betting was 9 to 10), and Master Bob came in second (the betting was 43 to 10).

Evan Shipman (q.v.) described Héros XII as "certainly the greatest steeplechase horse of his time on the Continent, and his name is still [in 1950] mentioned in hushed and reverent tones by the initiated."[272]

The narrator recalls the steeplechaser Héros XII with admiration (5).

Homosexuals. Hemingway has traditionally been seen as disapproving of lesbians and homosexuals, perhaps even excessively so, with all that such excess implies. Scholes and Comley's recent study, however, argues convincingly that "Hemingway was . . . much more sensitive and complex in his consideration of . . . [t]he complexity of human sexuality—especially the potential bisexuality of all humans" (144). Throughout their book, and most impressively in their chapter on "Toros, Cojones, y Maricones," they use published and unpublished texts as well as biographical materials and contemporary attitudes to enrich their reading of this recurrent topic in *Death in the Afternoon*. *See* Androgyny, in this volume; and "Chulo" in *DS*.

Hemingway discusses several artists in terms of their recognized or presumed homosexuality: Cocteau, Firbank, Gide, el Greco, Leonardo da Vinci, Radiguet, Shakespeare, Wilde, and Whitman (qq.v.); two bullfighters are also suspected of being homosexuals (417–18). Two characters in a twice-told tale (by a newspaperman to the narrator and by the narrator to the Old Lady and thus to us) form a homosexual alliance (179–82), the conversion of the younger man to homosexuality being announced by his newly hennaed hair. As

Debra Moddelmog has pointed out, early in the twentieth century, dyed, bleached, and hennaed hair were markers for "effeminacy and male homosexuality."[273] Gertrude Stein and Alice B. Toklas's lesbian relationship, emphasized in *A Moveable Feast*, is not mentioned in *Death in the Afternoon*.

The narrator employs a variety of terms for homosexuals, in English and Spanish: *queer* (34), *fairy* (271), *espalda* and *sodomite* (*h:* 436, s.v. *Espalda*); the Glossary entry for *Maricón* begins with a virtuosic display of synonyms for *homosexual* (*h:* 447–48; *see also* 205). The words *unfortunate* and *abnormal* are also attached to homosexuals (179–80). Homosexual speaks: 181.

Horses, Horse Racing. Hemingway's horse-racing story, "My Old Man" (written in 1922, published in *Best Short Stories of 1923*), was seen as derivative from Sherwood Anderson—a comparison that angered Hemingway. In that story, and in several of Hemingway's later works, horse racing is associated with dishonesty; see, for example, the San Siro scene in *A Farewell to Arms* (128–31) and Santiago's criticism of John J. McGraw in *The Old Man and the Sea* (22). Rose Marie Burwell argues that in *A Moveable Feast*, horse and bicycle racing become metaphors for marital infidelity, "an indirect way of talking about his first and second marriages. . . . [I]nstead of including Pauline [in *MF*], Hemingway inscribed her in the complex feelings he had about horse racing—it is a false friend, beautiful, exciting, time-consuming, demanding and profitable; and it gave him material for writing."[274] In the biographical sketches at the end of *Death in the Afternoon*, Hemingway writes that P. M. (Pauline Marie Pfeiffer) likes horses and bicycle racing (*h:* 499).

Hemingway is too complex a writer to lock himself into any particular metaphor. Although in much of his work gambling and horse racing are fraught with negative associations, the narrator of *Death in the Afternoon* admires several race horses (5–8). Horses are also associated with war, both as pitiful victims (*see* Smyrna) and as dignified and brave warriors admired by Colonel Cantwell (*ARIT,* 52). Both Hemingway and his character Robert Jordan remember a mare called Bess.[275] *See also* Peto; Shipman, Evan; Sports; Victoria Eugenia; *and* individual horses: Epinard; Exterminator; Héros XII; Kzar; Man of War; Master Bob; Pinky; Uncas.

The narrator discusses his responses to horses in and out of the bullring (1–8). Horses participate in the ceremonies preceding the bullfight (58–59, 61). During the bullfight, they work with picadors (57, 114, 128–29, 184–89) and *rejoneadores* (26, *h:* 420–21, s.v. *Caballero en Plaza*; *h:* 473, s.v. *Rejón, Rejoneador*). Horses are often injured (1–8, 92–93, *h:* 286, 290, 292, *h:* 420, s.v. *Burriciegos*; 465); many are killed (114, 152, 213, 220, *h:* 404, 414, s.v. *Arrastre*). They are also associated with expensive sports like polo and horse racing (5, 109, 185, *h:* 499), and with war (2, 134, 135).

Host. A thin white wafer which, in Roman Catholic ritual, represents the body of Christ. The springtime Feast of Corpus Christi (body of Christ), in which the Host is shown to the faithful in procession, is observed the first Thursday after Trinity Sunday, late May or early June. It became an obligatory church festival through Urban IV's Papal Bull of 1264. In medieval times, church officials, princes, sovereigns, and trade and craft guilds participated in the colorful procession, which was followed by the performance of miracle plays and mysteries.

When Hemingway visited Spain in the 1920s and 1930s, the Civil Guard escorted religious processions like this one and, of course, the often rowdy annual July event in which Navarre's patron saint, San Fermín, is carried ceremoniously through the streets of Pamplona— hence Hemingway's linking of weapons and the Host. *See also* Guardia Civil.

The narrative links the Civil Guard's bayonets and belts with church trappings like candles and the Host (274).

Hotel Valencia. Current address: Convento San Francisco, 7, 46002 Valencia.

In 1928, the Hotel Restaurant Valencia was listed among the thirteen hotels and fifteen pensions approved by the Valencia Chamber of Commerce. Its address then was Plaza Emilio Castelar, 1, where the Bajada de San Francisco ran into the plaza. A map of the period indicates that this plaza was a small rectangular park or garden, separated from the larger Parque de Castelán by the Calle Barcas. The Valencia must have been a very pleasant hotel, facing the gardens and elegant buildings of the center of Valencia and conveniently close to the bullring. It charged ten pesetas for a room and full board, slightly more than the pensions but less than most of the other hotels, which charged between eleven and fifteen pesetas for full board. The Valencia is probably the hotel where Finito and Pilar "made love and then sent for another pitcher of beer with the drops of its coldness on the glass" (*FWTBT* 86; see also 85).

The remodeling of the two plazas and surrounding streets began in the late 1920s and by the early 1940s the whole area, from the Calle Barcelonina to the Calle Lauria, had been consolidated as the Plaza del Ayuntamiento. Much of it was paved over, though some greenery and a fountain still remain. The Bajada de San Francisco disappeared, and with it the buildings of the old Hotel Valencia. The hotel's owner built a new building to house the Hotel Valencia, at Calle Convento San Francisco, 7, also near the Plaza de Ayuntamiento and the bullring. Like its predecessor, the relocated Hotel Valencia also had a dining room.[276]

> The narrator of *Death in the Afternoon* recalls the fine food and the good, cold beer, served in pitchers, which he enjoyed at the Hotel Valencia. He mentions that the rooms are "very modest" (*h:* 425, s.v. *Cerveza*).

Hudson, W. H. Full name: William Henry Hudson. English naturalist and writer, 1841–1922. Hudson was born in Argentina, about which he wrote several books, including *The Purple Land that England Lost* (1885), *The Naturalist in La Plata* (1892), and *South American Sketches* (1909).

Three of Hemingway's characters, Robert Cohn, Jake Barnes, and David Bourne, have read Hudson (*The Sun Also Rises*, 9–10; *Garden of Eden*, 94–95). The protagonist of *Islands in the Stream* is named Thomas Hudson, no relation.

Like his characters, Hemingway owned many of Hudson's books. He remarked that Hudson "writes the best of anyone." Hemingway satirizes natural scientists whose writing is shaped by their religious "disposition to wonder and adore" (*DIA*, 134): he seems to admire Hudson. Beegel points out that of the four naturalists Hemingway mentions in *Death in the Afternoon*, only Hudson was writing after Darwin published *Origin of the Species* in 1859.[277] *See also* Humanism, Naturalism.

> The narrator claims he admires Hudson's "charming and sound" descriptions of Patagonia's plant and animal life (133).

Humanism, Naturalism. The late nineteenth century saw the emergence of the trend broadly called "realism," which aimed at accurate representation. Realism rejected the romantic or transcendental commitment to "morality," "beauty," or "civilization" in art, arguing that their insistence on positive values distorted the world and produced falseness, not art. Realism aimed at accuracy.

Realism expanded to include other movements, none of which painted "pretty" or uplifting pictures. Impressionism intensifies reality by representing the impression excited by the event rather than the event itself. Expressionism uses symbols and distortion in order to create or communicate the absolute rather than the physical reality. And naturalism attempts objective, scientific depiction of the biological, social, and environmental forces that shape human life.

The New Humanists, sometimes called Literary Humanists, found this focus distasteful. Raeburn defines these "humanists" as "a group of conservative critics calling for a return to moral values and for decorum in literature," a reactionary position reflecting the schism between pre- and post-World War I attitudes. Irving Babbitt and the other middle-aged academicians and members of the literary establishment who argued for the New Humanism were, as Beegel points out, a generation older than Hemingway: they subscribed to "prewar literary values not far divorced from Dr. and Mrs. Hemingway's moral values"—values that Hemingway rejected in his earlier fiction as well as in *Death in the Afternoon*.[278]

Hemingway's attack on the Humanists was triggered by Robert Herrick's review of *A Farewell to Arms*, which compared it unfavorably with Erich Marie Remarque's best-selling *All Quiet on the Western Front*, also published in 1929 and obviously Hemingway's major competition. Herrick was so put off by *A Farewell to Arms* that he didn't even finish reading it before penning his scathing review. He argued that although both books contain references to "certain common physiological functions" such as vomiting and sexual intercourse, "one [*All Quiet*] is literature and the other [*A Farewell to Arms*] it would not be too strong to call mere garbage," which should be suppressed by the censors. Herrick wrote that "Ardent naturalists or realists or expressionists (whatever from generation to generation they prefer to call themselves) seem to forget the elementary truth that while all human activities may have eternal significance and therefore an art value, few actually do bear the sacred mark. It is the fundamental duty of the creator to endow the activities he chooses to present with such an enduring quality. . . . Because a man often vomits after over-drinking of what human importance is it . . . ?" Raeburn argues that while Herrick himself "was not a Humanist, . . . his moralistic tone of disapproval [and] his publication in *The Bookman* . . . were enough for Hemingway." *The Bookman*, published from 1895 to 1933, was a conservative monthly which, under the editorship of John Farrar, presented "short, sometimes caustic sketches of contemporary writers" in a column called "The Literary Spotlight." It was a mouthpiece for the New Humanists, and the movement died with the journal.[279] Coincidentally, Irving Babbitt also died in 1933.

When Hemingway republished "A Natural History of the Dead" as a short story in *Winner Take Nothing*, he identified the Humanists in a footnote in which he called for "The reader's indulgence . . . for this mention of an extinct phenomenon . . . it is retained because of its mild historical interest and because its omission would spoil the rhythm" of his own work.

In addition to attacking the New Humanists, Hemingway rejects those natural scientists who, like the scientifically trained Mungo Park, the Reverend Gilbert White, and Bishop Edward Stanley (qq.v), read nature in the context of Christian optimism. Beegel writes that even Hemingway's father, a physician educated after the publication of Darwin's *Origin of the Species* (1859), "had no difficulty reconciling his scientific [training] with his religious faith."[280] Hemingway satirizes this blurring between science and the supernatural when he sets out to determine "what inspiration we may derive from the dead" (*DIA*, 134) using the methods of "Natural History." Hemingway's postwar literary naturalism offers no theological or even evolutionary optimism or comfort.

In the nineteenth century, a "naturalist" was a biologist, and "natural history" was the study of living organisms (plants and animals). The phrase can also be more widely defined as the study of all objects in nature (animal, vegetable, and mineral). Both definitions exclude the supernatural.

> The narrator rejects the Humanists and looks forward to the death of all such "self-styled" persons; he calls himself a "naturalist" (139).

Hurón. Hemingway's account of this bull is a complete, accurate translation of Carralero and Borge's entry for him in *Toros célebres*. Writing about the same bull, Martínez Salvatierra specifies that one person was killed and seventeen injured in the shooting; many more were hurt in the ensuing panic and stampede.[281] For information about the ranch which produced Hurón, *see* López Plata, don Antonio.

> The narrator reports that in 1904 this famous bull, whose exploits are chronicled in *Toros célebres*, fought and beat a Bengal tiger. He broke open the cage and the two animals charged the spectators; the police "fired several volleys" (111).

Huxley, Aldous. Full name: Aldous Leonard Huxley. English novelist, essayist and social critic, 1894–1963. Huxley's best known novels are *Crome Yellow* (1922), *Antic Hay* (1923), *Point Counter Point* (1928), *Brave New World* (1932), *Eyeless in Gaza* (1936), and *Ape and Essence* (1948). Hemingway quotes all of the first and most of the second paragraph of Huxley's essay, "Foreheads Villainous Low," which appeared in the collection *Music at Night and Other Essays*. In it, Huxley mentioned *A Farewell to Arms*, and the compliment Hemingway does not quote consists of a parenthetical phrase: "(for Mr. Hemingway is a most subtle and sensitive writer)" (Huxley, 201). It is interesting that while Huxley celebrates the reference to Mantegna in *A Farewell to Arms*, he does not mention that the characters of that novel are also familiar with Rubens and Titian (*AFTA*, 280).

In their analysis of Huxley's essays, "Meditation on El Greco" and "Foreheads Villainous Low," Scholes and Comley argue that just as Huxley used el Greco's painting as a pretext for his own discussion of the physical, so he used Hemingway as a starting point for his discussion of culture, education, and commercialism. Similarly, argue Scholes and Comley, Hemingway used Huxley's remarks about himself as a pretext for his own discussion of art (111–16).

Hemingway's carefully constructed public image highlighted his expertise in hunting, fishing, boxing, baseball, horse racing, drinking, and bullfighting. Several psychobiographers have argued that by emphasizing the so-called masculine arts, Hemingway was denying or downplaying the influence of his artistic mother, herself a musician and painter. More and more, Hemingway scholars are recognizing her positive influence on Hemingway's character and art. We need a book-length biography of this remarkable woman.

In spite of his anti-intellectual pose, Hemingway was well versed in music, painting, sculpture, architecture, history, and literature. He owned a dozen of Huxley's books, and claimed in *A Moveable Feast* that when he was not writing, he read Huxley for relaxation—a not-so-subtle putdown that is reinforced by his quoting of Gertrude Stein's advice that he not read Huxley at all, because Huxley is "a dead man" who writes "inflated trash" (*MF*, 26).

> The narrator inaccurately asserts that his book does not contain the phrase Huxley admires. His rejection of Huxley leads him to assert his own artistic principles (191–92). Later, the narrator embarks upon a discussion of art and art critics, "to please" Huxley (203).

– I –

Ibarra, Eduardo. Spanish bull breeder, late nineteenth and early twentieth centuries.

In 1884 or 1885, Eduardo Ibarra of Seville bought half of one of the Murube herds. It is probably this Murube-based herd, rich in Vistahermosa blood, that Ibarra presented to be fought in Madrid on 8 February 1885 (his herd's *antigüedad*, or seniority). In 1903 and 1904 Ibarra sold his holdings to two breeders: Manuel Fernández Peña, who seems never to have registered this stock in Madrid and who sold it in 1905 to the Count of Santa Coloma (q.v.); and Fernando Parladé, who later sold his animals to the Marquis of Tamarón, Francisco Correo, and Luis Gamero Cívico. Gamero Cívico's sons thus owned Parladé/Ibarra stock in the 1920s. In that decade Hemingway visited Spain frequently and saw Santa Coloma, Gamero Cívico, and Murube bulls (qq.v.), whose history connects them to Eduardo Ibarra.[282]

The Ibarra bulls were almost pure Vistahermosa and do not constitute a separate race or strain, as Hemingway writes. When Ibarra was dispossessing himself of his herd, one of the

Martínez heirs convinced him to sell them a seed bull. This was the famous Diano (q.v.).

After the Spanish Civil War, Spain had bull breeders by the name of doña Dolores Aguirre Ibarra (or Ybarra) and doña María Isabel Ibarra e Ibarra, but they are unrelated to the Eduardo Ibarra of a century ago. Today's Ibarra or Ybarra bulls are Mexican and also unrelated to the Ibarra whom Hemingway mentions. The Ibarra brand, an unadorned Y, was a variant of the more elaborate Y used by Juan Domínguez Ortiz (el Barbero de Utrera), and not an indication that Ibarra was spelled Ybarra. Later brands, resembling the original rather than Ibarra's plain Y, were used by Juan Guardiola Fantoni, Guardiola Soto, and Rancho Juliven. After various sales, the Guardiola brand, somewhat modified, belongs to Félix Hernández Barrera, although his herd's *antigüedad* is 12 July 1942. Today (2001) the Guardiolas have different brands.[283] For a discussion of the relationship between brand and *antigüedad*, see the essay on "Bulls and Bull Breeding," in the introduction to this volume.

> The narrator inaccurately identifies the Ibarra as one of the main strains of fighting bulls (132).

Iceberg Theory. The "iceberg theory" is so closely associated with Hemingway that we tend to think he invented it. But James Hinkle has pointed out that "the image had been used in a similar context by the sculptor Auguste Rodin (1840–1917): 'What is visible in the human body is but a fraction of that which lies below the surface. . . . What a man does displays only a part, and that the smaller part, of his character. . . . That which is manifest in action is to the unacted part as the visible peak of the iceberg to the submerged invisible mass.' " The image is also attached to Sigmund Freud, who reportedly wrote that "The mind is an iceberg—it floats with only one-seventh of its bulk above water."[284]

Closer to home, we have a letter Hadley Richardson wrote to Hemingway in August 1921, a few weeks before they were married: "If only one could find the theme behind any subject tackled. I found something like that in music a little once, but you've got a magnificent grip on it—a magnificent grip on the form back of the material no matter how strange it is, like icebergs."[285] In trying to discover when Hemingway himself first used the image, Michael Reynolds mentions a Hemingway "filler" entitled "The Ice-Berg Patrol," published on 1 October 1921 in *Co-operative Commonwealth*. The piece, "written completely from secondary sources," is unsigned and insignificant, but it does mention the submerged and invisible seven-eighths of an iceberg. "Years later," as Reynolds notes, "he would come back to that image as a metaphor for his own technique."[286]

The first definition of Hemingway's "iceberg theory" appeared in *Death in the Afternoon* (1932). He expanded upon the iceberg image in 1958: "I always try to write on the principle of the iceberg. There is seven-eighths of it underwater for every part that shows. Anything you know you can eliminate and it only strengthens your iceberg. It is the part that doesn't show. If a writer omits something because he does not know it then there is a hole in the story. . . . I have tried to eliminate everything unnecessary to conveying experience to the reader so that after he or she has read something it will become a part of his or her experience and seem actually to have happened. This is very hard to do and I've worked at it very hard.[287]"

In *A Moveable Feast*, Hemingway repeated that "you could omit anything if you knew that you omitted and the omitted part would strengthen the story and make people feel something more than they understood" (75).

Although explicators of Hemingway's work have often turned to the author's manuscripts and his life history to flesh out the missing seven-eighths, Susan Beegel points out that "The significant omission itself . . . Hemingway defines only vaguely. The thing eliminated that gives a story its 'dignity of movement' can be 'anything' the writer knows."[288] *See also* entries for Goya; Huxley, Aldous; *Mojigangas*.

> The narrator defines himself as a writer who communicates through omission (192).

Isabella. Isabella I (the Catholic Queen), 1451–1504; queen of Castile and Leon, 1474–1504. Isabella married Ferdinand II of Aragón (later Ferdinand V, q.v.) in 1469, and they ruled and conquered jointly.

Ronda was incorporated into their kingdom on 12 May 1485. To commemorate the event, the Church of the Holy Spirit was erected on the site where the sovereigns formally took possession.[289] For the history preceding the Catholic Monarchs, see Christian Kings in *DS*.

To commemorate its conquest by Ferdinand and Isabella, the town of Ronda has a bullfight and a fair every 20th of May (43).

Isidro, Saint. Full name: San Isidro Labrador (1082–1170). He is the patron saint of Madrid, his birth and burial place, which celebrates his feast day, 15 May, with one or more corridas. The celebrations were fairly modest until 1947, when the *feria* of San Isidro was more widely publicized as a major taurine event in Madrid. That year, it consisted of four consecutive corridas during which the Portuguese Manuel dos Santos, Luis Gómez (el Estudiante, q.v.), Antonio Mejías (Bienvenida, see in *DS*), and Luis Miguel Domingín (see in *DS*) were all gored. In 1959, the festivities lasted about ten days, by 1966 they had expanded to cover two weeks, and in the 1990s the inflated fiesta ran three and sometimes four weeks.[290] The 1998 *sanisidros*, for example, consisted of twenty-eight corridas. For the importance of Madrid and its *feria*, see "The Bullring," in the introduction to this volume. *See also* entries for Madrid, in this volume and in *DS*.

Many bullfights take place in the middle of May, including the *sanisidros* in Madrid (*h:* 509).

Italian Restaurant. Correct name: Buffet Italiano. Address: Carrera de San Jerónimo, 37, corner of Calle de Arlabán.[291] The restaurant was, as the narrator mentions, very near the Café Fornos. It was also close to the Aguilar and the Plaza de Canalejas (qq.v.).

The Italian restaurant seems to have been popular with politicians who, according to an unverifiable claim, drafted Spain's constitution "on a back table in the Buffet Italiano on Madrid's Carrera de San Jerónimo, which happened to be one of Hemingway's favorite drinking places."[292]

When the narrator and the Old Lady visit the Café Fornos, he offers to take her to a nearby Italian restaurant that is frequented by political figures (93).

– J –

James, Henry. American-born author, 1843–1916; became a British subject in 1915, a few months before he was awarded the Order of

Merit, a British honor restricted to twenty-four people at one time. His sophisticated stories, novels, and essays about fiction have earned him the title of "the Master." Much of his fiction deals with the experiences of naive, well-meaning Americans among sophisticated Europeans; see, for example, "Daisy Miller," *The Portrait of a Lady* (1881), *The Ambassadors* (1903), and *The Golden Bowl* (1904).

Reynolds reports that before 1921 Hemingway was ignorant of James (*The Young Hemingway*, 194) and that "Although both Ezra Pound and Gertrude Stein would tell Hemingway to read Henry James, Hadley was the first and closest person to tell him about the 'Master' " (*Paris Years*, 14). Before they were married, she compared Hemingway unfavorably to James: "Hadley admired Ernest's journalism but she was not impressed by the first short story he showed her . . . Years later she explained, 'I don't think I understood [his work] right away. It was not the kind of writing I adored. I adored Henry James.' " She recalls that when she told a reporter that James was her favorite author, Hemingway " 'Exploded. . . . *James* was a scurrilous word in our household.' "[293] Pauline Pfeiffer's admiration for James elicited another anti-James tirade from Ernest: "Pauline . . . has read Henry James (*The Awkward Age*) out loud—and knowing nothing about James it seems to me to be the shit."[294]

When the narrator of *A Moveable Feast* tells his wife about the wonders of Sylvia Beach's bookstore, she asks if Beach stocks James: "Her idea of a good writer was Henry James" (*MF* 38, 156). Hemingway praises Henry James in *Green Hills of Africa*, although he claims that James did not become wiser with age (22–24).

Clearly Hemingway read James: he owned at least thirteen volumes and mentioned James in two of his novels, *The Torrents of Spring* (38–39) and *The Sun Also Rises* (115–16).

Mrs. E. R. is Hemingway's first wife: *see* Hemingway, Hadley. For Hemingway's anti-intellectual pose, *see* Huxley, Aldous.

The narrator remarks that Mrs. E. R. admires Henry James (467).

Jaqueta. Professional nickname of two Spanish bullfighters: the *matador de toros* José Giráldez Díaz (1837–1902) and his grandson, Antonio Giráldez (d. 1912), both from Seville.

The grandfather's career was derailed by drink; he retired in 1890.

Hemingway's account of an event that took place in 1908 clearly refers to the grandson, a minor *novillero* active in the early years of the twentieth century.

This younger Jaqueta showed promise and was popular in the provinces and in Venezuela, but he did not impress the Madrid crowds: his performances were desultory and, to make matters worse, he was frequently gored. He was even gored in the stands: on 30 June 1912, four years after the misadventure with Víbora (q.v.), another *novillo* jumped out of the bullring in the Tetuán plaza (Madrid), clambered up into the stands, and gored the hapless Jaqueta, who was in the plaza as a spectator, though not fatally.[295] This event is so peculiar that it has entered the history books, thus undermining Hemingway's claim that the incident with Víbora was Jaqueta's only claim to fame.

> The narrator identifies Jaqueta as the bullfighter who was not able to kill Víbora in 1908 (110).

Jeffries, James Jackson (Jim, The Boilermaker). U.S. prizefighter, 1875–1953; world heavyweight champion, from June 1899, when he defeated Robert Fitzsimmons (q.v.), until 1905, when he retired undefeated. He came out of retirement to fight the black boxer Jack (John Arthur) Johnson (q.v.) in Reno, Nevada, on Independence Day, 4 July 1910. Jeffries, the "great white hope," was knocked out in the fifteenth round, and the event was followed by race riots. The bout earned Jeffries a large sum, $117,066 (about $1,842,000 in 1995 terms); the black victor received only slightly more, $120,600 ($1,898,000 in 1995). This was the only fight of his career that Jeffries lost. He was elected to the Boxing Hall of Fame in 1954.[296]

Hemingway and Jeffries. Hemingway apparently associated Jeffries with old age and outdated values. In a 1924 letter he compared Ford Madox Ford (1873–1939), whom he disdained as ridiculously out-of-date, with Jim Jeffries. In another letter, he defended his own work, writing his publisher, "I don't look on it in any way as a lost cause . . . it has a good gambling chance to sell . . . a good 3/1 chance. And I never bet on Jeffries at Reno nor Carpentier nor other sentimental causes."[297] Of course, in July 1910 Hemingway was eleven years old and too young to bet on a boxing match.

Jeffries is mentioned in *Green Hills of Africa*, but physical similarity rather than racial difference is emphasized: as old men, both the "white hope" Jeffries and the black character M'Cola have "fallen pectoral muscles" (48). In another boxing passage, however, the narrator of *Green Hills of Africa* reveals his longing for an untarnished, white, "all-American" champion to represent "us" against "them," and bemoans the death of Harry Greb, who might have filled that role (*GHOA*, 166). Neither *Death in the Afternoon* nor *Green Hills of Africa* mentions that the black Johnson defeated the white Jeffries in that racially charged match; it was such a famous event that identifying the winner was perhaps unnecessary for the contemporary audience.

The narrator's remark that Luis Freg (q.v.) was promoted to *matador de toros* in 1910, the same year of the Johnson-Jeffries fight, is accurate. The Fourth of July fight preceded Freg's *alternativa* (on 23 October 1910) by only three months.

The narrator mentions that Jeffries fought Johnson in 1910 (263).

J. H. *See* Hemingway, John Hadley Nicanor.

Jiminiz, Manuel (Chicuelo). Correct spelling: Jiménez. Alternate spelling: Giménez. Full name: Manuel Jiménez Moreno (Chicuelo, Chicuelo II). Spanish bullfighter, 1902–67. Investiture as *matador de toros* in Seville, 28 September 1919, granted by Belmonte; confirmed by Rafael Gómez Ortega, in Madrid, 18 June 1920. In 1919, Seville had two plazas: Chicuelo was promoted at the Maestranza on the same day that Juan Luis de la Rosa (q.v.) was promoted at the Monumental (see Seville in *DS*).

Chicuelo was the son and nephew of bullfighters. His father, also named Manuel Jiménez (Chicuelo, 1879–1907) was a matador who died of tuberculosis when his son was five years old. The boy was brought up by his childless uncle, the banderillero Zocato (q.v.), whose encouragement and support smoothed the talented boy's way. Popular and well received, he was the leading *novillero* of 1919 (fifty-seven *novilladas* in spite of a goring which cost him a month's performances) and was promoted to *matador de toros* at the end of that season: he was seventeen years old.

1920 was a successful season for Chicuelo (sixty-three corridas), and 1921 was even better (seventy corridas). He was sick much of 1922, but again enjoyed critically successful seasons 1923–26, years in which Hemingway visited Spain. Although Chicuelo limited the number of his appearances to forty-four corridas in 1923, Cossío calls this a "temporada triunfal" (a triumphant season). The numbers remained fairly consistent: thirty-nine in 1924, forty-one in 1925 and again in 1926. In the winters of 1923, 1924, and 1925 Chicuelo also went to Mexico, where he was the most successful of the Spanish matadors who fought there in those years—and many did, since the American tours were lucrative.

These cold statistics do not express Chicuelo's artistry, which drew incredible rave reviews. As one critic explains, "Chicuelo es ante todo y sobre todo un artista" (first and foremost an artist), whose performance depends on inspiration and encouragement, and not just on physical factors like the bull and the weather. Chicuelo was not always inspired, and even on good afternoons he could easily be thrown off his stride by an antagonistic public, or simply by his perception, correct or not, that the public was antagonistic.[298] But when he was good, which was quite often, he was incandescent.

In reviewing the 1926 season, Tomás Orts Ramos (Uno al Sesgo) was puzzled by the discrepancy between what he saw (consistently magnificent performances) and what he read in the press. He concludes that Chicuelo "no tiene 'buena Prensa' " (doesn't have a good [relationship with the] press).[299] Another critic remarks that, unlike other bullfighters, Chicuelo does not concern himself with contracts, money, publicity, or reputation. He seems not to care who his fellow performers will be, doesn't demand the usual "right of refusal," has no preference for this or that breed of bull, accepts contracts in third-rate plazas as readily as for the first-rank bullrings of Madrid, Seville and Valencia, and generally approaches bullfighting in an uncalculating, offhand manner. And yet, the critic claims, every year he manages to impress critics and audience, to chalk up a respectable number of corridas, and to earn large sums.[300]

Chicuelo was sick for part of 1926 and again in 1927; the illness, "derivada del ácido úrico" (derived from uric acid), sounds like gout.[301] It caused him to limit himself to twenty-four corridas, most but not all to glowing reviews. He married a famous singer, Dorita la Cordobesa, at the end of that season and refused the usual South American tour, leading his public to suspect that his retirement would soon be announced.

With his usual unpredictability, Chicuelo surprised everyone by fighting eighty-one corridas in 1928 (Hemingway did not go to Spain that year), more than anyone else that season and fourteen more than Gitanillo de Triana, who ranked second. After this triumphant season, Chicuelo risked everything by simply disappearing, for no apparent reason, from a festival where he was scheduled to perform with Cayetano Ordóñez and Julio García (Palmeño). The unusual incident occurred in Almodóvar del Río (Córdoba), in December 1928, after the taurine season was officially over. All three matadors and their *cuadrillas* duly showed up in their suits of lights. The announcement that the *novillos* originally scheduled for this event were going to be replaced by others caused some commotion and confusion among the public. When order was restored, Chicuelo's absence was noted: he had simply walked away. The other two bullfighters offered to kill all six *novillos* and the management was ready to refund the customers' money, but Chicuelo's behavior had so enraged the crowd that they refused all offers, rioted for several hours, and set fire to a section of the bullring, almost burning down the bullring impresario's house in the process.[302]

In spite of this and other contretemps, the magnificent 1928 season yielded many contracts for 1929, Chicuelo's tenth year as a full *matador de toros*. But his season was cut short by two serious gorings, and Chicuelo performed in thirty-six corridas that year. He did not perform at all between 14 April, when he was gored in Barcelona, and 12 May; or after 1 September, when he was gored in Málaga; both these gorings were described as "grave."[303] In 1930, without suffering injuries, he cut his season down to thirty corridas. In 1931 his performances were so few (eighteen corridas) and so lackluster, that one critic curtly dismissed Chicuelo: "No quiere ya toros" (he no longer wants [to fight] bulls).[304] But in accordance with the unpredictability that characterized his career, he more than doubled the number the next year, fighting forty-three corridas in 1932. On the whole, however, Chicuelo limited the number of his appearances during the 1930s, although he remained popular and continued to enjoy good reviews.[305]

During and after the Spanish Civil War (1936–39) Chicuelo continued to perform, though infrequently. When the war ended, however, he enjoyed "una de las más brillantes temporadas de su brillante historia torera" (one of the most brilliant seasons of his brilliant taurine career).[306] Chicuelo continued to perform, although infrequently, in the early 1940s; stayed away from the ring in 1945, 1946 and 1947; appeared only occasionally 1948–50; and retired in 1951, at the age of forty-nine, thirty-two years after his promotion to *matador de toros*.

A skillful, talented performer, Chicuelo had the benefit of being carefully educated and well-connected. He excelled in all aspects of the fight and in spite of bouts of illness and indifference (both of which preceded the goring to which Hemingway attaches so much importance), he enjoyed a long career. Cossío admires Chicuelo's "gran técnica" and writes that he had "una gran facilidad en todas las suertes, incluso en la de matar; un extraordinario conocimiento y dominio de su profesión y de los toros" (he could perform all maneuvers easily, including that of killing; [he had] an extraordinary knowledge and command of his profession and of the bulls). He died in his native Seville.[307]

Throughout his career Chicuelo was careless about contracts. Most bullfighters, realizing that their time may be short and that the public is fickle, struggle to fight as often as possible, even returning to the ring before their wounds are fully healed. Chicuelo frequently and inexplicably refused contracts and, even when he accepted them, did not always exert himself. But since he produced spellbinding performances more often than not, he had no difficulty obtaining contracts whenever he wanted—impresarios knew the public would flock to see him.[308]

Although Chicuelo mastered all aspects of bullfighting, his muleta work requires another word or two. Chicuelo's expertise with muleta passes known as *naturales* enabled him to link several of them together so that the bull is forced to circle the matador's body. This beautiful choreography highlighted his *faena*, the muleta work that precedes the final sword work and which had, in the early years of the bullfight, basically served the utilitarian purpose of positioning the bull for the kill.

Pepe Alameda writes that Rafael Guerra (Guerrita) "invented" or defined the possibility of *toreo en redondo*, by introducing innovations in foot and arm work that enabled the bullfighter to remain fairly static and use the muleta to force the bull to move around him (*toreo en redondo*, or *toreo* in the round). Joselito also linked muleta passes, but his *toreo en redondo* was limited to two or three *naturales*, as preparation for what was then still the highlight of the bullfight, the kill. Thanks in part to Chicuelo's graceful and extended *toreo en redondo*—he could link together as many as eighteen *naturales*—the *faena* achieved the prominence it enjoys today.

The emergence of the bullfight's three *tercios* is a slow historical process, not the work of one person, but Chicuelo's name figures largely in the literature of the bullfight's last act. As Nestor Luján wrote, "Chicuelo es creador del ritmo de torear moderno, del encadenamiento suave y fluente de las faenas" (Chicuelo created the rhythm of modern *toreo*, the smooth and fluid linking of the *faenas*).[309] Like Belmonte, Chicuelo shifted the public's attention from the sword to the muleta.

Hemingway and Chicuelo. Hemingway saw Chicuelo quite often. He identifies Chicuelo, Gitanillo, and Villalta as the first bullfighters he ever saw, May-June 1923, in Madrid. Although he admired the bull and Villalta's and Gitanillo's appearance and behavior, Hemingway seems to have been repelled by Chicuelo. Chicuelo was not physically impressive: "era pequeño y débil, con un cuerpo de muñeca, unos brazos cortos, las manos diminutas y una cara cérea, ambarina y triste" (small and weak, with a doll's body, short arms, tiny hands, and a waxen, amber-hued, sad face). Hemingway's diction—he describes Chicuelo as a "dough-faced," "chubby-faced" man who "flapped his cape"—reflects both the unattractiveness of the man and Hemingway's own immediate dislike of him.[310]

Chicuelo was not contracted for the 1923 *sanfermines*, but Hemingway saw him several times in Pamplona in July 1924, when he performed in four of that fiesta's six corridas (7, 9, 10, and 13 July 1924), one of which was a *corrida de prueba* (four bulls from the same ranch are fought by four bullfighters) so that Hemingway saw him fight a total of seven bulls in a few days. His performances with six of them were *fracasos* (thorough failures), all the more obvious because his fellow fighters in Pamplona that year—Maera, Fuentes Bejarano, Nacional, Nacional II, and Algabeño (qq.v.)—generally did well. But fighting the last bull of that fiesta, Chicuelo produced one of the performances which, as the reviewer remarks, made his audiences forget his earlier disasters: "Su faena en el cuarto [toro de esta tarde] fué la mejor de la feria de este año, repetimos con permiso de Maera" (we repeat, with his permission, Maera's remark that [Chicuelo's] *faena* with the fourth [bull of this afternoon] was the best of this year's *feria*).[311] Even so, Pamplona did not engage Chicuelo for its 1925 *feria*. However, Hemingway saw him that year in the Valencia *feria*, where Chicuelo performed on 26, 28, and 31 July (other stars at that *feria* were Litri, Ordóñez, Belmonte, Lalanda, Villalta, qq.v.). On the 28th, as he was preparing to kill a Murube bull, Chicuelo cut himself on the left leg with his own sword.[312]

Hemingway probably did not see Chicuelo in 1926 or 1927. Although in 1926 Hemingway was in Madrid most of May and went to the *ferias* of Pamplona and Valencia, Chicuelo did not perform at all in Madrid that May and was not contracted for any of the big *ferias* of July. In 1927 Chicuelo was unwell and was again absent from Hemingway's favorite fiestas. Hemingway did not come to Spain in 1928, Chicuelo's great year, but saw Chicuelo the next year, when he performed in Pamplona on 7, 9, and 10 July 1929; Hemingway may have seen him other times that year. In 1930 Hemingway was again absent from Spain, and in 1931, when he was in Spain from May to September, he may have seen Chicuelo in Madrid (31 May and 22 June) and Valencia (31 July). That year, Chicuelo was the third oldest active bullfighter in Spain (in terms of years since the *alternativa*) and his performances were, on the whole, listless. In addition to seeing Chicuelo several times, Hemingway also read about him, all through the 1920s and early 1930s.

Although Hemingway notes that Chicuelo was nothing if not unpredictable, he attempts to find a pattern to his behavior and to predict his future. Not surprisingly, Chicuelo proved Hemingway wrong. Hemingway suggests, for example, that Chicuelo was afraid of competition from Joselito and Belmonte and that his success was directly related to their absence from the bullring. But Chicuelo had made a name for himself before Belmonte's first retirement and while Joselito was still alive: he was the leading *novillero* of 1919 and had excellent seasons as a *matador de toros* in 1920, the year Joselito was killed, and in 1921. Belmonte retired twice during the 1920s: in 1922 and late in 1927. In 1924 and 1925, when Belmonte was again performing, Chicuelo had "triunfos resonantes" (resounding triumphs), both in Spain and in Mexico.[313] It is true, however, that in Belmonte's good years, 1926 and 1927, Chicuelo reduced the number of his appearances and that in 1928 and 1929, after Belmonte had retired, Chicuelo increased them. But in 1930, while Belmonte was still retired, he decreased the number again. Chicuelo did not plan his life in terms of the actions of other people: he acted as the spirit moved him. The ups and downs in the statistics, while more dramatic in Chicuelo's career, are not unusual among bullfighters.

In attacking Chicuelo, Hemingway seems to have adopted the negative attitude of the American Gin Bottle King, who first pointed Chicuelo out to him in Madrid in 1923, describing him as "The kid with the chubby face . . . They say he doesn't really like bullfighting, but the town's crazy about him." Soon after, Hemingway compares Chicuelo's cape to "a ballet dancer's skirt."[314] Hemingway remained faithful to this early opinion and image. Nearly ten years later, he used a similar image to define the *chicuelina*: the bullfighter "makes a pirouette in which the cape wraps itself around him" (*DIA*, 395). The feminine imagery is extended to the definition of the "delantal," another one of Chicuelo's famous passes: "the cape is swung in front of the man so that it billows out like an apron on a pregnant woman in a breeze" (*DIA*, 400). Elsewhere Chicuelo is described as "unhealthily plump" with "a bad complexion, tiny hands, and . . . the long eyelashes of a girl. . . . [He is] a miniature bullfighter . . . [like] a little porcelain statuette" (74). The attack is unrelenting, aimed not only at his "feminine" looks (84, 228–29, 276) but also at his personality and performance (76, 215, 276, 402). In the Glossary, Hemingway writes that two bullfighters are homosexuals: one of them may have been Chicuelo, who was both miserly and expert with the cape (*h:* 448, s.v. *Maricón*). The attack extends even to his uncle (74, 273) and intensifies in the short story "A Lack of Passion" (q.v.); *see also* Androgyny.

Hemingway's unkind prediction that Chicuelo was "finished" in 1931—an evaluation shared by other critics, including Uno al Sesgo in *Toros y toreros en 1931*—was disproved by Chicuelo's fine 1932 and 1939 seasons. (For other matadors with long careers who alternated slow seasons with longer ones, *see* Rafael Gómez Ortega and

Marcial Lalanda, both of whom Hemingway admires wholeheart-edly.) Chicuelo maintained a respectable standing until the Spanish Civil War broke out: he was then thirty-seven. In fact, he continued to perform until 1951, though he never regained the popularity he had enjoyed in the 1920s. As a *figura del toreo*, however, his position was firmly established well before the publication of *Death in the Afternoon*—and such taurine icons are never "finished."

Angel Capellán remarks that "Two of [Hemingway's] greatest mistakes are his near silence on Antonio Márquez . . . and his esti-mate of Manuel Jiménez, 'Chicuelo II,' both considered by critics among the very best matadors of the decade."[315] For other "mis-takes," *see* Ortega, Domingo, in this volume; and Rodríguez Sán-chez, Manuel (Manolete), in *DS*.

> The narrator scornfully describes the famous Chicuelo as a short, fat bull-fighter from Seville who rose to prominence in the "decadent" 1920s. The narrator concedes that Chicuelo had "beautiful execution" and an exten-sive repertoire with the muleta, but claims that he lacked both a feeling for the art and the height necessary for graceful killing. His first goring (Hemingway probably means the one of April 1929) made him "utterly cowardly" and after that his performance was unpredictable; his career was over by 1931 (267). The narrator mentions Chicuelo often and usually dis-paragingly (73–74, 75, 76, 84, 178, 214–15, 217, 229, 267, 273, *h:* 425, s.v. *Chicuelinas*; *h:* 430, s.v. *Delantal*; *h:* 432, s.v. *Descabellar*; photo-graphs *h:* 290, 354–71 passim).

Johnson, John Arthur (Jack). African-American prizefighter, c. 1876–1946. Johnson became the world heavyweight champion in 1908, when he defeated Tommy Burns. Because of racial prejudice in the United States, the fight took place in Sydney, Australia. John-son won in the fourteenth round to become the first black man to hold the world heavyweight title.

Exuberant and proud, Johnson led a flashy life, defying his soci-ety's prejudices: three of his four wives were white. He was the ob-ject of so much racial hatred that the white champion James J. Jeffries (q.v.), who had retired undefeated in 1905, was brought out of retire-ment to challenge him. The racially fraught contest took place in Reno, Nevada, on 4 July 1910. It lasted fifteen rounds, and race riots erupted when Johnson defeated the "great white hope." Johnson earned $120,600 for this fight (about $1,898,000 in 1995 terms), one of the most important bouts of his career.

In 1913 Johnson was convicted of violating the Mann Act (interstate transportation of a female for the purposes of prostitution; he claimed it was a trumped-up charge), given a jail sentence, and forbidden to fight in the United States. He left the United States in order to continue fighting. In 1915, he lost the heavyweight title to another "white hope," Jess Willard, in Havana, Cuba; the fight lasted twenty-six rounds. He had been champion from 1908 to 1915. Johnson lived abroad a few more years but finally, in 1920, returned to the United States, served his jail sentence, and continued boxing, though without regaining his title.

Johnson retired in 1927, having fought a total of 114 professional fights, of which he only lost seven.[316] He engaged in exhibition matches for many years after his retirement, even as late as 1945, one year before he died in an automobile crash. He was elected to the Boxing Hall of Fame in 1954. His two books are *Mes combats* (1914) and *Jack Johnson in the Ring and Out* (1927; rpt. 1975).

As Hemingway indicates, Luis Freg (q.v.) was promoted to *matador de toros* in Mexico City on 23 October 1910, the year of the Johnson-Jeffries fight. Freg's Spanish *alternativa* (q.v.) took place in Alcalá de Henares, on 25 August 1911, and was confirmed in Madrid a month later. Spanish resistance to Mexican fighters, like white American resistance to black fighters, links Johnson and Freg, two racial outsiders who became champions and endured great physical suffering during their long careers.

> The narrator mentions that Luis Freg has been a *matador de toros* for two decades, since the 1910 fight between Johnson and Jeffries (263).

Jokes. *See* Altrock, Nick; Circus; Fratellinis, the; *Mojigangas.*

Jones, Bobby. Full name: Robert Tyre Jones, Jr. American lawyer and golfer, 1902–71.

An amateur golfer, Bobby Jones won the U.S. and British championships with impressive regularity, often winning more than one tournament in the same year: the U.S. Open four times (1923, 1926, 1929, and 1930), the British Open three times (1926, 1927, and 1930), and the U.S. Amateur five times (1924, 1925, 1927, 1928, and

1930). In 1930 he also won the British Amateur, thus becoming the first man to complete a Grand Slam (winning all four major tournaments in the same year). He never became a professional golfer and seldom played in championship competitions after 1930. He lived and practiced law in Atlanta, Georgia, the city of his birth and death.

To define and assess a Spanish art for a non-Spanish audience, Hemingway frequently mentions writers, painters, boxers, and other people whose work is part of the cultural background of the (mostly American) audience he is addressing. This indicates, of course, that he knows something about them himself and expects his audience to recognize them as well. But in comparing Bobby Jones and Cayetano Ordóñez, Hemingway crosses not only international borders but also areas of personal interest or expertise. Hemingway himself knew very little about golf, but even so, he knew about Bobby Jones and the city that, through him, became associated with golf. Hemingway knew far more about other sports, like fishing, boxing, and baseball, and therefore, for him, a fisherman or boxer or baseball player would have been a less apt figure to exemplify fame that crosses boundaries or areas of interest. Similarly, Ordóñez had achieved such fame that even Spaniards with no interest in bullfighting would know about him and would associate him and his birthplace, Ronda, with excellence in bullfighting.

> To explain how, in Spain, a certain person (Cayetano) and a certain place (Ronda) signify excellence in bullfighting, the narrator translates the equation into terms that would be familiar to his U.S. audience, to whom Atlanta and Bobby Jones signify excellence in golf (89).

José, San. St. Joseph, a carpenter, was the husband of Mary, the mother of Jesus. His feast day, 19 March, is celebrated with corridas in Barcelona, Valencia, Madrid, and other cities; often this is the arena's opening corrida.

By mentioning the promotion of Luis Gómez (el Estudiante, q.v.), which occurred on 19 March 1932, Hemingway reveals that he was keeping up with last minute taurine details: *Death in the Afternoon* was already in galleys on that date. *See also* Roman Catholic.

> The narrator mentions that Luis Gómez (el Estudiante) was promoted during the fiesta of San José (229).

Joselito. *See* Gómez Ortega, José.

Jota Contests. *See* Zaragossa.

Juanito. *See* Martín-Caro, Juanito; Quintana, Juan.

– K –

Kutz, Café Kutz. In Hemingway's day, Luis Kutz owned and managed four successful cafés: two in Madrid, one in Pamplona, and another in San Sebastian. Address in Pamplona: Plaza de la Constitución (the name was later changed to Plaza del Castillo), next to the Café Iruña. Addresses in Madrid: 24 Avenida del Conde de Peñalver, and Caballero de Gracia (no number).[317] Hemingway does not mention the Madrid branches in *Death in the Afternoon*.

The Pamplona café was established by Luis Kutz in 1912 and run after his death by his wife and children; it closed its doors in 1961.[318] For more detail on the fight that Hemingway mentions (272–73), *see* David, Alfredo.

> The narrator praises the beer served at the San Sebastián and Pamplona branches of the Café Kutz (*h:* 425, s.v. *Cerveza*). In Pamplona, bullfighters drink, talk, and quarrel (154, 272–73).

Kzar. Usually spelled Ksar. Foaled in 1918, Ksar had "fine breeding: his sire Bruleur, and his dam Kizil-Kourgan both won the Grand Prix de Paris." Ksar was a fine chestnut horse.

As a two-year-old, Ksar ran two races in the fall of 1920, winning one and coming in second in the other. The next year he ran seven races and won six: the Prix Hocquart, the Prix Lupin, the French Derby (or Prix du Jockey Club), the Prix Royal Oak, the Prix de l'Arc de Triomphe (probably the most prestigious race in Europe, with a prize of 300,000 francs), and the Prix Edgar-Gillois. He lost the Grand Prix de Paris, coming in second to last, but that year won several other races: the Prix Cadran, the Prix du Prince d'Orange, and the classic Prix de l'Arc de Triomphe, which he won two years in succession (1921 and 1922). In 1922 he also won the Prix des Sablons, the Prix Cadran, and the Prix du Prince d'Orange.

When he was three and four years old, Ksar won all the major prizes in flat racing. He was almost unbeatable.[319]

In Hemingway's story, "My Old Man" (written in 1922), Kzar is described as a beautiful, "great big yellow horse . . . There never was such a wonderful, lean, running built horse" (*In Our Time*, 160).[320] If Hemingway bet on Ksar, which is likely, he probably won.

The narrator recalls Kzar (*sic*) with affection (5).

– L –

"A Lack of Passion." Three manuscript versions, a corrected typescript version, and four manuscript fragments of this story, as well as the story as edited by Susan Beegel, were published posthumously in *The Hemingway Review* 9.2 (1990): 57–93. The main character is a disgraced matador variously named Tomás Jiminez, Chicuelo, Manuel, Luis López, Luis Alvarez (Quinito), and Francisco Ortega (Gavira); Hemingway seems to prefer the nickname Gavira. His uncle is called Zocato and, sometimes, Paco; the nickname is often changed to Paquiro. Beegel identifies the historical prototypes for these two characters as Manuel Jiménez (Chicuelo) and his uncle Zocato (qq.v.). She reports that Hemingway worked on the story between September and November 1924 and again "sometime during or after the winter of 1924–25 . . . and before the summer of 1926. . . . By 17 August 1927, Hemingway had abandoned 'A Lack of Passion' " because it "would not come right."[321]

The narrator mentions that he wrote a story called "A Lack of Passion," but was dissatisfied with it and refused to publish it (273).

Lagartijo. *See* Molina Sánchez, Rafael.

Lagartito. *See* Royo Turón, Francisco.

Lalanda, Marcial. Full name: Marcial Lalanda del Pino. Spanish bullfighter, 1903–90. Investiture as *matador de toros*, in Seville, September 1921; confirmed in Madrid, May 1922.

The younger brother of two bullfighters,[322] Marcial was a child prodigy who fought his first *becerro* (yearling) at the age of nine and killed his first bull one month before his eleventh birthday. He performed often with his cousin Pablo Lalanda (1902–36); the two *novilleros* were a popular team. Marcial fought in thirty-five *novilladas* in 1920 and fifty-two in 1921, having a well-established reputation before his *alternativa* (q.v.) late that season. The occasion of the confirmation of his *alternativa* in Madrid on 7 May 1922 was rendered tragic by the fatal goring of Manuel Granero (q.v.) by the bull Pocapena, whom Lalanda managed to distract from the stricken Granero, though it was too late to save him.[323]

In 1922, his first full season as a graduated *matador de toros*, Lalanda went from success to success. He fought seventy-nine corridas and increased his already large following. Minor accidents reduced his appearances to fifty in 1923; a serious wound in 1924 kept him out of the ring for a month so that, although he had started the season with more contracts than anyone else, he actually performed in only forty-eight corridas (but we must remember that thirty corridas mark a quite respectable season, even for an uninjured fighter). In 1925 he fought seventy-five engagements, more than any other bullfighter that year. The following year, however, a long illness reduced his appearances to fifty-four (he had been contracted for about seventy). That year he was ranked third among matadors, after Cayetano Ordóñez, who fought seventy-eight corridas, and Antonio Márquez, who fought fifty-eight. Two serious gorings in 1927, one on 8 May (in Toledo) and the second on 26 July (in Valencia) kept him from fulfilling all his contracts; even so, he performed in fifty-one corridas and was ranked fourth nationwide. In 1928, dispirited and ill, he kept his performances down to forty-one. As had happened earlier, this relatively slow season did not damage his career, and the next few years re-established him as one of the all-time masters of the art. His 1929 season was full (eighty-five corridas) and brilliant; he ranked first nationwide. In 1930 he fought eighty-seven engagements, again heading the list. In 1931 the taurine critics, never given to understatement, were hard put to describe his masterful performances. He performed in sixty-eight corridas, another twelve contracts having been canceled because of illness and rain.

Lalanda's enormous success allowed him to charge enormous fees, and he consequently reduced the number of his appearances to thirty-five in 1933, forty-one in 1934, and forty-three in 1935. He performed in forty-eight bullfights during the three years of the Spanish Civil War, after which he returned to his more usual schedule of between forty and fifty fights a year until his retirement in 1942, more than twenty years after his promotion to *matador de alternativa*.

From the beginning to the end of his career, Lalanda was an acknowledged master, admired for his control, discipline, courage, and great knowledge of the bull, whom he could dominate even when fighting *de rodillas* (on his knees). After his retirement, he dedicated himself to the bull-breeding ranch he had bought in 1931, and to charitable work: the *Montepío de Toreros* (Beneficent Association of Matadors) in particular benefited from his patronage. For a brief period in the 1940s he also managed the career of Luis Miguel Dominguín (see in *DS*) and other matadors.[324]

Hemingway and Lalanda. Lalanda performed in many corridas during the years in which Hemingway visited Spain, so that Hemingway had plenty of opportunities to see him during his first decade as a *matador de alternativa*. Absent from Spain in 1928, Hemingway missed Lalanda's weakest year.

Lalanda performed frequently in Pamplona, where Hemingway saw him in 1925 (on 8, 9, 11, and 12 July),[325] in 1926 (7 and 11 July),[326] in 1927 (8, 9, and 12 July), and in 1929 (8 July). On 2 September 1929 Lalanda fought on the same bill with Vicente Barrera and Félix Rodríguez (qq.v.), in Palencia, a fight that Hemingway saw. He probably saw Lalanda several times in 1931 as well.[327] Hemingway's remarks about Lalanda's courage (215) repeat contemporary judgment so closely that I quote at length:

> Es muy significativo el doble hecho de que detrás de sus dos cogidas haya vuelto a la pelea con más ardimiento y mayores entusiasmos que nunca; las cornadas siempre dejan alguna huella en el ánimo de quienes las sufren; ello es tan humano, que nos parece cruel no acatarlo y reconocerlo; pero en Marcial Lalanda ha ocurrido todo lo contrario, y por eso su reputación, ya muy alta, acusa hoy [1927] más vigorosos trazos que nunca (It's very significant that after each one of his two *cogidas* he has returned to the fray more passionately and enthusiastically than ever; gorings always leave their mark on the spirit of those who suffer them: this is so human, that it seems cruel not to recognize it and take it into account; but in Marcial Lalanda the absolute opposite has happened, and therefore his reputation, always excellent, is today [1927 season] at its peak).[328]

Hemingway mentions Lalanda in two of his novels, one written before *Death in the Afternoon* (*The Sun Also Rises*, 171, 212, 215, 219) and one after (*For Whom the Bell Tolls*, 251–52).

The narrator correctly identifies Lalanda as a bullfighter from Madrid (267) who was hailed as Joselito's successor in the early 1920s. The narrator claims that, although at that time he was "technically skillful and completely intelligent," his early performances were often "mediocre and uninteresting" (74).[329] Over the years he has improved both in terms of style and courage (215) and has developed into superb bullfighter (84) who dominated the seasons of 1929, 1930, and 1931 (84, 248). He had great knowledge of the bulls, because his father had been overseer of the Veragua breeding ranch (74; but Cossío says the father supervised the ranch of don Enrique Salamanca) and the boy grew up in a very taurine environment.[330] The narrator admires Lalanda's work with the banderillas (200), with the cape and muleta (176–77, 215, 418), and with the sword (247–48). In addition to the occasions already cited, the narrator mentions Lalanda often and admiringly (20, 162, 169, 218, 224, 244, 262, *h:* 505; photographs, *h:* 376–83).

Lausín López, Braulio (Gitanillo, Gitanillo de Ricla, el león de Ricla). Spanish bullfighter, 1898–1967. Investiture as *matador de toros*, in Santander, August 1922; confirmed in Madrid, September that same season.

Gitanillo's interest in the bullfight developed relatively late, when he was about twenty years old. He was famous for his bravery and for the many injuries he suffered: he was thrown by a bull even at his investiture. His first years as a full-fledged matador were successful, and Hemingway first saw him perform at this bright period of his career. His 1923 season was successful enough to land him a goodly number of contracts for 1924, but a terrific goring in mid-May 1924 practically destroyed his left leg and kept him out of the ring for more than four months (including July, when Hemingway was in Spain). His return on 20 September was indicative both of his physical strength—the wound had been expected to cripple him permanently—and of his determination to succeed. Fans were relieved to see that his courage was undiminished and that he remained skillful and daring with the muleta.[331]

The next two seasons were his most successful, with thirty-six corridas in 1925 and thirty-two in 1926, usually with famous matadors and in prestigious bullrings. On 15 May 1927, in his fourth corrida of the season (in Madrid), another terrible goring, involving his face, lungs, and ribs, effectively ended his career; he was in and out of the hospital for over five months. In 1928 he appeared in four farewell corridas and then resumed his former profession as horse and mule dealer. The narrator identifies this matador simply as "Gitanillo," but gives sufficient details about his nickname ("In spite of the name he was no gypsy") and career to make the exact identification possible.[332]

Hemingway and Gitanillo. Hemingway saw Gitanillo in Madrid, on Sunday 27 May 1923 (when he was awarded the afternoon's only ear), and again in Pamplona, on Friday, 12 July 1923 (the corrida, originally scheduled for 10 July, had been postponed twice because of rain), when the bulls were Pérez Tabernero. Gitanillo was applauded in both his bulls, but his performance paled beside those of his fellow matadors, Maera and Algabeño, both of whom were awarded ears.[333]

Hemingway may have seen Gitanillo again, though not in Pamplona, which did not invite him back, or in Valencia, which never contracted him for its July fiesta. None of the critics I have read comment on his height (*see* the entry for Isidoro Todó for a discussion of height).

> The narrator believes Gitanillo to have been a second-rate bullfighter. He describes him as "short, arrogant and really brave" but "unskillful at everything" so that he was often gored and eventually crippled. He relied on tricks to impress the audience (76–77; *see also* 271).

League of Nations. An international organization to promote international cooperation, security, and peace, established in 1920. Although President Woodrow Wilson (1856–1924) was awarded the 1919 Nobel Peace Prize for advocating the establishment of the League of Nations, the United States Congress refused to ratify the League's covenant and the United States never became a member state. In 1946, aware of its failure to prevent war, the League of Nations voted to dissolve itself. Its aims, organization, and property were adopted by its successor, the United Nations.

Spain was a member of the League from its founding until 1939.

The narrator argues that Spain's membership in the League of Nations has strengthened the anti-taurine lobby (268).

Leonardo da Vinci. Italian painter, sculptor, architect, and scientist, great Renaissance genius, 1452–1519. His best-known works include the Milan fresco *The Last Supper* and the *Mona Lisa*. Most biographers say that he was a homosexual. On the topic of the impermanent arts, *see* Cézanne, Paul.

> The narrator writes that bullfighting "is an impermanent art . . . one of those that Leonardo advised men to avoid" (99; *see also* 418).

Lesaca. Full name: Pedro José Picavea de Lesaca. Alternate spellings of this Basque name: Pikabia or Pikabea.[334] Spanish bull breeder, d. about 1830.

In the 1820s, when Luisa, who had inherited the Vistahermosa (q.v.) herds from her brother, the last Count of Vistahermosa, began selling off the stock, one of the principal buyers was Salvador Varea. Soon after, Varea's holdings were acquired by don Pedro José Picavea de Lesaca. On 2 July 1832, Lesaca's widow, Isabel Montemayor, was listed as the owner of the herd; her son, José Picavea de Lesaca, inherited the herd from her. In the early 1850s, he sold practically all of his holdings (eight hundred head) of the herd, as well as the rights to the brand, colors (sky blue and white) and *antigüedad* (14 July 1845) to Antonio Rueda de Quintanilla, the sixth Marquis of Saltillo.

 When Saltillo died in 1880, the herd was inherited by his widow and, upon her death, by their son, the seventh Marquis, who seems not to have registered his bulls in Madrid. *Toros y toreros en 1931* castigates this Marquis del Saltillo for allowing his excellent herd to deteriorate during the twenty-five or thirty years that he owned it. When he died in 1918, his heirs sold it, with all its rights, to the excellent breeder don Félix Moreno Ardanuy (q.v.). The Moreno family still owns the Lesaca-Saltillo herd; their ranches are in Córdoba (Andalucía).[335]

Toros y toreros en 1931 remarks that the animals produced under the careful stewardship of the two generations of the Picavea de Les-

aca family were of such excellent quality—almost pure Vistahermosa—and achieved such fame "que dejaron de llamarse 'condesos'
. . . para ser conocidos con el nombre de 'lesaqueños' " (that they
became known as Lesaca bulls instead of 'condesos'—i.e., the Count
of Vistahermosa's bulls). This may account for Hemingway's mistake in listing them as a separate strain.[336] Bull breeds and genealo-
gies are complicated: for more detail, see the essay on "Bulls and
Bull Breeding," in the introduction to this volume.

The narrator lists Lesaca as a "strain," like Vistahermosa (132).

Lesireas. This Portuguese place name does not appear in most histories of bullbreeding ranches. The Portuguese spelling is *lezíria*, and it
refers to the marshes near Lisbon, where bulls are raised (*see* Palha,
don José).[337] Carralero and Borge spell the name Lesirias (*Toros célebres*, 321), and Cossío has a single reference to the Portuguese bull-
breeding enterprises called Compañías Das Licerias—Lisboa
(Cossío [1943–97] I: 305). The bull Zaragoza escaped while being
taken to the Plaza de Moetía (Portugal), October 1898. I have not
been able to find details beyond what Carralero and Borge and
Cossío offer. Hemingway's translation of the original account is accurate. *See also* Zaragoza.

The narrator repeats the account from *Toros célebres*, identifying Lesireas
(*sic*) as the ranch which produced the bull Zaragoza (110).

La Libertad **(Liberty, Freedom).** Subtitle: Diario nacional sindicalis-
ta. Madrid daily newspaper, 1919–34.

The Biblioteca Nacional, Madrid, holds a variety of nineteenth-
century newspapers and journals called *La Libertad*, most of them
short-lived. Hemingway's reference is to the longest-lived of these
publications, an eight-page Madrid daily established in 1919. It was
such an outspoken opposition paper that it was quickly outlawed. It
appeared for a short time under a new name, *El Popular*, after which
the original title was restored. Hemingway's friend Rafael Hernández
Ramírez (q.v.), a Republican sympathizer, wrote many taurine reviews and other essays for *La Libertad*, hence Hemingway's linking
of "Rafael" and the newspaper (277–78).

In a letter to John Dos Passos dated 26 June 1931, Hemingway commented upon the unrest that preceded (and followed) the Spanish elections which established Spain's second Republic (1931–39). The Republicans had steadily gained ground, their increased power forcing the resignation of Miguel Primo de Rivera (q.v.) early in 1930, the restoration of the constitution in February 1931, the Republican victories in the municipal elections on 12 April of that year, and the departure of King Alfonso XIII (q.v.) two days later. The elections of 28 June gave the Republican-Socialist coalition a huge majority in the Spanish *Cortes* (Parliament).

Two days before this national election, Hemingway wrote Dos Passos that "La Libertad is now Le Temps—consequently all my buddies are prosperous." He was referring to the Republicans of various stripes who had supported *La Libertad* during its lean years as an opposition paper ("my buddies") and who now found themselves increasingly in power ("prosperous"). The newspaper itself changed focus: formerly it had attacked the monarchy, clergy, army, and other right wing elements, but as these grew weaker it turned its attention to the various factions among the newly empowered but always fractious Republicans (separatists, socialists, communists, anarchists, syndicalists). Needless to say, it alienated much of its readership. *La Libertad* ceased publication in 1934.[338]

Longer-lived than *La Libertad*, the French newspaper *Le Temps* (q.v.) maintained an oppositional stance during the nineteenth century and well into the twentieth. "Although . . . not an anti-government publication, it had the courage to displease the government on particular issues." Throughout its history it featured a modest format ("small headlines, no photographs") and offered "serious and even scholarly coverage of social, political, and diplomatic affairs."[339] As the Republican *La Libertad* moved from the margins into the mainstream of power, it too maintained its political independence, attacking the government it generally supported. Hence Hemingway's remark that "*La Libertad . . .* is getting like *Le Temps*" (278).

During the Spanish Civil War, after the publication of *Death in the Afternoon*, the name *Libertad* was used for at least two other Republican papers. The Biblioteca Nacional, Madrid, holds a single, undated issue of a wartime weekly by that name, published by the Defense Committee and offering news about Division "D" of Cuenca. An underground newspaper of this name was put out by the Federación Anárquica Ibérica (F.A.I.).[340]

Hemingway also linked *libertad* with American journalism. He argued that the concept of "liberty" had become so devalued that its meaning was restricted to the five-cent weekly miscellany called *Liberty: A Weekly for Everybody*, founded in 1924 and acquired by the notorious Bernarr MacFadden in 1931.[341] MacFadden (1868–1955), who began his career by displaying his muscular body to promote his physical culture studio, broke into the publishing world in the 1920s with the magazines *Physical Culture, Health and Beauty*, and the successful, lurid *True Story Magazine*. His sensationalist tabloid, the New York *Daily Graphic* (soon and predictably nicknamed the *Daily Pornographic*), had a large circulation in the late 1920s and perished in 1932, during the "holy war" against such sensationalism. In 1931, when MacFadden acquired *Liberty* as part of a large deal involving the Detroit *Daily* newspaper, Hemingway was writing *Death in the Afternoon*. He also mourned the devalued word in an unpublished manuscript and in the story "The Gambler, the Nun, and the Radio," both written as he was finishing *Death in the Afternoon*: "Liberty, what we believed in, now the name of a MacFadden publication."

In 1926, *Liberty* had turned down Hemingway's "Fifty Grand." Hemingway never submitted another story to *Liberty*, but he obviously and unforgivingly kept track of it.[342]

> The narrator praises *La Libertad* for its accurate taurine reviews (*h:* 463, s.v. *Periódicos*) and claims that in the new political atmosphere, the leftist *La Libertad* has become a mainline paper like *Le Temps* (277–78).

Liceaga, David. Full name: David Liceaga Maciel. Mexican bullfighter, 1913–96. Investiture as *matador de toros* in Mexico City, January 1931; in Barcelona, June 1931, his first season in Spain; confirmed in Madrid, 25 September that same year.

Liceaga began his career at age thirteen, as a banderillero. He showed promise as a *becerrista* and *novillero* (fifty-six *novilladas* in Mexico), and received his Mexican *alternativa* (q.v.) at age seventeen. He came to Spain that same year (1931) and was so impressive that he was awarded the Spanish *alternativa* only a few months after arriving. His first year in Spain was successful but not spectacular: he appeared in seven *novilladas* and four *corridas de toros*, in almost all of which he was awarded the bull's ear. He was wounded early in the 1932 season, had to cancel many contracts and consequently had a weak season: six undistinguished corridas. After the 1932 Spanish season, he returned to Mexico and never fought in Spain again.

In 1933 rumors surfaced that Liceaga had resigned the *alternativa* altogether and was fighting as a *novillero*,[343] but in 1935 he fought as *matador de toros* in Mexico and several South American countries and had a fairly successful season. In July 1938, however, Liceaga did renounce his *alternativa*; he retook it in December, in Mexico. In the early 1940s he continued to fight, mostly in Mexico and occasionally in Portugal. But his career was winding down. In 1945 he was seriously wounded (but he still managed to kill the bull); in 1946 he fought only three corridas, all in Mexico; and in 1947 he retired, becoming, among other things, a teacher of *toreo*.

In short, Liceaga's career did not fulfill the promise of his Spanish appearances in 1931. Evaluating Liceaga's debut in Spain, Tomás Orts Ramos (Uno al Sesgo) had written that the banderillas and the muleta were his strong points, the cape his weakest, and that in general he was still "en período de formación . . . no está aún vigorosamente definida su personalidad" (he is still developing . . . his personality is not yet fully defined).[344] Cossío repeats this judgment when, summarizing Liceaga's entire career, he writes that he was elegant with the banderillas, effective with the muleta, weaker with the cape, and generally lacking in personality.[345] This praise for his work with the banderillas contrasts with Hemingway's report.

> The narrator, who has not yet seen Liceaga perform (1931), has heard that the young Mexican matador was reputed to be unimpressive with the cape and banderillas but "enormously skillful" with the muleta. He adds that Liceaga is very popular in Mexico and was promoted to full matador in Madrid in October 1931 (225–26).

La Lidia (**fight, combat**). Founded in 1881 or 1882 and published in Madrid, this bullfight journal excelled in the quality of its printing and drawing. Its founder, don Julián Palacios, was an experienced publisher who acquired the most modern machinery of his time for color printing. The periodical offered reliable reviews of the fights as well as essays on taurine history. It ceased publication at the turn of the century and resumed publication about a decade later, as a weekly under the editorship of Adolfo Durá, painter and photoengraver.[346]

The Biblioteca Nacional, Madrid, has the 1925 issues: they are usually eight pages long, printed on glossy paper, with many color illustrations and double-page center photos of matadors. The journal also offers editorials and other articles (obituaries, interviews) about taurine critics and writers as well as bullfighters. The 1925 issues cost 30 *céntimos*; back issues were available for 60 *céntimos*. It had no advertisements. Hemingway saved several back issues of *La Lidia*, including a double issue dated 16 June 1920 (dedicated to the recently killed Joselito), and several issues from 1887, 1889, and 1892.[347]

> The narrator describes *La Lidia* as a serious bullfight magazine although, like most publications of its kind, its taurine reviews are influenced by financial considerations (*h:* 475, s.v. *Revistas*; mentioned, *h:* 445, s.v. *Lidia*).

The Lieutenant. The lieutenant of artillery is a character in the story "A Natural History of the Dead" (q.v.). Susan Beegel argues that the lieutenant "is afraid to confront death," to see the "nothing—the terrifying emptiness of death," and that when he is blinded by the iodine, he is "taught . . . to see nothing." Similarly, the shocking details of the story "A Natural History of the Dead" should reveal "the terrifying emptiness of death" to its readers, thus cleansing them of the optimistic readings of the Christian natural historians mentioned at the beginning of the story (133–34).[348]

> Wounded in the arm, the lieutenant is waiting for treatment at the dressing station. He demands mercy killing for another wounded man. When he threatens the doctor, the doctor throws iodine in his face, temporarily blinding him, and disarms him. The Lieutenant speaks: 141–44.

Litri. *See* Báez, Manuel.

Longfellow, Henry Wadsworth. American poet, 1807–82.

Longfellow taught at Bowdoin College and was later Smith Professor at Harvard. Interested in foreign languages and literatures, he visited Germany, Spain, France, and Italy. His poetry was popular at home and abroad. His first book of poetry, *Voices of the Night*, included "A Psalm of Life," from which Hemingway quotes. The poem begins:

> Tell me not, in mournful numbers,
> Life is but an empty dream!—
> For the soul is dead that slumbers,
> And things are not what they seem.
>
> Life is real! Life is earnest!
> And the grave is not its goal;
> Dust thou art, to dust returnest,
> Was not spoken of the soul.

It ends with the same earnest, optimistic call to duty, achievement, and immortality:

> Lives of great men all remind us
> We can make our lives sublime,
> And, departing, leave behind us
> Footprints on the sands of time;
> . . . .
> Let us, then, be up and doing,
> With a heart for any fate;
> Still achieving, still pursuing,
> Learn to labor and to wait.

Longfellow's later books include *Ballads and Other Poems* (1842), *Evangeline* (1847), *The Song of Hiawatha* (1855), *The Courtship of Miles Standish* (1858), and *Tales of a Wayside Inn* (1863).

Longfellow also appears in Hemingway's complicated, understudied satire, *The Torrents of Spring*, in which Hiawatha's prophecy that his people will accept the culture of the white man ironically seems to come true in a variety of ways. The Native Americans, for example, establish an English-type club, complete with class snobbery, thus enshrining not only the white "civilizers" who oppress them but the religiously, socially oppressive British society that those white "civilizers" themselves had sought to escape. Hanging a picture of Longfellow in their club, the Indians pay homage to a poet who had argued for their submission to their surrounding civilization, particularly to the optimistic Christian thought which assumed that Christianity would eventually and inevitably replace all other religions and philosophies (*TS*, 61, 65). *See also* Humanism, Naturalism.

> The narrator quotes but does not name Longfellow, whose philosophy he obviously abhors (266).

Lope de Vega. Full name: Félix Lope de Vega y Carpio. Prolific and popular Spanish playwright and poet, 1562–1635.

Lope de Vega's exciting life included two marriages, several mistresses, a stint in the Spanish Armada, and various skirmishes with the law. In 1613 he became a priest whose enthusiastic self-flagellation spattered the walls of his cell with blood. He was one of bullfighting's most influential opponents, which may account for Hemingway's negative comments about him.

Lope de Vega wrote many volumes of verse and prose novels but is best known for his drama, which he produced at a furious rate, without much revision. He is reputed to have written over 1,500 plays. Among his best-known works are *Los ramilletes de Madrid*, *El perro del hortelano*, and *La viuda de Valencia*. Hemingway's character Robert Jordan has read Lope de Vega's famous play *Fuenteovejuna* (*For Whom the Bell Tolls*, 231; *see also FWTBT*, 164–65) and shares Hemingway's reservations about this major Spanish author.

> To emphasize the achievements of Joselito and Belmonte in the art of bullfighting, the narrator compares them to Cervantes and Lope de Vega in literature or Velázquez and Goya in painting. He adds that he does not like Lope de Vega (73).

López Plata, don Antonio. Twentieth-century Spanish bull breeder. Antonio López, the father of the bull breeder Hemingway mentions, established a herd with stock from Fernando Freire, later adding a seed bull from the Orozco ranch. Because Antonio never presented his bulls to be fought in Madrid, his herd had no registered *antigüedad*, or seniority. In 1902, when his son, Antonio López Plata, inherited the herd, he enlarged it considerably by acquiring both halves of the Clemente herd (as described below), including the rights to its colors (sky blue and white), brand, and *antigüedad* (14 October 1888). At the time of the writing of *Death in the Afternoon*, it was the son, Antonio López Plata, who owned the ranch in Seville, much expanded from what it had been in his father's day.

The pedigree of the Clemente herds that López Plata bought can be traced back to 1817, when Domingo Varela bought out all of the Marquis de Casa-Ulloa's stock, adding Cabrera (q.v.) cows and bulls to it. After Varela died, the herd changed hands several times before being acquired by José Clemente Rivera, and the herd's *antigüedad* dates from Clemente's registration of his bulls for a corrida in Madrid, on 14 October 1888.[349] Clemente sold half his stock to García Becerra but kept the other half as well as its colors, brand, and seniority. In the early 1900s, López Plata acquired both these halves of the Clemente stock, as well as its seniority.

When López Plata died, his widow, Concepción Soto, inherited the herd. She willed it to her nephew, José María Soto de la Fuente, who owned it from 1944 to 1974, when it was sold to a company called "Soto de Luis." Today (2000), the herd carries the name "Soto de la Fuente."[350] For more detail on the relationship between pedigree and ownership, see the essay on "Bulls and Bull Breeding," in the introduction to this volume.

López Plata started presenting *toros de lidia* in 1917, and was the owner of the herd in the years Hemingway visited Spain. His fierce bull Hurón (q.v.) was presented in a spectacle in the early years of his ownership of the herd.

The narrator repeats Carralero and Borge's identification of Antonio López Plata as the owner of the ranch that produced the bull Hurón (111).

Loyola, Ignatius of. Spanish soldier, courtier, theologian, and saint, c. 1491–1556.

As a young man, Ignatius "was free in his relations with women, gambled and fought" but in May 1521, as a member of the garrison defending Pamplona from the French who were besieging it, "the claims of religion reasserted themselves on the young solder, and . . . he made his confession." A few days later, on the 19th or 20th of May, he was injured by a cannon ball that broke his left leg and burned his right leg. Two weeks later, the leg had to be broken again and reset, a difficult procedure: "Ignatius was very ill, and the pain very severe . . . His condition grew steadily worse, until on June 28th, the vigil of the feast of St. Peter and St. Paul, the crisis came" and he received the last sacraments. After this, Loyola recovered quickly.

During his convalescence, Ignatius read religious tracts and turned away from worldly pursuits. Inspired by the first of the many visions he was to experience throughout his life, he decided early in 1522 to make a pilgrimage to the great Benedictine Abbey at Montserrat. He stayed at a hospice in nearby Manresa. Weakened by doubt, penitential fasting, and thrice-daily self-flagellation, he contemplated suicide. According to one of Ignatius's biographers, this is not an unusual sequence: "First comes conversion . . . Next follows the purgative way . . . The repentant man by means of prayer, meditation, scourging and privation, strives to wash from his soul the stains of sin; and, as if physical pain were not enough, black thoughts . . . crowd upon his spirit. But after repentance, discipline and mental torment have cleansed the soul, then the grace of God descends . . . in blessings. . . . This stage is called the illuminative way."[351]

Like other sixteenth-century Spanish mystics, such as Teresa of Avila (1515–82) and Juan de la Cruz (1542–91; co-founders of the Order of the Discalced Carmelites), Ignatius had many visions, illnesses, and doubts. He came into conflict with the Inquisition and eventually joined with several other men to found the Society of Jesus (Jesuits), which defines its members as "soldiers of Christ." Leaders of the Catholic Reform, the Society's founders focused on the education of young people rather than on the conversion of Protestants to Catholicism. Loyola's system of asceticism is explained in *The Spiritual Exercises*: "This little book is said to have converted more souls than it contains letters."[352] Ignatius was beatified in 1609 and canonized in 1622. His feast day is 31 July.

The narrator explains that Loyola was wounded while defending Pamplona, the capital of Navarre (274–75).

Luck. Bullfighters are predominantly Roman Catholic and notoriously superstitious. It is considered bad luck to deviate from standard procedure during certain moments of the fight (*see* Proverbs), to take the place of an injured matador, to have any last-minute change in the program (see Linares in *DS*), or to speak of death. See also Luck in

DS. One scholar concludes that "Hemingway's vision of the world is
. . . one in which chance in the form of luck or random combinations
of circumstances, rather than any rational or easily comprehensible
principle, dominates and determines the course of events,"[353] but
characters like Santiago in *The Old Man and the Sea* and the narrators of *Death in the Afternoon* and *A Moveable Feast* prefer to rely
on a combination of luck, skill, and commitment, whether in bullfighting, writing, betting, or maintaining a marriage. *See also* Roman
Catholic.

> The narrator recognizes the role of luck in a bullfighter's life (90, 238; *see
> also h:* 481, s.v. *Suertes*), refers frequently to bad luck (224, 226–27, 277,
> *h:* 488, s.v. *Tuerto*; *h:* 500), less frequently to good luck (171, 236, 241),
> and mentions luck in connection with several bullfighters: Fuentes Bejar-
> ano (223), Franklin (*h:* 450), Gitanillo de Triana (219–20), Luis Gómez
> (229), Litri (254), Martínez (260), Mazquiarán (223, 259–60), and Zurito
> (256–58).

Luis and the Unsuccessful Matadors. James Mellow identifies Luis
as Luis Crovetto, Sidney Franklin's *mozo de estoques* (his sword handler and confidential assistant). Paul Smith's identification of Luis as
Luis Ortiz (Picardías; a picador active in the 1920s) is inaccurate.[354]

The other, unnamed "unsuccessful matadors" are probably some
of the men portrayed in an unpublished Hemingway fragment, "Portrait of Three, or The Paella," which recounts a similar picnic. There
they are referred to as Paco (probably Francisco Royo Turón, q.v.);
another character variously called Paco, Paco Aldeano, and Aldeano,
and clearly based on Francisco Gómez (q.v.); and Paco Curro or
Curro Prieto (two nicknames for the same person), described as a
young bullfighter from Málaga and thus identifiable as Francisco
Prieto Domínguez, a minor matador born in 1894 in Málaga—all
told, three unsuccessful bullfighters.[355]

With the three "unsuccessful matadors" are three other, more successful men. They are Ernesto (Ernest Hemingway); Sidney (Sidney
Franklin, q.v.) who was much better versed in the taurine arts than
his companions; and an unnamed young man who wanted to be a
bullfighter but was working as a photographer: this is probably Antonio Calvache (1896–1984), whose studio was near the Hotel Aguilar
(q.v.), where Hemingway often stayed when he came to Madrid in
the 1920s.

Calvache was the son of the photographer Diego Calvache, who moved his family to Madrid in 1909. They settled at 16 Carrera de San Jerónimo (the Hotel Aguilar was at number 32), taking over a photography studio formerly owned by Valentín Gómez. All the Calvaches were photographers: Diego Calvache's oldest son, also named Diego, worked with him, and the second, José, set up an independent studio known as Walken (after its previous owner). Antonio, the third son, was also educated by his father, but he was more attracted by the bulls. He was a *novillero* from 1914 to 1919, made his Madrid debut on 9 August 1917, and spent most of 1918 in Barcelona without, apparently, much hope for an *alternativa* (q.v.). When his brother Diego died in 1919, Antonio gave up the bulls and took over the Calvache studio and its clientele.

Antonio photographed Madrid's high society, including politicians, aristocrats, theater personalities, and bullfighters. The catalogue of the 1994 exhibit, *Calvache*, reproduces some of his stylish photographs, with dates. Hemingway readers will recognize Pastora Imperio (1920), Rafael Gómez Ortega (1921), Antonio Márquez (1924), Alfonso XIII (1925), and Jesús Solórzano (1930). Antonio and his brother José (Walken) also got involved in movies, writing scripts, filming, and producing. Antonio even acted the role of a bullfighter, Antonio Romero, in *La España trágica* (1919 or 1920). When Hemingway first came to Madrid, in the spring of 1923, Calvache had been working as a photographer for almost four years and was, just as Hemingway describes him, at the beginning of his career as a photographer. He was still passionate about the bulls.[356] Hemingway probably also met Antonio Calvache's brother José, who photographed Hemingway's friend Sidney Franklin in 1929 or 1930. They probably frequented the Café Fornos (q.v.).

Two other bullfighters who became photographers were José Fernández Aguayo (Pepito, 1911–99) and Francisco Cano Lorenzo (Paco Cano, Curro Cano, b. 1912). They are twelve to fifteen years younger than the other people at the picnic (in the fragment). Aguayo did not take up photography until after *Death in the Afternoon* was published, and Cano did not meet Hemingway until 1959.[357] There seems little doubt that Calvache is the bullfighter-photographer in the fragment.

Photographs at the Hemingway Collection depict a group of happy young men, scantily dressed, enjoying a picnic that features a paella. Hemingway, Sidney Franklin, and Luis Crovetto are among them.[358]

The narrator regrets that he lacks space to discuss Luis and "the unsuccessful matadors" at a picnic where they swam, cooked, and played ball (271).

– M –

Machaquito. *See* González Madrid, Rafael.

MacLeish, Archibald. American lawyer, poet, playwright, and statesman, 1892–1982. During his five years in Europe, from 1923 to 1928, MacLeish published a book almost every year: *The Happy Marriage* (1924); *The Pot of Earth* and *Nobodaddy* (verse play, 1925); *Streets in the Moon* (1926); and *The Hamlet of A. MacLeish* (1928). After his return to the United States he wrote his most famous poems, such as "Ars Poetica" and "You, Andrew Marvell." MacLeish was awarded three Pulitzer Prizes: for the narrative poem *Conquistador* (1933), for the *Collected Works* (1953), and for *J. B.*, a verse drama based on the Book of Job (1958). His last works were a collection of poems, *The Wild Old Wicked Man* (1968), and the verse drama *Scratch* (1971).

MacLeish, an outspoken political activist, held several prestigious federal appointments under Franklin Delano Roosevelt. He was Librarian of Congress (1939–45), assistant director of the Office of War Information (1942–43), and Assistant Secretary of State (1944–45). He helped write the UNESCO constitution in 1945 and became a member of that organization's executive board in 1946. He was Boylston Professor at Harvard from 1949 to 1962.

Although the published version of *Death in the Afternoon* refers to *A. U.*, in the manuscript version the second initial looks like an *M*.[359] The description of *A. U.* corresponds to facts from MacLeish's life. During World War I, MacLeish "served in the field artillery, first as a private, then as a captain,"[360] which would have required him to ride horses, as Hemingway mentions. By then he had already graduated from Yale, where he had been "a member of the Freshman and University Football Teams" and "Captain of Water Polo," as well as Class Poet for his Class of 1915.[361]

When Hemingway met MacLeish in Paris, in 1925, the latter had earned his law degree from Harvard University and made the fateful decision to give up a lucrative career in law for the uncertain profession of poetry. The MacLeishes went to Paris, where Archibald read and wrote poetry and Ada, a trained singer, supported the family.

Hemingway and MacLeish. In October 1926, MacLeish and Hemingway saw at least two corridas in Zaragoza (q.v.);[362] MacLeish seems to have seen no other bullfight since "that fall," when Hemingway was separating from Hadley and preparing to marry Pauline, and MacLeish himself had had an affair and suspected that his wife was unfaithful as well.

It is not clear whether Hemingway knew all the details about the MacLeishes's problems, but MacLeish knew about and disapproved of Hemingway's decision to divorce Hadley, perhaps because he himself was so stressfully attempting to save his own marriage. The tension was exacerbated by an argument over James Joyce: "MacLeish said that Hemingway 'should relax a little and give Joyce credit,' for 'there were some aspects of Joyce's work that Ernest ought to think about.' Hemingway exploded with an anger more intense than the discussion warranted or MacLeish could understand."[363] The Zaragoza experience is recalled in MacLeish's "Cinema of a Man":

He walks with Ernest in the streets in Saragossa
They are drunk their mouths are hard they say *qué cosa*
They say the cruel words they hurt each other
Their elbows touch their shoulders touch their feet go on and on together.[364]

In spite of the quarrels and tension that marred this trip, the friendship survived and Hemingway dedicated *Winner Take Nothing* (1933) to A. MacLeish, thus "acknowledg[ing] a debt to Ada as well as to Archie."[365] The two men quarreled again in 1934. When Hemingway apologized, their friendship was resumed, albeit with less warmth. They collaborated on the making of the film *The Spanish Earth*, to raise funds for the Republicans in the Spanish Civil War.

In *A Moveable Feast*, Hemingway recalls a party given by the Murphys and attended by the Fitzgeralds, the MacLeishes, and the Hemingways, in May 1926, when Ernest, Hadley, and Pauline were living together near the Murphys (*MF*, 185). Although Ada MacLeish went to that party, her husband was then still in Persia (modern Iran) at the time and could not have been at the party, as Hemingway says.[366]

In 1926 MacLeish was thirty-four years old, not thirty-two as Hemingway claims. He may have seen bullfights before going to Zaragoza with Hemingway "that fall," but it is more likely that in this entry, as in several others, Hemingway is inaccurate about age. *See also* Zaragossa.

> The narrator describes A. U. [A. M.] and his responses to the bullfight (*h:* 499).

Madame. *See* Old Lady.

Madrid. Madrid's is the premier bullring of Spain and, therefore, of the taurine world. For a discussion of the city's bullrings, their significance in a bullfighter's life and a bull breeder's reputation, see "The Bullfighter," "Bulls and Bull Breeding," and "The Bullring" in the introduction to this volume. For Madrid's fiestas, *see* Isidro, Saint. For impresarios of the Madrid bullring, *see* Mosquera; see also Madrid in *DS*.

> The narrator mentions Madrid's large *plaza de toros* in passing (28, 36, 55, 204, 241) and names the city's two smaller plazas, Tetuán de las Victorias (168, 272, *h:* 508) and Vista Alegre (110, *h:* 508).

Madrid, Paco. Full name: Francisco Madrid Villatoro. Spanish bullfighter, 1889–1957. Investiture as *matador de toros*, Madrid, September 1912, granted by Rafael Gómez Ortega (el Gallo).

As Hemingway indicates, Paco Madrid was from Málaga. He learned his art in the south of Spain, mostly in Seville, and made his debut in Madrid (Carabanchel) as a *novillero* in September 1911, being promoted to *matador de toros* a year later. His first full year as *matador de toros* confirmed the fine reputation he had earned as a *novillero*. He was applauded in the best Spanish rings, performed in forty-four corridas, and capped the season when a colleague failed to show up and the announced *mano a mano* became a spectacular solo performance: he fought six bulls to almost constant applause in Logroño, on 23 September 1913. The following year saw a slight increase in the number of performances, to forty-nine, but a decrease in skill and, consequently, popularity.

Madrid and Joselito became *matadores de toros* in the same month, and the younger genius's spectacular career only emphasized Madrid's decline so that, in spite of his always-excellent swordword, Madrid performed in only twenty corridas in the years from 1915 to 1919. In 1920, with Joselito gone, Madrid fought twenty-eight corridas and received good reviews, particularly for the afternoon of 10 September, when Sánchez Mejías failed to show up and Madrid again fought all six bulls by himself. This was his last good year, and although he performed a few times each year for the next few years, his career was over several years before he finally retired at the end of the decade. A promising comeback in 1935 was aborted by the Spanish Civil War, which practically closed the bullrings from 1936 to 1939. His last performances, one in 1937 and the other in 1938, were both in his hometown of Málaga, where he lived during the twenty years of his retirement.[367]

Paco Madrid and the Photographs in Death in the Afternoon. Although Rafael el Gallo, Joselito, and Paco Madrid were photographed when they performed together in Madrid, the photograph in *Death in the Afternoon* (*h:* 331) does not represent that corrida, as its caption claims. Instead, it shows the three Gómez Ortega brothers: on the far left, we see Rafael el Gallo and Joselito; on the far right, we see Fernando Gómez Ortega (Gallito), and not Paco Madrid. But Paco Madrid does appear in another photograph, though he is not named in the caption (*h:* 293): he is in the center of the photograph, just behind the fallen horse. The matador on the right, just behind the bull, is Francisco Martín Vázquez.[368]

> The caption incorrectly identifies Paco Madrid as the bullfighter shown in a photograph (*h:* 330–31) with the Gómez Ortega brothers and Enrique Berenguet (qq.v.).

Maera. *See* García, Manuel.

Magdalena, Saint. Mary Magdalen (also known as Mary of Magdala) watched the crucifixion of Jesus, waited near the tomb, and witnessed the resurrection (Matt. 27:56 and 28:9; John 19:25 and 20:11–18). She is usually identified with the unnamed prostitute who washed Jesus's feet with her tears, dried them with her hair, and then anointed them (Luke 7:38). "No good evidence has survived for calling this

woman Mary Magdalene but . . . the equation has been widely believed" since the sixth century.[369] The account presented in John 11:2
and 12:3 indicates that the woman who wiped Jesus's feet with her
hair was Mary of Bethany. The feast day of Mary Magdalen is 22
July, but the annual March *feria* in Castellón de la Plana is called
"La Magdalena." It is one of the earliest, but not always the first,
bullfight of the taurine season.

> The narrator defines the fiesta of the Magdalena as the opening event of
> the taurine season (37, *h:* 508).

Magritas. *See* Suárez, Luis.

Man of War. Usually spelled Man o' War. Foaled in 1917, this famous
American racehorse was sired by Fair Play out of Mahubah, and
trained by Louis Feustel. He was bred by August Belmont, and Mrs.
Belmont, who usually named their foals, called him "My Man of
War" in honor of her husband's recent enlistment. By 1918, when
Samuel Riddle bought him, the name had been shortened to Man o'
War. He was a blazing chestnut, of so brilliant a hue that he was nick-
named "Big Red."

As a two-year-old, Man o' War was ridden by Johnny Loftus; as a
three-year-old, by Clarence Kummer, Earl Sande, and Andrew
(Andy) Shuttinger. These jockeys rode him to victory in twenty of
the twenty-one races he ran during his two seasons (1919–20), when
he established five track records.[370]

Man o' War lost only one race, the Sanford Memorial Stakes, at
Saratoga Springs, New York, on 13 August 1919. The victor of that
race was appropriately named Upset. In 1920 Man o' War won the
Preakness and Belmont stakes; he did not race in the Kentucky Derby
that year. He ran his last race in Canada, on 12 October 1920.

At the end of the 1920 season, the handicapper for the Jockey
Club, Walter Vosburgh, informed Mr. Riddle that in the following
season Man o' War would have to carry " 'the heaviest weight . . .
ever carried by a Thoroughbred.' . . . The chance of injury or un-
soundness under such weight is great and it would have been, any-
way, a sorry spectacle to see a horse of Man o' War's stature beaten
by an inferior animal to which he might be giving as much as fifty

pounds. So Mr. Riddle, quite properly, retired Man o' War at his peak."

Riddle bred Man o' War sparingly. Over the next quarter century, he produced 386 foals, of which 289 raced. Many of them were given war names (e.g., War Hero, War Glory, War Relic), and several were champions (e.g., American Flag, winner of the 1924 Belmont; Crusader, winner of the 1925 Belmont and named best horse of the year; and War Admiral, triple crown winner in 1937). In 1943, their winnings passed the $3,000,000 mark: "Man o' War's get had earned more money than those of any other sire in any country, living or dead."

Riddle resisted all attempts to turn Man o' War into a commercial venture. He refused a $1,000,000 offer made on behalf of the Hollywood magnate Louis B. Mayer and tore up a signed blank check tossed on his desk by another would-be owner. He did allow Man o' War to be shown to visitors who traveled to Faraway Farm.

Man o' War died on 1 November 1947. He was an extraordinary horse who brought fame to his owner, groom, trainer, jockeys, and indeed all who came into contact with him. He ran with such exuberance and extravagant energy that he endeared himself to all his publics. He was a legendary champion, the standard of excellence with which only very few horses, like Citation and Secretariat, can be compared.

It is not likely that Hemingway bet on Man o' War, but even if he had, he would not have profited greatly on this odds-on favorite. On three occasions the betting on him ran 1 to 100.[371]

The narrator remembers Man o' War with admiration (5).

Manager. To handle their complicated financial, legal, and professional affairs, matadors need a manager, or *apoderado*, who is often a relative or trusted friend empowered to negotiate contracts, arrange schedules, handle publicity, and generally speak for his matador. Their names and addresses were listed in the back pages of taurine journals. Managers who manage several important bullfighters acquire a great deal of clout. Among the more powerful managers of Hemingway's day were Matías Retana, who managed Nicanor Villalta and was the brother of Manuel Martín Retana, the impresario of Madrid's bullring; and Eduardo Pagés, whose clients in 1926 included Rafael Gómez Ortega (el Gallo), Juan Belmonte (Pagés had lured him out of retirement in 1925), and Ignacio Sánchez Mejías (qq.v.). Hemingway mentions Domingo González (Dominguín, q.v.), who managed Joaquín Rodríguez (Cagancho) in the late 1920s and Domingo Ortega and Fermín Espinosa (Armillita, qq.v.) in the early 1930s; he was a bullring impresario as well.

In 1925 and 1926, the newly established Union of Bullring Impresarios attempted to set ceilings for matadors's fees. Since several powerful impresarios also managed or were related to bullfighters, they in fact created monopolies which simply excluded bullfighters who wanted higher fees. This of course damaged several careers, although some bullfighters, like Ignacio Sánchez Mejías, managed to circumvent the boycott.[372] For a fuller discussion, see "Impresarios, Managers, and the Rise of *los Trusts*" in the introduction to *DS*.

> The narrator identifies Dominguín (93, 168, 170), Manuel Mejías (165–68), and Zocato (74) as bullfighters who were also managers. He refers to other bullfighters' managers (90) and bullring impresarios (60, 165), often commenting on their sharp financial dealings.

Manzanares, Joachin (Mella). His first name is usually spelled "Joaquín." Full name: Joaquín Manzanares Antón. Spanish bullfighter, 1899–1971. This banderillero worked in the *cuadrilla* of the famous Nicanor Villalta, 1922–23, and afterwards with several other first-rank matadors. He was very able and popular with the public.[373]

> The narrator correctly ranks Manzanares among the best banderilleros of his day (201).

Manzanares River. *See* Bombilla.

Marlowe, Christopher. English dramatist and poet, 1564–93. Among his famous plays, most of them published posthumously, are *Tamburlaine the Great* (1590), *Edward II* (1594), *Tragedy of Dr. Faustus* (1601), and *The Jew of Malta* (1633), from which Bill Gorton "quotes" in *The Sun Also Rises* (75) and from which Hemingway's short story "In Another Country" (composed in 1926) takes its title.

> The narrator classes Marlowe and Shakespeare among the great English writers (73).

Márquez, Antonio. Full name: Antonio Márquez Serrano (el Belmonte rubio, the blond Belmonte). Spanish bullfighter, 1898–1988. Investiture as *matador de toros*, in Barcelona, September 1921; confirmed in Madrid, May 1923.

Like many bullfighters before him, Márquez had to overcome his family's resistance to his desire to be a bullfighter. He became a *novillero* in 1915, performed more frequently and with growing skill as the years passed, and was the leading *novillero* of 1921, with thirty-two *novilladas*. He was promoted to full *matador de toros* by Belmonte at the end of that season. Thus far, his is the standard success story, capped by a prestigious *alternativa* (q.v.).

In 1922, Márquez had to interrupt his taurine career to do military service in Morocco, which damaged his health. He returned to the bullring for two moderately successful seasons: twenty-two corridas in 1923 and thirty-three in 1924, when he was ranked eighth nationwide, earned rave reviews,[374] was often carried out of the ring on shoulders, and was awarded the year's "Medalla de Oro" (gold medal given by the bullfighters' benevolent association, Montepío).

In 1925, however, illness forced Márquez to cancel most of his June performances, and he was still not in good form when Hemingway saw him in July, in Pamplona's *sanfermines*. In general, however, 1925 was a full and successful season for Márquez: fifty-four corridas (ranked fourth nationwide for that season).

Márquez improved even this high standing in the next two years, with fifty-eight corridas in 1926 and fifty-four or fifty-five (reports vary) in 1927. He was ranked second for both those years, in which Cayetano Ordóñez (q.v.) headed the lists, with seventy-eight and sixty-five corridas. These may be considered Márquez's best years, even though some of the 1927 performances were disappointing.

Márquez married in December and announced that he would cut short the next season: in 1928 he fought only twenty-eight or twenty-nine corridas, almost all of which were highly praised. In 1929 he again decided to accept fewer engagements, and his season was further shortened by a serious goring that removed him from the ring for six weeks (3 August to 13 September)—altogether, thirty-seven corridas for that year. In spite of these shortened seasons, the excellence of his performances kept Márquez in the forefront of his profession and in 1930 he fought fifty-one corridas (tying with Gitanillo de Triana for fifth place), although ill health affected the quality of his performances. After three performances early in the 1931 season, he announced his retirement.

Márquez did not perform in 1932 but, as Hemingway predicted, he did return to the bulls, giving seven special performances (galas and benefits), all impressive, in 1933. In 1934 and 1935 he again acceded to his worried family's demands that he not fight; but in 1936 he embarked upon a full season, which was cut short by the outbreak of the Spanish Civil War in July. He fought a very few times in 1937 and 1938, under Nationalist auspices, and then retired. After the Civil War he dedicated himself to furthering the careers of his wife, Conchita Piquer, and their daughter Conchi, both singers.

Márquez was widely acclaimed as a master of the cape, banderillas, and muleta; the adjectives most often applied to him by the critics are "elegant" and "classic" (he is often compared with Fuentes and the later Belmonte). Cossío particularly admires his *verónicas*, his work with the banderillas, and his "miraculous" left wrist, which enabled him to perform such aesthetically satisfying *faenas*. He remarks that the sword work was occasionally deficient, but another respected critic, Tomás Orts Ramos (Uno al Sesgo), insisted that Márquez was accomplished in all aspects of bullfighting and was one of the leading lights of his day.[375] Cossío ascribes Márquez's decision to accept fewer engagements to recurring health problems and adds that Márquez's repeated withdrawals from the profession cost him the "triunfo definitivo, completo, absoluto a que pudo y debió llegar, dadas sus cualidades, aptitudes y condiciones artísticas" (definitive, complete and absolute triumph that he could and should have achieved, given his talent and artistic capabilities).

Márquez's health problems have not been identified. Bagüés thinks Márquez suffered from a lack of *afición* (passion for the bullfight), not illness. In spite of the occasional shortened season, however, Bagüés rates Márquez "entre las figuras más sobresalientes de los años que corren desde 1921 a 1930" (among the outstanding figures of the 1920s).[376]

Hemingway and Márquez. Hemingway had plenty of opportunity to see Márquez. The two coincided in Pamplona in 1923 (6 and 8 July), 1925 (7, 8, 9, and 12 July),[377] 1927 (7, 8, 10, and 12 July), and 1929 (7, 9, and 10 July). Márquez did not perform in Pamplona in

1924, 1926 or 1931, and Hemingway missed the *ferias* of 1928 and 1930. He saw Márquez several times in Zaragoza in October 1926, a great year for Márquez (*see* Zaragossa).

Hemingway's prediction (that Márquez's retirement would be short) may have been based on Márquez's own announcement, late in 1931, that he would return to the bullring in 1932. The announcement was published before *Death in the Afternoon* was finished (see *Toros y toreros en 1931*, 236 n.). In fact, however, Márquez performed only seldom after 1930, and not at all in 1932.

The incident in which Márquez's sword killed a spectator occurred on 2 September 1923; the victim was Carlos Aguirre. As Márquez was trying to administer the *descabello* to his second bull, the sword apparently hit bone and flew out of Márquez's hand and into the stands. The bull came from the ranch of Félix Moreno (q.v.) and the event, as Hemingway mentions, occurred in Bayonne.[378] There was no trial. In a similar event, another spectator, Juan Genovart, was killed in 1930 (*see* Martínez, Manuel). And the same thing happened again in 1934: this time the place was La Coruña, the bullfighter Ignacio Sánchez Mejías (q.v.), the bulls Albaserrada, and the victim Cándido Roig, who died in the stands. Again, there was no trial.[379] Hemingway did not attend the bullfights in which these spectators were killed, but the events were widely reported. For bullfighters injured in the stands by fellow spectators or by bulls, *see* the entries for Anlló, Juan (who died of his injury); and for Jaqueta (gored but not killed).

Angel Capellán, one of Hemingway's most ardent admirers, feels that Hemingway's "near silence on Antonio Márquez" is one of the few weaknesses of *Death in the Afternoon*.[380] Hemingway's very qualified praise of Márquez and the repeated accusation of "tricks" (see in *DS*) seems to be at odds with most taurine authorities.

The narrator admires this matador from Madrid, though not without reservations. He considers Márquez to be excellent but not consistently so with the muleta (215); his work with the banderillas is "very interesting" but marred by tricks (200, 380, *h:* 411, s.v. *Adorno*). He reports that Márquez was tried for and acquitted of manslaughter when his sword killed a spectator (*h:* 431–32, s.v. *Descabellar*). In 1931 he was in ill health but the narrator predicts he will soon return to the ring (217, 267).

Martín-Caro, Juanito (Chiquito de la Audiencia). Full name: Juan Martín-Caro Cases. Spanish bullfighter, b. 1910. Investiture as *matador de toros*, in Ciudad Real, April 1932; confirmed in Madrid, May 1932; renounced c. 1939.

After four or five years as a *becerrista*, Martín-Caro became a *novillero* in 1930. In 1931 he performed in thirty-two *novilladas*. Cossío remarks that as a *novillero* Juan was skillful with the cape and muleta but weak with the sword, a weakness which became more pronounced after his investiture.

Martín-Caro was a minor bullfighter. Bagüés plays on his nickname, noting that in spite of the occasional good performance with the cape, he was "Chiquito en todo, o sea artística y físicamente" (small in every way, artistically and physically). In his four Spanish seasons as matador (1932–35), he fought an unimpressive total of twenty-eight corridas. He enjoyed some successes abroad during the Spanish Civil War, after which he appeared a few more times in Spain, though no longer as *matador de toros*: he acted as banderillero in the *cuadrillas* of his younger brothers.[381] Of the four Caro brothers, three were bullfighters: Francisco (1915–76, known as Curro Caro), was the most successful. But Chiquito de la Audiencia's career was practically over at the time that Hemingway wrote that it would be "very interesting to follow" it.

> The narrator admires Chiquito and predicts that he will have an "interesting" career (276, 228–29).

Martínez, Manuel (Manolo). Full name: Manuel Martínez Solaz (el tigre de Ruzafa). Spanish bullfighter, 1897–1966. Investiture as *matador de toros*, in Madrid, September 1924.

In 1925, his first season as a full *matador de toros*, Martínez fought six corridas before suffering a terrible wound in the right thigh on 31 July in Valencia, which caused him to lose the rest of the season. In 1926 he fought fourteen corridas without making much of an impression in any area except his sword work.[382] In 1927 he fought seventeen, with successful performances in the July fiesta in his native Valencia (witnessed by Hemingway, who was fond of this *feria*; see below). In 1928 he fought sixteen corridas (five of them in Valencia), fourteen in 1929 (four in Valencia), and twenty-one in 1930 (his best season). On 10 May 1931, after three corridas in Valencia, Martínez appeared in Madrid, where he was so terribly gored that he did not fight for a month. The sixteen corridas of 1931 (eight in Valencia) were uniformly undistinguished. In the 1930s and 1940s he performed mostly in France and in Central and South America. His farewell performance took place in Valencia in April 1948.

Martínez was, as the narrator correctly remarks, popular in his hometown of Ruzafa, in Valencia (although he failed even there in the 1931 *feria*) but he never became a first-rate matador. Although he was showily brave and an accomplished swordsman, he lacked the personality and style that define the best matadors. His fighting did not mature over the years, and his courage, his most admirable trait, started to waver in 1930. Bagüés classifies him as "de tercera fila" (third-rank). Most of the narrator's predictions about this bullfighter, whose aggressive courage impressed him, were not realized: Martínez did not make the expected comeback after the 1931 goring, which effectively marked the end of his career in Spain.[383] Martínez lived to be sixty-eight years old and died of natural causes and not, as the narrator predicted, at the horns of a bull.

Hemingway expands upon three dramatic incidents in Martínez's career, two of which he probably witnessed: "the terrible cornada . . . in Valencia" (*DIA*, 260–62) occurred in 1925. Martínez was injured in the right thigh by a bull from the ranch of Antonio Flores; the serious wound kept him out of the bullrings for the rest of the season. The blood loss was described as "alarmante."[384] Hemingway also attended the July 1927 Valencia fair, which was a huge success for Martínez, who took over as one bullfighter after another was disabled. In all, seven bullfighters were hurt in that terrible fair: Simâo da Veiga on 25 July; Marcial Lalanda on 26 July (badly gored in the right thigh); Juan Belmonte (injured in the right hand) and Cayetano Ordóñez on 27 July; and Martín Agüero and Valencia II on 29 July. Martínez performed on 24, 25, and 29 July of that star-studded fair, escaped injury as all around him fell, and was clearly the star of the *feria*.[385] Hemingway did not, however, see the fatal stabbing of a spectator, Juan Genovart (1898–1930), which occurred on 8 September 1930, because he did not go to Spain that year. This strange accident—the bull shook off Martínez's ill-placed sword, which flew through the air and pierced Genovart—occurred in Tortosa (south

262 • MARTÍNEZ, DON VICENTE

of Tarragona) and not in Tolosa (northwest of Pamplona), as the narrator claims (*DIA*, 402).[386] In 1923 and 1934, similar incidents also proved fatal to spectators; see Márquez, Antonio; Sánchez Mejías, Ignacio.

> The narrator ranks Martínez among the top killers of his period (223; *see also* 253). He finds that Martínez performs best in his home city of Valencia (262; *see also* 267), and remarks that his terrible horn wounds resulted from his insufficient skill with the cape and muleta, combined with a bravery that led him to take risks (262). It was thought that his 1931 wound would end his career, but the narrator predicts that he will recover although it is "inevitable" that some day a bull will destroy him (223; *see also* 260–62, *h:* 432, s.v. *Descabellar*).

Martínez, don Vicente. Spanish bull breeder, d. 1894.

The Vicente Martínez herd traces its pedigree to the eighteenth century, when don Julián de Fuentes acquired eighty head from the well-established herd of don José Jijón.[387] Fuentes's careful breeding produced such good results that some of his bulls were bought by don Manuel Gaviria, the manager of King Fernando VII's herds. On 16 September 1822, Fuentes's bulls were fought for the first time in the Madrid bullring; their *antigüedad*, or seniority, dates from that corrida. After Fuentes's death, the breed remained in the family, but the son managed it less expertly than the father, so that it was at a low point when it was acquired by don Vicente Martínez in 1852.

Vicente Martínez was a careful breeder, however, and in the forty years that he owned the herd, it improved considerably. In 1894, don Vicente's two sons-in-law, Julián Fernández and Luis Gutiérrez Gómez, inherited his holdings. Julián died within a few years, and his three sons—Julián, Pedro, and Alberto Fernández Martínez—joined their uncle, Luis Gutiérrez Gómez, as co-owners of the herd. Luis Gutiérrez reshaped the herd, most notably by introducing Vistahermosa blood in 1904 (via Diano, the famous Ibarra seed bull, q.v.), which produced the smoother, more pliable bull that would be demanded by Joselito, Belmonte, and the new style of bullfighting they created. Luis Gutiérrez died in 1907, before seeing the results of his acquisition.

In 1925 the three nephews divided the herd. The two younger brothers sold their shares—one to a conglomerate of breeders, the other to don Antonio Pérez Tabernero (q.v.)—and the oldest brother, Julián Fernández Martínez, who had been managing the business since the turn of the century, retained the family's colors, brand, and *antigüedad* (16 September 1822). Thus in Hemingway's day the breed was variously listed as belonging to the grandfather, Vicente Martínez, and to this grandson, who carefully maximized the benefits Diano had brought to the herd. The Martínez bulls were much in demand in the post-Joselito days when Hemingway went to the bullfights.

The Spanish Civil War decimated the herd, and when don Julián died unexpectedly in 1938 (of natural causes, not a victim of war), the family sold what was left, about forty head, to the Duke of Pinohermoso, who added other stock to it and then sold the enlarged herd to the Arribas Sancho family (no relation of the Arribas Hermanos discussed previously). The Arribas Sancho heirs have kept the herd, with its brand and *antigüedad* (16 September 1822) in the family until today (2000).[388]

In 1959, twenty years after the herd had passed out of the family's hands, Julián's son, Luis Fernández Salcedo, an engineer, wrote a book about the acquisition of Diano. For a definition of *antigüedad*, see "Bulls and Bull Breeding," in the introduction to this volume; for another breed based on the *casta jijona*, *see* Pablo Romero.

The narrator correctly reports that the current owner of the herd (in 1932) is don Julián Fernández Martínez (132; photograph, *h:* 374).

Marvell, Andrew. English politician and poet, 1621–78. Marvell was tutor to the daughter of Lord Fairfax and later to Cromwell's ward. In 1657 he was appointed secretary to John Milton and in 1659 he was elected to Parliament. Most of his famous poems, including "To His Coy Mistress," were published posthumously. The main character of *A Farewell to Arms*, Frederic Henry, is clearly familiar with the poem (*AFTA*, 154, 311); the narrator of *Death in the Afternoon* refers to its second section:

> then worms shall try
> That long-preserved virginity,

>And your quaint honor turn to dust,
>And into ashes all my lust.

Hemingway's many unidentified allusions and direct quotes show him to be as much a high modernist as T. S. Eliot (q.v.), whom he pretends to despise.

The narrator puns on Marvell's poem (139).

Master Bob. A chestnut colt, foaled in France, c. 1914. His breeding was Chulo and Morelos, his trainer was John Dutton, and his owner was H. Roux de Bézieux. He was a steeplechaser who generously rewarded bettors who had confidence in him.

The odds on Master Bob are always interesting. In 1922, he ran eight races and won two, both at Auteuil: the Prix La Vague, on 1 November (the betting was 3 to 2), and the Prix Firino on 5 November (the betting was 8 to 1). Hemingway saw him race at Auteuil on 19 November 1922, where Master Bob came in third in the 5,500 meter, Prix Montgomery race. The odds on Master Bob were 16 to 1, so even if Hemingway had only bet on him to place, he would still have won nicely. Héros XII (q.v.) ran in the same race.

In 1923 Master Bob ran thirteen races, placing in four and winning two. Both victories were at Auteuil: the Prix Arthur O'Connor, on 25 March, when the betting on him was 31 to 10; and the Prix du Cinquantenaire, on 1 November, with the betting on him at 14 to 1.[389] In June, Hemingway saw him run in the Grand Steeplechase de Paris, which was won by L'Yser, paying 53 to 10. Master Bob came in second, at 13 to 1, and Héros XII third, at 17 to 10; Ernest and Hadley had bet on Master Bob and won 250 francs on the exciting race. On 22 June 1923, when Master Bob came in second, the odds on him were a profitable 43 to 10.

Master Bob's earnings for 1923 were much higher than for 1922: only L'Yser and Onyx II won more money than he did that year. In 1924, Master Bob headed the chart for moneymaking champions. That year, he ran four races and won two, both of them important races with big stakes, at Auteuil: the Président de la République, on 30 March (the odds were again 43 to 10) and the Grand Steeplechase de Paris, on 22 June. The Hemingways were in Paris on those dates.

In 1925, Master Bob ran two races, not winning either. This was the last racing season of this steeplechaser.[390]

Even though Master Bob was a top moneymaker in 1923 and 1924, the betting public did not have much confidence in him. Not being a favorite to win, he paid handsomely.

> The narrator identifies the steeplechaser Master Bob as one of the several horses he bet on and admired (5).

Maupassant, Guy de. French novelist and short story writer, 1850–93. Among his many famous stories are "The Necklace," "The Piece of String," and "Miss Harriet." By 1891, he was insane, probably a result of syphilis.

Hemingway owned several volumes of Maupassant's work, mostly collections of short stories, which he seems to have read in the original French, and displays his familiarity with his fiction when he describes a favorite Parisian restaurant as "a place out of a Maupassant story" (*A Moveable Feast*, 43).[391] *See* Authors; Boxing.

Hemingway describes at least two other eateries in high-culture terms: see Simenon and Sisley in *DS*. Such comparisons would have gladdened Aldous Huxley (q.v.).

> The narrator indicates that Maupassant went mad and died of syphilis, a disease prevalent among bullfighters (102).

Mazquiarán, Diego (Fortuna). Full name: Diego Mazquiarán Torróntegui. Spanish bullfighter, 1895–1940. Investiture as *matador de toros*, September 1916, in Madrid. He acquired his nickname because of his good luck in surviving a train accident when he and his friend, equally poor and equally fascinated by the bulls, were jumping on a train to catch a free ride to the next bullfight. The friend was killed, but Fortuna recovered fully from his injuries.

Fortuna's passion for the bulls took him south, from Sestao (Vizcaya), where he was born, and Bilbao, where he grew up, to Salamanca and finally to Andalucía, where he had the good luck to befriend the famous Gallos (q.v.) who were among his customers when he worked as delivery boy for a bakery and who recognized his talents.

In 1914 Fortuna made his Madrid debut as a *novillero*. He already had a good reputation and performed in twenty-two *novilladas* that year, many in important plazas. Clearly a first-rate *novillero*, he was watched with great interest. In 1915 he was "el novillero de moda"; in 1916 he performed in thirty-one *novilladas* before his promotion to *matador de toros* at the end of the season.

Fortuna's first two seasons as *matador de toros* were very successful (fifty-one corridas a year, in spite of injuries that forced him to cancel some contracts). But illness and injury produced weaker performances, and he lost some of his appeal. The number of corridas decreased to thirty-six in 1919 and thirty-one in 1920. In 1921 he enjoyed some triumphs and recovered ground; in 1922 he performed in thirty-five corridas, most of them excellent performances. He was free of illness and injuries that year.

Although he was a reliably fine swordsman, his reputation for uneven performances with the cape, banderillas, and muleta reduced the number of contracts he was offered. In the years during which Hemingway visited Spain before publishing *Death in the Afternoon* (1923–31), Fortuna was clearly in decline. In 1924 he was down to fifteen corridas, seventeen in 1925, six spiritless performances in 1926, and three in 1927 (all in September).

An unusual event in January 1928 revived interest in this talented but unsuccessful performer. An escaped bull terrorized Madrid for an entire morning, injuring several people. Fortuna happened to be strolling on the Gran Vía when the bull suddenly appeared; the matador took off his coat, sent someone off to fetch his sword, fought the bull until the sword arrived, and dispatched him quickly and artfully, to the acclaim of the crowd that had gathered. Fortuna was decorated for this unusual feat, and in October 1928 he was awarded the Press Association's "golden ear." All this revived his career somewhat: he performed in fourteen corridas in 1929, eighteen in 1930, and ten in 1931 (six of them in Madrid, including the inaugural corrida of Las Ventas, which Hemingway probably saw). But in the 1930s, as in the 1920s, his performances were frequently unattractive, he was often gored, and he was unable to hold on to the public's attention. When the Spanish Civil War broke out, Fortuna left Spain for Peru, where he had enjoyed several successful tours. In Peru he was institutionalized in a mental hospital, where he died at age forty-five.

Taurine critics speculate that mental illness may have been the reason for the unevenness of Fortuna's performances. With his skills and art, he could and should have been a consistently fine performer. Cossío writes that he was perhaps the best killer of his time—and Fortuna was Joselito's contemporary. He was capable with the cape, fine with the muleta, and a master of the *volapié*, the method of killing which earned him many trophies: "Dominaba y ejecutaba la suerte con perfección" (he dominated and performed this technique perfectly).[392] Early in his career he did share top billing with the great Joselito and Belmonte. But in spite of his nickname, Fortuna suffered frequent illness and injury.[393] Hemingway saw Fortuna in Valencia on 25 July 1925; he may have seen him a few times in Madrid as well. Hemingway doesn't often comment on a bullfighter's intelligence, but he emphasizes that Fortuna is stupid and Martín-Caro intelligent: neither made it into the first ranks of bullfighting.

> The narrator defines Fortuna as one of the flawed bullfighters who dominated the bullring after Joselito's death in 1920. He describes him as brave, lucky, and technically competent (222–23) but adds that his style is old-fashioned, his method of killing is graceless, and his stupidity makes him an uninteresting bullfighter (259–60; *see also* 70, 75, 262).
>
> Fortuna speaks: 259–60.

Mazzantini, Luis. Full name: Luis Mazzantini Eguía. Spanish bullfighter, 1856–1926. Investiture as *matador de toros*, in Seville, April 1884; confirmed in Madrid in May that year.

Mazzantini's father, an Italian, came to northern Spain to supervise the construction of railroads in the Basque provinces. Although he married a Spanish woman and settled in Spain, his work often took him and his family to France and Italy. Luis became, like his father, an employee of the railroads, but his international outlook, his university degree, and his ambition made him restless and dissatisfied with the modest living the railroads offered. He delivered himself of the famous sentence, "En este país de los prosaicos garbanzos no se puede ser más que dos cosas: o tenor del Teatro Real o matador de toros" (In this land of prosaic chickpea-eaters, one can be only one of two things: a tenor in the Royal Theatre, or a *matador de toros*).[394] Having tried and failed as a singer, Mazzantini began his training as a bullfighter in the late 1870s.

In the early 1880s he finally quit (or was fired from) the railroads, and his bullfighting career took off. He was promoted to *matador de toros* in 1884 in Seville, and both this performance and the confirmation in Madrid were so fine that the spectators carried him out of the ring. Tall, strong, ambitious, and a fine swordsman, he became enormously rich and popular, fighting in France, Cuba, and Mexico as well as in Spain. He was the first of the bullring's pop stars: Mazzantini neckties, handkerchiefs, and walking sticks became the rage, a popular novelist wrote a book about him, and the press reported his every move.[395]

Mazzantini's popularity evoked a negative reaction: he was said to be a Freemason, a serious accusation in a Roman Catholic country; his international fame was attributed to Masonic support or a Masonic conspiracy. By the late 1880s his audiences were frequently abusive, shouting insults and throwing fruits and vegetables into the ring even as the bullfight was in process. In 1889 a rioting audience pelted him with bottles and stones: Mazzantini had to be taken to the infirmary and the bullfight was canceled. In the early 1890s Mazzantini regained much of his popularity, but by the end of the decade his age (he was in his forties) and his increasing girth were slowing him down. He performed seldom and not well and relied more and more on his younger brother Tomás (1862–1919), his banderillero, to get him out of tight spots. In 1905, shortly after the death of his wife, Mazzantini finally retired from the bullring. He devoted the rest of life to politics.[396]

Even in the early 1880s, at the beginning of his career, Mazzantini was recognized as an "estoqueador formidable."[397]

> The narrator contends that, critics being what they are, Mazzantini was vilified while alive for his work with the cape and muleta, but revered after his death for his work with the sword (240–41).

Meier-Graefe, Julius. German art critic, 1867–1935.

Meier-Graefe was an early admirer of Impressionists and author of books on Renoir, Manet, Delacroix, and Degas. Translations of several of his books were available in Hemingway's time: *Modern Art, Being a Contribution to a New System of Aesthetics* (1908), *Cézanne* (1927), *Pyramids and Temple* (1930), *Vincent Van Gogh: A Biographical Study* (1922), and *The Spanish Journey* (1927). Reynolds points out that Hemingway owned the book on Van Gogh and borrowed *The Spanish Journey* from Sylvia Beach. Brasch and Sigman indicate that J. Holroyd-Reece's English translation of *The Spanish Journey* was in Hemingway's library in Key West and that he took the book to the Finca Vigía in Cuba.[398]

Scholes and Comley examine Hemingway's reference to Meier-Graefe closely and conclude that Hemingway's "idea of treating the dead precisely in terms of natural history seems to have been stimulated by Meier-Graefe's reading of Goya's sketch [from the *Desastres de la guerra*, in Meier-Graefe's *The Spanish Journey*], just as the idea of taking the dead as a subject for art was certainly supported by Goya's own work" (115). They add that Hemingway "is using the art historian for his own purposes, much as Huxley [q.v.] used Hemingway" and that by mentioning Meier-Graefe Hemingway may have been "acknowledging and concealing a debt to the art historian for stimulating his thinking about a book on Spain in which bullfighting is treated in the language of art."[399] We need to remember, however, that Hemingway read Meier-Graefe in December 1926, but his correspondence with Maxwell Perkins reveals that he was thinking of a bullfight book as early as April 1925 (*see* entry for *Death in the Afternoon*).

As a matter of fact, Hemingway had written about bullfighting even before he saw his first bullfights in May and June 1923. Talking to other aficionados, reading bullfight papers and journals, and browsing in bookstores, he realized very quickly that bullfighting was a very proper subject for book-length treatment; he did not need Meier-Graefe's example for this. Bullfighting is not only an art form in itself, it is also the subject of much folklore and art (sculpture, literature, and music as well as painting), and taurine writers and critics, whose foreheads are generally not "villainous low," often speak of bullfighting in aesthetic terms: color, form, movement, classicism, decadence, *temple* (harmony, rhythm), control, balance, composition, order, temperament, and so on (see, for example, Gregorio Corrochano's reviews in *ABC* and his books, especially *¿Qué es torear?*).

Hemingway read and responded to Meier-Graefe, who may certainly be considered an influence in this respect, but he was also influenced by the "2077 books and pamphlets in Spanish dealing with or touching on tauromaquia," many of which he read before he read

Meier-Graefe; and by Waldo Frank (q.v.), who wrote about the subject in English and whose *Virgin Spain* (1926, q.v.) was also an unacknowledged and concealed source. Still, Scholes and Comley's "deep reading" of Hemingway's reference to Meier-Graefe is valuable in that it encourages additional intense scrutiny of the many other names in this book. Hemingway's name-studded texts richly repay such attention.

> The narrator, always on the defensive about critics and apparently stung by Huxley's remarks about him, attacks Meier-Graefe for applying unfair and irrelevant criteria "to exalt Greco" at the expense of Velázquez and Goya (203).

Mejías, José (Pepe Bienvenida). Full name: José Mejías Jiménez. Spanish bullfighter, 1914–68. Investiture as *matador de toros*, Madrid, 5 July 1931, at age seventeen.

Pepe Bienvenida was born into a decidedly taurine environment (*see* Bienvenida). A child prodigy, he performed abroad with his older brother Manuel (q.v.), returning with him to Spain late in 1928, when Manuel turned sixteen (the minimum legal age for performing in Spanish bullrings). In 1929 he fought seventeen *novilladas* in Spain, often sharing the bill with Alfredo Corrochano (q.v.). All these teenagers attracted attention because of their family connections as well as their talent. In 1930 an injury reduced his season to twenty-one *novilladas*; his *alternativa* (q.v.) the next year was preceded by eleven *novilladas* and followed by twenty-one corridas, most of them quite impressive. From then until the outbreak of the Spanish Civil War, he appeared regularly about twenty times a season, impressing the public and critics with his skill, knowledge of the bulls, and large repertoire of techniques, but without achieving his brother's standing or increasing his own popularity.

Pepe Bienvenida performed in Nationalist-controlled territories throughout the Spanish Civil War and was invited to perform in the *Corrida de la Victoria*, 24 May 1939. He fought in thirty-three corridas in 1940, forty-one in 1941, fifty-four in 1942, fifty-three in 1943 and fifty-nine in 1944, probably his best year: he was ranked third nationwide. He continued to fight, though less and less frequently and occasionally even skipping a season altogether, for the rest of the 1940s and the early 1950s, retiring in 1957. After that he performed occasionally in special festivals. He died suddenly in Lima, Peru, on one such occasion: he had a heart attack just after he placed a pair of banderillas. Cossío praises Pepe Bienvenida's work with the cape, the banderillas, the muleta, and the sword, calling him "un excelente torero," but notes that even early in his career he lacked the enthusiasm, ambition, and commitment that characterize the superstars of this profession. Bagüés repeats the criticism, noting inaccurately that he never made it to the top of his profession even though he had a long career and was "un torero completísimo . . . uno de los diestros más completos de su época" (one of the most accomplished matadors of his time), so skilled and intelligent that he was seldom gored.[400] Both Pepe and Manolo performed in the lighthearted, graceful *estilo sevillano*, and both were fine banderilleros.

Hemingway and Pepe Bienvenida. Hemingway may have seen Pepe Bienvenida as a fifteen-year-old *novillero*, perhaps on 11 July 1929, at a Pamplona *novillada*; but he did not see him in 1930 (Hemingway did not go to Spain that summer) or in 1931, the year Bienvenida was promoted to *matador de toros* (Bienvenida did not perform in any of the fiestas Hemingway saw). Hemingway undoubtedly read reviews, most of them glowing, as Pepe and Manolo Bienvenida were a sensation, both together and individually.[401]

The narrator finds that the seventeen-year-old Pepe Bienvenida is a promising but inexperienced bullfighter (225; alluded to 165, 230, 267).

Mejías, Manolo (Bienvenida). Full name: Manuel Mejías Jiménez. Spanish bullfighter, 1912–38. Investiture as *matador de toros*, in Zaragoza, 30 June 1929; confirmed in Madrid that October.

Grandson, nephew, son, and brother of bullfighters, Manolo, like his younger brother José (Pepe, q.v. above), was a child prodigy. The brothers early overcame their parents' objections and left school in order to begin performing, aged twelve and eleven, as *becerristas* (fighting *becerros*, bulls about one year old). Because a recently passed law barred children younger than sixteen from performing in Spain's bullrings, the boys fought in France, Peru, Venezuela, and Mexico in 1926, 1927, and 1928, returning to Spain when Manolo reached the requisite age. Manolo became a *matador de toros* in June 1929, at sixteen.[402]

From his investiture to his premature death, Manolo Bienvenida was one of the stars of the ring, often awarded ears and tails and maintaining his popularity with the critics and the public, as the numbers indicate: thirty-one corridas in 1929, seventy-three in 1930 (he ended this season by fighting two corridas singlehandedly and was carried triumphantly out of the ring on both occasions), eighty-four in 1931 (he had been contracted for eleven more; only Domingo Ortega [q.v.] performed more often that season), fifty-seven in 1932 (he had been contracted for more than seventy, but canceled several, for reasons unknown). His first life-threatening goring reduced the 1933 season to forty-five corridas without, as the narrator of *Death in the Afternoon* fears, breaking his spirit. The numbers continue to be impressive: forty-one corridas in 1934, sixty-four in 1935, and fewer, of course during the Spanish Civil War, when bullfights were few, and held only in Nationalist controlled areas. Manuel often appeared *mano a mano* (in which two rather than three matadors kill the six bulls) with his brother Pepe; in 1936 he fought a series of *mano a manos* with Domingo Ortega.

Bienvenida was good with the cape, banderillas, and muleta, but not with the sword, although his sword work improved with time. Thanks to his own gifts and his father's excellent training, Manuel (like Pepe) was seldom injured in the ring. His education and discipline helped him achieve and maintain his standing among the top-ranked bullfighters for his whole career. Unlike his brother, he was completely committed to bullfighting: it was "su pasión favorita . . . su único vicio" (his favorite passion, his only vice). Cossío applies to him the phrase usually reserved for Joselito: "Todo para él era fácil" (he did everything easily).[403] His early death has been attributed to a number of causes: tuberculosis, cancer, or an operation to remove a cyst or tumor. He was twenty-six years old when he died in 1938.[404] *See also* Bienvenida.

Hemingway and Manolo Bienvenida. Hemingway did not come to Spain in 1930, but he saw Manolo Bienvenida in 1929 (on 11 July, in Pamplona, and probably on several other occasions) and in 1931 (on July 7, 8, and 12 in Pamplona, and on 27, 29, and 30 July and 1 August in Valencia).[405] Unfortunately, these were all uncharacteristically poor performances. Even an admiring biographer had to admit that in the generally good year of 1931, "Se le dan mal los Sanfermines. . . . También se le da floja la feria de Valencia" (it went badly during the *sanfermines* [in Pamplona] and the Valencia *feria*). Bienvenida did well with only one bull in Pamplona and with none in Valencia.[406]

In 1931 Manolo Bienvenida fought in eighty-four corridas and killed 174 bulls. Hemingway claims to have seen him kill twenty-four bulls that season, only two of them "decently" (249–50). At a minimum of two bulls per corrida, this suggests that Hemingway saw Bienvenida in about twelve corridas: the three in Pamplona and four in Valencia, as well as several others, probably in Madrid, where the two men coincided on 16 May and on 1, 17, and 23 June and perhaps on 5 July.[407]

Hemingway was in Spain for several months during the 1929 and 1931 seasons, and Bienvenida fought frequently during those seasons. But the string of failures in July caused Hemingway to retain his suspicions about Bienvenida, as he did about Domingo Ortega, the two top-ranked bullfighters of 1931.

Hemingway, Bienvenida, and Agrarian Reform. Hemingway argues that Manolo Bienvenida performed poorly because he was more worried about the damage being done to his houses and lands back home than he was about the bulls he had been contracted to kill in Pamplona (*DIA*, 251). There may be some truth to this. Thanks to Pepe's and especially Manolo's success, the Bienvenidas had recently become important landowners. By 1931 they had a house in the city of Seville; a *finca* called San Rafael, in Dos Hermanas (Seville); and another property, "La Gloria," also in Dos Hermanas, which included a large house, several outbuildings, olive groves, pasture for a few bulls, and a small bullring. Like most landowners, they suffered losses in the pilferage and riots against landowners that accompanied the Spanish Republic's attempts at Agrarian Reform (q.v.).[408]

The narrator accurately summarizes Manolo Bienvenida's early career, reporting that in his second season as *matador de toros* (1930) Bienvenida was triumphant and he was hailed as "the local Redeemer of bullfighting" (166–68). The narrator claims he will not make up his mind about Manolo until after he has endured his first goring, although he undercuts this wait-and-see attitude with his thoroughly negative remark, "I do not believe in this particular Messiah" (167; *see also* 166, 171). Meanwhile, he finds him to be excellent with the banderillas (200) and the muleta (215) but cowardly and ineffective as a killer (249–50; photograph, *h:* 376–77, 390–91). He is obviously not impressed with Bienvenida's 1931 season (249–52).

Mejías, Manuel (Manolo Bienvenida, el Papa Negro). Full name: Manuel Mejías Rapela. Spanish bullfighter, 1884–1964. Investiture as *matador de toros*, in Zaragoza, October 1905; confirmed in Madrid, March 1906.

The son and brother of bullfighters, Manolo Bienvenida was, like his sons after him, a child prodigy. In his years as *novillero* (1902–05) he was recognized as an outstanding performer; he was the top-ranked *novillero* of 1905.

Manolo Bienvenida's first seasons as *matador de toros* were controversial. He was graceful and skilled but his occasional deficiencies at the important moment of the kill troubled his public. Although he had resounding successes in Madrid, he performed seldom and with less enthusiasm in the provinces; much of his reputation, therefore, was based on hearsay.

The next few years were uneven. In 1907 he fought a respectable twenty-nine corridas, but none in the important plazas of Madrid and Seville. In 1908 the number grew to thirty-three, including appearances in all the important bullrings. In this year, he also improved his sword work a good deal. In 1909 the number decreased to twenty-eight, almost all of them lackluster, but in the spring of 1910 his performances were again so magnificent that he was nicknamed *el Papa Negro* (the Black Pope, the title often given to the black-garbed head of the Jesuits, so powerful in the Catholic hierarchy as to be second only to *el papa*, the pope) to distinguish him from Ricardo Torres Reina (Bombita, q.v.), called "the pope" of the taurine "church," both because of his authoritative performances and because of his various campaigns to improve conditions for bullfighters.[409]

On 10 July of 1910, after twenty spectacular corridas in what was shaping up to be his best season, Bienvenida attempted a solo corrida in Madrid. The third bull of the afternoon, Viajero, ripped and tore the bullfighter's left leg so vehemently that the leg pained Bienvenida for the rest of his life. Cossío, who (like most taurine critics) does not share Hemingway's belief that the first goring is decisive, does indicate that in this case, the Madrid goring, which happened to be

Manolo's first, marked a downward turn in a promising career. Hemingway focuses on the psychological and emotional consequences of the first goring, but clearly, a bullfighter with a weakened leg is at a serious physical disadvantage.[410]

Bienvenida's career certainly declined after this. He lost the rest of the 1910 season, and although the thirty-one corridas of 1911 included a few great ones, the year's summary acknowledged a general decline in quality. He began the 1912 season with a fine success in Madrid early in April, which quickly translated into fifty-six contracts, but was soon again gored, in the same place where Viajero had done so much damage, and had to cancel many appearances. When he returned to Madrid, on 26 May, his leg failed him and he was seriously gored again: his total for the season of 1912 was eighteen corridas. Bienvenida's financial situation was so precarious that he had to continue performing, but he had lost all hope of fame: he had only twenty-four corridas in 1913, seventeen in 1914, and six in 1915. In 1917 he left Spain for South America, where he continued to perform, although he spent more and more time educating and managing his sons, five of whom became matadors (*see also* Manager). He returned to Spain for one performance in 1924; it was his last corrida. The next generation of Bienvenidas brought the family wealth and success; see Mejías, José (Pepe) and Mejías, Manolo, in this volume; see also Mejías Jiménez, Antonio in *DS*.

> The narrator describes Manolo Bienvenida as an old-fashioned matador whose first goring "deflated" him (167). He adds that Bienvenida educated his three sons (*sic*; *see* Bienvenida) in the arts of bullfighting, having them perform widely in Mexico, France, and South America before bringing them to Madrid (165).

Mella. *See* Manzanares, Joachin.

Las Meninas. *See* Velázquez.

Mercédes. Correct spelling: Mercedes. Mercedes was Sidney Franklin's (q.v.) Spanish cook, who "always prepared enough for six or eight guests who dropped in at almost every meal." On the day Franklin met Hemingway, he invited him home for lunch. The meal Mercedes served them lasted "five and a half hours." Franklin praises her as "one of the most wonderful cooks in the country, and Spain is noted for her good cooks."[411]

The narrative correctly identifies Mercedes as a servant of the American bullfighter Sidney Franklin (277).

Mérida, Andrés. Full name: Andrés Leiva Mérida. Spanish bull-fighter, 1905–39. Investiture as *matador de toros* in Seville, April 1930; confirmed in Madrid, October 1930; renounced late in 1934 or 1935.

As a *novillero*, Mérida attracted considerable attention, thanks to some spectacular performances in 1925 and 1926. These were probably his best two seasons: he was ranked seventh among *novilleros* in 1925, with twenty-five *novilladas*, and fifteenth in 1926, with eighteen *novilladas*. It soon became clear, however, that his failures were as spectacular as his successes, so that the public and, more damagingly, the managers of taurine affairs became wary of him. The negative impression was strengthened by the seasons of 1927 (eleven *novilladas*, all lackluster) and 1928 (thirteen unimpressive *novilladas*). In 1929 he seems to have exerted himself, and after fifteen *novilladas*, some quite impressive, he was promoted to *matador de toros* early in the 1930 season.

At this rank Mérida also give dispirited, disappointing performances: eleven in 1930, three in 1931, and only one a year for 1932, 1933, and 1934, in which year he was wounded and was unable to kill his bull. After this failure he renounced his *alternativa* (q.v.) and in 1935 fought as a *novillero*. The outbreak of the Spanish Civil War ended his career at this rank.[412]

Hemingway is more generous to Mérida than other taurine critics, who had washed their hands of him long before his promotion. Even in 1925 the critic Tomás Orts Ramos (Uno al Sesgo) remarked upon "una desigualdad grande" (a great unevenness) in his performances which boded ill for his future.[413] The usually generous Cossío dismisses him as uneven, unreliable, and disappointing, agreeing with Hemingway that at times he displayed great fear. Bagüés says flatly that "algunos creyeron que iba a ser algo, pero sufrieron un error" (some people thought he was going to amount to something, but they were wrong).[414]

Mérida's father was a gypsy.

The narrator correctly identifies Mérida as a matador from Málaga, perhaps a gypsy, who was active (though barely) in 1931. The narrator praises his cape and muleta work and remarks upon his "completely absentminded air in the ring." Like Cagancho, he succumbs to fear and is an erratic performer (223).

Merino, Félix. Full name: Félix Merino Obanos. Spanish bullfighter, 1894–1927. Investiture as *matador de toros*, in Madrid, October 1917; renounced in 1925.

Merino was born into a middle-class family with no taurine interests or connections, but his *afición* was strong and his art sufficient to convince people in his native Valladolid to sponsor *novilladas* for him. He began modestly, with three or four *novilladas* a year, from 1914 to 1917, all in minor plazas in and around Valladolid. By the end of the 1917 season, he had matured sufficiently to warrant an *alternativa* (q.v.), unwillingly conceded by Joselito and witnessed by Belmonte.

Although Merino excelled in cape work, his career was, on the whole, disappointing: seven corridas in 1918, although in major plazas; nine corridas in 1919, with some success, which led to seventeen contracts in 1920, his most successful year. The numbers declined so dramatically that he renounced the rank of *matador de toros* in 1925, performing as *matador de novillos* in 1926 (fifteen *novilladas*) and 1927 (six *novilladas*). On 4 October 1927 he was gored and died soon after, apparently from infection in the wound.[415] By the time Hemingway came to Spain to see his first bullfights, in 1923, Merino was already in decline.[416]

The narrator remembers Merino and wishes he could include him in his book (272).

Mexican Feather Work. The museum at the monastery of San Lorenzo de El Escorial (q.v.) houses a bishop's mitre decorated with scenes of the Passion and Resurrection of Christ that are worked in tropical bird feathers ("mosaico de plumas," feather mosaic). The exquisite feather work, which completely covers the red silk background, permits great detail (drops of blood on the body of Christ, ragged fringes to his loincloth). The color gold predominates, probably from the gold thread used to attach the feathers to the silk. Some of the feathers may be gilded.

Spanish colonizers, much impressed by Aztec feather art, sent several samples to their aristocratic patrons back home. Philip II (q.v.) commissioned this particle mitre. Today it is in such delicate condition that it is seldom displayed.[417]

> The narrator pays a graceful compliment to Rafael Gómez Ortega (el Gallo, q.v.) when he compares his work to the delicacy of the antique Mexican feather work held by the museum at El Escorial (159).

Mexicans. In Hemingway's day, Mexican *alternativas* (q.v.: promotions to the rank of *matador de toros*) were not valid in Spain, and Mexican bullfighters often had difficulty obtaining contracts in the jealous, competitive world of the Spanish bullfight. A few Mexican bullfighters did manage to succeed in Spain; many more worked in *cuadrillas*. In 1931 Tomás Orts Ramos (Uno al Sesgo) wrote of David Liceaga that "Como todos los mexicanos es un excelente banderillero" (like all Mexicans he is an excellent banderillero),[418] a generalization Hemingway repeats with his comment about "the overwhelming excellence of all Mexican bullfighters with the banderillas" (*DIA*, 198).

The beginning of the Mexican bullfight season overlaps with the end of the Spanish one and lasts until April. Today as in Hemingway's day, Spanish bullfighters who wish to work the winter months do so in Mexico, Venezuela, Peru, and other Latin American countries. Since disabling gorings may end a career suddenly and without warning, bullfighters are under pressure to make as much money as possible in their good years.

> The narrator praises Mexican banderilleros (198; *see also* 224, 225), mentions several Mexican bullfighters (Fermín and Juan Espinosa, Luis Freg, Rodolfo Gaona, Heriberto García, José González, David Liceaga, Jesús Solórzano, qq.v.), refers to a Mexican politician (Porfirio Díaz, q.v.), gives some details about the Mexican season (477–79, 484–85; *see also* 37, 226), distinguishes between Indian and non-Indian Mexicans (75, 163, 220, 224), and states that Sidney Franklin was trained by a Mexican bullfighter, Rodolfo Gaona (*h:* 504).

Miguel, San. The Archangel Michael, traditionally represented as a prince or warrior, is credited with the defeat of Satan. His feast day, Michaelmas, is September 29.

In describing the bullfight calendar, Hemingway correctly points out that bullfights honoring San Miguel are held in Seville, late in September (*h:* 513).

Milan. *See* Munition Factory.

Miró, Joan. Spanish (Catalan) surrealist painter, 1893–1983.

Miró came to Paris in 1919 and affiliated himself with the Dadaists. In 1925 he exhibited with the surrealists and was acclaimed by the critic Bernard Dorival as "the best and perhaps the only great painter" of the group. When Paris fell to the Germans in 1940, Miró returned to Spain, then ruled by Franco; in 1947 he went to the United States. His paintings are abstract, full of bright color and humor. Famous canvases include *The Farm* (1922), *The Tilled Field* (1924), *Dog Barking at the Moon* (1926), and *Women and Kite among the Constellations* (1939). Miró is also noted for book illustrations, prints, tapestries, ballet designs, and two pairs of huge mosaic murals: *Night* and *Day*, and *Sun* and *Moon*, the latter two at the UNESCO building in Paris.

Miró's The Farm: In about 1910, Miró's father bought a country house just outside Montroig del Camp, in his native Tarragona, in southern Cataluña, where the family spent most of its summers. Miró frequently painted the city and landscapes of Montroig, including his family's and neighbors' old-fashioned country houses: *Montroig, Sant Ramon*, 1916; *Hort amb ase*, 1918; *La casa de la Palmera* (*The Farm-House with the Palm Tree*), 1918; *Poble i església de Montroig* (*Town and Church of Montroig*), 1919. The famous large oil painting, *La masia* (*The Farm*, 123 × 147 cm, 1921–22), has been described as "the culmination of his early period . . . every detail is linked to the rhythm of the shapes surrounding it, reminiscent of the arabesques and bold calligraphy found in the Spanish peasant tradition . . . The innovative achievement of this painting [resides in] the linking of . . . folk painting to the simplification of form urged by cubism." The critic Ramón Barnils writes that the painting not only summarizes painting styles but also catalogues a vanishing lifestyle by presenting a realistic, literal inventory of the everyday items necessary for life in an isolated country house. He reports that Miró, working on the painting in Paris, had his family send him a package of grasses from home, to wipe out the influence of the greenery of the Bois du Boulogne.[419]

Miró himself gives a long, somewhat different account of the composition of the painting: "I began that painting in Montroig . . . in the days when I used to work out-of-doors—like Cézanne, in fact . . . Everything you see was actually there, even if I made changes or jumps in scale and rearranged things here and there. When a cactus interested me, for instance, I made it as big as a tree trunk, and when I wanted to show the inside of the chicken coop, I just left out the wire netting. It took me nine months, that painting—and I worked at it eight hours a day, like a farm laborer. I began it at Montroig, went on with it in Barcelona, and finished it in Paris. I even took grasses from Montroig to Paris in an envelope to make sure that I got it right. They dried up, so I had to go to the Bois de Boulogne and pick up some more.

"No one liked the picture in Paris. I was very poor, but I would take it in a taxi to dealers, and then I'd have to take another taxi to get it home again. Paul Rosenberg said, 'Why don't you cut it into several pieces? People don't have room for such a big picture nowadays.' Then Ernest Hemingway bought it—for pennies actually, but he really did like it very much."[420]

Hemingway and the Farm. Sean O'Rourke writes that Ezra Pound introduced Hemingway to Miró's work, and Michael Reynolds suggests that Hemingway bought the painting on the advice of Gertrude Stein, but Hemingway's own account of his acquisition of the painting, written a decade after the fact and probably romanticized, doesn't give either of them any credit. Instead, Hemingway writes that "[Evan] Shipman, who found him [Miró] the dealer, made the dealer put a price on it and agree to sell it to him. This was probably the only good business move that Shipman ever did in his life. But doing a good business move must have made him uncomfortable because he came to me the same day and said, 'Hem, you should have *The Farm.* I do not love anything as much as you care for that picture and you ought to have it.'

"I argued against this explaining to him that it was not only how much I cared about it. There was the value to consider. . . . So we rolled dice and I won and made the first payment."

At this point of the story Shipman offers a different account, claiming that they tossed a coin for it and that Shipman won, but that "When I saw Ernest still felt worse about than I would have if I had lost, I said: 'Ernest you can have it.' " Hemingway was obviously sensitive to the painting's emotional content: "It has in it all that you feel about Spain when you are there and all that you feel when you are away and cannot go there. . . . I would not trade it for any picture in the world." Hemingway recalls that Miró saw the picture in Hemingway's apartment and approved of its owner: " 'I am very content that you have *The Farm.*' "[421]

Hemingway's claim that he bought *The Farm* in 1925 as a birthday present for Hadley is supported by the fact that he gave it to her when they separated in 1926. He "borrowed" the painting from her in 1934 and kept it for the rest of his life; it was obviously one of his favorites. Early in 1959, after extended correspondence, Hemingway gave permission for *The Farm* to be shipped to the Museum of Modern Art, New York, for a Miró exhibit. The artist and the museum's restorer discovered that the painting was "in extremely poor condition" and "should be treated as soon as possible." Hemingway agreed to the restoration, which took considerable time. In September the status of the painting was changed to "extended loan" to the Museum of Modern Art.[422] Hemingway's widow Mary claimed it upon his death and donated it to the National Gallery of Art, Washington, D.C., in 1987.

The Farm and *Death in the Afternoon.* Like Miró's painting, *Death in the Afternoon* is a nostalgic, detailed catalogue that attempts to capture a disappearing way of life. The political upheaval (the ousting of King Alfonso XIII and the rise of the republic) necessarily affected all aspects of Spain's cultural life. Spain's more European outlook strengthened the opponents of the bullfight (see *Peto*). Hemingway feared that bullfighting as he knew it was disappearing. He intended his description of it to stand as a record "for anyone who should ever be interested in knowing what it was like."[423]

Like Miró, Hemingway needed distance from his subject (he wrote about Spain while in the United States), and he also needed to freshen sense and memory through physical contact: between 1923, when he saw his first bullfight, and 1932, when *Death in the Afternoon* was published, Hemingway attended the bullfights every season but two: seven seasons in nine years. *Death in the Afternoon* is also a highly self-conscious catalogue of the various genres Hemingway had attempted separately in the past (e.g., journalism, short fiction, novels, poetry) and an expansion into new areas, such as lexicography, criticism, and biography. It shows its author attempting to define and explain his own art—hence the many references to the art of writing (2–3, 190–92, 278; *see also* 20, 52–54, 63, 122, 173, 269, *h:* 506), to other writers (*see* Authors), and to other arts (sculpture, painting, architecture). Like *The Farm*, then, Hemingway's *Death in the Afternoon* is both a summary and a new beginning.

Ernest and Hadley Hemingway planned to visit Joan Miró and his wife, Pilar Juncosa de Miró, in July 1926, but the visit was canceled when Miró's father died suddenly.[424] Hemingway did visit the Mirós in 1929, as recounted in *Death in the Afternoon*, and the Hemingways and the Mirós maintained friendly relations over the years; Hemingway received letters and cards from Joan and Pilar Miró in the 1930s, 1940s, and 1950s.

In 1959, after months of negotiation about insurance and transportation, Hemingway lent *The Farm* for the Miró exhibit, which ran from mid-March to 10 May 1959. On 30 April Miró wrote Ernest and Mary to arrange a meeting in New York, but by then the Hemingways had already sailed for Spain.

Hemingway drove to Miró's farm during that summer of 1959, but the Mirós were not in residence and the Hemingways were denied admittance by the caretakers, one of whom, Hemingway claimed, remembered him.[425]

Miró's daughter recalls her mother's speaking of the Hemingways' pleasant visit. She says that wooden barrels, not "earthen jars," were used to store wine. She also reports that the woman and the girl who killed the duck were probably the wife and daughter of the farmer who cared for the Miró vines and gardens; this is probably the woman who recognized Hemingway, remembering his earlier visit. The house and lands still belong to the family.[426]

Hemingway mentions Miró in *Islands in the Stream* (71) and in the preface to *A Moveable Feast*.

The narrator recalls his visit to Miró's farm (275–76).

Miura, don Eduardo. Recurring name in this family of Spanish bull breeders.

The Founder: Juan Miura Rodríguez. In 1841, the wealthy hat-maker and landowner Juan Miura established the family's first ranch in Seville. He presented his bulls to be fought under his brand and colors (scarlet and black) in Madrid for the first time at a corrida held on 30 April 1849 (still the date of their *antigüedad*, or seniority). Among the more important of his acquisitions were the lots of Cabrera stock he bought in 1850 and 1852; he crossed these with two Saavedra seed bulls in 1854.[427] Juan Miura died in 1860, and his widow, who inherited the ranch, died the following year.

Juan's Older Son, Antonio. In 1861, Antonio Miura, who had managed the holdings during the last years of his parents' lives, became the owner of the ranch and the official head of the family. A careful breeder, he tested his cows thoroughly and was wary of change. Still, it was under his tutelage that Navarrese blood entered the herd, via Murciélago, fought by Rafael Molina (Lagartijo, q.v.) in 1879 and given an *indulto* (pardon, i.e., allowed to live) because Lagartijo thought the bull was too brave to be killed: Antonio Miura acquired the bull. He also introduced a Veragua seed bull, though that cross-breeding had minimal effects, and another seed bull may have come from the Conde de la Corte (q.v.). After more than forty years of careful management, don Antonio died in 1893.

Juan's Younger Son, Eduardo. Antonio's brother and heir, Eduardo Miura, held the ranch, brand, colors, and *antigüedad* for about two decades, from the close of the nineteenth century until he died in 1917.

Don Eduardo's Sons: Antonio and José. When don Eduardo's sons, Antonio and José Miura Hontoria, inherited the Miura holdings in 1917, they kept the property in their father's name, calling themselves the "señores hijos de don Eduardo Miura" (sons of Eduardo Miura). They crossed the herd with Tamarón seed bulls (these were Parladé, representing the more pliable Vistahermosa strain), but *Toros y toreros en 1931* remarks that they quickly abandoned this attempt to reform the herd. This is probably the crossbreeding to which Hemingway refers.

After 1940. In 1940 or 1941, the two brothers ceded all rights to the herd to Antonio's son, Eduardo Miura Fernández (1914–96), who managed the family enterprise for more than fifty years. For an evaluation of the bulls under Eduardo's stewardship, see Miura in *DS*. Don Eduardo gradually turned over some aspects of the business to his sons, Eduardo and Antonio José Miura Martínez. This youngest Eduardo now represents the family.

Thus, the breed has been under the Miura family's control from its inception. Vera describes it as "la vacada más famosa de todos los tiempos" (the most famous herd or breed of all time).[428] The most recent book about the Miuras is José María Sotomayor's *Miura: Siglo y medio de casta 1842–1992* (Madrid: Espasa-Calpe, 1992). Earlier books include José Carralero Burgos's *Los toros de la muerte, o sea la ganadería de D. Eduardo Miura* (Madrid, 1909) and Enrique Vila's two volumes: *Miuras: Cien años de gloria y de tragedia* (Seville, 1941) and *Miuras: Más de cien años de tragedia y gloria* (Madrid: Escelicer, 1968). All these books discuss the family, the *ganadería*, the several bullfighters killed by Miura bulls, great performances featuring Miuras, the boycott of the Miuras, and the Miura colors.

The Miura Colors. The Miuras are unique in that they perform under two sets of colors: scarlet and black in Madrid and scarlet and green elsewhere. According to one story, when don Antonio brought his bulls to Madrid on 20 April 1862, he wanted to use the colors green and black. But another bull breeder was already displaying these colors, and so don Antonio chose scarlet and green (or, according to Sotomayor, scarlet and lilac) for his bulls. A more romantic but less accurate story reports that the black in the Madrid colors is a sign of mourning for the matador José Rodríguez (Pepete, 1824–62), killed by the Miura bull Jocinero during don Antonio's inaugural Madrid corrida.[429] For more detail about the death of Pepete, see endnote 251 in this volume.

The Miura Boycott. The Cabrera and Veragua blood made the Miuras so strong, aggressive, and fierce that in 1908 many bullfighters, led by the stars of the day, Ricardo Torres Reina (Bombita) and, less enthusiastically, by Rafael González Madrid (Machaquito, q.v.), demanded higher wages for matadors when they fought Miuras. This is the so-called *pleito de los Miura* (the Miura dispute or boycott). To their surprise, Indalecio Mosquera (q.v.), the manager of the Madrid ring, stood firm against the powerful bullfighters' demands. As a result, the striking bullfighters did not appear in Madrid for two seasons, during which other bullfighters, including Rafael Gómez Ortega (el Gallo), Rodolfo Gaona, and Vicente Pastor (qq.v.) had freer access to the Madrid bullring, where they ostentatiously fought the dreaded Miuras and thus advanced their careers. At about the same time, a different kind of boycott was called against the Veraguas: bullfighters refused to fight them, complaining that they did not respond well to the muleta. The Veraguas responded by exiting from the taurine world in which they had lived for almost a century (*see* Veragua, Duke of). One effect of "el pleito de los Miura" and "la cuestión de los Veragua" was an addendum to the statutes of the *Unión de criadores de toros de lidia* that stipulates that none of its members would provide corridas for any bullfighter who boycotts any one of its members (a reverse boycott).[430]

Victims of Miura Bulls. José Rodríguez (Pepete), fatally gored in Madrid on 20 April 1862, was the first Miura victim. Probably the most famous bullfighters killed by Miuras are Manuel García (el Espartero, q.v.), killed by Perdigón on 27 May 1894; and, years after the publication of *Death in the Afternoon*, Manuel Rodríguez (Manolete, see in *DS*), gored by Islero on 28 August 1947. Two of these victims, Pepete and Manolete, were members of the same family. Hemingway mentions Pedro Carreño, killed in 1930, but does not identify the *novillo* as a Miura.[431] Typically fast learners, Miuras come to understand the difference between the *engaño* (the deceitful lure that takes the bull away from the man) and the person wielding it. This sense, or *sentido*, makes them fearsome opponents. Although other breeds have claimed more victims, the Miuras inspire more than the usual fear.

Hemingway and Miuras. Hemingway undoubtedly saw many generations of Miuras. The difficult corrida of Miuras he saw in Pamplona (*DIA*, 154) were unloaded on 4 July 1925 and fought on 8 July 1925 (they needed time to recover from their long journey). The local taurine reviewer described them as big but not particularly brave. They may be famous and expensive, he wrote, but let Miura keep them. Although they were a disappointment in the ring, they had provided plenty of excitement during that morning's 6:00 A.M. *encierro*, almost goring two young men on Calle Estafeta.[432] *See also* Cabrera;

Saavedra; Passchendaele; Veragua. For the later history of the Miuras, see *DS*.

The narrator accuses don Eduardo Miura's sons of attempting to breed
some of the deadliness out of their famous Miura bulls (129–30; Miuras
are also mentioned on pages 45, 132, 154; photograph, *h:* 334).

Mojigangas. These are pantomimes and comic performances presented in the bullring, as lighthearted interludes between bullfights.
Based on historical, folklore, literary, and other motifs, they featured
clowns, dwarves, musicians, and trained animals. Sometimes a *novillo* was worked into the end of the routine, and sometimes the entire
routine was combined with bullfighting to produce *toreo bufo*. *Mojigangas* were offered at afternoon shows for children or at *novilladas*,
not at *corridas de toros*, and were popular throughout the nineteenth
century. *Novilleros* who had not yet attracted a sufficient following
to appear by themselves occasionally found work with these bands.

In the twentieth century, the *charlotadas*, based on the figure and
work of Charlie Chaplin (1889–1977; known in Europe as Charlot),
drew good audiences. In 1916, the innovative impresario Eduardo
Pagés brought a trio of well-known taurine comics (Llapisera, Charlot, and Charlot's sidekick Botones) to the Madrid bullring, billing
them as a *cuadrilla* of comic bullfighters. All three were trained and
innovative bullfighters, and their performances, a parody on serious
bullfighting, spawned many imitators, like "El bombero torero,"
"Los enanos toreros," and "El guardia torero" (The bullfighting
fireman, the bullfighting dwarves, the bullfighting policeman).[433]
These differed from *mojigangas* in that the bull and the techniques
of bullfighting became the central subject of the performance. *See
also* Dutrús; *El Empastre.*

The glossary of *Death in the Afternoon* is interesting for what it
repeats from the main text, for what it adds (detailed entries on food
and drink, s.v. *Cerveza* and *Mariscos*), and for what it excludes (no
entries for gangrene or for the matador's wrist, both identified in the
text as important concerns). In his entry for *Mojiganga*, for example,
Hemingway does not make any reference to other clowns mentioned
in the text (e.g., Altrock, Fratellini, qq.v.) or to his discussions of
comedy, comic relief, and tragedy (6–9, 16, 20–21, 206–207). The
Glossary has its own jokes and wit, however: see its entries for *Abur-*

rimiento (*h:* 409), *Botellazo* (*h:* 418), *Tacones* (*h:* 481–82), and *Tal* (*h:* 482). *See also* Iceberg Theory.

The narrator presents a short discussion of comic bullfighting under the entry *Mojiganga* in "An Explanatory Glossary" (*h:* 451).

Molina Sánchez, Rafael (Lagartijo). Spanish bullfighter, 1841–1900. Investiture as matador, in Ubeda, 29 September 1865; confirmed in Madrid two weeks later.

This nineteenth-century master had one of the longest and most successful careers in the history of bullfighting: he was nine years old when he first performed, twenty-three when he was promoted to *matador de toros*, and over fifty when he retired. He performed in 1,645 corridas, although the number cannot be verified (for a discussion of what constitutes a long career, see "The Bullfighter," in the introduction to this volume).

Cossío divides Lagartijo's long career into four stages. The long apprenticeship, from about 1850 to 1865, included work in the *cuadrilla* of the Carmona brothers, Manuel and Antonio, and ended with the promotion to *matador de toros*. The struggle to reach the top, from 1865 to about 1871, included performances with and challenges to the famous bullfighters of his day, such as Antonio Sánchez (el Tato, 1831–95); his former sponsor, Antonio Carmona (el Gordito, c. 1838–1920); and the older masters, Francisco Arjona (Cúchares, 1818–68) and Cayetano Sanz (q.v.). This period was marked by some brash behavior both in and out of the ring. By 1868 Lagartijo considered himself the undisputed master: el Tato had been forced to retire because of a serious goring; Antonio Carmona had been vanquished; the older Cayetano Sanz was clearly in decline; and Cúchares died that year. 1868 also marks the first joint appearance of Lagartijo and his contemporary Salvador Sánchez (Frascuelo, q.v.); their two-decade long rivalry dates from that first meeting.

During Lagartijo's championship years, the 1870s and early 1880s, Frascuelo was his only serious rival. Lagartijo was a great favorite in Madrid, which forgave him the occasional poor performance and even the absence, for the whole 1886 season, from its bullring. He was, however, unpopular in Seville.

In the many years during which he shared top billing with Frascuelo, Lagartijo produced only occasional poor performances. He was a brave, elegant, proud matador, skillful and artistic in all aspects of the fight. His method of killing (taking a step back before moving forward to meet the bull in the *volapié*) was first criticized and then widely imitated: it was called a *media lagartijera*. But as he grew older he took fewer chances, doing the old spectacular passes only when the bull presented less danger.

The fourth period of his career, the decline, began in the mid-1880s. By this time, he had spent almost forty years fighting bulls, half of them as a *matador de toros*. Frascuelo had retired in 1889, but Lagartijo, still ambitious and bellicose, attempted to maintain his position against the younger crop of matadors, in the forefront of whom stood Guerra (whom Lagartijo attempted to kill in a café in 1891), Mazzantini, and Fernando Gómez (qq.v.). But even though his performances became increasingly erratic, Lagartijo refused to retire until 1893, by which time his reputation was in tatters. The public which had eulogized him for so many years jeered the flawed performances that were all he could offer at the end. He gave several retirement performances—in Zaragoza, Bilbao, Barcelona, Valencia and Madrid; note the absence of Seville—in which he performed solo. All of them were disasters. The Bilbao performance was such a *fracaso* (failure) that the Guardia Civil and local police had to be brought in to control the crowds. The same thing happened on 1 June, in Madrid, as Hemingway notes (*DIA*, 240).[434]

Lagartijo and Frascuelo were the reigning bullfighters of their day; both received plenty of praise during their careers. The rivalry divided the public so thoroughly that it affected the next generation: *see* entries for Rafael Guerra Bejarano (Guerrita) and Manuel García Cuesta (el Espartero), in this volume; see also Rivalry in *DS*.

> The narrator correctly defines Lagartijo as a matador of the golden age of bullfighting and mentions that although the Madrid public was hostile at his last performance (240), he was deified by the critics after his death. The narrator ranks him and his contemporary Frascuelo as the best bullfighters before José Gómez Ortega (Joselito) and Juan Belmonte (243; *see also* 247, 248).

Money. Money is a loud subtext in much of Hemingway's writing, fiction as well as nonfiction. In the world of the bulls, money is the topic of much rumor and little truth—and always worth discussing. Hemingway's narrator discusses beggars, bribes, fines, the cost of tickets, and the financial position of spectators as well as performers, their families, and the various professionals associated with the bullfight. Money also dominates Hemingway's 1930 essay "Bullfighting, Sport and Industry," published in *Fortune* magazine, and figures prominently in *The Dangerous Summer*, where the narrator frequently comments on the matadors' finances and on their ability to fill the house. In *Cuando suena el clarín* (1961), Gregorio Corrochano theorizes that these remarks about money reveal Hemingway's own worries about his finances and his public. As Hemingway's physical and mental health deteriorated, his worries about money intensified.

For a well-documented study of money and the bullfight, see Adrian Shubert's *Death and Money in the Afternoon: A History of the Spanish Bullfight*.

The narrator mentions money when discussing bullring servants (188), substitute fighters (*h:* 480, s.v. *Sobresaliente*), banderilleros (201–202, *h:* 417, s.v. *Banderillero*), picadors (185–89, *h:* 466, s.v. *Picador*), *matadores de novillos* (159, *h:* 457, s.v. *Novillero*; *h:* 504, 505), and *matadores de toros* (49–50, 78, 82, 201, 207, 222, *h:* 384, 448). Money is also an issue for spectators (29–30, 32–36, 50, 167, *h:* 480–81, s.v. *Sol y sombra*), critics (163–64), managers (168, 170), and horse contractors (57–58, 185–87, *h:* 465, s.v. *Pica*). He also speaks about writers making money (191) and about coins (*h:* 434, s.v. *Duro*; 442, s.v. *Kilos*; 479–80, s.v. *Sevillano*).

Montes, Antonio. Full name: Antonio Montes Vico. Spanish bullfighter, 1876–1907. Investiture as *matador de toros*, April 1899, in Seville; confirmed in Madrid in May.

At age eighteen, Montes realized that his profession—he was a carpenter—condemned him to lifelong poverty and, in spite of his family's opposition, he opted for bullfighting. Poverty made the apprenticeship difficult, but slowly he attracted attention and reached the first-class bullrings. As a *novillero*, in 1898, he got rave reviews for his "toreo genuinamente clásico y rondeño" (genuinely classic *toreo*, in the Ronda style [of Pedro Romero]). Audiences were surprised, however, that this disciplined, elegant torero could at times be graceless, cowardly, and awkward with the sword. The successes of

290 • MONTES, ANTONIO

1898 were followed by mediocre performances for most of 1899; even the important corrida of his promotion was marred by poor sword work.

In 1900 Montes performed in thirty-five corridas; the number fell to thirty-one in 1901, and in 1902 he again disappointed his audiences. Realizing that his career was evaporating, he avoided the stern audiences of Madrid in the 1903 season and dedicated himself to rebuilding his reputation in the Spanish provinces and in Mexico. In 1904 and 1905 he performed well, was contracted for first-class rings and did not disappoint. The next year, 1906, was his triumphant year (thirty-eight corridas, mostly to rave reviews). In January 1907 he was fighting at the top of his form in Mexico when he was gored as he killed his second bull; he died four days later.

The Mexicans gave Montes an elaborate memorial service and placed his body in Mexico's Spanish Pantheon until it could be shipped to Spain. The large memorial candles started a fire that burned his coffin and charred his body.

Hemingway and the Critics. Hemingway's simplification of the critics' treatment of bullfighters inevitably leads him into inaccuracy and error. Montes received enormous praise both as a *novillero* (in 1898) and then as a *matador de toros* (in 1905 and 1906). In the years between these two high points, however, he gave weak performances which, reasonably enough, elicited bleak reviews. But even though his successful comeback was cut short—he was thirty-one when he was killed—he had already achieved a firm reputation as a serene fighter who stood still and relied upon his cape work to control the bull. His close attention to detail and his pitched concentration may have been the result of his deafness, which forced him to rely more heavily on visual cues. Whatever the reason, his elegant cape work was certainly admired during his lifetime. Cossío quotes several contemporary critics who recognized Antonio Montes's contributions to the art of bullfighting.[435] Later critics saw his elegant cape work as foreshadowing that of Belmonte.[436]

> The narrator correctly identifies Montes as a matador working in the early twentieth century. He adds that although the bullfighter was "serious and masterly," he was not appreciated by the critics and the public until he died of a horn wound in Mexico, when he was praised as the foremost fighter of his period (241–42; *see also* 253).

Montes, Francisco. Full name: Francisco Montes Reina (Paquiro). Spanish bullfighter, 1805–51. Investiture as *matador de toros*, April 1831, in Madrid.

Montes, whose family suffered financial reverses while he was still a child, was trained as a bricklayer. Financial need combined with an early interest in bullfighting to determine the career of this great torero. He studied briefly in the newly established Real Escuela de Tauromaquia (Royal Training Institute) in Seville, where Pedro Romero commented that Montes "carecía de miedo y estaba adornado de mucho vigor en las piernas y brazos" (was fearless and was blessed with strong legs and arms).[437] His quick reflexes and fine coordination enabled him not only to rise quickly through the ranks but also to distinguish himself by performing unusual feats, such as vaulting over the bull from horn to tail. His skill with the cape developed from corrida to corrida, as he tried new and unusual combinations and variations that charmed the public. The seasons from 1832 to 1836 were sensational, Montes performing frequently and always to great acclaim.

Paquiro ran afoul of the Madrid establishment when he began to insist that he always be billed as senior matador regardless of his fellow bullfighters' date of *alternativa* (q.v.). The Madrid management attempted to exclude him from the Madrid ring, but his popularity was such that the impresarios had to back down, and Montes continued to perform, albeit less frequently, in Madrid. His performances were consistently artistic and frequently unusual. He often came into direct contact with the bull, grabbing him by the horns or the tail. In an 1839 corrida he knocked out (with his fist) an enraged bull that had refused to be distracted from a prone bullfighter he had been attacking. He was not only an agile, expert performer, but also an able master of his *cuadrilla*, which he picked carefully and used to maximum advantage. He was also a fine judge of *ganado bravo*, often being called in to settle disputes about the age and fitness of bulls.

Paquiro's energetic performances, demanding schedule, and almost constant travel began to take their toll. In the mid-1840s he suffered several minor gorings; his drinking also increased markedly. In 1845, 1846, and 1847 he accepted fewer and fewer engagements, in order to reduce the travel, the strain, and the possibility of failure. He retired in 1848 and attempted to start a business, but financial difficulties returned him to the ring in 1850. He was received with great pomp and enthusiasm and gave fine performances until he was gored in the lower part of the left leg, in July 1850. He recovered very slowly from this wound, suffering several setbacks and infections. The injury seems to have weakened his system; he never fought again, and he died less than a year later.

Like his life, Montes's death was spectacular: there was great disagreement about whether he was really dead or not, and his burial was delayed for quite some time. Finally he was taken to the cemetery, where he was left, above ground, under the surveillance of guards. After twenty-four hours of observation in those dismal surroundings, he was finally pronounced fully dead and the funeral took place.[438]

Montes's Tauromaquia. In 1836 Montes's *Tauromaquia completa* defined his views of the art and recommended changes and improvements. The book was commissioned by and then mostly ghostwritten by Paquiro's friend and admirer, the author and taurine critic Santos López Pelegrín (Abenamar). It set down Paquiro's reformist views on the function, organization, and management of the *cuadrilla*, redesigned the torero's dress, and defined new ethics and new standards for the bullfight. The book established Paquiro as a leading theorist as well as practitioner of *toreo*.[439]

Hemingway quotes from the *Tauromaquia completa*, in which Paquiro declares that "Las condiciones indispensables al torero son: valor, ligereza y un perfecto conocimiento de su profesión. Las dos primeras nacen con el individuo, la última se adquiere" (Hemingway's translation of the first sentence is accurate. Montes's second sentence elaborates: "The first two [of these qualities] are innate; the last must be acquired."[440] In the next several paragraphs, Montes expands upon these qualities and also defines the qualities a bull must possess in order to qualify for the bullring.

Hemingway evaluates Montes's *Tauromaquia* according to his own literary criteria and defines Montes as the author (but see above). Many years later, when writing *The Dangerous Summer*, Hemingway misremembered the last part of Montes's famous dictum, saying of Dominguín that "he had the three great requisites for a matador: courage, skill in his profession and grace in the presence of the danger of death" (*TDS*, 51). Here Hemingway replaces Montes's "ligereza" (agility) with a variant of his own famous phrase, "Grace under pressure."[441] The lapse of memory and style reveals Hemingway's decline; his self-aggrandizement indicates his need to still feel himself an authority. For another important Hemingway tenet, *see* Iceberg Theory.

The narrator refers to Montes's dictum about bullfighters and applies it to pickpockets (*h:* 445, s.v. *Ligereza*; *h:* 446, s.v. *Maleante*). He admires Montes's *Tauromaquia* as being "the clearest and simplest" (*h:* 483, s.v. *Tauromachia*).

Montes, Mariano. Full name: Mariano Montes Mora. Spanish bullfighter, 1894–1926. Investiture as *matador de toros*, September 1921, in Córdoba; confirmed in Madrid, May 1922. Of the four bullfighting Montes Mora brothers, only Mariano attained the highest rank; the other three (Luis, b. 1891; Pedro, q.v.; and Jerónimo, b. 1910) were *matadores de novillos*. Both Mariano and Pedro were killed by bulls.

A very brave bullfighter, Mariano Montes attracted considerable attention as a *novillero*, performing in nineteen *novilladas* in 1919, 26 in 1920 and the same number in 1921, many of them in important plazas. One afternoon in particular won him critical approval: in August 1920, in Madrid, he was one of four bullfighters scheduled to fight eight Palha bulls. One by one the other three men were carted off to the infirmary, leaving Montes to fight and kill all eight: he left the bullring on the shoulders of screaming fans and admirers. But on the whole, Cossío remarks, Montes was an undistinguished performer. In spite of his long apprenticeship (he fought as *novillero* from 1914 to 1921), he had a limited repertoire of techniques and only a superficial understanding of the bull.

Unable to dominate the bull through skill, Montes faced enormous danger and was often injured during the final third of the corrida, when he had to get in close enough to kill. After his promotion, he fought in ten corridas in 1922, eighteen in 1924, but only six in 1925, and some of these were in France. He was more successful in Mexico and South America, where he fought a few winter seasons, but the general consensus was that "Mariano Montes no fué nunca un gran torero" (he was never a great bullfighter). He was killed on 13 June 1926 by a bull named Gallego, in Vista-Alegre (Carabanchel), Madrid, and not at Tetuán de las Victorias, as Hemingway reports (*DIA*, 272).[442]

Bullfighters who display an aggressive, even daredevil bravery (e.g., Barrera, Freg, and the early Belmonte) generally attract attention early in their careers. But if their bravery is unaccompanied by skill, personality, or art, they quickly lose their public, which doesn't enjoy seeing a matador gored. Frequent injuries also make them chancy for impresarios, as they cause too many cancellations of scheduled fights. Such "toreros machos" are too often "toreros cortos" (short in repertoire). Mariano Montes was such a bullfighter: "Un torero valiente que a donde no llega con sus conocimientos quiere llegar con su voluntad" (a brave bullfighter who attempts to succeed by force of will instead of skill).[443]

> The narrator, who erroneously claims that Mariano Montes was killed in Tetuán, wishes he could discuss this bullfighter more fully (272). He mentions his brother Pedro Montes.

Montes, Pedro. Full name: Pedro Montes Mora. Spanish bullfighter, 1905–30.

This *novillero* appeared in Madrid for the first time shortly after his older brother Mariano had been killed in the ring. He also was a brave but unskilled fighter; his career was already in decline when he was fatally gored on 25 July 1930, at a *novillada* in Escalona, outside Toledo. He had been awarded an ear for his work with the first *novillo*. The second *novillo*, named Español, injured a banderillero before goring Pedro fatally: the horn entered the right thigh, destroying the femoral artery, and extended into the abdomen. The announcement that Pedro had died came during the *lidia* of the third *novillo*, and the *novillada* was canceled by public demand. Pedro's two surviving brothers witnessed the fatal goring: Luis had been serving his brother as banderillero, and Jerónimo was a spectator.[444]

The fates of Mariano and Pedro Montes recall Hemingway's story "The Undefeated," in which a bullfighter contemplates the stuffed bull's head in the impresario's office: "He felt a certain family interest in it. It had killed his brother, the promising one."

> The narrator accurately defines Pedro as a "brave, awkward" bullfighter whose brother Mariano was killed. He adds that when Mariano was killed

Pedro promised his mother that he would retire; he did not keep that promise (272).

Moreno Ardanuy, don Félix. Spanish bull breeder, d. 1960.

In 1918 don Félix, who already owned several herds, acquired another one: he bought it from the Marquis of Saltillo, whose father had bought it in the early 1850s from Pedro José Picavea de Lesaca (q.v.). The herd's brand (a circle enclosing two horizontal parallel lines), colors (sky blue and white), and *antigüedad* (q.v.), or seniority (14 July 1845) were established under Lesaca's heirs, under whose expert tutelage, the herd maintained its fine reputation; they had become almost pure Vistahermosa (q.v.).

 Unfortunately, the Lesaca herd and its seniority came to be owned by the son of the Marquis of Saltillo who had originally bought the herd in 1854. This later Marquis de Saltillo was a careless breeder who kept poor records, and the fine Lesaca herd deteriorated rapidly. When he died, his widow sold the herd to don Félix Moreno Ardanuy, considered one of the most intelligent and knowledgeable bull breeders of Andalucía, and he carefully restored it to its former glory. In the first years of his ownership, he slaughtered more than half of the four hundred cows that had comprised the herd when he acquired it in 1918. In 1931, when he presented twenty-seven bulls and nine *novillos* to be fought, most of them obtained good marks and some won prizes.

Félix Moreno Ardanuy owned the Lesaca-Saltillo herd from 1918 until his death in 1960, leaving his heirs in possession of a very prestigious property, much in demand by bullfighters and bull breeders. A portion of the herd was transferred to Mexico, where it quickly became one of that country's leading herds. Don Félix's son, Félix Moreno de la Cova, is currently (1998) the owner of the herd, whose *antigüedad* still dates from 14 July 1845.[445]

For a curious incident involving one of Félix Moreno's bulls, *see* Márquez, Antonio. Don Félix's wife, Enriqueta de la Cova (q.v.), also owned an important herd.

The narrative correctly identifies don Félix Moreno as an important bull breeder from Seville (132).

Mosquera, don Indalecio. Impresario of the Madrid bullring, c. 1850–1928.

Mosquera managed the large old Madrid bullring at the Carretera de Aragón in the first decade of the twentieth century. He was a canny businessman, "aunque sin saber una palabra de toros" (although he knew nothing about bulls), who managed to put the ring on sound financial footing in the few years of his tenure.

One of Mosquera's major innovations involved the hiring of substitute bullfighters on occasions when the originally contracted bullfighter was injured and unable to perform. Formerly, the injured bullfighter himself contracted a cheap substitute, paying him and pocketing the difference between his own salary and that paid out to the substitute. After a bitter struggle with the bullfighters, Mosquera assumed control of the hiring and paying of substitutes and thus raised the quality of performances in Madrid. Joining forces with fellow-impresario Manuel Martín Retana (for many years impresario of Madrid's large plaza on the Aragón Road and later in charge of the smaller plaza at Tetuán de las Victorias), he was similarly able to defeat those bullfighters who demanded higher wages for fighting Miuras, in view of the greater danger these bulls offered and the higher prices charged to the public for corridas with Miura bulls (*see* Miura).

Unlike Domingo González (q.v.) and others who had been bullfighters before they turned to administration, Mosquera was a professional manager, whose main concern was his bullring. He was succeeded as impresario by Eduardo Pagés and Manuel Martín Retana.[446] *See also* Fulano. For more detail about the Madrid bullrings and about the size of bulls at different periods and in different cities, see "The Bullring" and "Bulls and Bullbreeding," in the introduction to this volume.

> The narrator mentions that Mosquera was a promoter of the Madrid bullring in the early twentieth century who prided himself on obtaining the biggest bulls for the Madrid ring. He argues that the critics who denigrated the bullfighters of that period (Pastor, Fuentes, Bombita, Machaquito, and Rafael Gómez Ortega) by insisting that their bulls were younger and smaller than those fought by the previous generations (Lagartijo, Frascuelo, Guerrita, Mazzantini) were wrong (241).

Mrs. A. B. *See* Bird, Sarah Costello.

Mrs. E. R. *See* Hemingway, Hadley.

Mrs. M. W. *See* Murphy, Sara.

Mrs. S. T. *See* Twysden, Mrs. Stirling.

Munition Factory. On 7 June 1918, there was an explosion at the munitions factory of the Swiss firm Sutter & Thevenot, at Bollate, a small town about twelve miles outside Milan. Thirty-five people were killed; the explosion was so violent that fourteen of the victims were dismembered.

Red Cross volunteers were sent to Bollate to help in the rescue work. Hemingway had just arrived in Milan on his way to the Italian battlefront, and his vivid description suggests that he may have gone to Bollate, or that he knew some of the volunteers who went and who told him what they had seen. A contingent of the American Red Cross attended the funeral at the Bollate cemetery.

To forestall the accusation of sabotage and arson, the Italian government immediately launched an investigation. Within twenty-four hours, the committee of inquiry declared the explosion an accident.[447]

The narrator describes the terrible aftermath of the explosion at a munition factory near Milan (135–36).

Muñoz, Bernard[o] (Carnicerito). Full name: Bernardo Muñoz Marín. Spanish bullfighter, 1895–1969. Investiture as *matador de toros*, August 1920, in his native Málaga; confirmed in Madrid, October 1920. As his nickname indicates, his family were butchers.

Muñoz's *afición* showed itself early, and as a boy he attracted the patronage of the powerful bull-breeding house of Domecq. At age sixteen he was performing as a *novillero*, and as word spread, he was invited to appear in increasingly important plazas, finally making his Madrid debut in 1915. In 1918 he fought in thirty-seven *novilladas*; the number increased to forty in 1919 and after twenty-eight more *novilladas* in 1920 he was promoted, adding fourteen *corridas de toros* to the season's tally. This was his most successful season, with some remarkable performances, including the one of 6 June, in Madrid, where he was tossed, bumped, and generally thrown about by the bull, who ripped his suit but somehow did not injure him. His *cuadrilla* wrapped him in a cape, took him to the infirmary where he was pronounced capable of continuing the fight, and found him some clothes in which to resume the performance. The fans were beside themselves.

In 1921 Muñoz performed twenty-one times, participating in another dramatic event: on the afternoon of the confirmation of his *alternativa* (q.v.), both his fellow fighters, Luis Freg and José Roger Serrano (Valencia), were injured. Although Muñoz was still recovering from an injury sustained only a few days earlier, he killed four of the afternoon's six bulls. But his luck turned sour that year. The next year he had only seven corridas, only one in 1923 (the year in which Hemingway saw his first bullfights), and six in 1924.

Then the numbers began to improve, though not spectacularly: eleven appearances in 1925, thirteen in 1926, fifteen in 1927, ten in 1928, and fourteen in 1929—all very respectable. During these years he had also been building up a solid reputation in South America, being particularly popular in Venezuela and Peru. But in 1926 rumors circulated that he was accepting employment in *novilladas*, and in 1927 he was castigated in print for this behavior.[448]

In 1929, as in 1921, Muñoz was left alone in the ring with more than his normal share of bulls. He had been engaged as a *sobresaliente* (substitute or backup bullfighter) for Luis Freg, who was going to give a solo performance. Freg was injured early in the afternoon, and Muñoz killed all six Palha bulls by himself.[449] That afternoon brought him valuable publicity but did not really revive his faltering career, especially as Muñoz arrived late in Spain for the 1930 season, after canceling several of his contracts. Even so, his eleven corridas that year were successful enough to land him fifteen contracts for 1931. Again, Muñoz failed to capitalize on these achievements: he absented himself from Spain in 1932, preferring to spend that year in Venezuela. As a result, he had only four Spanish corridas in 1933 and the same number in 1934. The number rose to six in 1935, the year in which he resigned the rank of matador.

From then on, Muñoz worked as a banderillero. In this profession he was not particularly successful either, and was reduced to freelancing, mostly for *novilleros*. He did finally achieve a good position, in the *cuadrilla* of Manuel Rodríguez (Manolete, see in *DS*), being present at Linares when that famous matador was killed in 1947.[450]

Muñoz had a long, respectable, but far from brilliant career as a bullfighter. By 1931, Hemingway's last year in Spain before the publication of *Death in the Afternoon*, he had been a *matador de toros* for a decade, and his best years were clearly behind him.

> The narrator accurately defines Muñoz as having been a promising young matador who although "really brave" did not achieve greatness because of his insufficient repertoire and his lack of "artistic ability" (224).

Murphy, Sara. Full name: Sara Sherman Wiborg Murphy, 1883–1975.

Both Sara and her husband, Gerald (1888–1964), came from well-established, rich families; they married at the end of 1915. Opting for an artistic lifestyle (Gerald was a painter), the Murphys spent most of the 1920s in France, where they befriended the Picassos, the Mac-Leishes, the Hemingways, the Fitzgeralds, Donald Ogden Stewart, John Dos Passos, and other painters and writers. They expended a great deal of time, energy, and money to make their and their friends' lives pleasant. Their home, Villa America, saw a constant stream of visitors.

Sara Murphy as Mother. The Murphy's three children were born in quick succession: Honoria in 1917, Baoth in 1919, and Patrick in 1920. Baoth died suddenly in 1935, of meningitis following an attack of measles, and Patrick died of tuberculosis in 1937, after many years of illness. Sara always worried about her children's health, even before Patrick was diagnosed. In her adulatory biography of her parents, the sole surviving child, Honoria, concedes that "If there is anything about our upbringing that might be faulted, it is that we were overprotected. Mother . . . was excessively afraid of germs, and she went to extremes to protect us from them. . . . My father supported my mother . . . I would have to admit that we had a sheltered childhood."[451] When Hadley and her son visited the Murphys in June 1926, they were isolated from the Murphy family because Bumby had whooping cough, and Sara was afraid for her children. Hemingway's remark that Sara was a "very good mother" may veil his displeasure at her quarantine of his family.

Hemingway and Sara Murphy. In *A Moveable Feast*, Hemingway mentions a party hosted by the Murphys; later in the same book he blames them for destroying his austere, disciplined way of life and, indirectly, his marriage to Hadley (*MF*, 185–86, 207–11). The Murphys approved his relationship with Pauline and lent him Gerald's Paris studio when he and Hadley separated. *See also* Skull and Bones.

The Murphys went to the July 1926 fiesta in Pamplona where Ernest, "already caught in a triangle with Hadley and Pauline . . . seemed compelled to flirt with Sara."[452] Sara's "revulsion at the spectacle in the bullring was apparent. On the first day of the corrida, bothered especially by the sight of the broken-down horses . . . being gored by the bulls, she stalked out of the arena in disgust, though she returned the next day and actually enjoyed herself." A week after the end of the fiesta, Sara wrote Hadley and Ernest that "no one has anything on me about liking bullfights—, even if I don't like seeing bowels."[453] As he does with the women he likes, Hemingway makes Sara younger: in 1926 she was forty-two years old (she turned forty-three that November), and not forty, as Hemingway reports.

The narrator describes Mrs. M. W. [Murphy-Wiborg] and her reaction to the bullfights (*h:* 500; *see also* 34).

Murube. In the nineteenth century the well-established Murube family of bull breeders bought a Vistahermosa herd from Manuel Suárez, the grandson of Manuel Suárez Cordero. When Dolores Monje, as Murube's widow, inherited the herd, she bought the rights to the colors, brand, and seniority, which had remained with Manuel Suárez, from his son and heir. She also strengthened the Vistahermosa strain by buying more Saavedra stock (two hundred cows and fifty bulls). On 1 April 1868, she presented the resulting *toros de lidia* in her

name (variously spelled Monje or Monge, with the addition of the phrase "viuda de Murube," the widow of Murube) in Madrid. She kept the Suárez brand and colors (scarlet and black), thus retaining the herd's *antigüedad* (13 October 1848).

Murube bulls were much in demand, and over the years Dolores Monje sold stock to various breeders (most notably to Eduardo Ibarra, q.v.). When she died, her sons, Joaquín and Faustino Murube Monje, inherited the herd. Faustino sold his share to his brother Joaquín, and in 1917 Joaquín's widow sold the entire Murube holdings, including the seniority, to Juan Manuel de Urquijo, who registered it in the name of his wife, Carmen de Federico (q.v.). For more detail on the relationship between pedigree, ownership, and *antigüedad*, see the essay on "Bulls and Bull Breeding," in the introduction to this volume.

> The narrator correctly reports that the Murube bulls are "today" (i.e., at the time of the writing of *Death in the Afternoon*) owned by Carmen de Federico (132).

M. W., Mrs. *See* Murphy, Sara.

– N –

Nacional. Professional name of the four Anlló brothers, who made their careers as bullfighters in the 1920s: Ricardo (Nacional) and Juan (Nacional II) (qq.v.) were matadors, Eduardo (Nacional III) was a skillful banderillero, and Ramiro (Nacional IV) a *matador de novillos* (killer of three-year-old bulls).

Narratee. The narrator uses the pronoun *you* to suggest that he is addressing an unnamed or implied narratee, who is foreign to Spain and inexperienced in bullfighting: "If you are in a town and know you are going to the bullfight buy your seats as soon as you are decided. . . . You should, as a spectator, show your appreciation of the good and valuable work that is essential but not brilliant" (36, 162–63).[454] This imagined narratee, sometimes called "the spectator," is occasionally enlarged into the plural, dramatized, and allowed to speak (63–64, *h:* 318; *see also* The Old Lady); sometimes words are put into its mouth (194). The text implies that some of these narratees or would-be spectators exist within the text (they go to a bullfight and are asked if they liked it), but the readers of *Death in the Afternoon* can also be defined as narratees, who "listen" to the narrator as he imparts fact and philosophy.

The text defines all these narratees (would-be spectators, both in and out of the book) as people who are ignorant of the bullfight, occasionally dense, and probably non-Spaniards, which makes them fine foils to the more knowledgeable, usually patient narrator (q.v.), the "I" who speaks and instructs. The narratee's function is to accept the narrator's instruction and thus, one hopes, become an educated devotee of the art.

The narrator is aware that his narratees are difficult to convince. The in-text narratees who go to the bullfight do not, with the exception of the Old Lady, like it. The narratees who exist outside the text (literary critics and contemporary readers who are repelled by bullfighting) are the literary equivalents of the unteachable, insensitive tourist who goes to the bullfight with a closed mind and leaves the ring (or closes the book) before the performance is ended. To counteract this hostility to his subject, the narrator tries reason (he distinguishes between humanitarians and animalarians, paying particular attention to the goring of the horses, the aspect of the bullfight that most distresses the uninitiated [1–8]); and simile (the bullfight is an acquired taste, like wine [10–12]). But aware that some readers will remain unconvinced, he heaps scorn upon the unteachable (34).

Past experience has taught the narrator to expect hostility to his style as well. He preemptively attacks those who he feels attacked him in the past (Huxley, Woolf, qq.v.), those who would prefer a different kind of writing (e.g., admirers of *Virgin Spain*, q.v.), those who are his rivals (e.g., Faulkner, q.v.), and those who withhold recognition from contemporary artists (the diatribe against taurine critics and historians [240–44]). These attacks seek to control or at least to defuse expected criticism of *Death in the Afternoon*, which was actually quite well received on both sides of the Atlantic. *See also* Authors; Critics.

The text also presents spectators who are not narratees (that is, the narrator doesn't address them). They are mostly Spanish, attend the bullfights regularly, have strong opinions, and are usually members of large crowds: "the public." They are described but not instructed by the narrator, although he does not always approve of them. Whereas the narratees are addressed in the second person (you), these spectators are treated in the third person (they): "The public did not like it" (257). See also Spectators in *DS*.

Although spectators speak occasionally in *Death in the Afternoon*

(63–64, and in a photograph caption, *h:* 318), the Old Lady is the only narratee with a real speaking part. In contrast to the resisting readers, she is open-minded on important matters such as death, sex, the bullfight, and literature, on all of which she accepts the narrator as an authority from whom she is willing to take instruction. As Hemingway's brother pointed out, Ernest always "needed someone he could show off to as well as teach."[455]

> The narrator's audience is composed of the narratees who exist within the text and the readers who are reading the book. They are indistinguishably addressed as "you" (passim).

Narrator. The narrator of *Death in the Afternoon* is a foreigner to Spain who admires the bullfight and attempts to communicate its complexity to a novice narratee (q.v.). He has long experience of Spain, speaks Spanish, and knows and loves the Spanish countryside, food, wine, art, and literature. To display this knowledge, he tends to make lists and catalogues, most notably in Chapter Twenty. He uses all the pronouns, his favorite being the first person singular with which he presents himself as a self-conscious narrator/writer ("I will not describe" . . . "I tried to describe" . . . "I wrote a story about it" . . . "If I could have made this enough of a book" [176, 89, 273, 270]) and an authoritative witness ("Many times I have seen a bull attack the inch-thick wooden planks" . . . "I saw him in most of his fights" . . . "I have seen a horn wound in the thigh" [109, 89, 255]), although occasionally he aligns himself with other knowledgeable aficionados (presumably Spaniards who accept him as an equal) and assumes the plural: "We sat in the first row behind the wooden barrier" . . . "We all spoke of him as carne de toro" (17, 254). In an attempt to make the experience more immediate, and thus to draw his audience into the text, he also uses the second person when he means "one" or "I": "You read of bulls in the old days" . . . Then you could walk across the town and to the café" (183, 277).

Despite his conversational manner, the narrator, like Hemingway, is a writer. He tells several stories: "A Natural History of the Dead" (q.v.), the story of the homosexuals (q.v.), the story of the brother and sister who eat the bull's testicles. In his conversations with the Old Lady, he even dramatizes himself as Author. That is, the published author Hemingway and the unnamed narrator of *Death in the*

Afternoon converge in terms of literary production, enabling us to supply absent titles: both have refused to publish a bullfighting story ("A Lack of Passion," q.v.) and have written two unidentified books (*The Sun Also Rises* and *A Farewell to Arms*, qq.v.), and are writing another (the book we are reading). The narrator discusses travel literature (40, 52–54; mentioned, *h:* 436, s.v. *Estoque*) and mentions a variety of English, Spanish, American, French, and German authors. He comments on writing (2–3, 190–92, 278; see also 20, 52–54, 63, 122, 173, 269, 476) and has a strong interest in dialogue (71, 120, 132–33, 228). He is also interested in sports and art.

Although it seems that Hemingway makes no attempt to disguise himself, his narrator is a construct he presents to his narratees, both the fictional listeners he creates and controls within the text and the actual readers and critics of *Death in the Afternoon* who exist outside the text. The narrator differs from Hemingway in significant details: there is no indication, for example, that he is divorced and now married to a second wife, that his wife is pregnant, that he never saw Joselito, and so on. See also Spectators in *DS*.

> While discussing his subjects (bullfighting, art, life) and manipulating/controlling his narratees, the narrator is in turn humorous, angry, disdainful, compassionate, philosophical, and admiring.

"A Natural History of the Dead." In the nineteenth century and in the early years of the twentieth, when Hemingway was educated, a "naturalist" was a biologist, and "natural history" was the study of living organisms, which makes "A Natural History of the Dead" a grimly ironic phrase. Today, "natural history" is defined as "the study of animal life, and sometimes also of plant life, usually in a popular manner" (*The New Lexicon Webster's Dictionary of the English Language*, 1987 ed.).

Citing manuscript fragments, Paul Smith argues that Hemingway originally thought of this piece as an independent story, that he revised it for inclusion in *Death in the Afternoon* (1932), and that he published it again, as an independent story, in *Winner Take Nothing* (1933). Smith details the alterations: for *Death in the Afternoon* Hemingway added the dialogue between the Old Lady (q.v.) and the Author and the section on Spanish influenza (q.v.). For *Winner Take Nothing*, he removed the dialogue, kept the influenza, and added "a petulant footnote" about the previous publication. The footnote was later dropped, but another one, calling the Humanists "an extinct phenomenon," was added.[456] For a fine discussion of the long coda Hemingway decided not to publish, see Susan F. Beegel, *Hemingway's Craft of Omission*, 31–49. *See also Generals Die in Bed*; Hudson, W. H.; Humanism, Naturalism; Munition Factory; Park, Mungo; Spanish Influenza; Stanley, Edward; White, the Reverend Gilbert; and under individual fictional characters: Adjutant; Doctors; the Lieutenant; the Sergeant; Stretcher-Bearers.

> After a long preamble, the Narrator tells the Old Lady a story entitled "A Natural History of the Dead" (141–44).

Naturalism, Naturalist. *See* Humanism, Naturalism.

New York Herald, **Paris edition.** In 1924 the daily *New York Herald,* founded in 1887, merged with the *Tribune* to become the *New York Herald Tribune* and as such launched a European edition (1924–66), which eventually merged with the *New York Times International* to form the *International Herald Tribune* (1967-present). In *Death in the Afternoon,* the homosexuals (q.v.) read the Paris *New York Herald.* Other Hemingway characters also read the Paris edition of this paper (see *The Garden of Eden,* 59, 209, 210; and *Across the River and Into the Trees,* 164, 166–67).

> The narrator tells the Old Lady a story about a young man being initiated into homosexuality. After a noisy, tearful night the homosexual couple are obviously happy as they read the Paris *New York Herald* (182).

The Newspaperman. Robert W. Lewis, who looked at the manuscript of *Death in the Afternoon* at the University of Texas at Austin, writes that a "hard-to-read marginal note . . . seems to identify the newsman who told him the story of the homosexuals as William Nash, a Paris acquaintance of the 1920s and a reporter for the *Chicago Daily News.*"[457]

> The narrator identifies the Newspaperman as a friend, although he is boring and unintelligent. The Newspaperman is the source for the story about the two homosexuals (q.v.) that the narrator tells the Old Lady (180 ff). The Newspaperman speaks: 181.

Nicknames. Nicknames are so frequently used in Spanish that several nouns exist to distinguish among different kinds: *apodo*, *alias*, *mote*, *remoquete*, *alcuña*, *seudónimo*, *título*, *cédula*. In small communities or clans, nicknames distinguish among people with the same name. In bullfighting, fathers, sons, grandsons, and nephews may share not only the same name and patronymic but even the same nickname, so that generation after generation, the same names and *apodos* appear on bullfight posters: *see also* Taurine Dynasties.

Just as Bob and Joe are standard English nicknames for Robert and Joseph, so Spanish has standard nicknames like Pepe for José, and Paco or Curro for Francisco. But nicknames may also be descriptive, alluding to physical characteristics (el Rubio, el Gordo), place of origin (Alcalareño, Algabeño, el Trianero), ethnic background (Gitanillo), the father's profession (el Niño del Matadero, Carnicerito), or some other characteristic (Mazquiarán's luck resulted in his being called Fortuna). Diminutives of a name or surname are also popular; they indicate youth, small size, or affection (Joselito for José Gómez Ortega, Varelito for Manuel Varé). Nicknames of famous bullfighters persist not only in their families but sometimes in the families of their in-laws and even in their fellow townsfolk: Antonio García (Bombita IV), for example, was not related to the famous Bombitas (the three Torres Reina brothers) but took their nickname because he came from the same town, Tomares, near the city of Seville.

Some nicknames are very popular: *see* the various entries for Niño, below. For Hemingway's own fondness for nicknames, *see* Smith, William Benjamin in this volume; and Papa in *DS*.

Translating Taurine Nicknames into Names. Because bullfighters are so often known by their nicknames rather than their names, Cossío offers an "Indice alfabético de apodos" (alphabetic listing of nicknames) to enable researchers to find the relevant entries in each one of the several volumes that offer taurine biographies (the biographies themselves are arranged alphabetically by patronymic, not by nickname). The index of nicknames most relevant to the bullfighters mentioned in *Death in the Afternoon* appears at the end of Cossío's Volume III: there are some eighty Niños, and not three hundred, as Hemingway claims (*h:* 455–56, s.v. *Niño*), but even without Hemingway's exaggeration it is obvious that the nickname was popular in the 1920s. Post-Civil War bullfighters are treated in Cossío's Volumes IV, V, and VI.[458]

Spanish names, which feature both the mother's and father's family names, or sometimes one, or sometimes the other, can be as confusing as nicknames; see "User's Guide," in the introduction to this volume. Cossío's encyclopedia presents bullfighters alphabetically according to the patronymic, but other authorities organize their materials differently, so that in order to locate a particular bullfighter, one must also know his birth date, or the date of his Madrid debut as *novillero*, or of his promotion to *matador de alternativa* (q.v.).

> The narrator uses names and nicknames interchangeably in the text. He explains a few nicknames or professional names in the Glossary (*h:* 439, s.v. *Gallo*; *h:* 455–56, s.v. *Niño*).

El Niño de la Palma. Cayetano Ordóñez (q.v.), was called el Niño de la Palma because his father, a shoemaker, called his shop La Palma; it was located in Ronda's Plaza de Alarcón. Cayetano's older brother, who died young, was called Antonio de la Palma; one of his sons fought under the name of Juan de la Palma. *See also* Jones, Bobby; and Ronda.

El Niño de la Sierra Nevada. Like musicians, bullfighters often achieve fame as children, and few bullfighters would object to being taken for younger than they are. As Hemingway notes, many grown-up bullfighters are known as Niño: Cossío identifies almost eighty such instances.[459] "Niño de la Sierra Nevada," however, does not appear in Cossío's comprehensive list; it seems to be Hemingway's own invention.

> The narrator discusses the use of "Chico" and "Niño" as part of a bull-fighter's nickname (*h:* 455–56, s.v. *Niño*).

El Niño del Matadero. (The boy or son of the slaughterhouse, or of the butcher). Often located inside the bullring itself, the town *matadero* is obviously a fine training ground for would-be matadors: it offers beasts to practice on, as well as the opportunity to study the bull's anatomy. Many butchers have had bullfighting sons, whether or not the boys were nicknamed el Niño del Matadero. See, for example, Vasquez, Pepe Luis, in *DS*.

Several *novilleros* were called "el Niño del Matadero," among them Antonio Cuadrado Morgado, Antonio Gil Maroto, Manuel Jiménez, Luis Lara, and Agustín García. The banderillero José Pérez, of Huelva, worked in the 1940s under this same nickname. The one who best fits Hemingway's time frame was a *matador de novillos*: *see* Pino Suárez, Manuel del.

El Niño del Seguridad. (The boy or son of the security guard). The father of Enrique Torres was a guard for Seguridad, a security company; hence the son's nickname. *See* Torres, Enrique.

Niños Cordobeses. (The boys or the kids from Córdoba). The late nineteenth century saw several *cuadrillas juveniles*, groups of teenaged bullfighters who performed together. Most of the groups were short-lived, lasting two or three years and disbanded when the boys became old or experienced enough to embark upon independent careers.

One of the earliest of these groups was established c. 1876 by a banderillero, Francisco Rodríguez (Caniqui), and composed entirely of boys from Córdoba. In 1878 the *cuadrilla* consisted of eight boys who generally performed as a group. Occasionally only two or three of them were engaged together, as Hemingway notes, their affiliation with the *cuadrilla* being noted on the *cartel*; and a few of them sometimes fought young bulls (*becerros*, *utreros*, and *novillos*) on their own. The *cuadrilla* was dissolved in late 1879.[460] It had served "the kids" well, bringing them publicity and contracts. The publicity was due not only to the novelty of such a *cuadrilla*, but also to the already obvious talent of one of the members, Rafael Guerra Bejarano (q.v.).

Other *cuadrillas* of *niños cordobeses* soon followed. José Rodríguez (Bebé chico, 1870–1902) belonged to a short-lived *cuadrilla juvenil cordobesa* organized by Manuel Fuentes Rodríguez (Bocanegra), in the late 1880s.[461] In April 1898 the retired banderillero Caniqui organized another *cuadrilla de niños cordobeses*, which worked for the *matador de toros* Rafael Sánchez (Bebé). This *cuadrilla* included the well-connected Rafael Molina (Lagartijo chico), who was the son of a bullfighter and nephew of the famous Rafael Molina (Lagartijo, q.v.); and Rafael González Madrid (Machaquito, q.v., who was also a member of the *cuadrilla de niños sev-*

illanos, see below). These two "boys" or "kids" were eighteen years old at the time and had already performed as *novilleros*. This *cuadrilla*, perhaps the most famous group of *niños cordobeses*, did not last long, as its two leading members became *matadores de toros* themselves in 1900.

The narrator refers to the fad, prevalent in the nineteenth century but since abandoned, of youthful *cuadrillas* (*h:* 455–56, s.v. *Niño*).

Niños Sevillanos. (The boys or the kids from Seville). In imitation of the youthful *cuadrillas* organized in Córdoba, rival *cuadrillas* of boys were formed in Seville. Although the boys in most juvenile *cuadrillas* usually fought as banderilleros under the orders of a *novillero* or *matador*, several groups of *niños sevillanos* featured *becerristas* (bullfighters who fight *becerros*, bulls less than three years old). One such group, captained by Faíco and Minuto, was established in November 1889 and toured most of Spain. Another famous *cuadrilla de niños sevillanos* was established in 1895 by the matadors Fernando Gómez (Gallo), Antonio Reverte, and Emilio Torres Reina (Bombita, qq.v.); the *cuadrilla* was contracted for *becerradas* and even occasional *novilladas* in important plazas. This 1895 *cuadrilla*, popular until it was disbanded in 1899, featured young performers with considerable followings of their own, such as Fernando's son Rafael Gómez Ortega (el Gallo, who belonged to it from age thirteen until he was almost eighteen years old) and, at various times, such figures as Manuel García (nephew of Reverte), Rafael González (Machaquito, who was from Córdoba and who joined the *cuadrilla de niños cordobeses* in 1898), Emilio Torres Reina's younger brother Ricardo (qq.v.), and several others.[462]

A few years later, in 1908, José Martínez, a retired policeman, organized another *cuadrilla de niños sevillanos*. It included several boys whom he had seen fighting *becerros*: José Puerta (Pepete), José Gárate (Limeño), Antonio Marroco, and José Gómez Ortega (Joselito, then twelve or thirteen years old). They performed in Portugal for a few months. When this *cuadrilla* was disbanded, another was formed in 1909, featuring Joselito and Limeño. Like the earlier *cuadrilla* of *sevillanos*, which had featured Joselito's older brother, these boys fought mainly as *becerristas*. The *cuadrilla* was disbanded in

1911, because its two leading members had become *novilleros* by that time.[463] The competing *cuadrillas* often appeared in each other's plazas and, in spite of the natural rivalry, were cheered both in Seville and Córdoba.

Hemingway saved an article from the taurine journal *El Clarín* that objected to the proliferation of *niños sevillanos*, *niños malagueños*, *niños valencianos*, and so on, claiming that most of the boys lacked talent and were thrust into the limelight by lustreless fathers seeking fame through their sons. Only "pocos, muy pocos" (few, very few) such children became serious artists: "Faíco y Minuto, Pepete y Varelito, Joselito y Limeño, Eladio Amorós, Granero y Pacorro, todos niños prodigios" (all child prodigies). But, the article complained, the popularity of juvenile *cuadrillas* exposed too many boys to danger and deprived them of a proper school education.[464]

The narrator mentions the juvenile *cuadrillas* that were famous at the end of the nineteenth century and the beginning of the twentieth (*h:* 455–56, s.v. *Niño*).

El Noticiero de Lunes (The Monday Bulletin). Original name: *Hoja oficial del lunes* (Official Monday Newssheet). As Hemingway notes, in the 1920s Spain's newspapers did not put out Sunday evening or Monday morning editions. The *Hoja oficial del lunes* filled that gap.

For its first two years, from 7 January 1924 to 4 January 1926, the weekly *Hoja oficial*, published in Madrid,[465] consisted of one sheet and was distributed free of charge to the population in order to provide "official" information and thus avoid rumors, panics, and alarms concerning Spain's military intervention in Morocco. Most of that period's sheets reassure the public that Morocco is quiet (e.g., "Sin novedad en nuestra zona de Marruecos" (no new developments in the Spanish-controlled zone of Morocco, 12 January 1925) or that uprisings have been easily put down, with many casualties among the local population and none or few among the Spanish forces.

In 1926 the weekly began to experiment with size and format. On 4 January a four-page issue appeared, the pages being twice as big (almost modern newspaper size) and offering information about countries other than Morocco. It cost ten *céntimos* an issue and carried ads on the last page. By the next week the publication returned to its original page size, but offered sixteen pages and the new title,

El noticiero del lunes.[466] Pretty landscapes and important Spanish personalities soon began to appear on the front cover, the illustrations spreading to the inside pages as well. News from Morocco occupied less space and was relegated to the back pages, ads got larger and were scattered throughout the issue, and taurine news began to appear.

The first taurine items I saw offered details about the forthcoming Spanish season and reported that Rafael Gómez (el Gallo) had fought in a corrida in Tampa, Florida (8 February 1926, pages 16, 17). Fiction, poetry and cartoons enlarged the February and March issues to twenty-four pages, and taurine reports occupied more space during the season itself (March to September). A few editorials protested the goring of horses and the practice of pic-ing in general (a hot issue: *see* Peto).

But other matters soon took precedence. Very patriotic covers appeared on 17 May 1926 (the fortieth birthday of King Alfonso XIII, q.v.) and 3 May 1926 (victory over Morocco). On 7 June 1926 the newspaper expanded its page size and doubled its price to twenty *céntimos*. Ads appeared on every page except the cover. But by January 1929 the number of pages had been reduced to eight, with foreign and national news on the front page, two pages dedicated to sports, a good number of obituaries, and large ads for movies, theaters, concerts, and other events; the price was reduced to ten *céntimos*. Pictures of the royal family and of Primo de Rivera (q.v.) appeared with increasing frequency on the front page (on 16 September Primo de Rivera's pronouncements occupied the entire first four pages), and the 1929 International Exposition in Barcelona figured heavily in the news.

By September 1929 the newspaper pages had again been reduced in size but the number of pages doubled to sixteen; the price remained stable. On 23 September, taurine news took up two whole pages, because there had been many injuries; but by November the taurine section had disappeared. Hemingway's claim that the paper offered bullfight news every week is accurate only for some periods of this variable newspaper's life.

The eminent taurine critic, Ventura Bagüés, co-compiler (with Tomás Orts Ramos [Uno al Sesgo]) of the annual *Toros y toreros en* . . . , wrote for the *Hoja Oficial del Lunes* under his pseudonym, don Ventura. His reports are accurate and less biased than the political reporting found elsewhere in the paper. The Biblioteca Nacional, Madrid, has a fairly good run of this paper, from 1924 to 1929, 1936, 1939–45, and 1978–82.

El noticiero de lunes is defined in the glossary as the weekly publication that reports taurine as well as political events (*h:* 456, s.v. *Noticiero*).

Noy de Sucre. Literally, the boy of sugar. The correct spelling of the Catalan word for *boy* is *noi*.[467] Real name: Salvador Seguí i Rubinat. Seguí was called "el Noi del Sucre" because, as a youth, he had worked in a sugar factory.[468] He is sometimes referred to as "de Sucre" (of sugar), and sometimes "del Sucre" (of the sugar). He was a Spanish painter and union activist, 1886–1923.

Seguí was one of the founders and most eloquent defenders of the Confederación Nacional del Trabajo (C.N.T.), a national umbrella organization founded in 1910 by several local anarcho-syndicalist organizations, some of which later split off to join the Communist Party of Spain. In 1915 he helped unite twenty disparate construction unions into a single, more powerful union. In 1918 he was elected secretary-general of the C.N.T. and called for the C.N.T and the Unión General de Trabajadores (U.G.T.) to join forces. Working with the U.G.T., he helped organize the strikes of 1919. With other labor leaders, he was jailed by the repressive governor Martínez Anido.

During his sixteen months in jail (1920–21), Seguí wrote *Anarquismo y sindicalismo*, in which he argued that in the short term an anarchistic attitude would lead to greater acceptance of well-organized, powerful, nationwide unions that would regulate the economy. He even advocated the formation of a workers' political party. As he was preparing for a trip to meet with the leadership of the Portuguese U.G.T., he was murdered, in Barcelona, on 10 March 1923.[469] The murder was front-page news: *La campana de gracia*, a Barcelona publication with nationwide distribution, carried three illustrations of "L'assassinat d'En Salvador Seguí 'Noi del Sucre' " (issue of 17 March 1923, one week after the event). Seguí is the subject of two biographies: *Salvador Seguí, el Noi del Sucre* by Manuel Cruells, and *El Noi del Sucre, materials per a una biografia*, by J. M. Huertas Clavería, both books appearing in 1974. His essays were collected and published by Isidre Molas (1975).

In 1923, when the Noy de Sucre was killed, Hemingway visited Spain twice, first in late May and early June, and then again in July. His reference to this important incident, like his references to Deva, Garibaldi, *La Libertad* (qq.v.), and the fight between David and Maera (discussed in the entry for David, Alfredo) expand Chapter Twenty into the political and labor unrest that preceded the formation of Spain's second Republic. If we read this chapter carefully, we realize how close Hemingway came to his goal of putting "everything in it" (270).

The narrator regrets that he is unable to write about the Noy de Sucre (272).

Noya. Modern Galician spelling: Noia. The two-story bullring in Noya, a town in La Coruña, was built in 1894. It seats about four thousand spectators. Its traditional fiestas occur at the end of April (fiestas de San Marco) and the end of August.

Pauline and Ernest Hemingway, who went to Santiago de Compostela in August of 1927, 1929, and 1931, could easily have traveled to Noya for the August bullfights. The fact that Noya is mentioned in the same paragraph as the visit to Montroig suggests that the year is 1929: the Hemingways visited Miró in mid-July 1929, went to Valencia for the *feria* late in July, and arrived in Santiago de Compostela by 3 August, staying there until the end of the month.

Chicuelo and Valencia II (qq.v.), mentioned in the same paragraph, performed together in San Sebastián on 11 August 1929; Hemingway probably read about that corrida. Chicuelo and Valencia II appeared several times in the Valencia *feria* of 1929, where Hemingway would have seen them perform within days of each other, if not actually on the same day. He might also have seen Chicuelo perform in La Coruña on 4 August (with Cagancho and Maera II) and 6 August (with Lalanda, Cagancho, and Maera II, qq.v.) of that year.

Toros y toreros' annual listings of *corridas de toros* and *corridas de novillos* do not mention Noya among the bullrings which hosted such events in April and August, 1929 or 1931. This suggests that Hemingway saw *novilladas* with such minor fighters that the event did not reach the compilers of *Toros y toreros* for that year, or that he saw lesser spectacles, such as *festivales, concursos, becerradas,* or *capeas* (even though these were outlawed in 1929).[470] The fact that he recalls a "temporary wooden ring in Noya" further supports this.

> The narrator recalls the smell of the wood used in building the temporary bullring in Noya (276) and the bullfighters he saw at that time (though not necessarily in Noya) (276).

– O –

Oficial. Hemingway's anecdote about the bull named Oficial varies from that offered by his source, Carralero and Borge's *Toros célebres*, only in that Hemingway omits the name of the gored banderillero: Avalos. Cossío confirms Carralero and Borge's account, adding that Oficial was third bull of the day.[471] *See also* Alonso Bertolí, Rafael (el Chato), the injured banderillero; and Arribas Brothers, who bred the bull.

> The narrator correctly identifies the bull, the date and the venue of the event. He also indicates his approval of Oficial as a "police-hating" creature (111–12).

The Old Lady (Madame). The Old Lady was an afterthought—a happy one, to my mind—added to the original manuscript as *Death in the Afternoon* was nearing completion. She is a fictional, dramatized narratee (q.v.), ignorant of bullfighting but with good instincts and a quick understanding. By developing her into a lively, speaking character, Hemingway emphasizes the importance of his generally silent and invisible narratees. She speaks for them—and us (the narratees/readers who are outside the text)—and thus brings the narratees into equality with the narrator (q.v.), as evidenced by the fact that just before he introduces her and immediately after he abandons her, the narrator addresses his narratees more directly, as "you."

The Old Lady's age and the fact that she has a speaking part mark her as the literary descendant of the "venerable harridan" who converses with the narrator of Richard Ford's *Gatherings from Spain*. Ford's description of his "worthy old lady" is venomous: she is "a greedily-biting pike" with "a dead and shrivelled face, which evil passions had furrowed like the lava-seared sides of an extinct volcano, and dried up, like a cat starved behind a wainscot, into a thing of fur and bones, in which gender was obliterated." Ford's "old lady" appears twice: first to interrupt Ford's discussion of the dead horses and then, at the very end of the bullfight, to draw his attention to the beauty of the bull (Ford, 163, 165). She is a Spaniard and knowledgeable about the bullfight, but Ford dismisses her ("let her pass," 163), just as Hemingway, almost a century later, threw his Old Lady "out of the book, finally" (190). Ford, whose "predominant sensation" at the bullfights was "bore[dom]" (170), would have done well to take instruction from the woman sitting near him at the bull-fight.

Hemingway's Old Lady has been variously read. Stanton thinks she is based on Hemingway's mother, Grace Hall Hemingway, whom Hemingway disliked, and is therefore "wacky, despised." Portz calls her "the Little Old Lady" and finds that "her shockable qualities, representative of the genteel tradition," align her with "the innocent, religious naturalists and nature lovers finding pretty designs in . . . nature," whom Hemingway attacks in "A Natural History of the Dead" (q.v.). Junkins supports my more positive reading: she "has the necessary objectivity . . . is impatient with literary talk . . . remains curious . . . has the clearheadedness of cynicism . . . [is] earthy but not prurient."[472]

The Old Lady is perceptive. When the narrator recalls the mules "at Smyrna [q.v.], where the Greeks broke the legs of all their baggage animals," she points out that "You wrote about those mules before" (135). She is correct: Hemingway wrote about them twice before, first in *In Our Time* (1930) and then on page 2 of *Death in the Afternoon*.[473] This suggests that she has read his earlier, published work and/or the very work-in-progress in which she appears. Her familiarity with Hemingway's work defines her as the ideal Hemingway reader: one who reads attentively enough to recall details of his work, but has barely heard of his rival, Faulkner (q.v.; *see also* Authors; Boxing; Critics). The Old Lady is also the only one of the in-text narratees to like her first bullfight, which further endears her to the narrator.

The Old Lady's First Bullfight. Hemingway is a meticulous artist for whom every detail is important. He carefully chooses the first bullfight that his narratees attend, and just as carefully enables us to figure out which one it was. By naming "the most valorous and manly chaps" who performed that day—Nicanor Villalta, Luis Fuentes Bejarano, and Diego Mazquiarán (Fortuna)—he points us to the inagural bullfight of Madrid's new bullring, Las Ventas: the only occasion when these three bullfighters performed together. This was a historic event and the proper occasion for the Old Lady's initiation into the taurine arts. The date was Wednesday, 17 June 1931.[474] Hemingway was in Madrid that day, and probaby went to that bullfight himself. *See also* Women.

> The Old Lady catches the narrator's attention because she is the only one of his fictionalized audience (63) who enjoyed the bullfight. She stays with the narrator from Chapter Seven through Chapter Fifteen (63–182, 190). The Old Lady speaks: 64, 70–72, 82, 92–95, 103–104, 120–23, 132–33, 135, 137–40, 144, 171–73, 179–80, 182.

Old Zurito. The father of Antonio de la Haba (q.v.). *See* Zurito.

Ordóñez, Cayetano. Full name: Cayetano Ordóñez Aguilera (Niño de la Palma). Spanish bullfighter, 1904–61. Investiture as *matador de toros*, in Seville, 11 June 1925, granted by Juan Belmonte; confirmed in Madrid, July 1925.

Cayetano's generation was the first in the Ordóñez family to take up bullfighting: five of the seven brothers attempted it, but only Cayetano achieved the rank of *matador de toros*.[475]

Without money or taurine connections, Cayetano began, like so many others, to build his reputation locally, in minor rings in his native Andalucía and in Ceuta. But he was incredibly gifted and his career took off quickly. By 1923 he was making a national stir, and his triumphs in 1924 led to contracts in the important plazas of Seville (three *novilladas*) and Valencia (two *novilladas*): in Seville he cut two ears and a tail and was carried out of the bullfight on the shoulders of admirers. Although Cayetano had not yet made his Madrid debut, *Toros y toreros en 1924* describes him as "el 'fenómeno' del año" and insinuated that he might become "una gran figura de la Tauromaquia" (a great figure).[476]

The next year, 1925, was arguably his best, but he got off to a poor start, with a serious goring in the left thigh, incurred on 1 March, in Barcelona, which cost him three weeks of the season. He returned to the ring on 22 March, in Valencia, but was carted off to the infirmary when the still-unhealed wound opened up again: he did not kill his bulls that afternoon. Hemingway's claims to the contrary, Cayetano's first serious goring did not affect his courage or determination. Once the wound healed he fought frequently and well all through April and May. His Madrid debut as *novillero* took place on 28 May (a weak performance, see below). To the twenty-one *novilladas* of 1925, some very poor, others excellent, Cayetano added forty-nine triumphant *corridas de toros* and was ranked sixth among *matadores de toros* that year (Lalanda was first, with seventy-five corridas), even though his season as full *matador de toros* did not begin until after his *alternativa* (q.v.) on 11 June.[477]

Cayetano's triumphs of 1924 and 1925 inevitably led to comparisons with Joselito and other great *figuras* of the past. Gregorio Corrochano (q.v.) coined the famous phrase, "Se llama Cayetano y es de Ronda" (which Hemingway quotes and explains, *DIA*, 89). In their enthusiasm, most critics glossed over the fact that he was frequently (but lightly) caught by the bulls throughout that year, which indicated that he was not yet fully in control of his art.

With seventy-eight corridas, Cayetano was Spain's top-ranked *matador de toros* of 1926 (Antonio Márquez, q.v., ranked second),[478] but the reviews were less positive than they had been: critics claimed that Cayetano lacked the stamina, the self-confidence, the steadfast commitment or passion (*afición*) required of great bullfighters. As Abad Ojuel puts it, Cayetano is "un hombre aplastado por su arte, que parece demasiado grande para sus ánimos" (a man crushed by his art, which seems too great for his spirit).[479] This combination of great natural gifts with psychological weakness made his an uneven and interesting career. The problem had come to light while he was still a *novillero*: his beautiful performances drew multitudes of expectant critics and fans to his Madrid debut, but on that important occasion he produced a weak, lackluster performance that alienated them. This waning and waxing persisted: his triumphant investiture and the incandescent season of 1925 were followed by artistically disappointing performances in 1926. Iribarren writes that on 7, 8, and 9 July, Cayetano's performances in Pamplona (which Hemingway witnessed, see below) were so dreadful that the police had to escort him to the Hotel Quintana, to protect him from the crowd. On 9 July the enraged crowd broke into the hotel, and Cayetano took refuge in

Marcial Lalanda's room. When the crowd burst in, Lalanda falsely claimed that Cayetano was not there, and Cayetano was able to sneak out a back door, still in his bullfighting suit.[480]

The formerly adulatory press turned against Cayetano. As one critic remarked, "El torero de Ronda, como Chicuelo, tiene mala prensa" (The Ronda bullfighter, like Chicuelo, has a bad press).[481] In an unprecedented move, Cayetano retaliated, challenging the critics; the face-off between the famous bullfighter and the critics became a *cause célèbre*, to be settled in the Madrid bullring. Although he had staked reputation and career on a Madrid corrida, Cayetano's fighting on that day was merely competent, devoid of character, logic, or fire.

In 1927 he still had sufficient reputation to have more contracts than any other matador (sixty-five corridas put him in first place; Antonio Márquez again placed second, with fifty-four). He began the season energetically, but apathetic performances became frequent. The occasional fine performances, which showed what he was capable of, made the poor ones all the more distressing. The critics were severe: Tomás Orts Ramos (Uno al Sesgo) remarked that "si él quisiera, podría ser la gran figura de estos tiempos . . . sería el indiscutible número uno . . . pero no quiere, y este es un gran pecado" (if he wished, he could be the great figure of our times . . . the indisputable number one . . . but he doesn't want to, and this is a great sin).[482]

Cayetano retired in mid-July 1928, after twenty-seven corridas. In 1929 he returned to the ring, began his season with fire, but was unable to maintain the pace or his public. The forty-three corridas of that year were reduced to thirty-one in 1930 and twenty-two in 1931 (including four in Madrid, all disastrous).[483]

Hemingway and Ordóñez. Hemingway saw Cayetano often. In 1925, Cayetano performed in Hemingway's two favorite fiestas: in Pamplona on 7, 9, 11, and 12 July and in Valencia on 26, 27, and 29 July. The narrator of *Death in the Afternoon* claims to have been present at Cayetano's "first presentation as a matador in Madrid" (89): Hemingway was in Paris when Cayetano made his debut as *matador de novillos* on 28 May (a poor performance), but he was in Madrid when Cayetano confirmed his *alternativa* on 16 July, (a resounding success). In 1926, Hemingway saw Cayetano at the same festivals again (7, 8, 9, and 11 July in Pamplona; 26, 27, 28, and 30 in Valencia) and in Zaragoza, on 14 October. He saw him again in

1927, when Cayetano performed in Pamplona (9 July) and Valencia (26, 27, 28, and 29 July). *See also* Hemingway, Hadley.

Hemingway did not come to Spain in 1928, but in 1929 he and Cayetano coincided in Valencia on 25, 27, and 31 July. Hemingway missed the 1930 season but probably saw Cayetano in Pamplona, 9 and 12 July 1931. Cayetano's performance on 12 July surely confirmed his low opinion of Cayetano. Ordóñez was pelted with sandwiches, bottles, and even stones for his poor work with his first bull. Things got worse with the second bull, and the police and several high officials had to intervene to quell the twenty-minute riot, the worst seen in Pamplona's notoriously riotous plaza.[484]

Starting with 1925, Hemingway's visits to Spain were quite long, from two to five months, and he may have seen Cayetano in Madrid and in various other cities.[485] In addition to seeing him, Hemingway undoubtedly read a great deal about him as well: Cayetano was big news. But *Death in the Afternoon* was published before Cayetano would show, in his fine seasons of 1934 and 1935, that he was not yet "finished."[486]

In *Death in the Afternoon*, Hemingway blames Cayetano's descent on the thigh wound he received "At the end of the season" (89). This is probably the goring of 24 August 1925, in Almagro, in the right thigh; it kept him out of the ring until 10 September, but was followed by twenty-two corridas in which he did not display the "shameful" fear Hemingway claims resulted from that wound (89). Cayetano had been badly injured earlier in the 1925 season (see above), also in the thigh: that wound certainly did not dampen his courage.[487]

Hemingway's excessive praise and later condemnation of the early Ordóñez reveal as much about him as they do about the taurine artist about whom he wrote. Even in 1925 there were plenty of cooler heads around. *ABC*'s taurine critic Gregorio Corrochano, for example, advocated a wait-and-see attitude with Ordóñez. In spite of its resonant title, "Es de Ronda y se llama Cayetano," his famous 1925 review avoids excesses and tells a cautionary tale to warn Cayetano and his fans not to confuse ability (which he grants Ordóñez possessed in abundance) with achievement (which can only be assessed after many years of performance).[488] Similarly, Tomás Orts Ramos (Uno al Sesgo) wrote, at the end of that stellar 1925 campaign, that "no se improvisa una primera figura en un dos por tres . . . su encum-bramiento . . . es tal vez algo prematuro" (premier figures are not created with the snap of a finger . . . his enthronement is perhaps somewhat premature).[489] Perhaps because he had praised Cayetano Ordóñez so lavishly and publicly by making him into the Pedro Ro-mero of *The Sun Also Rises* (q.v.), Hemingway could not forgive his hero's clay feet. He venomously describes 1926 as "the most shame-ful season any matador had ever had up until that year in bullfight-ing" (89–90) and damns Cayetano (and not the critics, as he usually does) for having "raised the most false hopes and proved the greatest disappointment" of any matador in the 1920s (88). His disappoint-ment with Cayetano leads him to attack his appearance ("fat rumped, prematurely bald," 88) and to make dogmatic predictions about a twenty-seven-year-old bullfighter: "That was the end of him . . . He never got it [his valor] back . . . he was never the same" (89–90, 222; *see also* 267).

Having erred about Cayetano in 1925, Hemingway thereafter was wary of endorsing any but established bullfighters such as Lalanda and Villalta, who each boasted a decade of successful seasons by 1931. He touchily refused to share the current enthusiasm for the new stars, Manolo Bienvenida and Domingo Ortega (qq.v.).

Cayetano's five sons—Cayetano, Juan, Alfonso, Antonio, and José —all became bullfighters. His daughter, Anita, married a Mexican bullfighter, Feliciano (Chano) Ramos. For more detail on Ordóñez's later career and those of his children, see *DS*.

> The narrator notes that in 1925 Cayetano Ordóñez was hailed as the savi-our of bullfighting (88) after the death of Joselito. The narrator had been impressed by Cayetano's beautiful cape and muleta work and his elegant attempts to kill *recibiendo* (standing still and waiting for the bull, 89, 238) and mentions that he had described him in one of his earlier books (89; that book, not named, is *The Sun Also Rises*, q.v.). The narrator finds that a severe goring at the end of that magnificent season destroyed his spirit and that by 1931 he was "finished" (89, 267). He mentions Cayetano's cowardice repeatedly (89–90, 250, 402), usually attributing it to that wound (43, 167, 171, 222). The unnamed bald bullfighter who gave Hadley Hemingway the ear he cut off a bull is Cayetano (270).

Ortega, Domingo (the Hayseed of Borox). Full name: Domingo López Ortega. Spanish bullfighter and bull breeder, 1908–88. Investiture as *matador de toros* in Barcelona, on March 1931; confirmed in Madrid, June 1931. Ortega was called "el pardillo de Borox" and, less frequently, "el paleto de Borox" because he was born in Borox, a small town near Toledo, and was therefore a rustic or provincial. He did not use these nicknames himself, preferring to be known as Domingo Ortega.

Unlike most of the great figures of bullfighting, Domingo Ortega was neither a child prodigy nor an early success. He showed scant interest in bullfighting until he was nineteen or twenty years old, and from then until 1930 he appeared only in very minor rings. Cossío emphasizes that of the several contemporary *novilleros* who later became major figures, Ortega was the only one whom no one noticed in 1928, 1929, and most of 1930. An ex-banderillero from Ortega's neighborhood, however, recommended the *novillero* to Domingo González (Dominguín, q.v. in this volume and in *DS*), who liked his style, liked him personally, signed him on, and introduced him to important plazas at the end of the 1930 season (see, for example, the photograph that shows Ortega at Aranjuez, on 6 September 1930, *h:* 376–77).[490] Ortega was a success, showing that he could fight difficult bulls with great coolness. He was quickly booked for more corridas in September, October, and November 1930 and suddenly found himself that year's most talked-about *novillero*.

Cossío remarks that the most astonishing thing about Ortega was that, practically self-taught, he emerged from small town *capeas* and *ferias* as a mature, powerful bullfighter, not showing the mannerisms or awkwardness often seen in provincial *novilleros*. The always perceptive Tomás Orts Ramos (Uno al Sesgo) described him as "la revelación del año . . . tales cosas ha hecho de gran torero que es difícil resistir a la tentación de profetizar que en el *pardillo* de Borox hay algo más que una esperanza de gran figura del toreo: hay un torero excepcional" (the discovery of the year . . . he has done such things that one is tempted to call the Hayseed of Borox something more than a potentially great bullfighter: he is already an exceptional bullfighter).[491] At his first appearance the next year, Ortega was promoted to *matador de toros*.

During this first season of *alternativa* (q.v.), Ortega was so extravagantly successful—he headed the year's ranking with an astounding ninety-three corridas, only a very few of which fell short of being spectacular—that Uno al Sesgo wrote in *Toros y toreros*, "No hay precedente en la historia del toreo de caso semejante" (no such thing has been recorded in the history of bullfighting, a phrase which also appears in a very negative review, see below, and which Hemingway repeats, *DIA*, 168).[492]

In 1932 Ortega was contracted for 116 fights and performed in ninety-one, more than any other matador. Except for one disastrous performance in Barcelona, he seems to have been consistently magnificent the whole season, triumphing even in Madrid. He maintained his position as the most polished and effective matador, as well as the one who appeared most often, through much of the 1930s, with sixty-nine corridas in 1933 (an injury kept him out of the ring from 9 September until 12 October); eighty in 1934; fifty-six in 1935 (an injury on 13 September forced him to cancel the rest of his contracts); and forty-five in 1936 (the season was cut short by the Spanish Civil War, which broke out in July). He was ranked first nationwide for four successive years, 1931–34, and again in 1936 and 1937.

Ortega continued to perform during the Spanish Civil War and, with the exception of 1941, throughout the 1940s (for the numbers, see *DS*). Although he appeared less frequently in this decade than in the preceding one, his appearances were generally as highly acclaimed.

Ortega retired in 1950 but, as most famous matadors do, appeared in festivals and benefits. In 1953, at the age of forty-seven, "con la cabeza totalmente blanca, más con bríos juveniles" (with his hair completely white, but full of youthful energy),[493] he emerged from retirement, performing fourteen times that year and twelve the next. He retired again at the end of the 1954 season, although he continued to fight in scattered festivals and fund-raisers until 1958. In 1955 he performed with Antonio Mejías Jiménez (Antonio Bienvenida, see in *DS*) and Enrique Vera in the movie *Tarde de toros*: tall, slim, and white-haired, he played an arrogant, unsympathetic senior matador who mistreats his young mistress. In real life, Ortega maintained his reputation and prestige to the end of his long career.

While acknowledging Ortega's power and presence, Cossío reports the complaints that were made against him: Ortega relies too heavily on his right hand, does not appear often enough in Madrid, and, more damningly, takes more or less the same tack with all the bulls (the same complaint that was later lodged against another great bullfighter, Manuel Rodríguez (Manolete, see in *DS*). Such consistency is often a mark of strength, because it is possible only when the bullfighter is powerful enough to control his bulls so thoroughly that he does not need to adjust his performance according to the bull's strengths or weaknesses. On the other hand, it makes the bullfighter predictable and perhaps boring.

But not all critics agree. Corrochano insists that Ortega's greatness derives from the fact that he tailors each fight to the bull's characteristics, not to the public's demands or his own strengths; he finds Ortega a moving, exciting performer. Corrochano also finds that, like Joselito and like all great artists, Ortega competes against himself, always attempting to improve, not repeat, his performance. Bagüés closes his evaluation of Ortega by claiming that "Su nombre suscita siempre los mayores elogios y nadie podrá negar que durante su época fué el eje de la fiesta taurina" (His name always elicits the highest praise and no one can deny that he was the defining bullfighter of his era).[494]

Hemingway and Ortega. Hemingway was not in Spain in 1930, when Ortega first burst into fame. But he had plenty of opportunity to see him in 1931, when bullring schedules all over Spain were juggled to bring Ortega to the major plazas and festivals. Hemingway saw him on two afternoons in Pamplona (July 8 and 11) and seven in Valencia (July 25, 27, 28, 29, 30, 31, and August 1). These performances all got rave reviews. Ortega's less successful performances included the confirmation of his *alternativa*, two more corridas later that June, and two more in September; all these took place in Madrid and might explain Hemingway's negative response.

Reviewing Ortega's first three Madrid performances (16, 23, and 28 March 1931, which Hemingway didn't see, though he probably heard or read about them when he arrived in Madrid), *El eco taurino* complains that Ortega failed to convince the Madrid public of his worth: although he had good bulls, the three afternoons were uneven, each corrida producing one satisfactory and one dreadful performance. Although Ortega clearly displays the self-confidence, power, and courage that mark the best of bullfighters, writes the critic, these

Madrid performances indicate that the glowing reports from the provinces were obviously doctored by his free-spending manager.[495]

Another reviewer, Gregorio Corrochano, wrote of the Madrid corrida of 16 March 1931, that it was disappointing because expectations had been so extraordinarily high. In his review of Ortega's second Madrid performance, however, Corrochano compares Ortega to Belmonte, in that both fight close to the bull, in the elegant style of the great Antonio Montes (q.v.). Even in these early Madrid performances (Ortega's weakest ones), Corrochano saw in Ortega a mature master of the bullfight. He adds that the initially hostile Madrid public was won over later in the season, and that in the *Corrida de la Prensa* of 8 October 1931, Ortega cut an ear and finally and completely won over Madrid. He praises Ortega's quiet, elegant fighting; his well-placed, unmoving feet; the quality, seriousness, and intensity of his work; his "faena de artista."[496] Bagüés insists that "nadie puede negar que durante su época [Ortega] fué el eje de la fiesta taurina" (no one can deny that in his time [Ortega] was the defining power, or touchstone, of bullfighting).[497] Hemingway probably read these reviews too.

Hemingway saw the confirmation of Ortega's *alternativa*, at the Madrid corrida of 16 June 1931. According to *El Clarín*, it was "Un fracaso como no se registró jamás en la historia del toreo, y una dura lección para Dominguín y para Ortega" (a failure unprecedented in the history of bullfighting, and a harsh lesson for Dominguín and Ortega).

It is interesting that Hemingway, who rails at critics and historians for withholding praise until after the bullfighter is dead (*DIA*, 240–44), here tries to discredit both the living artist and the critics who praise him. Hemingway chides Ortega for relying too heavily on his left hand (169, 170–71), exaggerates his age (168; in 1931 Ortega was either twenty-three or twenty-five years old, reports vary, but not thirty-two),[498] and disparages his face and body (169, 276). He claims that positive reviews indicated the smooth workings of Dominguín's propaganda machine, not the skill of Domingo Ortega (*see* the entry for *El Heraldo de Madrid*).

Hemingway's disparagement of Ortega is valuable for what it suggests about Hemingway as aficionado, artist, and man; it offers very little that is useful about Ortega himself. The fact that Dominguín, like all managers, promoted his client, does not diminish Ortega's achievements but might explain Hemingway's rejection of him. Perhaps he felt that at the beginning of his own career, he had not had financial and emotional support from his parents, or aggressive enough advertising from his publisher, and consequently resented another young man's good luck in finding a committed backer. Or perhaps, angered by or jealous of the young Ortega's early and spectacular success, Hemingway judged him too harshly, as he later did Manuel Rodríguez (Manolete) in *The Dangerous Summer*. Or perhaps Hemingway simply disliked the very vertical, unbending style of both Ortega and Manolete.

In January 1934, Hemingway resumed his attack on Ortega, noting that although Ortega "has . . . learned how to fight bulls, . . . [h]e is desperately monotonous" and superficial, building his popularity on crowd-pleasing theatricals, "his attitudes, his false tragedy."[499] In later years Hemingway seems to have wanted to rectify his vicious assessment, but he never fully recanted it (see Domingo Ortega in *DS*). In any case, Ortega's career proved Hemingway completely wrong. Fortunately, Hemingway had hedged his bets, grudgingly admitting that Ortega might last the course (*see* Fitzsimmons, Robert).

Other contemporary taurine critics, like Corrochano, Bagüés, and Uno al Sesgo, all recognized Ortega's greatness and praised him wholeheartedly. Cossío found him a limited but still indisputably important figure. *See also* Authors; *El Clarín*; Critics; Manolo Mejías, the "messiah" of 1930; and Cayetano Ordóñez, the "messiah" of 1925.

Ortega is the subject of at least three full-length biographies: Ventura Bagüés's folksy *Domingo Ortega, el torero de la armonía* (1931), Antonio Díaz Cañabate's effusive *La fábula de Domingo Ortega* (1950), and Antonio Santainés Cirés's more formal *Domingo Ortega: Ochenta años de vida y toros* (1986). Gregorio Corrochano analyzes Ortega's art in *¿Qué es torear?* Ortega has inspired a long list of poems, articles, and songs, including a famous *pasodoble*, and is himself the author of several well-regarded works, including *El toreo y la bravura del toro* (1961). *See also* Quintana, Juan.

The narrator claims that it is only due to his manager Domingo González, who bribed the critics, that Domingo Ortega was hailed as "the great phenomenon" and the "new messiah" of bullfighting in 1931. The narrator, who saw him perform that year in Aranjuez [30 May 1931], Toledo [4 June], Madrid [his weakest performances, see above], Pamplona, and several other places, formed a negative opinion of him (168–71; mentioned 93, 224, 226, 267, 276; photographs, *h:* 376–77).

Ortega, widow of. Full name: María Josefa Corrochano Sánchez de Ortega. Spanish bull breeder, 1848–1924. She was cousin to the taurine critic and theoretician Gregorio Corrochano (q.v.), and she was married to Vicente María Adrián Ortega (1846–94), whom she survived by thirty years. When she and her son became bull breeders, she was already a widow.

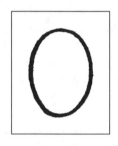

The Ortega herd was established in 1909, when the widow's son, Venancio Ortega Corrochano (1871–1936), bought twenty-five heifers from the Duke of Veragua (q.v.), which he augmented with another twenty-five the following year. The Ortegas' first seed bull proved defective, but in 1914 they were able to acquire a fine specimen, *Canastillo*, from the Count of Santa Coloma (q.v.). The first corrida that the Ortegas sold was fought on 25 August 1919; the second, which was fought on 16 May 1920, included the five-year-old bull *Bailaor* (son of *Bailaora* and *Canastillo*), who killed the great matador José Gómez Ortega (q.v.; no relation to the widow) at Talavera de la Reina.[500] This terrible event wrote the widow, her herd, and the town into the history of tauromachy.

In Hemingway's day two organizations registered fighting bulls: the well-established Unión de Criadores de Toros de Lidia (U.C.T.L., founded in 1905 and powerful to this day) and the younger Asociación de Ganaderos Libres de Reses Bravas (the Association of Unaffiliated Breeders of Fighting Stock), based in Salamanca. This Asociación took its membership from breeders who lacked the credentials to be accepted into the U.C.T.L. and therefore had to accept low prices. They also found it difficult to acquire stock from registered breeders, who were afraid of losing their affiliation in U.C.T.L. The Asociación tried to empower these breeders, but it never achieved the clout of the U.C.T.L.

Although the Ortega herd was "de casta conocida y cuidada y seleccionada con esmero" (of good pedigree, well bred, and carefully tended), it was never accredited by either organization and is therefore not well documented. *Toros y toreros en . . .* occasionally mentions nonaffiliated herds, but merely to list their annual output. Thus we know, for example, that in 1925, the Ortega ranch provided good bulls for the corrida in Talavera, which seems to have been the *ganadería*'s main outlet, as well as *novillos* for other plazas.

Ortega bulls were fought for the last time in 1935, in Talavera de la Reina: the matadors were Fermín Espinosa (Armillita Chico), Luis Gómez (el Estudiante), and Antonio García (Maravilla).[501]

The herd's brand (*hierro*) was an O, and its colors (*divisa*) blue and white. See also Talavera de la Reina in *DS*.

The narrator reports that in his day the widow of Ortega's bulls were in bad repute not only because they were dangerous and dull, but also because one of them killed the great José Gómez Ortega (Joselito; 39).

Ortega Monge, Enrique (Alamendro). Correct spelling: Almendro. Spanish bullfighter, 1892–1959.

There were at least three bullfighters named Enrique Ortega, sons of Gabriela Ortega's three brothers and therefore cousins of Gabriela's fabled sons Rafael (el Gallo) and José (Joselito) Gómez Ortega (qq.v.), and in-laws of Ignacio Sánchez Mejías (q.v.), who married one of Joselito's sisters. The three bullfighters named Enrique Ortega are distinguished by their second family names, which derive from their mothers, and by their nicknames. Enrique Ortega Jiménez (Lillo) was a *matador de novillos*; Enrique Ortega Ezpeleta (el Cuco) and Enrique Ortega Monge (Almendro) were banderilleros. At various times, all three worked in the *cuadrillas* of their famous cousins and in-laws. In 1920, when Joselito was killed, two of them were present: el Cuco, who was a member of Joselito's *cuadrilla* that year, and Almendro, who worked for Ignacio Sánchez Mejías, the matador who killed the bull that had killed Joselito.

Almendro's service in Joselito's *cuadrilla* (1912–18) marked the most successful years of his career. Afterwards Almendro worked for Sánchez Mejías (1918–22 and again in 1926), and for Maera (1923 and 1924). After some freelancing, he joined Cagancho's *cuadrilla* in 1927, where he worked until his retirement in 1931.[502]

I have seen no photographs like the one Hemingway mentions, with Joselito's brother-in-law holding a handkerchief to his eyes or with gypsies weeping over their dead master. One famous photograph, not reproduced in *Death in the Afternoon*, shows the dead Joselito surrounded by his cuadrilla, but Almendro (who was then working for Sánchez Mejías) is not in the picture. He does appear in the picture of the farewell brindis of his cousin Rafael Gómez Ortega (el Gallo), although the caption does not identify him by name (*h:* 400). As the photograph indicates, Almendro (seen clearly on the left) was rather heavy.[503]

> The narrator claims that Almendro was one of the gypsy bullfighters who wept over Joselito's corpse in Talavera de la Reina, May 1920 (243).

– P –

Pablo Romero. Full name: Felipe de Pablo Romero y Llosent. Spanish bull breeder, d. 1906.

Don Felipe de Pablo Romero founded his ranch in Seville in 1885, acquiring stock that already boasted a long and complicated pedigree: the Pablo Romero bulls are modern representatives of the *casta jijona*, developed by José Jijón in the early 1700s and distinguished by their large size, their strong heads, and their red color.[504] For another herd based on the *casta jijona*, *see* Martínez, don Vicente, in this volume. The Pablo Romero pedigree also contains Cabrera (q.v.) blood.

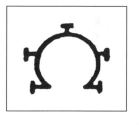 Don Felipe first presented his bulls for a Madrid corrida on 8 April 1888; the brand and colors (sky blue and white) have remained unchanged since then. When don Felipe died in 1906, his son and namesake inherited the carefully bred herd. This Felipe (1859–1943) brought his own two sons into the business, and in the 1920s and early 1930s, when Hemingway visited Spain frequently, it was the sons, José Luis and Felipe de Pablo Romero y Arloitia, who managed the property. They were the grandsons of the founder.[505] For the later history of the Pablo Romeros, see *DS*.

The narrator lists the Pablo Romero family of Seville among the best modern breeders of bulls (132).

Palace Hotel. Address: Plaza de las Cortes, 7, Madrid (near the Prado, the Ritz, and the Palacio Villahermosa, which today houses the fine Thyssen-Bornemisza Collection).

The Palace Hotel was established at the request of King Alfonso XIII (q.v.), who convinced millionaire Georges Marquet that Madrid needed such a luxury establishment. Construction began in 1912 and the five-hundred-room hotel opened fifteen months later, on 12 October 1913. It was then the largest hotel in Europe. It houses magnificent gardens, a variety of boutiques, several restaurants and conference rooms, including the Salón Hemingway/Mata-Hari. The Palace Bar boasts that Hemingway was a frequent customer. The hotel's central lobby is covered by a huge dome made of stained glass. Like all such establishments, the Palace Hotel has hosted many celebrities.[506]

Hemingway and the Palace Hotel. Hemingway mentioned the Palace in several of his books. One of the last scenes of *The Sun Also Rises* takes place in the bar of the Palace Hotel (*SAR*, 243–45); Catherine and David Bourne stay in a "big room in The Palace in Madrid" (*The Garden of Eden*, 59); and the narrator of *The Dangerous Summer* mentions that he stayed there in 1954 (*TDS*, 54). In *Death in the Afternoon*, the reference to the "beer place" near the Palace is probably the hotel's own "café-cervecería restaurant y billares," located at 5, Plaza de las Cortes, at the corner of Plaza de Cánovas and part of the Palace Hotel itself. By 1930, that address housed the "Sociedad Española de Automóviles Citroën," or "Citroën-Palace."[507]

In the list of places the narrator wishes he could include in his book is the bar near the Palace that became a Citroën show room (272).

Palencia. Capital of the province of Palencia, in Castilla-León. Its *feria* takes place early in September.

Hemingway in Palencia. In 1929, Ernest and Pauline saw "Two *swell* bull fights in Palencia—me in bed between fights with a busted gut": Ernest had "tor[n] a muscle badly in my groin." The Hemingways "stayed 3 days in the hottest room you ever saw 115 in the shade—room on the hot side of the house and no shade—only a small single bed for two and I couldn't move. Hotel full for the bull fights in Palencia. Really hot."[508]

The narrator wishes he could discuss the heat and other discomforts of Palencia (272; mentioned, 119, *h:* 425, 512).

Palha, don José. Full name: José Pereira Palha Blanco. Portuguese bull breeder, 1854–1937.

The Palha family ranch was established in Vila Franca de Xira, Portugal, c. 1850 (Hemingway misspells the name of the city, *DIA*, 132). Don Antonio José Pereira Palha first registered the breed under his name (Pereira), brand, and colors in Madrid in 1862. His son don José Pereira Palha Blanco presented the bulls to be fought in Madrid under his brand and colors (blue and white) on 4 November 1883; they kept this *antigüedad* (q.v.), or seniority, for the better part of a century.

The Pereira Palha family introduced a variety of seed bulls to the herd: Concha y Sierra bulls in 1875 and again in the late 1880s; Miura bulls in 1884, 1886, and 1888; and Veragua bulls in 1896 (qq.v.).[509] In 1931, the Palhas were described as "muy duras y difíciles" (very strong, stubborn, and difficult), which made them dangerous and "indeseables" (undesirable). Palhas are so skittish and unmanageable that one critic said they have "pulgas en las pezuñas" (fleas in their hooves).[510]

For the Palha's later history, see Palha in *DS*.

The narrator correctly identifies don José Palha as a Portuguese bull breeder whose bulls boast Miura blood (130; *see also* 132).

Palmeño. The nickname indicates that he comes from Palma del Río (Córdoba). *See* García, Julio.

Pamplona. Although Pamplona has a long history of bullfighting, documented as far back as the fourteenth century, its first bullring was not built until 1843.[511] It burned down on 10 August 1921, about three weeks after the end of the traditional Pamplona fiestas of San

Fermín. The fire broke out in three locations at the same time, suggesting arson. A new, larger bullring, with a seating capacity of thirteen thousand, was constructed on the same site. It was finished in time for the fiestas of 1922, so that there was no break in the annual celebrations. When Hemingway first visited Pamplona, in July 1923, this bullring was only one year old.

Hemingway and Pamplona. Before publishing *Death in the Afternoon*, Hemingway went to the Pamplona July bullfights, the *sanfermines*, in 1923, 1924, 1925, 1926, 1927, 1929, and 1931. After the Spanish Civil War, he did not visit Spain until the 1950s, when Franco, anxious to renew commercial and diplomatic ties with other countries, allowed the United States to open a base in Spain. Eisenhower's visit to Spain in 1953 marked a turning point. Tempted by a favorable exchange rate, tourists (see in *DS*) flowed into Spain (Hemingway among them) and, inevitably, to the Pamplona fiesta, the setting for much of the action of *The Sun Also Rises* (q.v.).

In 1959, the city honored its famous literary friend with a lunch hosted by the mayor, Miguel Javier Urmeneta.[512] Today a handsome bust of Hemingway stands in the Paseo Hemingway, near the bullring. It is decorated every July with the obligatory red neckerchief.

> The narrator mentions the Pamplona fiestas of 1923 (161), 1924 (*h:* 318), 1925 (154), 1930 (224), and 1931 (251–52). He remarks that Pamplona has changed (273, 278).

Parachute Jumper. *See* Zaragossa.

Park, Mungo. Scottish explorer in Africa, 1771–1806.

The son of a farmer who wanted his son to become a clergyman, Park studied medicine, as did Hemingway's father. He is the only one of the "naturalists" Hemingway derides who was scientifically trained.

Park was the first European to explore the Niger River. During his first expedition he suffered many illnesses and hardships, including four months' imprisonment by an Arab chief. These adventures are recorded in *Travels in the Interior Districts of Africa: Performed under the Direction and Patronage of the African Association in the Years 1795–1796, and 1797*, which was printed privately in 1799 and became a popular success. The book is written in the third person and flatters Park with flowery remarks like "The honour of having given birth to Mungo Park belongs to Scotland," and does not name any author other than Park himself. But John Portz reveals that it was "in part ghost-written by Byron Edwards, Secretary for the African Association which sponsored Park's two explorations. Park's biographers conclude that most of the rhapsodic, sententious, and religious passages—such as the one incorporated into 'A Natural History of the Dead'—are really the work of Edwards, although this is impossible to prove."[513]

Portz also claims that Hemingway did not read Park's *Travels*—a claim supported by the absence of the book from Hemingway's library—and that his material on Park derives from Bishop Edward Stanley's (q.v.) "Introduction" to his *Familiar History of the Birds*, where Stanley "quoted the passage [about the moss flower] from Park's text . . . In working the paragraph into his story, Hemingway . . . used several lines from Stanley's accompanying introduction as key phrases in his story. They are: '. . . a disposition to wonder and adore,' 'a few rational and interesting facts,' and especially the phrase by which he repeatedly derides Park, 'that persevering traveller.' " Portz claims that, by not reading all of Park's *Travels*, Hemingway "falls, ironically, into a number of misapprehensions . . . The . . . irony of Hemingway's rude and uninformed treatment of Park is that Park, undergoing appalling hardships and slipping through great dangers, is exactly the kind of man Hemingway always admired."[514]

But Park's book did contain the passage of the moss flower, which clearly expresses belief in God's benevolence, a belief Hemingway, like much of his generation, found offensive. He strenuously rejected Park, Bishop Stanley, the Reverend Gilbert White (q.v.), and his own father, all of whom read Christian theology into natural events.[515]

The large profits of *Travels in the Interior Districts of Africa* financed Park's second expedition (1805), from which he never returned. He either drowned or was murdered, probably in early 1806. *See also* The Lieutenant; "A Natural History of the Dead."

"A Natural History of the Dead" examines Mungo Park's pious claim that a study of nature will lead man to reject despair (134, 138, 139).

Pasaje Alvarez, Madrid. In modern maps this short street is called the Calle de Alvarez Gato; in 1923 it was known as Calle del Gato. It is not directly off the Calle Victoria (q.v.), but it is very near. If one walks along the Calle de la Cruz, starting at the Plaza de Canalejas (q.v.) and heading towards the Calle de Atocha, one will soon see the Calle Victoria to the right and, one block later, the Calle de Alvarez Gato on the left. This alley or passage (Hemingway calls it Pasaje Alvarez) leads into the Plaza Santa Ana, where the Cervecería Alemana and the Cervecería Alvarez (qq.v.) have operated for most of the twentieth century. The walk, from the Hotel Aguilar (q.v.) on the Carrera San Jerónimo, where Hemingway stayed, to the Pasaje Alvarez or the Cervecería Alemana, takes only a few minutes.

> The narrator remembers the neighborhood of the Pasaje Alvarez and the Calle Victoria (34, 40; *see also* 38, 55; *h*: 424, s.v. *Cerveza*).

Passchendaele. Also spelled Passchendale. A small town near Ypres, Belgium, site of enormous casualties when it was taken by the British (1917) and retaken by the Germans (1918). Passchendaele is usually associated with the British attack, but the battles demonstrated the strength of the defensive position, which can withstand the most courageous attempt to dislodge it. Passchendale is also known as the third battle of Ypres.

The Miura corrida in Pamplona that Hemingway compares to the battle of Passchendaele took place on 8 July 1925, that is, six or seven years before *Death in the Afternoon* (depending on whether one counts back from Hemingway's last visit to Spain, in 1931, or from the publication of *Death in the Afternoon*, in 1932) but not ten years ago, as Hemingway remarks.[516] The six Miura bulls of that corrida were large, cowardly, and, therefore, very dangerous; they killed eight horses and frightened the three bullfighters, Antonio Márquez, Marcial Lalanda, and Martín Agüero (qq.v.), who gave dreadful performances.[517] The taurine reviewer of *El pensamiento navarro* wrote that the Miuras were big, famous, cowardly, and too expensive: he suggested that henceforward Pamplona should let Miura keep them home on the ranch.[518] The same "very bad bullfight" of Miuras appears in *The Sun Also Rises*, page 169. *See* Miura, don Eduardo.

> The narrator compares a long, harsh corrida of Miura bulls to the terrible military action at Passchendaele, "with apologies" for the comparison. The defensive bulls presented such difficulties that the bullfighters were

reduced to killing them any which way, instead of fighting them artistically (154).

Pastor, Vicente. Full name: Vicente Pastor Durán. Spanish bullfighter, 1879–1966. Investiture as *matador de toros*, September 1902, in Madrid.

Pastor was said to be a typical Castilian bullfighter: dry, serious, disciplined, and disdainful of audience-pleasing novelties. The public responded coolly to Pastor's sober style, and after three meager seasons, 1904–06, he decided to try the more generous audiences of Peru. The South American rave reviews influenced the Spaniards, and the tide turned. Pastor was signed up for twenty-one corridas for 1907; all were successful and his career took off.

Pastor was very attached to Madrid, his birthplace, and during the Miura controversy (1908–09) he defied the boycott imposed by Machaquito and Bombita in order to continue appearing in the Madrid ring. His fame and following increased for the next several years. The Madrid impresarios rewarded his loyalty to them during the Miura controversy by contracting him to appear frequently in that bullring. In 1910 he was awarded the first "serious" ear ever cut in a Madrid bullring (see Trophies in *DS*).

Pastor's best seasons were 1911 and 1912 (fifty-one and fifty-six corridas). In the next two years his performances began to fall off, to forty and thirty-six corridas: he was thirty-five years old, and by then audiences were increasingly enchanted by Joselito and Belmonte. In 1917 Pastor was gored by a Miura bull. He recovered and finished that season but retired early in the 1918 season. He lived the rest of his long life in Madrid.[519]

Pastor's contemporaries include Machaquito, Bombita, and Antonio Fuentes (qq.v.). None of the critics I've read comment upon Pastor's fear of bulls, and in any case, it is neither unusual nor to his discredit for a bullfighter to be frightened before the fight.

The narrator correctly identifies Pastor's birth place as Madrid. He defines him as one of "the minor greats" (267) of the early twentieth century (241; *see also* 243; photographs, *h:* 370–71).

Patti, Adelina Juana María. Spanish-born soprano, 1843–1919.
"Possessed of one of the most beautiful voices of modern times,"

Patti became the highest paid opera singer of her day. She began singing professionally at age seven: "Her wonderful voice . . . was nearly ruined by overwork . . . and she only retired from the concert stage in time to save it." Her first "comeback" was probably her New York opera debut in 1859, when she was sixteen. She retired from the opera in the 1880s, but performed at the private theater on her Welsh estate and occasionally at the Albert Hall, London, "her singing of 'Home, Sweet Home' becoming peculiarly associated with those events."[520]

In 1903 Patti emerged from retirement for a two-month-long American concert tour "which was a great financial success, and which showed that her vocal powers were only slightly impaired" at age sixty. She gave a farewell concert in London in 1906, followed this with a provincial tour, and came out of retirement again in 1914, when she was already in her seventies, to gave a charity concert.[521]

> The narrator remarks that Rafael Gómez Ortega (el Gallo, q.v.) "gave more farewell performances than Patti" (157). A veiled reference to Patti appears in the Glossary (*h:* 433, s.v. *Despedida*).

Pepe-Hillo. *See* Delgado, José.

Perea, Bonifacio (Boni). Also known as El Boni. Full name: Bonifacio Perea Rapel. Spanish bullfighter, b. 1896.

As a boy Perea studied singing; he turned to bullfighting fairly late, at age seventeen. After several years of apprenticeship he reached the rank of *matador de novillos*. In 1925 he abandoned the dream of becoming a *matador de toros* and opted to be a banderillero. He had found his calling, and was soon hailed as one of the bravest and most distinguished of his profession.

Boni served the famous Manuel Mejías Jiménez (Bienvenida) in the years 1929–33, and did all the banderilla work for Marcial Lalanda and other famous matadors. His three sons, several nephews, and other relatives became bullfighters, many under the nickname Boni, Boni Chico, and so on.[522]

> The narrator correctly identifies Perea as the top-ranking member of Bienvenida's *cuadrilla*, noted for his excellent work with the cape and the banderillas (201).

Pereira Palha, don José. *See* Palha, don José.

Pérez Tabernero. Spanish bull breeders. The three Pérez Tabernero brothers whom Hemingway names—he does not mention the fourth brother, Alipio—were the sons of Fernando Pérez Tabernero and his wife, Lucía Sanchón, the daughter of the wealthy breeder Casimiro Manuel Sanchón, much of whose holdings she and Fernando inherited. Fernando and Lucía added their inherited stock to their own much smaller herd, which they had started c. 1885 with twenty-five cows from the Duke of Veragua and a Miura (qq.v.) seed bull.

Don Fernando and doña Lucía nurtured their herd for more than twenty years. When he died in 1909, his holdings went first to his widow and then to their four sons. These brothers used slightly different versions of the family name, calling themselves Graciliano Pérez Tabernero, Argimiro Pérez, Antonio Pérez de San Fernando (San Fernando being the family ranch), and Alipio Pérez T. Sanchón.

 Alipio, the brother Hemingway does not mention, was a prestigious bull breeder who kept his herd separately but worked closely with his brother Graciliano. Graciliano and Argimiro pooled their holdings, including the rights to the brand, colors (sky blue, pink, and yellow) and *antigüedad* (q.v.): 17 February 1895. They added two Miura seed bulls before dissolving their partnership. When Argimiro ceded his portion to Graciliano, this brother became the major owner of his family's enormous holdings. Argimiro died in 1936, his brother Graciliano retaining all rights to the brand, though Alipio's herd continued to hold the same *antigüedad.*

 In 1920, dissatisfied with the results obtained from the Miura bulls, Graciliano acquired 130 Santa Coloma and Albaserrada cows as well as one seed bull from each of those closely related ranches.[523] He bred out the Veragua-Miura strain, focusing instead on his new Vistahermosa (q.v.) stock. In 1931, thirty-one of his bulls and six of his *novillos* were fought in important plazas in Spain, al-

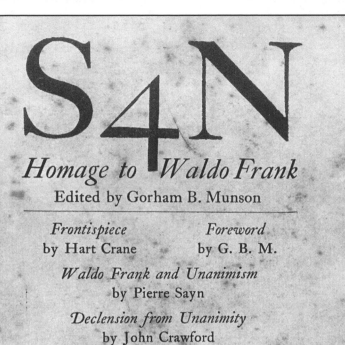

S4N

Homage to Waldo Frank

Edited by Gorham B. Munson

Frontispiece   *Foreword*
by Hart Crane   by G. B. M.

Waldo Frank and Unanimism
by Pierre Sayn

Declension from Unanimity
by John Crawford

From the Note-Books of Waldo Frank

A Note on the Language of Waldo Frank
by Gorham B. Munson

The Critic of Waldo Frank
by Jean Toomer

Front cover of a double issue of the literary journal *S4N* (*Space for Name*), September 1923 to January 1924. The journal's celebration of another writer angered the competitive Hemingway, who attacked Waldo Frank, his immigrant background, his flowery style, and his popular book *Virgin Spain* (1926). Courtesy John F. Kennedy Library, Boston.

A *cartel* of Hemingway's first corrida in Madrid, 27 May 1923. Hemingway and McAlmon paid scalper's price for *barrera* (first row) tickets in the shade (*sombra*). Courtesy Anthony Brand Collection, Seville.

Rafael Gómez Ortega (el Gallo) in Mexico, early 1900s. His suit is stiff with sequins and gold thread embroidery in a fashionable vine-and-leaf design. The *capote de paseo* (parade cape) is carefully arranged over his left arm to show off the matching handwork. Courtesy Anthony Brand Collection, Seville.

Ignacio Sánchez Mejías as *novillero*, c. 1918. He served a long apprenticeship in the *cuadrillas* of Belmonte, Rafael el Gallo, and Joselito before his promotion to the final rank of *matador de toros* at the relatively late age of twenty-eight. The *alamares* (appliqued bead work) on the vest do not match the ones on his jacket, an eccentricity expressive of his strong personality. Courtesy Anthony Brand Collection, Seville.

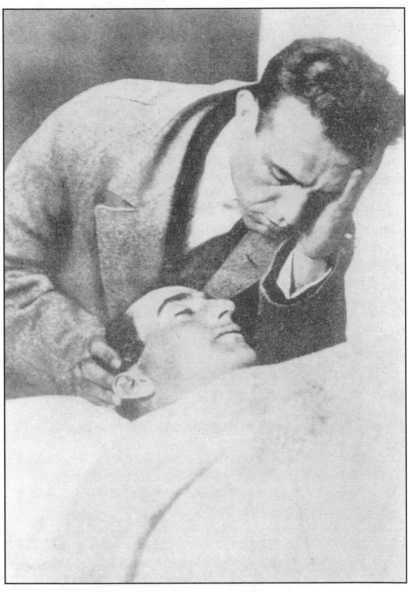

Talavera de la Reina, 16 May 1920. Ignacio Sánchez Mejías mourns his friend, colleague, and brother-in-law, José Gómez Ortega (Joselito). Sánchez Mejías killed Bailaor, the bull that had fatally gored Joselito. Courtesy Anthony Brand Collection, Seville.

Juan Anlló (Nacional II) takes a triumphal tour of the ring, early in his career. The shape and size of the *alamares* on his jacket, sleeves, and *taleguilla* (trousers) date the photo to the early 1920s. Promoted to *matador de toros* in 1921, Nacional II had only four good seasons before he died in a ring-side brawl. Courtesy Anthony Brand Collection, Seville.

Manuel Granero on the day he was killed by the Veragua bull Pocapena in Madrid, 7 May 1922. Typically heavy gold embroidery adorns his stylish suit, replacing even the *alamares* usually seen on toreros' *trajes de luces*. Suits without *alamares* enjoyed a vogue in the 1920s, but *alamares* made a quick comeback. The fashion of Granero's day also called for smaller *hombreras* (epaulettes) and *caireles* (beadwork around the epaulettes) than those worn by Rafael el Gallo a decade earlier. Courtesy Anthony Brand Collection, Seville.

José García Carranza (Algabeño *hijo*), c. 1923. Toreros dress handsomely even when off-duty. Algabeño wears a wide-brimmed Cordoban hat, four-stud collar, and custom-made, lace-fronted shirt. Courtesy Anthony Brand Collection, Seville.

Cayetano Ordóñez (Niño de la Palma) in Pamplona, July 1925. Seen here less than a month after his Seville *alternativa* (investiture), Niño de la Palma wears a suit without *alamares*. His *capote de paseo* is folded and draped around him as he prepares to enter the bullring during his first feria in Pamplona. In *The Sun Also Rises*, Hemingway wrote Cayetano Ordóñez into American literature. In *The Dangerous Summer*, he did the same for Cayetano's son Antonio. Courtesy John F. Kennedy Library, Boston.

Enrique Torres, 1928. Valencia saw two of its promising *novilleros*, Enrique Torres and Vicente Barrera, promoted to *matadores de toros* late in the 1927 season when they were only nineteen years old. Torres's best years were 1926 to 1930. At that time, the *alamares* tended to be rather angular and the *caireles* quite narrow. Courtesy Anthony Brand Collection, Seville.

Marcial Lalanda (upper right) confers upon Saturio Torón the rank of
matador de toros in Pamplona, 8 July 1930. In 1930 Lalanda was Spain's
top-ranked matador, with eighty-seven *corridas*. Torón was injured by his
second bull on the afternoon of his *alternativa*, which Lalanda killed.
Injuries plagued Torón, who resigned his *alternativa* in 1933. Lalanda
favored the *traje de luces* without *alamares*, which was fashionable at the
time of his *alternativa* in 1921 (confirmed in Madrid on 7 May 1922, at
the *corrida* in which Granero was killed). He wore such suits during the
twenty years of his career. Torón wears a more modern suit, with white-
tufted *alamares* visible at wrist, knee, and back. Courtesy John F.
Kennedy Library, Boston.

Fermín Espinosa (Armillita Chico) in Spain, c. 1930. The costume is typically Mexican, with butterfly-shaped *alamares* and bright *pasmanería* (colored thread embroidery) on the *capote de paseo*. In twenty-five years of fighting bulls, the "Mexican Joselito" suffered only one serious goring. Courtesy Anthony Brand Collection, Seville.

Sidney Franklin, c. 1930. Born in Brooklyn and trained in Mexico,
Franklin wears a Mexican-style *traje de luces* practically indistinguish-
able from Armillita's, down to the butterfly-shaped *alamares*. Armillita
wears the very *torero*, Andalusian four-stud collar; Franklin's pedestrian
collar lacks grace. Courtesy Anthony Brand Collection, Seville.

Nicanor Villalta, c. 1931. The carefully posed photograph minimizes Villalta's long neck and reveals a scar on his cheek, a reminder of the goring he suffered on 26 May 1923. When Hemingway first saw Villalta in Madrid at the sixth subscription bullfight, 10 June 1923, a bandage covered this wound. Villalta's *capote* reflects his early training in Mexico and his popularity in that country. Courtesy Anthony Brand Collection, Seville.

Manuel Mejías (Manolo Bienvenida), c. 1931. From his investiture in
June 1929 at age sixteen to his untimely death of cancer in 1938, Manolo
Bienvenida was one of the stars of the ring. In 1931 he was ranked second nationwide, having fought 84 corridas and killed 174 bulls. His first
serious goring, which occurred in 1933, did not, as the narrator of *Death
in the Afternoon* fears, break his spirit or diminish his *afición*. The photograph shows an interesting sartorial innovation: the *caireles* and *alamares*
end in dark rather than light tufts. Courtesy Anthony Brand Collection,
Seville.

The *Peto*: 1917 and 1993. In 1917, the retired matador Enrique Vargas (Minuto) designed one of the earliest versions of the *peto* (protective carapace worn by the horse during the pic-ing). Many other versions were tested before the *peto* was incorporated into the taurine code in 1928. The *peto* continued to evolve, however. The modern *peto*, seen in the bottom photo, is a solid, continuous shield that protects the horse's chest, right side, and hindquarters. Hemingway, who began to follow the bulls in 1923, saw many horses killed in the ring; today's spectator expects that no horses will die. Courtesy Anthony Brand Collection, Seville.

most all of them earning high marks. *Toros y toreros* summarizes his herd's performance that year: "Otra camada superior de este inteligente y afortunadísimo ganadero, que ha logrado colocar y mantener su divisa a una altura envidiable, que se disputan los toreros y por lo tanto las empresas. . . . ¡Enhorabuena y siempre así!" (Another fine litter from this intelligent and lucky breeder, who has achieved and maintains an enviable position, his bulls being much in demand among bullfighters and, consequently, among impresarios. . . . Congratulations, and keep it up!).[524]

After the Spanish Civil War, which decimated most herds and fortunes, Graciliano sold much of his stock to José Escobar, whose ranch is in Seville. Graciliano retained the rights to the brand, colors, and *antigüedad*, as well as twenty-five carefully chosen cows and one seed bull, with which to begin anew.

Having ceded his share of his father's herd to his brother, Argimiro established his own herd in 1914, basing it on Vistahermosa stock, most of it purchased from Dionisio Peláez's fine collection of Santa Coloma and Tovar stock. He registered it under his name, brand, and colors (yellow and pink) on 6 June 1919. In 1931 he presented sixteen bulls and two *novillos* to be fought in bullrings. Most performed well, but they did not earn the kudos enjoyed by Graciliano's stock. Even so, his herd was described as "magnífica." Most of it was lost during the Spanish Civil War.[525]

Antonio, the third brother Hemingway mentions, was also a much respected bull breeder. Rejecting his share of his father's herd, in 1911 he acquired a Murube-based herd built up by the Portuguese bull breeder Luis de Gama. He crossed it with Parladé and Tamarón seed bulls and added Gamero Cívico cows (all Vistahermosa strain). By 1931 he had "una de las mejores vacadas de España" (one of the finest herds in Spain); his bulls were highly prized by bullfighters.[526] The descendants of these four brothers are still a major force in the Salamancan fields.

The narrator counts the three Pérez Tabernero brothers—don Argimiro, don Gracialano (*sic*), and don Antonio—among the top bull breeders of his day (132).

Peto. Padded carapace, weighing between twenty-five and thirty kilograms, worn by the picador's horse to protect its chest and right side, which are presented to the bull during pic-ing. It is occasionally called *caperuza* and *caparazón*, or, when it is ceremonial rather than functional, *gualdrapas*.[527]

Before the Peto. The bull's charges on the mounted picador were applauded by the audience as evidence of *bravura* (bravery), which is measured by the bull's willingness to charge even after he discovers that the charge will cause him pain. These charges often killed the picador's horse, and pre-*peto* audiences expected that a good set of brave bulls would leave many gored horses scattered about the ring. The sight elicited the following description from Byron:

> One gallant steed is stretch'd a mangled corse;
> Another, hideous sight! unseam'd appears,
> His gory chest unveils life's panting source;
> Though death-struck, still his feeble frame he rears;
> Staggering, but stemming all, his lord unharm'd he bears.
> (*Childe Harold's Pilgrimage*, Canto the First, LXXVII, ll. 769–73)

When Hemingway started going to the bullfights in 1923, the *peto* was not yet in use, and he saw plenty of gored horses: "The horse's entrails hung down in a blue bunch and swung backward and forward as he began to canter. . . . Blood pumped regularly from between the horse's front legs" (*In Our Time*, Chapter Ten).

Hemingway's descriptions of the hasty repairs that returned the horses to the bullring, and of the disgust of foreign tourists who were attending bullfights in increasing numbers, are accurate accounts of the situation before the *peto* was introduced in 1927. At that time, the picadors were in the ring for more time than they are today and had far more opportunities for pic-ing. In fact, they were in the ring before the bull himself entered it, and stayed until the *suerte de banderillas*. For a discussion of this and other changes in the evolution of bullfighting, including the introduction of the *peto*, see "The Corrida," in the introduction to this volume.

The Peto Controversy. The *peto* was first proposed in 1906, by the taurine critic Mariano de Cavia (Sobaquillo), who suggested that it be used that year in the fiestas held in the honor of the royal wedding of Alfonso XIII and the English-born Victoria Eugenia (qq.v.), who would undoubtedly be shocked at the spectacle of disembowelled horses. Sobaquillo's proposal unleashed such a hot debate that the *peto* did not appear in Spanish rings until the late 1920s.

Purists rejected the *peto* outright, arguing that it would change the basic nature of the bullfight so drastically that the nation would have to decide between preserving the bullfight as it was or else canceling the whole thing. Between these two extremes, many possibilities emerged. Some aficionados suggested a variety of changes in the pic, or *vara*, such as modifying the point, shortening the pole (which is about eight feet long), or substituting the shorter *rejón* (about five feet long, used when the entire bullfight is performed by a mounted bullfighter or *rejoneador*) for the pic. In fact, *rejoneo*, in which the well-bred, carefully trained horse moves around the ring instead of standing still, as happens in pic-ing, was also suggested as a substitute for the *suerte de varas*; few horses are injured in *rejoneo*.

Counter proposals included reducing the number of pics inflicted or changing the position of the horse or the length of its stay in the plaza. Tomás Orts Ramos (Uno al Sesgo) argued that the best protection for the horse resided in the person who made his living from the horses, and that if the horse contractor, and not the matador, were in charge of hiring the picadors, the picadors would be motivated to protect the horse. According to his plan, never adopted, both horses and picadors would be supplied by the ring. Another suggestion was that the matador himself should supply his picadors' horses, although the problems of transporting horses from corrida to corrida would be enormous.

Some people insisted that stricter supervision of the picador would force him to abide by already-existing regulations, which offered sufficient protection both for him and for the horse. Another proposal gave more authority to the veterinarian, providing a horse-clinic in the plaza itself, and writing stricter rules for returning horses to the ring. Others said that the kindest thing would be to kill the injured horses immediately, not to heal them in order to expose them to injury again.

Clearly, the eviscerated and dying horses were becoming increasingly repugnant to the public, and the 1923 *Reglamento*, cognizant of the change in taste, called for the removal of injured animals from public view.[528]

Design and Effects of the Peto. In 1917, the retired matador Enrique Vargas (Minuto) designed what is probably the earliest version of the *peto*; other designs followed. In 1926, a government commission was established to study the *suerte de varas* (the pic-ing),[529] and the debate over the *peto* intensified. The Society for the Protection of Animals lobbied strongly for its introduction, as did tourist agencies and other sectors of the population. But even the pro-*peto* factions argued among themselves: the very design of the *peto* was controversial. Some worried that the early designs offered insufficient protection; such a *peto* might make the horse's injuries less visible to the public, but it would not help the horse. Others predicted it would make the horse more clumsy and difficult to manage and would therefore increase the danger to the picador. And others thought it would enable the picador to inflict excessive punishment on the bull and thus weaken him; this would not only dilute the artistic and emotional possibilities of the last third of the bullfight, but might even endanger the bullfighter, as a weakened, uncertain bull would be more likely to embark upon wild, sudden rushes.

Several models of the *peto* were tested on ranches, but the carapace was not used in a bullfight until the Madrid *novillada* on 6 March 1927, almost a decade after Vargas displayed his design. The *peto* was added to the bullfight code on 18 June 1928, as Article 85.[530] It was incorporated into the body of the *Reglamento* itself in the 1930 edition. Obviously, the various aspects of the *peto* were much discussed in the years Hemingway visited Spain, and he saw bullfights both before and after the introduction of the *peto*.

The design of the *peto* and the rules governing its use continued to be modified for several years.[531] The 1930 *Reglamento* did not specify its size, construction, or weight. The next edition, the 1962 *Reglamento*, defined its design and weight (twenty-five kg., with leeway for an additional five kg., unchanged in later editions). Regulations governing the *peto* appear in all subsequent editions of the *Reglamento*.[532]

The Post-Peto Situation. The *peto* drastically reduced the number of horses killed by the charging bull. The 1930 *Reglamento*, the first to include the new ruling, specified that the bullring must provide four horses per bull to be fought, with twelve of them saddled and waiting in the *patio de caballos* ready to enter the ring if needed; a codicil soon reduced the number to three per bull, and by 1947 one commentator wrote that eight or ten horses would probably suffice for the whole corrida.[533] And indeed, the 1962 *Reglamento* lowered the number to a minimum of eight horses for the whole corrida, and that number was lowered again in the 1992 *Reglamento*, which requires six in first-rank plazas and four in all others—that is, one or fewer horses per bull.[534] Hemingway saw many dead horses in the ring; the modern spectator expects that no horses will be killed.

Always resistant to change, Hemingway argues against the *peto*. He was not alone: the *peto* completely changed the *suerte de varas* and, unavoidably, all that follows it. For a discussion of the evolution of all three acts of the bullfight, see "The Corrida," in the introduction to this volume. *See also* the entry for Primo de Rivera, Miguel, in this volume, and Redondel and Seville in *DS*.

> The narrator defines the *peto* (*h:* 423, s.v. *Caparacón*; 464, s.v. *Peto*). He disapproves of it: it endangers the picador, it allows horse contractors to return injured horses to the ring, and it detracts from the spectator's experience of the bullfight (7–8, 12, 184–85, *h:* 464–66, s.v. *Pica*). He is aware of the controversy surrounding the *peto* and the different proposals put forward to protect the horses (186–89).

Pfeiffer, Virginia Ruth (Jinny, V. R.). American heiress, 1902–73. Like her older sister, Pauline, Virginia was educated at the Visitation Convent in St. Louis. She spent a year at the University of Missouri and then traveled to Paris with Pauline. The two sisters were dark, good-looking, well educated, cosmopolitan, and clever, and several biographers have mentioned that when Hemingway first met them, he was more impressed with Virginia.

Hemingway retained his fondness for his sister-in-law during the early years of his marriage to Pauline: she traveled with them, wrote and visited frequently, and often took care of the Hemingway boys. Hemingway encouraged her writing, none of which achieved publication. As the marriage soured, however, she openly expressed her disapproval of his unfaithfulness and his rudeness to her sister, and he in turn accused her of turning Pauline against him. He also became less tolerant of her bisexuality.

The two sisters remained close friends until Pauline's death. In the 1940s Jinny maintained a stylish home in Hollywood, California, which she shared with Laura Archera, who later married Aldous Huxley (q.v.). Attractive, rich, "spirited and adventurous," Jinny had many friends. She adopted two children.[535]

Jinny was seven, not three, years younger than Pauline.

Hemingway describes V. R.'s response to the bullfights (*h:* 499).

P. H. *See* Hemingway, Patrick.

Philip II. Spanish ruler, 1527–98; king of Spain, 1556–98, and of Portugal, 1581–98 (as Philip I).

From his father, the Emperor Charles V, Philip II inherited Spain, Naples, and Sicily, and through his mother, Isabel, the daughter of the king of Portugal, he inherited the throne of Portugal. During his forty-year reign, Spain had large Italian, American, and African holdings and was one of the superpowers of Europe. Philip II strengthened his ties with other important nations through treaties and through his four marriages: to Mary of Portugal, Mary Tudor of England, Isabel of Valois of France, and Anna of Austria. He has been implicated in the deaths of his oldest son and of his half-brother.

Philip II's reign was marked by war, both on the religious and political, or national, fronts. He acquired the Philippine Islands, expelled the Moors, defeated the Turks, failed to maintain Spain's hold on the Netherlands and Tunis, and sent the Spanish Armada on its ill-fated mission against England (1588). When he died, Spain was still at war with Britain and France. *See also* El Escorial.

The Monarchy and the Bullfight. Spain's monarchy has had a complicated relationship with the bullfight. In its early days, bullfighting was an aristocratic entertainment, and royal births, birthdays, weddings, and accessions were traditionally celebrated with bullfights. But Philip II, a committed Catholic and an unbending, hardworking monarch, disdained such public entertainments. One of his many biographers reports that "Like his great-grandmother Isabella of Castile, he disliked bull-runs and usually avoided them."[536] In 1567, during Philip II's reign, Pope Pius V (q.v.) forbade bullfighting upon pain of excommunication. But the king argued that the bullfight was so deeply embedded in Spain's "blood" that it could not be eradicated. He pressured Pope Gregory XIII (1572–85) to soften his predecessor's edict forbidding it.

Influenced by the Church and related interests, however, later monarchs occasionally attempted to ban the bullfight. Their attempts were only slightly more successful than those of the papacy. King Philip V (1683–1746) and his son Ferdinand VI (1712–59) forbade the bullfight, but their edicts were so widely disregarded that they hastily rescinded them. In 1785 Charles III (1716–88) permitted only those bullfights that raised funds for worthy organizations, and his son Charles IV (1748–1819) finally managed to impose a complete three-year ban, from 1805 to 1808.

A weak king, Charles IV was much aided in his anti-taurine efforts by his corrupt minister, Manuel de Godoy (1767–1851), and by Godoy's friend, the essayist Pedro Rodríguez, Count of Campomanes (1723–1802) who argued, among other things, that the bullfight weakened Spain economically, spiritually, and politically. Campomanes wrote that the breeding of bulls and horses occupied huge tracts of land that could be more profitably employed in agriculture. In addition, taurine spectacles drew workers away from their workplaces and encouraged idleness and violence, thus damaging both the economy and the national character. And finally, the bloody spectacle strengthened her neighbors' antipathy to the Spanish people, a particularly potent claim in view of Napoleon's power. It is ironic that the unpopular ban was lifted in 1808 by Napoleon's brother Joseph Bonaparte (appointed King of Spain, 1808–13), who hoped thus to endear himself to his Spanish subjects.[537] Throughout the centuries, important bullfighters have been court favorites, a tradition continued by Franco, who enjoyed hunting and chatting with Luis Miguel Dominguín (see in *DS*) and other taurine luminaries of his day.

The Alguacil's Costume. Hemingway traces the extravagant costume of the *alguacilillo* or *alguacil* to the reign of the stern, empire-building Philip II, but the basic, most authoritative taurine dictionaries (e.g., those of Sánchez de Neira and Nieto Manjón) date it to the seventeenth century, that is, the reign of the pleasure-loving Philip

IV (1605–65). Philip IV relinquished most of his authority to his trusted advisor, the Conde-Duque de Olivares (1587–1645), who mismanaged Spain's affairs while encouraging the king to cultivate his amusements. Philip IV had a well-developed artistic sense: he was the patron of Velázquez, Lope de Vega (qq.v.), and Calderón de la Barca. It is more likely that uniforms and costumes were more elaborate in his time than in the days of his grandfather, Philip II, who in any case disliked the bullfight. But the costume probably evolved and was modified over time, with some details dating to the sixteenth and others to the seventeenth century.

Today, in some plazas, *alguacilillos* wear a modern *traje campero* (formal country dress). But they are more often seen in the old-fashioned black velvet outfit adorned with panels of yellow or red taffeta, wide sleeves, ruffled neckpiece, long gloves, and spurred boots. The most spectacular item of the costume is the black hat, with its pinned-up brim, black and colored ribbons, and eye-catching tall plume.[538] This *sombrero chambergo* derives its name from Friedrich Hermann Schomberg (c. 1615–90), the French marshal who introduced the fashion. Items of that military uniform, most notably the hat, were adopted by the personal guard of Charles II (1661–1700), son and successor of Philip IV.

> Describing the ceremonies and costumes of the bullring, the narrator claims that the mounted bailiffs' costumes date from the reign of Philip II (59, *h:* 413, s.v. *Alguacil*).

Pilar, Virgen del Pilar. Pilar is the patron saint of the province of Aragón. Tradition has it that the Virgin appeared to St. James the Apostle (Santiago) as he prayed at Zaragoza. A large, richly decorated basilica stands at the site of the shrine built by James the Apostle to commemorate the miracle. An image of the Virgin stands on a marble pillar (Spanish *pilar*) that supposedly marks the precise location of the vision.

Zaragoza (*see* Zaragossa), celebrates Pilar's feast day, 12 October, with a *feria*. Hemingway used the name Pilar as a code name or nickname for Pauline during their affair, and especially when they were separated, waiting for Hadley to agree to a divorce.[539] Hemingway also gave this name to his boat and to a character in *For Whom the Bell Tolls*. See also Pilar in *DS*.

Hemingway and his friends often used nicknames (q.v.) for themselves and for each other: *see*, for example, Smith, William Benjamin
in this volume; and Davis, Bill; *Papa* in *DS*. The practice was extended to his sisters, brother, wives, sons, and friends.

The calendar of important fiestas remarks that the taurine season ends in
October with the Zaragoza festival in honor of Pilar (*h:* 478, *h:* 514).

Pinky. Baker mentions two horses at the Nordquist ranch, where Hem-
ingway, Pauline, and John (Bumby) spent the summer of 1930:
Goofy and Bess (a mare who is also mentioned in *For Whom the Bell
Tolls* [337]).[540] There is no mention of a Pinky.

Pinky is a horse at a Wyoming ranch (228).

Pino Suárez, Manuel del (el Niño del Matadero). Spanish bullfighter, d. 1964.

After several years in fighting in minor bullrings, Manuel del Pino,
a Southerner from El Puerto de Santa María (Cádiz), began to break
into the more important bullrings of Andalucía, where he was quite
popular by the end of the 1920s. But his Madrid debut as *novillero*
on 25 March 1931 was a disaster: injured by his first bull, he was
unable to complete his performance. That year he appeared in fifteen
or twenty-eight *novilladas* (reports vary), the number descending to
nineteen in 1933, six in 1934, four in 1935. The Spanish Civil War
seems to have ended his sorry career.

He was never promoted to *matador de toros*.[541]

The narrator identifies "the kid of the slaughterhouse" as one of large crop
of "Niños" in the mid- and late 1920s (*h:* 455, s.v. *Niño*).

Pius the Fifth. Secular name: Michele Ghislieri. Italian churchman,
pope, and saint, 1504–72. He became pope in 1566, holding the position, as is usual, until his death. He was canonized in 1712; his feast
day is 5 May.

Ghislieri was such an aggressive Inquisitor and later Grand Inquisitor that even some of his colleagues were "repelled by his excessive
severity, . . . censoriousness and obstinacy." His election as Pope
marked "the enthronement of the Inquisition."

In short order, Pius V reformed the catechism, breviary and missal, and published a Papal Bull, *In Coena Domini* (1568), which "re-asserted the Holy See's supremacy over the civil power." He established the Index to identify and proscribe "heretical literature"; expelled the Jews from all Church-controlled lands and offices; and in general "issued . . . decrees and ordinances . . . with astonishing rapidity," including "severe penalties . . . [for] Sunday desecration, profanity and animal baiting." The edict Hemingway mentions was entitled *De salutis gregis dominici* (1567), which forbade bullfights under the threat of excommunication to participants and spectators.[542]

In August 1575, the recently installed Pope Gregory XIII, who lacked "the savage vehemence of his predecessor" and who was pressured by Philip II (q.v.), published the Papal Bull *Expone Nobis*, which exempted all lay people from Pope Pius V's edict and its punishment. Subsequent popes continued to condemn the bullfight, but with decreasing severity: in 1583, Pope Sixtus V decried it as dangerous, and in January 1596 Pope Clement VIII completely lifted the decree of excommunication in another Papal Bull, *Suscepti Numeris*. In subsequent centuries, including the present, the Church has had to accommodate the bullfight.[543]

As the narrator points out, Pope Pius V forcefully opposed the bullfight (22).

Plaza de Canalejas. The Plaza de Canalejas was named for José Canalejas (1854–1912), the radical, liberal, pragmatic prime minister of Spain, 1910–12, assassinated by an anarchist in the streets of Madrid. The plaza is near Madrid's Puerta del Sol, on the Carrera de San Jerónimo. It marks the confluence of the Calle del Príncipe, the Calle de la Cruz, and the Calle de Sevilla (which leads to the Calle de Alcalá). It is very near the Hotel Aguilar (q.v.). At 28, Plaza de Canalejas, off the Carrera de San Jerónimo, Madrid, stood La Teatral, which sold tickets for public spectacles such as circuses and bullfights. It was run by José Antonio Peypoch. The same building housed the Reina Victoria Theater and a ladies' dress shop. A few doors down was the Buffet Italiano (Italian Restaurant, q.v.).[544] *See also* Pasaje Alvarez.

The narrator describes a café on the Plaza de Canalejas that advertises bullfights all over Spain (38, 40; *see also* 33–34).

P. M. Pauline Marie Pfeiffer became Hemingway's second wife on 10 May 1927. *See* Hemingway, Pauline.

Pocol. A small town near Cortina d'Ampezzo, in the province of Belluno, in the Dolomite Mountains of the northern Veneto province, at the headwaters of the Piave River. It is the site of a World War I war cemetery, the *Ossario di Pocol*, where thousands of soldiers from both the Italian and Austro-Hungarian sides were buried. In 1935 a monument and crypt were built at the site. Almost ten thousand soldiers, including General Antonio Cantore, were reburied in its crypt.[545] *See also* the General.

> The narrator mentions but does not name the general who was buried in the beautiful cemetery in Pocol (140).

Police. *See* Guardia Civil.

Porcellian. The Porcellian Club of Harvard College is a secret undergraduate society established in the 1780s. It began as a small group that met in each other's rooms on alternate Friday evenings and who called themselves The Argonauts, The Pig Club (because a young pig roasted whole was traditional fare at the banquets), and The Gentlemen's Society. In 1794, they finally settled on the current name, "Porcellian"; their symbol is a boar's head.

The club has honorary members (alumni) and immediate members (current undergraduates). The grand marshal presides over meetings which include the entire membership, and the deputy marshal runs the more frequent ones attended only by the undergraduates. Other officers are the trustees, the librarian, and the secretary. The club, which seems to serve a purely social function, has been described as "Harvard's snootiest social club."[546] *See also* Skull and Bones.

> The narrator mocks "porcellian-ed" socialites who buy expensive seats for the bullfight but don't stay until the end (34).

Prado. Full name: Museo del Prado de San Jerónimo (the Meadow of St. Jerome).

Madrid's premier museum was built on the grounds of the St. Jerome Monastery and of the Palace of Buen Retiro, at the end of the eighteenth century, according to a design by the architect Juan de

Villanueva. Originally intended as a natural history museum, it was opened as an art museum in 1819. The royal collections of art works formed the basis for what has become one of the world's great art museums. Additional buildings have been added as the collection quickly grew. Masters like el Greco, Goya, and Velázquez (qq.v.) are well represented in the Prado, where Hemingway saw them. See also *DS*.

> The narrator admires the organization and presentation of the Prado's collection (51–52; mentioned, 33, 270).

President. For a summary of the duties and privileges of the president of the bullfight, see President in *DS*.

> The narrator mentions the corrida's president frequently but does not express an opinion about the office or any particular incumbent (58–59, 61, 96, 97, *h:* 412, 419, 425, 437, 454, 458–59, 460, 468).

Primo de Rivera, Miguel (Marqués de Estella). Spanish lawyer, general, and politician, 1870–1930.

Primo de Rivera's early military service was in the Spanish provinces of Cuba, the Philippines, and Spanish Morocco. After the military coup on 13 September 1923, Primo became the head of the government and the military. For the rest of the 1920s (that is, for most of the years that Hemingway followed the bulls), Spain was a dictatorship, plagued by social unrest and political uprisings (*see* Civil Guard; Deva; Rotonde). Finally even the military turned against Primo de Rivera, and the king convinced him to resign.

Primo de Rivera left the political scene on 30 January 1930. When the Republicans won the election later that year, he went into exile in France, where he died.

Primo de Rivera's son, José Antonio Primo de Rivera (1903–36), established the Falangist party, closely allied with Franco after the Spanish Civil War. Another son, Fernando, was also killed in the early days of the Spanish Civil War. For details about a son who survived the war, see Primo de Rivera, Miguel, in *DS*.

The *peto* (q.v.) was instituted during Primo de Rivera's dictatorship, although it had been proposed twenty years earlier. *See also* Victoria Eugenia.

The narrator correctly reports that the law requiring horses to wear the *peto* was passed under Primo de Rivera's rule (7; *h:* 426, s.v. *Cojones*; 464, s.v. *Peto*; 473, s.v. *Reglamento*).

Proverbs. Religious talismans are the subject of the proverb, "A quien no hace la cruz, se lo lleva el diablo" (he who doesn't make the cross is taken by the devil), which Hemingway translates for his readers (*h:* 399, s.v. *Cruz*).[547] Women are also the subject of proverbs such as "más cornadas dan las mujeres" (women inflict more wounds [than the horns of the bull], a reference to "giving horns" or cuckolding a man and to the generally held belief that sexual intercourse weakens or slows a man and should be avoided before a bullfight). The narrator seems to like this proverb: he quotes it twice (103, *h:* 488, s.v. *Uretritis*; *see also* Women and Girls, in this volume and in *DS*).[548] The saying is a variant of "más cornadas da el hambre" (hunger inflicts more wounds [because it makes the bullfighter take risks]), attributed to Manuel García (el Espartero, q.v.).[549] Probably the oldest version is Pedro Romero's "más cogidas da el miedo que los toros" (fear inflicts more wounds). *See also* Luck; Roman Catholic, in this volume; and Proverbs in *DS*.

Puerta del Sol, Madrid. *See* Pasaje Alvarez.

– Q –

Quintana, Juan (Juanito). Full name: Juan Quintana Urra. Spanish hotelier and bullfight aficionado, c. 1891–1974.

In July 1923, when Hadley and Ernest first came to Pamplona, they had not yet met Quintana. But the following year, following the recommendation of their friend Rafael Hernández Ramírez (q.v.), the Hemingways and their friends (Chink Dorman-Smith, Bill and Sally Bird, Bob McAlmon, George O'Neil, Donald Ogden Stewart, and John Dos Passos) stayed at the Hotel Quintana, Pamplona. Hemingway patronized the hotel during the next several fiestas of San Fermín, and both Quintana and his hotel appear under the name Montoya in *The Sun Also Rises*.

Quintana had known the Gómez Ortega brothers (Rafael and Joselito) and was friends with Juan Belmonte, Cayetano Ordóñez, Marcial Lalanda (qq.v.), and many other bullfighters who lodged in the Hotel Quintana and to whom he introduced Hemingway. He "had been an impresario of means in Pamplona before the Civil War, when he ran the bullring" as well as the hotel.[550] But he was openly Republican in Nationalist territory (hence Hemingway's remark about Quintana's brave patriotism). When Franco defeated the Republicans, Quintana left Pamplona for San Sebastián.

Quintana and Hemingway were good friends. For their relationship in the 1950s, see Quintana in *DS*.

> Quintana owns and manages a hotel in Pamplona that is popular with bullfighters (271). The narrator admires him for his commitment to the bullfight and to Spain (274). Quintana shares the narrator's disgust with Domingo Ortega (q.v., 170).

Quintanilla, Luis. Full name: León Gerardo Luis Quintanilla Isasi Cagigal Cerrajería. Spanish painter, 1893–1978.

Born in Santander, northern Spain, Quintanilla went to Paris in 1912 and met Gris, Picasso, and other painters whose influence led him into Cubism. Returning to Spain in 1915, Quintanilla became interested in large murals; the one which decorates the entrance of the Museum of Modern Art, Madrid, still survives. In 1922 he returned to Paris, where he met several other artists and writers, including Ernest Hemingway. Two years later he returned to Spain and opened a studio in Madrid (address: 68, Calle Fernando el Católico); by 1924 the peripatetic artist was on his way to Italy to study the techniques of painting and restoring murals. In 1927, back in Spain, he joined the Socialist Workers' Party, under the leadership of Pablo Iglesias. Art and politics became inextricably intertwined in his life. His Civil War drawings, commissioned by the Republican Government, were exhibited in the Hotel Ritz of Barcelona and, with Hemingway's help, in the Museum of Modern Art in New York.

After the Spanish Civil War, Quintanilla moved to New York, married an American, Jane Speirs, had a son, and executed commissions in Kansas City (frescoes based on Don Quijote), Hollywood (movie sets), and San Juan, Puerto Rico (a portrait of Pablo Casals, in the Casals Museum). His work was exhibited in several prestigious American galleries, but his socialism made it difficult for him to adjust to American society and impossible to return to his beloved Spain. He moved to France, wrote his memoirs, and produced increasingly bitter drawings and paintings. Franco died in 1975; Quintanilla moved to Spain in 1976 and died only two years later.

Retrospective exhibitions were presented in Santander (in 1978) and in Madrid (posthumously, in 1979).[551]

Hemingway and Quintanilla. Hemingway and Quintanilla met in 1922 were good enough friends for Hemingway to write advertisements, reviews, and prefaces for Quintanilla's books and for at least two of his New York exhibitions (at the Pierre Matisse Gallery, 1934, and at the Museum of Modern Art, 1938). Hemingway clearly admired Quintanilla, both for his Republican activism, which landed him in jail, and for his etchings which, according to Hemingway, "make a world where there is light and depth and space, humor, pity and understanding, and a sound earthy knowledge that gives us the first true Madrid that we have seen since Goya."[552]

Hemingway wrote three prefaces for Quintanilla's *All the Brave* (1939). The first, written in Key West and dated March 10, 1938, reports that Quintanilla's studio, the many drawings it contained, several of his large frescoes, and much of his work for the monument to Pablo Iglesias had been destroyed during the Civil War. Hemingway describes these lost pieces as "great Spanish works of art" and Quintanilla himself as "not only a great artist but a great man." The other two prefaces, while repeating the praise for Quintanilla, focus on Hemingway himself. They were written "Somewhere in Spain" and dated 18 April 1938 and May 1938. In April Hemingway described Quintanilla as "a great Spanish artist and an old friend" and remarks bitterly that having "all his life's work destroyed" (the subtext of Hemingway's stolen suitcase can be clearly discerned) is "unfortunate." He then interviews himself, surveying his opinion on war (it is "unpleasant . . . I have never liked it. But I have a small talent for it"), on war drawings, on his style, and on his role as warrior. He refers frequently to the publisher's demand that he produce a thousand-word introduction. In May he describes the April preface as "particularly churlish . . . a good example of the peculiar, unattractive, surly righteousness which certain phases of war can produce in people." He describes Quintanilla as "one of the bravest men that I have ever known" but most of the preface is devoted to an elaboration of his own earlier remarks and a discussion of the war as it affects him and his writing.

The three prefaces (pages 7–10) are followed by Jay Allen's essay, "All the Brave" (12–29); the title is taken from Wordsworth's 1810 sonnet, "Indignation of a High-Minded Spaniard." Elliot Paul's well-written "Running Commentary" accompanies the black-and-white drawings.

Other collections of Quintanilla drawings include *La cárcel por dentro: Cincuenta dibujos por Luis Quintanilla* (Madrid: Editorial España, 1935; Imprenta Sáez Hermanos, 1936), *Intoxication Made Easy* (1941), *With a Hay Nonny Nonny* (1942), and *Franco's Black Spain* (New York: Reynal & Hitchcock, 1946). He also illustrated an edition of Jonathan Swift's *Gulliver's Travels* (New York: Crown, 1947).

Quintanilla's Studio. Carlos Baker identifies the view Hemingway mentions as being from Quintanilla's Madrid apartment.[553] The precise address, as listed under Quintanilla's name in the 1931 Madrid guide, *Anuarios Bailly-Baillière*, is 68, Fernando el Católico, between Gaztambide and Hilarión Eslava Streets.[554] The even-numbered buildings on the street face south and west, and in the days before skyscrapers, the uphill street offered a clear view of the Manzanares River below and the chalk hills of Carabanchel on the other side. Hemingway mentions their color twice: "the bare white mud hills [when one is] looking across toward Carabanchel" (*DIA*, 270) and "the clay white ground" which one sees when "looking beyond from Quintanilla's window [toward] the mountains" (*DIA*, 274). In 1931, Carabanchel was on the outskirts of Madrid. Not yet built up, it was the site of the Vista Alegre bullring (in Carabanchel Bajo, or the lower Carabanchel) and a firing range, the noise of which could be heard, as Hemingway says, from Quintanilla's studio.[555]

The narrator mentions the view from Quintanilla's window (270, 274).

— R —

Radiguet, Raymond (Bebe). French poet and novelist, 1902 or 1903–23.

Radiguet's poems (*Les joues en feu*, 1920) attracted and influenced

Cocteau and his circle. Radiguet and Cocteau were lovers and collaborators (*Le gendarme incompris*, 1921, music by Poulenc). Radiguet's first novel, *Le diable au corps* (1923) was translated by Kay Boyle (*Devil in the Flesh*, 1932). Another novel, *Le bal du Comte d'Orgel*, was published posthumously, with a preface by Cocteau; it was translated into English by Malcolm Cowley (*The Count's Ball*, 1929) and by Violet Schiff (*Count d'Orgel Opens the Ball*, 1952). Radiguet's work, including a small collection of *Vers libres* (Champigny: Au Panier Fleuri, 1925), originally appeared in limited editions of one hundred to one hundred twenty-five copies, mostly published under the patronage of Cocteau.

Radiguet and Women. Wiser confirms that Radiguet was bisexual—he "was constantly slipping away from Cocteau for heterosexual rendezvous; even, it was said, with Cocteau's own patron and beloved friend, Coco Chanel"—and that he "died in the arms of his Polish mistress," whom O'Rourke identifies as the Polish-Jewish Bronia Perlmutter. Bronia and her older sister Tylia had come to Paris from Amsterdam in 1922, when they were sixteen and eighteen years old, respectively. They worked as actresses and couturier models and are the historical prototypes for the "two sisters who were then working as models in the quarter" (*DIA*, 71).[556] Radiguet also had affairs with Beatrice Hastings and Marie Beerbohm.[557] There seems to have been no shortage of women in Radiguet's short life.

Radiguet's Death. Wiser writes that Radiguet died of "typhoid fever . . . misdiagnosed as grippe." O'Rourke claims that the typhoid came from tainted oysters, and the *Encyclopaedia Britannica* comments disapprovingly that Radiguet "died of typhoid, his body wasted by dissipation and alcoholism."[558] *See also* Authors; Homosexuals.

> The narrator identifies Radiguet as Cocteau's lover, whom Cocteau denounced as "decadent" for sleeping with women. He adds that Radiguet died of typhoid while still young (71–72).

Rafael. *See* Hernández Ramírez, Rafael.

Rafaelillo. *See* Valera, Rafael.

Recaseus, Juan. The narrator takes his material from Carralero and Borge's *Toros célebres*, where the name is spelled Recasens and his wound, but not his death, is reported. For a comparison between Hemingway's and Carralero and Borge's accounts, *see* the entry on Comisario.

The narrative describes Recaseus as a bullring servant killed in a freak accident at a bullfight (111).

Republican Convention. At the Republican convention of 15 June 1928, Herbert Hoover was elected on the first ballot to be his party's candidate for the presidency. Calvin Coolidge, the sitting president, had announced in August 1927 that he would refuse his party's nomination. Hoover defeated the Democratic candidate, Alfred E. Smith, to become the thirty-first president of the United States.

Hemingway and the Republican Convention. Hemingway and his second wife, Pauline Pfeiffer, drove into Kansas City on 14 June, the day before the Republican convention. They were coming from Piggott, Arkansas, to visit Malcolm and Ruth White Lowry. Ruth was Hemingway's cousin; she and her husband had a large house on Indian Lane, and the Hemingways stayed with them to wait for the birth of their son Patrick, on 28 June. They left Kansas City about 20 July.[559]

Hemingway visited the convention center briefly.[560]

The narrator recalls a trip to visit his cousins in June 1928 (48).

Rerre. *See* Aguilar, Manuel.

Ripamilán, don Victoriano. This Spanish bull breeder registered stock in Madrid under his name for a corrida fought on 27 July 1890. He and his heirs managed the herd until the early twentieth century, when the whole fine enterprise, including the Ripamilán brand,

colors, and *antigüedad* (q.v.), was acquired by Manuel Lozano. Lozano had also acquired the herd of the Marquis of Fuente el Sol, as well as that herd's brand, colors, and seniority (20 October 1912).

Lozano died in 1929, and his heirs mismanaged the stock. In 1931 not one bull or *novillo* was sold to a bullring; a few animals were fought in local, largely illegal *capeas*. Alvaro Domecq Díez writes that in 1929 or 1930, his family acquired the Lozano stock, and Mira reports that the brand became extinct.[561]

The Ripamilán bull Comisario was tall, red, and sported impressive horns.[562] Hemingway does not mention that he was being fought by Antonio Fuentes (q.v.), who followed him out of the bullring, subdued him in the stands, and thus enabled the police to shoot him. For a detailed comparison between Hemingway's and Carralero and Borge's accounts of this event, *see* Comisario.

> The narrator repeats Carralero and Borge's account of the Ripamilán bull Comisario (111).

Rivalry. For historical taurine rivalries, *see* Guerra Bejarano, Rafael; Molina Sánchez, Rafael (Lagartijo); Rodríguez, Joaquín (Costillares); and Romero, Pedro, in this volume; see also Rivalry in *DS*.

> The narrator mentions that professional rivalry may prod a bullfighter to risk injury (49).

Roberto, don Roberto. *See* Domingo, Roberto.

"Rock of Ages." Subtitle: "A Living and Dying Prayer for the Holiest Believer in the World." Popular hymn, penned by the Calvinist minister Augustus Montague Toplady in 1776, and set to music by the American hymnist, Thomas Hastings, in 1833. One version reads as follows:

> Rock of ages, cleft for me,
> Let me hide myself in Thee;
> Let the water and the blood,
> From Thy riven side which flowed
> Be of sin the double cure,
> Cleanse me from its guilt and power.[563]

In Christian iconography, the Rock of Ages is usually represented as a large rock (symbolizing Peter or the Church), with Christ positioned at its center.

> The narrator describes himself hanging on to the bull's horns with the same passion as "the figure" clings to the Rock of Ages "in the old picture" (172).

Rodalito. *See* Rubio Oltra, Rafael. His nickname derives from his birthplace, La Roda, Albacete.[564]

Rodero. Full name: Aurelio Rodero Reca. Spanish taurine photographer, d. 1936. First studio location: San Bernardo 17, Madrid. In 1926, Rodero moved his studio to the Carrera de San Jerónimo 36, Madrid, near the Pensión Aguilar (q.v.).

Rodero published his photographs in taurine magazines such as *Los toros*, *Toros y toreros*, *La lidia* (later *La lidia taurina*), and *Sol y sombra*. At one point he became graphic director of the weekly *Toros y toreros*, for whom he did an exclusive report of the Seville *feria*. He published a book of photos, *Postales de todas las corridas de toros: Variación inmensa*.

On 25 July 1936, one week after the start of the Spanish Civil War, Rodero was shot dead as he was crossing the Puerta del Sol, probably by anticlerical Republican sympathizers (his brother was a dean of the Cathedral of Burgos). Rodero's archive passed into the hands of his colleague and friend, the photographer Manuel Vaquero (d. 1980).[565]

Hemingway acknowledges the photographers Vandel and Rodero, whose photographs he reproduced in *Death in the Afternoon* (*h:* 408).

Rodríguez, Félix. Full name: Félix Rodríguez Ruiz. Spanish bullfighter, 1905–43. Investiture as *matador de toros*, 3 April 1927, in Barcelona; confirmed in Madrid on the 24th of that same month.

As a *novillero* Rodríguez drew a great deal of favorable attention. In 1924 he performed in twenty-two *novilladas* (ranked ninth nationwide); in 1925 and 1926, with thirty-eight and forty-seven performances, respectively, he was ranked first. After three *novilladas* in 1927, he was promoted to *matador de toros*; his forty-two corridas placed him eighth for that year.

Rodríguez was at the height of his powers in 1926 and 1927. But he contracted syphilis in the winter of 1927–28, and by March of 1928 was already displaying locomotor ataxia (uneven gait). He had excellent medical advice—Paco Serra (q.v.) was one of his physicians—but he didn't follow it. He abandoned treatment as soon as the symptoms were alleviated, and would not be deterred from the riotous life style that his success encouraged. The syphilis advanced rapidly, and during the 1928 season he suffered intermittently from visual disturbances, dizziness, nausea, arthritic inflammation of the joints, and pains in the legs. He was forced to cancel seventy performances and performed in only twenty-three corridas. The number rose to sixty-five in 1929 (he had been contracted for six more), but his work was uneven, and even his best performances lacked the brilliance of earlier seasons. Tomás Orts Ramos (Uno al Sesgo) writes that "en nada ha bajado su cartel, porque como a todos los toreros de su clase y estilo, el público les concede un margen amplio de crédito, sabiendo que pueden volver por sus fueros y prestigios cuando se les antoje" (his popularity has not decreased, because the public makes allowance for bullfighters of his class and style, knowing that they can display their power and authority whenever they want).[566] This assessment proved to be overly optimistic: in 1930 he was contracted for only twenty-six corridas. Weakened by his illness, he was badly gored in 1931 and decided to retire in 1932. He was poor and bedridden for most of the last ten years of his life. As a colleague said of him, "él vivió su vida y la vivió a tope. Tuvo mala suerte, fue víctima de una enfermedad muy grave y poco controlada" (he lived his life to the hilt, had bad luck, and succumbed to a terrible, uncontrolled disease).[567]

Rodríguez was such an extraordinary bullfighter that he was often compared to José Gómez (Joselito). Cossío wrote of Rodríguez that "todo lo intenta y todo lo hace, y lo hace bien, con inteligencia y dominio, y al mismo tiempo con gracia y buen estilo" (he tries everything and can do everything, and do it well, with intelligence and authority, with grace and good style).[568] One critic praised him as "excelente con la capa . . . un extraordinario banderillero y un verdadero maestro en torear con la muleta" (excellent with the cape . . . an extraordinary banderillero and a true master with the muleta).[569] Bagüés joins the chorus of praise: "tuvo un conocimiento extenso . . . una intuición extraordinaria, una afición muy grande y un mayor deseo de triunfar" (he had enormous knowledge . . . extraordinary intuition, a great passion for the bullfight and a greater drive to succeed).[570]

Hemingway and Rodríguez. As Hemingway notes, Rodríguez was born in Santander, but his family moved to Valencia while he was still very young (*DIA*, 267). Because Valencia considered him a native son, he was often contracted for the Valencia *feria*, which Hemingway regularly attended.

In 1927, Rodríguez's first season as *matador de alternativa* (q.v.), Hemingway saw him in Valencia on 25 and 29 July, and in San Sebastián as well, on 18 September. Hemingway missed the 1928 and 1930 seasons, but in 1929 he saw him frequently: in Pamplona, on 9, 10, and 14 July; in Valencia, on 27, 28, 28, and 30 July; and in Palencia, on 1 September. And in 1931 he and Rodríguez again coincided in the Valencia *feria*, 25, 27, and 28 July. He may have seen Rodríguez at other times as well, both as *novillero* and as *matador de toros*.[571]

> The narrator greatly admires Rodríguez for his work with the cape (14, *h:* 296), banderillas (200), and muleta (215). When he faced a brave, aggressive bull who knew how to use his horns, Rodríguez gave a master lesson in bullfighting (127–28; *see also* 219, 267). The narrator refers to Rodríguez's illness (200, 216); the unnamed excellent bullfighter who suffers from veneral disease (100, 171) is probably Rodríguez. Rodríguez's muleta work can be seen in a beautiful photograph (*h:* 396–97).

Rodríguez, Joaquín (Cagancho). Full name: Joaquín Rodríguez Ortega. Spanish bullfighter, 1903–84. Investiture as *matador de toros*, in Murcia, 17 April 1927; confirmed in June that year, in Madrid. The promotion was granted by Rafael Gómez Ortega (el Gallo), the witness was Manuel Jiménez (Chicuelo), so that the afternoon brought together three stellar, temperamental bullfighters. Cagancho took his nickname from his grandfather, a flamenco singer; in Sevillian gypsy argot, *cagancho* means a song bird.

Cagancho himself was a great bullfighter. He was from the gypsy barrio of Triana (q.v.) and developed a passion for bullfighting in childhood. His first *novillada* took place in 1923, the year of Hemingway's first visit to Spain, and he gradually developed his scope and audience, performing in important plazas: Seville in 1924, Valencia in 1925, and Zaragoza, Barcelona, and his Madrid debut in 1926. Although the Zaragoza performance was a disaster, the others drew rave reviews and he became that year's *novillero de moda*, even though he was badly wounded (on 10 September, in Madrid) and had to cancel many appearances.[572]

Cagancho's eagerly awaited investiture at the beginning of the

1927 season was disappointingly colorless, but the year produced some extraordinary performances as well, establishing the pattern that was to characterize most of his career (see endnote 575). As Silva Aramburu remarks, Cagancho was "absolutamente desigual" (absolutely uneven). In 1927, his first year as *matador de alternativa*, he was ranked fifth, with forty-five corridas. Even in that fine year, Cagancho did dreadful things: on 5 June, in Bilbao, for example, he suddenly proclaimed himself unfit to finish a fight because of pains all over his body, mainly in the legs; the police had to protect him from the irate public. On 1 May and again on 25 August, he was carted off to jail for failure to kill the bull.[573] The season was composed of "triunfos clamorosos, a nada comparables . . . [triunfos] parciales . . . [y] fracasos rotundos que tampoco admiten comparación" (incomparable triumphs . . . partial [triumphs] . . . [and] thorough failures, also incomparable).[574]

In 1928 Cagancho had forty-nine corridas and in 1929, thirty-one corridas, only one or two of which were successful. But during the next year, probably his best, he appeared sixty-eight times and was ranked fourth nationwide; and his critical successes far outnumbered the failures. A serious wound on 7 May 1931 kept him out of the ring for months; when he returned to bullfighting in August his performances lacked style, and style was Cagancho's strong point. He performed in only twenty-eight corridas that season, and the next three seasons were unmitigated disasters.

In 1935, however, Cagancho's energy seems to have revived, and he was at the top of his form for the thirty corridas he fought that year. During the Spanish Civil War (1936–39) and in the early 1940s he fought about a dozen corridas a year, the number decreasing in the next few years until he retired in 1953. Cagancho's grace with the cape and the muleta, his *salsa gitana* (gypsy spice and lightness), could bring the whole plaza to its feet. But at any point in a fight, he might perform as badly as any ignorant beginner. Because of this unevenness, also typical of gypsies, he was often compared to Rafael Gómez Ortega, the main difference being that Cagancho performed in the more modern, post-Joselito, post-Belmonte style. One writer explained that Cagancho, like Chicuelo and Rafael, has the poet's temperament and dependence on "inspiration." When there is no inspiration, Cagancho is mediocre; when he is afraid he simply refuses to perform; and when he is inspired, he is magnificent, and can even be compared to Belmonte. The standards that apply to other bull-fighters—discipline, courage, *pundonor*—are simply irrelevant to a man whose psychology is so different.[575] Hemingway's attacks on Chicuelo and Cagancho indicate an intolerance for the temperament which defines these two bullfighters, and this intolerance expressed itself in attacks on the men as well as on their art. His two sentences about Cagancho's crude table manners (276), for example, are obviously an unkind exaggeration. In fact, Cagancho was a sophisticated man who dressed impeccably and dined at elegant tables.[576] And in spite of Hemingway's complaints, Cagancho often killed in a very classic way.

An interesting aspect of Cagancho's uneven career is that he was consistently successful in Mexico, where he was idolized. He lived in Mexico after his retirement, and died there in 1984.[577] His son, Joaquín Rodríguez Sánchez (Cagancho hijo, or son of Cagancho) was a bullfighter of no importance.

Hemingway and Cagancho. Hemingway probably saw Cagancho in 1926, his last year as *novillero*, and several times in 1927, including the Pamplona corrida of 12 July 1927, when he appeared with Antonio Márquez and Marcial Lalanda (qq.v.) and outperformed them both: Cagancho was awarded two ears and a tail for his fine *faena* with his second bull, and was carried on the shoulders of his audience, all the way from the bullring to his hotel.[578] Cagancho performed again in Pamplona on 14 July 1929. Hemingway did not go to Spain in 1928 or in 1930, which is generally considered Cagancho's best year; in 1929 and 1931, when Hemingway did spend the summer in Spain, Cagancho seldom had a good day.

> The narrator admires Cagancho's grace and skill (13–14, 216–17, 250; *see also* 223) but despises his "cynical cowardice" (250; *see also* 13, 159, 251–52, *h:* 432, s.v. *Descabellar*) and his table manners (276). He writes that Cagancho is still ranked among the top ten fighters of 1931 although he is already "finished" (267). He compares him to Rafael el Gallo (216) and to Belmonte (14). *See also* photographs, *h:* 300–301, *h:* 308–309, *h:* 384–85).

Rodríguez, Joaquín (Costillares). Hemingway also spells the first name as Joachin. Full name: Joaquín Rodríguez Castro. Eighteenth-century Spanish bullfighter, whose dates are highly disputed: he may have been born in 1729 or 1748; he died c. 1805. One authority claims he was born in 1746 and that his godfather, also a bullfighter, allowed him to kill a bull in 1762, thus promoting him to *matador de toros* at age sixteen. Cossío cites documents that variously claim he was twenty or twenty-five years old when he became a *matador de toros*.

The confusion in dates may be due to the fact that several bull-fighters in the same family were nicknamed "Costillares." The first was the matador Juan Rodríguez; his two sons Juan Miguel and Joa-quín were also bullfighters, the latter being the father of the famous Joaquín Rodríguez (Costillares) Hemingway mentions.[579]

Costillares's best years were 1775–85, during which he main-tained a rivalry with Pedro Romero (q.v.); this rivalry was immortal-ized in verse and on the stage, with Pedro Romero usually represented as the honest hero of the masses and Costillares the so-phisticated darling of the aristocracy. Costillares charged enormous fees and attempted to impose conditions on the other bullfighters who appeared with him, including Romero, who of course refused to be dictated to. In 1776 Madrid, which wanted Romero and Costillares to appear together, conducted long negotiations with Costillares but, unable to agree to his terms, lost him to the Seville ring. In 1777 Costillares came to Madrid, but Romero refused to appear. In 1778 Costillares threatened to resign from the ring. In 1779, Costillares and Romero were prevailed upon to appear together, after extended and delicate negotiations to settle such matters as salary and senior-ity. The royal family, the minister of war, and the courts were all involved in these long, complicated disputes. In the early 1780s, the emergence of a new star, José Delgado (Pepe-Hillo, q.v.), defused the rivalry between Romero and Costillares.

In 1786 Costillares's health began to falter. In 1788 he was badly gored in his first corrida of the season; in the next year a tumor ap-peared on one of his hands.[580] After 1790 he appeared seldom and irregularly. Romero, whose career lasted longer than that of Costil-lares, continued the rivalry with Costillares's protégé, Pepe-Hillo.

Costillares's impact on bullfighting is enormous. He redesigned the bullfighter's uniform; he raised the muleta from an incidental to a basic part of the fight; he shaped and formalized various aspects of cape and sword work; and he perfected the *volapié* and the *verónica*, which are invariably associated with his name. A contemporary described him as tall, violent, and irascible.[581]

> The narrator correctly associates Costillares with the important technique of *volapié* (*h:* 492–93, s.v. *Volapié*) in which the bullfighter, instead of waiting motionless for the bull, moves towards it to kill it (237). His claim that Costillares was promoted to full matador at the age of sixteen (88) is controversial.

Roger, Victoriano (Valencia II, Chato). Full name: Victoriano Roger Serrano. Spanish bullfighter, 1898–1936, killed in the Spanish Civil War. Investiture as *matador de toros*, 17 September 1921, in Madrid.

The son and brother of bullfighters (see below), Valencia II practically grew up in the Madrid bullrings. In 1916 and 1917, his early years as *novillero*, he displayed the enormous courage and enthusiasm that were to make him so popular. He was a fine swordsman, and he was obviously committed to his art, his audiences, and his career. In 1919 he was contracted for twenty-five *novilladas*, in 1920 for twenty-seven, and in 1921 for fourteen, after which he was promoted to *matador de toros* by the Valencian Manuel Granero (q.v.).

As a top-ranked matador, Valencia performed in thirty corridas in 1922 and a similar number in 1923, even though he was seriously injured on 13 May and again on 28 June and had to cancel many contracts. He still managed to appear in all of Spain's important bullrings and to earn favorable reviews. Of the fifty contracts he signed for 1924, he kept only twenty-nine, having been gored in April.[582] Such gorings were almost annual events with him, as his bravery exceeded his repertoire and abilities. A goring in April 1925 forced him to cancel his appearances at the Seville *feria*, and that year he again performed on only twenty-nine afternoons, although he had been scheduled for many more. Gored again in July 1926, in Madrid, he appeared only thirty-eight times. In 1927, 1928, and 1929 he performed on forty-five (ranked sixth nationwide), forty-six, and forty-three afternoons, respectively, but in that last season he displayed less spirit and energy than he had formerly, and his uninspired performances reduced the number of his contracts to eighteen for 1930. When he retired in 1931, after only seven corridas, he had fourteen disfiguring scars. His comeback, begun modestly in 1935, was derailed by the outbreak of the Spanish Civil War the following year.

Cossío's estimate of Valencia II is that he was excellent with the cape; quite good with the muleta, although his repertoire was limited, particularly as he used only his right hand; and a fine, accurate swordsman. His greatest strength, however, was his character: his bravery and temperament enabled him to continue in spite of his technical deficiencies. His courage and self-confidence gave him elegance, a quality that his Madrid audiences appreciated, and their affection for him was enhanced by the fact of his being a loyal and affectionate native of Madrid (in spite of his nickname), who frequently performed in benefit of local charities.[583] (He was popular in South American countries as well.) Uno al Sesgo also remarks upon Valencia's courage and energy, saying, as do most of the critics I've read, that although he was "un torero corto" (had a short repertoire), his personality enabled him to overcome his shortcomings. Néstor Luján is less generous, claiming that Valencia lacked style and art, having nothing but bravery to recommend him.[584]

Hemingway and Valencia II. Victoriano Roger did not perform in Pamplona or Valencia in the early 1920s, when he was at his spirited best. Hemingway saw Valencia on 28 and 29 July 1927, Roger's first appearance in the Valencia *feria*, and on 18 September in San Sebastián. He saw him in 1929, when Roger performed often but with less spirit: in Pamplona on 7, 8, and 9 July, and in Valencia on 25, 27, and 31 July. Hemingway skipped the 1928 and 1930 seasons and probably saw the worn-out Roger perform in Madrid on 7, 14, 28, and 30 June 1931.[585] Hemingway probably also saw Roger in Madrid in his more spectacular years, and contrasted these earlier performances with the less impressive ones of Pamplona and Valencia in 1929. Whatever the reason, Hemingway stands alone in accusing Valencia of selective bravery.[586]

For a later Valencia, see Cuevas Roger, Victoriano, in *DS.*

The narrator identifies Valencia II as a flawed matador of the 1920s. He claims that Valencia II concentrated all his efforts on Madrid where he bravely took great risks and was inevitably gored (76, 219, *h:* 364); elsewhere he failed to control his nerves and gave lesser performances (75, 85). The narrator admires his cape work but finds him weak with the muleta (75, 85, 222). He mentions that his face was disfigured by the bull's horn (84, 276) and concludes that by 1931 he was "nearly through" (85).[587]

Roger Durán, José (Valencia). Spanish bullfighter, 1867–1924. He was called Valencia because he was born there, though he moved to Madrid as a child, and his sons, Victoriano and José Roger Serrano (qq.v.), both nicknamed Valencia, were born in Madrid.

José Roger, originally apprenticed to a painter, became a bullfighter who worked in several *cuadrillas*, including those of Manuel García (el Espartero), Emilio Torres Reina (Bombita), and Luis Mazzantini (qq.v.). He did not keep any of these positions very long, for he was not a top-notch banderillero. He retired from the ring at the turn of the century and from then on made his living as a manufacturer.[588]

The narrative correctly identifies Valencia as a banderillero and the father of Victoriano Roger (75).

Roger Serrano, José (Valencia, Pepe Valencia). Spanish bullfighter, 1894–1971. Investiture as *matador de toros*, 5 September 1919, in Madrid.

Originally apprenticed to a carpenter, Pepe Valencia insisted that he wanted to be a bullfighter, and in 1913 he gave several very impressive performances in Madrid (including that of his debut as *novillero*), which suggested that he was headed for stardom. In 1914, however, he did so poorly that he was forced to return to carpentry. In 1918 he tried the bulls again, and a succession of triumphs brought him quickly to the major bullrings. He finished the season with twenty-six *novilladas* and was among the most promising and popular *novilleros* of the year. The next year was similarly successful, and he was promoted to *matador de toros* in September. All told, in 1919 he performed in twenty-six *novilladas* and five *corridas de toros*.

As a matador, however, Pepe Valencia went steadily downhill: his best year was 1920, with twenty-five corridas. After that, he was never able to perform more than ten or eleven afternoons a season.[589] Although he continued to fight for more than ten years, and although he was skillful and well-versed in the profession, he did not succeed. Cossío remarks that "Lo hacía todo y todo lo ejecutaba con perfección" (he could do everything and he did it all to perfection), but because he lacked spirit and enthusiasm his fine work gave the impression of being merely mechanical and his audiences did not warm to him. He retired from the Spanish bullring in 1929.

Valencia was more popular in Venezuela, where he had performed in several winter seasons in the 1920s. After his retirement, he spent several years in Venezuela, fighting occasionally but mostly working as a taurine impresario. He eventually returned to Spain, where he died in 1971. In his last years he was the technical advisor to the president of the Madrid bullring. His son, José Roger Martín (Valencia III, 1922–78) was also a matador.[590]

Pepe Valencia is an interesting contrast to his younger brother Victoriano Roger (Valencia II, q.v.). The critics unanimously praise Pepe Valencia's work with the cape, the banderillas, the muleta, and the sword: they find him to be a *torero largo*, a knowledgeable, capable matador. Most agree that he was technically more accomplished and had a larger repertoire than Victoriano, and that there was no weakness in Pepe Valencia, only a lack of will. What the younger Valencia lacked in expertise, however, he more than made up with his courage and passion, qualities that turn the bullfighter into an artist.

> The narrator identifies Pepe Valencia merely as Victoriano Roger's unsuccessful older brother (75).

Roman Catholic. The Roman Catholic church and the bullfight are closely connected, bullfights being the central entertainment at the many fairs which celebrate a saint's feast day (e.g., the May *sanisidros* of Madrid; the March corridas in honor of San José in Valencia, Barcelona, and other cities; the June *ferias* in honor of San Juan in Barco de Avila; the July *sanfermines* of Pamplona; the late July *ferias* of San Jaime (Santiago) in Valencia; the September *feria* of San Miguel in Seville; the October *feria* of Pilar in Zaragoza. The classic pass with the cape, the *verónica*, is named after St. Verónica, who holds the cloth with which she wiped the face of Christ with her two hands, as the cape is held in that pass.

Most bullfighters are Roman Catholics, and the narrator correlates their various degrees of piety (59). For the church's opposition to the bullfight, *see* the entry for Pius the Fifth; *see also* Luck. For the saints and virgins Hemingway mentions, *see* Fermín; Gabriel; Isidro; José; Loyola, Ignatius of; Magdalena; Miguel; Pilar; Sebastián; Soledad; Verónica.

Biographers and critics have examined Hemingway's Protestant background, his conversion to Roman Catholicism, and the religious elements in his work in scores of articles and several books, such as Larry Grimes's *The Religious Design of Hemingway's Early Fiction* (Ann Arbor: UMI Research Press, 1985).

Romero, Pablo. *See* Pablo Romero.

Romero, Pedro. Spanish matador, 1754–1839, native of Ronda (q.v.).

Pedro Romero Martínez was trained by his father, Juan Romero, himself an outstanding matador. Juan was an organizational genius, both for the bullfight—he introduced formal order into the *cuadrillas* by defining their duties and the order of their entry into the fight— and for the political intricacies involved in managing a bullfighter's career. He trained and advised all his sons, and carefully managed the career of his most gifted son, Pedro.[591]

Pedro Romero acted independently as *matador de toros* for the first time in Ronda in 1771, in other plazas starting in 1774, and in Madrid in 1775. It wasn't long before the son eclipsed the father and was compared with Joaquín Rodríguez (Costillares, q.v.), with whom he probably performed for the first time in 1777. The rivalry between them was bitter, pitting the Madrid bullring against those of Seville and Cádiz, with the two masters refusing to perform together, as each insisted on seniority, higher wages, and more control over future contracts and the conduct of the bullfight. Romero was younger than Costillares, and the rivalry carried over to Costillares's disciple, José Delgado (Pepe-Hillo, q.v.). Romero and Delgado also demanded concessions from each other and occasionally refused to perform together.

Romero's career was long and impressive. He retired in 1799, without having suffered any injury in over twenty-five years of bullfighting. He is said to have killed all his bulls on the first try and to have saved many of his fellow performers from injury and even death. An interesting statistic is the rise of casualties in the bullring after he retired.

In 1830, finding himself in straitened circumstances and still physically strong, he asked to be appointed to the faculty of the newly formed bullfighting school in Seville (founded under the auspices of Fernando VII and the Conde de la Estrella). When a student found himself in difficulties, the seventy-six-year old Romero attracted the bull away from the student and toward himself, stood motionless when the bull charged, and dispatched him on the first try. The school was disbanded in 1834, but Pedro Romero was still not done with the bullfight. On a trip to Madrid, he was invited to appear once again in that city's bullring: he performed with his usual straightforward efficiency.

Romero is considered one of the masters of all time, legendary for his strength, stamina, and longevity in the profession, "the insuperable master of the eighteenth century."[592] In summarizing his career, Romero wrote a friend of his that "en el espacio de veintiocho años, desde el 71 hasta el 99, me parece se pueden arreglar que habré matado en cada uno de los dichos años, doscientos toros por año que a mi suma hace 5,600 toros, y estoy persuadido en que quizás serán más, pues como después de las funciones de esta Corte iba a . . . varios pueblos" (in the period of twenty-eight years, from '71 to '99, I estimate I killed two hundred bulls a year, which to my reckoning comes to 5,600 bulls, and I believe that the number is probably higher, since after performing in this Court I performed in . . . other towns).[593] He is said to have killed all his bulls *recibiendo* (standing still and waiting for the bull, as opposed to moving towards the bull to kill it, as Costillares did).

The dates published in *Death in the Afternoon* for Romero's career—"between the years of 1771 and 1791" (239)—are incorrect. In manuscript Hemingway had written the correct dates, 1771 and 1799. Romero was eighty-four when he died, and not ninety-five, as Hemingway writes. The Goya (q.v.) portrait of Romero is in the collection of the Duke of Veragua (q.v.).[594]

Hemingway used the name and fame of Pedro Romero, as well as the achievements of Cayetano Ordóñez (q.v.) in creating his fictional bullfighter in *The Sun Also Rises*. He also mentioned Pedro Romero in *The Dangerous Summer* (*TDS*, 112, 203).

The narrator's summary of Pedro Romero's life and career is not entirely accurate (43, 239; *see also* 243).

Ronda. Ronda (Andalucía) was incorporated into the kingdom of Ferdinand and Isabella (qq.v.) on 12 May 1485. The Church of the Holy

Spirit was erected on the site where Ferdinand placed his royal standards.[595] The city's extraordinary scenery includes a dramatic gorge in the middle of the town. Hemingway admired both the town and its mountainous surroundings when he first visited Ronda in June 1923.

Hotel Reina Victoria. Address: 25, Paseo Dr. Fleming, Ronda. The Hotel Reina Victoria was built in 1906 by the British company that was laying the railroad between Bobadilla and Algeciras. The British owner of the railroad company, Lord Alexander Henderson, named the hotel in honor of Spain's new queen (*see* Victoria Eugenia). Recognizing that tourism and railroads are closely related, Henderson had earlier built a sister hotel, named after another Spanish queen, at Algeciras (see María Cristina in *DS*).

In June 1923, the Hotel Reina Victoria was the only one in town. Then as now, it offered spectacular views and excellent facilities and services. Hemingway's admiration for the hotel's management is a compliment to Mrs. Law, who managed the Ronda hotel from its early years until she left Spain when the Civil War broke out in 1936.[596] Another famous writer who stayed at the Reina Victoria was Rainer Maria Rilke, several of whose personal effects can be seen in Room 203, kept as the Museo Rilke. A life-size statue of Rilke stands on the grounds. In 1997, Ronda named the road bordering the bullring Paseo Hemingway.

Valencia also has a Hotel Reina Victoria; Hemingway stayed there in 1959 (see Victoria in *DS*).

Ronda's Bullring. Ronda boasts one of the oldest, prettiest, and best-preserved bullrings in Spain. Built c. 1785, it is the subject of at least two books: Adolfo Lozano Serna's *Anales de la plaza de toros de la Real Maestranza de Caballería* (1948; 2nd ed. Ronda: Hermanos Vega, 1954) and Francisco Garrido Domínguez's *La plaza de toros de la Real Maestranza de Ronda* (Ronda and Málaga: Impresión Gráficas Urania, 1985).

The Romero family, important figures of the early history of bullfighting, were *rondeños*, and Ronda is often called the birthplace of *toreo a pie* (on foot, as opposed to *rejoneo*, in which the bullfighter performs on horseback). Francisco Romero (born c. 1700) is credited with inventing the muleta, a much disputed claim. His son Juan was the best-paid fighter of his day and the father of five bullfighters of renown, the most famous being Pedro Romero (q.v.).

In the twentieth century, Ronda produced another great bullfighting family, whose portraits Hemingway drew in *The Sun Also Rises*, *Death in the Afternoon*, and *The Dangerous Summer*. *See* Ordóñez, Cayetano, in this volume; and the entries for the Ordóñez Araujo brothers, the Mayor of Ronda, and Ronda in *DS*.

The narrator summarizes the history of Ronda and enthusiastically recommends the town to his narratees (42–43). He mentions Ronda in connection with its bullring and bullfights (39, 40, 479) and its most famous bullfighters (43, 267). He describes the Ronda school or style of bullfighting (446–47; see also 382, 449).

Rosa, Juan Luis de la. Full name: Juan Luis de la Rosa y de la Garquén. Spanish bullfighter, 1901–36. Investiture as *matador de toros*, 28 September 1919, in Seville; confirmed in Madrid, May 1920. In 1919, Seville celebrated bullfights in two plazas, the old Maestranza and the new Monumental (see Sevilla in *DS*). On the same day and at the same time that Rosa was promoted to *matador de toros* by Joselito in the new plaza, his friend Chicuelo was promoted by Belmonte in the old one. Belmonte confirmed Rosa's *alternativa* (q.v.) in Madrid on 24 May 1920; Chicuelo's was confirmed by Joselito's brother, Rafael Gómez Ortega (el Gallo) on 18 June 1920.

Another of the many matadors who were child prodigies, Rosa was famous at age fourteen and won over the tough public of Madrid at fifteen, while still fighting *becerros* (bulls about one year old). As *novillero* he was impressive with the cape and spectacular with the muleta, especially with the *pase natural*. At that stage, his sword work was uncertain, but it was hoped that it would improve with experience. Meanwhile, the statistics record the happy progress of his career. In 1918 he performed in seventeen *novilladas*, including several impressive triumphs in the important plaza of Seville. The number rose to forty-one in 1919, with a resounding triumph at his Madrid debut in July, and ending with his promotion to *matador de toros* a few months later.

After such an auspicious beginning, Rosa's first season as a *matador de alternativa* was disappointing, his sword work in particular being severely criticized. Rosa claimed his health prevented him from performing well or frequently. He improved in 1921 and 1922 (thirty-two and thirty-eight corridas, respectively, mostly well received), but in 1923 he was doing military service, was seldom in the bullring, and when he was, gave weak performances, as he was out of training. Rosa signed only seven contracts for 1924. Cossío describes his descent as "vertiginoso" (dizzying).

Early in 1924 Rosa injured his hand and was unable to train or perform for some weeks, after which he gave the appearance of being "sin voluntad, indiferente" (without spirit, indifferent). This suggests that he was already "finished" before the terrible abdominal wound he suffered on 25 May 1924, his fourth corrida of the season.[597] After that miserable 1924 season, Rosa spent more and more time in Venezuela, where he had a modest following. He was not seen in the Spanish rings from 1927 until 1936, when a series of disastrous performances in Barcelona clearly indicated that his career was over. He was murdered a few days after his last bullfight, in the early months of the Spanish Civil War.[598] To reinforce his pet theory about the almost mystical significance of the first goring, Hemingway omits certain interesting facts about Rosa: that he and Chicuelo were promoted to *matador de toros* in the same city and on the same day; that Rosa was in the ring when Granero was killed; that his career was interrupted by military service; and that he suffered from physical illness, apparently aggravated by heavy drinking—both Bagüés and Cossío describe his private life as "disorderly." But in suppressing these facts, as well as their attendant psychological and financial pressures, Hemingway flattens and distorts his portrait of Rosa. Hemingway's dislike of Chicuelo also taints his presentation of Rosa, causing him to attribute to one man the faults he sees in the other: preciosity of style, physical unattractiveness, suspected homosexuality, and cowardice. This is not to say that Hemingway is inaccurate in presenting Rosa as a disappointing flash in the pan—Rosa's career did not live up to its early promise—but that his explanation of the downward spiral is uncharacteristically flat.

Hemingway has several pet theories and passions, and they frequently led him into distortion and simplification. For a discussion of his idea that a short bullfighter is doomed, *see* the entry for Isidoro Todó; for his diatribe against what he calls premature promotions, see "The Bullfighter," in the introduction to this volume. In addition to Chicuelo, Hemingway treated several other bullfighters with excessive harshness; *see*, for example, the entries for Cayetano Ordóñez, Domingo Ortega, and Ignacio Sánchez Mejías, in this volume; and González Lucas, Luis Miguel (Dominguín) and Rodríguez Sánchez, Manuel (Manolete) in *DS*.

The narrator counts Juan Luis de la Rosa among the best bullfighters who appeared after the death of Joselito in 1920. He recognizes his talent and good "Belmontistic" technique but claims that his first goring "frightened" him and he retired to South America, where he successfully pursued a double career (bullfighting and sexual services, 76). The narrator is scornful of Juan Luis de la Rosa (73–74, 76).

Rotonde, Café Rotonde. Address: 103 Boulevard du Montparnasse, Paris.

In 1922 Hemingway berated the Rotonde's clientele, most of them foreigners and would-be artists, as "the scum of Greenwich Village . . . the thickest scum and the scummiest scum has come across the ocean, somehow, and . . . has made the Rotonde the . . . showplace for tourists."[599] This negative attitude surfaces in *The Sun Also Rises*, when Jake Barnes walks past "the sad tables of the Rotonde" (42), consistently preferring other bars (29, 78). But the Rotonde's clientele was not all noise and frivolity: it was also a "centro de artistas y de conspiradores de todo el mundo; gentes de los países más remotos; vidas inquietas, abrazadas a un noble ideal" (center for artists and conspirators from all over the world, people from the remotest lands, restless spirits committed to a noble ideal).[600] Among them were Spanish philosophers, academics, writers, publishers, politicians—people like Miguel de Unamuno, Eduardo Ortega y Gasset, Vicente Blasco Ibáñez, and Francisco Madrid—who plotted the overthrow of the dictator Primo de Rivera (q.v.).[601] *See also* Deva.

The narrator mentions the revolutionaries who came to Deva (*sic*) from the Café Rotonde (274).

Royo Turón, Francisco (Lagartito). Spanish bullfighter, 1902–66. Investiture as *matador de toros*, September 1926, in Barcelona; confirmed in Madrid, October 1926.

Lagartito began his career unobtrusively in 1920, fighting in and around his native Zaragoza (Aragón) and slowly working up to more important plazas. He appeared in the first-rank Barcelona plaza in 1922, attracted favorable attention towards the end of the 1923 season, and made his Madrid debut as *novillero* in March 1924, where his obvious nervousness resulted in a miserable performance. The failure was preceded and followed by great successes in Barcelona, and these mitigating circumstances, as well as his solid reputation (twenty-one good *novilladas* in spite of a wound which kept him out of the ring for seven weeks in the middle of the season) enabled him to engineer a return visit to Madrid in 1925. This was a successful afternoon and, combined with his other spirited performances of that year, established him as one of the up-and-coming bullfighters: with twenty-seven performances he was ranked third that season among *novilleros* by *El Clarín* and first by Uno al Sesgo (in his annual report, *Toros y toreros en 1925*).

In 1926 Lagartito again enjoyed resounding successes, sweeping the first-rank plazas of Madrid, Seville, and Barcelona. On 30 July 1926, in Madrid, he cut an ear for his performance with his first bull and dedicated his second one to the popular Victoriano Roger (Valencia II, q.v.), who was to promote him to *matador de toros* two months later. The *ABC* review of that day's performance recorded that he was knocked over twice by his second bull, but that he continued his work unshaken and killed the bull with a single, accurate sword stroke.[602] We see in this performance some similarities to his unfortunate Madrid debut in 1924. But *Toros y toreros en 1926* summarizes Lagartito's performances that year as "una larga y continuada serie de éxitos" (a long, and continued series of triumphs), and he was promoted to *matador de toros* towards the end of that season, adding six *corridas de toros* to the thirty-four *novilladas* which preceded the promotion.

From this impressive run of forty performances in 1926, Lagartito descended to eighteen in 1927, his first full season as *matador de alternativa* being cut short by the injuries that often attend brave bullfighters with insufficent technique. One critic remarked that the terrible *cornada* (goring) he suffered on 17 April 1927, in Málaga (not his first, see above) "le quitó ánimos, facultades y afición" (diminished his courage, abilities, and commitment)—the very qualities upon which his career was based. That injury cost him a month of corridas, and when he was sufficiently recovered to perform again, on 15 May, he was injured again, so severely that he was unable to finish the fight. In 1927, he had eighteen corridas. The number dropped drastically to three in 1928, and rose to six in 1929 (all poor performances, and none of the plazas in which he appeared contracted him for the next year). After this descent, Lagartito performed only in France (where he was seen as late as 1942) and South America; he also bred bulls for *novilladas*.

Attracted into the profession by their older brother's successes in 1925 and 1926, Francisco's two younger brothers failed even more quickly: neither one achieved the rank of *matador de toros*. José (Lagartito II, 1906–68), a *matador de novillos*, disgraced himself at his Madrid debut in 1930, retired, came out of retirement in 1931, disgraced himself again, and retired permanently; he was twenty-five. The youngest brother, Eduardo (Lagartito III) was a *matador de novillos* with an even shorter career: after one unimpressive *novillada* in 1928 and another in 1929, he retired.[603] By 1931 all three had failed in their profession, but only Francisco had enjoyed sufficient success to warrant the "real" smile Hemingway mentions.

It seems that Hemingway had intended to write more about Francisco's descent into failure. A character in the unpublished manuscript fragment entitled "Portrait of Three" is a bullfighter named Paco (the standard nickname for Francisco), who showed great promise but whose career foundered on his cowardice. Unlike his historical prototype, this Paco had only one scar: Hemingway was foregrounding his theory that courage or *afición* sometimes evaporates with the first wound.[604] *See also* the entry for Luis and the Unsuccessful Matadors.

> Among the things the narrator regrets he cannot include in this book is the history of the change in Lagartito's smile (271).

R. S. *See* Stewart, R.

Rubio Oltra, Rafael (Rodalito). Spanish bullfighter, 1894–1979. Investiture as *matador de toros*, in Yecla (Murcia), on 1 October 1922; confirmed in Madrid in 23 August 1925; renounced in 1927.

Rodalito's career seems to have begun in 1913 and to have peaked in 1919, when as *novillero* he performed in thirty-six generally unremarkable and unremarked *novilladas*, including the mediocre one of his Madrid debut in March. The numbers dropped to twenty-seven *novilladas* in 1920 and twenty in 1921 and 1922. Rodalito was promoted to *matador de toros* in a very minor plaza at the end of the 1922 season. In 1923, his first year at the higher rank, he performed in a dozen corridas, the numbers descending to nine in 1924 (only four of which were in Spain), five in 1925, and six in 1926. The following year he renounced his rank and became a *novillero* once again, continuing to perform at this level until he retired from the Spanish ring in 1930.

Throughout his career, Rodalito's performances impressed neither the critics nor the public. Understanding that he was unequal to Spanish competition, Rodalito tried his luck in foreign plazas as early in 1921. He performed with modest success in Mexico, Guatemala, and Italy, though he fought in several other European and Latin American countries as well. In 1925 he married Ana Maria Tedeschi, the younger daughter of a minor Italian aristocrat, and after the Spanish Civil War he settled in Italy. He died in Rome.[605] A totally unremarkable performer, Rodalito spent his life on the fringes of the bullfight world, including nocturnal and comic bullfights. Probably his major claim to fame is that he shared the *cartel* with Rodolfo Gaona (q.v.) at the latter's farewell performance, on 12 April 1925, in Mexico: Gaona probably chose him because he offered no competition. Rodalito, who resembled Gaona, was sometimes called "el Gaona español."

Rodalito and the Fight. The fight Hemingway wishes he could include in his last chapter occurred on 28 August 1930, when Hemingway was in the United States. The comic bullfighter was Joaquín Chamorro Gaitero, and the fight occurred in Madrid. Rodalito had twelve *novilladas* before the August stabbing and none after: he seems to have disappeared from the bullrings.[606]

The narrator refers to a fight between Rodalito and a comic bullfighter (276).

– S –

S 4 N. Monthly magazine published by the S 4 N Society in Northampton, Massachusetts, from November 1919 to July 1925. In August 1926 it merged with the *Modern Review* to become the *Modern S 4 N Review*. The journal's name, *S 4 N*, is explained as follows: "no title for the magazine had yet been decided upon when the first issue was ready to be sent out. On the cover of the magazine the editor and printer had written 'Space for Name' which became *S 4 N* and remained as the final name of the magazine." The journal fostered controversy, taking the position "That out of a comparison of opposed viewpoints . . . comes aesthetic progress."[607]

An entire double issue, which actually covers five months (September 1923-January 1924, Issues 30 and 31, sixty unnumbered pages) was devoted to Waldo Frank (q.v.). It was edited by Gorham B. Munson, author of *Waldo Frank: A Study* (Boni & Liveright) and reflects his opinion that Frank is "America's most significant novelist" ("Foreword")—an opinion he reissued in his 1961 essay, "Herald of the Twenties: A Tribute to Waldo Frank."[608] The issue contains Hart Crane's pencil drawing of Frank, a foreword by the editor, excerpts from Frank's notebooks, and four essays (see illustration 1). As befits an issue subtitled "Homage to Waldo Frank," all the contributors have something flattering to say about Frank or about Munson.

Pierre Sayn praises Frank's *Our America*; finds that *The Dark Mother* is flawed, "a rough draft"; but admires *Rahab* as "a complete artistic creation" (unnumbered pages 22–23). All three works, he says, deal with the relationship between the individual and the community: "sometimes [Frank's] vision expands; the group, divorced from the individual and enlarged to infinity, embraces the entire universe" (22). This merging of individual, community, and universe, advocated by Frank as a healthy replacement for the narrow, stultifying American passion for economic and social success, is called "unanimism" by Sayn. The three novels of Waldo Frank that Sayn discusses are, he claims, all concerned with this philosophy, which Frank expresses with increasing clarity and beauty. About half of Sayn's essay consists of quotes from these novels.

John Crawford's much shorter essay deals with Frank's *Holiday*, a book set in Nazareth, a town in the American South whose white residents are "dry, bloodless, they lean to death"; and whose black population enjoys "a complete release of spirit"—the same stereotypes that underlie Anderson's *Dark Laughter* and that Hemingway parodied in *The Torrents of Spring*. The races are personified by "John Cloud, Negro, and Virginia Hade, Girl of the Old South"; John is, inevitably, lynched. Crawford's essay, like Sayn's, relies heavily on plot summary, quotation, and effusion.

The section to which Hemingway refers is the central piece of *S 4 N*. It is entitled "From the Note-Books of Waldo Frank," dated February 1921, and it runs four pages, during which Frank is, as Hemingway notes, lying in bed naked and thinking of God. Frank experiences several "planes" while falling asleep: "My mind seemed to run along a thin dimension of Truth that was for all its inadequacy marvelously palpably cöordinate with a deeper REAL, so that I saw that always I and All were one. All was a sort of sphere, a form created by the curving and thrusting beyond themselves and beyond the dimensions and realms of themselves of many spheres, until they joined in one as in a globe curves and flatnesses thrust and join and mount" (unnumbered page 30).

Frank sleeps three hours, from five to eight, and then recognizes that he has had a mystic experience (relevant to unanimism): "The Hand of God had moved me, so silently, so terribly, through the Domain of Himself: and had placed me again in that Part of Himself which is man. I prayed and looked upon the journey which the Hand of God had led me" (unnumbered page 35).

Just as Hemingway's reproduction of Frank's remarks is followed by a comment on his language (Frank writes "so badly he cannot make a clear statement"), so the excerpt from Frank's diaries in *S 4 N* is followed by "A Note on the Language of Waldo Frank" in which Munson bemoans the fact that English publishers rejected all of Frank's submissions, claiming that "Frank seemed to have an interesting talent, but it was unfortunately impossible to publish his works until he learned to write." Munson claims that such rejections were "probably a greater misfortune for British readers than . . . for Mr. Frank" and then defends Frank's "unique language" by quoting "the Russian logician of a higher consciousness, P. D. Ouspensky" to explain the various problems encountered by Frank and other writers who enjoy an expanded consciousness that exceeds the powers of language to express it. That Hemingway read Munson's apologia is clear from his remarks about "breaking so-called rules of syntax or grammar to make an effect" (*DIA*, 54).

In the issue's concluding essay, Jean Toomer reviews Munson's *Waldo Frank: A Study*. She reports that this book reveals Munson's own "cultural program [which posits] three factors in the spiritual life of man: man himself, Nature, and the Machine" (unnumbered page 53). Munson argues that Frank has created a form and language appropriate for this new tripartite reality; he likens Frank to Joyce. Toomer, who admires Frank even more than Munson does, complains that Munson's analysis of the early Frank is "incomplete." But she praises Munson for having found the proper tools for evaluating Frank and for applying them with "fine intelligence and enthusiasm" (unnumbered page 52). Munson's *Study*, she claims, "is an art product in the critical form" (unnumbered page 45).

Hemingway and S 4 N. Robert Lewis points out that in referring to *S 4 N*, Hemingway contradicts himself, first saying that he doesn't have the issue at hand, and then quoting directly from it. Lewis explains that "The first draft [of *Death in the Afternoon*] is consistent, and apparently Hemingway revised it, including direct quotes, after he did in fact find a copy of the article. Hemingway's quotes of Frank's materials are accurate except for one detail: Frank capitalizes the word 'All'."

Lewis also points out that Hemingway originally referred to *S 4 N* as "a now happily dead little magazine." Although this insult to the magazine was removed in later drafts, the antipathy to Frank was allowed to remain.[609] For further discussion of Hemingway's attacks on literary competition, *see* the entry for Humanism, Naturalism.

The narrator refers to an article in *S 4 N* in which Waldo Frank describes "how he did his writing" (53).

S. A. *See* Asch, Sholem.

Saavedra. Full name: José Arias de Saavedra. Spanish bull breeder, active c. 1830–70.

Like Ibarra and Lesaca (qq.v.), Saavedra was a nineteenth-century bull breeder. But the pedigree of the Saavedra herd can be traced back to the famous Vistahermosa family of breeders (q.v.) of the eighteenth century. When the Vistahermosas sold off their stock in 1822 and 1823, one of the main buyers was don Juan Domínguez Ortiz, known as "el Barbero de Utrera" (the Barber of the city of Utrera [Seville]), who registered his Vistahermosa bulls under his name, colors, and brand in Madrid for the corrida of 23 June 1828, thus establishing their *antigüedad*, or seniority. Domínguez's son-in-law, José Arias de Saavedra, inherited this herd, registering it in his name in Madrid on 17 July 1837. In 1863, the Murube (q.v.) family acquired a large Saavedra lot, and in 1868 the rest went to Ildefonso Núñez de Prado (the heir of the Cabrera herd, q.v.). At this point Saavedra seems to have withdrawn from bull breeding, and his brand, though certainly not his herd's influence, disappeared. Part of the

Murube holdings were later sold to Eduardo Ibarra (q.v.); the rest of it came to doña Carmen de Federico (q.v.) in 1927.⁶¹⁰

The Saavedra's stock had been Vistahermosa. Saavedra is not, as Hemingway claims, a separate caste or race of *toros de lidia*. He was simply an important link in the Vistahermosa history. For more detail on the relationship between pedigree, ownership, and *antigüedad*, see the essay on "Bulls and Bull Breeding," in the introduction to this volume.

> The narrator lists several strains or castes of *toros de lidia*, including Saavedra (132).

Saiz, Julián (Saleri II). Usually accented: Sáiz. Alternate spelling: Sáinz.⁶¹¹ Full name: Julián Sáiz Martínez. Spanish bullfighter, 1891–1958. Investiture as *matador de toros*, September 1914, in Madrid. Cossío claims that Sáiz is the seventh, not the second bullfighter to be nicknamed Saleri; Uno al Sesgo says he is the fifth. Sáiz was unrelated to the preceding Saleris, and it is not clear why he chose this nickname to replace his earlier, equally inexplicable nickname, el Posadero (the Innkeeper, which he wasn't). Both Cossío and Orts Ramos (Uno al Sesgo) remark that his misappropriation of someone else's nickname is typical of his lack of individuality.⁶¹²

In 1906, at age fifteen, Sáiz quit his job as a butcher to become a bullfighter. By 1913 he was a well-established *novillero*, performing frequently and to generally good reviews. Among his forty *novilladas* of that year was his Madrid debut, on 2 May: this important event was an embarrassing failure but when he returned to Madrid in August of that year he got fine reviews. All told, 1913 was a successful season. Sáiz spent the winter season of 1913–14 in Venezuela and was among the leading *novilleros* of 1914, with thirty-eight successful appearances, most of them in Madrid, before his promotion in September.

After his promotion, Sáiz had an uninterrupted run of successful seasons, performing between forty-six and seventy-two corridas a year until a complicated operation for a liver disease caused him to cancel many of the performances scheduled for 1922. Sáiz's numbers for those seven fat years are: forty-six corridas in 1915, fifty in 1916, sixty-two in 1917, seventy-two in 1918, fifty in 1919 (five of these were in South America), forty-eight in 1920, and fifty-seven in 1921 (he canceled eight contracts because of illness). These statistics are remarkable not only in that they indicate a long streak of successful seasons, but that this continued success occurred during the golden age of Joselito and Belmonte, with whom he often appeared as the "third man" on the program.

1922 was dominated by illness, surgery, and a long convalescence. He managed thirty-four corridas that year, but he seems not to have regained his strength or ambition and in the following years refused many contracts and had to cancel many of those that he had signed. His performances were disappointing, as the numbers for the following seven lean years indicate: three corridas in 1923 and the same low number in 1924,[613] twenty-four in 1925, eleven in 1926, ten in 1927 (two of these were in Portugal and one in France; only seven were in Spain), eight in 1928, and two in 1929. During many of these years, he fought in South America during the winter season, and in the last year or two of the 1920s he also tried his hand at being a bullring impresario, both in the smaller plazas of Spain and in those of South America. This venture didn't prosper, and financial need forced him to continue performing, though infrequently and mostly in foreign rings, in the early 1930s.

The general consensus is that Sáiz was a *torero largo* (possessed of a varied repertoire, technically skillful) and therefore able to give consistently satisfying performances, to avoid injury, and to hold his own against younger bullfighters. In his best years he was graceful with the cape, extraordinary with the banderillas, artistic with the muleta, and precise with the sword, often killing *recibiendo*. Throughout his long career he was a reliable performer, and even after his operation would produce the occasional glowing performances. Increasingly, however, the charge of dullness was raised against him, and his refusal to retire tarnished what had been a brilliant career. Like Hemingway, Cossío ascribes this decline to a "falta de originalidad, de personalidad" (lack of originality, of personality).[614] Like most *toreros largos* he was seldom injured.

Hemingway and Saleri II. When Hemingway first came to Spain in 1923, Saleri II was already afflicted with his liver complaint. Although he was only thirty-two then, he was past his prime. Good reports were heard of his performances in Mexico and South America, but these were belied by what he did in the Spanish ring. In 1923 and 1924 Saleri performed so seldom that it is unlikely that Hemingway saw him, but he may have seen him in 1925, Saleri's most prolific season in the years Hemingway visited Spain. In a revisionist summary of Saleri's career, *Toros y toreros en 1926* writes that even in his good years he had been merely a journeyman without artistic refinement and asserts that his retirement is imminent.[615]

Like Cayetano Ordóñez (q.v.), Sáiz acted as a banderillero for other bullfighters in his later years, but Hemingway's claim that Saleri II would be retired by the time *Death in the Afternoon* would be published (in 1932) is basically accurate. Sáiz did not appear as *matador de toros* in Spanish rings after 1929, and in that year he appeared only twice, in a very minor plaza of which he was impresario.

> Although he was "a very complete bullfighter" and an excellent banderillero, Saleri was now too cautious to be interesting (75). The narrator thinks Saleri is close to retirement (201).

Saleri II. *See* Saiz, Julián.

San Sebastián. Although this seaside resort town had bullfights as early as 1587, it did not have a permanent bullring until the mid-nineteenth century, when three small wooden bullrings were built in quick succession, one in 1851, one in 1870 (it burned down in 1878), and one in 1876 (renovated in 1882 and 1888). At the turn of the century the town decided it had outgrown these facilities, and built a well-appointed bullring that could hold nine thousand spectators. This bullring, "El Chofre," inaugurated in 1903, was the one Hemingway knew. It was torn down in the early 1960s. More than three decades later, the city built another one, with a capacity of 11,200, inaugurated in 1998.[616] San Sebastián's fiesta, or *Semana Grande* (big week), is held in the middle of August. *See also* Sebastian, Saint. In *The Sun Also Rises*, several of Hemingway's characters go to San Sebastián. Hemingway visited the city several times, but he usually stayed in nearby Hendaye, which is smaller, less fashionable, and therefore not as crowded or expensive.

The narrator disparages the tourists who attend the bullfights in San Sebastián (33–34; mentioned, 87, 111, 187, 257, *h:* 500, 504; for dates of bullfights, *see h:* 510–13).

Sánchez, don Francisco (Paco Coquilla). Twentieth century Spanish bull breeder.

Francisco's father, don Andrés Sánchez, established a ranch in 1901, with Udaeta, Veragua, and Carreros stock. Don Andrés died in 1912; the following year the herd was registered in the name of the "hijos de (sons of) Andrés Sánchez Rodríguez." On 20 September 1914, their bulls made their official debut in the Madrid bullring, displaying the family's brand and colors (yellow and green); this corrida established the herd's *antigüedad*, or seniority.

The mixture don Andrés had established seems to have displeased his heirs, who soon got rid of almost all of it. In 1916 his son Francisco, who had become the herd's sole owner, began to rebuild it with Santa Coloma and Albaserrada stock, the combination yielding such good results that his bulls were soon in great demand. In 1931, Hemingway's last bullfight season before the publication of *Death in the Afternoon*, Francisco presented fifty-four bulls and six *novillos* to be fought in Spanish and French plazas; they were "toros de primera calidad, bravos y nobles" (first class bulls, brave and noble).

Francisco Sánchez sold his herd in 1934 to various breeders, including Arturo Sánchez Cobaleda, Justo Sánchez Tabernero, the Marquis of Villagodio, and don Santiago Ubago; Ubago also obtained the rights to the brand, colors, and *antigüedad*. Subsequent owners were Julio Garrido and Daniel Ruiz Yagüe, of Albacete.[617] For more detail on the relationship between pedigree, ownership, and *antigüedad*, see the essay on "Bulls and Bull Breeding," in the introduction to this volume.

The narrator accurately identifies Francisco Sánchez as a well-known bull breeder from Coquilla, Salamanca (132).

Sánchez, Salvador (Frascuelo, el Negro). Full name: Salvador Sánchez Povedano. Spanish bullfighter, 1842–98. Investiture as *matador de toros*, in Madrid, October 1867. Frascuelo was called "el Negro" because he was so dark-skinned. His brother, Francisco (Paco Frascuelo, 1843–1924) was also a *matador de toros*, though not a successful one. For many years he served in his brother's *cuadrilla* as banderillero.

This nineteenth-century master, born in Churriana (Granada) began his career in poverty. His father, a retired military man and a gambler, died when Salvador was eleven. His widow could barely support the family, let alone supply the finery and status Salvador craved, and it was the lure of fame and money, rather than a love of the art, that propelled him into the bullring. His courage and his flamboyant personality were the defining factors of his career.

At the beginning of his career, Frascuelo performed as often as he could, working indiscriminately in *mojigangas* (q.v.); in *cuadrillas*, including that of Cayetano Sanz (q.v.); and as a *novillero*. He tried all sorts of techniques with great enthusiasm and strength, if not always with polish. One critic wrote of him at this stage, "que todo lo intentaba, que todo lo quería hacer y que nada sabía" (that he tried everything, that he wanted to do everything, and that he knew nothing).[618] Nothing fazed him. In 1866, for example, he was having difficulties killing a bull, stabbing it repeatedly, when another bull suddenly broke through the *toril* and entered the ring. Frascuelo killed this fresh bull with one incredible stroke, and returned to the other bull, which was still tottering about the ring, and finished him off as well. More than once, he dragged a chair into the middle of the bullring and conducted the *suerte de banderillas* while seated, leaping up at the very last moment to place the banderillas. He quickly attracted attention, improved his technique with practice, and was promoted to *matador de toros* in his early twenties.

In these years, Frascuelo became very popular in Madrid, particularly with the aristocracy. In economic and social terms, he had achieved his goal. But in the process he had developed into a top-notch bullfighter, able to challenge the elegant virtuoso Rafael Molina Sánchez (Lagartijo, q.v.), with whom he first appeared in the bullring in 1868. The competition with Lagartijo continued throughout Frascuelo's career. Their supporters were fanatically partisan: Lagartijo was more popular with the public and press of Madrid; Frascuelo was feted by the aristocracy and other trendsetters, which, of course, elicited the charge that he was turning his back on the lower class from which he came.

The bullfighters themselves displayed no animosity towards each other and were frequently scheduled together, especially on important occasions such as the corrida in benefit of the famous Antonio Sánchez (el Tato, 1831–95) who had been crippled by a bull in 1869. They closed the season of 1872 with a pair of corridas, each of them killing six bulls by himself, with the other standing by in case of mishap. At the end of the season, one critic claimed they were "ambos necesarios en la plaza de Madrid" (both necessary in the Madrid plaza) since they were the best bullfighters, and neither one was better than the other. They also appeared together at the last corrida of the old bullring at the Plaza de Alcalá, 18 July 1974.

But Lagartijo's Madrid fans made life so miserable for Frascuelo that early in 1875 he angrily announced a boycott against the Madrid ring—an outrageous move that exacerbated the situation. (For the importance of Madrid, see "The Bullring" and "The Bullfighter," in the introduction to this volume.) He returned to Madrid in 1876, but he boycotted the city again in 1877, and from 1881 to 1884 he performed there only once. One of his first performances in 1885 was a *mano a mano* with Lagartijo, at which some spectators unfurled a huge white banner, hoping "Que no se vayan nunca Lagartijo, Frascuelo y sus cuadrillas" (May Lagartijo, Frascuelo and their *cuadrillas* never leave us).[619] Frascuelo continued to perform often with Lagartijo, in Madrid as well as elsewhere, in 1885, 1886, and 1887. Frascuelo also appeared in Madrid on his own, as on the afternoon of 26 May 1887, when he obtained "un triunfo señaladísimo" (a most outstanding triumph) in a long afternoon during which he fought and killed six Veragua bulls by himself, "de modo insuperable."

Fracuelo was injured at a charity performance in November 1887, and the next year he was visibly weaker. He was injured again in Barcelona, May 1888 and, after the necessary absence from the ring, even his most devoted admirers had to agree that his powers were waning. He retired in May 1889, at age forty-six, with a *mano a mano* with Lagartijo, with Rafael Guerra (q.v.) performing as banderillero and many other stars showing up to honor him. During his long career—he retired twenty-two years after his investiture—he maintained his position at the top of his profession.

Frascuelo was a colorful and distinctive performer, original with the cape and muleta and spectacular with the sword. His courage, pride, and self-confidence were enormous and unshaken by fairly frequent injuries; prudence and moderation were noticeably lacking in his character. His pride and exuberance, combined with an enormous talent, resulted in many magnificent performances inside the ring and not a few brawls outside it.

Just as his passion for the bulls did not abate with success or maturity, the attention-getting behavior that had characterized his earlier years persisted even when he had achieved fame. In the 1870s, for example, he inexplicably decided he didn't want to fight the last bull of the afternoon; on days when he was the youngest professional on the bill (i.e., the bullfighter who had been promoted to *matador de toros* most recently and who would therefore work with the sixth, or last, bull), a seventh bull had to be added to the program, to be fought by someone else. Each time this happened, of course, heated discussions broke out in the ring, the press, the cafés, and the bars. In 1874, he punched the editor of the journal *El Toreo* and then offered to run him through with his sword. Although he was an indisputably fine bullfighter, such shenanigans affected his audiences' responses to him.[620]

Like Pedro Romero and Joaquín Rodríguez (Costillares) in the eighteenth century, Cayetano Sanz and Manuel Domínguez just before them, and José Gómez Ortega (Joselito) and Juan Belmonte (qq.v.) after them, Frascuelo and Lagartijo dominated the art in their time.[621] They were very different in appearance, character, and behavior.[622] Each had thousands of passionate admirers and was celebrated in print, music, and art. Most critics would agree that they were the "greatest" figures of their time, though not at the expense of later "greats." Taurine historians recognize that insisting that one epoch or style was "greater" than another is a highly dubious proposition, as indefensible as Hemingway's claim that "Historians speak highly of all dead bullfighters" (240). See also Toledo in *DS*.

For Fracuelo's banderillero (474), Saturnino Frutos (Ojitos, 1855–1913), *see* Gaona, Rodolfo.

The narrator has read that Frascuelo was a "truly great" matador, a fine killer. He is dissatisfied with taurine historians who exaggerate the virtues of dead bullfighters at the expense of the living, that is to say, those who denigrate the living Joselito and Belmonte by proclaiming the era of Frascuelo and Lagartijo as "the golden age of all golden ages" of bullfighting (240). He mentions Frascuelo often (240, 241, 243, 267, 474).

Sánchez Mejías, Ignacio. Spanish bullfighter and writer, 1891–1934. Investiture as *matador de toros*, March 1919, in Barcelona; confirmed more than a year later, in Madrid, April 1920.

Sánchez Mejías was a complicated personality, attracted both by the active and the literary life. The son of a well-to-do physician, he was interested in the bulls even as a child, playing and practicing with his good friend José Gómez Ortega (Joselito). But Ignacio's father insisted that he study medicine, as his older brother José had, and at age eighteen Ignacio escaped parental pressure by stowing away in a boat, in the company of a friend, Enrique Ortega (el Cuco, a cousin of Joselito). After several difficulties and adventures, they ended up in the care of Ignacio's brother Aurelio (not a physician), in Mexico.

Ignacio had a difficult time making his way into the Mexican bullfight world, but he found part-time employment in the *cuadrilla* of the minor Spanish matador Fermín Muñoz (Corchaíto, 1882–1914), with whom he traveled the bullfighting circuit, in Spain and Mexico, in 1911 and 1912. In 1913 he appeared as a *novillero* in Mexico, and in 1914 he performed in Spain, receiving praise for some of his performances but not enough contracts to continue as *novillero* for the next season. From 1915 to 1918 he worked in the *cuadrillas* of Belmonte, Rafael Gómez Ortega (el Gallo) and Joselito. After this protracted apprenticeship as a *peón de brega*, he reappeared as *novillero* in August 1918. A few performances convinced the public that he was ready for the next step, and early in 1919 he was promoted by Joselito, now his brother-in-law, to *matador de toros*. He was twenty-eight years old.

In spite of his undeniable talent and expertise, Sánchez Mejías had to struggle to win over his audiences: many saw him as riding Joselito's coattails to fame, and others objected to his rude manners in and out of the ring. He also faced the problem of defining a style for himself, to distinguish himself in a field dominated by Joselito and Belmonte. Sánchez Mejías responded to these challenges by deliberately courting danger in the ring. He would put himself in difficult positions, such as fighting with his back against the barrera or sitting on its railing, and then flaunt the intellectual and technical powers that enabled him to survive such situations. The taurine public was fascinated, as he knew they would be, and he was soon drawing large audiences, demanding high fees, and publicizing his quarrels with the managers and administrators who refused to pay. He usually got his way, because he could always fill a bullring: he made money for everyone associated with him. In 1919 Ignacio had contracts for eighty corridas, but performed on only fifty afternoons: he had consistently magnificent reviews. His promotion was confirmed (also by Joselito, who was killed a month later) in 1920, another excellent season (ninety performances); he was ranked first nationwide.

Illness caused Sánchez Mejías to miss a good part of the 1921 season, but between mid-July and the end of the season in October he performed more than forty times. During these good years he spent the winter seasons in Mexico, where he had a great following as well. But for some reason Ignacio shunned the Madrid rings, causing that influential public to doubt the glowing reports that flowed in from the provinces. On 26 September 1921, he quelled the rumors about him by giving a dazzling performance at a Madrid benefit. In 1922, having established a great reputation and amassed a fortune, he retired.

Some analysts argue that the death of Joselito prompted this retirement. Heartrending photographs show Ignacio grieving his childhood friend. They had been friends, colleagues, and brothers-in-law, and had been in the bullring together on 16 May 1920. Sánchez Mejías killed the bull that had fatally gored Joselito, accompanied the body from Talavera de la Reina to Seville, and served as pallbearer. He was eventually buried in the same grave. (For details about another fatal *mano a mano*, see Linares.)

Ignacio returned to the ring late in the 1924 season, immediately resuming his position as a leading performer: with forty-two corridas, he was ranked fourth. Several times during that year, he asked for and got more than the maximum seven thousand pesetas established as a ceiling by the Unión de Empresarios de Plazas de Toros (Union of Bullring Impresarios), which no doubt led to his being elected, in November 1924, as president of the Unión de Matadores de Toros y Novillos. In 1925, with sixty-one corridas, he was ranked second nationwide (behind Lalanda, who had seventy-five corridas), and continued to defy the Unión de Empresarios, who had imposed a fine of 5,000 pesetas on any bullring manager who contracted him. Ignacio obviously overrode the boycott, performing in all of Spain's major plazas, including Madrid, Barcelona, Valencia, and Seville, and charging high fees.

Ignacio's preoccupation with literature distracted him from the ring. In 1926 he worked on a novel (unfinished), wrote for a bullfight magazine, and was active in the theater. That year he performed in thirty-six corridas, earned rave reviews, and was not injured. Obviously, he could have fought more often if he had wanted to. In 1927 he chose to perform in the ring only three times, announcing his retirement at the third performance. In 1928 two of his plays, *Sinrazón* (about mental disease) and *Zayas* (about a retired bullfighter), were successfully produced. He wrote two other plays, the surreal *Ni más ni menos* and *Soledad*, which examines men's and women's attitudes toward work; neither one of these was staged. He also wrote for and produced a musical extravaganza featuring his lover, Encarnación López (la Argentinita); hosted famous writers and literary conferences at his estate, Pino Montano; was president of Seville's branch of the Red Cross and of a football team; and wrote for a newspaper (including taurine reviews).

All these activities ceased, however, in 1934, when he returned to the ring. His skills, his pride, his bravery, and his disregard for danger remained unchanged; he shared the limelight with the best fighters of the 1930s and performed with distinction. But he was in his forties, his reflexes had slowed, and he was heavy: he was fatally wounded in his sixth fight.[623] For more details about his death, see *DS*.

Ignacio was mourned more by the literary than by the taurine world. Although poems, songs, and even novels and plays are frequently written about bullfighters, no bullfighter has inspired as great a poem as García Lorca's passionate and frequently reprinted lament for his friend, "Llanto por [Lament for] Ignacio Sánchez Mejías." It has been translated into dozens of languages; John Fulton, the American matador and painter, illustrated a beautiful bilingual edition of this poem; in the 1950s Mauricio Ohana set it to music; more recently it has been choreographed for dance. It is one of García Lorca's most famous works.

Ignacio Sánchez Mejías was a brave, skilled, aggressive, and inventive bullfighter. His slow, thorough training gave him a technical precision which, combined with his pride and his intellectual approach, resulted in what many criticized as a cold, detached style. He deliberately took great risks and then devised ingenious solutions to the desperate problems he had created for himself. The audiences got a sense of great danger, but Ignacio's own detachment and insolent fearlessness defused the feeling. As a result, he was admired but not loved by his audiences: he was a great bullfighter who had to win over his audience with each performance.[624] Hemingway was among those who were not won over.

Hemingway and Sánchez Mejías. Sánchez Mejías was retired the first year Hemingway came to Spain, 1923, and again from 1927 until after *Death in the Afternoon* was published. In 1924 Hemingway was in Spain only for the Pamplona fiesta, at which Sánchez Mejías did not perform. In 1925 Hemingway was in Spain for a longer time, and Ignacio performed in sixty-one corridas, but the two men seem not to have been in the same places at the same time. In 1926 Sánchez Mejías performed in Pamplona on 7 and 10 July and in Valencia on 25 and 26 July; Hemingway saw him on these occasions and perhaps on others as well.[625]

Hemingway mentions Sánchez Mejías's comeback and death in *For Whom the Bell Tolls* (253–54) and in *The Dangerous Summer* (68).

Sánchez Mejías married Dolores (Lola) Gómez Ortega. Their son, José Ignacio Sánchez Mejías (1917–66), was a *matador de toros* and, more successfully, a taurine manager.

A famous photograph, not reproduced in *Death in the Afternoon*, shows Sánchez Mejías mourning Joselito, his colleague, friend, and brother-in-law: there are no tears or handkerchief, as Hemingway claims (*DIA*, 243), only a bent head and a terrible grief (illustration 5).

The narrator correctly reports that Ignacio was married to Joselito's sister (229–30) and recognizes Sánchez Mejías as one of the major figures of the golden age of Joselito and Belmonte. He grants that he is a fine banderillero (94, 95, 201) but dislikes him for his theatrical bravery and therefore says he will not discuss him at any length (94–95). Thereafter, however, he offers descriptions of his work (201) and his relationship with Alfredo Corrochano (q.v.; Hemingway's emphasis on Gregorio Corrochano's "attacks" on Joselito implies that training Alfredo is tantamount to treachery on Ignacio's part). He completes his attack on Sánchez Mejías by claiming that his grief when Joselito was killed is ostentatious and self-servingly camera-conscious (243; photographs, h: 322–25).[626]

Sandhurst. Prestigious English military academy, established in 1799 under the patronage of the Duke of York in High Wycombe. In 1802, the school was moved to Great Marlow, and in 1812 it was moved again, to Sandhurst, whereupon it became the Sandhurst Royal Military College (RMC). It is now known as the Royal Military Academy Sandhurst.

Dorman-Smith and Sandhurst. Eric Edward was the oldest son of Major Edward Patrick Smith (later Dorman-Smith) of Bellamont Forest, County Cavan. In 1910 he was sent to Uppingham, a public (i.e., private) school established in 1534, where he was not very happy. His father, chafing at the expenses involved in educating his sons, insisted that Eric take the entrance examination to Sandhurst in December 1912, although Eric's teachers argued that he was unprepared and needed another full year at Uppingham. Eric "swotted" for the difficult examinations, passed them, and entered Sandhurst in February 1913. At Sandhurst, academic success enabled him to receive his commission after two instead of the customary three terms. He left on 17 December 1913, and his first commission, as second lieutenant in the Northumberland Fusiliers, is dated 25 February 1914.[627] *See also* Dorman-Smith.

Hemingway and Sandhurst. Hemingway mentions that Dorman-Smith was educated at Sandhurst in *A Moveable Feast* (55). He reveals his sensitivity about his own lack of academic degrees when he reports the academic backgrounds of almost all of the twelve adults he mentions in "Some Reactions." *See also* Porcellian; Skull and Bones; Yale, in this volume; and West Point in *DS*.

The narrator correctly reports that D.S. was educated in British public schools and at Sandhurst (466).

Santa Coloma, Conde de. Full name: Enrique de Queralt y Fernández Maquieira, Conde de Santa Coloma. Spanish bull breeder, d. 1933.

Although the Count of Santa Coloma became a bull breeder in the twentieth century, the pedigree of the herd he bought reaches back to the eighteenth century Vistahermosa (q.v.) ranch. This particular Vistahermosa herd had passed through a number of skillful hands, including such respected bull breeders as (in chronological order) Lesaca, Suárez Cordero, Dolores Monge vda. de Murube, Eduardo Ibarra, and Manuel Fernández Peña, before Santa Coloma acquired it in 1905.[628]

The Count presented his new bulls under his name, brand and colors (turquoise and crimson) for the Madrid corrida on 17 May 1906, thus establishing the date of their new *antigüedad* (q.v.), or seniority. He continued the work of the previous owners by adding Vistahermosa stock from the Ibarra and the Saltillo ranches.

Throughout their history, the Santa Coloma bulls have performed well in the ring. The Count's ownership of the herd coincided with the *época de oro* (*edad de oro*, golden age) of Joselito and Belmonte (qq.v.), and their obvious preference for his bulls contributed to their achieving "un cartel verdaderamente extraordinario" (a truly extraordinary popularity): the herd was "francamente magnífica." In the 1920s and 1930s, the *edad de plata* (silver age) and the years of Hemingway's most intense involvement in tauromachy, the Santa Colomas were in great demand not only by the leading bullfighters, but also by bull breeders looking to improve their herds.

In 1932, Santa Coloma sold his herd to Felipe Bartolomé (d. 1959) and to Joaquín Buendía Peña, both of Seville.[629] Buendía also acquired the colors and *antigüedad*, which are still (in 1999) in the Buendía family.[630] *See also* Ibarra, Eduardo; Lesaca; Saavedra; Vistahermosa.

The narrator counts the Count of Santa Coloma among the leading bull breeders of his day (132).

Santiago de Compostela. After he married Pauline, Hemingway added Santiago de Compostela, an important Catholic pilgrimage site, to the places he visited regularly. In 1927, 1929, and 1931, they went to Santiago de Compostela and La Coruña after the July *ferias* of Pamplona and Valencia, spending much of the hot month of August in this cool part of Spain.[631]

The feast day of Santiago, or St. James, is 25 July. He is Spain's patron saint.

In his catalogue of the places and sensations that signify Spain to him, the narrator includes Santiago de Compostela (271, 276, 278).

Sanz, Cayetano. Full name: Cayetano Sanz Pozas. Spanish bullfighter, 1821–91. Investiture as *matador de toros*, November 1848, in Madrid.

Sanz was born to a widowed mother and, after she remarried, was brought up by his paternal grandparents. When he was ten years old, he was apprenticed to a cobbler, a profession that was almost a guarantee of lifelong poverty. He quickly grasped this and, looking for other venues, discovered his aptitude for bullfighting. He spent most of his free time practicing at local *capeas* and *mojigangas* (q.v.) and in the *matadero* (slaughterhouse, the training ground for many bullfighters). By age sixteen the strong-willed boy had overcome his grandparents' objections to this dangerous profession and was able to devote himself fulltime to bullfighting.

His progress was slow. In 1844, however, his skill and style attracted the patronage of the Duke of Veragua and, through him, introductions to the day's leading teacher and theoretician, José Antonio Calderón (Capita), whom Cossío credits for Sanz's elegance with the cape and muleta. Sanz also became an excellent banderillero and was thus able to work regularly, most profitably in the *cuadrilla* of José Redondo (el Chiclanero, 1819–53), a fine, accomplished matador who was very popular 1845–50 and under whose tutelage Sanz enlarged his repertoire. Chiclanero's rival Francisco Arjona (Cúchares, 1818–68, born in Madrid but raised in Seville, whose hero he became) put obstacles in the way of Sanz's *alternativa* (q.v.), but after an extended apprenticeship, Sanz managed to be promoted to *matador de toros*. He was in his late twenties.

Sanz became the darling not only of his native Madrid but of all the major plazas of Spain, including that of Seville, stronghold of

Cúchares fans whose chauvinism was overcome by Sanz's art in 1851. He performed at all important corridas attended by the Spanish monarchs and was the first Spanish bullfighter to perform in France where, in 1854, he appeared in a series of corridas held in honor of the wedding of Napoleon III and the Countess of Teba. Throughout the 1850s much of the 1860s he performed successfully with all the other first-ranked matadors, including Manuel Domínguez (Desperdicios, 1816–86),[632] and the younger stars, Antonio Sánchez (el Tato, 1831–95) and Antonio Carmona (el Gordito, 1838–1920).[633]

Like most *toreros largos* (well-educated, with a varied repertoire), Sanz suffered few serious injuries. But injuries are inescapable: his more serious gorings were probably those of June 1856 and September 1859. He was more frequently though less seriously hurt in the 1860s. In a physically demanding profession, Sanz displayed remarkable staying powers. In 1869 one contemporary critic marveled that unlike other bullfighters at his stage of life, Sanz was still fighting full schedules, with no diminution of strength or energy (he was then forty-eight and had started fighting bulls in childhood). In his mid-fifties, however, Sanz did begin to slow down. When he found himself unable to kill his second bull, in May 1877, he retired.

In 1878, thirty years after his *alternativa*, Sanz performed at a gala corrida to honor the wedding of Alfonso XII and María de las Mercedes: he was fifty-six, but he performed with distinction with the cape and muleta, being less sure with the sword. Sanz was so confident of his cape and muleta work that he often cleared the ring so he could face the bull entirely alone. But he often hesitated visibly before attempting the kill, and occasionally found himself in trouble in the last stage of the fight. Bagüés calls him "uno de los toreros más elegantes que han pisado los ruedos . . . un verdadero artista" (one of the most elegant bullfighters to step out into the ring . . . a true artist) and repeats the usual criticisms: occasional weakness with the sword and generally undistinguished performances with difficult (i.e., spiritless or cowardly) bulls.[634] Sanz was always true to his motto: "Más vale no intentar una suerte que ejecutarla mal" (Better not to try than to fail).

A lovely story about the older Cayetano Sanz recalls Pedro Romero's enduring powers. It involves a *novillada* in Villamantilla, attended by some young hopefuls from Madrid. One of them, angered by the advice being shouted at him by an old gentleman in the stands, challenged him rudely to take up a muleta himself. The old gentleman clambered down, entered the improvised ring, and gave a virtuosic display that brought the audience to its feet: he was, of course, Cayetano Sanz. The *novillero* humbly apologized.

The narrator praises Sanz (89, 267).

The Saturday Evening Post. Published 1821–1969. Originally a news weekly which offered both news and fiction, the *Post* slowly increased its emphasis on fiction. Under the ownership of Cyrus H. K. Curtis and in the decades of George Horace Lorimer's editorship (1899–1936), it became very popular (circulation of three million) and carried a lot of advertising, which enabled it to pay high prices for popular fiction.[635] It published F. Scott Fitzgerald regularly but rejected all the short stories the young Hemingway submitted. In *The Torrents of Spring*, Hemingway's character Scripps was well paid for the story he published in *The Saturday Evening Post*, but he approves of a restaurant because it does not advertise in that slick weekly (*TOS*, 16–18).

Without embarrassment, Sidney Franklin writes that "I never . . . read anything that wasn't directly concerned with bullfighting, except *The Saturday Evening Post*. I had no idea that [Hemingway] had already written *A Farewell to Arms* and *The Sun Also Rises* and was world-famous. When he offered to get me some of his books, I told him I wasn't interested."[636] By mentioning the lowbrow Franklin's attachment to *The Saturday Evening Post*, Hemingway insults that publication, getting back at editors who had rejected his submissions. Similarly, in *Green Hills of Africa*, Hemingway writes that the white hunter, Phillips, whose literary taste is unsophisticated, likes lion-hunting stories, which he reads in *The Saturday Evening Post* (197).

Although Hemingway insults *The Saturday Evening Post* in *A Moveable Feast* (for publishing Fitzgerald's formulaic stories, 155), Hemingway had in fact subscribed to the magazine. Writing from Italy in the fall of 1918, Ernest had asked his father to "subscribe to the Sat. Eve. Post for me and have it sent to my address here. They will forward it to me wherever I am." Clarence seems to have done so, and Ernest took the magazine with him on a vacation in late September.[637] He quickly outgrew such reading once he came to Paris.

The Saturday Evening Post is Sidney Franklin's only reading material (*h:* 505–506).

Sebastian, Saint. Roman martyr of the late third century. When the Emperor Diocletian learned that Sebastian was a Christian, he ordered him killed. His archers shot Sebastian with arrows and left him for dead. Sebastian recovered and was then beaten to death on Diocletian's orders. He is usually depicted in his martyrdom, his body pierced by many arrows and his eyes cast upwards. The Louvre displays two such portraits, by the fifteenth century painters Le Pérugin and Andrea Mantegna. Titian painted the saint in the same position: his large portrait (210 cm. × 115 cm., full body, five arrows) hangs in the Hermitage in St. Petersburg, which also has a smaller portrait, by Perugino (face and chest, one arrow). Hemingway saw el Greco's paintings at the Louvre and at the Prado, which has many Grecos, including the large *St. Sebastian* (115 cm. × 85 cm.). St. Sebastian's feast day is January 20.

Scholes and Comley, arguing that Hemingway was remarkably sensitive to gender issues, point out "how readily Hemingway noted that images of Saint Sebastian are regularly androgynous, an observation confirmed by the current status of that saint as something of a gay icon" (119). The young Sebastian was so beautiful that Diocletian became enamored of him, which may explain his repeated violence against Sebastian when the youth turned to the spiritual life.

Sebastian appears in a simile in *Islands in the Stream*: the expression on the face of Thomas Hudson's houseboy recalls that of St. Sebastian (*IITS*, 232). *See also* San Sebastián, the city named for this saint.

The narrator mentions St. Sebastian in his discussion of androgyny (q.v.), homosexuality, and painting (204).

Seniority. For definitions of this important concept, which applies both to herds (*antigüedad*) and to bullfighters (counting from the date of the *alternativa*, or promotion to the rank of *matador de toros*), *see* "Bulls and Bull Breeding" and "The Bullfighter," in the introduction to this volume.

The Sergeant. A character in the story "A Natural History of the Dead" (q.v.).

The sergeant assists the doctor at the dressing station (143). The sergeant speaks: 143.

Serna, Victoriano de la. Full name: Victoriano de la Serna Gil. Spanish bullfighter, 1910–81 (died by his own hand). Investiture as *matador de toros*, in Madrid, 29 October 1931.[638] Graduated from medical school, 1933.

Victoriano de la Serna was an unusual bullfighter. His *afición* manifested itself rather late, when he was well into his medical studies. His well-to-do family, uninterested in taurine matters, was shocked by his sudden desire to abandon his studies. As young men usually do, he prevailed over their objections. He learned quickly and rose rapidly in the ranks. He mesmerized the critics and the public with his unusual work with the cape and the muleta, both held very low: it was revolutionary.

Victoriano's management of his career was as unusual as his style. Even as a *novillero*, he insisted on such high prices that few rings were able to afford him. As late as 1930, the year before his promotion to *matador de toros*, he was contracted for fewer than ten *novilladas*, not enough for him to rate an individual entry in that year's bullfighting annual, *Toros y toreros en 1930*—a very unusual situation, since *novilleros*, like young actors, are hungry for audiences.[639] But his (relatively) few performances were striking. He conquered the Madrid audience with his debut there as *novillero*, on 27 August 1931. After sixteen more *novilladas*, he took the *alternativa* (q.v.) just two months later, on 29 October 1931. On that important afternoon his performance was decidedly unspectacular.

In spite of his high fees and his disappointing *alternativa* performance, Victoriano was offered a goodly number of contracts for 1932, of which he accepted only thirty-four. A serious goring early in the season forced him to cancel half of those; he ended the 1932 season with seventeen performances. But Victoriano was able to maintain public interest, and his performances in 1933 and 1934, his best seasons, were spectacular often enough to for him to survive his few failures. Even at his high prices he performed fifty-three times each year (twenty marks a successful season; Domingo Ortega, q.v., was top-ranked both those years, with sixty-nine and eighty corridas, respectively). Victoriano found time in 1933 to finish medical school.

Victoriano fought less often and less brilliantly in 1935 (thirty-five corridas) and the next year was gored twice in the leg, on 10 and 29 May 1936. He worked in Pamplona as a physician during the Spanish Civil War (1936–39). As a Nationalist, he was invited to participate in the *Corrida de la Victoria* of 24 May 1939, but his displeasure with the bull that was assigned him led him to refuse the honor, though he performed in Madrid on other occasions that year, being injured in the Madrid corrida of 29 June 1939.

There were not many bullfights in the first postwar years, but Victoriano performed in several festivals in 1940 and in a few corridas at the beginning of the 1941 season, after which he seems to have retired, although he issued no formal announcement. He continued inactive in 1942, had short but triumphant seasons in 1943 (eighteen corridas) and 1944 (six corridas), and then retired again and finally, with the famous explanation, applied also to his occasional poor performances, "No se puede estar ni valiente ni inspirado todos los días a las cinco en punto de la tarde" (One can't be brave and inspired every day at five o'clock sharp).[640]

Victoriano was an excellent bullfighter, capable and intelligent in all aspects of the bullfight and innovative and supremely stylish with the cape and muleta, inventing or perfecting several showy muleta passes, like the *manoletina* (so named because it was popularized by Manuel Rodríguez [Manolete, see in *DS*] and the *giraldilla*; these are sometimes called *lasernista* passes. He ranks among the best and most original fighters of his time. The late and sudden awakening of his *afición*, his completed medical education, and his early and successful insistence on high fees all point to his "enorme personalidad"; he was unpredictable and original ("personalidad impredecible y genial").[641]

Victoriano's two younger brothers, Ramón and Rafael, followed him into the bullring: because of him and because of their own similar gifts, they were watched carefully. Ramón quickly became a successful *novillero*, was hailed in 1934 as a bullfighter "de exceptional calidad . . . continuador . . . del arte de su hermano Victoriano" (of exceptional gifts . . . perpetuating . . . the art of his brother Victoriano), and then retired suddenly in 1935, without taking the *alternativa*. He became a lawyer. The youngest brother, Rafael, somewhat less talented but still very promising, also quit the profession before being promoted to *matador de toros*. Victoriano's son, Victoriano de la Serna Ernst, was also a bullfighter.[642]

Hemingway and de la Serna. Like his contemporary Domingo Ortega (q.v.), Victoriano leapt to fame just as Hemingway was finishing *Death in the Afternoon*: when Hemingway left Spain in September 1931, Victoriano had not yet taken the *alternativa*. Hemingway's predictions about both these new stars missed the mark. His claim that he saw Victoriano in September 1931 is inaccurate: Victoriano did not perform in Madrid that month. Hemingway probably means Victoriano's Madrid debut as *novillero*, on 27 August, which Hemingway probably saw and which was, as he writes, "a great afternoon." Alfredo Corrochano and Juan Martín-Caro (Chiquito de la Audiencia) shared the bill; the *novillos* were supplied by Lacerda Pinto Barreiros. After that first Madrid performance, Victoriano performed in three more *novilladas* (13, 20, and 29 September) before being promoted to *matador de toros* in Madrid, on 29 October 1931: this date marks his first (and not his second, as Hemingway writes) "appearance as a full matador." Although Hemingway was in Spain and probably in Madrid at the time of the debut, he returned to the United States before Victoriano's *alternativa*, which was Victoriano's single corrida (as opposed to *novillada*) for 1931.[643] For the difference between these ranks and ceremonies, see "The Bullfighter," in the introduction to this volume. Hemingway saw Victoriano de la Serna in 1933 and did not like his performances that year (see below).

Hemingway's assessment that de la Serna was "green, insufficiently grounded in his profession" (*DIA*, 231) is decidedly a minority opinion. In 1934, writing about the corridas he had seen in August and September 1933, Hemingway resumes his attack on Victoriano, delicately ascribing to Victoriano's "enemies" the shocking accusation that "his bursts of extraordinary courage originate in a hypodermic syringe and that if he does not care to fight he knows the secret of producing a high fever and frothing at the mouth." He describes him as "intelligent . . . unsound, enigmatic, interesting, and highly irritating."[644]

Although de la Serna had his share of failures, Cossío's review of the 1933 season offers a more accurate summary of Victoriano's early career: "con su clara inteligencia se hace cargo de la parte técnica del toreo, conoce sus secretos y martingalas y al aficionado exigente le da la sensación que en él hay un auténtico lidiador, desbordado por un estilista singular" (with his clear intelligence he controls the technical aspects of *toreo*, knows its secrets and techniques, and he gives the demanding aficionado the feeling that in him we have a classic performer, overtaken by an original style).[645]

The narrator recognizes Victoriano de la Serna's "phenomenal natural ability" but thinks that he was promoted prematurely and predicts that the setbacks of 1932 mark the end of a promising career (230–31).

Serra, Dr. Paco. Full name: Francisco (Paco) Serra Juan. Spanish physician, 1886–1958.

Serra graduated medical school in June 1913 in internal medicine and became a specialist in *taurotraumatología* (injuries suffered during the bullfight). He was appointed to the medical staff of the Valencia bullring in 1915 and served as its Chief Surgeon for many years.[646]

Serra in the 1920s. Manuel Martínez (q.v.), who was gored often, was usually attended by Dr. Serra, a fellow Valencian and a great bullfight aficionado. The goring that Hemingway dramatizes was suffered by Martínez in the July 1925 *feria* in Valencia, with Dr. Serra in attendance. In 1927, when Martínez was gored in Barcelona, Dr. Serra rushed to that city to treat him. Barcelona's taurine weekly, *La fiesta brava*, hailed him as "sabio" and a "verdadero 'as' en eso de curar traumas de toreros" (wise and a real ace in treating bullfighters' wounds).[647] *See also* Doctors.

Serra in the 1940s: Penicillin. On 14 October 1944, Dr. Serra used penicillin in the treatment of Manuel Cortés, a *novillero* who had been badly gored in the left thigh on 28 September 1944, in Algemesí. The local infirmary applied a tourniquet and the young man was put into a car en route to better medical facilities in Valencia. The car broke down on the way, and with one thing and another, Cortés didn't arrive to Valencia until 9:00 P.M. Needless to say, he was in pretty poor condition. Dr. Serra gave him three blood transfusions and finally came to the painful conclusion that the leg had to be amputated. He hesitated, because he recognized that "tal decisión representaba la muerte del torero, aunque se salvara el hombre" (this decision spelled death for the bullfighter, even if it saved the man), but the situation was desperate.

Cortés survived the drastic surgery and even showed some improvement. But the wound became septic, whereupon Serra ordered penicillin. The patient improved markedly, but that night he suddenly lost consciousness (probably a blood clot or heart attack) and died.[648]

This seems to be the first time that "esta nueva medicación" was used to treat a bullfight wound. What is remarkable is that penicillin had only recently been released for use. Although it was discovered in 1928, British and American scientists spent more than a decade learning to grow, purify, and concentrate it, to perform clinical tests, and to obtain government approval. The outbreak of World War II gave urgency to the research, but by 1943 only "200 patients had been treated with the drug. The results were so impressive that the surgeon general of the United States Army authorized trial of the antibiotic in a military hospital. Soon thereafter, penicillin was adopted throughout the medical services of the United States Armed Forces."[649] Thus, "the present antibiotic era may be said to date from 1940, when the first account of the properties of an extract of cultures of *Penicillium notatum* appeared."[650] Dr. Serra was clearly aware of this research: he ordered the recently released drug for Cortés in 1944.

In 1959, Hemingway discussed the importance of penicillin in the taurine world: "Strangers to bullfighting are always puzzled why so many fighters are wounded and so few are killed. The answer is antibiotics and modern surgery. Penicillin and the other antibiotics are as important to a bullfighter, if he is to survive, as his confidential banderillero is. Penicillin is the unseen member of the cuadrilla. Without antibiotics there would have been at least twenty matadors and novilleros killed last season. With antibiotics and modern surgery many famous matadors who died in the past would have been saved."[651]

Or, as Nicanor Villalta put it, "Esto es lo que divide precisamente el toreo en dos épocas: antes y después del doctor Fleming" (This clearly divides bullfighting into two periods: before and after Dr. Fleming).[652]

In the typescript of *The Dangerous Summer*, Antonio Ordóñez tells Hemingway that "They're going to put up a statue to the man who invented penicillina [*sic*] out at the ring."[653] The statue of Dr. Alexander Fleming (1881–1955) stands in the front courtyard of Las Ventas, Madrid's bullring.

In 1955 Valencia honored Dr. Serra for his forty years of uninterrupted service to his native city. A plaque on the outside of the bullring, near the ticket office, bears his likeness, and Valencia's lovely taurine museum is located in a nearby arcade, called the Pasaje Serra. Dr. Serra is the author of *Taurotraumatología, precedida de un diseño histórico sobre la fiesta de los toros*, from which the above account of Manuel Cortés is taken. See also Quintana, Juan, in *DS*.

For another doctor with close ties to bullfighters, see Tamames in *DS*.

> When Manolo Martínez was gored in Valencia, he was attended by Dr. Paco Serra (261–62; the doctor is alluded to but not named, 255).

Seville. Although Hemingway has no particular bone to pick with Seville in *Death in the Afternoon* (37, 44, 268, *h:* 508), he seems to have turned against this city in later years: see Seville in *DS*.

Shakespeare, William. English poet and dramatist, 1564–1616. Hemingway frequently refers to Shakespeare's plays and characters. In works preceding *Death in the Afternoon*, for example, references to *The Tempest* and *A Midsummer Night's Dream* appear in *Torrents of Spring* (39); and to *Julius Caesar* and *Othello*, in *A Farewell to Arms* (139–40, 257). The short story "The Sea Change," written while Hemingway was working on *Death in the Afternoon*, takes its title from *The Tempest*, and the characters in "The Short Happy Life of Francis Macomber," composed between 1934 and 1936, quote *Henry IV, Part II*. *Green Hills of Africa* (1935) mentions *Othello* and several Shakespearean actors. References to Shakespeare continue to appear in almost all of Hemingway's books, but it is *Across the River and Into the Trees*, the last novel Hemingway supervised into print, that offers the most references to Shakespeare: *Othello* (230), *King Lear* (171), *Richard II* (236), *Henry IV, Part I* (171) and, indirectly, to *Romeo and Juliet* (179) and *As You Like It* (18). *The Dangerous Summer* refers to *Hamlet* (54).

The narrators of Hemingway's "Prizefight Women" (*Toronto Star*, 15 May 1920) and of *Death in the Afternoon* quote the same line:

"He jests at scars that never felt a wound" (*Romeo and Juliet*, II, ii). Several scholars have traced the influence of Shakespeare in Hemingway, most recently Ernest Lockridge, "*Othello* as Key to Hemingway."

The narrator mentions Shakespeare (73, *h:* 448, s.v. *Maricón*) and quotes him (102).

Shipman, Evan. Full name: Evan Biddle Shipman. American writer and soldier, 1904–57.

As a boy, Shipman occasionally ran away from home and even from Salisbury, one of the exclusive schools to which his well-educated, well-descended parents sent him. In 1923, he was sent for a year to the University of Louvain, Belgium, to improve his French and complete his preparation for Harvard University, the school his father, Louis, had attended but not graduated from. Shipman became proficient in French, but instead of returning home to take the Harvard entrance examination, he went to Paris in 1924. There he met American poets and writers, including Hemingway, who admired his writing and shared his interest in literature, war, drink, and horse racing.

Shipman and War. Shipman was too young to fight in World War I, but he was attracted to the other two major conflicts of his lifetime, the Spanish Civil War and World War II.

In close touch with Hemingway during the Spanish Civil War, he helped him negotiate ambulances through French customs. He then joined a group of volunteers and attempted to enter Spain himself, but the French, signatories to the nonintervention pact, arrested them at the border. After several weeks of imprisonment Shipman was released, made it into Spain, and joined the International Brigades. He was wounded in Brunete, July 1937, and endured a long convalescence complicated by pneumonia.

Shipman also volunteered to fight in World War II, but as a veteran of the International Brigades during the Spanish Civil War he was suspected of being a communist and was prevented from going overseas: he spent most of the war at Fort Knox, Kentucky. His unit arrived in Europe just before the German surrender. His obituary reports that "In World War II he was sergeant major of the Sixteenth

Armored Division's Sixteenth Regiment and was also with the 787th Tank Battalion," but Sean O'Rourke finds that Shipman's pay records show that he was a sergeant and that his letters to Hemingway specify that he was the battalion intelligence sergeant.[654]

Shipman, Horses, and Writing. Both before and after the Spanish Civil War, Shipman was a well-known racing columnist, writing for the *Morning Telegraph* and the *Daily Racing Form.* An informal biography reports that "His reputation grew to the point where he was regarded with considerable reverence at race tracks around the country for his style and erudition."[655] He "frequently traveled with racers, acting as a groom and general handyman when track assignments took him to Europe or across the American continent . . . His tall, angular figure was as familiar at trotting tracks as it was at thoroughbred courses."[656] In 1981, the New York Racing Association honored Shipman by naming a race in honor of "one of the world's greatest authorities on thoroughbred and harness racing and breeding." The Evan Shipman Handicap, run at Belmont Park, New York, is open to New York-bred horses, three years old and up.[657]

Shipman worked on his long, sad poem, *Mazeppa,* for a decade. The autobiographical poem reports his banishment from home and from school and incarceration in a hospital-cum-cemetery where he suffers an opium-nightmare, riding through a "bleak plateau" on a horse "like Pegassus." In *A Moveable Feast,* Shipman mentions to the narrator that his *Mazeppa* is almost finished (*MF,* 136), which suggests that Shipman completed the poem in the 1920s. But Shipman really worked on it until at least 1934, when he wrote to Josephson that at last "I am satisfied it says what I wanted to say." He may have worked on it longer: *Mazeppa* was published in the 1936 edition of the annual anthology of poetry, *American Caravan.*[658]

Shipman's loosely constructed novel, *Free for All,* is a thinly disguised morality tale in which old racehorses, like their broken-down trainers, suffer humiliation but are finally saved when their courage and loyalty are recognized and rewarded.[659] The novel was published in 1935, but Shipman probably discussed it with Hemingway during its composition. He is also the author of "a privately printed biography of John D. Hertz, breeder and owner of a famous racing stable."[660]

Hemingway and Shipman. Hemingway, who admired Shipman's

writing as well as his knowledge of horses, arranged for two of Shipman's poems to be published in the January 1925 issue of the *Transatlantic Review*. He also encouraged his own publisher to publish *Free for All* (New York: Scribner, 1935), of which Hemingway owned two copies.[661]

Hemingway dedicated *Men Without Women* (1927) to Shipman, and considered dedicating *A Farewell to Arms* (1929) to him as well, though he finally decided to pay that compliment to his uncle-in-law and generous patron, Gus Pfeiffer.[662] In his "Introduction" to *Men at War*, Hemingway praised Shipman as "one of my oldest friends, a fine poet and good prose writer . . . [and a] truly brave man."[663] *A Moveable Feast* presents a long, loving portrait of Shipman.

Shipman's reports about horses were reliable, and Hemingway would have been wise to bet on Shipman's tips. *See also* Epinard; Uncas.

Shipman gives the narrator updated information about the fate of Uncas (footnote, page 6).

Sidney. *See* Franklin, Sidney.

Silva, Isidro. A civil guard who attempted to kill the bull Comisario (q.v.) and killed a man instead (111).

Simâo da Veiga. *See* Veiga, Simâo da.

Skull and Bones. Established in the 1830s, Skull and Bones is the oldest and most prestigious of the secret student societies at Yale University. Some of these private undergraduate societies were devoted to a particular interest, like journalism, sport, drama, or music. Other, more exclusive societies were restricted to seniors, and membership was an important indicator of student success. Yale's three leading secret senior societies—Wolf's Head, Scroll and Key, and Skull and Bones—provide their members with valuable connections in the academic, professional, and business worlds. Though somewhat more open today (2000), they still operate on exclusionary principles. In 1991, when Yale seniors invited six women into Skull and Bones, irate "alumni . . . sneaked into the sepulchral clubhouse . . . and changed the locks."[664]

Hemingway, who did not go to college, sometimes mocked college graduates, especially those who, like MacLeish, Fitzgerald, and Stewart, had attended Ivy League schools.[665] The narrator's jibe at the rich tourist who wears a Panama hat, is a member of Skull and Bones, and follows his wife out of the bullring (*DIA*, 34) was aimed at Gerald Murphy, who had consulted Hemingway about wearing a Panama hat in Pamplona (he wore a golf cap instead) and did not like to be reminded of his lack of academic success at Yale or his membership in Skull and Bones.[666] In *To Have and Have Not* (1937), Hemingway also mocks characters for belonging to this exclusive society (239–40). *See also* Murphy, Sara; Porcellian; Yale.

> The narrator disdains "skull and bones-ed" tourists who buy expensive seats for the bullfight but don't understand or appreciate it (34).

Smith, William Benjamin (W. G.). The manuscripts at the Hemingway Collection, in the John F. Kennedy Library, Boston, indicate that the initials *W. G.* were originally inscribed as *W. B.*;[667] they refer to William Benjamin Smith Jr. (Bill, Boid, 1895–1972), the brother of Katherine Foster Smith (Katy, later Mrs. John Dos Passos), whom Hemingway met in 1916. The friends had many nicknames for each other. In his letters, Bill addresses Ernest as Miller, Millersonski, Millee, Hemenway, We-madge, W. E. Madge, Wemedge, Wemage, Hollowbones, Trobe Glotter (i.e., Globe Trotter), Woppian Wonder, Stine and Boid (his own nickname), or Avis. He signs himself Honest Will, H. Will and, occasionally, Garcon [*sic*] or Kellner (French and German for waiter).[668] *See also* Nicknames, in this volume and in *DS*.

Katy and Bill summered with Hemingway in Upper Michigan. Katy and Hadley Richardson had gone to school together, and Hadley met Hemingway when she went to visit Katy at the Chicago home of the oldest Smith sibling, Kenley. Kate was present and "Bill served as best man when Hemingway married Hadley Richardson . . . in 1921."[669]

Hemingway reported in February 1925 that Bill "had a hell of a time . . . the toughest breaks on family, health, jack, and everything else" and was depressed. Reynolds explains that in 1925 Bill Smith wrote Hemingway that "The last three years had been a series of disappointments . . . he had never found his proper profession nor the wife that he needed. His older brother Merrill and his beloved Aunt Charles, who raised him, had both died, and Bill had spent months in a sanitarium for diagnosed tuberculosis."[670] Smith came to Paris that summer, and Hemingway tried but failed to get his friend a job on the staff of *This Quarter*, a journal that had published his own work.[671] Smith went fishing with Don Stewart and Hemingway in Burguete before going on to the Pamplona fiesta of July 1925. He is one of the historical prototypes for Hemingway's character Bill Gorton, who appears in *The Sun Also Rises*; the superinscribed second initial of W. G. may stand for Gorton.

In 1925, when he saw his first bullfight, Smith would have been about thirty years old, and not twenty-seven as Hemingway reports. Smith often wrote to Hemingway about boxers, but not about bullfighters. The only bullfighter he mentions in his letters is Belmonte.

The narrator reports that W. G. did not enjoy the bullfights (*h:* 498).

Smyrna. Today the name of this Turkish city is Izmir; it is on the Gulf of Izmir, an arm of the Aegean Sea.

In August and early September 1922, the city was fought over by the Greeks, who were backed by the British, and the Turks, who were aided by France and Italy and had the tacit support of Russia. The Turks vanquished the Greeks, and on 14 September, they set the city on fire, sparing only the Turkish and Jewish quarters. The British evacuated some Greeks, but the situation of the refugees was desperate.

At the time of these events, Hemingway was still in Paris. Although his description of what happened "On the Quai at Smyrna" is very detailed and vivid, it is not an eye-witness account. It derives from his newspaper reading about Smyrna and from his own journalistic report of later events (see "A Silent, Ghastly Procession" about the Christian refugees at Adrianople, published in *The Toronto Daily Star*, 20 October 1922). In writing "On the Quai at Smyrna," Hemingway filtered his own earlier reading and writing through the voice and diction of a stoic British officer (probably based on Dorman-Smith, q.v.) and added the awful detail of the mules. He used the piece as an introduction to *In Our Time* (1930), although it was written earlier, perhaps in 1924 or 1925.[672]

In *Death in the Afternoon*, the narrator implies that he witnessed the violence done to the mules. The power of this invented detail is reinforced by the Old Lady (q.v.) who, by commenting on its recurrence, indicates that it was vivid enough for her to remember its earlier appearance. What sounds like her criticism of the narrator is actually flattery.

The narrator mentions the evil done to the mules at Smyrna (2, 135).

Snow Bound. Subtitle: *A Winter Idyl.* This long poem, written in 1866 by John Greenleaf Whittier (q.v.), is dedicated "To the Memory of the Household It Describes." The members of the Household are carefully identified in Whittier's "Introduction" as "my father, mother, my brother and two sisters, and my uncle and aunt both unmarried. In addition there was the district schoolmaster who boarded with us." The poem sentimentally extols their frugal lifestyle and simple virtues, but casts a less-approving eye on two strong-minded women, Harriet Livermore and the "strained and fantastic" Lady Hester Lucy Stanhope. Other minor characters appear at the end, when the snow is cleared away and the family greets its neighbors.[673]

Although the poem recalls fireside evenings filled with storytelling and conversation, we hear mainly the narrator's voice as he nostalgically recalls "the winter joys his boyhood knew" in the company of these now-dead characters, who still give him the feeling of "sweetness near." The poem is written in iambic tetrameter, more popular in the nineteenth century than in the twentieth, and its rhymed couplets are as uncomplicated as its characters. As one commentator remarks, "It would be injudicious to rank Whittier among the great poets."[674]

The character of the schoolmaster is (like Whittier himself) an ardent abolitionist, but there are no Civil War scenes, even though the poem was written during that war. Some of the characters witnessed Indian massacres, and the newspaper that they read mentions battles between the Greeks and Turks, but this violence hardly disturbs the "winter idyl" the narrator remembers. In contrast, Hemingway's narrator focuses directly on the horrors of war and dramatizes the situation, letting all the characters speak and act their pain.

In *Green Hills of Africa*, Hemingway dismisses Whittier, along with Hawthorne and Emerson, as "very good men . . . all very respectable" but disembodied and cut off from reality and therefore unable to write great literature (*GHOA*, 20–21). Barbara Lounsberry suggests that Hemingway's title echoes a line from "Snow Bound": "Green hills of life that slope to death" (l. 725). Lounsberry points out that "The speaker of the poem, however, triumphs over the snowstorm by retreating to the hearth and fire of memory which alone can conquer death. . . . It would be ironic if, in this book celebrating memory, Hemingway actually did not remember the source of 'Green hills of life.' . . . However, it may be even more intriguing to imagine that Hemingway clearly recognized the similarity of his vision to Whittier's . . . but, disparaging the poet in general, chose to take the line, disparage the source, and prove instead his statement that 'a new classic does not bear any resemblance to the classics that have preceded it' (21)."[675] I am not aware of any other attempt to identify the source of Hemingway's title for *Green Hills of Africa*.

> The narrator recommends the story "A Natural History of the Dead" (q.v.), with its graphic presentation of war and of the effects of war on men, as the "*Snow Bound* of our time" (133, 144).

Sol y Sombra. Subtitle: *Semanario taurino ilustrado*. Established in 1896 or 1897, this taurine weekly enjoyed two runs: from its founding until 1926 it was published by the Hermanos Carrión, and in the 1940s it had a second, shorter run under Valentín Bejarano. The Biblioteca Nacional, Madrid, has a fairly complete collection of issues, 1897–1926 and 1941–43.

Although published in Madrid, *Sol y sombra* maintained correspondents in practically all Spanish cities with important plazas and reviewed French and Latin American bullfights as well. It offered feature stories on individual fighters, serious essays on a variety of taurine topics, a sober style, and high-quality illustrations. Hemingway saved the double issue, 20 and 27 March 1924, which features a long essay on Nacional II.[676]

> The narrator enjoys reading *Sol y sombra* (h: 475, s.v. *Revistas*).

Soledad, Virgen de la Soledad (solitude, loneliness). The image of the Virgin Mary mourning the death of Christ in the time between the Crucifixion and the Resurrection, is known as the *Virgen de la Soledad*. Unlike the more familiar images of the seated Pietà holding the dead Jesus on her lap, the *Virgen de la Soledad* is presented alone. In Seville's Church of San Lorenzo, for example, a fifteenth-century life-size image called the *Virgen de la Soledad de San Lorenzo*, shows her with tears running down her face, holding the crown of thorns, and clad in black. She is brought out of the church in procession in the three days between the Crucifixion and the Resurrection. On Easter Sunday, her black mourning garb is changed for white. Another image, *Nuestra Señora del Mayor Dolor en su Soledad* (Our Lady of the Greatest Sorrow in her Desolation), is at the Church of San Cayetano, Cofradía de Córdoba.

This image of the mourning Virgin is the subject of the hymn *Stabat Mater Dolorosa*, which has been set to music by Pergolesi, Palestrina, and many other composers.

Bullfighters ask for the protection of a variety of holy images, but I have not been able to confirm Hemingway's claims that this Virgin is "the patron of all bullfighters" or that her image was displayed in the chapel of the Madrid bullring. Bullfighters are notoriously superstitious and studiously avoid references to death; this Virgin seems an unlikely choice. She is more appropriately the patron saint of the bullfighters' relatives.

> The narrator identifies the *Virgen de la Soledad* as the patron of bullfighters (*h:* 418, s.v. *Santo*).

Solórzano, Jesús (Chucho). Full name: Jesús Solórzano Dávalos. Mexican bullfighter, 1908–83. Investiture as *matador de toros*, 1929, in Mexico; investiture in Seville, September 1930; confirmed in Madrid, April 1931. His nickname, Chucho, is a common diminutive for Jesús.

Solórzano came to bullfighting in his late teens, had a generally lackluster career as a *novillero*, and then gave a great performance in 1929, which brought him into the limelight and earned him the promotion to *matador de toros* in Mexico. He came to Spain in 1930 and, as Mexican *alternativas* (q.v.) were not valid there, he performed as *novillero*. He was promoted to *matador de toros* near the end of that season, with time left to add three corridas to the eighteen successful *novilladas* that had preceded the promotion. He was said to have a great future.

In 1931 Solórzano fought twenty-three corridas, but his performances were uneven. Many were splendid, including one tremendous success in Madrid, in June, but on some afternoons he seemed totally uninterested in the bull, the art, or the audience. Because these weaker performances came at the beginning of the season, explains one critic, he was not offered additional contracts for the later months of the season, although his personality and style certainly suggest he has the makings of a first-class *torero*.[677] Most of his twenty corridas of 1932 were undistinguished, and the better ones were marred by nervousness and uncertainty with the sword. After a bad goring in the Mexican winter season, early in 1933, he was able to perform in only five Spanish corridas in 1933. Undisciplined and uncommitted, he lived like a rich playboy while his bullfighting deteriorated. He retired from the Spanish bullring in 1935 but continued to perform sporadically in Mexico until 1949.[678]

Solórzano's younger brother Eduardo (b. 1912) was also a *matador de toros*, but with a Mexican, not a Spanish degree. His son, Jesús Solórzano Pesado (Chuchito, b. 1942), like his father, was capable of occasional great performances but could not sustain the high level required for a first-class reputation.[679]

Hemingway and Solórzano. Hemingway did not visit Spain in 1930, but he probably saw Solórzano in 1931. Because he was finishing *Death in the Afternoon*, Hemingway stayed in Spain for almost the whole season—he was there from May until September—and since Solórzano was such a hot item, he probably made an effort to see him. He undoubtedly read and heard a good bit about him. His assessment echoes the majority opinion of the day.

> The narrator echoes the general critical view that in 1929 and 1930 the Mexican Solórzano was the "most promising" young bullfighter (224). He admires him as "brave, artistic, intelligent" and impressive with the banderillas, cape, and muleta (200, 225), but finds him lacking in spirit (225; *see also* 267).

Soria. Soria has a small plaza, built in the early 1850s, which seats about four thousand spectators.[680] Soria celebrates two annual *ferias*, one in honor of San Juan (24 June), the second in honor of San Saturio (2 October). *See also* Anlló, Juan, who was killed in Soria.

The narrator mentions the "red dust" of Soria (77, 275) and the October *feria* (*h:* 514).

Sotomayor, don Florentino. Spanish bull breeder, d. 1934.

In 1911 and 1912, Florentino Sotomayor established a herd with Miura and Parladé stock. Their first batch of offspring were fought mostly in Córdoba, in bullrings close to Sotomayor's ranch, and were criticized for excessive size and insufficient bravery. To correct these problems, Sotomayor added more Miura blood, producing fierce but uncontrollable bulls that still tended to be too heavy. He then increased the Parladé strain, and his careful, selective breeding finally paid off and Sotomayor bulls reached the Madrid bullring on 23 May 1919. By the mid-1920s his southern bulls were being bought by other prestigious bullrings, some as far away as Barcelona and San Sebastián, and the reviews were consistently glowing.

In 1931, in a complicated deal, Sotomayor acquired a large number of fine animals from the Martín Alonso brothers. Part of the trade agreement involved the transfer of Sotomayor's brand, colors and seniority to the Martín Alonso brothers, who registered the Sotomayor herd in Fermín's name (the other brother, Manuel, had a Veragua herd). Fermín kept his herd for only a few years, selling them in 1935 to the bullfighter Marcial Lalanda (q.v.), who also acquired the herd's seniority. Lalanda registered the property in the name of his wife, Emilia Mejía de Lalanda.

The herd was decimated during the Spanish Civil War (1936–39), but after the war Lalanda invested heavily in it, adding Albaserrada stock to what remained of his original holdings. In 1945, the herd and the rights to its brand, colors, and seniority were acquired by Tomás Prieto de la Cal, who enriched the herd with Veragua (q.v.) stock. This don Tomás died in 1975, and his son is the current owner of the herd which, in Hemingway's day, had been owned by Florentino Sotomayor.

As part of the 1931 transaction that transferred the Sotomayor brand, colors, and *antigüedad* (seniority) to Fermín Martín Alonso, Sotomayor himself acquired the herd that the Martín Alonso family had themselves recently acquired from the Arauz brothers, as well as the Arauz brand, colors (white, pink, and green), and seniority, or *antigüedad* (4 October 1924). When Florentino Sotomayor died in 1934, this herd was inherited by his son, Eduardo Sotomayor Criado. Like many other such properties, it was decimated by the Spanish Civil War, and don Eduardo was left with sixty-three head with which to begin again. In 1955 he sold his herd and retired from bull breeding. In 1960 the herd was sold again, to don Fernando Vázquez de Troya.[681] For a discussion of the complicated relationship between pedigree, ownership, and *antigüedad*, see the essay on "Bulls and Bull Breeding," in the introduction to this volume.

The narrator correctly identifies Sotomayor as an important bull breeder from Córdoba (132).

Spanish-American War. The United States was drawn into Spanish affairs by the 1895 insurrection in Cuba, which interested the American yellow press (they agitated for military intervention). In February 1898 the USS *Maine* was blown up in Havana Harbor, war was formally declared on 24 April 1898, and the Peace Protocol was signed on 12 August. In the peace treaty, signed on 10 December 1898, Spain ceded Cuba, Puerto Rico, Guam, and the Philippines. The American victories in the Caribbean and the Pacific helped establish the United States as a world power and brought the accusation of colonization and empire building.

The years leading up to the Spanish-American War were difficult for Rafael Guerra Bejarano (Guerrita, 1862–1941, q.v.), Spain's leading bullfighter. Frustrated by taurine politics and the extremely hostile Madrid public and press, Guerrita retired in April 1899, after twelve tempestuous years as a *matador de alternativa*.

The narrator places Guerrita in the time frame of the Spanish-American War (240).

Spanish Influenza. A highly infectious respiratory disease that swept through most of the world in 1917 and 1918, causing an estimated twenty to forty million deaths: it was a " 'demographic catastrophe' which killed more people in such a short time than any other disease in the history of the world."[682]

According to Peter Griffin, Hemingway saw a patient die of Spanish influenza in the American Red Cross hospital in Milan, where he fell in love with Agnes von Kurowsky, a Bellevue-trained nurse. In an unpublished story written late in 1918, the first-person narrator's fear of the disease makes him unwilling to kiss the nurse who has given mouth-to-mouth resuscitation to a patient dying of Spanish influenza. Obviously unafraid herself, she goes out to gargle "To please you" and then they kiss, "but we were never as close again as we had been (something was over between us)."[683]

The narrator describes death from Spanish influenza (139).

Spectator. *See* Narratee, in this volume; see also Spectators in *DS*.

Sports. The narrator mentions a variety of sports: baseball (202, 213, 276, *h:* 498; *see also* Altrock, Nick), bicycle racing (*h:* 499), boxing (q.v.), diving (14), fencing (127, 150), fishing (*h:* 499), football (183, 276, *h:* 499), game stalking (233), golf (89, 104, *h:* 499; *see also* Jones, Bobby), horse racing (*see* Horses, Horse Racing), polo (109), shooting (165, 232–33, *h:* 499, 512), skiing (63, *h:* 497), and tennis (*h:* 497). See also Sports in *DS*.

S. T., Mrs. *See* Twysden, Mrs. Stirling.

Stanley, Edward. English clergyman and naturalist, 1779–1849. As a child Stanley was interested in the sea, but his father insisted that his second son make his career in the Church. Stanley became rector of Alderley (1805–37) and bishop of Norwich (1837–49). He wrote several treatises on parochial education, such as *A Series of Questions on the Bible* (1815).

Stanley's avocation, natural history, led him to study the geology, mineralogy, botany, entomology, and ornithology of his parish and to publish scientific essays in various magazines. His popular *A Familiar History of Birds, their Nature, Habits and Instincts* (2 vols., 1835) went through eight editions in thirty years. The "new" 1865 edition, also "published under the direction of the Committee of General Literature and Education Appointed by the Society for Promoting Christian Knowledge," presented the entire work in one volume: the first chapter deals with classification; chapters two to five with the structure, organs, musculature, and plumage of birds; chapters six to thirteen with various groups of land birds; and chapters fourteen to twenty with water fowl. Many of the chapters report the observations of unidentified travelers in foreign lands (frequently African) as well as the folklore and traditions associated with birds. As Stanley emphasizes, "we are not writing a regular book upon the natural history of birds, but confining ourselves chiefly to anecdotes connected with their habits."[684] Unlike the Reverend Gilbert White (q.v.), Stanley was often, though not always, careless about distinguishing between his own and others' observations, and about identifying or evaluating his sources (a traveler, a gentleman, some boys). *A Familiar History of Birds* was Stanley's major scientific work, accomplished while he was rector. His duties as Lord Bishop of Norwich apparently precluded further study of natural history.

Hemingway and Stanley. Hemingway owned *A Familiar History of Birds* and his "direct and lengthy quotation from Bishop Stanley [re Mungo Park, q.v.] makes it likely that he actually had a copy of *A Familiar History of the Birds* beside him during the lengthy period . . . when he was writing *Death in the Afternoon.*"[685] Stanley's "Introduction" begins with the following sentence: "Our object being rather to furnish the reader with rational and interesting facts, than systematic arrangements, it is not intended to treat the subject of Ornithology scientifically" (1). Hemingway lifted some of the first half of that sentence, and most of Stanley's long second paragraph—from the words "When that persevering traveller, Mungo Park" through the phrase "our journey through that wilderness of life" (Stanley, 1–2)—almost verbatim into *Death in the Afternoon* (134): he changed Stanley's "And with the disposition" to "With a disposition" and added a question mark after "wilderness of life."

Stanley finds that "every branch of the creation . . . prov[es] beyond contradiction that 'as the works of the Lord are manifold, so in wisdom hath He made them all' " and that a study of "visible creation . . . may impart not only instruction to the head, but consolation to the heart" ("Introduction," 1)—a position Hemingway thoroughly rejected. *See also* Humanism, Naturalism.

In "A Natural History of the Dead," the narrator names Bishop Stanley's book and then sets out to undermine the cleric's pious claims about "Natural History" (134).

Stein, Gertrude. American writer and art collector, 1874–1946.

After studying philosophy at Harvard University and medicine at Johns Hopkins University, Stein moved to Paris in 1903, living first with her brother Leo and then with her lover Alice B. Toklas (1877–1967). Her early work includes stories (*Three Lives*, 1909), poems (*Tender Buttons*, 1914), *The Making of Americans* (1925), and theoretical and critical essays collected into several volumes: *Composition and Explanation* (1926), *How to Write* (1931), and *Narration* (1935). In the early 1930s, Stein and Toklas set up their own small publishing house, Plain Editions, to publish Stein's increasingly difficult work, such as *Lucy Church Amiably*, *Before the Flowers of Friendship Faded Friendship Faded*, and *Opera and Plays*. The commercially published *Autobiography of Alice B. Toklas* (Harcourt Brace, 1933) enjoyed a wide readership and facilitated further publication.

Hemingway and Stein. Sherwood Anderson gave Hemingway a letter of introduction which enabled him to meet Stein soon after he arrived in Paris. They quickly became good friends. She read and commented on his early prose, and he was instrumental in convincing Ford Madox Ford to publish *The Making of Americans* in the *Transatlantic Review*. Stein even became godmother to Hemingway's first son, John (Bumby).

But the friendship soured. As one of Stein's biographers points out, "Hemingway's impressions of *The Making of Americans* and of Gertrude's writing were to change noticeably during the course of his transcribing and proofreading sessions." And Hemingway was angered by Stein's claim that she and Anderson were responsible for his style and that "they were both a little proud and a little ashamed of the work of their minds . . . They admitted that Hemingway was yellow."[686] In *Green Hills of Africa*, Hemingway retaliates, claiming that he, not she, was the teacher: "She learned how to do it [dialogue] from my stuff" (65–66). He continues the attack by parodying her in *For Whom the Bell Tolls* (289), and has the last word about their troubled relationship in the three chapters he devotes to her in *A Moveable Feast* (1964). *See also* Authors; Homosexuals.

Stein and Toklas had traveled to Spain during World War I and admired José Gómez Ortega (Joselito) and his older brother, Rafael (el Gallo), of whom she wrote: "I forget war and fear and courage and dancing. I forget standing and refusing. I believe choices. I choose Gallo. He is a cock. He moves plainly."[687] Stein's enthusiasm for what she had seen influenced Hemingway to write a short piece, "The first matador got the horns," in March 1923, several months before he ever saw his first bullfight.[688]

Stein admired Joselito and bullfighting before the narrator became acquainted with the taurine arts (1, 2).

Stendhal. Pseudonym of Marie Henri Beyle. French writer, 1783–1842. Under various pseudonyms, Stendhal wrote about Haydn, Mozart, Rossini, Racine, Shakespeare, Napoleon, the history of painting, and other subjects. His first novel, *Armance* (1827), is seldom read; Stendhal is best known for his psychologically insightful novels *The Red and the Black* (1830) and *The Charterhouse of Parma* (1839).

Hemingway and Stendhal. Hemingway admired Stendhal's descriptions of battle so much that he reprinted the second half of chapter two, all of chapters three and four, and the beginning of chapter five of *The Charterhouse of Parma* in *Men at War* (1942). In *A Moveable Feast* he referred to these descriptions of battle as Stendhal's "wonderful Waterloo account" (134). In *Green Hills of Africa*, Hemingway also praised Stendhal's war scenes (71), as well as the seduction episodes of *The Red and the Black* (108). Stendhal's strong "anti-clerical" strain, apparent in both his great novels, dominates the chapters of *The Red and the Black* which are set at the seminary.

Hemingway's admiration for Stendhal led to his unfortunate pugilistic metaphor (*see* Boxing).

The narrator admires Stendhal for, among other things, being a "good anti-clerical" (204).

Stewart, R. Hemingway's manuscript originally read D. S.[689] Full name: Donald Ogden Stewart. American author and screenwriter, 1894–1980.

Stewart was educated at Yale (Class of 1916). His books include *Parody Outline of History* (1921), *Perfect Behavior* (1922), *Aunt Polly's Story of Mankind* (1923), *Mr. and Mrs. Haddock Abroad* (1924), its sequel *Mr. and Mrs. Haddock in Paris France* (1926), *Father William: A Comedy of Father and Son* (1929), and *By a Stroke of Luck:*

An Autobiography (1975). He also wrote screenplays for several successful movies: *The Philadelphia Story* (for which he won an Oscar in 1940), *Keeper of the Flame*, *The Barretts of Wimpole Street*, *Dinner at Eight*, and *Kitty Foyle*. "In Hollywood Mr. Stewart was an articulate spokesman for labor and liberal causes, especially civil liberties, and he became involved in virtually every issue, to the point that it was said that when President Franklin D. Roosevelt got up in the morning, he ordered orange juice, coffee and his first 10 telegrams of protest from Donald Stewart."[690] During the McCarthy period, Stewart was blackballed in Hollywood. He spent the last three decades of his life in England.

Hemingway and Stewart. Stewart accompanied Hemingway and Hadley to Pamplona in July 1924 and 1925. On the first trip he was enticed into the bullring after the morning *encierro*; the experience cost him two cracked ribs. Even so, he enjoyed that first trip more than the second, which was marred by sexual jealousies and temperamental outbursts. He did not join the tense Hemingways, whose marriage was dissolving, for the fiesta of 1926; it was Pauline Pfeiffer and the Murphys (qq.v.) who came to Pamplona that year.

Stewart married Beatrice Ames in July 1926; the newlyweds visited Hemingway, by now separated from Hadley, in August 1926. Hemingway had read and liked Stewart's books and described him as "a swell guy" and his future wife as "awfully nice and good looking."[691] But in August 1926, Hemingway turned away from Stewart, whose brand-new marriage emphasized his own marital failure.

Stewart's Ivy League education, membership in Skull and Bones (q.v.), impressive publication record (five successful books in six years), and financial success fueled Hemingway's jealousy. Stewart writes that the friendship ended when he expressed disapproval of Hemingway's 1926 poem "To a Tragic Poetess," an anti-Semitic attack on Dorothy Parker.

In 1929, although already a successful author himself, Hemingway was "bilious" when he heard that Don Stewart had signed a $25,000 contract.[692] *See also* Authors.

The narrator reports that R. S. stopped going to the bullfights after he married and became money-conscious (*h:* 498–99).

S. T., Mrs. *See* Twysden, Mrs. Stirling.

Stockyards. The terrible fire at Warehouse Number 7 of the Nelson Morris and Company's Plant at the Chicago Union Stock Yards began at about 4:00 A.M. on 22 December 1910 and was not extinguished until 6:30 A.M. of the next day. More than fifty fire engines fought the blaze, which killed twenty-one firemen and caused tremendous property loss.[693] Hemingway was then eleven years old and living in Oak Park: even though the fire was about four miles from Oak Park, the sky glow from the enormous fire would have been clearly visible all through the long winter night. In 1910, Chicago was burning more than ten thousand tons of soft coal a day. The city's skies were full of particulate matter to capture and reflect light, creating ideal conditions for sky glow. Oak Park's skies were relatively clear, making it easier to see the faraway glow.[694]

The narrator recalls the glow of the fire at the Chicago stockyards (48–49).

Stretcher-Bearers. Characters in the story "A Natural History of the Dead" (q.v.).

The stretcher-bearers' task is to transport the wounded into the dressing station and the dead into a nearby cave; they are disturbed to discover that one of the men in the cave is still alive. Their request to move him out precipitates the argument between the lieutenant and the doctor. The ensuing violence could have been avoided if the doctor had allowed the stretcher-bearers to speak when they first tried to announce that the man had died (141, 143–44). Stretcher-bearers speak: 141, 143–44.

Suárez, Luis (Magritas). Spanish bullfighter, 1889–1957. Magritas was an excellent banderillero and performed elegantly with the cape, but his attempts to become a *matador de novillos*, first in 1913 and again in 1922 and 1923, were foiled by his incompetence with the sword. As a banderillero, however, he was superb, and the list of matadors whom he served reads like a taurine who's who: Vicente Pastor (1913–14), Rafael Gómez Ortega (1915), José Gómez Ortega (1916), Juan Belmonte (1917–19), Manuel Jiménez (1920–23), Diego Mazquiarán, Martín Agüero, Antonio Márquez, Joaquín Rodríguez, Alfredo Corrochano, and Domingo Ortega (qq.v.). Since

Belmonte's weak legs prevented him from placing the banderillas himself, his star banderilleros, Maera and Magritas, performed often in the many corridas where Joselito and Belmonte acted together. Clearly these banderilleros had reached a high degree of proficiency, to hold their own against Joselito.

Magritas was so admired that, like the more popular *matadores de toros*, he had a fan club, Club Magritas, which occasionally organized bullfighting festivals in his honor. During his long career he suffered three major gorings.[695]

Hemingway and Magritas. Hemingway probably saw Magritas perform in the years he visited Spain, 1923–31.

> The narrator accurately describes Magritas as one of the best banderilleros working in Spain in the 1920s and early 1930s (203). Although good matadors are over-paid, even the best of banderilleros are denied a share of the wealth (201).

The Sun Also Rises. Novel by Ernest Hemingway, set in France and Spain during the mid-1920s; published in 1926. The novel's bullfighter, Pedro Romero, is based on Cayetano Ordóñez (q.v.). The two performances the narrator claims to have seen are probably the Madrid confirmation of Cayetano Ordóñez's *alternativa*, 16 July 1925 (a resounding success; the other bullfighters were Luis Freg, Villalta, and Manuel Báez [Litri], qq.v.) and the Valencia corrida of 29 July 1925, in which Ordóñez and Belmonte (q.v.) shared the bill. Hemingway also saw them in Pamplona on 11 July 1925. *See also* Romero, Pedro, in this volume; and *The Sun Also Rises* in *DS*.

> The narrator refers to *The Sun Also Rises* without naming it. He merely remarks that he had "tried to describe" two performances of Cayetano Ordóñez, one in Madrid and one in Valencia, in which Belmonte also fought (89).

– T –

Talavera de la Reina. José Gómez Ortega (Joselito) was fatally gored at Talavera de la Reina on 16 May 1920. For details about this event, *see* Gómez Ortega, José; and Ortega, widow of, in this volume; see also Talavera de la Reina in *DS*.

The narrator mentions the death of Joselito in Talavera de la Reina (39, 242–43) and the annual bullfights held in the town (*h:* 509, 513).

Tamarit, Francisco (Chaves). Spanish bullfighter, 1897–1964. Investiture as *matador de toros*, 26 September 1925, in Valencia, with Marcial Lalanda officiating and Cayetano Ordóñez acting as witness; confirmed in Madrid, May 1927.

Tamarit entered bullfighting when he was already in his twenties. Like younger aspirants, he worked in and around home—he was Valencian—until he had sufficient reputation to attract contracts from other bullrings in Spain. By 1924 his obvious talent took him to several first-rank plazas, but the increased exposure brought the criticism that too many of his performances were weak, both in terms of technique and of commitment: and such uneven performers are always suspect. He seems to have heeded the criticism, and the mixed reviews of his fifteen *novilladas* of 1924 gave way to more widespread praise for the thirty-seven *novilladas* of 1925, which justified his promotion near the end of that season. He was as impressive on the afternoon of his *alternativa* (q.v.) as he was on the five additional corridas with which he closed the season. He signed many contracts for the next season.

On the voyage to South America for the 1925–26 winter season, Chaves got so sick that he was unable to fight until the end of December. At that corrida he was still so weak that he had to leave the ring without killing his bull. On 1 January, while training, he was gored. Back in Spain, his bad luck continued: another bout of illness in May caused him to lose many corridas, and then a catastrophic goring on 29 July (he almost lost his arm) ended his season after only sixteen corridas.[696] These mishaps noticeably diminished his strength and spirit and, consequently, his appeal. He performed in only eight or nine corridas in 1927 (reports vary), five in 1928 and again in 1929 (four of these were in his native Valencia), one in 1930, and two in 1931 (both in Valencia). He did, however, have several successful South American tours in the early 1930s.

Tamarit eventually took out Mexican citizenship, renounced his *alternativa*, and performed as banderillero for Jesús Solórzano (q.v.), in Mexico. After his retirement he opened a small business in Mexico, where he died in 1964.

Hemingway and Tamarit. Hemingway claims to have seen Chaves five times (45), probably at the Valencia fiestas in late July, where Chaves performed in 1926 and 1927 and which Hemingway attended. In 1929, Hemingway again attended the Valencia fiesta but Tamarit had not been invited to perform then. He did fight in Valencia on 17 and 26 May and on 3 and 4 August 1929, but Hemingway was elsewhere in May and left Valencia on 3 August; it is not likely that he saw Tamarit in 1929. In 1930 Hemingway did not come to Spain, and in 1931 Tamarit performed his only two corridas in Valencia, on 26 July and 2 August; Hemingway may have seen the first of these.[697] I have been unable to confirm Hemingway's remarks about Tamarit's physique or about the toilet that Valencia reportedly named after him.

> The narrator correctly identifies Tamarit as a cowardly bullfighter much admired for a time in his native Valencia [which had just lost its hero Granero and was hoping Chaves would take his place] and adds some colorful details about his stomach, buttocks, and reputation (45–46).

Taurine Dynasties. Not infrequently, several members of the same family become bullfighters or bull breeders. Hemingway mentions several such bullfighting families or dynasties: *see* Anlló (Nacional), Agüero, Espinosa (Armillita), Freg, García (Algabeño), Gómez (Gallo), González (Dominguín), Haba (Zurito), Jiménez (Chicuelo), Mejías (Bienvenida), Ordóñez, Ortega, Roger (Valencia).

In his fiction, Hemingway sometimes conflated generations of bullfighters. This intensification occurs when the two Algabeños, father and son, were joined in the creation of the fictional Algabeño of *The Sun Also Rises*, though Hemingway distinguished between them in *Death in the Afternoon*. He also conflated Pedro Romero and Cayetano Ordóñez (qq.v.), both from Ronda (q.v.), when he named his bullfighter in *The Sun Also Rises* after the former but modeled him on the latter.

> The narrator often discusses members of the same taurine family, recognizing biological connection (*h:* 478, s.v. *Sangre torera*). Some taurine dynasties appear both in *Death in the Afternoon* and in *The Dangerous Summer* (e.g., Bienvenida, Dominguín, Ordóñez).

Le Temps. French newspaper, established in the nineteenth century.

A sober paper, *Le Temps* supported socialist causes and became increasingly influential during the 1930s as the French left wing gained in popularity. In 1936, when the French Socialists came to power under the leadership of Leon Blum, it became the nation's official newspaper.

Both in his 1931 correspondence and in *Death in the Afternoon*, which he was finishing at that time, Hemingway compares the Spanish Republican newspaper *La Libertad* to *Le Temps*. In June 1931 he wrote John Dos Passos about the political upheaval that ushered in Spain's Second Republic, commenting that the certainty of victory causes Republicans to "shift from left to right faster even than in France" and that newspapers follow suit: "La Libertad is now Le Temps."[698] In *For Whom the Bell Tolls* (1940), Hemingway's character Agustín also talks about the general shift, among the Republican factions, from the left to the right (*FWTBT* 285).

Le Temps in the 1930s and 1940s. This movement towards the right became very pronounced in *Le Temps* in the years following the publication of *Death in the Afternoon*. In 1938, still a pro-government paper, *Le Temps* supported the Munich Pact, to which France was signatory. Several of *Le Temps*'s leading figures resigned in protest, including Hubert Beuve-Méry, who founded *Le Monde* after World War II. *Le Temps* continued to publish until 1942, when Nazi troops occupied southern France (Vichy government). After the war, the liberation forces did not allow the newspaper to resume operation, and its presses became the property of *Le Monde*.

The narrator finds that *La Libertad* increasingly resembles *Le Temps* (278).

Tiebas, Cándido (Obispo). Spanish bullfighter, d. 1930. Tiebas occasionally used the "poco reverente apodo" (irreverent nickname) of Obispo (bishop) in his years as *novillero*, though taurine critics consistently used his family name, not his nickname. It is an unusual nickname for a young man from Tafalla, as Navarre was (and is) very conservative and attached to the Church.

Tiebas began his career in small, local bullrings, developing a local reputation as a brave and skillful swordsman. By 1924 he was appearing in the more important *novilladas*, and in 1925 he sprang to national prominence with a fine performance, which led to his Madrid debut as *novillero* 19 July 1925. That year he performed in twenty-two *novilladas*, several in first-rank plazas like Madrid, Valencia, and Barcelona, and was ranked tenth among *novilleros*. 1925 was undoubtedly his best year.

Sick for most of 1926, Tiebas performed in only nine *novilladas*, mostly close to home. His next two seasons were worse (three *novilladas* in 1927, two in 1928) and, realizing that his star had faded, he resigned his rank as *novillero* in 1928 and became a banderillero for Saturio Torón (q.v.), a fellow Navarrese who was on his way up. On 9 March 1930 Tiebas died suddenly of a heart attack, while standing in the *callejón*. Saturio Torón and Ruiz Toledo were gored, quite seriously, in that same *novillada* in Valencia.[699]

Hemingway and Tiebas. With his strong interest in Navarre, it is not unlikely that Hemingway went to see Tiebas in a *novillada*. He would have been most likely to see him in 1925, when Tiebas performed most often and Hemingway paid a long visit to Spain. Hemingway's wording and punctuation differentiate between "a bishop" and the bullfighter, but the juxtaposition suggests that Hemingway knew that Tiebas's nickname was Obispo. Like bullfighters, ecclesiastical dignitaries were and are prominent figures in Navarre.

The narrator includes Tiebas in the catalogue of items he wishes he could describe vividly enough to enable the reader to experience Navarre (275).

Todó, Isidoro (Alcalareño II). Full name: Isidoro Todó de la Paz. Spanish bullfighter, 1893–1931. As his nickname indicates, Todó was from Alcalá de Henares, Madrid.

Todó started life as a baker, but turned to bullfighting in his late teens or early twenties. His first goring, endured in 1914, did not deter him, and he embarked upon a second-rate career, never attaining the rank of full *matador de toros*.

Todó made his Madrid debut as a *novillero* on 19 July 1923, one of his better years. On this important occasion, with the Madrid public and the critics watching, Todó was unimpressive with his first *novillo* and injured by his second. He did not improve with time, and in spite of a few triumphs in 1923 and 1924, by 1925 he was again one of the many unnoticed, unadmired *novilleros*, competent enough to find occasional employment in second- and third-rank plazas, but unable to achieve promotion to *matador de toros*.

The numbers tell the discouraging, familiar story: six *novilladas* in 1925, eleven in 1926, five or twelve in 1927 (accounts differ), five in 1928. The next year saw a sudden upsurge, to sixteen *novilladas*, including one in Madrid; in 1930 he had twelve *novilladas* and again appeared in Madrid. Just as things were brightening for him, Todó was mortally wounded in Madrid, on 23 August 1931, by a black *novillo* named Cartelero which gored him just as he prepared to kill him. Todó died within forty-five minutes.[700]

A detailed report of Todó's last afternoon does not mention his lack of height, to which Hemingway attributes the fatal goring. *El Clarín* writes that the bull, which had defective vision, was made even more dangerous by an *espontáneo* (a member of the audience who leaps into the ring and attempts a few passes; see Espontáneo in *DS*). The audience's wild cheers not only encouraged the intruder to resist all efforts to remove him but also inspired two more aficionados to follow him into the ring. The prolonged melee in the overpopulated bullring—three *cuadrillas* and several police officers attempted to remove one *espontáneo* after another—further disconcerted both the *novillo* and the man who had to fight him.

Todó had a difficult time throughout the *faena*, with a couple of close calls and a premature attempt to kill. The animal's head was still high, the bullfighter neglected to lower his muleta, and the goring was inevitable and fatal. Cartelero was killed by Finito de Valladolid while Todó was being rushed to the clinic, where the gaping chest wound rendered the doctors helpless. Todó's brother, brother-in-law, and three nephews witnessed the disaster and were allowed into the clinic to bid him farewell. Hemingway's remarks that Todó "was breathing through his chest . . . the wound too big to do anything with" though he was still "able to talk in the infirmary" before he died "within an hour" all agree with the newspaper report.[701]

In discussing Todó's finances and family, Hemingway echoes contemporary obituaries. *El eco taurino* defines Todó's household as composed of his wife, his sister, and "unos niños" (some children);[702] he was hard put to support them all.

Hemingway correctly identifies Todó's fellow performers as Alfonso Gómez (Finito de Valladolid) and Miguel Casielles (qq.v.). The *novillos* were from the Conradi ranch. The date was 23 August 1931; Todó was three months short of his thirty-eighth birthday; for once, Hemingway reports the age correctly. Hemingway was in Madrid at the time, and his wife Pauline and son John (Bumby) were probably with him. It is very likely that he and Sidney Franklin (q.v.) saw the bullfight together and that Franklin stayed on at the bullring to hear medical reports and discuss the event with his friends.

Hemingway, Height, and Todó. Cossío describes Todó as "el pequeño diestro" (the small or short bullfighter) and Tomás Orts Ramos (Uno al Sesgo) considers that "su pequeña estatura . . . constituía una seria dificultad" (his lack of height . . . was a serious obstacle). *La fiesta brava*, summarizing the unusually bloody 1931 Madrid season, notes that Todó, forced by financial need to fight, was gored "debido a su poco estatura" (due to his lack of height).[703] But the issue of height is controversial. The well-informed aficionado Kenneth Tynan notes that "many of the best modern toreros have been well below average height," including Belmonte and Chicuelo (qq.v.): "That their lack of inches might be a disqualification seems never to have crossed their minds"; *see also* González, Rafael (Machaquito), who was similarly unhampered by being short. Antonio Ordóñez (see in *DS*), a veteran of forty years of bullfighting, remarks that lack or excess of height may pose "un problema de estética" (an aesthetic problem), but he does not believe that being short necessarily hampers performance; it may even offer an advantage, as shorter men are often better coordinated and more agile.[704]

Hemingway's attitude to height is inconsistent. He treats Villalta's height as a problem, for example, but doesn't mention that Manuel García (Maera, q.v.) was tall. At one point he generalizes that lack of height is always a serious problem (253), and finds it endangers Julio García (224) and, of course, Todó. But sometimes lack of height is irrelevant to him: he doesn't mention, for example, Juan Martín-Caro (Chiquito de la Audiencia) or Alfredo Corrochano (qq.v.) were short. Sometimes he describes a bullfighter as short but does not factor that element into his performance. Occasionally, as in the cases of Barrera (referred to as the Valencian, 429) and Chicuelo (74), being short seems a moral or psychological defect, not just a detail of physique.

Other short bullfighters were gored for reasons unrelated to their lack of height: Gitanillo de Ricla was "unskillful at everything" and was consequently "gored badly nearly every season" (76). And in contrast to Todó, whose shortness "made it impossible for him to succeed as a matador" (227), Varé (q.v.) was "of only moderate height" but still managed to be "a consistently great killer." And Varé died of "almost the same wound" as Sidney Franklin, who was tall (253). Hemingway's inconsistencies and contradictions on this point of height are very interesting. Himself a tall man, and used to Americans who are generally taller than Spaniards, Hemingway may have associated lack of height with inferiority.

Hemingway's best treatment of the short bullfighter appears in *For Whom the Bell Tolls*. Pablo remarks that Finito de Palencia "was a good matador" but that "He was handicapped by his short stature" (184), and Pilar agrees that when Finito went in for the kill, "It was difficult for him to get out from over the horn because of his short stature" (188). But she does not think that lack of height is necessarily disastrous, and she scornfully rejects Primitivo's simple solution, that "If he was so short he should not have tried to be a matador" (188; *see also* 189). Finito de Palencia's career is ended by tuberculosis, not by a goring. The most likely historical prototype for Finito de Palencia was Alfonso Gómez (Finito de Valladolid, q.v.), who was tall.

Language and the Torero Corto. In taurine jargon a *torero corto* is one who is short of repertoire or faculties; the antonym, *torero largo*, refers to one who controls an extensive repertoire, who has mastered many techniques. In other contexts, *corto* and *largo* can mean short or long: a short trip is *un viaje corto* and and a long skirt is *una falda larga*. But in terms of height, a short person is *bajo* or *baja*, not *corto* or *corta*; and a tall one is *alto* or *alta*, not *largo* or *larga*. In the Glossary, Hemingway sometimes seems aware of this difference and sometimes not. His entry for *Corto* correctly explains that a *torero corto* is a "matador with a limited repertoire," but his entry for *Torerito* evades the distinction between height and skill by using the word *small*: "Torerito: a small bullfighter" (*h:* 487).[705] *Torerito*, spoken with a dismissive sneer, is a pejorative word, but it can also connote affection or admiration, as in *buen torerito*.

In the incident involving Todó, the narrator, and the narrator's son, Hemingway may be working with both meanings of the word *corto* (deficient, short) but misapplying it when referring to height, when the proper adjective would be *bajo*. The mistake may be due either to Hemingway's own imperfect Spanish at this stage of his life, or to his attempt to render his son's deficiencies in the language. For another instance of a child's fears being caused by imprecise translation, see Hemingway's short story "A Day's Wait" (1933).

The narrator considers Todó's lack of height an insuperable obstacle. He claims to have witnessed the fatal goring (227–28, 239).

Toklas, Alice. Full name: Alice Babette Toklas. American expatriate author, 1877–1967; companion to Gertrude Stein (q.v.), 1907 until Stein's death in 1946.

Toklas wrote *The Alice B. Toklas Cookbook* (1954), notorious for its hashish fudge; *Aromas and Flavors of Past and Present*, edited with Poppy Cannon (1958); *What Is Remembered* (1963); and *Staying on Alone* (1973), about her life after Stein's death. Toklas figures largely in all the biographies of Gertrude Stein and is herself the subject of Linda Simon's *The Biography of Alice B. Toklas* (1977; rpt. Lincoln: University of Nebraska Press, 1991). Both Toklas and Stein are attacked in *A Moveable Feast. See also* Authors; Homosexuals.

Toklas and Stein's admiration for the bullfights they saw during and after World War I convinced Hemingway to visit Spain himself, in May-June 1923: he went with the express purpose of learning about the bullfight.

Toklas attended bullfights with Gertrude Stein (1, 2).

Torerías. Originally subtitled *Semanario taurino bolcheviki* (Bolshevik taurine weekly), established in 1920, in Madrid. In 1933 the subtitle was changed to *Revista taurina de gran información* (Taurine journal [offering] full information) and in November 1954 the title itself was changed to *Toreros-Torerías*, though the 1933 subtitle was kept unaltered. The Biblioteca Nacional, Madrid, has the 1927–31 run.

Torerías adopts a slangy, jocose tone, full of "witticisms," exclamation marks, terrible poetry, rumors, and conjectures that often take up more room than the announcements, reviews, and other taurine news items. Its eight pages also offer photographs and cartoons, all for the 1930 price of ten *céntimos*.[706]

The narrator describes *Torerías* as a "scurrilous" but "always interesting" bullfight magazine (*h:* 475, s.v. *Revistas*).

Toreros y toros. Two journals with this name were published in Madrid, one established in 1916 and one in 1919. Another magazine of the same name appeared in Seville in 1919. All these seem to have been short-lived. By the time Hemingway became interested in the bullfight, there was only one journal called *Toreros y toros*. It had begun publication in Madrid in 1918 and was edited by Don Manué. By 1931, Hemingway's last taurine season before the publication of *Death in the Afternoon*, it was in its thirteenth year of uninterrupted publication.[707]

Toros y toreros. Similarly named journals, *Toros y toreros*, began publication in Madrid in 1915 or in 1917, and in Béziers, France, in 1924. The authoritative annual volumes, *Toros y toreros en . . .*, subtitled *Resumen crítico-estadístico de la temporada taurina* (Critical-statistical summary of the taurine season), covered all the years during which Hemingway visited Spain, except for 1923. Although Hemingway does not mention this annual in *Death in the Afternoon*, he owned the volumes for 1925, 1926, 1927, 1929, 1930, and 1934; they are invaluable references for anyone interested in the bullfight.[708]

Another authoritative annual was published by Enrique Minguet y Calderón de la Barca (Pensamientos). Hemingway owned Minguet's *Desde la grada: Anuario taurino* for the years 1913, 1918, 1925, 1928, 1957, and 1959.[709] Since Cossío's taurine encyclopedia had not yet been published at the time Hemingway wrote *Death in the Afternoon*, these annual publications offered the most complete and accurate record of taurine events for the years preceding the publication of *Death in the Afternoon*. There is no doubt that Hemingway consulted them. He does not always acknowledge his sources.

> The narrator describes *Toreros y toros* as an "interesting" bullfight magazine (*h:* 475, s.v. *Revistas*).

Le Toril. Subtitle: *Revue Tauromachique Indépendante Illustrée.* French bullfighting newspaper, established March 1922, in Toulouse, and edited by Aguilita. It was a four-page weekly during the long bullfighting season (spring through fall) and a monthly during the winter. A few articles are in Spanish or contain untranslated quotes from Spanish papers; most essays are in French, even when signed by taurine critics with Spanish pen names like Aguilita, Amarguras, and don Cándido. The articles cover Spanish, French, Portuguese, and Central and South American taurine events. A large drawing of a bull adorns the title of the newspaper; smaller illustrations accompany the headings of some of the articles. Hemingway subscribed to this taurine paper in 1925, 1926, and 1927 and saved about twenty issues from these years.[710] In *The Sun Also Rises*, Hemingway's character Jake Barnes reads this publication from cover to cover (*SAR*, 30).

> Although the narrator disagrees with *Le Toril*'s evaluation of Manuel Martínez, he admires its impartiality, maintained in spite of financial difficulties (260, *h:* 475, s.v. *Revistas*).

Torilero. The person who opens the *toril* door to admit the bull into the bullring. *See* Gabriel.

Toro de Lidia. The first bullfighting journal with this title was founded in Madrid, 1928, and is clearly not the journal Hemingway means. In a survey of current taurine periodicals, *Toros y toreros en 1924* identified *El toreo* as the oldest (est. 1874), followed by *El chiquero* (est. 1886). In its annual bibliography, *Toros y toreros en 1931* does not mention a periodical titled *Toro de lidia*, but does mention *La lidia* (q.v.).[711]

> The narrator describes a periodical named *Lidia* or *Toro de Lidia* as "the most famous and oldest" taurine weekly (*h:* 445, s.v. *Lidia*).

Torón, Saturio. Full name: Saturio Torón Goyanes. Spanish bullfighter, c. 1898–1937. Investiture as *matador de toros*, in Pamplona, July 1930; confirmed in Madrid, April 1931; renounced in 1933.

A very strong young man, Torón started out as a boxer, but he was soon drawn to bullfighting. After several years as banderillero, he attempted in 1926 to become a *novillero*; the failure returned him to the ranks of the banderilleros for another few years. He tried his luck as a *novillero* again, intermittently in 1928 and with more focus and success in 1929: he made his Madrid debut on 25 August and was contracted for ten *novilladas*, most of them in important plazas, for the next year. Torón was promoted to *matador de toros* by Marcial Lalanda on 8 July 1930, thus becoming "el primer espada navarro que se ha doctorado en Pamplona durante sus famosas fiestas de San Fermín" (the first Navarrese matador to be promoted to the final rank in Pamplona during its famous fiestas). During the ceremony he was injured by his second bull and had to cancel his next two corridas, both in Pamplona.[712] He was injured again in Cádiz, on 13 July, and in Ceuta, on 10 August.[713]

Torón had more courage than skill, and the several injuries he suffered in 1930, his best season, kept the number of his corridas down to six (in addition to the several *novilladas* which preceded the promotion).[714] He was similarly unable to avoid the bull's horns during the seasons of 1931 and 1932: he was well enough to appear in only eleven and nine corridas, respectively, and his audiences began to lose interest because he did not develop or improve. In 1933 he fought only two times, resigned his *alternativa* (rank as *matador de toros*), worked for a while as *novillero*, resigned that rank as well, and returned to his earlier profession, that of banderillero. He retired in 1935 and was killed in the Spanish Civil War; he was a Republican.

Cossío remarks that "Saturio Torón fué un ejemplo aleccionador de que sólo el valor no basta para alcanzar categoría de torero" (bravery alone does not make a bullfighter).[715] Like his fellow Navarrese Cándido Tiebas (who worked for him as banderillero), Torón enjoyed only a brief period in the limelight. *Torerías*, which called him "el león navarro" (the Navarrese lion), touted him in 1929 and 1930, but more sober publications realized that without technique and repertoire, he would not last long.

Hemingway and Torón. Hemingway didn't go to Spain for the 1930 season and thus missed Torón's Pamplona *alternativa*. But he correctly reports that Marcial Lalanda officiated at the event, although he neglects to add that Lalanda had to kill one of Torón's bulls, and he errs slightly when he says Torón was injured in his first three performances as *matador de toros*: he was actually injured on his first, second, and fourth fights (8 July, 13 July, and 10 August 1930, see above). The third fight, on 3 August, took place without untoward incident (in Estella, Navarre). Hemingway saw Torón in Pamplona the next year, when he performed on 7 and 9 July 1931. He may have seen him one or two other times as well.

The narrator claims he saw this brave new matador from Navarre in 1931. Although a fine banderillero, he lacked the skills necessary for survival. The narrator inaccurately reports that Torón was "severely gored in his first three fights" and concludes correctly that "his case looked hopeless" (223–24, 275; see also *h:* 495–96).

Toros célebres. An alphabetical listing of more than fifteen hundred famous bulls, compiled by José Carralero and Gonzalo Borge (cited in this volume as Carralero and Borge). As Hemingway indicates, the small book has 322 pages. Cossío also offers an "Indice de toros célebres," published in 1943 and updated in 1995.[716] There are many such listings in the taurine literature.

The narrator writes about several of the bulls described in *Toros célebres* (110–12).

Torres, Enrique. Full name: Enrique Torres Herrero (el Niño del Seguridad). Spanish bullfighter, 1908–80. Investiture as *matador de toros*, October 1927, in Valencia; confirmed in Madrid, May 1928; renounced in 1935; retaken in 1936. His nickname, the boy or kid of the security [guard], derives from his father's job in the Seguridad.

Born in Valencia, Enrique Torres was apprenticed to a jeweler but showed such aptitude for bullfighting that his father transferred the family to Seville so that the boy, then fourteen, could receive better training. By 1925 he was well-known in the south of Spain, and with twenty or so *novilladas*, he was ranked nineteenth nationwide. In 1926 he was ranked third among *novilleros* and hailed as the new star of the bullfight (thirty-four *novilladas*, several more being canceled because of two injuries). In 1927 he fought thirty *novilladas* before being promoted to *matador de toros* near the end of the season. Valencia saw two of its young men, Torres and Vicente Barrera (q.v.), both born in 1908, promoted to *matadores de toros* within weeks of each other: they were only nineteen years old. Félix Rodríguez, who was not born in Valencia but who grew up there, was also promoted that year: a fine crop of new fighters to comfort Valencia for its loss of Manuel Granero, killed in 1922.[717]

The next year, 1928, was Torres's first full season as *matador de toros*, and he was ranked among the nation's top ten, with forty-two corridas, the same number as Marcial Lalanda (q.v.). In 1929 he fought thirty-five corridas. These four seasons, his last two as a *novillero* and his first two as a *matador de toros* (1926–29), were his best, though in 1929 his performance was slipping (but see below). Torres appeared in only twenty-two corridas in 1930, with few good reviews. He managed a comeback in 1931 (twenty-eight corridas), but the decline both in number and quality of his appearances continued: fifteen corridas in 1932, fourteen in 1933, and ten in 1934. He was not contracted by the Madrid ring in any of these years. In 1935, a goring forced him to cancel some contracts so that altogether he performed in only eight corridas. At the end of that season he renounced his *alternativa* (q.v.), fighting as *novillero* at the beginning of the next season. He retook the rank of *matador de toros* early in the Spanish Civil War, after which he seems not have fought again in Spain, though he continued to perform in South America. A serious goring, in Caracas, 1949, injured his liver, and he retired, after a quarter century of bullfighting. He died in Mexico City.

At the peak of his career, Torres was praised for his elegance and courage, was extravagantly feted in his native Valencia, and was in demand throughout Spain. But his personality seems to have crumbled under the pressures of this demanding profession. His expertise with the cape, always his strong point, intoxicated the public, but in other areas of the fight he deteriorated instead of improving as the years passed. Even his cape work, insufficient by itself to maintain a reputation, became lusterless. Bagüés, like Hemingway, remarks that "con la muleta hizo pocos progresos" (he achieved very little with the muleta) and mourns that his promising career turned out to be "Un desastre" (a disaster).[718]

In their reporting of Enrique Torres, *Toros y toreros en . . .* make their usual thoughtful, perceptive, and accurate evaluation, all the more impressive in that they review all the season's bullfighters, more than a hundred figures. In 1926, the annual recognizes and cordially welcomes a great new talent. Two years later, it praises the year's work—"una bonita campaña" (a handsome campaign)—and offers a warning so perceptive that I quote at length: "Acaso este torero haya dado de sí cuanto podía dar y no pase de lo que es. . . . Sería un lástima, porque los mismos públicos que hoy le agasajan no tardarían en cansarse y en volverle la espalda. Tal vez sería conveniente que el buen torerito valenciano reflexionase sobre esto" (It may

be that this bullfighter has given his all and has no more to give . . .
That would be a pity, because the same public that lauds him today
will soon tire of him and abandon him. Perhaps this brave new Valencian bullfighter will heed this warning).

Hemingway and Torres. Hemingway saw Torres in his hometown
of Valencia, a city that features its own sons in the local fiestas and
treats them with great indulgence. Torres performed there every year,
and Hemingway came for several of those seasons.

Absent from Spain in 1928 and 1930, Hemingway most probably
saw Torres when he performed in Valencia as *matador de toros* on
25, 29, and 30 July 1929; and on 28, 29, and 30 July 1931. In 1929,
the reviews were not always good, and in 1931, they were somewhat
better.[719] He may have seen him in *novilladas* as well.

> The narrator accurately describes Enrique Torres as a matador from Valen-
> cia (267) who occasionally achieves greatness with the cape (14, 222) but
> is deficient with the muleta (222; photograph, *h:* 296–97; see also *h:* 455,
> s.v. *Niño*).

Torres Reina, Ricardo (Bombita [Chico]). Spanish bullfighter,
1879–1936. Investiture as *matador de toros*, 24 September 1899;
confirmed in Seville that same year. Two of his four brothers were
matadors: the older brother, Emilio (1874–1947), was the first Bombita; Ricardo fought as Bombita Chico or Bombita II; and a younger
brother, Manuel (1884–1936) was known as Bombita III. Both Ricardo and Manuel were killed in the early months of the Spanish
Civil War.

Emilio had a meteoric rise and a similar fall: his best years were
1893–96. Like Ricardo, he was weak with the sword and was often
gored; an untreated wound in May 1897 led to complications that
destroyed much of that season for him and marked the beginning of
the end of his career. In 1899 he was grotesquely gored by a Miura;
in 1903 he retired. The youngest brother had a short and insignificant
career.

Influenced and helped by Emilio, Ricardo (Bombita Chico) decided to become a bullfighter in spite of their mother's strenuous objections. In his early teens he traveled to various plazas with Emilio,
performed in a *cuadrilla* of Niños Sevillanos (q.v.), and made his
Madrid debut as *novillero* in 1897. Bombita Chico was accident-

prone, and his frequent injuries, not always inflicted by bull's horns, made him lose several weeks of each season. In 1898, for example, a splinter caused an infection that almost cost him an arm; once a bull stepped on his foot; another time he stepped on a pic. But his older brother's patronage, combined with his own talents, incredible courage, and disdain of pain, resulted in his working fairly constantly during his early years. With experience he improved his style and enlarged his repertoire, though his sword work seemed to be incurably inept. When he performed well he was outstanding, but accidents and injuries continued to plague him, even after his promotion to *matador de toros*, at age twenty.

By 1901, when his brother Emilio was clearly in decline, Bombita Chico decided he had outgrown his nickname: he began to be known simply as Bombita. That year he had some outstanding afternoons, including an impressive show of bravery in Madrid when, after a bull had tossed him and shredded his clothes, he borrowed a companion's trousers, returned to the ring, and killed the bull with a single, powerful sword thrust. 1902 was marred by some disgraceful performances and one major goring; it was the worst season of his career. But in 1903 he was in top form; that year he appeared with Rafael González (Machaquito, q.v.) for the first of what would be many joint performances. At the end of the season he was ranked the premier fighter of 1903, in spite of the stiff competition offered by Machaquito.

Bombita appeared in sixty-four events in 1904 and a similar number in 1905; in these years he was gored frequently but not seriously. Early in 1906 a major chest wound (broken ribs and a perforated lung) caused him to cancel much of his Mexican tour, but he recovered fully and the next three years he fought consistently between sixty and eighty times a season, in spite of frequent cancellations because of injury. Most critics consider him and Machaquito the leading matadors for the whole period from 1903 to 1909. Unlike Machaquito, who was seldom injured, Bombita continued to be plagued by frequent and often terrible injuries, but he returned to the ring each time with sufficient strength, courage and art to maintain his reputation.

In 1908 Bombita organized the famous "pleito de los Miura," demanding higher pay for bullfighters in corridas that featured these famously dangerous and expensive bulls. Because he himself had so often been injured (by Miuras and by other bulls), Bombita's boycott was attributed to fear, not to a desire to improve conditions for his fellow bullfighters. He convinced Machaquito, who was seldom injured, to join him, and together they led the struggle against the bull-breeders' union and the Madrid ring's management, which charged higher fees on Miura afternoons but did not pass the profits on to the bullfighters—a struggle which they lost (*see* Miura). Bombita also challenged the Madrid bullring's impresario, Indalecio Mosquera (q.v.), on other matters concerning bullfighters' rights and salaries, losing those struggles as well. Mosquera retaliated by not employing Bombita (until 1912), which of course injured his career but benefited those bullfighters who had continued to fight Miuras throughout (e.g., Rafael Gómez [el Gallo], Rodolfo Gaona, and Vicente Pastor, qq.v.).

Bombita was more successful in another one of his efforts to help his fellow bullfighters. The *Montepío de toreros* (formal name: *Asociación Benéfica de Auxilios Mutuos de Toreros*) is a mutual-aid society which he founded and to which he contributed heavily; he established the custom of benefit performances to fund it. The Society supplied (and still supplies) various kinds of financial aid, including disability, medical, pension and death benefits; it also owned and operated a sanatorium for bullfighters. The annual *corridas extraordinarias* that support the Montepío have become gala affairs. Because of his masterful performances and his activities to improve the lot of bullfighters, Bombita is sometimes called "el papa" (the Pope [of the taurine church]).[720]

In April 1912, Bombita's eagerly awaited return to Madrid— his first appearance in that bullring since 1908—was one of his best afternoons. Among the delirious spectators was King Alfonso XIII (q.v.), who supported the popular demand that Bombita be awarded an ear. This was only the third such trophy presented in Madrid (see Trophies in *DS*). But the next month, on 17 May 1912, he slipped while fighting a Miura. Though not injured by the bull, he hurt his ankle so badly that he had to cancel the remaining forty-seven contracts of his season. The loss of the season contributed to the erosion of his popularity with the Madrid public, from whom he had been absent while younger talents performed there, and who found it rather suspect that a mere ankle injury should result in so many cancellations. At this point, Bombita was thirty-three years old and, like others of his generation who recognized that they could not compete with Joselito and Belmonte, he retired the following year, in 1913. He donated all the income of his farewell corrida to the *Montepío*, to which he also dedicated most of his energies after his retirement.

Bombita was impressive not only for his skills and prowess as a fighter but also for the resilience that enabled him to overcome the physical and psychological effects of so many injuries. He was most skillful with the muleta, efficient but not impressive with the cape and banderillas, and inept with the sword. This description of his skills belies the important position he occupies in the history of bull-fighting, which is due more to his intelligence and character than to his mastery of any particular technique. His *tauromaquia*, entitled *Intimidades taurinas y arte de torear de Ricardo Torres "Bombita"* was written by Miguel A. Ródenas (for other ghostwritten *tauromaquias*, see Davis, Bill in *DS*).[721] Bombita received plenty of criticism during his lifetime, but his *toreo* was not, as Hemingway claims, described as "incomparable" after his death. He does, however, receive unanimous praise for founding the *Montepío*.

> The narrator explains that the current Spanish practice of reviling living bullfighters and praising them after their death is not new: Ricardo Bombita was unfavorably compared to his predecessor Mazzantini (q.v.), but "became incomparable" after he retired (241–42, *see also* 243).

Tovar. Full name: Rodrigo Figueroa de Torres, Duke of Tovar. Spanish bull breeder, d. 1929.

The Duke's Arribas Herd. Among the Duke of Tovar's many holdings was the valuable and venerable Vistahermosa (q.v.) herd he acquired from the Arribas family, whose pedigree can be traced back to the 1750s. Tovar registered these bulls under his own name on

12 May 1919, but since he had acquired the rights to the Arribas brand, colors (crimson and black), and *antigüedad*, their seniority dated back to 24 June 1883. The Duke sold this herd in 1927 (for a more detailed history of this herd, *see* Arribas Brothers).

The Duke's Suárez Herd. Shortly before he died, the Duke of Tovar acquired another herd, which had been established in 1918 by Félix Suárez with Santa Coloma and Albaserrada stock. These bulls were presented in Madrid on 6 May 1928; this became their new *antigüedad* (q.v.), as the family discarded the old Suárez brand and colors (crimson, sky blue, and white) in favor of their own (crimson and black). When the Duke died, his heirs did not divide this herd up among themselves; they called themselves "Herederos del señor Duque de Tovar" throughout the 1930s and 1940s. In 1930 and again in 1931, *Toros y toreros en . . .* remarks that this excellent herd was being mishandled by the heirs.

In 1947, the herd was divided into five equal lots. The rights to this herd's brand, colors, and its *antigüedad* (6 May 1928) remained with the lot that ended up as the property of the Portuguese bull breeder Antonio José da Veiga Teixeira: he has had them since 1959.[722]

Hemingway and the Tovar Novillos. Hemingway could have seen six Tovar *novillos* in Madrid only in 1925, when the *novillos* would have come from the Duke's Arribas herd, or in 1929, when they would have been from his Suárez herd, as these are only seasons in which the Tovar family sold *novillos* to the Madrid ring.[723] The fact that Hernandorena (q.v.) was gored by a Tovar *novillo* in Madrid establishes the date as 19 July 1925. By 1929 Hernandorena's career was such a shambles that he was not contracted to appear in Madrid.

The *novillo* was called Morito, and Hernandorena was gravely injured in the right thigh.[724] Hemingway reports seeing almost the entire length of the thigh bone (*DIA*, 19).

> The narrator recalls the six young Tovar bulls (*novillos*) in the Madrid *novillada* where Hernandorena was gored (17).

Triana. Situated on the banks of the Guadalquivir River, opposite the city of Seville, Triana gets its name from the Roman Emperor Trajan (Marcius Ulpius Nerva Trajanus, c. 53–117, Emperor, 98–117), who was reputed to have had a villa on the site. Recent excavations, however, conclude that the site was originally an Islamic burial ground upon which the Moors later constructed the fortification now known as the Castillo de San Jorge (Castle of St. George), in the late twelfth or early thirteenth centuries.[725]

In the twentieth century, Triana offered a lively street life, in sharp contrast to the staid, tradition-bound city of Seville. Triana is famous for its pottery, its gypsy population, many of them ironmongers, its flamenco bars and *cafés cantantes*, and its excellent bullfighters, among them Antonio Montes, Joaquín Rodríguez (Cagancho), Manuel García (Maera), and Francisco Vega de los Reyes (Gitanillo de Triana), qq.v. Although Juan Belmonte was sometimes called "El Pasmo de Triana" (the Wonder of Triana), he was not from Triana. He was born in Seville's Calle Feria and spent his boyhood there. The family did not move to Triana until he was eight or nine years old.

The narrator mentions bullfighters who are from Triana (77, 267).

Tricks. See Tricks in *DS*.

The narrator claims that he strives for honesty in his writing and therefore eschews the tricks that make journalism attractive and forceful (2).

Tunney, Gene. Full name: James Joseph Tunney. U.S. prizefighter, c. 1897–1978. Tunney became world heavyweight champion when he defeated Jack Dempsey in 1926. He defeated Dempsey again in 1928 and retired as undefeated champion the next year. Tunney served in both world wars: as a marine in World War I and as director of athletics and physical fitness for the United States Navy in World War II. He wrote *A Man Must Fight* (1932), a book that Hemingway owned, and *Arms for Living* (1941).[726] Tunney is mentioned in two of Hemingway's novels: *Across the River and Into the Trees* (171) and *Islands in the Stream* (299). The comparison between a boxer's fists and the bull's horns appears, though with less technical detail, in *The Sun Also Rises*: " 'Look how he knows how to use his horns,' I said. 'He's got a left and a right just like a boxer' " (139; *see also* 140).

The narrator compares the bull's use of his horns to Gene Tunney's punches (151).

Twysden, Mrs. Stirling. Full name: Mary Duff Stirling Byrom, married to Sir Roger Thomas Twysden in 1917 and therefore called Mrs. S. T. in *Death in the Afternoon*.

Hemingway and Duff Twysden. In 1925, when Hemingway met and was attracted to her, she was in the process of divorcing Twysden and was engaged to marry Pat Guthrie. Reynolds reports that she was then "Twice married . . . and [already] twice divorced" and engaged to Guthrie.[727] Critics and biographers agree that she and Guthrie were the historical prototypes for Hemingway's characters Brett Ashley and Mike Campbell in *The Sun Also Rises*. Born in 1893, she was more than thirty years old in 1925; she died in 1938.

The narrator reports that Mrs. S. T. drank heavily during the fiesta (*h:* 498).

– U –

Uncas. Pequot warrior, c. 1588-c. 1683. Uncas was "the ally of the English in all the wars against the Indians during his life." The English rewarded his services with gifts of land. In peacetime, however, Uncas "shielded many of the Pequots from the vengeance of the English . . . and for this was for a time in partial disgrace with the authorities; but he was soon received again into so great favor with the whites that several attempts were made by different Indians to assassinate him."[728] Uncas appeared as a character in James Fenimore Cooper's *The Last of the Mohicans* (1826), a popular novel about the French and Indian Wars.

Three racehorses were named Uncas: one was a bay colt foaled in Great Britain in 1865; his breeding is Stockwell-Nightingale by Mountain Deer. A second Uncas, foaled in 1876, has none of his bloodlines listed.[729] The Uncas Hemingway refers to was a half-bred gelding, sired by Melbourne out of Orage. Foaled in 1920 and owned by René Samaison, he ran often at Auteuil in the years when Hemingway was in Paris.

Uncas seems not to have run in France in 1922 or 1923, Hemingway's first years in Paris. In 1924 he ran five races and won two. In 1925, he ran eleven races and again won two, both at Auteuil. These were more prestigious than the ones he had won the year before, and Hemingway may have seen them: on the days of Uncas's victories, 26 November and 1 December, Hemingway was in Paris.

1926 was a remarkable year for this horse. He ran ten races and won five, including the prestigious Prix du Président de la République on 4 April 1926. The betting on him was 45 to 4.[730] Hemingway had spent February in New York, negotiating his first contracts with Scribners. He had spent most of March in Austria, but he and Hadley were back in Paris by early April. Hemingway was correcting page proofs for *Torrents of Spring*, had finished *The Sun Also Rises*, and may well have celebrated his achievements by going to the horse races. The Prix du Président of 4 April seems to be the race that endeared Uncas to him: at 45 to 4, the odds were, as he accurately recalls, "better than ten to one" (5).

In 1927, his last racing season, Uncas ran five races, winning none. Aged seven, he could have run several more seasons—steeplechasers can run until age ten or twelve—so it seems that he may have had an accident or, as Shipman reportedly informed the narrator, had somehow "broken down" (6, n. 1).

In 1931 and 1932, when Hemingway was finishing and revising *Death in the Afternoon*, Uncas was more than a decade old. Retired from steeplechasing and unsuited for studwork, the gelding may well have been sold into the Italian royal household as a "hack" or "hackney": a horse used for riding or to draw a light carriage. *See also* Shipman, Evan; Victor Emanuel.

> Although he is fond of Uncas, the narrator proclaims himself unaffected by the news that the horse has been sold to Victor Emanuel (5; 6, n. 1).

Uncle. The relative "in the lumber business" may be a reference to Hemingway's father-in-law Paul Pfeiffer, who started his successful business life in Piggott, Arkansas, by buying timberlands. Baker reports that he "at one time owned 60,000 acres, from which two hundred men cleared trees, pulled stumps, and later planted cotton, corn, wheat and soybeans."[731]

> The dramatised Author (q.v.), speaking to the Old Lady, remarks that his uncle's father-in-law "was in the lumber business" (139).

Unsuccessful Matadors. *See* Luis and the Unsuccessful Matadors.

– V –

V. R. *See* Pfeiffer, Virginia Ruth.

Valdapenas. Correct spelling: Valdepeñas. *See* Drinks.

Valencia. Valencia has two annual fairs, the springtime *fallas* and the important July *feria*, which Hemingway attended in 1925, 1926,

1927, 1929, and 1931. Hemingway mentions several Valencian bull-fighters, including Vicente Barrera, Manuel Granero, Manuel Martínez, Rosario Olmos, Francisco Tamarit ("Chaves"), and Enrique Torres (qq.v.). For Valencia's famous taurine doctor, *see* Serra, Dr. Paco, in this volume; for its beachfront restaurants, see Pepica in *DS*; for its taurine history, see Valencia in *DS*.

> The narrator discusses Valencia's weather, food, and *afición* (44–46; *see also* 23, 42) and mentions the city's bullring (1, 33), taurine museum (109–110), and a few unusual taurine incidents (23–25, 108–109).

Valencia, Valencia II. Professional nickname of the Roger family, acquired because the dynasty's founder, José Roger Durán (q.v.), was born in Valencia. He moved to Madrid, where all subsequent Valencias were born and bred. *See also* Roger, Victoriano (Valencia II) in this volume; and Cuevas Roger, Victoriano, in *DS*.

Valera, Rafael (Rafaelillo). Full name: Rafael Valera Jiménez. Spanish bullfighter, 1890–1956.

Growing up in Seville, with the Gómez Ortega brothers, Valera inevitably aspired to become a *matador de toros*. He fought as a *novillero* in the early 1920s, but his performances were so consistently unsatisfactory that he eventually renounced that position and concentrated on the banderillas, in the placing of which he had always excelled. He worked in the *cuadrillas* of the major bullfighters of the 1920s and 1930s: Belmonte, Ordóñez, Chicuelo, Cagancho, and Domingo Ortega (qq.v.). Cossío praises him as the best banderillero of all times, although several of the other banderilleros Hemingway names have been similarly praised.

After retiring in Spain, Valera worked intermittently in Peru, retiring from the South American bullrings in 1953. During his very long career, he suffered remarkably few injuries. After his retirement, he managed one of the major bull breeding ranches of Peru, where he died.[732]

Hemingway and Valera. Hemingway often saw this banderillero, who worked for many of the matadors whom Hemingway saw in the years he visited Spain (1923–31).

The narrator ranks Rafael Valera among the best banderilleros (201).

Vandel. Real name: Juan Pacheco. Spanish photographer, d. 1935. Studio address: Puerta del Sol, 3, Madrid, near the Carrera de San Jerónimo.

Vandel was already a published photographer by 1910. His action photos, like Rodero's, appeared in popular taurine magazines like *Sol y sombra*, *Toros y toreros*, *La lidia*, and *Círculo taurino*. In the 1920s he was a correspondent photographer for *La corrida de Barcelona* and *La afición de Zaragoza*, which published his work as late as 1934.

Vandel's work was included in a book written by José María Carretero Novillo (El Caballero Audaz) about the death of Manuel Granero. One of Vandel's most famous photographs was "Suerte de varas en San Sebastián, 1921."[733]

Hemingway acknowledges Vandel and Rodero, whose photographs he reproduced in *Death in the Afternoon* (h: 408).

Varé, Manuel (Varelito). Alternate spellings: Varés and Varest. Full name: Manuel Varé García. Spanish bullfighter, 1893–1922. Investiture as *matador de toros*, 26 September 1918, in Madrid. He was promoted by Joselito, who also promoted Domingo González (Dominguín, q.v.) on the same afternoon. A picture of the three men together shows Varé to be only a few inches shorter than his companions (see below).[734]

In gypsy language, *varé* is a monetary unit (a duro, or five pesetas), which caused one fan to write that "Varé, por sus volapieses / se hará dueño de millones / de vareses" (Varé, on the strength of your [or his] *volapieses* (a way of killing the bull) / will earn millions / of *vareses*.[735]

Varé made his Madrid debut as *novillero* in July 1913, a presentation that was judged somewhat unwarranted because of his lack of reputation. But Varelito soon began to be recognized for his excellent sword work. From about 1915 on he fought in the first-rank plazas, but he was gored frequently and therefore was absent from the ring for many weeks at a time. In 1918, his "triunfal temporada" (triumphant season), he was contracted for forty *novilladas*, although two injuries allowed him to perform in only twenty-eight, "con inmejorable resultado artístico" (with supreme artistry). He received his *alternativa* (promotion to *matador de toros*) at the end of that season. In spite of the five years that had elapsed between Varé's Madrid debut as *novillero* and his *alternativa*, Hemingway considers that he had not "served a proper apprenticeship" (254; for a critique of Hemingway's treatment of "premature promotions," see "The Bullfighter," in the introduction to this volume).

Varé's first three seasons as *matador de alternativa* were, like his career as *novillero*, marred by cancellations due to illness and injury. But his swordsmanship and personality enabled him to maintain a high profile, even at a time when Joselito and Belmonte eclipsed all other bullfighters: thirty-seven corridas in 1919, thirty-two in 1920, and forty-four in 1921—a more-than-respectable record. He was heavily contracted (more than sixty corridas) for 1922 but was fatally wounded during the Seville fiesta, 21 April 1922. He suffered, as Hemingway reports, for almost a month afterwards, dying on 13 May.[736]

Hemingway remarks that "Like all killers of only moderate height he took much punishment from the bulls" (253; for further discussion on the function of height in a matador's work, *see* Todó, Isidoro). Cossío doesn't mention Varé's height, attributing his many injuries to "mala fortuna" (bad luck). Bagüés notes that his signature method of killing, his famous *volapié*, did not come as easily to him as most critics claim: he blames Varé's many injuries on his insistence on applying the technique for which he was famous even when the conditions were not suited for it, "pundonor que le costó algunas cornadas" (a concept of honor that cost him several gorings).[737] But the audience wanted it: in the Seville fiesta of April 1922, when he had performed four afternoons and had been unable to produce one of his spectacular sword strokes, the audience egged him on so mercilessly that he attempted it on his last bull of the *feria*, with fatal results. As Hemingway reports, Varé cried out, "¡Ya me la ha pegao! ¡Ya os habéis salido ustedes con la suya!" (Now he's hit me! Now you've got what you wanted!).[738]

Varé and Juan Belmonte were contemporaries, both from Seville. It is not unlikely that they practiced passes together, as Hemingway writes (77). They performed together as *novilleros* in 1912, and Belmonte's influence smoothed the way for Varé's Madrid debut in 1913.[739]

Varé and Hemingway. Varé was killed the year before Hemingway saw his first bullfight. Hemingway obviously read about him but never saw him perform.

The narrator correctly describes Varé as a matador from Seville noted for his excellent sword work. Although "a consistently great killer," he was often injured because he was short and had not "served a proper apprenticeship" (254). He died four weeks after being badly gored in 1922 (253–54; *see also* 77; and photographs, *h:* 372–73, *h:* 394–95).

Varelito. *See* Varé, Manuel.

Vasquez. Usually spelled Vázquez. The venerable *casta vazqueña* takes its name from the Spanish bull breeder Gregorio Vázquez, who established the herd in 1757. Gregorio died in 1778, and his more famous son, Vicente José Vázquez (d. 1830), enriched the herd with some Vistahermosa animals as well as "los mejores ejemplares de las ganaderías existentes en Utrera" (the best specimens from the ranches of Utrera, in the province of Seville, Andalucía). His mix was very successful, and Vicente claimed for it the *antigüedad* (q.v.), or seniority, of 2 August 1790, which is the same as that of Vistahermosa. When Vicente José Vázquez died (without heirs), most of his carefully bred herd was acquired by King Ferdinand VII of Spain.[740]

Unlike the *casta jijona* (distinguished by their size, their red coat, and their large heads), which are grown in Salamanca, the Vázquez (or Vázquez-Veragua), Cabrera, and Vistahermosa (qq.v.) strains are all *castas andaluzas* (from Andalucía), and said to be the most appropriate model of the *toro de lidia* (fighting bull).

For subsequent owners of the Vázquez herds, *see* Veragua, in this volume; and Domecq in *DS*. The Vázquez-Veragua genealogical tree branches out into a bewildering multitude of families, ranches, and brands, but the Veragua-Domecq line is the most direct. *See also* Concha y Sierra, doña Concepción de la; and Villamarta, in this volume.

The narrator mentions several of the early strains from which contemporary bulls are descended, including Vasquez (*sic*, 132).

Vega de los Reyes, Francisco (Gitanillo de Triana). Spanish bullfighter, 1904–31. Investiture as matador, 28 August 1927, in El Puerto de Santa María; confirmed in Madrid, October 1927. His nickname reflects both his ethnic origin and the place of his birth, the gypsy barrio of Triana, Seville (which also produced Cagancho, q.v.). He was also known as Curro Puya, perhaps to distinguish him from his younger brothers, who were also called "Gitanillo de Triana." Rafael was a talented though uneven *matador de toros* who died in a car crash in 1969 at age fifty-four, and Vicente and José were *novilleros*.

In spite of the taurine atmosphere of his neighborhood—but not of his home: his father was a blacksmith—Francisco did not become interested in bullfighting until he was about twenty years old. His talents, particularly his graceful handling of the cape, were evident from the beginning, and he quickly attracted patrons and admirers, including Juan Belmonte. By 1926 he was ready for his Madrid debut as *novillero*; that year he racked up forty-five *novilladas*, appeared in all the major plazas, and was second only to Félix Rodríguez (q.v.) in the national ratings. In 1927, after thirty-two *novilladas* (three of them within twenty-four hours), he was promoted to *matador de toros* "con honores máximos" (with top honors), both because of the quality of his performance that afternoon and because of the personalities who conferred the degree on him. The fact that two great but antithetical matadors, Rafael el Gallo and Juan Belmonte (qq.v.) came together to confirm his promotion to *matador de alternativa* was no accident. Gitanillo fought eighteen corridas that year.

In 1928 Gitanillo was second only to Chicuelo in the number of corridas: Chicuelo performed in eighty-one, Gitanillo in sixty-seven. He followed this with a lustrous winter season in Mexico. In 1929 he suffered many "tropiezos con los toros" (skirmishes with the bulls)[741] which, while not serious enough to keep him out of the ring, were debilitating enough to mar his performances. On 3 June of that year a serious car accident lost him two months' work, and on 2 September a Pablo Romero bull gored him so badly that he lost the rest of the season: his total for 1929 was only twenty-four corridas, and they were not as good as those of the previous season. In 1930, the number rose to fifty-one, and although most of the performances were merely satisfactory, on more than a few afternoons he achieved the artistic level that had propelled him to fame.

Gitanillo began the 1931 season with an upsurge of energy and ambition, but was gored severely after only sixteen corridas, on 31 May, by a Graciliano Pérez Tabernero bull named Fandanguero. Marcial Lalanda and Chicuelo (qq.v), who shared the bill with Gitanillo, were unable to extricate him before the bull gored him in both thighs and a hip, this last horn wound "arrancando el nervio ciático" (ripping out the sciatic nerve), just as Hemingway writes. He died ten weeks later, on 14 August, after several hemorrhages, pneumonia, infection of the meninges, and other terrible complications.[742] Hemingway's description of Gitanillo's wounds and subsequent suffering is accurate.

Gitanillo was desperately mourned: he was a graceful, very talented artist who had provided unforgettable performances for thousands of people. His work with the cape, especially his long, slow *verónicas*, "provocaban una emoción artística de primer grado" (aroused an extremely intense artistic response).[743] He was usually elegant with the sword, if somewhat weaker with the muleta. With the cape "he fought with his hands very low, *cargando la suerte*, and with great *temple*. His *verónicas* have never been equalled."[744] His style, at first described as "intuitive," like Cagancho's, become more sober under the influence of Juan Belmonte. The fact that Gitanillo continued to grow and develop after his *alternativa* suggested that, stirring as he was, he had not yet realized all his potential. Fandanguero killed not only a talented young bullfighter, but the superb bullfighter he might have become. The violence of the goring and the extended suffering that preceded Gitanillo's death added to his public's devastating feeling of loss.

Hemingway and Gitanillo. Hemingway may have seen Gitanillo in one of the many *novilladas* of 1926 and 1927. He saw Gitanillo on 18 September 1927, in San Sebastián, less than a month after his promotion to *matador de toros*.[745] Hemingway was not in Spain in 1928 and 1930, the years in which Gitanillo performed most frequently, but he may have seen him in 1929, and he was probably in Madrid for Gitanillo's last corrida, on 31 May 1931.

The narrator describes Gitanillo de Triana as a tall, graceful gypsy matador who was an artist with the cape although in other areas his technique was "fundamentally unsound." He admires the bullfighter's personality, mentions his car accident, and adds that he witnessed the fatal goring on May 31, 1931 (217–20, 223; mentioned, 267, 271; photographs, *h:* 294–95).

Veiga, Simâo da. Portuguese bullfighter, 1903–59. Like his father, after whom he was named and with whom he trained and performed, Veiga was a *rejoneador* (mounted bullfighter, or *cavaleiro*, in Portuguese). He appeared in Spain for the first time in 1924, with his father, at a festival in honor of the Italian king and queen. First in Barcelona and then in Madrid, Veiga's fine horsemanship and energetic, acrobatic handling of the bulls taught the Spanish audiences to appreciate this kind of bullfighting, in which the elegant, specially bred and trained horses play an important part. (The old art of *rejoneo* had been displaced by *toreo de a pie*, in which horses are used only during the pic-ing—and, before the *peto*, frequently killed; see "The Corrida," in the introduction to this volume.)

Veiga was absent from Spain in 1926 but returned in 1927, performing in twenty-seven corridas (a record for *rejoneadores* in Spain). He performed every year from 1931 until the Spanish Civil War broke out in 1936. He returned to Spain after the war, was received by Franco, and continued to perform until 1959, when he died of a heart attack after a corrida.

Veiga was the premier *rejoneador* of his generation, with great followings in Spain, Portugal, and France: "Sus méritos de jinete y de toreador son indiscutibles, y una diestra propaganda favoreció su popularidad" (He is an indisputably fine horseman and a bullfighter, and skillful advertising enhanced his popularity).[746] The Peralta brothers, Angel (b. 1926) and Rafael (b. 1933), were the next generation of great *rejoneadores*. They are from Puebla del Río (Seville).

Hemingway and Simâo da Veiga. Veiga's peak years were the 1920s and 1930s, when Hemingway visited Spain. He saw Simâo da Veiga when in Pamplona on 8 July 1924, and may have seen him in 1927 and 1931 as well, when he performed often in important corridas. The taurine weekly *Zig Zag* offers a picture of Simâo da Veiga in action in Pamplona, 1924, leaning sharply towards the bull and holding banderillas in both hands. Another journal describes him as a "jinete diestro y espectacular en la suerte de banderillas a dos manos" (a skilled horseman and spectacular in placing the banderillas with both hands, i.e., controlling his horse only with his legs).[747]

The narrator mentions Simâo da Veiga's well trained horse (*h:* 441, s.v. *Jaca*).

Velázquez. Full name: Diego Velázquez Rodríguez de Silva. Major Spanish painter, 1599–1660. Among his most famous works are *The Surrender of Breda* (1625), *Las Meninas* (1656), and several court portraits, including those of dwarves and jesters, many of which hang in Madrid's Prado Museum. The Prado also displays Velázquez's *Christ Crucified*, a serene, graceful figure that emphasizes the humanity, rather than the suffering, spirituality or divinity of its subject. Robert Jordan is familiar with Velázquez's equine portraits (*FWTBT*, 13); Richard Cantwell also mentions this painter (*ARIT*, 146).

Las Meninas (*The Maids of Honor*, also known as *The Family of Philip IV*), painted in 1656, is perhaps Velázquez's most famous work. It presents the Infanta Margarita surrounded by her maids of honor, her guardian or duenna, a male figure, and two dwarves. The organization of the picture emphasizes depth, perspective, and the play of light: there are three sources of light, one to each side and one behind the Infanta, which open the canvas in three different directions. Several of the figures in the painting look directly out of the painting at the viewer, which adds a fourth perspective: that is, the painting opens out in all directions.

The relationship between the painting, its subject, its viewers, and the painter is also complex. The painter appears in the painting, painting a large unseen canvas which may depict the Infanta (in which case he is painting the painting we see), or the figure or figures standing in front of the painting (in which case he is painting the viewer, who may be the Infanta's parents, or may be any person interested in painting). Thus the painter himself, his subject (the Infanta), his patron (the Infanta's parents, the King and Queen, who are vaguely suggested in a mirror who may be the subjects of the painting within the painting), and all other viewers through the ages, are all privileged centers in this complicated, supremely intelligent work of art.[748]

The proud painter in the painting is said to be Velázquez himself. He wears a decoration upon his chest, the Order of Santiago, which is usually bestowed upon the highest nobility. According to one tradition, he painted the decoration on himself as a hint to the King that he deserved it. According to another, it was painted on him by the King himself, in recognition of the outstanding achievement of *Las Meninas*.

The narrator obviously admires Velázquez (39–40, 73, 203, 204–205), including his famous *Las Meninas* (52).

Veneno. *See* Granados, José (Veneno).

Veragua, Duke of. Spanish bull breeders, active in the nineteenth and early twentieth centuries. The three Dukes of Veragua were don Pedro Alcántara Colón, his son don Cristóbal Colón y de la Cerda, and his grandson Cristóbal Colón y Aguilera.[749] This grandson owned the Veragua herds when Hemingway visited Spain in the 1920s. He sold them in 1927.

Early History: Vázquez to Martín Alonso. The Veragua bulls are descended from bulls bred by Vicente José Vázquez (q.v.). When Vázquez died in 1830, part of his herd was acquired by King Ferdinand VII. In 1835, Ferdinand's widow sold his carefully bred herds to the Duke of Osuna (Mariano Tellez Girón) and the Duke of Veragua. In 1836, although the breed was co-owned by the two Dukes, the bulls were fought in the Madrid plaza under the brand and colors (crimson and white) of the Duke of Veragua, who became the sole owner of the stock in 1849. The three successive Dukes of Veragua owned the breed for almost a century, with minimal crossbreeding: they acquired only one outside seed bull, a Miura, but bred only a few cows to him. The Veragua animals were true *vazqueños*, although the animal Vázquez had created was itself a mix.

In 1927, the Veraguas sold their herds to don Manuel Martín Alonso.[750] At that time, the Duke of Veragua was the president of the Asociación de Ganaderos de Reses Bravas (Association of Bull Breeders), a post he resigned shortly before selling his holdings. The disappearance of the powerful Veragua family from all aspects of bull breeding was a major event.

The Veragua bulls had been controversial for some years preceding their sale because—so their detractors said—excessive inbreeding resulted in weak legs and lack of stamina. Matadors complained that the bulls' weakness made it impossible for them to perform well in the last third of the fight (this is the position Hemingway reports). Matadors powerful enough to dictate to the bullrings boycotted the Veraguas.

Defenders of the Veragua breed, however, blamed the matadors, not the bulls, for the animals' rapid weakening. One long editorial argued that if the matadors adapted their strategies (by moderating the cape work and restraining the picadors) to the capacity of the bull, they could preserve its strength and then take advantage of the breed's great courage and speed to make an impressive *faena*. These valuable Veragua qualities, the editorial argued, had been preserved because the Duke had steadfastly resisted the current trend to downbreed, and they were being wasted by ignorant and insensitive matadors who did not understand the differences among breeds and among individuals within the breed.

In any case, the barrage of complaints and financial pressures—the *cuestión de los Veraguas*, similar to the *pleito de los Miura* (q.v.)—led the Duke to resign his position and sell his holdings in 1927. Manuel Martín Alonso acquired the herd "con todos sus derechos" (with all its rights; i.e., the brand, colors, and venerable *antigüedad*, q.v.). (For the declining influence of bull breeders, see also "Bulls and Bullbreeding" and "The Corrida," in the introduction to this volume.)

Later History: Martín Alonso to Domecq. The Martín Alonso family held the Veragua stock for only three years, selling it and all its rights to Juan Pedro Domecq Núñez de Villavicencio in 1929 or 1930. Domecq moved the herd from southern Madrid to his ranches in Jerez de la Frontera, a month-long trek of almost seven hundred kilometers. The Domecqs added more Vistahermosa blood by acquiring cows and seed bulls from the Conde de la Corte in 1930, 1932, 1939, and 1940. The resulting herd was proclaimed "una de las mejores de España" (one of the best in Spain). The Domecqs registered the herd under their name in 1931; these are probably the "new owners" Hemingway mentions.[751] For the later history of this *ganadería*, see Domecq in *DS*. *See also* Vistahermosa in this volume. Manuel Granero (q.v.) was killed by a Veragua bull, *Pocapena*, in 1922, when the herd was still under Veragua ownership.

> The narrator correctly reports that Granero was killed by a Veragua bull (45). He claims that the Veragua bulls had degenerated because of inbreeding, and that they have been sold (130–31; see also 74).

Verónica, Saint. The name of this saint may derive from *vera icon* (true image), and is associated with an image of the face of Christ on a cloth as well as with the woman who wiped Christ's face with the cloth. Such a cloth was venerated in Rome in the late tenth and early eleventh centuries.

One of the oldest stories associated with the shadowy figure of Verónica says that, in gratitude for a miraculous cure, she was on her way to a painter to have the face of Christ painted upon a linen cloth when she met Christ. When he heard of her errand, he "caused his features to appear" on the cloth. Other stories variously report that Jesus pressed his face upon the cloth, or that she wiped his face with the cloth as he was carrying the cross, or that she handed him the cloth so that he could wipe his own face.

The pass named after this saint requires the bullfighter to hold the cape with both hands, which is the position in which Verónica is most frequently depicted (e.g., in the oil painting, *St. Veronica*, by the fifteenth-century artist Hans Memling). It is a basic, classic pass, said to have been invented by Joaquín Rodríguez (Costillares, q.v.). Many matadors, including Cagancho, Gitanillo de Triana, and Jesús Solórzano, have become famous for their *verónicas*. A more recent master, Antonio Ordóñez (see in *DS*) performed the pass to heart-stopping perfection.

The *verónica* is performed early in the fight, before the bull is piced; and in the *quite*, to distract the bull away from the horse and picador. If the bull is responsive, several of these passes can be performed in succession, the series to be finished with the *media-verónica*.[752]

> The narrator carefully describes the *verónica* and the *media-verónica* (65–66, *h:* 449–50, s.v. *Media verónica*; *h:* 489–91, s.v. *Verónica*; see also 175, 176), criticizes those who perform it badly (230), and praises those who do it well (*h:* 294–97, 503).

Víbora. Hemingway's account of this bull accurately reports all but two of the details supplied by Carralero and Borge in *Toros célebres*: Hemingway (1) changes the position of the carpenter's wound by mistranslating "el muslo izquierdo" (the left thigh), and (2) enlivens the event by making the bull jump the *barrera*. Carralero and Borge merely write that the bull injured González "Al salir del chiquero . . . dentro del callejón" (as he emerged from his stall . . . in the *callejón*, which is the alley between the *barrera* that encloses the bullring and the first rows of seats). This suggests that the event happened before the bull entered the arena itself. In order for the bull to jump the *barrera*, he would have had to enter the arena first.

The missing antecedent for the "he" who was returned to the corrals is the bull.[753] *See also* Bueno, don José; Jaqueta.

The narrator comments on the exploits of Víbora (110).

Victor Emanuel. Italian name: Vittorio Emmanuele III, 1869–1947; king of Italy, 1900–46.

A member of the royal house of Savoy, Vittorio Emmanuele III ascended to the throne when his father, Umberto I, was assassinated at Monza on 29 July 1900. He was king of Italy during both world wars. During World War I he spent much of his time near the front. When the Austrians broke through at Caporetto (q.v.), he urged the retreating Italian army to hold at the Piave River, where their desperate position attracted the aid of England and France.

Vittorio Emmanuele III was unable to check Mussolini's rise to power. Although he arrested Mussolini in 1943 and appointed his own son Umberto as lieutenant governor in 1944, he could not preserve the monarchy, which was defeated in a plebiscite in 1946. Both Vittorio Emmanuele and his son went into exile.[754]

Vittorio Emmanuele III owned a fine stable of horses. In addition, he commanded the mounted *carabinieri* (called "V. E. soldiers" because the unit was established by Vittorio Emmanuele I, and called "airplanes" because of their wide hats). These forces have historically been closely connected to the royal house of Savoy and to the head of state, for whom they serve as personal guard. They are empowered to keep civil and military order and in this capacity enjoyed special favor during Mussolini's fascistic regime.[755] Hemingway refers to both Vittorio Emmanuele III and the mounted *carabinieri* in *A Farewell to Arms* (4, 6, 36, 192, 224). He may have bet on the gelding Uncas (q.v.) in 1926.

The narrator has heard that Uncas, who won good money for him, "is now used as a hack by Mr. Victor Emanuel" (6, n. 1).

Victoria, Calle Victoria. This Madrid street runs from the Carrera de San Jerónimo to the Calle de la Cruz. *See* Pasaje Alvarez.

The narrator remembers the neighborhood of the Pasaje Alvarez and the Calle Victoria (34, 40; see also 38, 55, *h*: 424, s.v. *Cerveza*).

Victoria Eugenia. Full name: Victoria Eugenia Julia (Ena). British-born aristocrat, 1887–1969; Queen of Spain, 1906–31. On her mother's side, Victoria Eugenia was the grand-daughter of Britain's Queen Victoria; her father was Prince Henry of Battenberg. She was educated within the British royal family and became queen of Spain when she married Alfonso XIII on 31 May 1906. A skilled linguist, she spoke Spanish fluently.

During her reign she established public hospitals and schools, mostly in connection with the Anti-Tuberculosis League and the Spanish chapter of the Red Cross. She established the *Ropero de Santa Victoria*, which distributed clothes to the poor in the winter, and several schools for orphans and for the retraining of people injured in work accidents. When the Spanish Republic was proclaimed in April 1931, she followed her husband into exile. She visited Spain briefly in 1968, and she died the next year at her home in Switzerland.[756]

Hemingway and Victoria Eugenia. When Hemingway visited Spain in the 1920s (during Primo de Rivera's dictatorship), Victoria Eugenia was still queen. At the time of the final writing and revisions of *Death in the Afternoon*, she was already the ex-queen. She was born in Balmoral Castle, Scotland, not in England. Like most British aristocrats, she was fond of horses, and it distressed her to see them injured in the bullring. The *peto* was under discussion in Spain for several years before it was finally instituted in the late 1920s; *see* Peto; Ronda.

The narrator explains that the *peto* was introduced as a gesture to please Spain's now-deposed queen (*h:* 464, s.v. *Peto*).

Vigueres, Ubaldo. A Civil Guard (q.v.) who shot at the bull Comisario (q.v.) and accidentally killed a bullring servant (111).

Villalta, Nicanor. Full name: Nicanor Villalta Serris. Alternate spelling: Serres.[757] Spanish matador, 1897–1980. Investiture as *matador de toros*, in San Sebastián, 6 August 1922; confirmed in Madrid on 21 September that same year.

After a long but inauspicious apprenticeship, first in Mexico and then in Spain, Villalta had two outstanding afternoons in Madrid (2 April and 2 May 1922), and his career took off. After a few more *novilladas* in important plazas, he was promoted to *matador de toros* and electrified Spanish audiences with his idiosyncratic style and "muñeca mágica" (magic wrist). In 1923, his first full season after his promotion, he performed in forty-one corridas, including Madrid's annual *Corrida de la Prensa*, at which he was awarded the "golden ear." He was the first recipient of this prize.

In 1924 Villalta appeared in thirty-nine corridas, cutting four ears in what must have been an amazing corrida, 1 June, in Madrid. He was a top figure for the rest of the decade, performing in fifty-five corridas in 1925, fifty-one in 1926, twenty-six in 1927 (he suffered a long illness and then was gored in the groin in August: he had to cancel two-thirds of his contracts), fifty-two in 1928, forty in 1929, and forty-five in 1930. He was praised for his work with the muleta and for his excellent sword work, and was frequently contracted to appear in Madrid, where he invariably earned trophies and rave reviews. He holds the record for cutting ears most frequently in Madrid: thirty-two in a ten-year period, a fact that supplied the title for the biography written by his brother, Joaquín Villalta (Joaquinillo), *Treinta y dos orejas en Madrid: Diez años matando toros* (Madrid, 1932); and a total of fifty-two or fifty-four over his entire career (reports vary, but fifty-two is the more likely number, to which must be added three tails), a record which still stands, as of 2000.

Firmly entrenched as a master, Villalta performed less frequently in the 1930s: thirty-eight corridas in 1931, thirty-one in 1932, thirty-four in 1933, eighteen in 1934, and seventeen in 1935. In these last two years he was lackluster, and he retired at the end of the 1935 season.

Villalta performed occasionally during the Spanish Civil War, when bullfights were held only in Nationalist-controlled territory, and resumed an active role after the war. Although he was then in his forties, he had fine seasons in 1940, 1941, and 1942 (thirty-two corridas, all in important plazas and festivals, and most of them well-reviewed: an impressive season for the forty-five-year-old matador), finally ending his long career in 1943. In these years, he helped restore bullfighting and lent his prestige to an industry much weakened by the war. Not incidentally, he also restored his own finances to their pre-war level.

During his career, Villalta killed 1,236 bulls. A matador of the first rank for two decades, *una figura del toreo*, he was a serious, even solemn artist. His striking build was widely commented: Cossío reports that his height helped him at the moment of killing. Luján comments on his "figura alta y musculosa . . . piernas inacabables y gruesas . . . cuello desmesuradamento largo y unos movimientos inarmónicos" (tall, muscular physique . . . endless, thick legs . . . disproportionately long neck and jerky movements). Bagüés confirms Hemingway's criticism: "No era bonito toreando porque su figura se lo impedía" (his figure kept him from being an attractive [aesthetic] fighter), but he was brave, committed, and skillful, particularly with the muleta and the sword.[758] As Hemingway says, Villalta was Aragonese, having been born in Cretas, Teruel.

Hemingway and Villalta. Hemingway had plenty of opportunity to see Villalta and to read reviews of his performances. He saw Villalta when he first came to Madrid (corrida of 10 June 1923), as well as during his first Pamplona fiesta (corridas of 6 and 8 July 1923).[759] Villalta obviously impressed Hemingway and his pregnant wife, Hadley: they named their son after him. In 1925, Villalta performed on three of the six corridas of the Valencia fiesta. In 1926 he performed in Pamplona and Valencia on the days when the Hemingways were in those cities for the fiestas; he also performed on every day of the Zaragoza fiesta (13–17 October), which Hemingway attended with Archibald MacLeish (q.v.).

In 1927 Villalta performed less frequently, and in 1928 Hemingway did not go to Spain. In 1929, although Villalta did not perform in Pamplona or Valencia, Hemingway saw him at least once, on 1 September in Palencia. Hemingway missed the Spanish season of 1930, but the next year he was in Spain from May to September: he saw Villalta in Madrid on 24 May, early in his stay, and several times more during that long, intense season when he was gathering data in order to finish *Death in the Afternoon*. During all those years, Hemingway and Villalta frequently coincided in Madrid and Hemingway probably saw him in those important corridas.[760]

Like all famous bullfighters, Villalta is the subject of poems, songs, and at least one full-length novel, *Juramento baturro* by A. José Ullán Rodríguez (1930). Hemingway mentions Villalta briefly in *The Sun Also Rises* (176) and devotes two paragraphs to him in *In Our Time* (unnumbered page 137).

> The narrator admires this brave Aragonese matador, comments repeatedly on his height, his long neck, and his individual style of fighting. Although his work with the cape "is not good," he has complete control of the muleta and the sword and works closely with the bull. He considers Villalta "the bravest, most secure, and most consistent and emotional killer" of 1931 (85–87, 221–22, 252–53) but complains that Villalta is unintelligent and conceited (253, 260, 262). He mentions Villalta frequently (70, 267, *h:* 461–62, s.v. *Parón*; *h:* 496; photographs, *h:* 308–13) and alludes to him without naming him (*h:* 459, s.v. *Oreja*).

Villamarta, Marqués de. Full name: Alvaro Dávila y Agreda, Marquis of Villamarta. Spanish bull breeder, d. 1933.

In the 1880s, the Marquis of Villamarta, established a herd of 365 animals, acquired from Juan Vázquez's holdings (some of it via Concha y Sierra, q.v.) of Vistahermosa (q.v.) stock. He registered it in Madrid in 1895 and ten years later, the already-famous herd having increased to 874 head, he sold it to Eduardo Olea.

In 1914, the Marquis of Villamarta formed another herd with 360 cows, many of them Murube (q.v.), to which he continued to add stock, mostly Parladé and Santa Coloma. The resultant bulls were

first fought in Madrid under the Marquis's brand and colors (bottle green and old gold) on 22 April 1921.[761] The excellent herd won many prizes and expanded quickly, to more than fifteen hundred head in 1931.

When the Marquis died in 1933, the bulls were registered in his widow's name. Upon her death in 1941, their only son, Alvaro Dávila

Garvey, inherited the Villamarta title and the rights to the herd's brand, colors, and *antigüedad*; his three sisters inherited portions of the herd itself. The herd remained in the family until it was sold, with all its rights, to a company called "Garcibravo, S. A." in 1980.[762] For a discussion of the complicated relationship between breeds, ownership, and *antigüedad*, see the essay on "Bulls and Bull Breeding," in the introduction to this volume.

The narrator correctly reports that the Villamarta family's important bull-breeding ranches are registered in Seville (132).

Villar, Francisco and Victorio. Twentieth century Spanish bull breeders.

In 1914, the Villar brothers acquired almost all of a herd that José Vega had established in 1910 with sixty-five Veragua cows (*casta vazqueña*) and three Santa Coloma seed bulls (*casta Vistahermosa*). Vega's experiment produced a new kind of bull, which Vera lists separately as Vega-Villar and praises highly.[763] For other castes or types, *see* Cabrera, José Rafael; Vásquez; and Vistahermosa; for the *casta jijona*, which Hemingway doesn't mention, *see* Gómez, don Félix, widow of; Martínez, don Vicente; and Pablo Romero.

In 1922 or 1923, shortly before Hemingway first came to Spain, the Villar brothers dissolved their partnership, one portion of their herd remaining with Francisco and the other sold by Victorio to José Encinas Fernández del Campo. These may be the bulls Hemingway means when he writes that sometime before 1927, "The breeding stock was sold to another man" (*DIA*, 161). Even under the new Encinas ownership, they might still be known to aficionados as Villar or Vega-Villar bulls.

Encinas. Encinas registered his newly acquired Villar bulls on 8 June 1924. Hemingway saw eight Encinas bulls (officially listed under their new owner's name) in Pamplona on 10 July 1927; they were fought by Antonio Márquez, Pablo Lalanda, Martín Agüero (qq.v.), and Manuel del Pozo (Rayito). Hemingway did not go to Spain in 1928, but in 1929 he again saw Encinas bulls in Pamplona, on 7 July, when the matadors were Manuel Jiménez (Chicuelo), Victoriano Roger (Valencia II), and Antonio Márquez (qq.v.). *Toros y toreros en 1931* praises Encinas's breeding of the bulls he had bought from Victorio Villar: "en sus manos no han desmerecidos estos toros, sino todo lo contrario, han mejorado, alcanzando éxitos muy sonados el inteligente y entusiasta criador" (in his hands these bulls have not deteriorated; on the contrary, they have improved, this intelligent and enthusiastic breeder having achieved resounding successes).[764]

Francisco Villar. After the Villar brothers separated, Francisco Villar presented his bulls in Pamplona every year from 1923 to 1926. On 13 July 1923, the last corrida of the fiesta, the six Villar bulls were fought by Manuel García (Maera), Rosario Olmos, and José García (Algabeño, qq.v.). The local reviewer gave low marks to the bullfighters but praised the Villar bulls as "bravísimos." One of them in fact was given a turn around the ring for his brave performance.[765] Hemingway mentions this corrida, praising the bulls and claiming "the bullfighters did not care for them" (*DIA*, 161). One matador and two banderilleros had been injured.

 Francisco Villar first presented his share of the herd under his name, colors (purple and red), and brand in Madrid on 5 July 1924, thus establishing their new *antigüedad* (q.v.). In that year, he presented only ten bulls: four for the Madrid corrida of 5 July, and six in Pamplona, on 11 July 1924. Hemingway also saw Villar corridas on 7 July 1925, and on 11 July 1926 (when eight instead of the usual six bulls were fought).[766]

Toros y toreros en 1926, a publication which recognized that Belmonistic maneuvers required smaller, more agile bulls and which therefore tolerated occasional infractions of the law in terms of the age and weight of bulls, accused Francisco Villar of having crossed all permissible boundaries and harshly remarked that the animals which Villar had sent to the Vitoria *corrida de toros* of 5 August looked as if they were two to three years old, instead of the requisite minimum of four years for *toros de lidia*—an intolerable abuse of the law.[767] Francisco sold most of his herd in 1928. Because the herd had been mismanaged over the years, it took their new owner, Arturo

Sánchez Cobaleda (see in *DS*), some time to restore them to their former glory.

In 1929 Francisco Villar was criticized for other sharp dealings: having sold his stock and its *antigüedad* at a good price to Sánchez Cobaleda, he then bought lesser stock and presented it under his name. Although he gave them a new *divisa* (colors), he was still able to overcharge bullring impresarios who had not kept careful track of changes in ownership. Thus Villar undermined the reputation and value of the stock he had sold to Sánchez Cobaleda.

All of this suggests that the Villar bulls to which Hemingway objected came from Francisco Villar's herd, sold in 1928 to Sánchez Cobaleda—and not from his brother's portion, which had been sold to Encinas in the early 1920s and which had benefited from his expertise and careful breeding practices (Hemingway saw Encinas bulls on 14 October 1926; *see* Zaragossa).[768]

> The narrator recalls seeing wonderful, aggressive Villar bulls in Pamplona in 1923. He reports that in 1927, 1928, and 1929, under different ownership, they were less brave (161–62).

Vindel, Pedro. Spanish publisher, bookseller, and bibliographer. Address of Librería (book store) de Pedro Vindel: 31 Calle del Prado, Madrid (about a block from Madrid's Palace Hotel, q.v.). The family of Pedro Vindel maintained the business until about 1970.

Vindel specialized in catalogues and bibliographies, among them a compilation of titles dealing with fencing, bullfighting, and hunting (Madrid, c. 1897); a catalogue of the various contemporary editions of Goya's work, with dates and prices (Madrid, 1928); and two books that Hemingway owned: *Estampas de toros: Reproducción y descripción de las más importantes publicadas en los siglos XVIII y XIX relativas a la fiesta nacional* (a catalogue containing reproductions and descriptions of important taurine paintings of the eighteenth and nineteenth centuries; Madrid, 1931); and the taurine bibliography compiled by Díaz Arquer (q.v.).[769]

> The narrator correctly identifies Pedro Vindel as the publisher of *Libros y folletos de toros*, by Graciano Díaz Arquer (487).

Virgin Spain. Subtitle: *Scenes from the Spiritual Drama of a Great People* (New York: Boni & Liveright, 1926; rev. ed., 1942). Popular book about Spain by Waldo Frank (q.v.).

Frank's book is wide-ranging, historically oriented, well-informed, and carefully researched. In his acknowledgments, Frank thanks prominent Spanish intellectuals such as the philosopher Ortega y Gasset, the Nobel Laureate Juan Ramón Jiménez, the novelist Pío Baroja, and Professor Federico de Onís, the head of the Department of Spanish Literature at Columbia University, who advised him and then read the book in proof. In spite of its intellectual credentials, however, the book's conception and style are rather romantic. Frank writes that "What I have attempted might be called a Symphonic History."

Virgin Spain is divided into three sections. The first part contains six chapters that canvass Spain geographically. Part two, subtitled "The Tragedy of Spain," discusses the Catholic Kings; the "Saint and Sinner" (with chapters on Judah Ibn Gbirol, Loyola, the Lazarillo de Tormes, and Velázquez, among others); the hero (don Quijote); and God (with chapters on the bullfight, on "Man and Woman," and on Madrid). Part three, subtitled "Beyond Spain," discusses marginal or disaffected populations.

Frank's book is studded with names and titles. Its frequent references to Spain's history and literature, and especially the pervasive presence of *Don Quijote*, underscore the narrower scope of Hemingway's *Death in the Afternoon* and suggest why Hemingway feared an unfavorable comparison. *Virgin Spain* had sold well and had been much praised by the critics just six years before the publication of *Death in the Afternoon*. In most of his nonfiction, Hemingway writes with one eye on the competition and another on the critics. In *Death in the Afternoon*, he clearly has his eye on Frank. *See also* Authors; Critics.

In spite of Frank's penchant for sentence fragments, dramatic punctuation, long descriptions, and impressionistic similes, his prose is not as consistently unpalatable as Hemingway suggests. But silly patches do appear: "The sky of Spain is high. It is above earth very high. It is above Spain very high. It is separate from Spain . . . It is a clear white sky. Sunlight is white in it. And the clouds are white" (*Virgin Spain*, 7)—a passage that contrasts unfavorably with Hemingway's phrase, "The high blue windless sky" of Idaho. Such lapses may have resulted from Frank's haste in getting his work into print: according to Robert W. Lewis, "Frank's book was published shortly after his first visit to Spain, whereas Hemingway had been visiting Spain for nine years and laboring on his book for seven."[770] *Death in the Afternoon* is, obviously, a carefully crafted production. *See also S 4 N.*

> The narrator resents the popularity of *Virgin Spain* and condemns author's style and ignorance (53, *h:* 436, s.v. *Estoque*).

Virgins. The narrator mentions various virgins whose feast days are associated with bullfighting (90, *h:* 478, 513, 514). *See also* Pilar, Virgen del Pilar; Roman Catholic; Soledad; Women and Girls.

Vistahermosa. The three bull-breeding Counts of Vistahermosa were a father and two sons. Pedro Luis de Ulloa y Calis, the first Count of Vistahermosa (1697–1776) established the herd in Seville, with stock he acquired from the Rivas brothers in the 1750s. His two sons were Benito, the second Count of Vistahermosa (d. 1800); and Pedro Luis, the third Count of Vistahermosa (d. 1821). Benito presented bulls to be fought in Madrid on 2 August 1790; the Vistahermosa *antigüedad* (q.v.) dates back to that corrida.

When Pedro Luis died, his sister Luisa became the Countess of Vistahermosa, inherited the breed but not the rights to the brand, colors, and *antigüedad*, or seniority. She sold the herd to various breeders (*see*, for example, Murube; Saavedra). She died in 1831, and her cousin, Juan José Ulloa, became the Count of Vistahermosa. By this time, however, the pure Vistahermosa herds had been dispersed and the Vistahermosa brand had disappeared. (A curious aside: the Domecq herds, although they are descended from Cabreras and Vázquez, happen to have the same *antigüedad* as the Vistahermosa.)

Vera identifies the qualities of bravery (fearlessness, disdain of pain, courage, eagerness to charge) and nobility (honesty, giving a straightforward charge, following the muleta) as the Vistahermosa bulls' outstanding characteristics.[771] In the 1920s and indeed for the rest of the twentieth century, the Vistahermosa has been highly valued, so much so that most important breeds of *toros de lidia* boast Vistahermosa blood. For herds in which the Vistahermosa strain predominates, *see* Concha y Sierra, doña Concepción de la; Corte, Conde de la; Ibarra, Eduardo; Lesaca; Murube; Santa Coloma, Conde de; and Veragua, Duke of, all in this volume; see also Domecq in *DS*. Writing in 1925, Bagüés claimed that for the past fifty years, the best bulls were those produced by the ranches Saltillo, Murube, and Ibarra. These three types of bulls, although clearly defined and distinct from each other, all carry Vistahermosa blood.[772] In the later years of the twentieth century, with improved roads and methods of transport, crossbreeding has increasingly blurred the distinctions between the different strains, such as those derived from the herds of Cabrera and Vázquez. See the essay on "Bulls and Bull Breeding," in the introduction to this volume.

The narrator praises the Vistahermosa strain (129–30; see also 132).

Von Behr. *See* Behr, General von.

V. R. *See* Pfeiffer, Virginia Ruth.

– W –

W. A. *See* Bird, William Augustus, IV.

Waiter. Although waiters appear frequently in Hemingway's fiction and often represent a moral position, they appear less often and less prominently in *Death in the Afternoon*. *See also* Drinks.

Waiters hurry by (57, 64), take orders for food (93), and provide bullfight tickets (*h:* 418, s.v. *Billetes*).

Weather. The narrator remarks upon Spain's extreme weather (47–50), including the wind (90, 252, *h:* 370, *h:* 411, s.v. *Aire*; 491, s.v. *Viento*) and the heat (38, 40, 44, 47–50, 220). He recalls the wind and especially the heat he experienced in the United States, Europe, and Africa (38, 44, 138, 140; see also 263), and remarks that tension (90–91) and pain (80–81) also cause a bullfighter to sweat. *See also* Weather in *DS*.

W. G. *See* Smith, William Benjamin.

White, the Reverend Gilbert. English clergyman and naturalist, 1720–93.

Educated in Oriel College, Oxford, White spent most of his life as curate of his native village of Selborne, Hampshire, refusing appointments that would require him to live elsewhere. He wrote *Calendar of Flora and the Garden* (1765) and *Natural History and Antiquities of Selborne* (1789, owned by Hemingway), which "immediately met with the acclaim of major naturalists, who were impressed by White's methodical approach and keen sense of observation. . . . [It is the] first work on natural history to attain the status of an English classic."[773]

Natural History of Selborne is interestingly constructed: it is epistolary, consisting of forty-four letters addressed to Thomas Pennant, Esq., a zoologist of North Wales. The first nine letters, apparently composed post facto to serve as an introduction to the book, offer a general description of Selborne, its geography, soil, rock formations, trees, wells, rainfall, and population. They are undated. The next thirty letters, dated from 4 August 1767 to 30 November 1780, were actually sent to Pennant. They reveal that the two men exchanged information, anecdotes, and scholarly references, and sent each other specimens, books, drawings, and manuscripts. The last four letters, never sent, were added "to complete the work when Gilbert White had decided on publication." One of White's annotators reports that Pennant incorporated much of White's material into his own field notes without acknowledgment.[774]

Like *Death in the Afternoon*, the letters are conversational, frequently using the pronouns *I* and *you*. They contain very little biographical detail, but White is revealed indirectly by the style, organization, variety, and cautiousness of his long, detailed reports about the phenomena he observed. Like Hemingway, White extends his regional and temporal boundaries by citing the books, pamphlets, neighbors, friends, and relations he has consulted, though he is more careful than Hemingway in distinguishing between his own observations and those of others. Like Hemingway, White frequently provides lists and uses foreign languages (Latin and Greek). Again like Hemingway, White does not shy away from death, though he discusses it only in terms of animals, not humans. In an incident similar to Hemingway's careful examination of a decaying dog,[775] White examined and measured a dead female moose even though "it was in so putrid a state that the stench was hardly supportable" (120–21).

Although White occasionally mentions "Providence" (e.g., "Providence has been so indulgent to us as to allow of but one venomous reptile of the serpent kind in these kingdoms" [71]), these references are formulaic and the author returns immediately to factual description. Portz remarks that "Gilbert White is usually given credit for having been the first great English field naturalist, but his *Natural History of Selborne* has about it an eighteenth-century piety and benevolence, a tranquility and sententiousness which Hemingway would have found exasperatingly credulous" (30); I find the "piety and benevolence" to be remarkably infrequent in a book written by a churchman.

Birds are mentioned in almost every letter, and some letters are completely ornithological. The hoopoes to which Hemingway refers appear in Letter XI: "The most unusual birds I ever observed in these parts were a pair of *hoopoes* (*upupa*), which came several years ago in the summer, and frequented an ornamented piece of ground, which joins to my garden, for some weeks. They used to march about in a stately manner, feeding in the walks, many times in the day; and seemed disposed to breed in my outlet; but were frighted and persecuted by idle boys, who would never let them be at rest" (Gilbert White, 40–41). Hemingway seems to have had a lifelong interest in the hoopoe. When he returned to Spain in 1953, he "look[ed] along the road all morning for a bird he particularly associated with Spain, the hoopoe bird with its long curved bill and big crest. 'They're rare,' he said. 'But they weren't extinct during the war here.' " On a visit to the Prado, "Ernest found a hoopoe bird in Hieronymus Bosch's *Garden of Eden* painting. No discovery in Madrid pleased him more."[776]

The *Natural History* has gone through many editions, most of them heavily footnoted and lavishly illustrated. Two additional books by White, *A Naturalist's Calendar* (1795) and his *Journals* (1931), were published posthumously. The Selborne Society, dedicated to the preservation of the area's wildlife, was founded in 1885 in White's memory. *See also* Humanism, Naturalism.

> The narrator reports that White "has written most interestingly of the Hoopoe on its occasional and not at all common visits to Selborne," where White spent most of his happy, uneventful life (133).

Whitman, Walt. American editor and poet, 1819–92; his major works are *Leaves of Grass* (1855, 1856, 1892), *Drum Taps*, and *Sequel to Drum-Taps* (1865 and 1866).

Scholes and Comley remark that Hemingway's sensitivity to gender issues leads him to take "Whitman's [homosexuality] for granted at a time when many would have denied it fiercely" (121). *See also* Authors; Homosexuals.

> The narrator attacks Whitman for his homosexuality and sentimentality (205).

Whittier, John Greenleaf. American poet, reformer, and abolitionist, 1807–92.

Whittier was apprenticed to a cobbler when one of his poems was accepted for publication by William Lloyd Garrison, an abolitionist who became his friend. Under Garrison's influence, Whittier became a fervent anti-slavery propagandist. He was a delegate to the National Anti-Slavery Convention in Philadelphia and served one term in the Massachusetts legislature.

Garrison also encouraged Whittier to study, teach, and write. Whittier's early poetry was unsuccessful, but he wrote with more authority in his middle age and published many volumes of popular poetry, much of which documented his vision of the American past. He was a regional writer with a strong didactic and moral streak: his most famous work, *Snow Bound* (1866, q.v.) depicts his family and friends at Haverhill, Massachusetts, as uniformly generous, kind, cheerful, and good.

Whittier was a founding member of the *Atlantic Monthly* and an important literary figure of his time. His seventieth and eightieth birthdays were occasions for nationwide homage.

> When the Old Lady (q.v.) asks to be amused, the narrator offers her the bleak "Natural History of the Dead" (q.v.), a stark contrast to Whittier's *Snow Bound* (133, 144).

Whores. *See* Women and Girls.

Wilde, Oscar. Irish poet, dramatist, and novelist, 1854–1900; author of *The Portrait of Dorian Gray* (1891); his best-known plays are *Lady Windermere's Fan* (1892) and *The Importance of Being Earnest* (1895). Wilde's homosexuality led to a trial and imprisonment, a painful experience that resulted in the posthumously published *De Profundis* (1905). *See also* Homosexuals.

> As part of his diatribe against homosexuals, the narrator attacks Wilde (205).

Wind. *See* Weather.

Wine. *See* Drinks.

Wives. *See* Women and Girls.

Women and Girls. Muriel Feiner's book, *La mujer en el mundo del toro*, offers a well-documented and thorough historical survey of women in bullfighting, as performers, bull breeders, wives and mothers of bullfighters, and spectators. Unfortunately, Feiner's book has not yet been translated into English. Adrian Shubert offers briefer but accurate reports on the appeal of women bullfighters and the presence of aficionadas in the stands: see his *Death and Money in the Afternoon: A History of the Spanish Bullfight* (96–114). The narrator of *Death in the Afternoon*, although he mentions women quite often, does not recognize their participation in or contribution to the bullfight. In *Death in the Afternoon*, nameless women weaken bullfighters by distracting them from the task at hand, creating financial pressures, or infecting them with disease. *See also* Proverbs; Virgins, in this volume; and Women and Girls in *DS*.

> The narrator uses various classifications and languages when discussing women: daughter (104), *femmes* (71), girls (40–42), models (71), *mujeres* (103, *h:* 488, s.v. *Uretritis*), sisters (71), wives (103–104, 228, 257, *h:* 469, s.v. *Qué lástima!*), and whores (41, 64, 92, 271, 273, *h:* 439, s.v. *Gachís*, and, especially, 469, s.v. *Puta* and *Qué lástima!*). He also defines women, bulls, and men by hair color (*h:* 477, s.v. *Rubios*). Women betray men (103, 277), are blown up (135–36), and attend bullfights (1, 4–5, 33–34,

h: 497–501). They are clearly present, although not mentioned, in the first two pages of a long discussion about the promiscuity of bullfighters which leads to syphilis (101–105). They are associated with courage (222). Whore speaks: 273.

Woolf, Virginia. English novelist, essayist and critic, 1882–1941; author of *Mrs. Dalloway* (1925), *Orlando* (1928), and *The Waves* (1931). Her long essay, "A Room of Her Own," attacks the male establishment for excluding women from education and literary production. In 1926 or early 1927, Hemingway borrowed Virginia Woolf's *The Common Reader* from Sylvia Beach's bookstore, Shakespeare & Company.[777]

Virginia Woolf's remarks on Hemingway's work were thoroughly negative: she wrote that "nothing new is revealed" in *The Sun Also Rises*, and that his writing contains "something faked . . . which turns bad and gives an unpleasant feeling . . . the thing that is faked is character." Of *Men Without Women*, she offers a poisoned compliment: the collection contains "many stories which, if life were longer, one would wish to read again. Most of them are so competent, so efficient, and so bare of superfluity that one wonders why they do not make a deeper dent in the mind than they do." In her opinion, the stories offer a "superfluity of dialogue" and a "lack of proportion," and she finds that "compared with his novel his stories are a little dry and sterile." She concludes that "his talent has contracted rather than expanded" and, using his own bullfighting metaphor, accuses him of fakery: "Mr Hemingway leans against the flanks of that particular bull after the horns have passed."

Hemingway found Woolf's review "damned irritating" and suggested that it was inspired by an older writer's jealousy of a younger talent: the "Bloomsbury people who are all over 40 . . . dislike what they consider the intrusion of anybody much under 40 into their business." Woolf, who was then forty-five years old, had complained that Hemingway "is not modern . . . is not an advanced writer . . . he is modern in manner but not in vision." Responding to the publisher's blurb that "the softening feminine influence is absent," she wrote that "any emphasis laid upon sex is dangerous. . . . The greatest writers lay no stress upon sex one way or the other." Woolf bemoans contemporary authors' "display of self-conscious virility" and the fact that "Mr. Hemingway, but much less violently, follows suit."[778]

The narrator states that Virginia Woolf, being a feminist, would assume, albeit incorrectly, that cows are more intelligent than bulls (106).

Wounded Soldier. A character in the story "A Natural History of the Dead" (q.v.).

The mortally wounded soldier has been treated "skillfully" by the doctor, assumed to be dead, and deposited in a nearby cave that serves as a mortuary. The stretcher-bearers (q.v.) alert the doctor that the soldier is still alive, but the doctor, realizing that he cannot help him further, refuses to have him moved; he also refuses to have him killed. The wounded man dies while the doctor and the lieutenant (q.v.) argue about him (141–44). *See also* the entry for Doctors.

Wounds. Wounds, injuries, and gorings (*cornadas*) are discussed at length (238–39, 255–57). The narrator feels that the wounds the bullfighter suffers can produce cowardice and thus wreck his career (76, 89–90, 166–67), although the cowardice can be temporary and a wound may occasionally increase courage (76, 222). Bullfighters are sometimes injured in the arm pit (450) and frequently in the buttocks, abdomen, or thighs (424, 461, 475). These wounds cause great pain (9, 79–82, 195–96, 219–20), and gangrene may set in (255, 259, 475). *Death in the Afternoon* was written before penicillin became available (*see* Serra, Dr. Paco). *See also* under individual bullfighters' names.

Writers, Writing. *See* entries for Authors, in this volume and in *DS*.

– X –

X. Y. Carlos Baker identifies X. Y. as Robert (Bob) Menzies McAlmon (1896–1956). McAlmon, the tenth and last child of a Presbyterian minister, grew up in Kansas and South Dakota and was educated at the University of Minnesota and the University of Southern California. He married Winifred Bryher, a poet and novelist and the daughter of the wealthy Sir John Ellerman. They came to Europe in the early 1920s, separated in 1926, and divorced in 1927.[779]

Between 1922 and 1929, McAlmon's publishing house, Contact

Editions, published several important writers of the period, including Hemingway's first book, *Three Stories and Ten Poems*. He was a writer himself, author of *Village: As It Happened through a Fifteen Year Period* (1925, reissued 1990), *A Hasty Bunch* (short stories, 1922; reissued 1977), *Not Alone Lost* (poems, 1937), and *Being Geniuses Together* (a memoir of the 1920s, 1938; reissued 1968). McAlmon was bisexual, a heavy drinker, and a generous man.

McAlmon accompanied Hemingway on his first trip to the bullfights in the spring of 1923, a trip for which he "was footing all the bills and buying all the Scotch." His report of that trip mentions Hemingway's "bullfight book," and repeats many of the details Hemingway mentions, such as the drinking and the "screeching intake of breath." McAlmon writes:

> We had a bottle of whisky with us, with the understanding that if shocked we would gulp down a quantity to calm ourselves. My reactions to the bullfight were not at all what one had anticipated. . . .
>
> The first bull charged into the ring with tremendous violence, and did not refuse a charge. When the horses were brought in the bull charged head-on and lifted the horse over its head. The horns did not penetrate.
>
> Instead of a shock of disgust I rose in my seat and let out a yell. . . . Later, however, when one of the horses was galloping in hysteria about the ring, treading on its own entrails, I decidedly didn't like it and looked away. . . .
>
> I resented the crowd's brutality. . . . The crowd was taking no chances. The bull was . . . a magnificent animal, a snorting engine of black velocity and force. The matadors moved beautifully and did their dance well, and played seriously with death. The horses I decided to overlook. . . . The wonderful matadors and their fights are rare and I recall too many degrading exhibitions.[780]

McAlmon's memoirs, written several years after the fact, are often inaccurate—he misdates his and Hemingway's first bullfight, for example—but they indicate that McAlmon saw other bullfights, and that he particularly liked *rejoneo*: "It has always been the Portuguese bullfight which I prefer, for the bull is properly killed from on horseback, and the horse is a magnificent Arabian mare or stallion, and beautifully trained and never injured by the bull without disgrace to the 'rejoneador' or rider. In this there is breathless speed and terrifying beauty of power and velocity. It is not so intricate or so daring an art as Spanish bullfighting, but it has more throbbing and breathtaking excitement, for me, generally."[781]

Apparently recognizing himself as X. Y., McAlmon expands upon Hemingway's remark that McAlmon "Doubted genuineness of my enthusiasm for bullfights" (*DIA, h:* 496). He wrote that Hemingway's admiration for bullfighting derives not from the art itself but "from Gertrude Stein's praise of [the bullfights], as well as from his belief in the value of self-hardening . . . his bullfight book takes a belligerent attitude defending his right to love bullfighting," which suggests that ulterior motives lead Hemingway to pretend admiration.[782]

In 1923 when he and Hemingway saw their first bullfight, McAlmon was twenty-seven years old, as the sketch reports, and indulged in all the activities attributed to X. Y.

> Hemingway reports disdainfully that because X. Y. did not like bullfighting himself, he could not believe that any one else could (*h:* 496).

– Y –

Yale, Yale in China. The institution that began as the Collegiate School of Connecticut in 1701 became Yale College in 1716 and Yale University in 1887. Since 1716 it has been located at New Haven, Connecticut. Established as an all-male, religiously oriented institution, the school was shaped by profoundly Christian theologians like Ezra Stiles (1727–95; president of Yale 1778–95) and Timothy Dwight (1752–1817; president of Yale, 1795–1817).

Yale in China. Several members of the Yale Class of 1898, all active members of the Yale Christian Association (commonly called Dwight Hall), organized the Yale Mission in China. It took a few years of meetings and speaking tours, but by 1902 the group had written a charter, convinced the university to give its backing, and raised sufficient funds, mostly from like-minded faculty and alumni, to finance their first trip to China. The Christian ideals that motivated the young men reflected a widespread Victorian phenomenon, a vigorous Christian zeal that expressed itself in the establishment of institutions like the YMCA (q.v.) and the Salvation Army (mocked in *The Torrents of Spring*), and in the activism of local churches which supported charitable works at home and sent missionaries abroad. That spirit was strong in Oak Park while Hemingway was growing up, and he objected to it in much of his writing.

In spite of its religious association and missionary connections, the primary purpose of the Yale Mission in China was to establish an educational institution, an oriental outpost of Yale University. To reflect this aim, the name was changed to Yale in China and, later, to Yali, a name that "derived from Yale's interest and from the two Chinese words meaning 'elegant propriety'." Yali tried to respect the local culture: the faculty members spent their first two years in China studying Chinese language and culture, the school's language of instruction was Chinese, Chinese as well as Christian holidays were celebrated, and local instructors were hired to teach Chinese language, literature, and history. In spite of these attempts to fit into the local environment, Yali's negotiations with Changsha's administrators were difficult, as Hunan Province was strongly anti-foreign. Eventually, however, land was acquired, buildings were constructed, and students were enrolled.

Before the envisioned college could open, however, students had to be prepared for university work. The program's first venture, therefore, was a small, private nondenominational middle or preparatory school for boys, with a strong emphasis on academic subjects, including science, mathematics, and Chinese and English language and history. The middle school opened in November 1906. In 1914, the first college class began work, "to interpret Yale traditions and ideals to the Orient." A medical department, teaching hospital, and school of nursing were added during the next decade.

The growth of nationalism, communism, anti-Western and anti-Christian forces resulted in the closing of Yali and other Western-backed institutions, most of them mission-affiliated, late in 1926. The students dispersed, and most of the staff returned to their home countries. By the spring of 1928, when the first revolutionary fervor had subsided and the institutions were invited to reopen their doors, they had lost both faculty and students. They reorganized, jointly forming the Hua Chung University. Because of the strength of its medical facilities and faculty, Yale in China was put in charge of the Faculty of Science. The middle school also remained in its Changsha campus.

As early as 1931, the unrest that preceded the Sino-Japanese war began to affect Yale in China. Yali withstood drills, sporadic attacks, several evacuations and, finally, the resettlement of the middle school to a new campus. Much of the Changsha campus was destroyed by bombing and fires during the war, but Yale in China, still strongly supported by Yale University, Yale alumni, and associated missionary and Chinese groups, rebuilt, restaffed, and reopened Yali in 1946. But the program's days were numbered: communism marginalized and finally paralyzed Yali. The government took over the Changsha campus in 1951, renaming it the Hunan Private Liberation Middle School. By 1954 Hua Chung University had become Central China Normal College. Soon after, hoping to maintain its Chinese connections, Yale in China decided to support the New Asia College in Hong Kong.[783]

Several of Hemingway's friends, including Archibald MacLeish, Gerald Murphy, and Donald Ogden Stewart (qq.v.), were Yale educated, but none served as a "bachelor," a volunteer teacher in China, supported by his classmates during his stint abroad. Hemingway's grandparents, uncles, and parents, committed Christians all, were active in church affairs. His uncle Willoughby Hemingway was a medical missionary in Shansi Province, China. For other societies Hemingway mocks, *see* Christian Endeavor; Skull and Bones; and YMCA.

> The narrator mocks puritanical education that produces chaste young men committed to converting and educating others but ill-prepared to deal with their own sexuality (101–102; see also 103).

YMCA. The Young Men's Christian Association was established in England in 1844 to promote social and religious work among young Christian men who, drawn away from their towns and villages to the opportunities presented by urban centers, might be tempted to go astray. The YMCA grew quickly and soon had branches around the world. The U.S. movement was begun in 1851.

The YMCA typically constructs or acquires large buildings with gymnasiums, reading rooms, libraries, and large halls in which the association offers church services, lectures, concerts, and social and sports events. It offers young men inexpensive food and lodging as well as contacts with like-minded business, clerical, and political leaders who might help them advance professionally. It is the model for the Young Women's Christian Association (YWCA) and the Young Men's Hebrew Association (YMHA).

During World War I, American branches of the YMCA raised money to support the war effort, but the soldiers were often alienated by the organization's focus on "matters of faith and conduct" and its high-minded, "scrub-faced proselytizing" by "churchy" men who spoke from the safety of their civilian positions. Reynolds writes that at the end of the war, the YMCA was in possession of more than "one hundred million undistributed dollars . . . had begun to smell a little tainted . . . [and] had lost credibility."[784]

Hemingway's family were very much in favor of the YMCA. Ernest's paternal grandfather, Anson Tyler Hemingway, a religious man, founded the Chicago YMCA and served as its general secretary for ten years before moving to Oak Park. In 1920, Ernest joined both the Oak Park and the Toronto YMCAs, perhaps to please his father, who had "urged him to associate with YMCA men, strong Christians all." In later years, however, Hemingway mocked the institution: he "often used it as a shorthand way of demeaning trendy salvationists."[785] *See also* Christian Endeavor; Skull and Bones; Yale.

The narrator connects the YMCA with "clean living" (103).

– Z –

Zaragossa. Usually spelled Zaragoza, sometimes Saragossa, capital of the province of Zaragoza (Aragón). Zaragoza's week-long October fiesta, in honor of Pilar (q.v.) is still, as it was in Hemingway's day, "the last important feria of the season" (*DIA*, 514). On 11 October 1926, Hemingway and Archibald MacLeish took the late night train from Paris, arriving in Zaragoza late on the 12th, which is the *Día de la raza*, or Columbus Day, as well as Pilar's feast day—the first official day of the fiesta.[786]

The city offered decorated streets and storefronts, agricultural and livestock exhibits, daily concerts and theatrical performances, parades featuring local beauty queens and their entourages as well as giants and dwarves (papier-maché figures inhabited by people who make them walk and dance), *jota* concerts and a *jota* contest (the *jota* is a popular regional dance; the word also denotes the music and the lyrics of the dance music), and the requisite bullfights and religious processions. The fiesta's schedule for 1926:

Monday, 11 October: Ringing of the church bells, masses, concerts, theater performances, parades, banquets, and the arrival of special trains from Madrid and Barcelona.

Tuesday, 12 October (Pilar's feast day): Marching bands, parades, masses, strolling folk musicians (*chistularis*); at 4:00 P.M., a religious procession featuring the city's civil and religious potentates, and in the evening, a concert which included a *jota* singer known as "la Sardana de las Monjas."

Wednesday, 13 October: Masses, processions, parades of giants and dwarves, banquets, display of hot air balloons, ceremonies honoring teachers and pupils at various schools (the first day of the Fiesta del Maestro), bicycle races, and the fiesta's first bullfight, in which Antonio Márquez, Marcial Lalanda, Nicanor Villalta, and Cayetano Ordóñez (Niño de la Palma) fought eight Concha y Sierra bulls. At six in the evening, another great religious procession, the colorful *gran Rosario del Pilar*, accompanied by choirs and lit by lamps and candles; and at 10:00 P.M., two concerts.

Thursday, 14 October: Masses, the usual street and musical festivities; the second day of the Fiesta del Maestro, with ceremonies memorializing deceased teachers; the opening concert of the annual Fiesta de la Jota (featuring the winners of previous *jota* contests); and the second bullfight, featuring Márquez, Lalanda, Villalta, and Niño de la Palma, with six bulls of Encinas and two of Díaz. In the evening, fireworks and two concerts.

Friday, 15 October: Marching bands and performances by *chistularis*; parades of giants, dwarves, and beauty queens; a public lecture on agriculture (the newspaper announced that women were allowed to attend); displays of hot air balloons; the second *jota* concert, again at the Teatro Principal; and the third bullfight, featuring Márquez, Villalta, and Niño de la Palma, with six Miura bulls. Fireworks and a concert at 7:00 P.M.; another concert at 10:00.

Saturday, 16 October: Street music, sailing and swimming contests followed by prize-giving ceremonies and a concert, horse races, displays of hot air balloons, a second lecture on agriculture, a series of five boxing matches, an aviation display featuring a parachutist, the regional *jota* contest at 5:30 P.M. (see below), and fireworks at seven in the evening.

Sunday, 17 October: Parades of giants, dwarves, and beauty queens; bicycle and horse races; street musicians, a soccer match, and the fourth and last bullfight of the fiesta, featuring Márquez, Lalanda, and Villalta, with six Carmen de Federico bulls (Murube). At 10:00 P.M., a concert.

Monday, 18 October: The fiesta wound down with two concerts, a final parade of the giants and dwarves, and evening fireworks.[787]

There was another bullfight on Sunday, 24 October (one *matador de toros*, Morenito de Zaragoza; and four *novilleros*),[788] but by then Hemingway was back in Paris, lonely for Hadley, the wife he was leaving, and Pauline, the wife he was soon to acquire.

The Annual Jota Contest. Like other Aragonese cities, Zaragoza hosted an annual *jota* contest with prizes going to the best *jota* singers (duos and soloists) and dancing couples, both adults and children ("the wonderful boy and girl pairs," *DIA*, 272). More than a thousand *pesetas* were distributed in prizes, and each year's winners performed in subsequent *fiestas de jota*. The contest, like the two sold-out performances which preceded it, was held at the Teatro Principal on Saturday afternoon, 16 October. Like the bullfights, religious processions, and other major events of the fiesta, the *jota* festival was publicized and reviewed in the local papers.[789] Today's *jota* concerts and competition, basically unchanged from when Hemingway saw them, are held in the same theater, whose "old red plush" decor (*DIA*, 272) has been carefully preserved over its more than two hundred years of existence.[790]

The Airplane and the Parachute Jumper: A Novelty. The sports arena variously called Campo del Iberia or the Campo de Torrero was the site for soccer games, bicycle races, boxing matches, and other sports events. On 16 October 1926, for the first time, it presented demonstration fly-overs of a Junker F. 13, an aircraft belonging to the Compañía Unión Aérea Española, which became Iberia, Spain's national airline. The six-seater German-built Junker and its crew of two pilots and a mechanic arrived Thursday afternoon; the crew gave newspapers interviews and invited the public, for whom flying was a great novelty, to take panoramic flights on Friday afternoon, at the considerable cost of twenty-five *pesetas* per person.

The stunt parachutist Hemingway mentions was Sr. Fernández Moreno, who floated down to the spectators from a height of a thousand meters: "Se vió perfectamente al temerario paracaidista lanzarse al campo, descender vertiginosamente, en medio de la mayor ansiedad, mientras el paracaídas se desplegaba y luego más reposado ir a caer en el velódromo del Iberia con toda felicidad" (The daring parachutist could be seen clearly as he plummeted dizzyingly, much to the public's anxiety, while the parachute slowly unfolded, enabling him to finish his descent more sedately and to land safely in the bicycle racing track of the Iberia sports field).[791] Urban sprawl has since overtaken the Campo del Iberia.

For a history of the city's bullring, see Zaragoza in *DS*. For more detail on Hemingway's experiences in Zaragoza's *fiesta del Pilar*, October 1926, *see* MacLeish, Archibald.

The narrator would have liked to provide more details about his experiences in Zaragoza (272; *see also* 119).

Zaragoza. Hemingway's account of this bull's adventures repeats Carralero and Borge's report in all details (*Toros célebres*, 321). *See also* Lesireas.

The narrator relates Zaragoza's exploits (110–11).

Zig Zag. Subtitle: *Tragicomedia taurina*. Published from May 1923 until November 1924, in Madrid.

Zig Zag occasionally featured pictures of girls in provocative poses (both in the magazine and on the cover), as well as cartoons and pictures of bulls, bullfighters, and bullfighters' families. It offered jokes, riddles, letters from readers, editorials, poems, anecdotes, gossip, and occasional theater reviews in addition to reports on bullfights, taurine art, and taurine history. It also carried many advertisements (taurine tailors, restaurants, photographers, and so on). The Biblioteca Nacional, Madrid, has the complete run, 1923–24.[792]

The narrative describes *Zig Zag* as a generally reliable bullfight magazine, no longer published in 1931 (*h:* 475, s.v. *Revistas*).

Zocato. Professional nickname of Eduardo Borrego Vega, Spanish banderillero, 1878–1932.

Zocato worked for his wife's brother, the torero Manuel Jiménez (Chicuelo). When this brother-in-law died, the childless Zocato dedicated himself to his niece and nephew. The boy, who had the same name and nickname as his father, became a famous bullfighter, and Zocato is remembered as his trainer and manager.[793] *See* Jiminiz (*sic*), Manuel; "A Lack of Passion."

The narrator describes Zocato as a heavy drinker (273) and remarks correctly that Zocato trained his nephew, Chicuelo (74).

Zurito. Professional nickname of the Haba family. The father was Manuel de la Haba Bejarano, 1868–1936, whom many critics consider the best picador of his time. Manuel worked in the *cuadrilla* of Rafael Guerra (Guerrita, q.v.) from 1893 until Guerra's retirement in 1899, after which he worked for another star, Rafael González (Machaquito, q.v.), from 1902 to 1912. His three sons, all known as Zurito, became bullfighters: Antonio de la Haba (q.v.) was a matador, and José (1899–1977) and Francisco (1905–49) were picadors. Antonio's three sons were also bullfighters: Gabriel de la Haba Vargas was a *matador de toros* and his brothers Antonio and Manuel were banderilleros—three generations of Zuritos, spanning most of the twentieth century.[794]

The narrator describes Zurito as an excellent picador (254; photograph, *h:* 286–87) and mentions the two sons who practiced the same trade, but less successfully (258).

Notes

In the interest of saving space, short references are used in this notes section. Complete bibliographical details are provided in the list of Works Cited. In the notes as in the text, references to entries in this volume are indicated by q.v. or the italicized *see* or *see also*. References to entries in the companion volume, *Hemingway's* The Dangerous Summer: *The Complete Annotations*, are presented in roman type (see Barcelona, in *DS*; see also Ostos, Julio in *DS*). The abbreviation JFK stands for the Ernest Hemingway Collection, which is housed at the John F. Kennedy Library, Columbia Point, Boston, Massachusetts.

Preface

1. Fitzgerald to John Peale Bishop, August 1925; in Bruccoli, ed., *F. Scott Fitzgerald: A Life in Letters*, 126.

User's Guide

1. To readers who find Spanish names confusing, I would like to remark that this is still the simplest way of finding an individual bullfighter in a reference work. In this respect, the Cossío encyclopedia, *Los toros*, is the easiest for beginners to use: it alphabetizes the entries first according to the bullfighter's patronymic and then according to his first name, relying on the mother's name only when several bullfighters have the same patronymic and first name. But Ventura Bagüés (don Ventura) requires the users of his excellent *Historia de los matadores de toros* to know more than the alphabet or the occasional mother: he presents the bullfighters chronologically, so that one must know their birth dates. And in his index, he lists many of them only by nickname (no indication at all of family names), sometimes offering only initials or family relationship to distinguish between individuals who share the same nickname: e.g., Chicuelo (*abuelo*, grandfather), Chicuelo (*padre*, father), Chicuelo (*nieto*, grandson). The indispensable *Toros y toreros en . . .* uses yet another system: it arranges its annual reviews of individual bullfighters accord-

ing to their seniority, with separate listings for *matadores de alternativa* and *novilleros*, so that one must know not only the rank of a particular bullfighter in any particular year, but the day and month he achieved that rank. Yet other reference books, especially those dealing with bull breeders, arrange their entries by geographical area, so that the seeker cannot find what she is seeking unless she already knows where it is.

Let us be grateful for Spanish patronymics, alphabetically arranged.

2. In Spain and France, Hemingway regularly read bullfighting journals, papers, and books. He also collected a considerable taurine library. For further detail on his generally unacknowledged sources, *see* the entry for Díaz Arquer.

Introduction

1. The Ernest Hemingway Collection, John F. Kennedy Library, Item 39, un-numbered page 3; the Hemingway Collection is cited hereafter as JFK. Hemingway's refrain, "in the old days," refers to the mid-1920s, *his* old days, when he first became enamored of the bullfight.

2. This golden age, defined by the collaborative rivalry between Joselito and Belmonte, began with their first joint performances, in 1914, and ended with Joselito's death on 16 May 1920.

3. The two most glaring misjudgments in *Death in the Afternoon*, the attacks on Manolo Bienvenida and Domingo Ortega, stem from the same cause. In 1931, Hemingway's last season before the publication of *Death in the Afternoon*, these two fighters were poised to take the bullfight beyond the norms Hemingway was committed to. For Hemingway, the future is bleak territory, and he refuses to speak well of it and its harbingers—hence his rejection of the emergent "new Messiahs."

4. Not to be outdone by Málaga and Madrid (which modified and adopted the Málaga code in 1852), Seville issued its own code in 1858. These early codes had limited, local authority; different rules obtained in different bullrings. The 1917 *Reglamento* was the first to apply nationwide, but it was restricted to first-class plazas. Needless to say, the national *Reglamento* is the product of much negotiation and political accommodation. Attempting to strengthen central government and national unity, the 1923 *Reglamento* expanded its jurisdiction to all plazas. But that very clause caused it to be rejected. The revised edition, issued early in 1924, returned more or less to the 1917 parameters.

This restriction of the code's authority to first-rank plazas was merely a politically motivated compliment to local governments. In fact, the 1917 and 1923 *Reglamentos* carried great authority in all bullrings. For an excellent study of the social, financial and political interests that shaped the taurine code in the twentieth century, see chapter five of Tomás-Ramón Fernández's *Reglamentación de las corridas de toros. Note*: When I speak of the 1923 *Reglamento* I mean its revised form, which went into effect in 1924.

The life spans of the *Reglamentos* reveal their strength: the *Reglamentos* of 1930 and of 1962 each lasted three decades, though royal orders and codicils modified them periodically. To its shame, the politically motivated *Reglamento* of 1992 had to be replaced only four years later, by the *Reglamento* of 1996.

5. Hemingway to Perkins, qtd. in Trogdon, "Hemingway and Scribners," 204.

6. *DIA*, 473, s.v. *Reglamento*; see also Trogdon, "Hemingway and Scribners," 220–21. The 1930 *Reglamento* was the first to be translated into English; the translation, prepared by Anthony Brand, appears in Barnaby Conrad's 1961 *Encyclopedia of Bullfighting*, 257–69.

7. *Artículo* 85 of the 1917 *Reglamento*, *Artículo* 86 of 1923 *Reglamento*, *Artículo* 94 of the 1930 *Reglamento*, *Artículo* 116 of the 1962 *Reglamento*, *Artículo* 82 of the 1992 *Reglamento*, and *Artículo* 80 of 1996 *Reglamento*.

8. Fulton, *Bullfighting*, 4.

9. Unsuccessful specimens of both sexes (*desechos de tienta y cerrado*) are usually killed for meat, although if the animal's deficiency is minor, it might be sold for breeding or for a bullfight. The animal's condition as *desecho de tienta y defectuoso* (discarded and defective) must, however, be publicly announced.

10. *Artículo* 2 of the 1930 *Reglamento* required the bull breeder to provide a signed affidavit stating not only that his *novillos* or *toros* had the requisite weight and age, but that they had never been fought.

11. The full-grown *toro* is also known as a *cuatreño* (four years old) or a *cinqueño* (five years old). See Cossío (1995), "Vocabulario taurino autorizado," I: 343–88, 413; Nieto Manjón, *Diccionario ilustrado de términos taurinos*; and Sánchez de Neira, *El toreo: Gran diccionario taurómaco*.

12. As soon as they are killed, bulls are sent to the bullring's *desolladero* or *abattoir* to be stripped of skin, horns, organs, and fat. The weight of the bones and flesh (*en canal*) is considered a more accurate indication of the bull's age and strength, because extra fat and water can cause younger bulls to weigh in as full-grown *toros*. The minimal flesh-and-bones weight of a fighting bull is 258 kilograms.

13. One of the important innovations of the 1917 *Reglamento* was to prescribe the postmortem examination to settle the question of the animal's age (*Artículo* 19). But see Fernández, who finds a precedent for this ruling in the 1896 *Reglamento* for the plaza of Seville, specifying not only a postmortem examination of the teeth but also a fine for the bull breeder who failed to meet the minimum age requirement (qtd. in Fernández, *Reglamentación de las corridas de toros*, 119, n. 227). *Artículos* 74, 121, and 122 of the 1962 *Reglamento* clarify that the postmortem examination will rely on the dental development to determine the animal's age (for corridas, *novilladas*, and *becerradas*, respectively).

14. Minimum weights are defined in *Artículo* 20 of the 1917 *Reglamento*, *Artículo* 23 of the 1923 *Reglamento*, and Vera's glosses on *Artículos* 26 and 27 of the 1930 *Reglamento*, in his *Reglamento taurino comentado*, 33, 37.

15. *See* the entry for Diano, the long-lived seed bull who died in 1919. He fa-

thered the smaller, more agile bull needed for the new kind of *toreo* defined by José Gómez Ortega (Joselito) and Juan Belmonte.

16. Tomás Orts Ramos (Uno al Sesgo), "Los toros en 1926," *Toros y toreros en 1926*, 45, 49. The criticism occurs twice: on page 45 the Villar bulls are defined as three years old (i.e., *novillos*, not yet *toros de lidia*), and on page 49 they are dismissed as *becerros* (even younger, not yet *novillos* and certainly not fit to be fought). Uno al Sesgo repeats his complaint in 1927, when too many underage and underweight bulls were fought. He explains that both bullfighters and bull breeders prefer to send younger animals to corridas, the former because they are livelier and enable a showy *faena*, the latter because selling them earlier saves the breeder an expensive year of pasturage. Uno al Sesgo claims that in 1927, as in the previous year, even *utreros* were fought (*Toros y toreros en 1927*, 48). Although he advocates an occasional bending of the rules in order to produce a beautiful performance, he objects to making the undersized bull the norm.

17. Cossío (1995) I: 746; *Artículo* 27 of the 1930 *Reglamento*.

18. Knowing who the bullfighters were and which *ganaderías* were supplying bulls, each bull breeder knew when his own animals would enter the ring and who would fight them. He could then decide which of his animals he would assign to that bullfighter. If he provided all the bulls for a corrida, as was usually the case then, he had that much more control, both for good (matching the bull to the bullfighter who could play it most effectively) and for ill (dumping difficult bulls on bullfighters of less renown or skill). Bull breeders could thus affect the bullfighter's reputation and the course of his career.

19. The *sorteo* is defined in *Artículo* 30 of the 1923 *Reglamento* and in *Artículo* 36 of the 1930 *Reglamento*.

20. Ortiz Blasco and Sotomayor, *Tauromaquia A-Z*, I: 622, my italics.

21. The Villar bulls that Sánchez Cobaleda bought in 1928 carried the old Villar colors, purple and red, and dated their *antigüedad* to 5 July 1924. The new Villar animals, not having been fought in the Madrid ring, lacked *antigüedad* or seniority. The fraud was described in 1929 ("Compuesto y sin ganadería," *El eco taurino*, 14 January 1929, 3) and probably ceased soon after. Later records do not indicate that this new Villar herd, carrying the new green and crimson *divisa*, supplied bulls or *novillos* in 1929, 1930, or 1931 (*Toros y toreros en 1929*, 175; *Toros y toreros en 1930*, 207; *Toros y toreros en 1931*, 191).

In the 1930s, the Gamero Cívico family sold their prestigious herd and its *antigüedad*, but continued to deal in bulls. The family's name and reputation enabled them to demand high prices for their new herds, even though these lacked the famous pedigree and *antigüedad*. For more detail, see the entry for Gamero Cívico in *DS*.

22. "Los tratantes," *Unión de criadores de toros de lidia* (1978), 109–13. For other events that worked against the bull breeder, *see* the discussion concerning the boycott against the Miuras (*el pleito de los Miura*, under the entry for Miura) and the challenge to the Veragua family, which drove them out of bull breeding and which Hemingway commented upon (*see* the entry for Veragua, in this volume).

23. I am grateful to Eduardo Gismera and to Miguel Angel García of the U.C.T.L., who gave me a great deal of information as well as several of the organization's publications. In addition, Miguel Angel took a long list of my questions to don Manuel García-Aleas Carrasco, whose family (called simply Aleas in the definition above) owned Spain's most senior bull breeding ranch from its inception until 1983, when the herd and its *antigüedad* (5 May 1788) were sold to its current owner. Don Manuel, an authority on taurine genealogy and breeding, served as National Secretary of the U.C.T.L. from 1946 to 1985. Although aged and ill, he generously answered my questions (interviews, Madrid, 20–24 August 1997). Also helpful in these technical matters was taurine expert Anthony Brand (interviews and correspondence, 1998–2001). For rival organizations that tried unsuccessfully to challenge the U.C.T.L.'s hegemony, *see* the entry for Ortega, widow of.

24. There was still some overlap, in that a president who deemed the bull insufficiently pic-ed could order *banderillas de castigo*. By causing the bull to toss his head, these banderillas might tire his *morrillo* somewhat, but an insufficiently pic-ed bull remains insufficiently pic-ed, and no banderillas can remedy the situation.

25. Although the word *peones* literally means unskilled or day laborers, banderilleros are skilled professionals.

26. For more details, *see* the entry entitled Manager.

27. The ban against child performers appears in *Artículo* 96 of the 1917 *Reglamento* and *Artículo* 100 of the 1923 *Reglamento*. The same articles prevent women from performing.

28. In 1940 Luis Miguel's father, Domingo Dominguín, obtained permission from Madrid's Director General de Seguridad for his fifteen-year-old son to perform in local *becerradas*. Since other cities would not allow this exemption, Domingo Dominguín took his sons to Latin America late in 1940. Luis Miguel celebrated his sixteenth birthday in December 1941; the family returned to Spain in the spring of 1942 (Abella, *Luis Miguel Dominguín*, 89, 93–94).

29. For more detail, see *Espontáneo* in *DS*.

30. James Michener writes that "precedence among matadors is determined by when the man first fought as a full matador in Madrid" ("Introduction" to *The Dangerous Summer*, 18). This definition of seniority, or precedence, is accurate only in Madrid. In all other bullrings, it is the promotion to *matador de toros*, the *alternativa* itself, which determines seniority, regardless of where it is taken. In the 1920s, foreign *alternativas*, like those taken in Mexico, were not recognized in Spain, but all Spanish *alternativas* transformed a *matador de novillos* into a *matador de toros* and thus determined his seniority. Today, Mexican and French *alternativas*, like the one taken by Cristina Sánchez in Nîmes in May 1996, are valid in Spain.

Having clarified that, I must remark that all rules have their exceptions. On the rare occasions when two *matadores de toros* who took their *alternativas* on the same day appear on the same *cartel*, precedence would, as Michener says, have to be "determined by when the man first fought as a full matador in Madrid." The

Madrid *confirmación de alternativa* would, for example, have been the determining factor when Manuel Jiménez (Chicuelo) and Juan Luis de la Rosa performed together. They were promoted on the same day, 28 September 1919, but Rosa's *alternativa* was confirmed on 24 May 1920 and Chicuelo's on 18 June 1920. Fulton identifies another occasion when the Madrid confirmation would determine seniority: if only one of the three bullfighters has had his *alternativa* confirmed in Madrid, he would be considered the senior fighter on the bill (*Bullfighting*, 73).

31. Proper procedure for the *alternativa* was not written into the taurine code until 1930 (*Artículo* 99 of the 1930 *Reglamento*). The next *Reglamento* (1962) kept the same wording (*Artículo* 119) but dropped the articles that had dealt with the *alternativas* of banderilleros and picadors; these two ceremonies were rarely performed even then.

32. The *matador de novillos*'s qualifications are spelled out in *Artículo* 5 of the 1992 *Reglamento*.

33. The perennial problem of when a *matador de novillos* is ready to become a *matador de toros* was addressed by taurine expert Alberto Vera (Areva) in his 1949 gloss on the 1930 taurine code. Areva argued that promotions were awarded too liberally and prematurely, and recommended "un brillante aprendizaje novilleril, por lo menos de tres o cuatro temporadas" (a brilliant apprenticeship as a *novillero*, lasting at least three or four seasons; *Reglamento taurino comentado*, see the gloss on *Artículo* 101, *Reglamento* of 1930).

34. Modern examples of taurine longevity include Antonio Chenel (Antoñete, *alternativa* in 1953) and Curro Romero (*alternativa* in 1959), both still performing in 2000.

35. *See*, for example, the entry for Mejías, Manuel (Manuel Mejías Rapela, known as Manolo Bienvenida and el Papa Negro). Hemingway, for whom initiation carried almost mystical significance, argued that a bullfighter's first serious wound (initiation by blood) revealed his courage and *afición*. For further discussion on this topic, *see* the entries for Ordóñez, Cayetano (Niño de la Palma); and Mejías, Manolo (Manuel Mejías Jiménez, also known as Bienvenida, son of el Papa Negro), all in this volume.

36. Absences and retirements are so common that *Toros y toreros en . . .* regularly listed "Los que no han toreado" (those who have not fought). The list includes those who have not been able to find employment as well as those who have stayed away by choice.

37. *See*, for example, the entries for Vicente Barrera, Juan Belmonte, Antonio Fuentes, Rafael Gómez Ortega, Antonio Márquez, Domingo Ortega, in this volume; *and* Julio Aparicio, Luis Miguel Domínguín, Manuel Jiménez (Chicuelo II), Antonio Mejías (Bienvenida), Antonio Ordóñez, Jaime Ostos, and José Luis Vázquez, in *DS*. Belmonte, for example, abandoned bullfighting in 1911, announced his retirement at the end of the 1914 season (but didn't retire); stayed away from the Spanish plazas the entire seasons of 1918, 1922, 1923, and 1924 (he occasionally performed in *festivales* or as *rejoneador*, but not in corridas); reappeared in 1925,

retired again in 1927, and returned to the bullrings in 1934. These breaks inspired the charge that Belmonte had only a weak *afición* (passion for the bulls), a most peculiar complaint to be lodged against a *figura* who was so intensely involved with the bulls for all of his long life, both as matador and as bull breeder.

38. For *matadores de toros* who died of non-taurine causes, I consulted "Matadores de toros fallecidos trágicamente sin vestir el traje de luces," *Aplausos*, 7 November 1983. The statistics include Latin American as well as Spanish *matadores de toros*. They do not include deaths from illness or old age, listing only unusual or accidental demises. The list is updated periodically: the *Aplausos* issue of 18 November 1985 lists sixty such deaths between 1837 and 1985; in the same time period, forty-six matadors were killed in the bullring ("Matadores de toros fallecidos trágicamente sin vestir el traje de luces," 85; "Nombres de toros que causaron la muerte a espadas de alternativa," 87).

39. The first-class bullrings are listed in *Artículo* 109 of the 1923 *Reglamento*, which was binding for these but not for second- or third-rank plazas.

40. 1923 *Reglamento*, as summarized in Cossío (1943–97) V: 512–14; *Artículo* 16 of the 1930 *Reglamento*; *Artículo* 22 of the 1962 *Reglamento*; and *Artículo* 24, Items 1–4 of the 1992 *Reglamento*. Today all of Barcelona's corridas take place in the Plaza Monumental.

41. *Life*, 5 September 1960, 97; qtd. in DeFazio, "The HemHotch Letters," 1357. The size of the bullring was not legislated until the 1962 *Reglamento* specified that the diameter of the arena of all bullrings, regardless of ranking, must be between forty-five and sixty meters (*Artículo* 9). *Artículo* 19 of the 1992 *Reglamento* also specifies this size for all permanent plazas.

42. For additional details on *el pleito de los Miura*, *see* the entry for Miura, don Eduardo.

43. The bullfighters were, in order of *antigüedad*, or seniority: Diego Mazquiarán (Fortuna), Marcial Lalanda, Nicanor Villalta, Fausto Barajas, Luis Fuentes Bejarano, Vicente Barrera, Fermín Espinosa (Armillita Chico), and Manuel Mejías (Bienvenida). They fought bulls bred by Juan Pedro Domecq, Julián Fernández, Manuel García (formerly Aleas), the widow of Concha y Sierra, Graciliano Pérez Tabernero, the sons of Andrés Coquilla, the Count de la Corte, and Indalecio García. *Toros y toreros en 1931* adds that Juan Manuel Puente supplied two *sobreros* (substitute bulls), and these replaced the bulls of Manuel García and the Count de la Corte, both of which had been disqualified (*Toros y toreros en 1931*, 173, 347; see also Cossío [1943–97], "Las plazas de toros," I: 519). Thus, only seven *ganaderías* were represented.

44. Hemingway was in Madrid on 17 June 1931, the day of Las Ventas's inaugural bullfight. On 16 June, he wrote that he and Pauline were already in Madrid and would stay there until the 22nd, when they were going to the Sierra de Gredos for a few days (EH to Guy Hickok, private collection). On 26 and 29 June 1931, Hemingway again sent letters from Madrid: "Plenty of bull fights but they haven't been very good" (*Selected Letters*, 343). In *Death in the Afternoon*, he refers to

three of the bullfighters who performed at the inaugural corrida (*DIA*, 70); these three did not perform together on any other afternoon that year.

45. Mexico City's La Monumental has the largest capacity—between forty-six thousand and fifty thousand spectators—and the Plaza de Acho, Lima, boasts the largest arena, slightly more than sixty meters in diameter, and seats about thirteen thousand. Las Ventas seats about twenty-three thousand and has a diameter of about sixty meters.

46. Cossío (1943–97), "Las plazas de toros," I: 512–24 and Cossío (1995) I: 633–38; Pinto Maeso, *Plazas de toros de España*, 64–65, 70–71; *Toros y toreros en 1931*, 347. The *Guía taurina, 1966*, variously claims that the ring seats 24,900 (51) and 22,900 (72). In addition to the bullrings of the city of Madrid, the province of Madrid has forty-seven other bullrings of various sizes: the one in La Cabrera seats only eight hundred, while the Aranjuez ring, the largest one in the province outside of Madrid proper, seats about nine thousand.

47. The eight matadors were scheduled to fight bulls from eight *ganaderías*, but in the end only seven were represented. The bullfighters and bull breeders are identified in note 43, above.

48. The *Corrida de Beneficencia* benefits the *Montepío de la Asociación Benéfica de Auxilios Mutuos de Toreros*, a charitable organization founded by Ricardo Torres Reina (Bombita, q.v.) to finance medical treatment for bullfighters, provide pensions for their dependents, and so on. The organization is also known as the *Asociación Benéfica de Toreros* or, more simply, *el Montepío*. Pamplona's *sanfermines* help support the *Casa de Misericordia*, which subsidizes hospitalization and other health care for the needy.

49. We find instances in Hemingway's fiction. The *capea* is mentioned in *For Whom the Bell Tolls* and is the metaphorical model for the slaughter of the fascists organized by Pablo in that novel. A *corrida nocturna* is the decisive event in the short story, "The Undefeated." *Toreo bufo* or comic bullfighting was more popular in Hemingway's day than today (*see Mojigangas* and related entries).

50. *Artículo* 40 of the 1930 *Reglamento*.

51. *Artículos* 49 and 98 of the 1917 *Reglamento*; *Artículo* 48 of the 1923 *Reglamento*.

52. The ring would have been drawn on the morning of the day of the bullfight; see *Artículo* 34 of the 1923 *Reglamento*.

53. The prohibition appears in *Artículo* 40 of the 1930 *Reglamento*.

54. Formerly, three picadors were in the ring. Today, the bull usually enters an empty ring, as the off-duty bullfighters are standing behind the *barrera*, the on-duty team is behind the *burladeros*, and the picadors are waiting in the *patio de caballos*. Occasionally a matador will position himself in front of the closed *toril*, often on his knees, to greet the bull with spectacular cape work. Luis Miguel Dominguín was famous for his *larga cambiada de rodillas*, a dangerous opening ploy sure to impress the audience.

55. *Artículo* 50 of the 1917 *Reglamento* defines the positions the picadors are

to assume before the bull enters the ring; they are marked with white paint on the *barrera*. *Artículo* 56 requires the picadors to remain in the ring for the entire *tercio de varas*, and *Artículo* 57 enjoins them to stay in position and not ride away to evade the bull's charge.

56. *Artículo* 64 of the 1917 *Reglamento* and *Artículos* 79 and 81 of the 1923 *Reglamento* forbid the use of the cape to attract the bull when he first enters the ring: "No podrá echarse el capote al toro antes de que haya concluído de recibir el puyazo en toda regla, a no ser en caso de peligro" (except in emergencies, the cape can not be deployed until the bull has received the pic as mandated). See also Cossío (1995) I: 145–46. The prohibition indicates that the cape was being used early in the corrida, before and between pic-ing; it is no surprise to see that this prohibition does not appear in the 1930 *Reglamento*.

57. "Bull Fighting a Tragedy," *Toronto Star*, 20 October 1923.

58. In the 1923 *Reglamento*, ten articles dealt with the horses (19–24 and 74–77), two with the pic and the *puya*, or barb (32–33), one with the line drawn on the ring to mark out the picador's territory (40), and ten with the picadors themselves (64–73)—a total of twenty-three.

59. In the 1962 *Reglamento*, one article dealt with the circle marked on the arena (81), four dealt with the horses (83–84 and 97–98), one with the horses' equipment (85), three with the barbs (86–87 and 121), and seven with the picadors (90–96)—a total of sixteen.

60. The number of horses is specified in *Artículo* 13 in Melchor Ordóñez's 1847 document, in *Artículo* 13 of the 1917 *Reglamento*, in *Artículos* 16 and 67 of the 1923 *Reglamento*, in *Artículos* 19 and 74 of the 1930 *Reglamento*, in *Artículo* 83 of the 1962 *Reglamento*, and in *Artículo* 62, section 4 of the 1992 *Reglamento*.

61. The 1923 and 1930 *Reglamentos* continued to demand the *arandela* (*Artículos* 27 and 32, respectively). The 1962 *Reglamento* was the first to incorporate the *cruceta* (*Artículo* 86), which continues to be mandated in subsequent *Reglamentos* (*Artículo* 66 of the 1992 *Reglamento* and *Artículo* 64 of the 1996 *Reglamento*).

62. *Artículo* 34 of the 1923 *Reglamento*. Individual bullrings had experimented with circles earlier. On 11 October 1908, the Seville bullring decided to clarify matters by making the distance visible: a circle was drawn in green sawdust. A few days later, on 16 October 1908, a circle was drawn in Zaragoza, in red, for the picador Zurito (q.v.).

63. The picador's spaces are defined in *Artículo* 53 of 1917 *Reglamento*, *Artículo* 34 of the 1923 *Reglamento*, and *Artículo* 40 of the 1930 *Reglamento*.

64. Corrochano, "De la necesidad de picar los toros," in his *Teoría de las corridas de toros*, 81.

65. Both *Artículo* 53 of the 1923 *Reglamento* and *Artículo* 61 of the 1930 *Reglamento* specify that the president may ask for *banderillas de fuego* for bulls who had received fewer than the required four pics. An extra pair of regular banderillas was required for an insufficiently pic-ed bull, and a black ribbon was attached to his horns after he was killed, as a rebuke to the bull breeder who had bred an insuf-

ficiently brave bull (bravery is revealed by the bull's willingness to charge and attack an object, such as, for example, a picador or his mount).

66. *Banderillas de fuego* were outlawed in Spain in 1950, to be replaced by *banderillas de castigo*, whose use is defined in *Artículo* 67 of the 1962 *Reglamento*, *Artículo* 77 of the 1992 *Reglamento*, and *Artículo* 75 of the 1996 *Reglamento*.

67. The banderillas used in Portuguese *rejoneo* are called *farpas*.

68. In the eighteenth and early nineteenth centuries, when breeding was in its infancy, bulls tended to be rougher and less predictable. This factor, combined with the less concentrated pic-ing, made it extremely difficult to dominate, let alone kill, the bull. Mounted bullfighters, who were at some distance from the bull, faced even greater difficulties. The distasteful *media luna* (scythe-shaped blade at the end of a long pole, used to hamstring the bull), and the *perros de presa* (hunting dogs who worried and tired the bull by making him jump and toss his head), were measures of last resort, to weaken a bull until it could be killed by a swordstroke. The dogs and the *media luna* survived well into the nineteenth century but had disappeared from the bullring by the time Hemingway arrived.

69. *Artículo* 12 specifies that there should be sufficient *banderillas comunes* (regular, single-barbed banderillas) and *banderillas de fuego* (double-barbed banderillas with explosives at the tip, to be used on insufficiently pic-ed bulls), as well as two *medias lunas* (for bulls that cannot be pic-ed and therefore need to be removed from the ring). *Artículo* 14 regulates the use of the *banderillas de fuego*. *Artículo* 2 merely mentions the banderilleros in passing, when it decrees that all performers need to be properly dressed.

70. *Artículo* 103 of the 1917 *Reglamento* calls for *banderillas de fuego* for bulls who have not received four regulation pics; *Artículo* 74 of the 1923 *Reglamento* empowers the president to call for these banderillas.

71. Qtd. in García-Ramos and Narbona, *Ignacio Sánchez Mejías*, 178.

72. The *banderillas de fuego* were forbidden by a royal decree dated 15 June 1928. Instead, the *manso* (cowardly bull who refused to charge) was required to receive four pairs of regular banderillas, with the added embarrassment of a black linen hood or bow on the horns when he was dragged out of the ring, a public censure for the bull breeder who produced him. *Artículo* 28 of the 1923 *Reglamento* and *Artículo* 34 of the 1930 *Reglamento* both required the bullring to provide five pairs of regular banderillas and four *de fuego* for each bull to be fought in a corrida.

73. In collecting illustrations for *Death in the Afternoon*, Hemingway acquired several pictures of *banderillas de fuego*, which testify to his interest in this *suerte* (Hemingway Collection, JFK). His definition in the Glossary is slightly misleading, in that he says that these banderillas "are placed in bulls which have not charged the picadors" (*DIA, h:* 416, s.v. *Banderillas de fuego*). More precisely, *banderillas de fuego* were prescribed for bulls which were insufficiently pic-ed. They may have charged the picadors, but may have veered off, backed away, or refused to charge again.

74. The 1962 *Reglamento* required that five pairs of regular banderillas and

four *de castigo* be available on the premises for each bull to be fought (*Artículo* 88). The 1992 *Reglamento* required four pairs of regular and only two of black banderillas per bull (*Artículo* 64, Item 3).

75. The 1917 *Reglamento* has a separate section entitled "De los picadores" (*Artículos* 50–61) and another one for defining the duties "De los espadas, banderilleros y peones" (which defines the work of all the other performers and includes additional remarks about the picadors; see *Artículos* 62–88). Subsequent *Reglamentos* separate the performers more clearly, with individual sections entitled "De los peones," "De los banderilleros," and "De los espadas." *Artículo* 73 of the 1923 *Reglamento* defines the position of the matador at the time his banderilleros are placing the sticks.

76. *Artículo* 81 of the 1930 *Reglamento*, *Artículo* 101 of the 1962 *Reglamento*, and *Artículo* 78 of the 1992 *Reglamento*.

77. Hemingway claims four pairs are usual (*DIA*, 97). A number of factors affected the number: the matador's wish, the tradition at the plaza, the quality of the bull, and so on.

78. *Artículo* 78 of the 1992 *Reglamento*; repeated in *Artículo* 76 of the 1996 *Reglamento*.

79. Cossío (1995), "La muleta," I: 770–71.

80. De la Riestra Sanz writes, "La decadencia de la última suerte comenzó en la época de Joselito y Belmonte; entonces se empezó a dar mayor importancia a la muleta, bastándole al espada coger cualquier tranquillo que terminara con el toro para triunfar y ganar orejas" (the decadence of the sword began in the time of Joselito and Belmonte; then the muleta began to attract more attention, and the matador could take any shortcut to finish off the bull, and still garner kudos and ears; 47).

81. Walter Johnston, *Brave Employment*, 160.

82. *Artículos* 69 and 84 of the 1917 *Reglamento* limit the banderillero to three minutes for placing each pair of sticks; this generally disregarded time limit was dropped in subsequent *Reglamentos*.

83. The timing of the *avisos*, or warnings, is regulated by *Artículo* 75 of the 1917 *Reglamento*, *Artículo* 87 of the 1923 *Reglamento*, *Artículo* 95 of the 1930 *Reglamento*, *Artículo* 117 of the 1962 *Reglamento*, *Artículo* 83 of the 1992 *Reglamento*, and *Artículo* 81 of the 1996 *Reglamento*.

84. The 1996 *Reglamento* repeats the 1992 ruling on this point, so that, unfortunately, *faenas* tend to be rushed. It is to be hoped that the next *Reglamento* will remedy the situation.

85. *Artículo* 68 of the 1962 *Reglamento*. *Artículo* 84 of the 1992 *Reglamento* and *Artículo* 82 of the 1996 *Reglamento* also mandate a minimum of two ears, but omit the ruling about the three hundred meters.

86. In Seville, the main portal is called *la puerta del Príncipe* (the Prince's door), and three ears are required.

87. Hemingway understood the significance of taurine addresses. In *The Sun Also Rises*, he used the taurine Hotel Montoya in several scenes, first to show that

Jake Barnes is an insider, and later, when the hotel owner snubs him, to show that Jake has violated a moral norm and is therefore no longer "one of us" (one of the bullfight crowd).

Annotations to *Death in the Afternoon*

1. Rubio Cabeza, "ABC (*diario de Madrid*)," and "ABC (*diario de Sevilla*)," *Diccionario de la guerra civil española*, 12. The Seville edition was inaugurated in 1928 (according to Rubio Cabeza, 12) or in 1929 (according to Cortada, *Historical Dictionary of the Spanish Civil War*, 5). Both editions of *ABC* are still widely read and respected.

2. Kern points out in Cortada's *Historical Dictionary of Modern Spain* that the redistribution of land "theoretically would have affected about 50 percent of the cultivated land in Andalusia" (26–27). Kern's word *theoretically* is important because, as Cortada points out (in the same *Historical Dictionary of Modern Spain*), only one hundred and twenty thousand hectares were actually seized between 1931 and February 1936, when the leftist Popular Front won the elections. At this point, expropriation intensified, but in September 1936 a new decree nullified all the seizures that had taken place since February (Cortada, 9).

The Nationalists' answer to the Republicans' Agrarian Reform was the *Servicio Nacional de Reforma Económica Social de la Tierra* (April 1938), which "For a long time" concentrated on "the return of seized properties to their former owners" (Cortada, 9). The uncertainty, fear, and unrest that plagued the Andalusian countryside in 1931 and 1932 were real enough, but in the end there was no redistribution and the conditions of the peasantry were, if anything, worse.

3. Kern, *Historical Dictionary of Modern Spain*, 27.

4. Cortada, *Historical Dictionary of the Spanish Civil War*, 308.

5. Cossío (1943–97), "Agüero Ereño (Martín)," III: 7–8 and V: 582. Tapia writes that Agüero retired in 1930 (*Breve historial del toreo*, 392–93); Bagüés agrees (*Historia de los matadores*, 184).

6. The corridas of the 1925 San Fermín fiesta were reviewed in the local paper, *El pensamiento navarro*. The corrida of Tuesday 7 July, the first of the fiesta, was reviewed the next day, 8 July 1925, p. 1, cols. 3–4. The corrida of 9 July was reviewed on Friday, 10 July, p. 1, cols. 3–5.

7. Cossío (1943–97), "Agüero Ereño (José)" and "Agüero Ereño (Manuel)," III: 7; "Agüero Ereño (Manuel)," XII: 458.

8. The Aguilar's address is variously given as 32, 34, and 37 Carrera de San Jerónimo. The 1923 Madrid guide, *Anuarios Bailly-Baillière*, lists the Pensión Aguilar at both 34 and 37 Carrera de San Jerónimo: odd and even numbers make up two different lists, and the Pensión Aguilar appears on both lists (147, 148). In that year's listing, under "Huéspedes, Casas de," the Aguilar is listed at 37 Carrera de San Jerónimo (768).

The 1927 edition of the same guide places the Pensión Aguilar at 34 Carrera de San Jerónimo (150). The 1930 guide lists the establishment as Hotel Aguilar and the address as 34 Carrera de San Jerónimo (163); and the 1959 guide has the Hotel Aguilar at number 32 (309). Although the street numbers have shifted, the Aguilar has remained in situ for the better part of a century, and the large building that houses it is easy to find. The Carrera de San Jerónimo starts at the Puerta del Sol, and the Aguilar is an easy walk from that plaza. Since Hemingway's day, the Aguilar has been downgraded to a "Hostal." For Hemingway's visits to the Aguilar, see Baker, *A Life Story*, 110, 151, 169, 186; for other information I am indebted to the Hostal Aguilar's current manager and owner, Simón Hernández Hernández (interviews, 10 and 12 August 1997, Madrid).

9. *Anuarios Bailly-Baillière* (1923), 714, 715; *Anuarios Bailly-Baillière* (1930), 958.

10. Cossío (1943–97), "Aguilar González (Manuel), Rerre," III: 9–10.

11. Cossío (1943–97), "Albayda, señor Marqués de," I: 260; *Toros y toreros en 1931*, 95–96; Vera, *Orígenes e historial*, 163–64; "Albayda (Hros. del Excmo. Sr. Marqués de)," *Unión de criadores de toros de lidia* (1995), 80.

12. Hemingway, *Selected Letters*, 97; Baker, *A Life Story*, 117; Hemingway, *By-Line*, 101.

13. Cossío (1943–97), "Alonso Bertolí (Rafael), el Chato," III: 27–28.

14. "Altrock, 88, Dies; Baseball Comic," *New York Times*, 21 January 1965, 31: 1; and Obituaries, *Britannica Book of the Year*, 1966.

15. "Bullfighting a Tragedy," *The Toronto Star Weekly* (20 October 1923); rpt. in White, ed. *Ernest Hemingway: Dateline Toronto*, 341.

16. "Alternativas prematuras," *La fiesta brava*, 14 November 1930.

17. "José Amorós Cervigón," in Bagüés, *Historia de los matadores*, 208; Cossío (1943–97) III: 36 and IV: 355; *Toros y toreros en 1930*, 283; *Toros y toreros en 1931*, 16, 19, 262–63; Cossío (1995) II: 268–69. Some writers give Amorós's birthdate as 1913, but 1911 seems to be the correct date. When Amorós's death was announced in *Anuario taurino 1998 de la Corrida de la Prensa*, he was described as being eighty-six.

18. Cossío (1943–97) III: 39–40; quoted evaluation supplied by Anthony Brand (letter to author, April 1998).

19. Cossío (1943–97), "Anlló y Orrío (Juan), Nacional II," III: 39–40; Cossío (1995) II: 271; Tapia, *Breve historial del toreo*, 382–83; *Toros y toreros en 1924*, 139–41; *Toros y toreros en 1925*, 156–58. Cossío incorrectly reports his birthdate as 1897; Bagüés and *Toros y toreros en 1925* write that Nacional II was born 11 January 1898 (Bagüés, *Historia de los matadores*, 168).

20. Cossío (1943–97), "Méndez Sanz (Emilio)," III: 590–91, IV: 581, and VI: 93. In the 1930s Méndez worked in Portugal, France, and Latin America, often as a freelance banderillero. Apparently a Republican, he did not perform in Spain during the Civil War. In 1939 he left Spain for Mexico, where he spent the rest of his life.

21. Emilio Méndez is identified as the performer on the day when Nacional II was fatally wounded in *Toros y toreros en 1925*, 156. His sad career is detailed in Cossío (1943–97) III: 590–91, IV: 581, and VI: 93; and in *Toros y toreros en 1924*, 133–34; *Toros y toreros en 1926*, 185; *Toros y toreros en 1927*, 155; *Toros y toreros en 1928*, 172; and *Toros y toreros en 1929*, 213. My thanks to Anthony Brand for drawing my attention to Carmelo Pérez Fernández de Velasco's *Juan Anlló*, a book-length account of the events in Soria, 1925–27.

22. The Pamplona bullfights were reviewed in the local paper, *El pensamiento navarro*, on 10, 11, 12, and 15 July 1924.

23. Nacional II performed in Madrid on 3 April; 23 and 24 May; 11, 14, and 18 June; and 27 September 1925. Hemingway came to Spain for the July fiestas of Pamplona and returned to Paris in August.

24. Cossío (1943–97), "Anlló y Orrío (Ricardo), Nacional," III: 41–42; Bagüés, *Historia de los matadores*, 156; *Toros y toreros en 1924*, 123–24; *Toros y toreros en 1925*, 148; *Toros y toreros en 1926*, 180. The Pamplona performances of 1924 were reviewed in *El pensamiento navarro*, 9 and 11 July 1924.

25. "La corrida de San Fernando en Aranjuez," *Zig Zag*, 7 June 1923, 7; "Seis toros de Veragua, Marcial y Pablo Lalanda y Gitanillo," *ABC*, 31 May 1923, 27, col. 1; "Toros y toreros en provincias," *Heraldo de Madrid*, 31 May 1923, unnumbered page 5, col. 5.

26. JFK, Bullfight Materials: Schedules.

27. For brief biographies of these two brothers, see Cossío (1943–97), "Espinosa Saucedo, José," III: 265, and "Espinosa Saucedo, Zenaido" (also spelled Cenaido), III: 262. In his *Enciclopedia taurina*, Silva Aramburu mentions only three of the brothers: José, Juan, and Fermín (279–80). Anthony Brand reports that José was known both as Armillita and as "el Chato Armilla" and that he worked as a *mozo de espadas* (sword handler) for his brother Fermín (telephone interview, April 1998).

28. Rodríguez, *Armillita, el maestro*, 25, 26; Cossío (1943–97), "Aznar y Ros (Matías), Armillita," III: 72.

29. Francisco Giráldez's son sold the herd to Plácido Comesaña, who sold it to General Rosa, who in turn sold it c. 1855 to the Arribas brothers, from whom the Duke of Tovar acquired it in 1912 ("Tovar, Sr. Duque de," *Toros y toreros en 1925*, 105–06).

30. "Vistahermosa" and "Bernaldo de Quirós (señores herederos de don Luis)," in Vera, *Orígenes e historial*, 20, 281. *Toros y toreros en 1931* discusses the three bull breeders who owned the Arribas herd at the time Hemingway was finishing his book: "Bernaldo de Quirós, D. Luis," 102–03; "González, D. Gabriel," 135–36; "Villaroel, D. Nemesio," 192. The Bernaldo de Quirós family is also closely allied with the Gallardo caste: in the middle of the eighteenth century, don Marcelino Bernaldo de Quirós developed a new breed by crossing Andalucian cows with Navarre bulls. Some of these offspring were sold to the Gallardo brothers (hence the caste name), who improved and strengthened the breed enormously. Ga-

llardo bulls were known for their bravery, responsiveness, and stamina. The caste is almost extinct today ("Gallardo," in Vera, *Orígenes e historial*, 18–19).

31. Hemingway owned *Moskau: Roman*, *The Mother*, and *The Nazarene* (Brasch and Sigman, *Hemingway's Library*, 14). For material on Sholem Asch, I consulted the *Encyclopaedia Judaica*, III: 684–87; Ben Siegel, *The Controversial Sholem Asch* (1976); and the *New York Times* obituary, "Sholem Asch, 76, Is Dead in London," 11 July 1957, 25 and D18, D44. For Asch's interest in bullfighting, see Sholem Asch, "Der Ochsen-Kampf" ("The Bullfight"); and Hemingway's *Selected Letters*, 861–62.

My thanks to David Mazower, of London, who spoke to me about his family. His grandmother, Sholem's daughter, recalls her father's and brother's meetings with Hemingway. Hemingway met Sholem Asch's son, Nathan Asch, in Paris, and included his short story, "Marc Kranz," in the August 1924 issue of the *Transatlantic Review*, which he edited. It was Nathan Asch who introduced Hemingway to his father, Sholem Asch.

32. Cossío (1943–97) III: 76. The same tic is described, in the same words, in Luján, *Historia del toreo*, 318–19.

33. "Manuel Báez, Litri," *Toros y toreros en 1925*, 177–78.

34. Cossío (1943–97), "Báez (Manuel) Litri," III: 74–78; Abella, *Historia II*: 43–44 and III: 194–98. Bagüés gives his birthdate as 2 August 1904 and reports (incorrectly, it seems to me) that his full name was Manuel Gómez Fernández, the surname Báez deriving from his godmother (185).

35. Cossío (1943–97), "Barajas, Fausto," III: 88–89; *Toros y toreros en 1924*, 154; *Toros y toreros en 1926*, 195–96; *Toros y toreros en 1931*, 240; JFK, Bullfight Materials: Ticket stubs. On 27 May 1923, Barajas did not receive good reviews; see Mandel, "The Birth of Hemingway's *Afición*," especially 136–37. He was the first *matador de toros* to die in a car crash; many others followed.

36. He was imitating Rafael Guerra Bejarano (q.v.) (Guerrita), who fought three *corridas de toros* (not *novilladas*) on 19 May 1895.

37. The review of his promotion enumerates the many injuries Barrera suffered as *novillero*, including the most recent one of 31 July 1927, which had not yet fully healed by 17 September (*La fiesta brava*, 14 July 1927, 15; and 22 September 1927, 4, 5). As a *matador de toros*, however, Barrera was seldom gored. Barrera's *padrino* (godfather, the man who grants the promotion) was Juan Belmonte; he cut four ears off his two bulls.

38. Bagüés, *Historia de los matadores*, 197; Silva Aramburu, *Enciclopedia taurina*, 281; Corrochano's remark is qtd. in Bagüés, 196–97; *Toros y toreros en 1931*, 254.

39. Cossío (1943–97), "Barrera Cambra, (Vicente)," III: 92–95 and IV: 373. Barrera and Torres fought *mano a mano* on 28 July 1927, in the Plaza Monumental of Barcelona. The full-page review was highly complimentary, especially to Barrera (*La fiesta brava*, 4 August 1927, 10).

40. A couple of weeks later both Barrera and Ortega were injured at Vitoria, 5 August (*Toros y toreros en 1931*, 348–49).

41. Barrera had been contracted for eighty-six corridas in 1931 but lost several to illness, injuries, and rain (*Toros y toreros en 1931*, 251–53). For bullfight schedules, I consulted the annual *Toros y toreros en* . . . for the years in which Hemingway was in Spain, as well as the relevant almanac issues of *El Clarín*, which also offer annual summaries of each bullfight season. Their statistics disagree only rarely. The ticket stubs at the Hemingway Collection (JFK) enable us to identify some of the bullfights Hemingway saw; obviously he did not save all stubs.

42. For the citation of Lt. Gen. Albert von Berrer's decoration, see Hammelman, *The History of the Prussian Pour le Mérite Order*, III: 503. The quoted information was provided by David Penn, Keeper of the Department of Exhibits and Firearms, Imperial War Museum, London (letter to author, 29 November 1995). Michael Reynolds also identifies Hemingway's von Behr as General von Berrer, although he gives the date of the general's death as 27 October 1917 (*Hemingway's First War*, 121–22). I have been able to find two other Generals von Behr: the first was the German General Christian Friedrich von Behr (1739–1831), who lived a century earlier, fought in the Seven Years' War, was taken prisoner in Fulda, and was released upon his promise to refrain from hostilities. The Duke of Wurtenberg appointed him chamberlain and president of his Grand Council. He died at age ninety-one and is obviously not the general killed at Caporetto in 1917. The second was the commander of an Infantry Brigade but was not killed during World War I; Hemingway may have confused the names Behr and Behrer (see *Ehren-Rangliste des ehemaligen Deutschen Heeres* [Osnabrück: Biblio Verlag, 1987], Vol. I: 82). My thanks to Kapitänleutnant Sander-Nagashima of the Militärgeschichtliches Forschungsamt, Potsdam (letter to author and enclosures, 28 November 1996).

43. In 1945, the Mexican Carlos Arruza, the first man capable of breaking that record, stopped at 108 out of respect for Belmonte: 104 of Arruza's corridas were in Spain, and four in Mexico. In 1965, Manuel Benítez (el Cordobés) fought 111 corridas and then broke his own record in 1970, with 121 corridas (including those he fought in France). In 1977 the Mexican Eloy Cavazos (b. 1950) set a new record with 127 corridas (126 in Mexico and one in Venezuela). This record was unbroken until 1994, when Jesús Janeiro (Jesulín de Ubrique) fought 153 corridas. Jesulín broke his own record the next year, with 161 or 163 corridas (reports vary). Cavazos also holds the record for most corridas in one day: on 2 October 1977, in Mexico, he fought four corridas. For annual listings of corridas, see *Aplausos*, 10 November 1986 and 20 November 2000; the weekly *6 Toros 6* credits Jesulín with 163 corridas for 1995 (15 January 2001, 39). For material on Cavazos, see Torres Martínez's biography, *La predestinación de un hombre*, especially pages 221–22. As I've remarked elsewhere, statistics are highly variable: most Spanish books count only Spanish *corridas*; a few include those of neighboring France and Portugal; almost none dignify those fought in Latin America. My thanks to Anthony Brand, for supplying details and the supporting bibliography.

44. *Toros y toreros en 1925*, 27.

45. Cossío (1943–97) III: 116.

46. Belmonte's 1925 performances in Pamplona were reviewed in the local daily *El pensamiento navarro*, 12 July 1925, 1: 1–6, and in the Madrid daily *ABC*, 12 July 1925, 31: 1 and 3. *Toros y toreros en 1925* does not mention his ill health.

47. Bagüés, for example, writes "el tiempo y la práctica hicieron de su arte una obra dócil y serena cuya hondura producía encendido arrebato, sobre todo en su segunda época, o sea a partir del año 1925" (with time and practice his art became controlled and serene, with a depth that produced a fiery ecstasy [in the audience], especially in his second period, that is, from 1925 on; Bagüés, *Historia de los matadores*, 149).

48. Cossío (1943–97), "Belmonte García, Juan," III: 108–18 and IV: 375; Cossío (1943–97), "Sobre el toreo de Belmonte," IV: 963–69; Silva Aramburu, "Belmonte," *Enciclopedia taurina*, 268–69; Martínez Salvatierra, "Juan Belmonte y García," *Los toros: La fiesta nacional española*, 195; Tapia, *Breve historial del toreo*, 355–64. Bagüés writes that most of Belmonte's performances during and after the Spanish Civil War were on horseback (*rejoneo*, 149–50). During his retirement he also performed as *rejoneador* (as early as 1923 and 1924) and in *festivales*.

49. JFK, Item 39, Folder 59, 195–96.

50. Cossío (1943–97), "Belenguer Soler, (Enrique) Blanquet," III: 104–05; *Toros y toreros en 1926*, 311; "Los que mueren: Enrique Belenguer 'Blanquet'," *La fiesta brava*, 19 August 1926, 5. The anecdote about the "smell of wax" and Blanquet's own death is told by Barnaby Conrad, *How to Fight a Bull*, 166–69. Blanquet was the subject of a short novel by Agustín de Foxá (see Cossío [1943–97] VI: 929).

51. On 17 March 1933, the teenager Rafael Mejías was murdered by Antonio Fernández Gallego, a servant of the Bienvenida family. Rafael was an aspiring bullfighter who, after his death, was described as talented (*Toros y toreros en 1933*, 322).

52. Baker, *A Life Story*, 129; Reynolds, *Paris Years*, 218.

53. Hemingway, *Selected Letters*, 119.

54. Williams, *Autobiography*, 227, 192. Williams writes that he heard Sally "sing in her teacher's studio. She did marvelously well. *Figaro* and *Bohème* . . . Sally has been perpetually on the threshold of an Opéra Comique debut" but refused to sleep her way to a role (227). Other information about Mrs. Bird is scarce. She was born in New York and seems not to have been a college graduate. The Birds had two children: their daughter, Ann France (Francie), married Thomas W. Wilson Jr. in 1938, in Paris; their son, William, died in 1926, at the age of five. These details were supplied by Alesandra M. Schmidt, Watkinson Library, Trinity College, Hartford, Connecticut (E-mail communication, 30 October 1995; letter and enclosures, 31 October 1995). William Carlos Williams reports that his son "did not thrive" as a baby and was cared for by a nurse, Miss Nelson, who took him with her to Denmark (193).

55. Alesandra M. Schmidt, of the Watkinson Library, Trinity College, Hartford Connecticut, supplied details about Bird's early life. Bird's Paris years are docu-

mented in the many biographies of his contemporaries, and his later career is summarized in, among other sources, the long obituary, "William Bird, 74, Newsman, Is Dead," *New York Times*, 6 August 1963, 31. Bird had been a *New York Times* correspondent.

56. Williams, *Autobiography*, 209–11, 229.

57. On the 1922 Black Forest trip, the Hemingways and Birds were joined by Lewis Galantière and Dorothy Butler. The Birds did not go to Pamplona in July 1923, as Meyers claims (Meyers, *Hemingway: A Biography*, 141); Hadley and Ernest made that trip by themselves. The Birds did join the Hemingways on the 1924 Pamplona trip, as did Eric Dorman-Smith, John Dos Passos, Crystal Ross, Don Stewart, Bob McAlmon, and George O'Neil (Reynolds, *Paris Years*, 212). Alessandra M. Schmidt, of the Wilkinson Library, Trinity College, Hartford, Connecticut, supplied a necrology of Trinity alumnus William Bird (letter to author and enclosures, 31 October 1995).

58. The miracle focuses on St. Anthony's father, who had been wrongly accused of murdering a man. St. Anthony caused the murdered man to rise from his grave, and the corpse spoke and exonerated the saint's father. The circular fresco shows St. Anthony, his parents, the speaking corpse, the back of the real murderer (he has turned away and is trying to flee), and a variety of spectators.

59. *Anuarios Bailly-Baillière* (1923), 280, 852; *Anuarios Bailly-Baillière* (1927), 320; *Anuarios Bailly-Baillière* (1930), 360; *Anuarios Bailly-Baillière* (1959), 1011.

60. Botín's menu details the restaurant's history. The restaurant has been so successful that the family opened a branch in Toledo, the Hostal del Cardenal, which offers lodgings as well as a bar and restaurant. The advertisement for the Toledo Hostal, given to Botín's Madrid patrons, reads as follows: "Framed by the ancient city wall, and set like a jewel amidst lovely gardens, the Hostal awaits you. The Restaurant, built by Botín of Madrid, has only one aim—to make your visit to wonderful Toledo a memory you will always cherish." Allen Josephs describes the Madrid Botín in "At the Heart of Madrid."

61. The famous boxing image is qtd. in Ross, "How Do You Like It Now, Gentlemen?" 35.

62. Watts, *Hemingway and the Arts*, 122.

63. Alfred H. Barr Jr., as qtd. in Peggy Guggenheim, ed., *Art of This Century*, 36.

64. The Marquis of Albaserrada and the Count of Santa Coloma were brothers. Vera writes that José Bueno acquired the Albaserrada herd in 1921, a year or two after the Marquis had died.

65. "Bueno (D. José)," *Toros y toreros en 1924*, 33–34; *Toros y toreros en 1925*, 37; Cossío (1943–97), "Calvo, doña Juliana, viuda de Bueno," I: 265; *Toros y toreros en 1931*, 105–106; Cossío (1943–97), "Escudero Bueno, don Bernardo," I: 270; *Toros y toreros en 1931*, 119; Cossío (1943–97), "Escudero Calvo, Hermanos (sobrinos de doña Juliana Calvo)," IV: 209; "Martín Andrés (don Victor-

ino)," *Unión de criadores de toros de lidia* (1995), 129; Vera, *Orígenes e historial,* "Escudero Calvo Hermanos," 186; short obituary of José Bueno in "Efemérides," *Toros y toreros en 1928,* 243.

66. It is surprising how often nephews inherit important *ganaderías,* as Ildefonso did. Ildefonso, who had his own herds, seems to have been uninterested in the Cabreras (*see* Saavedra). Quite often, as in this case, the herd goes to the widow's relatives, who sometimes keep it in their uncle's name, which is well known but, of course, different from their own.

In Ildefonso's case, history repeated itself: Ildefonso was a bachelor, and two of his nephews inherited his herd, which they sold (Mira, *El toro bravo,* 178). For other fortunate nephews and nieces, see the entries for Bueno, don José; Concha y Sierra; López Plata, don Antonio; and Martínez, don Vicente.

67. Vera, "Cabrera," *Orígenes e historial,* 19; Vera, "Miura Fernández (don Eduardo)," *Orígenes e historial,* 101; "Casta cabrera," in "Ganaderías de toros de lidia," *Gran enciclopedia Rialp* XXII: 604; Sotomayor, *Miura,* 17–27. Like Sotomayor, Mira writes that Ildefonso Núñez de Prado inherited the Cabrera herd and sold it to Miura shortly after his aunt Jerónima died (*El toro bravo,* 132).

68. Cossío (1943–97), "Cano Iriborne (Enrique), Gavira," III: 155–56; Bagüés, *Historia de los matadores,* 177; "La mujer del muerto," *El eco taurino,* 11 July 1927, 2; "El entierro de Gavira," *El eco taurino,* 18 July 1927, 7; *Toros y toreros en 1924,* 156; *Toros y toreros en 1926,* 197; *Toros y toreros en 1927,* 246–48.

69. At the time, there were eight military regions: I Madrid, II Seville, III Valencia, IV Barcelona, V Zaragoza, VI Burgos, VII Valladolid, and VIII La Coruña. In the 1940s, a ninth Region was added: Granada. For information on Burguete, I consulted "Burguete (Ricardo)," *Enciclopedia universal ilustrada, Apéndice,* II: 716.

70. Obituary, *New York Times,* 30 June 1967, 37, 40. The *Encyclopaedia Britannica,* 1994 ed., writes that Carnera fought only ninety-nine bouts, winning eighty-six, of which sixty-six were knockouts (II: 881).

71. Hemingway to Arthur Mizener, 22 April 1950 (*Selected Letters,* 690).

72. Cossío (1943–97), "Carrato Baquedano, Mariano," III: 174, IV: 403, and V: 762.

73. In addition to the obituary in *Toros y toreros en 1930* (339), Carreño's death was reported in *El eco taurino,* 26 May 1930, 5, cols. 1–2; and in *Torerías,* 25 May 1930, 6, col. 3); see also Cossío (1943–97), "Carreño Martínez (Pedro)," III: 174–75. Both Cossío and *Toros y toreros en 1929* credit him with fifteen *novilladas* in 1929; *El Clarín* puts the number at eighteen.

Carreño's hometown, Huelva, was also the home and final resting place of Litri, whose funeral in 1926 was probably attended by many of the same people who buried Carreño.

74. The *Encyclopaedia Britannica,* 11th ed., describes the *Mémoires* as "clever, well written and, above all, cynical, and interesting as a trustworthy picture

of the morals and manners of the times." *The Oxford Companion of English Literature*, 3rd ed., remarks that "Casanova's veracity has been much questioned."

75. Miguel Casielles was such a minor figure that information about him is difficult to obtain, but see Cossío (1943–97), "Casielles Puerta (Miguel)," III: 180; "Casielles (Miguel)," *Toros y toreros en 1924*, 210, 219; "Casielles," *Toros y toreros en 1926*, 260; and the Obituary, *Toros y toreros en 1934*, 331–32. Cossío gives the date of Miguel Casielles's Madrid debut as *novillero* as 11 July 1926, which seems incorrect. For his brother, see Cossío (1943–97), "Casielles Puerta (Bernardo)," III: 180; and Cossío (1995) II: 363. By 1925 Bernardo was "definitivamente terminado" (*Toros y toreros en 1925*, 195). For a review of the *novillada* in which Todó was killed, see "En la plaza de toros de Madrid, el novillo Cartelero, de la ganadería de Conradi, causó la muerte a Isidoro Todó (Alcalareño II)" (*El Clarín*, 14 November 1931).

76. The street was called Príncipe Alfonso in the years before the dethronement of Alfonso XIII and the establishment of the Republic (*Anuarios Bailly-Baillière* [1923], 714; *Anuarios Bailly-Baillière* [1930], 958).

77. Ernest Hemingway, "The Dangerous Summer, Part I," *Life* (5 September 1960), 87. Pepe Dominguín gives the family's address as Calle Príncipe 35 (*Mi gente*, 109), a two-minute walk from the café. He writes that "La Alemana era el punto de partida de nuestras cuadrillas" (the *cuadrillas* of the various Dominguíns left on their journeys from the café). All the men, their equipment, and their cars gathered there to receive final instructions from their matadors (*Mi gente*, 212).

78. Mary Hemingway, *How It Was*, 335. When queried about Hemingway in 1998, the present owner-manager would say nothing except that to him, like to his father, Hemingway was persona non grata. I assume this was because Hemingway had insulted Luis Miguel Dominguín in *Life en español* and in the other versions of *The Dangerous Summer*.

In *Death in the Afternoon* Hemingway had, of course, spoken ill of both Domingo Ortega and the elder Dominguín (qq.v.), whom Mary Hemingway claims as friends.

79. *Anuarios Bailly-Baillière* (1923), 714; *Anuarios Bailly-Baillière* (1930), 958.

80. For extended discussions of Cézanne's influence on Hemingway, *see* Meyly Chin Hagemann, "Hemingway's Secret" and Emily Stipes Watts, *Ernest Hemingway and the Arts*.

81. "Christian Endeavour Societies" and "Clark, Francis Edward," *Encyclopaedia Britannica*, 11th ed., VI: 279 and 441–42.

82. Sanford, *At the Hemingways*, 1999 ed., 134–35, 147.

83. Cossío (1943–97), "Apéndice II: Periódicos taurinos," II: 533, 548; Silva Aramburu, *Enciclopedia taurina*, 321.

84. Because the journal carried few advertisements, the price rose sharply, from ten *céntimos* in the mid-1920s to thirty *céntimos* by 1931. The Hemingway Collection has receipts for Hemingway's 1932 subscription to *El Clarín* (JFK,

Other Materials, Box 1, folder labeled "Book Lists") as well as several issues that Hemingway saved.

85. JFK, Hemingway Collection, Bullfight Materials.

86. Carralero, "Comisario," in *Los toros de la muerte*, 92; Cossío (1943–97) I: 348–49; Silva Aramburu, *Enciclopedia taurina*, 213. For Fuentes's part in the Comisario episode, see Cossío (1943–97) III: 295. The statement about Ferrer's fearlessness is from *El arte de los toros* (1897), qtd. in Cossío (1943–97), "Ferrer y Armengol (Vicente), Pollito," III: 285. Born in 1867, Ferrer was twenty-eight years old at the time of his exploit with Comisario.

87. Bredendick, "*Toros célebres*," 69, 70.

88. "Pérez de la Concha (Sres. Hijos de don Tomás)," *Unión de criadores de toros de lidia* (1995), 254; Vera, *Orígenes e historial*, 130; Cossío (1943–97) I: 287; Vera, "Concha y Sierra (doña Concepción de la)," in *Orígenes e historial*, 42–43; Cossío I: 267; *Toros y toreros en 1931*, 110–11; "Concha y Sierra (Ganadería de)," *Unión de criadores de toros de lidia* (1995), 193. After doña Concepción's death in 1966, the breed was sold several times: Juan de Dios Pareja Obregón García acquired it in 1966, José Luis Martín Berrocal in 1968, "King Ranch España, S. A. in 1970, and Miguel Báez Espuny (Litri) in 1979. Fifteen years later, it was acquired by María Luisa, S. A. (Explotaciones Agropecuarias). The last two owners reinstated the name Concha y Sierra.

89. Bagüés reports that Corrochano appeared in thirty-five corridas in 1935, not thirteen as Cossío claims. See Bagüés, *Historia de los matadores*, 217–18; Cossío (1943–97), "Corrochano Miranda (Alfredo)," III: 203–05 and IV: 421. See also Abella, *Historia*, II: 75–76. With the deaths of Luis Fuentes Bejarano in 1999 and Alfredo Corrochano in 2000, we lost the last of the matadors whom Hemingway mentions in *Death in the Afternoon*.

90. Cossío (1943–97), "Corrochano, Gregorio," II: 559 and VI: 911.

91. "El caso de Corrochano," *La fiesta brava*, 31 July 1931, unnumbered page 3; Julio Montés, "Gregorio Corrochano y su mundo en el toreo," *Toro bravo* 3 (1995): 17–19.

92. I summarize Corrochano's views on the second circle, to govern the distance between bull and picador, in the entry for Silvestre Gómez, Enrique, in *DS*. Corrochano's books discuss this issue, and others, with unequaled authority.

93. Brasch and Sigman, *Hemingway's Library*, 85.

94. Cossío (1943–97), "Corte, señor Conde de la," I: 267–68; Vera, *Orígenes e historial*, 43–45; *Toros y toreros en 1931*, 113; *Unión de criadores de toros de lidia* (1995), 92.

95. The buying and selling of expensive pedigreed animals involves many factors other than the financial. The owners' names are attached to their herds, and maintaining a good reputation requires the bull breeder to sell as carefully as he buys. Doña Enriqueta's herd went through several hands in the early years of the twentieth century: Collantes's son sold his father's herd to don Rodrigo Solís, who joined it to his own considerable holdings; he presented his bulls in the Madrid

bullring in August 1911. The herd was subsequently acquired by Pedro Salvador Oliva, of Seville; Oliva sold part of it in 1921 to don Antonio Velasco Zapata who, in the same year, sold it to don Félix Moreno Ardanuy. To keep this herd separate from his own, Moreno Ardanuy registered it in the name of his wife, doña Enriqueta de la Cova; see Vera, "Cova (doña Enriqueta de la)," *Orígenes e historial*, 45–46 and Cossío (1943–97) I: 268. Most of this history is repeated under the name of the herd's present owner; see "Moreno de Silva (don José Joaquín)," *Unión de criadores de toros de lidia* (1997), 284.

    96. "Cova (doña Enriqueta de la)," *Toros y toreros en 1931*, 113–14.

    97. Hemingway, *Selected Letters*, 128–29; see also Reynolds, *Paris Years*, 152, 233–34.

    98. For a fine discussion of the more subtle, because submerged, attack on the critics in that same book, see Robert W. Trogdon, " 'Forms of Combat.' "

    99. *Anuarios Bailly-Baillière* (1923), 762; *Anuarios Bailly-Baillière* (1959), 762.

    100. Qtd. by Burwell, *Postwar Years*, 195–96, n. 17. For the correspondence between Hemingway and Perkins on the "words," see Bruccoli, *The Only Thing That Counts*, 88–112.

    101. Qtd. in Bruccoli, *The Only Thing That Counts*, 179. Bruccoli adds that the letter was never used.

    102. Corrochano takes the title of his book from the basic, overriding question, "¿Qué es torear?" and adds, "Yo no lo sé. Creí que lo sabía Joselito y vi cómo le mató un toro" (What is bullfighting? I don't know. I thought Joselito knew, and yet I saw him killed by a bull (*¿Qué es torear?* 203). Belmonte speaks about his and the public's reactions to Joselito's death in his *Killer of Bulls: The Autobiography of a Matador*, 292–94.

    103. Cossío (1943–97), "David Puchades (Alfredo)," III: 218 and V: 847–48; "Alfredo David Puchades," *El Clarín* (Valencia), 1 August 1931.

El Clarín gives David's birthdate as 1895, Cossío as 1891. Himself from Valencia, David liked to work for fellow Valencians like Barrera and Granero.

    104. Qtd. in *Sanfermines*, 196. Iribarren also dates the fight to 1924 (*Hemingway y los sanfermines*, 166, n. 10). To check who was in Pamplona when, I also consulted the Pamplona daily, *El pensamiento navarro*, for July 1923 and 1924; the annual *Toros y toreros* for the same years; and the Pamplona Bullfight Schedules for 1924 (JFK); the latter confirms that David was still in Algabeño's cuadrilla in July 1924. For Juan de Lucas, see Cossío (1943–97), III: 521. Rafael Hernández connects the banderilleros' and picadors' strike to the labor unrest spearheaded by the Noy de Sucre (*Historia de la plaza de toros,* 341).

    105. Hemingway, *Selected Letters*, 156, 236–37. The genesis of *Death in the Afternoon* has been surveyed by Robert W. Lewis in "The Making of *Death in the Afternoon*," and by Peter Hays in *Ernest Hemingway*.

    106. In *La fiesta brava*, Uno al Sesgo objected to Hemingway's evaluation of Domingo Ortega—clearly one of Hemingway's few and always interesting mis-

takes—but thought the book an extraordinary performance for a foreigner. Hemingway saved the review in *La fiesta brava*, which shows a picture of Sidney Franklin and Eddie Cantor, dressed as bullfighters and reading *Death in the Afternoon* (JFK). Uno al Sesgo's annotated bibliography appears in *Toros y toreros en 1933*, 333–34.

107. Cossío (1943–97), "Delgado Guerra (José), Pepe-Hillo," III: 221–31; Cossío (1995) II: 402–405; Bagüés, *Historia de los matadores*, 29–30; Tapia, *Breve historial del toreo*, 74–85; *Enciclopedia Universal, Suplemento 1953–1954*, 638–39.

108. Anthony Brand and María Victoria Rodríguez (Librería Rodríguez, Libros Antiguos y Coleccionismo Taurino, 31 Paseo Marqués de Zafra, Madrid) supplied details about Desperdicios (faxes, 5, 15, and 16 May 2000).

109. Blanco, *La dictadura*, 55.

110. *Diario de Navarra*, 6 December 1924, 2.

111. For the text of the strongly worded letter they signed, see Ortega y Gasset, *España encadenada*, Chapter XVIII.

112. Marco Miranda, *Las conspiraciones*, 39.

113. Vila-San-Juan names some government agents who, he suspects, infiltrated the planning committee in Paris (*La vida cotidiana*, 265).

114. Vila-San-Juan, *La vida cotidiana*, 263.

115. Vila-San-Juan, *La vida cotidiana*, 263, 278, n. 4; Marco Miranda, *Las conspiraciones*, 34, 38–39.

116. JFK, Item 239a.

117. JFK, Item 39, Folder 52, Galley 81, 2–3; and the typescript, JFK, Item 49–9, 1.

118. Had she done so, I would not have had to lavish so much time on Deva. My thanks to Anthony Brand, who first realized that the events at Vera matched the details of Hemingway's narrative; to Paul Preston, who supplied information and bibliography; to José Gabriel Rodríguez Pazos, who sent me contemporary accounts from several Navarrese newspapers: *Diario de Navarra*, 11–16 November and 2–7 December 1924, and *La voz de Navarra*, 7 December 1924. My thanks also to the librarians at the Archivo General Militar de Madrid: Col. Eduardo Bravo Garrido, Ignacio Pérez-Ugena y Coromina, and Juan Manuel Flores Retamar.

The most thorough and professional account of the events at Vera appears in Blanco, *La dictadura y los procesos militares*, 19–72; see also Marco Miranda's memoir, *Las conspiraciones contra la dictadura*, 28–40, and his more general discussion, 56–63; and Vila-San-Juan's succinct account, *La vida cotidiana en España durante la dictadura de Primo de Rivera*, 264–66, 278–79. More technical but less relevant is Navajas Zubeldia's *Ejército, estado y sociedad en España (1923–1930)*, 39–73.

119. Many decades after his death, Diano is recalled in the entry for "Sancho, viuda de Arribas (doña Francisca)," Vera, *Orígenes e historial*, 256; for "Montalvo (Ganadería de)," *Unión de criadores de toros de lidia* (1995), 310; and in the essay, "Los Toros," Cossío (1943–97) VII: 216.

120. Fernández Salcedo identifies the photographer of Diano (*Diano* [1988], 373). My thanks to Anthony Brand, who recognized that Diano's descendants were photographed in the corrals of the San Sebastián bullring and was thus able to date the photograph and trace their relation to Diano. Brand also identified Vandel as the photographer of the grandsons (interviews, July and August 2000).

121. *Encyclopaedia Britannica*, 1911 ed., VIII: 172; *Encyclopedia Americana*, 1961 ed., XVIII: 829–30.

122. The book's six sections are named, as if they were the six bulls fought in a bullfight, with a seventh, the *sobrero* (substitute bull), dedicated to the foreigner. The six sections present a historical survey, a discussion of the relationship between the church and the bullfight, secular regulations affecting the bullfight, economic factors, the bullfight in literature and the fine arts, and the effect of the bullfight on society.

123. Díaz Arquer's book was announced in the annual "Bibliografía" of *Toros y toreros en 1931*, 356. It was favorably reviewed as soon as it came out, in "Una nueva bibliografía de la tauromaquia," *La fiesta brava* (28 August 1931), n.p. Brasch and Sigman record it as Item 1763 of their listing of Hemingway's books, *Hemingway's Library: A Composite Record*.

Hemingway owned *Toros y toreros en . . .* for 1920 and 1921 (Reynolds, *Hemingway's Reading*, 89). *Toros y toreros* was not published in 1923. He also had the volumes for 1925, 1926, 1927, 1929, 1930, and 1934; the book by the Conde de las Navas mentioned in my text; and the 1913, 1918, 1925, 1957, and 1959 volumes of *Desde la grada: Anuario taurino* (Madrid, various publishers), compiled by Enrique Minguet y Calderón de la Barca (Pensamientos). He also owned Sánchez de Neira's *El toreo: Gran diccionario taurómaco* (Madrid: Guijarro, 1879) and its expanded, revised edition, *Gran diccionario taurómaco* (Madrid: Velasco, 1896) (Brasch and Sigman, *Hemingway's Library*, 279–80, 223, 255, 324). In short: Hemingway researched tauromachy thoroughly, just as he researched World War I before writing *A Farewell to Arms*, and the history and techniques of hunting before writing *Green Hills of Africa*.

124. See "Doctors" in Mandel, *Reading Hemingway*, 128–29.

125. The signed photos of the Domingo paintings are in the Hemingway Collection, JFK, Box 27, Folder 15. Hemingway mentioned the Domingo paintings and gouaches in his letters to Perkins, 4 April and 9 August 1932, and 31 March 1933 (qtd. in Bruccoli, *The Only Thing that Counts* 162, 177, 185). My thanks to Anthony Brand, who first identified Roberto as Roberto Domingo (fax, 13 May 2000).

126. Abella explains Dominguín's nickname in *Luis Miguel Dominguín*, 78.

127. Greacen, *Chink*, 55.

128. After 1924, the two men lost touch, not meeting again until 1950. Some aspects of Hemingway's fictional Colonel Cantwell, the main character in *Across the River and Into the Trees*, are based on the later career of General Dorman-Smith. Dorman-Smith, who had been stationed in India when World War II broke out, was reassigned to the Middle East Staff College in Haifa, Palestine. In April

1942 he was reassigned to Cairo, where he was director of Military Operations and then acting deputy chief of the General Staff of the 8th Army. He was highly successful in the first battle of El Alamein but was demoted for supporting General Auchinleck's resistance to Churchill's call for "a premature offensive" in north Africa. In the so-called Cairo purge of August 1942, Generals Auchinleck, Corbett, and Dorman-Smith were dismissed, ostensibly for the Allied defeats at Tobruk and Gazala (Meyers, *Hemingway*, 473–74). For two years Dorman-Smith tried to remake his career, but his efforts were resisted and he retired in 1944.

129. Reynolds, *Paris Years*, 379 nn. 13, 15, 20; and E-mail communication 24 August 1995. The two volumes of the *R.M.C. Magazine & Record* are in the Hemingway Collection (JFK). The first essay is unsigned; the second is signed "Chink." In both, Spanish words are misspelled and even misused. The second article is less tolerant and thoughtful than the first: it contains references to "the happy scallywags of Pamplona" and remarks like "no Spaniard will do an egg properly" (88, 92). It ends as follows: "We foreigners who go down amongst their scallywags and chance getting hurt are a great joke. Everybody's happy . . . Spain is a wonderful country!" (92).

130. Greacen, *Chink*, 58.

131. Greacen, who argues that Hemingway's friendship was a significant factor in Dorman-Smith's life, quotes Hemingway's 1924 poem, "To Chink Whose Trade Is Soldiering," as the epigraph of her book. Spilka identifies Marryat as a source for Wilson's Shakespearean line in "A Source for the Macomber 'Accident' "; Hutton discusses the implications of the fact that the line is spoken by Francis Feeble, a fool (Hutton, "The Short Happy Life of Macomber").

132. For Hemingway's poetry, see *Complete Poems: Ernest Hemingway*, ed. Nicholas Gerogiannis.

133. Cossío (1943–97), "Duarte y Acuña (Antonio)," III: 255–56 and V: 872; Cossío (1943–97), "Duarte y Acuña (José)," III: 256. The quoted evaluation appears in Cossío (1943–97) III: 256.

134. Brasch and Sigman, *Hemingway's Library*, 108.

135. Cossío (1943–97), "Dutrús Zamora (Rafael), Llapisera," IV: 437 and V: 875.

Although some taurine historians claim that Colomer began his career as *torero bufo* with Llapisera, he is more frequently associated with Charlot. When Llapisera and Charlot broke up their partnership, Colomer continued performing with Charlot. Born in Valencia, Colomer was among the first to recognize and encourage Manuel Granero (q.v.); he also sponsored other Valencian bullfighters. Colomer had a limp that prevented him from becoming a regular bullfighter. His character of Botones inspired many imitators. See Cossío (1943–97), "Colomer (José)," III: 197; Colomer's obituary, "El Botones de Llapisera," in *El eco taurino*, 11 October 1931; and the shorter death notice in *Toros y toreros en 1931*, 353 (s.v. 7 October 1931).

For Tusquellas (Charlot), see Cossío (1943–97) II: 770 and VI: 531–32. The injuries of comic bullfighters were reported in the taurine press: "El Chispa" was gored in the chest on 13 July 1924 ("Cogidas y otros percances," *Toros y toreros en 1924*, 251); "Don José" had a rib broken during a performance on 21 May 1925 ("Cogidas y otros percances," *Toros y toreros en 1925*, 250); and Dutrús himself was gored on 1 August 1926 ("Cogidas y otros percances," *Toros y toreros en 1926*, 323. The performances of these troupes are detailed in "Toreros cómicos," *Toros y toreros en 1924*, 225–26; the royal performance is described on p. 240 of this same issue (*s.v.* 11 June 1924).

136. Cossío (1943–97) II: 582, 584.

137. JFK, Bullfight Materials, Other Materials: Book lists. Hemingway also saved the 1 February 1927 issue of a small Mexican magazine with the same name, founded in 1926 (Cossío [1943–97] VI: 1035). This issue reported that, the Spanish season being over, Valencia II, Chicuelo, and Nicanor Villalta were fighting successfully in Mexico.

138. For Eliot's influence on Hemingway see, for example, Malcolm Cowley, ed. *The Portable Hemingway*, xxi; Baker, *The Writer as Artist* (1952 ed.), 90; Peter Hays, "Hemingway and the Fisher King," 225–28; and Nicholas Joost and Alan Brown, "T. S. Eliot and Ernest Hemingway: A Literary Relationship," 425–29.

139. Cossío (1943–97) VII: 110; "Toreros bufos," *Toros y toreros en 1931*, 333–34.

140. Hervey, *Racing in America*, 41.

141. Hervey, *Racing in America*, 46.

142. My thanks to Thomas Gilcoyne, Research Librarian of the National Museum of Racing and Hall of Fame, Saratoga Springs, New York (interview, 15 December 1997); and Howard Bass, Thoroughbred Racing Communications, Inc. (E-mail communication, 14 September 1995). For a history and evaluation of Epinard, see "Stud and Turf in U.S.A.," *The Bloodstock Breeders' Review* (published by the British Bloodstock Agency, London), XIII (1924): 143–46; and Hervey, *Racing in America*, 38–46. For statistics about the Prix Yacoulef, Deauville, 1922, see *Annuaire de la Chronique du Turf, 1922*, 504.

143. Evan Shipman, "It'll be Trotters for Hemingway: Famous Writer Must Take Part in Action," *The Morning Telegraph* (8 April 1950). I am grateful to Sean O'Rourke for forwarding this newspaper clipping to me. Hemingway was very interested in the horses in the summer of 1922 and wrote "My Old Man" late that summer. He did not see Epinard race at Deauville. According to Reynolds, "on August 23 . . . Ernest and Hadley were stil in Germany" (*The Paris Years*, 69). Hemingway may have placed his bet before he left France, or Shipman may have misremembered. Shipman's details about the odds on Epinard are correct.

144. Bagüés, *Historia de los matadores*, 199. Uno al Sesgo uses almost the same words in 1931, defining this coldness as the only complaint that can be lodged against this "torero completísimo" (*Toros y toreros en 1931*, 255).

145. Padilla gives a reliable account of the beginning and end of the boycotts (*Historia de la plaza El Toreo*, 151–53 and 368–70).

146. Cossío (1943–97), "Espinosa Saucedo (Fermín), Armillita chico," III: 262–65, IV: 444, and V: 889; Silva Aramburu, *Enciclopedia taurina*, 279–80; Abella, *Historia* II: 67–71; Bagüés, *Historia de los matadores*, 199; JFK, Bullfight Materials: Schedules and Bullfight Programs (Madrid).

147. Hemingway, "The Friend of Spain," *By-Line*, 148–49.

148. Cossío (1943–97), "Espinosa Saucedo (Juan), Armillita," III: 265–66, IV: 444 and V: 889; Tapia, *Breve historia del toreo*, 470–71; *Toros y toreros en 1925*, 181–82; *Toros y toreros en 1926*, 205–06; *Toros y toreros en 1927*, 171–72; *Toros y toreros en 1929*, 224. Bagüés claims that Juan resigned his *alternativa* and became a banderillero for his brother in 1928 (*Historia de los matadores*, 186); Cossío sets the date of the resignation at 1932.

149. Cossío (1943–97), "Gómez Calleja (Luis), el Estudiante," III: 382–83 and IV: 479–80. While he fought bulls, Luis Gómez practiced no other profession. After he retired from the ring, he became an important figure in the administrative and ceremonial aspects of bullfighting.

150. Exterminator was such a famous horse that his biography and statistics are easy to come by; see, for example, Mildred Mastin Pace, *Kentucky Derby Champion*. Thomas Gilcoyne, Research Librarian of the National Museum of Racing and Hall of Fame, Saratoga Springs, New York, made available his holdings on Exterminator (interview, 15 December 1997).

151. Hemingway to Scribner, 1948; qtd. in Voss, *Picturing Hemingway*, 76.

152. See, for example, Peter Hays, "Exchange between Rivals: Faulkner's Influence on *The Old Man and the Sea*, in Nagel, *The Writer in Context*, 147–64.

153. Lewis disagees, arguing that Hemingway praises Faulkner in a letter and in an unpublished section of *DIA*. Lewis argues, unconvincingly it seems to me, that Hemingway excised his short phrase of praise "perhaps because he did not want to clutter the introduction, perhaps because he saw no need to give his admired contemporary any more praise" ("The Making of *Death in the Afternoon*," 44–45). Hemingway admired Faulkner, but he was not about to praise his competition in print.

154. George Monteiro's essay, " 'Between Grief and Nothing': Hemingway and Faulkner," points out mutual borrowings; his paper on "Hemingway and Faulkner" points out the Nobel Prize connection.

155. "Federico, doña Carmen de," *Toros y toreros en 1931*, 120–21; Cossío (1943–97) I: 271; "Martín, don José Anastasio," *Toros y toreros en 1931*, 146–47; Cossío (1943–97) I: 281; Cossío (1943–97), "Urquijo de Federico, don Antonio y don Carlos," IV: 218 and also Vera, *Orígenes e historial*, 266–68; "Murube (ganadería de)," *Unión de criadores de toros de lidia* (1995), 238. Cossío mistakenly reports that Carmen de Federico acquired the Murube holdings in 1927 (Cossío [1943–97]I: 271). All other sources consistently report the date as 1917.

As the *Enciclopedia universal* notes, Antonio Ordóñez's acquisition of Carlos Urquijo de Federico's herd was a coup "digno de mención" (worthy of note), since "las vacadas de abolengo no suelen desprenderse de la propiedad de una misma familia" (prestigious herds are not easily relinquished by the family) (*Suplemento 1979–1980*: 1104).

156. "Ronda," *Enciclopedia universal ilustrada* LII: 256.

157. "Fermín, San," *Gran Enciclopedia Navarra* V: 91; "Sanfermines," *Gran Enciclopedia Navarra* X: 172–80, esp. 172 and 177; "Fermín, San," *Gran Enciclopedia Rialp* X: 21–22; "San Fermín's Cult," *Sanfermines*, 31–39. The *Diccionario Enciclopédico Abreviado* (1954 ed.) also mentions a French saint by the same name, a fourth-century prelate who was the bishop of Amiens. His feast day is the first of September.

158. Cossío (1943–97), "Martínez, don Vicente (hoy don Julián Fernández Martínez)," I: 282–83; *Toros y toreros en 1930*, 166–67; *Toros y toreros en 1931*, 149–51. *Toros y toreros* mistakenly reports that Ibarra sold Diano to Luis Gutiérrez Gómez in 1903; the correct date is 1904.

159. JFK, Bullfight Materials, Other Materials: Book Lists.

160. "Firbank," *Cassells Encyclopaedia of World Literature* (1953 ed.) II: 1781; Connolly, *Enemies of Promise*, 33–34, 36.

161. *National Union Catalog, s.v.* "Ford, Richard."

162. Brasch and Sigman, *Hemingway's Library*, 129; Reynolds, *Hemingway's Reading*, 126.

163. *Anuarios Bailly-Baillière* (1923), 99, 699; *Anuarios Bailly-Baillière* (1930), 92; Torrente Fortuño, "Contar, recordar" (unpublished ms), 1290–91. Torrente Fortuño recalls that the Fornos, like the Suizo and the Inglés, were frequented by bankers.

164. Hemingway, "The Friend of Spain: A Spanish Letter," *Esquire*, January 1934; rpt. *By-Line*, 151.

165. Bleu, *Antes y después*, 215.

166. The *contertulianos* are identified by De Miguel and Márquez (*Adios, Madrid*, 34) and García-Ramos and Narbona (*Ignacio Sánchez Mejías*, 140). Belmonte at first felt himself out of his depth, but soon realized that both he and the artists defied conventional society and thus were more similar than different. He remarked that the "abstrusos problemas de filosofía" required a great effort on his part and that he felt shy among the intellectuals (qtd. in García-Ramos and Narbona, *Ignacio Sánchez Mejías*, 140).

167. "Waldo, Frank," *Oxford Companion to American Literature* (4th ed.).

168. Reynolds, *Hemingway's Reading*, 127; Brasch and Sigman, *Hemingway's Library*, 132.

169. For the unpublished attack and the retraction, see JFK, Item 22, folder 24b, 3; and JFK, Item 39, folder 49 (9), galley 83.3404. For an excellent discussion of Hemingway's treatment of Waldo Frank, supported by long quotes from unpublished materials about Frank, see Beegel, *Hemingway's Craft of Omission*, 59–67. Beegel concludes that Hemingway cut the material not because he repented of its harsh tone, but because it "violated his own rules of composition" by defining rather than evoking the desired response from the reader (66–67).

170. Because Lee was not promoted or confirmed in Spain, Cossío describes him as a "matador de novillos" ([1943–97] IV: 528). Obviously, Lee's biographer errs when he claims that his subject "is not even listed by J. M. Cossío, the great Spanish encyclopedist" (Hail, *Knight in the Sun*, xviii).

Lee lived from 1884 to 1941 and was promoted to *matador de toros* on 20 February 1910, in Monterrey, Mexico. He was active from 1908 to the end of the 1911 season, when he was seriously gored. His short career consisted of fifty-two corridas and he killed one hundred bulls (Hail, *Knight in the Sun*, 227–29). My thanks to Anthony Brand for bringing Lee to my attention (letter to author, April 1998).

171. Hail, *Knight in the Sun*, xii.

172. Franklin, *Bullfighter from Brooklyn*, 205.

173. Cossío (1943–97), "Francklin [*sic*] (Sidney)," III: 288–89, IV: 454, and V: 924; Sidney Franklin, *Bullfighter from Brooklyn* (1952); "El diestro Franklin," *El eco taurino* (23 March 1930): 5. Bagüés exclaims, "¡Un yanqui matador de toros! No nos asombremos. Ha de recordarse que cada uno de nosotros tiene en su inconsciente facultades para realizar cosas superiores a cuanto pueda imaginarse" (A Yankee bullfighter! Let's not be amazed. We must remember that each one of us is capable of far more than could be imagined" [*Historia de los matadores*, 270]).

Cossío (1943–97) gives his birthdate as 1903 (III: 288), but this was later changed to 1905 (Cossío [1995] II: 440). The earlier date is probably correct, although Franklin at one point gave his birthdate as 1904 ("Un rato de charla con el neoyorquino Sidney Franklin," *La fiesta brava*, 11 October 1929, unnumbered p. 3). But the *New York Times* obituary, "Sidney Franklin, 72, Dies; Matador from Brooklyn" (2 May 1976) says that he was born on 11 July 1903 and was seventy-two when he died in May 1976. The *Los Angeles Times* agrees ("Jewish Bullfighter Sidney Franklin Dies," *Los Angeles Times*, 2 May 1976).

174. JFK, Item 354a, 7–8.

175. "Circo," *Enciclopedia Universal, Suplemento 1969–70*, 351; Albert Fratellini, *Nous, les Fratellini*.

176. Cossío (1943–97), "Freg (Luis)," III: 289–91. Cossío is uncertain about Freg's birth date, suggesting 1888, a date repeated by Tapia (*Breve historial del toreo*, 343); both Bagüés and Linares report it as 21 June 1890 (142). Because Freg suffered such terrible wounds and still returned to the bullring, Uno al Sesgo wrote admiringly that he is "matador de toros y mártir" (*Toros y toreros en 1924*, 117). Of Luis's three brothers, Miguel, a promising *novillero*, was fatally gored in the Madrid bullring in 1914; Salvador became a *matador de toros* who had a short career; and Alfredo, who was only a mediocre *matador de novillos*, usually worked for Luis and Salvador as a banderillero. A nephew, Ricardo Romero Freg, invented the "Fregolina" cape pass.

177. JFK, Item 22, Folder 24, 18.

178. Fuentes's performances on the afternoon of Espartero's death recalled Cayetano Sanz's fine work when Pepete was killed. Half a century later, in 1947, Luis Miguel Dominguín also distinguished himself when Manolete (see *DS*) was fatally

gored. Such afternoons, which mark the loss of one great artist and the emergence of another, are not forgotten in the taurine calendar.

179. Guerrita's famous remark is qtd. in Silva Aramburu, *Enciclopedia taurina*, 259.

180. Anthony Brand reports that Fuentes's last performance was in Mexico City, 19 March 1922 (telephone interview, April 1998).

181. Cossío (1943–97), "Fuentes Zurita (Antonio)," III: 293–97 and IV: 455; Bagüés, *Historia de los matadores*, 100; Tapia, *Breve historial del toreo*, 311–12.

182. Cossío (1943–97), "Fuentes Bejarano (Luis), Bejarano," III: 300–302 and IV: 455; Tapia, *Breve historial del toreo*, 400; Abella, *Historia* II: 27–28. The unidentified critic is quoted by Abella, who also reports that Fuentes Bejarano's real name is Luis Moragas Fuertes. This detail is repeated by Bagüés (*Historia de los matadores*, 180) and Cossío (1995) II: 443, 607. Fuentes Bejarano died on 25 April 1999 (Obituary, "Muere en Sevilla Luis Fuentes Bejarano," *ABC*, 26 April 1999, 102).

183. The corridas were reviewed in *El pensamiento navarro*, 8, 9, and 10 July 1924.

184. Rafael had several farewell corridas in 1918, and in one of them he may have dedicated his bull to the friend and protector whom Hemingway does not name. This may have been Indalecio Mosquera (q.v.) or, more likely, Manuel Martín Retana, who succeeded Mosquera as impresario of the Madrid bullring on the Aragón Road and held that position for almost two decades, from 1907 or 1908 until late 1926. In the early years of Retana's tenure, Rafael Gómez Ortega performed often in Madrid (*see* Miura, don Eduardo) while other bullfighters boycotted that ring.

In an interview, Rafael recalls Retana's early kindness to him. In the 1890s, having seen the young Rafael perform in a *novillada* in an ill-fitting borrowed suit, Retana had inquired about his finances, outfitted him thoroughly, and told him to pay him back for the *traje de luces* and cape when his financial situation improved, which he predicted would be very soon, as indeed it was. See Sánchez Carrere, *Rafael Gómez (Gallo)*, 17. This pamphlet, owned by Hemingway, is now part of the Hemingway Collection (JFK). The Rafael-Retana connection seems to have impressed Hemingway, who mentions them together in *For Whom the Bell Tolls* (187). Retana also appears in Hemingway's story "The Undefeated," in *Men Without Women*.

185. Aguado, *El rey de los toreros*, 292.

186. Cossío (1943–97), "La fiesta a través de las crónicas (1883–1920)," IX: 990–94; "Rafael Gómez, El Gallo" and "José Gómez, Joselito o Gallito," *Toros y toreros en 1918*, 95–97 and 109–111.

187. Anthony Brand identified the ring (interviews, 20–22 August 1999).

188. Rafael marked his 1918 retirement with a series of farewell performances. In September he appeared five times, ending the month in Sevilla, where he killed both his bulls. The Madrid corrida of 10 October was the only one for that month:

Rafael was scheduled for one more farewell performance, at Zaragoza, but it was canceled because of the influenza epidemic. Instead, his mother cut off his pigtail, or *coleta*, on 24 October. See "Rafael Gómez, El Gallo" and "José Gómez, Joselito o Gallito," *Toros y toreros en 1918*, 95–97 and 109–111; see also Cossío (1943–97) III: 387.

The bull Rafael had refused to kill in 1899 had been dedicated to Agustín Luque, who magnanimously arranged for his release (Cossío [1943–97] III: 386). The scandal at the retirement corrida occurred in Madrid in 1918, and the 1924 incident (the unkilled bull at the Corrida de la Prensa) took place in Santander (*Toros y toreros en 1924*, 233). Both in 1899 and in 1924, the animals were Concha y Sierra; the 1918 bull in Seville was also a Concha y Sierra; the unkilled bull from the Madrid farewell corrida was from the ranch of Juan Contreras.

189. "Gabriel," *The Oxford Companion to the Bible*, 238; *The Catholic Encyclopedia*, VI: 330; New Testament, King James version.

190. *El Ruedo*, 13 September 1944. Information about Madrid's *torileros* was supplied by the indefatigable Anthony Brand.

191. Gabriel is mentioned in the caption to the photograph of Hidalgo that accompanies a brief summary of the 1948 season ("Una temporada sin desgracias," *El Ruedo*, 4 November 1948). See also "El Buñolero fué sesenta años torilero de las Plazas de Madrid," *El Ruedo*, 3 January 1946; "Germán Hidalgo, torilero de la Plaza, lleva veintidós años abriendo los chiqueros," *El Ruedo*, 13 September 1944; Santiago Córdoba, "Ha muerto el torilero de la Plaza de Las Ventas," *El Ruedo*, 20 September 1956; Cossío (1943–97), "Sierra, Antonio (Morenito)," III: 921.

192. As bullring servant, Gabriel's duties included handing the banderillas to the banderilleros and, in the absence of a full-time *torilero*, opening the door of the *toril*. While performing these duties, he was required to wear a *traje de luces* (see Artículo 35 of the 1917 *Reglamento*: "Los sirvientes que den las banderillas y abran las puertas del toril . . . vestirán el traje de torero" (the servants who proffer the banderillas and open the *toril* doors . . . will wear the bullfighter's suit). Gabriel's duties, looks, and *traje de luces* are described in F. Serrano Anguita, "Las diversiones que hemos perdido," *El Ruedo*, 11 July 1946, 10–11.

193. JFK, Item 60.

194. Eloisa married Manuel Blanco (Blanquito), Dolores married Ignacio Sánchez Mejías (q.v.), Trinidad married Manuel Martín Vázquez (Vázquez II), and Gabriela married her cousin, Enrique Ortega Ezpeleta (el Cuco). These alliances have been reported in various sources; see, for example, Aguado, *El rey de los toreros*, 27–28.

195. Saturnino Frutos worked in various cuadrillas until he joined Frascuelo, for whom he worked from 1885 to 1889. He then went to León, Mexico, where he established a taurine academy whose most distinguished pupil was Rodolfo Gaona. Frutos accompanied Gaona to Spain, serving him as manager and advisor and making a fortune in the process, though he died alone and broke in Mexico. Guillermo Padilla's biography of Saturnino Frutos is called *El maestro de Gaona*. See Cossío

(1943–97), "Frutos (Saturnino), Ojitos," III: 293 and 313; and Tapia, *Breve historial del toreo*, 345, 402.

196. Cossío (1943–97) III: 315.

197. Cossío (1943–97), "Gaona y Jiménez (Rodolfo)," III: 313–15 and V: 948; Silva Aramburu, *Enciclopedia taurina*, 270–71; Bagüés, *Historia de los matadores*, 134–35; Tapia, *Breve historial del toreo*, 347.

198. Cossío (1943–97), "García Bermúdez (Antonio), Bombita IV," III: 320, IV: 461, and V: 955; Hernández Ramírez, *Historia de la plaza de toros de Madrid*, 341–42.

199. Cossío (1943–97), "García Espejel (Heriberto)," III: 326–27 and IV: 463; Bagüés claims he was born in 1906 (*Historia de los matadores*, 203). Tapia confirms Cossío's 1907 date (*Breve historial del toreo*, 471).

200. *Toros y toreros en 1929*, 240; JFK, Bullfight Materials: Schedules.

201. Cossío (1943–97), "García López (José), Maera II," III: 334; Jalón, *Memorias de "Clarito,"* 161.

202. Cossío (1943–97), "García Fuillerat (Julio), Palmeño," III: 336; Bagüés, *Historia de los matadores de toros*, 201. García's 1931 performances are listed in *Toros y toreros en 1931*, 257.

203. Cossío (1943–97), "García López (Manuel), Maera," III: 343–45; Bagüés, *Historia de los matadores*, 167–68; Tapia, *Breve historial del toreo*, 381–82; *Toros y toreros en 1924*, 135–37. Bagüés reports that in 1922 Maera had been engaged for fifty-eight corridas and performed in forty-nine; in 1923 he performed more than any other matador, sixty-four corridas; and in 1924 he fought in fifty-six corridas and was awarded the coveted Golden Ear award at the corrida for the Asociación de la Prensa, 5 July 1924 (*Historia de los matadores*, 168). Maera's son, also known as Maera, was a flamenco singer, popular in the 1950s and 1960s, partially because of his famous father.

204. "Su estatura, elevada, que le da facilidades para las suertes, le quita gracia, finura, estética. Esto a veces rebaja sus entusiasmos, pero no los apaga" (His excessive height gives him an advantage while fighting, but reduces the grace, elegance, and aesthetic appeal of his performance. This sometimes reduces—but doesn't extinguish—his public's enthusiasm for him; Cossío [1943–97] III: 343). Similarly, Bagüés refers to his height, gracelessness, and the other disadvantages of his physical appearance—in spite of which he was able to provide highly charged performances that endeared him to his public (*Historia de los matadores*, 167). *Toros y toreros en 1924* describes him as "Largo, desgarbado" (tall, awkward or graceless) but able nonetheless to win over his audiences and become a "primera figura indiscutible" (a leading light, a major figure; 135). Luján mentions "ojos hundidos . . . rostro azulado, arrogante y sombrío, con una seriedad claustral" (sunken eyes . . . a blue-tinged, arrogant, and somber countenance) and says he was daring and miraculous with the banderillas (*Historia del toreo*, 314). *Zig Zag* refers to his "ventajosas facultades físicas" (physical advantages) and praises his ability to kill *recibiendo* as well as his work with the banderillas (14 June 1924, 19).

205. In 1923 rain delayed Maera's first appearance, scheduled for 10 July, to 12 July: he shared the bill with Algabeño and Gitanillo (qq.v.). The next day he performed with Olmos and Algabeño. In 1924 he performed with Chicuelo and Fuentes Bejarano on 7 July; with Chicuelo, Nacional, and Fuentes Bejarano (qq.v.) on 9 July (this was a *corrida de prueba*, in which four matadors fought four bulls); and with Nacional and Algabeño on 11 July. For reviews of these corridas and other events of the Pamplona fiestas of those years, I consulted the local newspaper, *El pensamiento navarro*, as well as several taurine journals and the Bullfight Schedules, Hemingway Collection (JFK).

206. Anthony Brand relayed this undocumentable but generally accepted gossip (personal interview, 2 August 1999).

207. Cayetano Ordóñez (el Niño de la Palma, q.v.) took Algabeño's place in the 1925 Pamplona fiesta, with important consequences for American fiction and for Pamplona's reputation.

208. Pepe Algabeño was seriously wounded on 8 September 1929 in Bayonne; this marked his last performance for 1929, and rumors were rife that he was going to retire (*Toros y toreros en 1929*, 296). Cossío (1995) claims that Pepe Algabeño retired in 1930; *Toros y toreros en 1930* does not list any performances for Algabeño that year (291). Cossío (1995) describes Algabeño's *toreo* as old-fashioned, rough, and coarse, but grants that he was an excellent horseman and swordsman (II: 452–53).

209. Cossío (1943–97) III: 331.

210. Cossío (1943–97), "García Carranza (José), Algabeño," III: 329–31 and V: 968; Abella, *Historia*, 22–24; *Toros y toreros en 1924*, 157–58; *Toros y toreros en 1925*, 170–71; *Toros y toreros en 1926*, 198–99; JFK, Bullfight Materials: Schedules. Pamplona's local newspaper, *El pensamiento navarro*, carried reviews of all the corridas of the fiestas of 1923 and 1924.

211. Cossío (1943–97), "García y Cuesta (Manuel), Espartero," III: 337–42; Silva Aramburu, *Enciclopedia taurina*, 254; Bagüés, *Historia de los matadores*, 89–90; Tapia, *Breve historial del toreo*, 303–308. The quote at the end of the entry is from Cossío (1943–97) III: 342. Cossío and Tapia claim el Espartero was born 18 January 1865; both Silva Aramburu and Bagüés give the year as 1866.

Manuel García's career is usually linked with that of Rafael Guerra Bejarano (Guerrita, q.v.), just as Joselito and Belmonte are usually discussed together. Bagüés claims the pairing is unjust, as Guerra was a greater matador than el Espartero. But el Espartero, who worked extremely close to the bull (and consequently suffered many gorings), is considered a precursor to Belmonte, the father of modern bullfighting.

El Espartero, always disdainful of danger, is credited with having coined the phrase, "Más cornadas da el hambre" (Hunger injures more frequently [than the bulls]); *see also* the entry for Proverbs.

212. In *The Sun Also Rises*, Hemingway makes reference to this fact, although he conflates the brave, solid father with his more flighty son, José García Carranza (q.v.).

213. Cossío (1943–97), "García Rodríguez (José), Algabeño," III: 331–33 and IV: 466.

214. Barco de Avila annually celebrates the birthday of St. John the Baptist (San Juan Bautista) on 24 June. For the letter to Dos Passos, dated 26 June 1931, see Hemingway, *Selected Letters*, 342.

In unpublished sections of *Death in the Afternoon*, Hemingway mentions "the change that has come over just one name in our time, the name Garibaldi. . . . take what Garibaldi means now. . . . the proverb runs: the Garibaldi are like the potatoes; the good one is underground. But it is not the question of the individual nor the carrying on of the name but simply what the name its-self (*sic*) means. Bread still means bread, wheat means wheat, Garibaldi meant liberty and liberty was a great word and now it means nothing and neither does Garibaldi" (unpublished manuscript for Chapter Twenty of *Death in the Afternoon*, JFK, Item 22, Folder 24a, 75–76). In another unpublished passage, reminiscent of *A Farewell to Arms*, Hemingway wrote, "Anyhow I went to Spain from Italy via Paris trying to learn to write and well cured of all the abstract words. I knew that the Garibaldis were like the potatoes; the good ones are under the ground and much other practical information of a like nature. I no longer believed in revolution" (JFK, Item 22, folder 24, 6; qtd. in Beegel, *Hemingway's Craft of Omission*, 56). Beegel explicates the "anti-Fascist joke" about the two Garibaldis, the "good" father Guiseppe, now buried "under the ground" and his "nothing" son Riciotti, who "received Mussolini on his Caprera estate and hailed the Fascists as continuing the Redshirt tradition" (108, n. 23). In his essay, "King Business in Europe," Hemingway mentions the younger Garibaldi (*By-Line*, 101), but he cut the unflattering references out of *DIA*.

For Hemingway's commitment to the second Spanish Republic, see the entry for Spanish Civil War in *DS*.

215. Iribarren provides the information about the new and old Gayarre Theatres (*Hemingway y los sanfermines*, 166, n. 9).

216. Paul Montgomery, Luca Gandolfi, and Stefano Illing supplied information about Pocol and Antonio Cantore (E-mail communications, 29 and 31 March and 2 April 1999); and Colonel Enrico Pino, of the Stato Maggiore dell'esèrcito, Reparto Affari Generali, provided detailed reports of Cantore's military career (letter and enclosures, 26 April 1999).

217. Cossío (1943–97), "Vega de los Reyes (José), Gitanillo de Triana II" and "Vega de los Reyes (Rafael), Gitanillo de Triana," III: 980–81. José performed as *novillero* from 1930 (fewer than ten *novilladas*) to 1933 (fourteen *novilladas*), after which he abandoned the effort. Rafael had a promising career as a *novillero* and became a *matador de toros* in August 1933. By the time the Spanish Civil War broke out, however, it was obvious that he was a third-rate figure, relegated to minor plazas and to the mercies of more important matadors, such as Manuel Rodríguez (Manolete), who often included him in his own corridas during the 1940s. Rafael continued performing a few times a season until he retired in 1952. He died in a car crash, May 1969 (Cossío [1995] II: 793–94).

218. Cossío (1943–97), "Gómez Moro (Alfonso), Finito de Valladolid," III: 357–58 and V: 1001; *Toros y toreros en 1924*, 188–89; *Toros y toreros en 1925*, 203–04; *Toros y toreros en 1926*, 230; *Toros y toreros en 1927*, 200; *Toros y toreros en 1929*, 249; *Toros y toreros en 1931*, 288–89.

219. Personal interviews with Anthony Brand, Madrid, July 1998 and March 1999. Finito de Palencia (Pilar's lover in *FWBT*) was short, but both Antonio Ordóñez and Anthony Brand describe Alfonso Gómez as quite tall. Here as elsewhere, Hemingway modified fact to produce the necessary effect in fiction.

220. Cossío (1943–97), "Gómez, don Félix, señora viuda de," I: 275–76; *Toros y toreros en 1931*, 134; Vera, "Gómez (señores hijos de don Félix)," *Orígenes e historial*, 204–205; "Sanz Jiménez (don Mariano)," *Unión de criadores de toros de lidia* (1995), 154.

221. Rafael Menéndez de la Vega and his wife, Emilia Díaz del Castillo, were the godparents of Fernando's oldest son, Rafael Gómez Ortega (q.v.), born in Madrid in 1882 (Cossío [1943–97] III: 384).

222. Cossío (1943–97), "Gómez (Fernando), Gallo," III: 358–62; Silva Aramburu, *Enciclopedia taurina*, 249–50; Tapia, *Breve historial del toreo*, 268–74.

223. Cossío (1943–97), "Gómez Tarazona (Francisco), el Aldeano," III: 362–63 and V: 1004; "Francisco Gómez 'Aldeano,' " *Toros y toreros en 1929*, 260, 291, 294; *Toros y toreros en 1931*, 299.

224. Cossío (1943–97), "Gómez Calleja (Luis), el Estudiante," III: 382–83 and IV: 479–80; Tapia, *Breve historial del toreo*, 437; Abella, *Historia* II: 65–67 and III: 460; Bagüés, *Historia de los matadores*, 218. According to Abella, el Estudiante was the fourth oldest living matador as of January 1992 (*Historia* III: 460); he was eighty-four when he died. His coffin was covered with the embroidered *capote de paseo* that he had worn on the day of his *alternativa*, sixty-three years earlier (Cossío [1943–97] XII: 706).

225. For the paternal line, see the entries for Gallo and Gómez, Fernando; and for the list of bullfighters associated with the maternal line, Ortega, see Cossío (1943–97) III: 384. José's father died when he was still a small boy, barely two years old, and he was much attached to his mother, Gabriela Ortega Feria (daughter of Enrique Ortega and Carlota Feria). Her death on 25 January 1919 was a heavy blow: "Fué siempre Joselito un muchacho triste; pero desde la muerte de su madre se había acentuado su propensión hacia la melancolía" (he had always been a sad fellow, but after his mother's death his melancholic bent deepened; Cossío [1943–97] III: 375, 376).

226. On 3 July 1914, in Madrid, Joselito killed six Colmenar bulls and then acceded to the audience's demand that he fight the *sobrero* (the extra bull kept on hand in case one of the six proves defective). On 30 September 1915 he again killed six bulls, in Sevilla, and was awarded several ears, the first time such trophies were awarded in that city's bullring.

227. Interview with Filiberto Mira, 31 June 1998, Seville.

228. Cossío (1943–97), "Gómez Ortega (José), Gallito," III: 364–79 and IV:

959–63; Silva Aramburu, *Enciclopedia taurina*, 266–70; Martínez Salvatierra, *Los toros*, 193–94; Bagüés, *Historia de los matadores*, 146–47; Tapia, *Breve historial del toreo*, 370–79; Luján, *Historia del toreo*, 278–81; Belmonte, *Killer of Bulls*, 288–90.

229. Writing in the 1930s, Cossío states unequivocally that Joselito was "el lidiador de toros más grande de todos los tiempos" (the greatest bullfighter of all time; Cossío [1943–97] III: 377). Looking for faults, Cossío remarks that in 1912 Joselito was not yet perfect in the verónica, but that by 1916 he had an inexhaustible repertoire with the cape. As a banderillero he tended to prefer the right side, but he overcame this limitation as well, "banderilleando excelentemente por el otro lado." His sword work was occasionally weak, as he tended to lift his arm too high, but he was a quick and accurate killer and "Mató muchos toros recibiendo" (he killed many bulls *recibiendo*, that is, standing still and waiting for the bull to approach; Cossío [1943–97] III: 377–78). As we enter the twenty-first century, we can add other great names to the roster of taurine geniuses: Juan Belmonte, Manuel Rodríguez (Manolete), Luis Miguel González (Dominguín), Antonio Ordóñez, and Juan Antonio Ruiz Román (Espartaco). Of course, any such list represents a value judgment. Other aficionados would insist that Domingo Ortega, José Luis Vázquez, and many others need to be included.

230. Bagüés reports that Joselito was gored seriously on 1 September 1912, in Bilbao; on 5 July 1914, in Barcelona; and 19 August 1914, again in Bilbao (*Historia de los matadores*, 146). To these three injuries Cossío adds two other gorings and two illnesses: an injury suffered on May 1918, in Zaragoza, caused him to miss six corridas. On 1 May 1919 he was injured in Madrid, losing eighteen corridas. He also missed corridas in 1918 due to the influenza epidemic, which sometimes closed bullrings (*see* Spanish Influenza), and he was sick in August and missed ten engagements. He also developed a fever at the end of the San Fermín *feria* of 1919 (Cossío [1943–97] III: 375).

231. Agustín Luque is identified in Fernández Ortiz, *La Sevilla de Rafael el Gallo*, 21; Corrochano, "Las corridas de Bilbao: El último escándalo del 'Gallo'," *ABC*, 26 August 1917, rpt. in *La edad de oro*, 287.

232. *Toros y toreros en 1927*, 146.

233. Cossío (1943–97), "Gómez Ortega (Rafael), Gallo," III: 384–90; Silva Aramburu, *Enciclopedia taurina*, 262–63; Martínez Salvatierra, *Los toros*, 192–93; Bagüés, *Historia de los matadores*, 122; Tapia, *Breve historial del toreo*, 333–37; "Rafael Gómez 'El Gallo' celebra sus bodas de plata como matador de toros," *La fiesta brava*, 6 October 1927. Rafael's wife, Pastoria Imperio, is mentioned in Hemingway's *For Whom the Bell Tolls*, 185, 187.

234. The number and dates of el Gallo's appearances appear in *Toros y toreros* for the years 1924–31; the number of each Spanish matador's performances was also published in *El Clarín*'s annual almanac, which I consulted for those years. Hemingway attended the Pamplona and Valencia fairs regularly; a few ticket stubs for other bullfights are preserved in the Hemingway Collection (JFK).

235. In 1940 he bought the neighboring ranch, "El Macho," and made many expensive improvements on the property, including the addition of a bullring. He is buried nearby. Some years after his father's death, Luis Miguel sold "La Companza" (Olano, *Dinastías*, 34, 42).

236. Cossío (1943–97), "González Mateos (Domingo), Dominguín," III: 391–93 and IV: 482; Silva Aramburu, *Enciclopedia taurina*, 276; Tapia, *Breve historial del toreo*, 380–81; Bagüés, *Historia de los matadores*, 158; *Toros y toreros en 1924*, 124–25; *Toros y toreros en 1925*, 148–49.

237. Cossío (1943–97), "González-López (José), Carnicerito de Méjico," III: 397 and IV: 485; Tapia, *Breve historial del toreo*, 414–15; Abella, *Historia* II: 40–41; Bagüés gives his birth date as 1907 (*Historia de los matadores*, 215–16). For details about his performances in 1931, including his injuries, see *Toros y toreros en 1931*, 275–77, 343, 348.

238. For a discussion of height in connection with swordwork, *see* the entries for Todó, Isidoro; and García, Manuel (Maera).

239. *La estocada de la tarde* is in the Taurine Museum, Córdoba. The work of Mariano Benlliure (1866–1947) includes monuments to Christopher Columbus (Plaza Colón, Madrid), Velázquez (in front of the main entrance of the Prado Museum, Madrid), and Alfonso XII. Among his many important taurine pieces is the multifigured representation of the funeral of José Gómez Ortega (Joselito), in the San Fernando Cemetery, Seville.

240. Abella gives a more modest number: sixty-six corridas (in "Apéndice 2: Los diestros que más torearon en España y Francia a lo largo del siglo XX," *Historia* III: 378).

241. Machaquito was awarded the ear on 17 May 1911 for his work with a Miura bull named Zapatero.

242. Silva Aramburu writes that Fuentes was elegant, Bombita was cheerful and graceful, and Machaquito was known for his bravery, his disregard for his safety, and his extravagant personality (*Enciclopedia taurina*, 260).

243. Cossío (1943–97), "González Madrid (Rafael), Machaquito," III: 401–05 and IV: 493; Bagüés, *Historia de los matadores*, 113; Tapia, *Breve historial del toreo*, 331–32.

244. Stanton, *Hemingway and Spain*, 117–18.

245. Cossío (1943–97), "Granados (José), Veneno," III: 408. The other bullfighters nicknamed Veneno rate brief entries in Cossío (1943–97) III: little is known about them.

246. Cossío (1943–97), "Granero, Manuel," III: 409–11; Silva Aramburu, "Manolo Granero," *Enciclopedia taurina*, 278; Tapia, "Manuel Granero," *Breve historial del toreo*, 395–97; Bagüés, "Manuel Granero y Valls," *Historia de los matadores*, 164. Years after his death, Granero is frequently discussed and memorialized. On the twenty-fifth anniversary of his death, a life-size statue of Granero was placed on his tomb in the Municipal Cemetery of Valencia. The inscription reads: "A Manuel Granero, en el XXV aniversario de su muerte. Recuerdo de las

entidades taurinas valencianas. 7 mayo 1947." A plaque honors him at the entrance to Valencia's plaza de toros. See also "Manuel Granero, gran figura valenciana," *ABC*, 22 July 1992, 90–91.

247. Qtd. in Robertson, *Blue Guide: Spain, the Mainland*, 323.

248. Luca de Tena, *Guide to the Prado*, 57.

249. Stein, *The Autobiography of Alice B. Toklas*, 111, 259; for "The Life and Death of Juan Gris," see Dydo, *A Stein Reader*, 535–37.

250. Preston, *Franco: A Biography*, 27.

251. Just before Guerra was born, his uncle, José Rodríguez (Pepete, 1824–62), the family's only matador, was killed in Madrid, on April 1862. While attempting to attract the Miura bull Jocinero away from the banderillero he had injured, Pepete himself was gored dramatically. Jocinero inserted his right horn into Pepete's right hip. Grabbing the left horn, Pepete managed to disengage himself. He fell to the sand, and Jocinero gored him twice more, inflicting a deep chest wound. Pepete again disengaged himself from the bull's horns, stood up, brushed the sand off his uniform, and walked unaided to the edge of the bullring. There he keeled over, hitting his head and suddenly hemorrhaging violently from the chest wound. He was the second bullfighter to be killed in the Madrid bullring (the first had been Pepe Hillo), and his death was commemorated with poems and songs. Quite understandably, the family developed a great aversion to bullfighting (Tapia, *Breve historial del toreo*, 222–26). It is said that the Miura family displays green and black ribbons on the bulls they fight in Madrid as a sign of mourning for Pepete; in all other bullrings, their colors are green and crimson. For another, probably more accurate explanation of the double set of colors, *see* Miura, don Eduardo.

252. See the entry for Vicente Barrera, who in his last season as a *novillero* did the same thing: he even fought in two of the same cities where Guerra had fought: San Fernando and Seville. Barrera's third *novillada* of that day took place in Córdoba (*Toros y toreros en 1927*, 189).

253. Cossío (1943–97), "Guerra Bejarano (Rafael), Guerrita," III: 413–21 and IV: 497; Silva Aramburu, *Enciclopedia taurina*, 251–54; Martínez Salvatierra, *Los toros*, 191–92; Tapia, *Breve historial del toreo*, 298–303; Bagüés, *Historia de los matadores*, 91–92. Guerrita's famous remark is quoted in Cossío (1943–97) III: 421. Among the several books written about this master are *Espartero y Guerrita: Apuntes de Selipe* by José María Rey; *Guerrita* by Antonio Peña y Goñi; and *Antes y después del Guerra: Medio siglo de toreo* by F. Bleu. Hemingway owned the Cossío encyclopedia, the Guerra *Tauromaquia*, Peña y Goñi's books *Guerrita* (1894) and *Lagartijo y Frascuelo y su tiempo* (1887), the Bleu book (1914), and a great many other taurine titles (Brasch and Sigman, *Hemingway's Library*, 38, 85, 287, 382; Reynolds, *Hemingway's Reading*, 100, 168, 196). For the evolution of the fictional Pedro Romero's name, see Svoboda, *Hemingway and* The Sun Also Rises, 61–78. Guerrita was alive but long since retired when Hemingway began to see bullfights in 1923.

254. "Los faraones del toreo," *La fiesta brava* (10 October 1930). In *Heming-*

way and Spain: A Pursuit, Stanton argues that Hemingway dislikes gypsies: "EH not great admirer of gypsies: evident from several passages of *DIA*, and from the portrayal of the cowardly, irresponsible Rafael in *FWBT*" (226, 120–21). Rafael is sometimes a problem for his fellow characters in the novel, but he is useful to its author: through him, the stories about the blowing up of the train and the rescue of Maria are made available to Jordan and to the readers. And Hemingway treats him kindly: he endows Rafael (as he does Pilar) with a strong dramatic sense and a well-developed sense of humor to which most readers have responded favorably. Similarly, the narrator of *DIA* has both positive and negative things to say about the gypsies—and practically all the other bullfighters—whom he mentions. Hemingway being such an intelligent observer of human nature, generalizations like Stanton's are difficult to defend.

255. Cossío (1943–97), "Haba (Antonio de la), Zurito," III: 427–28 and V: 1104; Cossío (1995) II: 508–509; Bagüés, *Historia de los matadores*, 185–86; *Toros y toreros en 1924*, 174–76; *Toros y toreros en 1925*, 178–79; *Toros y toreros en 1926*, 204–205. The newspaper report, "Zurito Restablecido," indicates that the illness of 1927 required surgical intervention (*La fiesta brava*, 28 July 1927, 12). *Toros y toreros en 1927* mentions his fainting and places him firmly among bullfighters of the second rank (171); the short, dismissive report in *Toros y toreros en 1929* mistakenly reports Madrid as the plaza of his *alternativa* (271); and in 1931 the annual reported that Zurito still displayed "Gran estilo de matador; pero no interesa" (great killing style, but he no longer interests [the public]; *Toros y toreros en 1931*, 243).

256. "Antonio de la Haba, Zurito," *Toros y toreros en 1924*, 174–76.

257. Cossío (1943–97), "Hechicero," I: 366; Carralero and Borge, *Toros célebres*, 161; "Cárdeno," "Vocabulario taurino autorizado," Cossío (1995) I: 354; "Pérez de la Concha (señores hijos de don Tomás)," Vera, *Orígenes e historial*, 130–31.

258. Diliberto, *Hadley*, 9, 16. This is not unusual: Grace and Ed Hemingway kept all their daughters out of school for a year in their early teens. The Hemingways clearly felt that adolescence was less strenuous for boys and did not interrupt Ernest's and Clarence's schooling (Sanford, *At the Hemingways*, 111–112).

259. Mowrer (1887–1971) was a well-known newspaper correspondent. His early books focused on political analysis and were well received: *Hours of France in Peace and War* (1918), *Balkanized Europe* (1921), *Our Foreign Affairs* (1924), *Red Russia's Menace* (1925), and *The Foreign Relations of the United States* (1927). In 1929, when the Pulitzer Committee established an annual prize for the best foreign correspondent, Mowrer was the first recipient. He continued to write about the historical background of contemporary events (e.g., *The House of Europe*, published in 1945) and also wrote plays and several volumes of poetry.

260. Baker reports that Hadley wrapped the ear in Don Stewart's handkerchief (*A Life Story*, 224).

261. Reynolds points out that the lack of correspondence between Pauline and

Hemingway during this time period strongly suggests that they were together. When separated, they wrote each other almost daily (E-mail to author, 28 January 1998).

262. Baker, *A Life Story*, 221–22; Reynolds, *The 1930s*, 37, 73.

263. The bullfighters in Bayonne were Manuel Jiménez (Chicuelo), Joaquín Rodríguez (Cagancho), and Jesús Solórzano. In the months preceding the Bayonne bullfight, Bordeaux also had corridas on 10 May (the Hemingways were still en route to Europe), 28 June, 16 July, and 26 July 1931 (Pérez Maroto, *Estadística taurina*, 165, 171, 175, 179, 183, 198; fax from Anthony Brand, 14 June 1999).

264. Baker, *A Life Story*, 162–63; Reynolds, *Paris Years*, 287–88, 332; Kert, *Hemingway Women*, 171–77 *et passim*.

265. Cossío (1943–97) II: 559, 609; *Toros y toreros en 1927*, 237, 261. El Barquero died in December 1927.

266. *Toros y toreros en 1927*, 233.

267. Cossío lists two herds owned by the heirs of Esteban Hernández. One was acquired in 1932, the year *Death in the Afternoon* was published: it consisted of cattle bought from José Encinas (*see* Villar, Francisco and Victorio). It would seem that Hemingway means the family's older herd, acquired by Esteban Hernández himself in the early 1890s. See "Hernández, don Esteban, Herederos de," Cossío (1943–97) I: 277; *Toros y toreros en 1931*, 139; "Hernández Plá (don Esteban)," Cossío (1943–97) I: 278; Vera, *Orígenes e historial*, 211–12; "Hernández Plá (sres. Hrdos. de don Gabriel)," *Unión de criadores de toros de lidia* (1995), 112.

268. Cossío (1943–97), "Hernández, Rafael. *Rafael*," II: 633 and VI: 947; López de Zuazo Algar, *Catálogo de periodistas*, 278; Iribarren, *Hemingway y los sanfermines*, 39–40; see also Stanton, *Hemingway and Spain*, 123, 125; Mary Hemingway, *How It Was*, 333. Rafael Hernández is mentioned in the business correspondence between Hemingway and the Laboratorio y Comercio Substancia, S.A.: Rafael had helped arrange the purchase of books and journal subscriptions for Hemingway (JFK, Bullfight Materials: Book Lists). My thanks to Nancy Bredendick, who supplied the López de Zuazo Algar reference and a copy of Rafael's essay, "Míster Ernest Hemingway, el amigo de España."

269. Cossío (1943–97), "Hernandorena (Domingo)," III: 435 and IV: 503. He is such a minor figure that I have not been able to establish his birth date.

270. *Toros y toreros en 1925*, 253.

271. Louis Romanet, Direction des Relations Internationales, France Galop, Boulogne, supplied information about Héros XII's breeding and his 1921 and 1922 victories in a fax to author, 30 January 1996. Hemingway saved the program for the November 1922 race at Auteuil (JFK, Other Materials: Horse Racing). For statistics about Héros XII, I consulted the *Annuaire de la Chronique du Turf*, 1922 and 1923. For the 1923 race, see Reynolds, *The Paris Years*, 133.

272. Shipman, "It'll be Trotters for Hemingway: Famous Writer Must Take Part in Action," *The Morning Telegraph*, 8 April 1950.

273. Moddelmog, *Reading Desire*, 80. Moddelmog also mentions an unpub-

lished fragment, "There's One in Every Town" (JFK, Hemingway Collection, Item 743), in which "the narrator remembers the first time she saw one of the male homosexuals in the café, a man with hennaed hair. The narrator suspects that the man felt sexual excitement just by sitting there and showing off his hair" (*Reading Desire*, 80).

274. Burwell, 173. In addition to the published writing dealing with horses and horseracing, Hemingway wrote a fable, "The Great Black Horse," which remains unpublished. It was probably intended as a companion to "The Good Lion" and "The Faithful Bull," all written in 1950.

275. Baker writes that in the 1930s and 1940s, Hemingway rode "a horse that he loved, a black mare named Old Bess with a white streak on her face" (*A Life Story*, 214). Hemingway writes about her in "A Paris Letter, February 1934" (rpt. William White, *By-Line*, 169–70) and Robert Jordan recalls her in *For Whom the Bell Tolls* (337).

276. My thanks to Fernando E. Furio Martínez, Ajuntament de Valencia, for supplying maps and a history of the city (letter and enclosures, 8 April 1996); and to Mauro Soler Arnau, manager of the Hotel Valencia, who confirmed that the hotel had been moved to its present premises. Mr. Soler Arnau writes that the Hotel Valencia is now a one-star residential hotel, with forty-four rooms. It no longer has a restaurant (letter to author, 3 March 1998). Valencia also has another hotel with a similar name, the Hotel Valencia Palace, built in the early 1990s and clearly not the one Hemingway knew.

277. Hemingway's remark about Hudson is qtd. in Reynolds, *Hemingway's Reading*, 138–39; Smith, *A Reader's Guide*, 231–33; Beegel, *Hemingway's Craft of Omission*, 32.

278. Raeburn, *Fame Became of Him*, 34; Beegel, *Hemingway's Craft of Omission*, 35, but for her full argument, see 32–38.

279. Herrick, "What Is Dirt?" in *The Bookman* 70 (November 1929), 258–62; rpt. in Stephens, *Ernest Hemingway: The Critical Reception*, 86–89; Raeburn, *Fame Became of Him*, 34; "The Bookman," in Mott, *A History of American Magazines*, IV: 423–41, 458.

280. The most thorough discussions of Hemingway's attack on New Humanism are John A. Yunck's "The Natural History of a Dead Quarrel: Hemingway and the Humanists" and John Portz's "Hemingway's 'A Natural History of the Dead.' " Both identify *decorum* as a key word used to mean "values" or "principles" in the Humanists' creed. Yunck argues that Hemingway himself was heavily invested in artistic and moral values and that "Hemingway's was an intensely individualistic, flamboyant, hyper-athletic decorum, a trifle sentimental [but] . . . nevertheless a real decorum. . . . However much they differed . . . both Babbitt and Hemingway sought, and found, ordering principles among the splinters of life, and both men firmly believed that these principles were discoverable empirically" (39).

281. Martínez Salvatierra, *Los toros*, 151; "Hurón," in Carralero and Borge, *Toros célebres*, 164. On this same page, Carralero and Borge have an entry on an-

other bull named Hurón, a Miura who was part of such fine performances when he was fought in 1872 that both the banderillero and the matador were awarded ears. In 1957, another bull of this name, from the ranch of Alipio Pérez-Tabernero Sanchón, performed so well that he was awarded a turn around the ring and a prize (Cossío [1995] I: 553).

282. "Indice alfabético de ganaderos y fecha en que, por primera vez a su nombre, se han corrido toros, como nuevos, en las plazas de Madrid, desde el año 1765," Cossío (1943–97) I: 313–22; a similar listing in Vera, arranged chronologically instead of alphabetically, also mentions Eduardo Ibarra only once, for 8 February 1885 (Vera, *Orígenes e historial*, 382), the year in which he bought a large amount of stock from Dolores Monje, the famous widow of Murube who ran the Murube ranches after her husband died c. 1860. See also "Gamero Cívico" in *DS*; "Santa Coloma, Sr Conde de," *Toros y toreros en 1931*, 183; and "Historial," *Toros y toreros 1936 a 1940*, 144. Bagüés also traces the Vistahermosa-Murube-Ibarra connection in *Toros y toreros en 1925*, 28–29.

283. Mira shows the brands in his Vistahermosa genealogical trees (*El toro bravo*, 156, 180). The Hernández Barrera claim to the Guardiola brand is documented in the *Union de criadores de toros de lidia* (1997), 261. Other *ganaderías* also display variants of the Y, which is, to be fair, a fairly basic design. Since brands can be bought, sold, and imitated, older brands, or variants of older brands, sometimes show up in newer herds that have little or no connection to the original.

284. Hinkle, "Hemingway's Iceberg," 10. Freud's sentence appears in *Bartlett's Unfamiliar Quotations* (Chicago: Cowles, 1971), 185, but Kenneth Johnston insists that Freud himself "did not employ the iceberg analogy. . . . But popularizers of the new psychology frequently did" ("Hemingway and Freud: The Tip of the Iceberg," 69, 72 nn. 11, 12).

285. Qtd. in Griffin, *Along with Youth*, 212–13, 250.

286. Reynolds, *Young Hemingway*, 250.

287. Plimpton, "Art of Fiction," 84.

288. Beegel, *Hemingway's Craft of Omission*, 89.

289. "Ronda," *Enciclopedia universal ilustrada* LII: 256.

290. The impresario Livinio Stuyck first brought the San Isidro *feria* into prominence (Walter Johnston, *Brave Employment*, 180, 182). Both Johnston and Anthony Brand identify 1947 as the birth of the *sanisidros* we know today.

291. The Madrid guide for 1923 situates the Buffet Italiano at 37 Carrera de San Jerónimo. In 1930, the address is given as 37 Carrera San Jerónimo and 8 Arlabán. In 1959, the buildings seem to have been renumbered, or perhaps the restaurant moved: the address is 21 Carrera San Jerónimo (*Anuarios Bailly-Baillière* for 1923, 852; for 1930, 1108; for 1959, 1011).

292. Aronowitz and Hamill, *Life and Death*, 142.

293. Hadley's remarks on Henry James are qtd. in Diliberto, *Hadley*, 37, 204.

294. *Selected Letters*, 266.

295. Cossío (1943–97), "Giráldez (Antonio), Jaqueta" and "Giráldez y Díaz (José), Jaqueta," III: 355–56.

296. The purse for the fight was $101,000, 60 percent going to the winner. In addition, each fighter received $10,000 for training expenses. Jeffries sold his picture rights for $66,666; Johnson sold his for $50,000 (Menke, "Boxing," *Encyclopedia of Sports*, 245). To translate the dollar from 1910 to 1995, I used the "Composite Commodity Price Index" chart in Derks, *The Value of a Dollar*. To translate Derks's 1989 values into 1995 terms, I multiplied by 150/124 (CPI for 1995/CPI for 1989).

297. *Selected Letters*, 116, 155.

298. Orts Ramos (Uno al Sesgo), "Manuel Jiménez, Chicuelo," *Toros y toreros en 1924*, 130–32.

299. Orts Ramos (Uno al Sesgo), *Toros y toreros en 1926*, 182.

300. Don Clarines, "Glosas de la temporada: Chicuelo," *La fiesta brava*, 31 March 1927, 7.

301. *Toros y toreros en 1927*, 153.

302. "Cosas de Chicuelo," *El eco taurino*, 31 December 1928, 5. The incident is also reported in "Efemérides," *Toros y toreros en 1929*, 287. Because this was a festival, not a *corrida de toros*, the bullfighters were scheduled to fight *novillos*, not *toros de lidia*.

303. Cossío, who seems to be relying on *Toros y toreros en 1929* as a source, mistakenly reports sixty-nine corridas, decrying the "low" number in the same words as Uno al Sesgo. Chicuelo performed in thirty-six corridas but killed sixty-nine bulls (*Toros y toreros en 1929*, 213). For the injuries, see "Efemérides" for 14 April and 1 September, *Toros y toreros en 1929*, 291 and 295.

304. Uno al Sesgo, *Toros y toreros en 1931*, 233.

305. The numbers for the 1930s, before the Spanish Civil War, are: thirty corridas in 1930, eighteen in 1931, forty-three in 1932, twenty-nine in 1933, fourteen in 1934, and seven in 1935.

306. This was the season of 1939, twenty years after Chicuelo had been promoted to *matador de toros* (Cossío [1943–97] III: 464).

307. Cossío (1943–97), "Jiménez Moreno (Manuel), Chicuelo," III: 462–65, IV: 515, and V: 1106; Luján, *Historia del toreo*, 306–308. The quotation is taken from Cossío (1943–97) III: 464.

308. See, for example, Uno al Sesgo's review of the 1929 season, in which he explains that some bullfighters, having reached a comfortable position in terms of reputation and fees, rely on what they can do well and safely and still satisfy the public. He refuses to name such "especialistas" but is careful to indicate that Chicuelo is not to be included among them: Chicuelo is another story, a "personalidad inconfundible" (an original) in whose performances there is always something striking and artistic, which guarantees his "alta jerarquía" (preeminence; "Matadores," *Toros y toreros en 1929*, 208–209).

309. Alameda, "Sobre el pase natural y el toreo en redondo" and "Joselito y el toreo en redondo," in *El hilo del toreo*, 125–26 and 179–85; Luján is qtd. in Alameda, *El hilo del toreo*, 231. Anthony Brand defined Chicuelo's contribution (telephone interview, 2 May 1998).

310. Luján, *Historia del toreo*, 307; Hemingway, "Bullfighting a Tragedy," in *Dateline: Toronto*, 343–44. Bagüés confirms Hemingway's statement that Chicuelo was short (Bagüés notes he had short arms), but does not find that this diminished his performance: "con el capote y la muleta hizo verdaderas maravillas . . . [a pesar de sus] altibajos . . . siempre se le conceptuó como una primera figura" (with the cape and the muleta he performed real wonders . . . [in spite of his] ups and downs . . . he was always considered a first-rank performer; *Historia de los matadores*, 161). This judgment is shared by all other taurine critics. Mandel dates Hemingway's first bullfight (and thus of his dislike of Chicuelo) to 27 May 1923 ("The Birth of Hemingway's *Afición*," especially 129–34).

311. "Notas taurinas," *El pensamiento navarro*, 15 July 1924, 1, cols. 5–6. *El pensamiento navarro* reviewed all the corridas of the fiesta. At the end of the week the paper summarized the fiesta, complaining that the bulls had been too expensive and "los toreros de fama [han] estado mal" (the big-name bullfighters performed badly; "Despues de las fiestas," 15 July 1924). Most bullfight aficionados I've met are impressively tolerant and patient, willing to endure many boring afternoons in the hope of one artistic performance.

312. "Efemérides," *Toros y toreros en 1925*, 254.

313. Tapia, *Breve historial del toreo*, 399.

314. Hemingway, "Bullfighting a Tragedy," in *Dateline: Toronto*, 342, 343.

315. Capellán, *Hemingway and the Hispanic World*, 146–47.

316. Johnson's statistics are variously reported. His birthdate is given as 1876 and 1878, and the number of losses ranges from seven to thirty-four, probably because different encyclopedias look at different categories of fights.

317. *Anuarios Bailly-Baillière* (1923), 699. In the 1927 edition of the guide, the "café-cervecería y restaurant" belongs to Luis Kutz and was listed at Conde de Peñalver, 16. In 1930, this is the only one listed. The Café Kutz does not appear in the 1959 guide.

318. José Gabriel Rodríguez Pazos, of Pamplona, supplied information about the Café Kutz (E-mail, 21 June 1999).

319. "The Classic Races," *The Bloodstock Breeders' Review*, 1921 ed., X: 146–49 and XI: 182–83.

320. Howard Bass, of the Thoroughbred Racing Communications, writes that Ksar "was a chestnut, which is a reddish color, although an extremely light chestnut will seem yellow" (letter to author, 21 September 1990).

321. Beegel, " 'A Lack of Passion': Its Background Sources and Composition History." The identification of the matador as Manuel Jiménez is repeated in Beegel, "Ernest Hemingway's 'A Lack of Passion'," in Scafella, ed., *Hemingway: Essays of Reassessment*, 62–78. Beegel assumes that Chicuelo and Maera performed in Pamplona on July 1923, but the correct year is 1924. Maera appeared in Pamplona in 1923, but Chicuelo did not. *See* entries for García, Manuel; and Jiminez, Manuel.

322. Lalanda's oldest brother, Martín (1893–1922) was a promising *novillero*

but had to leave the profession because of illness (Cossío [1943–97] III: 480). The second brother, Eduardo (b. 1894), a banderillero, was a member of Marcial's *cuadrilla* (Cossío [1943–97] III: 475 and IV: 523).

323. Cossío writes that some "marcialófobos . . . crearon, sobre todo en Valencia, un ambiente desagradable en derredor de Marcial" (some Marcial-haters . . . created, especially in Valencia, a disagreeable feeling against Marcial) but that on the whole he was recognized as having acted quickly, intelligently, and bravely in Granero's defense, and that Valencia greatly loved and admired him (Cossío [1943–97] III: 476); *cf. DIA*, 74–75.

324. Cossío (1943–97), "Lalanda del Pino (Marcial)," III: 475–80 and IV: 523–24; "Marcial Lalanda," Silva Aramburu, *Enciclopedia taurina*, 277; *Toros y toreros en 1924*, 144–46; *Toros y toreros en 1926*, 189–90; *Toros y toreros en 1929*, 215–17; "El matador de toros Marcial Lalanda muere en Madrid a la edad de 87 años" and "El más grande," both articles published in the daily newspaper *El país* (26 October 1990): 41. For Lalanda's ranch, see Cossío (1943–97) I: 279–80.

325. For a review of the corrida of 8 July 1925 (Miura bulls), *see* Passchendaele. Contemporary reviews of the *corridas* of 9, 11, and 12 July are summarized in Mandel, *Reading Hemingway*, 88–89.

326. Lalanda had been contracted for four afternoons in Pamplona, but an injury incurred in the corrida of 7 July caused him to cancel the last two. Illness caused him to cancel the bullfights he had scheduled for 22 September-13 October (*Toros y toreros en 1926*, 190, 322).

327. Lalanda's bullfighting schedules, detailed in the annual *Toros y toreros en . . .* , have been tallied against the travel schedules and bullfight ticket stubs, Hemingway Collection (JFK).

328. Qtd. in Cossío (1943–97) III: 477.

329. Bagüés also compares Lalanda with Joselito and describes him, as Hemingway does, as "un torero cerebral." But Bagüés disagrees with Hemingway's negative evaluation of Lalanda's early performances. He writes that "desde que empezó a torear le aplicaron el apelativo de 'Joven maestro.' . . . He aquí un torero que fue primera figura desde que tomó la alternativa hasta que se retiró" (since he started to fight he was called the "young master." . . . Here's a bullfighter who was a premier figure from the day of his *alternativa* until he retired; Bagüés, *Historia de los matadores*, 170–71).

330. Cossío (1943–97) III: 475.

331. *Toros y toreros en 1924* reports that Gitanillo had been wounded on 11 May 1924 but fought again on the 16th. Both incidents occurred in Madrid, and I suspect that in his anxiety to right himself before that important public and not to miss an engagement in such a prestigious city, the young matador fought on the 16th before he was fully recovered, hence the terrific wound (151–53 and 249). The 1927 wound that finished his career also occurred in Madrid, during the fiesta of San Isidro; the bull, named Doradito, was from the ranch of Argimirio Pérez (*Toros y toreros en 1927*, 240).

332. Cossío (1943–97), "Lausín López (Braulio), Gitanillo de Ricla," III: 488–89 and V: 1124; Bagüés, *Historia de los matadodres*, 174; Tapia, *Breve historial del toreo*, 385–86; *Toros y toreros en 1927*, 240.

333. Mandel describes Hemingway's first exposure to Gitanillo in "The Birth of Hemingway's *Afición*," 130–40. The corrida was reviewed in *El pensamiento navarro*, 13 July 1923, 1, cols. 4–6.

334. Here and throughout I am grateful to Miguel Angel García and to don Manuel García-Aleas Carrasco, who supplied information about names, legal matters, and family relationships among bull breeders (Interviews, 20–24 August 1997, Madrid).

335. Vera, "Vistahermosa," *Orígenes e historial*, 20; "Moreno Ardanuy, D. Félix," *Toros y toreros en 1931*, 154–55; Cossío (1943–97) I: 284–85; Vera, "Moreno Ardanuy (hijos de don Félix)," *Orígenes e historial*, 107–108; "Saltillo (Ganadería de)," *Unión de criadores de toros de lidia* (1995), 263; "Indice alfabético de ganaderos y fecha en que, por primera vez a su nombre, se han corrido toros, como nuevos, en las plazas de Madrid, desde el año 1765," Cossío (1943–97) I: 313–22. The Santa Coloma (q.v.) bulls have Saltillo blood.

336. "Moreno Ardanuy, D. Félix," *Toros y toreros en 1931*, 154. Cossío repeats the remark ([1943–97] I: 284).

337. Claramunt López, "Marismas de Vila Franca de Xira," 15.

338. Cortada writes that in the years preceding the Spanish Civil War, the writer Victor de la Serna Espina, a Falangist, "directed the publication of various periodicals such as *El Imparcial* and *La Libertad*," but it is difficult to know if this is the same *La Libertad* (435).

339. *Selected Letters*, 341; Freiberg, *The French Press*, 84–85. Although *Le Temps* maintained a conciliatory position towards the Germans before the Munich accords, it opposed the Germans after the war broke out and "in no way collaborated" with the occupying forces or the German-controlled Vichy government. In fact, it "closed down when Nazi troops entered the 'Free French Zone' in 1942." Even so, it was not allowed to reopen after World War II, its presses being used to publish *Le Monde* (Freiberg, *The French Press*, 31).

340. Cortada, *Historical Dictionary of the Spanish Civil War*, 205. After the death of Franco in 1975, the Spanish Communist Party and several workers' unions again began publishing newspapers and journals called *Libertad*, without the article *La*.

341. Mott, *American Journalism*, 733.

342. JFK, Item 22, Folder 24a; "The Gambler, the Nun, and the Radio," *Winner Take Nothing*, 219. For the publication history of "Fifty Grand," see Smith, *Reader's Guide*, 126; and Hemingway, *Selected Letters*, 197. The unpublished manuscript is in JFK, Item 22, Folder 24a; for the reference to *Liberty* in "The Gambler, the Nun, and the Radio," see *Winner Take Nothing*, 219.

343. "David Liceaga," *Toros y toreros en 1933*, 268.

344. *Toros y toreros en 1931*, 271–72. Another 1931 report is much more enthu-

siastic, describing him as "formidable" with the muleta and predicting "un espléndido porvenir" (a splendid future); see "Un nuevo matador de toros mejicano: David Liceaga," *La fiesta brava*, 26 June 1931.

345. Cossío (1943–97), "Liceaga Macial (David)," III: 499 and IV: 528; Abella, *Historia* II: 79; Tapia, *Breve historial del toreo*, 448–49. Tapia reports that Liceaga's second last name was Maciel, a spelling confirmed by taurine expert Anthony Brand; Cossío (1943–97) spells the name Macial in volumes III and IV but corrects it to Maciel in XII: 770. Bagüés claims that Liceaga was born in 1912 (*Historia de los matadores*, 213–14). David's brother Mauro was also a *matador de toros* in Mexico but didn't take the Spanish *alternativa*. Their brother Eduardo, a promising *novillero*, was killed by a bull in August 1946, shortly before he was to take his Spanish *alternativa*. Their nephew, Anselmo Liceaga Rionda, was promoted to *matador de toros* in Granada, on 29 September 1951 (Cossío [1943–97] IV: 528). David Liceaga died on 2 November 1996 (Cossío [1943–97] XII: 1137).

346. Silva Aramburu spells the name Durán (*Enciclopedia taurina*, 321), as does Cossío in "Los toros y el periodismo," Cossío (1943–97) II: 551–52; *see also* Cossío (1943–97) VI: 1033 ff. The name appears as Durá on the masthead.

347. JFK, Bullfight Materials.

348. Beegel, *Hemingway's Craft of Omission*, 40–41.

349. Varela's widow sold all her cows and several bulls to Juan de Dios Romero, who sold most of his holdings to Angel González Nandín. Nandín in turn sold it to José Clemente Rivera, from whom López Plata acquired it.

350. Cossío (1943–97), "López Plata, don Antonio," I: 280; *Toros y toreros en 1931*, 144–45; "Soto de la Fuente, don José María," Cossío (1943–97) IV: 217; Vera, *Orígenes e historial*, 148.

351. Sedgwick, *Ignatius Loyola*, 33.

352. Quotations are from "Loyola, St. Ignatius of," *Encyclopaedia Britannica*, 1911 ed., XVII: 80–82; other details are from Sedgwick's *Ignatius Loyola*, 14–15, 32–33, *et passim*; *Encyclopedia Americana*, 1961 ed., XVII: 815. The 1911 *Britannica* claims the Society was founded by Loyola and six other men; the 1961 *Encyclopedia Americana* identifies "ten knights, all thoroughly educated university men" (XVII: 815).

353. Rao, "Motif of Luck," 35. Mandel discusses Luck in *The Old Man and the Sea* (*Reading Hemingway*, 353–54). Rao offers a fairly thorough review of references to luck in Hemingway's works generally.

354. Mellow, *Hemingway*, 407; Cossío (1943–97), "Ortiz (Luis), Picardías," VI: 218; Smith, *A Reader's Guide*, 264; "Portrait of Three, or The Paella," JFK, Item 660.

355. Cossío (1943–97), "Prieto Domínguez (Francisco)," III: 751. Francisco Prieto used the professional name Curro Prieto; he is the only bullfighter in Cossío's comprehensive encyclopedia with this nickname, so the identification is unequivocal. The usual nicknames for Francisco are Curro and Paco, which would explain his also being called Paco Curro.

Prieto made his professional debut in Madrid as *matador de novillos* on 12 June 1925, sharing the *cartel* with Francisco Royo (Lagartito), also mentioned in the fragment, and Sacristán Fuentes. His performances on that and subsequent afternoons were lackluster (Cossío [1943–97] III: 751).

"Portrait of Three" mentions other characters, who are more difficult to identify with any certainty. "The deformed one" is probably Francisco Gómez (Aldeano; q.v.), who was also much scarred. Both the young homosexual marquis who admires Sidney and the boxer who frequently accompanies him are unnamed.

356. Cossío writes that Calvache did quite well with the cape and banderillas but poorly with the sword; see Cossío (1943–97), "Calvache (Antonio)," III: 146; and the catalogue for the Calvache exhibit, Centro Cultural del Conde Duque (Madrid: Artes Gráficas Luis Pérez, S.A., 1994).

357. Cano was the son of a minor bullfighter and, as a young man, a *matador de novillos*; see "Cano Lorenzo (Francisco), Curro Cano," Cossío (1943–97) IV: 396. He was photographing Antonio Ordóñez in 1959 and thus met Hemingway (interview with author, 25 June 1998, Madrid); the photographs of the guests at La Cónsula (following *DS* 166) are his. Like Calvache, José Fernández Aguayo was the son and brother of famous photographers (both called Baldomero Fernández) who took up bullfighting. He was hampered by lack of talent and at 4′7″ was too short to fight full-grown bulls. He worked in Spain and Mexico as long as he could and then, recognizing the hopelessness of his situation, he went into the family business in 1933 or 1934, using the name Pepito Aguayo. For his career as a *becerrista* and *novillero*, see Alvaro Martínez-Novillo's catalogue for the 1991 exhibit, *Baldomero & Aguayo, fotógrafos taurinos*, 41–61. My thanks to Anthony Brand for bringing Calvache, Aguayo, and the two catalogues to my attention.

358. Hemingway is easy to recognize; Anthony Brand identified the others (interviews, March and August 1999).

359. Hemingway's handwritten "u" has a rounded bottom; the manuscript initial is spiky, like an "n" or an "m." Hemingway did not spot or correct the substitution of U for M (see JFK, Item 22, Folder 26, 8).

360. Obituary, "Archibald MacLeish Is Dead; Poet and Playwright Was 89," *New York Times*, 21 April 1982, 1: 5.

361. MacLeish's achievements are described in a variety of sources, but Sylvia Grinder, of the Association of Yale Alumni, gave me the most complete account of his education, publications, official postings, honors and awards, and family details (letter to author and enclosures, 8 September 1995).

362. Reynolds reports that Hemingway and MacLeish arrived in Zaragoza on 12 October 1926 (*American Homecoming*, 69–71). Bullfights took place on 13, 14, 15, and 17 October. The Hemingway Collection has the stubs Hemingway saved from the bullfight of Thursday, 14 October, and Sunday, 17 October (JFK, Bullfighting Materials: Schedules). The bullfighters on the 14th were, in order of seniority, Antonio Márquez, Marcial Lalanda, Nicanor Villalta, and Cayetano Ordóñez. The first three also appeared on the 17th (*Toros y toreros en 1926*, 24). No other bullfighters

performed in that year's Fiesta del Pilar. It is possible, of course, that Hemingway and MacLeish saw all four corridas of the 1926 Zaragoza fiesta. For more details, see the entry for Zaragoza.

363. Reynolds, *The American Homecoming*, 70.

364. MacLeish, "Cinema of a Man," from *New Found Land* (1930); rpt. in *New and Collected Poems, 1917–1976*, 146.

365. Donaldson reports that "The ambiguity was deliberate. When Archie thanked him for the dedication, Ernest said, 'What makes you think you're A. MacLeish?' " (qtd. in Donaldson, *Archibald MacLeish*, 248).

366. Vaill confirms that "Archie MacLeish didn't arrive in Antibes from Persia until June 16" (*Everybody Was So Young*, 407 n. 182).

367. Cossío (1943–97), "Madrid y Villatoro (Francisco)," III: 532–34 and IV: 545; Hagemann Collection, JFK, Item 568.

368. My thanks to Anthony Brand, who has worked extensively with the photographs.

369. Calvocoressi, *Who's Who in the Bible*, 155–56.

370. All these records have since been broken.

371. Thomas Gilcoyne, Research Librarian of the National Museum of Racing and Hall of Fame, Saratoga Springs, New York, supplied information on Man o' War (interviews, 15 December 1997 and 26 March 1998). Man o' War's groom was Will Harbut. Quotes are from the long obituary, "Man o' War," in Palmer, *American Race Horses*, 25, 31.

372. For Pagés, see *Toros y toreros en 1926*, 43. Matías Retana died in June 1929 (*Toros y toreros en 1929*, 293). For bullring managers/impresarios, see "Asociación de empresarios," *Toros y toreros en 1926*, 41.

373. Cossío (1943–97), "Manzanares Antón (Joaquín), Mella," III: 536, IV: 547, and VI: 19.

374. Cossío and *El Clarín*'s almanac give the number for 1924 as thirty-three corridas; *Toros y toreros en 1924* reports thirty-nine corridas (141–43) and heaps unqualified praise on Márquez (as does Cossío).

375. Márquez's *toreo* is usually described as "belmontino" or "post-belmontino." The contemporary critic Néstor Luján writes that Márquez's expertise and power enabled him to control the bull at close quarters, as Belmonte did, but without Belmonte's excesses. He adds that his intellectual, occasionally cold and aloof demeanor in the ring reduced the emotional power of his art (qtd. in Abella, II: 18). In 1929 the critic Uno al Sesgo called Márquez the "Torero . . . más completo de estos tiempos, con el capote, en banderillas, toreando de muleta y como estoqueador raya a tal altura, que en una tarde afortunada ningún otro espada puede aventajarle" (the most accomplished bullfighter of these times, with the cape, the banderillas, the muleta and sword he works at such heights that on a good afternoon no other matador can top him; *Toros y toreros en 1929*, 215).

376. Cossío (1943–97), "Márquez y Serrano (Antonio)," III: 542–45 and IV: 552; Cossío (1995) II: 568; Tapia, *Breve historial del toreo*, 386–87; Abella, *Hist-*

oria II: 17–18; Bagüés, *Historia de los matadores*, 169–70; *Toros y toreros en 1932*, 291; "Márquez 'en capilla'," *La fiesta brava*, 21 July 1927, 2; "Antonio Márquez: Este no torea; Esculpe," *La fiesta brava*, 10 October 1930.

377. In July 1925, two of Márquez's three afternoons in Pamplona were disappointing. On 7 July 1925, appearing with Martín Agüero and Cayetano Ordóñez (qq.v.), Márquez was awarded an ear. On 9 July he shared the bill with three other matadors (it was a *corrida de prueba*, with only four bulls), and he was the least successful of the four. On 12 July, performing with Lalanda (q.v.) and Ordóñez and fighting Pablo Romero bulls, he began the fight with his first bull well but ended it so badly that the bull had to be killed by Márquez's *puntillero*; the bull was applauded as it was dragged from the ring. On his second bull he was again disappointing, although this time he killed the bull on the second try and was applauded for this.

378. Minguet, *Desde la grada*, 151; "Efemérides," *Toros y toreros en 1924*, 233.

379. García-Ramos and Narbona, *Ignacio Sánchez Mejías*, 245–46.

380. Capellán, *Hispanic World*, 146–47.

381. Cossío (1943–97), "Martín-Caro Cases (Juan), Chiquito de la Audiencia," III: 553 and IV: 557; Bagüés, *Historia de los matadores*, 219.

382. Cossío reports eleven *corridas* in 1926, but these are the ones of the 1925–26 Mexican season. In Spain Martínez fought fourteen *corridas*.

383. Cossío (1943–97), "Martínez (Manuel)," III: 564–65, IV: 565, and VI: 66; "Martínez Solaz (Manuel)," Cossío (1995) II: 581; Abella, "Otros diestros olvidados" (other forgotten matadors), *Historia* II: 122; Bagüés, *Historia de los matadores*, 184; *Toros y toreros en 1924-Toros y toreros en 1931*. The Valencia publication *El Clarín* (q.v.) frequently raves about its native bullfighter (e.g., "Toques de Clarín: Está, sin más alegato, más valiente que un jabato," *El Clarín*, 31 August 1929).

384. Hemingway was in Valencia from July 23 until August 3 that year, writing *The Sun Also Rises* (Baker, *A Life Story*, 589). Martínez's 1925 wound is described in *Toros y toreros en 1925*, 176, 254.

385. Villalta and Chaves also performed in that fair, *Toros y toreros en 1927*, 15–16. Injuries are listed in "Los que han visitado el 'hule' en 1927," *El Clarín* (Almanaque 1928); see also *Toros y toreros en 1927*, 241.

386. Both the manuscript and the setting copy read Tolosa (JFK, Item 22, Folder 25–1, 36, and Folder 35, 27). The thirty-two-year-old Genovart died before reaching the infirmary (*Toros y toreros en 1931*, 361). The incident is also reported in *Torerías*, 14 September 1930, 7).

387. José Jijón gives his name to the *jijona* caste, distinguished for its red or reddish hide. This strain or caste of *toro de lidia* began to be recognized in the late sixteenth century but became associated with Jijón in the very early 1700s because he bought and bred stock to emphasize the breed's striking color. Unlike the more popular Vistahermosa and Cabrera strains, which are "castas andaluzas," the *ji-*

jones are from Castilla-La Mancha. Don José Jijón's ranch was in Villarrubia de los Ojos del Guadiana, province of Ciudad Real, in Castilla-La Mancha. Other herds that have a strong *jijona* strain are the Galache (formerly García Aleas) and the Pablo Romero (q.v.).

388. Cossío (1943–97), "Martínez, don Vicente (hoy don Julián Fernández Martínez)," I: 282–83; *Toros y toreros en 1930*, 166–67; *Toros y toreros en 1931*, 149–51. *See also* Vera, *Orígenes e historial*, 18; "Ganaderías de toros de lidia," *Gran enciclopedia Rialp* XXII: 603–605, s.v. section on "Casta jijona." For the herd's post-Civil War history, see "Sancho, viuda de Arribas (doña Francisca)," Vera, *Orígenes e historial*, 255–57; and her children, "Arribas Sancho (Hdros. de Don Antonio), *Unión de criadores de toros de lidia* (2000), 42. *Toros y toreros en 1930* incorrectly presents the brand with sloping sides, like an upside-down *W*, and *Toros y toreros en 1931* presents the brand upside-down, like a *W* instead of an *M*.

389. At the Cinquantenaire, Master Bob defeated Héros XII and L'Yser.

390. The "Programme Officiel, Courses a Auteuil, Réunion d'Automne," 19 November 1922, identifies Master Bob's breeding as Chulo and Morelos, his trainer as John Dutton, and his owner as H. Roux de Bézieux (JFK, Other Materials: Horse Racing). The *Annuaire de la chronique du turf, 1923* also identifies H. Roux de Bézieux as the owner, but the *Annuaire de la chronique du turf, 1924*, names Cte. du Crozet as the owner, although John Dutton continued as trainer.

Louis Romanet, who also gave me details about Master Bob's 1924 victory, identifies the horse's breeding as Master Robert-Welcor by Dick Welles, and his owner as M. le comte du Crozet (Louis Romanet, Direction des Relations Internationales, France Galop, Boulogne, fax, 30 January 1996), but this seems incorrect. Information was also supplied by Howard Bass, Thoroughbred Racing Communications (letter to author, 21 September 1990; and E-mail communication, 12 September 1995). Mr. Bass consulted the Jockey Club Information Systems' Equine Line (R), a computer database, as well as other sources. He reports that Master Bob was born in 1922, but the program in the Hemingway Collection indicates that in 1922 Master Bob was eight years old; M. Romanet also reports that Master Bob was born in 1914. Thomas Gilcoyne, Research Librarian of the National Museum of Racing and Hall of Fame, Saratoga Springs, New York, agrees with the earlier date (interview, 15 December 1997). For information about the June 1923 race, see Reynolds, *The Paris Years*, 133; for details about the other races of Master Bob's career, I consulted the *Annuaire de la chronique du turf, 1922–1925*.

391. Reynolds, *Hemingway's Reading*, 157.

392. Cossío (1943–97) III: 575.

393. Cossío (1943–97), "Mazquiarán Torróntegui (Diego), Fortuna," III: 573–75 and IV: 574; Bagüés, *Historia de los matadores*, 153; Tapia, *Breve historial del toreo*, 368–69; *Toros y toreros en 1924-Toros y toreros en 1931*. His nephew, Juan Mazquiarán (Fortuna chico, b. 1908), was never promoted to *matador de toros*.

394. Mazzantini's remark is qtd. in Cossío (1943–97) III: 576. Lozano writes

that Mazzantini was "very educated, linguistically versatile . . . his ambition was to become an opera singer" and adds that Mazzantini's choice of bullfighting as a profession brought dignity to the spectacle (24). The extent to which Mazzantini's remark entered daily language is revealed by Pilar's remark about "this country where no poor man can ever hope to make money unless he is criminal like Juan March, or a bullfighter, or a tenor in the opera" (*FWTBT*, 184).

395. Mazzantini had, or was said to have had, many affairs, with luminaries such as Sarah Bernhardt.

396. Cossío (1943–97), "Mazzantini y Eguía (Luis)," III: 576–79; Silva Aramburu, *Enciclopedia taurina*, 256–57. Bagüés particularly admires his sword work (*Historia de los matadores*, 88–89).

397. Tapia, *Breve historial del toreo*, 291.

398. Reynolds, *Hemingway's Reading*, 158; Brasch and Sigman, *Hemingway's Library*, 249; "Meier-Graefe," *Der Grosse Brockhaus*, 15th ed., XII (1932): 345; 16th ed., VII (1955): 649; *Enciclopedia Universal, Suplemento 1961–62*, 1334.

399. Scholes and Comley, *Hemingway's Genders*, 116.

400. Cossío (1943–97) III: 582; Bagüés, *Historia de los matadores*, 214. *Toros y toreros en . . .* praises Pepe Bienvenida in 1928, 1929, 1930, and 1931; Hemingway owned these volumes (see the entry for *Toreros y toros*).

401. Cossío (1943–97), "Mejías Jiménez (José), Bienvenida," III: 582, IV: 579, and VI: 87; Bagüés, *Historia de los matadores*, 214; Abella, *Historia* II: 126–27; "José Mejías 'Bienvenida'," *Toros y toreros en 1929*, 260–61; *Toros y toreros en 1931*, 273–74.

402. Hemingway writes that Manolo went directly from *becerrista* to *matador de toros* (166): this is true only in Spain. In Mexico and Peru, in the winter of 1928–29, he did perform as *novillero*. Hemingway also claims that Manolo's first Spanish season was a failure, but the facts argue otherwise. If one considers 1928 as his first Spanish season, Manolo was quite successful: he fought twenty-seven *becerradas* in the most important Spanish plazas, including three performances in Madrid. If one considers 1929 as his first Spanish season (I believe this is the one that Hemingway means, since he is speaking about mature bulls, not *becerros*), one needs to remember that Bienvenida was awarded both ears and the tail of his first, or *alternativa*, bull in Zaragoza, 30 June 1929. He was indeed unimpressive in Madrid at the end of that season, when he confirmed his *alternativa* on 12 October (Cossío blames this on bad luck: he drew weak bulls), but throughout the season he had enjoyed great success, performing in the most important ferias and plazas of Spain and obtaining an impressive seventy-three contracts for the next season— hardly the result of a weak season. Hemingway was not in Spain for the 1930 season. His remarks about Bienvenida were culled from taurine reviews of Bienvenida's performances.

403. Cossío (1943–97) III: 586.

404. Cossío (1943–97), "Mejías Jiménez (Manuel), Bienvenida," III: 582–86; Silva Aramburu, *Enciclopedia taurina*, 282. Bagüés, less enthusiastic, indicates that

Manolo Bienvenida's *toreo* lacked depth and recalls the occasional unimpressive performance, but even so, and in spite of his youth, he was "durante diez años una primera figura" (a top-ranked or first-class performer for ten years). Bagüés's statistics differ slightly from Cossío's: he claims that Manolo Bienvenida fought eighty-two corridas in 1931 (*Historia de los matadores*, 205–206). Cossío writes that Bienvenida had a cyst removed from his back a month before he died; Bagüés says Bienvenida suffered from lung cancer.

The errors in Hemingway's discussion of Manuel Bienvenida (about his sword work, his bravery, the quality of his early seasons, the age at which he started fighting, the bleak prediction about his future, etc.) suggest that he is confusing the son with his father, Manuel Mejías Rapela (q.v.).

405. The bullfighter's schedule is detailed in *Toros y toreros en 1929-Toros y toreros en 1931*. His reviews for those years are glowing: Uno al Sesgo writes that although he is too young to have a fully developed personality and style—at the end of 1931, Manolo Bienvenida was only nineteen—such development will only enhance his performances. Bienvenida already has a well-developed concept of what the art of the bullfight consists of, and he has grown and matured from season to season. He is "un gran torero hoy, lo será aún más" (a great torero today, he will be greater still; *Toros y toreros en 1931*, 260–61).

406. De la Hiz Flores, a friend of the family and obviously unwilling to say anything negative, provides the comment that the Pamplona and Valencia performances were almost unrelievedly poor, with only one "gran faena" (*Bienvenida*, 178). An ecstatic review of this 1931 Pamplona performance, for which he was awarded ears and carried out of the ring in triumph, can be seen in *El Clarín* (18 July 1931). De la Hiz Flores also reports that Gregorio Corrochano (q.v.), who had admired Manuel Bienvenida in his first years, also soured on him; she then quotes the many other critics who acclaim him (*Bienvenida*, 195–210) and clearly believes that Corrochano erred.

407. Hemingway and Bienvenida coincided in Madrid on those days. On 26 June 1931 Hemingway wrote to Dos Passos from Madrid: "Most bull displays lousy" (*Selected Letters*, 341).

408. Agrarian reform, aimed at improving conditions for the peasantry, was a major concern of Spain's Second Republic, proclaimed on 14 April 1931. For the Bienvenida holdings, see De la Hiz Flores, *Bienvenida*, 170, 176, 181, 247.

409. Manuel Mejías's nickname, "el Papa Negro" (the Black Pope), was bestowed on him by José de la Loma, the famous taurine critic known as Don Modesto, only a few days after this same critic had called Ricardo Torres (Bombita), "El Papa de la tauromaquia" (Mira, *Antonio Bienvenida*, 22).

410. Cossío (1943–97) III: 588. Biographical details are taken from Cossío (1943–97), "Mejías Rapela, Manuel," III: 586–88 and VI: 89; Silva Aramburu, *Enciclopedia taurina*, 265–66; Bagüés, *Historia de los matadores*, 128–29; Mira, *Antonio Bienvenida*, 20–32; and De la Hiz Flores, *Bienvenida*, 37–117, and especially 61 and 67, where she discusses the twice-gored left leg. His six sons all called

themselves Bienvenida, though most were born elsewhere (*see also* the entry for Bienvenida).

411. Franklin, *Bullfighter from Brooklyn*, 173, 176.

412. Cossío (1943–97), "Mérida (Andrés)," III: 595 and IV: 583; Cossío (1995), "Leiva Mérida, (Andrés)," II: 539. Bagüés also gives the bullfighter's full name as Andrés Leiva Mérida, noting that he was known as Mérida, his mother's last name (*Historia de los matadores*, 207). The numbers given by Cossío and by the annual almanacs of *El Clarín* differ occasionally.

413. *Toros y toreros en 1925*, 25–26.

414. Cossío (1943–97) III: 595.

415. Cossío (1943–97), "Merino Obanos (Félix)," III: 595–96; Bagüés, *Historia de los matadores*, 154; *El Clarín*, annual Almanacs for 1926 and 1927.

416. *Toros y toreros en 1927*, 252–53; this obituary reports that Merino was born in 1895.

417. The officers of the Patrimonio Nacional, Dirección de Actuaciones Histórico-Artísticas, Monasterio de El Escorial, kindly supplied information and color photographs of the mitre (letters and enclosures, 28 October, 20 November, and 9 December 1998).

418. *Toreros y toros en 1931*, 273.

419. Miró Obituary, *New York Times Annual Obituaries: 1983*, 611; Barnils, "L'artista i Mont-roig," 52–56.

420. Interview with Miró, qtd. in Bernier, "The Painter Miró," 105.

421. O'Rourke, "Evan Shipman and Hemingway's Farm," 156; Hemingway, "*The Farm*," 28. O'Rourke identifies Miró's new dealer (after Paul Rosenberg) as Jacques Viot, of the Galerie Pierre. Reynolds corrects Baker's price of 5,000 francs (Baker, *A Life Story*, 158), arguing that Hemingway bought the Miró for about $200 (3,500 francs; Reynolds, *Paris Years*, 40, 296). Baker probably based himself on Hemingway's own 1934 report that he had paid "five thousand francs for *The Farm* and that was four thousand two hundred and fifty francs more than I had ever paid for a picture. The picture naturally stayed with the dealer [until payment was completed]. When it was time to make the last payment the dealer came around and was very pleased because there was no money in the house or in the bank. If we did not pay the money that day he kept the picture. Dos Passos, Shipman and I finally borrowed the money around various bars and restaurants, got the picture and brought it home in a taxi. The dealer felt very bad because he had already been offered four times what we were paying. But we explained to him as it is so often explained to you in France, that business is business" (Hemingway, *The Farm*, 28). Dos Passos also remembers the event: "I had to rush around scrounging up cash. . . . He found he could buy it for two or maybe three thousand francs (damn little in dollars at the current exchange) and was in a fever for fear someone else would snap it up. He brought the picture home to the sawmill in triumph" (*The Best Times*, 144). Shipman's account of the coin tossing is quoted by Matthew Josephson in "Evan Shipman," 833. Although Hemingway does not mention Gertrude Stein in this ac-

count, the phrase "very pleased" recalls her, as does the emphasis on the investment value of the painting. Stein, a fine collector, often advised her friends to invest in painting.

422. Correspondence and contracts relating to the loan of *The Farm* to the Museum of Modern Art (JFK, Other Materials: Art Papers).

423. JFK, Item 39, Folder 47, unnumbered page 3.

424. Miró's letter to Hemingway, dated 17 July 1926, reports that his father had died suddenly (his body had been found in the garden) and consequently the Hemingways would not be able to visit as originally planned (JFK, Incoming Correspondence). In a letter to Archibald MacLeish, written in Montroig and dated 18 July 1929, Hemingway reports that he and Pauline are "Visiting Miró here" (*Selected Letters*, 300).

425. Hemingway described his unsuccessful attempt to gain entry in order to photograph the Miró house and farm (E. H. to J. T. Soby, 7 August 1959; JFK, Other Materials: Art Papers. When I visited Miró's farm in Montroich in the fall of 1995, I was similarly refused admittance by the resident caretakers.

426. Dolores Miró (María Dolores Miró de Punyet), letter to author, 11 March 1996. She reports that the Miró farmhouse has been painted and modernized since Hemingway's visit.

427. The Vistahermosa being such a superior caste, the Cabrera (like the Jijón) has been crossbred with it. Juan Miura and his heirs, however, have carefully bred Cabrera stock, keeping the herd separate from the stock they crossbred with Saavedra (Vistahermosa) bulls. The Miura family holdings represent the only true Cabrera herd in existence; their *antigüedad* dates to 1842, i.e., when the herd was still owned by Cabrera's widow. The Miura bull is a result of the crossbreeding between this Cabrera herd and Vistahermosa (qq.v.).

428. Vera, *Orígenes e historial*, 102.

429. Sotomayor, *Miura*, 70–72.

430. *Unión de criadores de toros de lidia* (1978), 122–23.

431. For the Miura family and their bulls, see Cossío (1943–97) I: 283–84, III: 952–53, and IV: 213; Vera, *Orígenes e historial*, 101–103; *Toros y toreros en 1931*, 152–53. For longer discussions of the great Miura controversy, see Cossío (1943–97), "Iniciativas y pleitos de Bombita," IV: 950–55; Cossío (1943–97), "Torres Reina (Ricardo), Bombita," III: 953–54; and Silva Aramburu, "El pleito de los Miuras," *Enciclopedia taurina*, 260–62; Silva Aramburu's date, 1808 (top page 262) is a typographical error, the correct date being 1908. Vera claims that the founder, Juan Miura, established his herd in 1842, not 1849 (*Orígenes e historial*, 101). Vera explains the matter of the two sets of colors in terms of a pre-existing claim (*Orígenes e historial*, 102); don Manuel Aleas explained that the black ribbon is a sign of mourning for the bullfighter Pepete (interview, Madrid, August 1997). Sotomayor agrees with Vera (*Miura*, 70–72).

432. *El pensamiento navarro*, 9 July 1925, 1.

433. "Mojiganga" and "Charlotada," Nieto Manjón, *Diccionario taurino ilus-*

trado, 157–58, 290; Cossío (1943–97), "En torno al toreo cómico y la mojiganga," V: 156–58. See also Cossío (1943–97) I: 721–23 and VII: 108–109.

434. Cossío (1943–97), "Molina Sánchez (Rafael), Lagartijo," III: 610–19; Martínez Salvatierra, *Los toros*, 191; Tapia, *Breve historial del toreo*, 246–53. Silva Aramburu describes Lagartijo as a dignified man and artist, the opposite of the passionate, fiery Frascuelo: they embodied contrasting national characteristics, and their rivalry captured the public and epitomized the age. He gives 1894 as the date of Lagartijo's retirement (*Enciclopedia taurina*, 247).

435. Cossío (1943–97), "Montes Vico (Antonio)," III: 625–27; Bagüés, *Historia de los matadores*, 107–108.

436. Montes and Belmonte shared the same mentor, a banderillero named Calderón (Anthony Brand, letter to author, April 1998).

437. Qtd. in Cossío (1943–97) III: 629.

438. Cossío (1943–97), "Montes (Francisco), Paquiro," III: 627–35; Silva Aramburu, *Enciclopedia taurina*, 242; Martínez Salvatierra, *Los toros*, 190–91.

439. For Abenamar's journalism, see Cossío (1943–97) VIII: 191–246.

440. Qtd. in Abella, *Historia* I: 172.

441. Hemingway coined his famous phrase, "grace under pressure," in 1926 (*Selected Letters*, 200).

442. Cossío (1943–97), "Montes Mora (Mariano)," III: 636–37; Bagüés, *Historia de los matadores*, 170; Obituary, "Mariano Montes," *Toros y toreros en 1926*, 329–30.

443. "Mariano Montes," *Toros y toreros en 1924*, 143.

444. Cossío (1943–97), "Montes Mora (Pedro)," III: 637; a full account of the *novillada* in which Pedro Montes was killed appears in *El eco taurino*, 28 July 1930, 2, col. 3 and 3, col. 1. The obituary describes the wound as more than twenty centimeters deep ("Pedro Montes Mora," *Toros y toreros en 1930*, 340–41).

445. Cossío (1943–97), "Moreno Ardanuy, D. Félix," *Toros y toreros en 1931*, 154–55; I: 284–85; Vera, "Moreno Ardanuy (hijos de don Félix)," *Orígenes e historial*, 107–108; "Saltillo (Ganadería de)," *Unión de criadores de toros de lidia* (1995), 263 (an incorrect date in this edition is corrected in the 1997 edition, on page 308); Cossío (1943–97), "Indice alfabético de ganaderos y fecha en que, por primera vez a su nombre, se han corrido toros, como nuevos, en las plazas de Madrid, desde el año 1765," I: 313–22. Bagüés also praises Moreno Ardanuy for having restored the decayed Saltillo herd to its "antiguo prestigio" in only seven years (qtd. in *Toros y toreros en 1925*, 30). Vera argues that the herd's *antigüedad* should be 25 July 1837 (*Orígenes e historial*, 107 n. 1). Anthony Brand writes that Ricardo Torres Reina (Bombita, q.v.) was instrumental in establishing the Mexican branch of the Lesaca-Saltillo; the ranch was San Mateo (letter to author, April 1998).

446. For Mosquera's brief career as bullring impresario, see Antonio Díaz Cañabate, "Panorama del toreo hasta 1979," in Cossío (1943–97) V: 127–28; Obituary, *El eco taurino*, 12 March 1928, 5, col. 3; "A los que metió en cintura Mosquera: Bombita—Machaquito," *Torerías: Semanario taurino bolcheviki*, 23 March 1930,

46; Silva Aramburu, *Enciclopedia taurina*, 260–61. See also Cossío (1943–97), "Torres Reina (Ricardo), Bombita," III: 952–53. Retana was impresario of the Madrid bullring for nineteen years, from 1907 until late 1926; he appears in Hemingway's story "The Undefeated" and in the novel *For Whom the Bell Tolls*.

447. Mellow, *Hemingway*, 57–58; Gandolfi, "The Outskirts of Literature," 105–08.

448. "Bernardo Muñoz," *Toros y toreros en 1926*, 184; *Toros y toreros en 1927*, 154–55.

449. "Bernardo Muñoz, Carnicerito," *Toros y toreros en 1929*, 213; *Toros y toreros en 1924-Toros y toreros en 1931*; *El Clarín*, annual almanacs, 1925–1928.

450. Cossío (1943–97), "Muñoz Marín (Bernardo), Carnicerito," III: 653–54, IV: 596, and VI: 151; Bagüés, *Historia de los matadores*, 161.

451. Donnelly, *Sara & Gerald*, 33, 32, 88–90.

452. Vaill, *Everybody Was So Young*, 179.

453. Donnelly, *Sara & Gerald*, 24; *see also* Reynolds, *American Homecoming*, 48; Linda Patterson Miller, *Letters*, 20.

454. In evaluating the revisions performed upon the manuscript that was posthumously published as *A Moveable Feast*, Tavernier-Courbin notes that "throughout the text, the editors deleted the indeterminate pronoun 'you' used as subject and replaced it by the determinate pronouns 'I' and 'we,' thus clearly modifying Hemingway's diction. This is done at least thirty times in the published text. . . . Moreover, numerous passages using 'you' as subject were deleted. . . . Such editing is double-edged, for it removes the psychological link Hemingway was trying to establish with his reader by making the reader part of his personal experience. . . . The use of 'I' or 'we' instead of 'you' isolates Hemingway within his own experience and from the reader, who no longer participates in his life" (Tavernier-Courbin, *Ernest Hemingway's* A Moveable Feast, 174).

455. Leicester Hemingway, *My Brother, Ernest Hemingway*, 36, 117, 170.

456. Smith, *Reader's Guide*, 231–39.

457. Lewis, "The Making of *Death in the Afternoon*," 51, n. 28.

458. Cossío (1995) also offers a discussion of "Apodos y tratamientos," II: 224–28.

459. The nicknames of bullfighters from the earliest times until the outbreak of the Spanish Civil War appear in an alphabetical listing at the end of Volume III of Cossío's encyclopedia, *Los toros: Tratado técnico e histórico*.

460. Among the members of this *cuadrilla juvenil* were the young banderilleros Rafael Rodríguez (Mojino, son of the *cuadrilla's* founder), Rafael Guerra (q.v.; he was then sixteen years old and "apenas tiene el alto de un abanico," is hardly as tall as a fan), Rafael Bejarano (nephew of the matador Manuel Fuentes Rodríguez [Bocanegra]), and José Diáñe (Cossío [1943–97] III: 414).

461. Cossío (1943–97) III: 800.

462. Cossío (1943–97) III: 385, 950. A more general discussion of the phenomenon of juvenile *cuadrillas* appears in the essay "Becerradas," Cossío (1943–97) I: 663–68, especially 666–68.

463. Cossío (1943–97) III: 365–67.

464. "Las cuadrillas de niños," *El Clarín*, n.d., unnumbered page 3 (JFK, Miscellaneous Bullfight Publications).

465. Different sections offered foreign news (pages 1–4), news about Spain and Morocco (5–6) and about different parts of Spain ("De provincias," 8–10), as well as many ads (12–16).

466. The *Enciclopedia Universal* claims the *Hoja Oficial* was published in Barcelona (*Suplemento 1953–1954*, 636). To expedite distribution, the paper may have been issued simultaneously from more than one city.

467. "Noi," "Sucre," *Diccionari General de la LLengua catalana*.

468. Anthony Brand's prodigious memory provided the given name of Noi del Sucre (fax to author, 22 August 1995).

469. "Seguí (Salvador)," *Nueva Enciclopedia Larousse* IX: 9017; "Seguí i Rubinat, Salvador," *Gran Enciclopèdia Catalana* XIII: 433. The Catalan encyclopedia gives Seguí's birth date as 1886. Other sources put it as late 23 December 1890.

470. Cossío (1943–97), "Las plazas de toros," I: 530; Pinto Maeso, *Plazas de toros de España*, 46–49; Reynolds, *Annotated Chronology*, 58, 64–65; *Toros y toreros en 1927*, 16–17; *Toros y toreros en 1929*, 24–25; *Toros y toreros en 1931*, 13–82 (the complete listing of all events for that year, when Hemingway spent many months in Spain).

471. Carralero and Borge, "Oficial," *Toros célebres*, 229; Cossío (1943–97) I: 382 and III: 27.

472. Stanton, *Hemingway and Spain*, 95; Portz, "Allusion and Structure," 35; Junkins, "Hemingway's Old Lady," 199.

473. The incidents reported in the "Introduction" to *In Our Time*, as well as the clipped British voice that reports them, are derived from Hemingway's friend, Eric Dorman-Smith (q.v.).

474. The Old Lady was a late addition to *Death in the Afternoon*, inserted early in 1932. Hemingway's last seasons in Spain before the publication of the book were 1929 and 1931, and the three bullfighters the Old Lady saw at her first bullfight appeared together only once in those years (*Toros y toreros en 1931*, 233, 239–41), when they performed with five other matadors at the inaugural corrida of Las Ventas. Hemingway does not list the matadors in the correct order of seniority: Diego Mazquiarán (Fortuna), the senior matador, should have been mentioned first; the other bullfighters, in descending order of seniority, were Marcial Lalanda, Nicanor Villalta, Fausto Barajas, Luis Fuentes Bejarano, Vicente Barrera, Fermín Espinosa (Armillita Chico), and Manuel Mejías (qq.v.). Eight ranches supplied bulls: Domecq, Concha y Sierra, Conde de la Corte, García Mateo, Julián Martínez, Manuel Aleas, Graciliano P. Tabernero, and Andrés Sánchez de Coquilla.

475. Cayetano's older brother, Antonio, died young as a consequence of injuries sustained while fighting a cow. His brother Manuel (b. 1901), a banderillero, worked in Cayetano's cuadrilla for many years. Rafael (b. 1906) and Alfonso (b. 1914) were *matadores de novillos* but abandoned bullfighting while they were still

in their twenties. Cayetano's other brothers were José (Pepe) and Manuel (Manolo). The seven brothers had two sisters, Consuelo (Concha) and María (Olano, *Dinastías*, 239). Cayetano's five sons all became bullfighters, the most famous being the great Antonio Ordóñez, see in *DS*. This Antonio's two daughters married prominent bullfighters, and Antonio's grandson (Cayetano's great-grandson) is Francisco Rivera Ordóñez, also a matador.

476. *Toros y toreros en 1924*, 199.

477. Hemingway does not present the full facts when he argues that Cayetano's investiture was premature, coming after only twenty-one performances in the ring (88). As a matter of fact, Cayetano was a *novillero* for five years: he performed as *novillero* for the first time in August 1921, in Ceuta, and was quite active in 1922 and 1923, mostly in Andalucía. In 1924 he fought in twenty-four *novilladas*, most of them in first-class rings; to these must be added the twenty-one of 1925 (the ones Hemingway seems to be referring to) before his *alternativa* in June, at which time he was twenty-one years old (Cossío [1943–97] III: 685; *Toros y toreros en 1924*, 200), and not sixteen as Hemingway implies. The annual almanacs do not record the performances of *novilleros* who have not yet made their Madrid debut, but their absence from these charts does not indicate inactivity. If Hemingway relied on these almanacs, he missed all of Cayetano's performances before his Madrid debut on 28 May 1925. I believe that Hemingway knew how to read these almanacs, and that his statistics, while not inaccurate, are skewed in order to make a point (about premature promotions).

If he wanted to make Cayetano's promotion look even hastier, Hemingway could have presented his statistics in a different way, saying that the promotion (11 June 1925) came only two weeks after the debut as *novillero*, and that in those two weeks Cayetano fought only three *novilladas* (*Toros y toreros en 1925*, 185). All that is true, and might have fooled some of his English-speaking readers, but not any aficionado worth his or her salt.

478. Cossío reports sixty-eight corridas for 1926, but the annual almanac of *El Clarín* and the reliable *Toros y toreros en 1926* both give the figure as seventy-eight. Even at sixty-eight corridas he would have been first-ranked: Antonio Márquez, who was ranked second, had fifty-eight corridas.

479. Abad Ojuel, *Estirpe y tauromaquia*, 126.

480. Iribarren, *Hemingway y los sanfermines*, 94–97. In a long footnote, Iribarren quotes and slightly amends R. Capdevila's account of this event, as reported in Capdevila's *Marcial Lalanda* (Madrid, 1943). *La fiesta brava* castigates both Cayetano for his poor performances and the crowd for its violence ("La feria de San Fermín, la debacle de un 'Niño' o la incultura de unas masas," 15 July 1926, 2).

481. *Toros y toreros en 1926*, 207.

482. *Toros y toreros en 1927*, 173.

483. Cossío (1943–97), "Ordóñez y Aguilera (Cayetano), Niño de la Palma," III: 684–89, IV: 611, and VI: 204; Silva Aramburu, *Enciclopedia taurina*, 280; Bagüés, *Historia de los matadores*, 187; *Toros y toreros en 1924—Toros y toreros*

en 1931; Olano, *Dinastías*, 239–68; Abad Ojuel, *Estirpe y tauromaquia*, 15–128. Abad Ojuel, who basically agrees with Hemingway's analysis of Cayetano, chides Hemingway for not mentioning Cayetano's successes in the years 1926–31 (119). He discusses the role of writers and critics (mainly Hemingway and Corrochano) in Cayetano's career, and identifies heavy drinking and financial irresponsibility as factors contributing to the disintegration of his career (118).

484. Iribarren, *Hemingway y los sanfermines*, 114.

485. Cayetano's schedules are presented in *Toros y toreros en 1925*, 165–86; *Toros y toreros en 1926*, 208–209; *Toros y toreros en 1927*, 174; *Toros y toreros en 1929*, 224–25; *Toros y toreros en 1931*, 246. Hemingway's schedule appears in Reynolds, *Chronology*, 39–65. Most of these years Cayetano fought in South America as well. The Hemingway Collection (JFK) holds many, but obviously not all, of the bullfight programs and ticket stubs of the fights Hemingway saw.

486. Hemingway made a similar claim about Manuel Jiménez (Chicuelo)—that he was "finished"—which is highly debatable, considering that he fought for many more years after the publication of *Death in the Afternoon*.

487. For Cayetano's two painful thigh wounds, see *Toros y toreros en 1925*, 248 and 256. Hemingway complained of several other bullfighters that their first wound drained them of courage (e.g., Bienvenida, Cagancho, Chaves, Chicuelo, Rosa, Valencia II; see *DIA*, 45–46, 76, 167), but the post-wound careers of most of these bullfighters contradict the charge.

488. Corrochano reports having come across an unpublished manuscript by Amós Salvador that tells the story of a young bullfighter who constantly pestered his master, Rafael Molina (Lagartijo, q.v.) to let him kill a bull. One day the opportunity arose, and the young man explained to Lagartijo exactly how he would set up the bull, face it, approach it, and kill it. Then he asked, "Am I missing anything, maestro?" And Lagartijo answered, "Just the doing of it." In the same manuscript, Salvador distinguishes between the bullfighter who controls the bull, forcing it to do as he wills, which is real *toreo*; and the one who adjusts himself to the bull, so that the bull is really in control (Hemingway makes this same distinction, *DIA*, 151–52). Corrochano discusses a few more details relevant to the art and theory of bullfighting that appeared in that manuscript, which, by "pure coincidence," he happened to stumble across at about the same time that Cayetano was performing in Madrid. He offers "estas puras ideas del arte del torear que acabo de leer" (these pure ideas about the art of bullfighting that I've just read) to Cayetano Ordóñez, who has hardly been mentioned in the whole review, "por si algo le sirviesen. . . . La teoría es clara y sencilla. ¿Falta algo? Contesto con la palabra de Lagartijo: hacerlo (in case they can be useful to him. . . . The theory is clear and simple. Is anything missing? I answer as Lagartijo did: just the doing of it).

489. *Toros y toreros en 1925*, 184.

490. Part of the bond between the two men undoubtedly derived from the fact that Dominguín was from Quismondo, a village near Borox. Spain's provinces, formerly independent kingdoms, have different histories, geographies, climates, cui-

sines, customs, accents and even languages. Even in the 1990s, after several decades of the equalizing power of television, regional distinctions and regional pride are striking, and bullfighters often choose or have bestowed upon them professional nicknames that recall their birthplaces. Jesús Janeiro (b. 1974), the bullring's pop star in the late 1990s, advertises himself as Jesulín de Ubrique, to indicate his birthplace in that town, to the west of Ronda, in the province of Cádiz.

Gregorio Sánchez (see in *DS*), the other great bullfighter to emerge from the province of Toledo, resembled Ortega in a number of ways, including his use of his mother's but not his father's surname.

491. Cossío (1943–97) III: 507; *Toros y toreros en 1930*, 297.

492. "Domingo López Ortega," *Toros y toreros en 1931*, 267.

493. Cossío (1943–97) IV: 531.

494. Cossío (1943–97) III: 508; Corrochano, "Me gusta el toreo de Ortega porque . . . ," in his *¿Qué es torear?* 224, 228; Bagüés, *Historia de los matadores*, 211–12.

495. *El eco taurino*, 6 July 1931, 2.

496. Corrochano reprinted his 1931 reviews as part of his "Introducción a la tauromaquia de Domingo Ortega," in *¿Qué es torear?* 215–41. Unlike Cossío, Corrochano wholeheartedly admires Ortega. *El Clarín* (q.v.), however, was unrelentingly anti-Ortega, even distorting the facts. On 25 July 1931, for example, *El Clarín* wrote that Ortega did not cut an ear in Barcelona, as the Madrid *Hoja oficial del lunes* (and other papers) reported.

497. Cossío (1943–97), "López Ortega (Domingo)," III: 504–08 and IV: 530–31; Cossío (1995) II: 549–51; Bagüés, *Historia de los matadores*, 211–12; *Toros y toreros en 1930*, 297–98; *Toros y toreros en 1931*, 267–69; Corrochano *¿Qué es torear?* 209–58; Cossío (1995), "Domingo Ortega y su *Arte de torear*," I: 230–33. For a description of Ortega's bull-breeding ranch, see Cossío (1943–97) IV: 260–61 and Vera, *Orígenes e historial*, 236–38.

498. Cossío gives his birth date as 1908, Bagüés as 1906. Hemingway frequently errs when giving people's ages, presenting himself as older than he is, and his wives and friends as younger. This is, of course, a transparent attempt to enhance his authority.

499. Hemingway, "The Friend of Spain," rpt. *By-Line*, 148–49.

500. Hernaiz, *La última corrida de Joselito*, 54–58. Cossío describes Bailaor (sometimes spelled more formally, Bailador), the bull that killed Joselito, as "negro y pequeño . . . bronco . . . peligroso . . . burriciego" (black and small, rough . . . dangerous . . . of defective . . . eyesight). Bulls with defective eyesight are particularly dangerous, because their responses cannot be predicted accurately. Before the corrida, the veterinarian filed the following report: "*Bailaor*, núm. 7, cinco años, negro mulato, bien puesto" (number 7, five years old, black with brown, with large, shapely horns; qtd. in Hernaiz, 59).

501. Cossío (1943–97) III: 376; "Ganaderías no asociadas," *Toros y toreros en 1924*, 106; *Toros y toreros en 1925*, 115–16; Serrano Labrador, *La Caprichosa*, 47.

My thanks to Rafael Gómez Díaz, Archivist of Talavera de la Reina, for providing details about the city and the Ortega family (letters and enclosures, 21 December 1998 and 13 May 1999).

502. Cossío (1943–97), "Ortega Monge (Enrique), Almendro," III: 692 and IV: 617; "Los subalternos: Enrique Ortega 'Almendro'," *El Clarín*, July 1931. Other bullfighters named Almendro (almond tree) were Miguel Almendro (a nineteenth-century *novillero* who acted as banderillero for Rafael Guerra and the elder Algabeño; Almendro was his family name, not a nickname) and Vicente Aznar (nicknamed Almendro, d. 1918).

For el Cuco, see Cossío (1943–97), "Ortega y Ezpeleta (Enrique), el Cuco," III: 692; Obituary, "Enrique Ortega 'Cuco'," *La fiesta brava*, 11 November 1926, 13; and *Toros y toreros en 1926*, 312. El Cuco was not only a cousin but also a brother-in-law to Joselito and Rafael, having married one of their sisters. After Joselito's death, this Enrique Ortega gave up all connection to the bullfight and became a nightclub impresario. Financial and other difficulties, including an arrest for beating his wife, led to his suicide, 23 October 1926.

The long parenthetical remark about Joselito's death (*DIA*, 242–43) does not appear in the manuscript (JFK, Item 22, Folder 22–4, 166). Hemingway added it in galley, as a typewritten insertion in which Almendro is clearly misspelled as "Alamendro" (JFK, Item 39, Folder 49–8, Galley 71, 3404).

503. Almendro was in the ring as a member of Joselito's *cuadrilla*. My thanks once again to Anthony Brand, who provided details about photographs (personal interview, 1 August 1999).

504. The *jijona* strain has been overpowered by the more popular Vistahermosa strain. By the twentieth century the word *jijón* denotes only the red color of the animal.

505. Cossío (1943–97), "Pablo Romero, don José Luis y don Felipe de," I: 286; "Pablo-Romero, S.A. (señores hijos de)," Vera, *Orígenes e historial*, 124–26; "Ganaderías de toros de lidia," *Gran enciclopedia Rialp* XXII: 603–605, see section on "Casta jijona"; "Jijona," Vera, *Orígenes e historial*, 18. Vera dates the herd's seniority back to 9 April 1888; the U.C.T.L. to 8 April 1888.

506. Carmen Castro, public relations manager of the Palace Hotel, Madrid, writes that "Hemingway was in Madrid several times and stayed at the Palace Hotel" and drank "his dry martinis at the Palace Bar where . . . he met . . . his Spanish friends" (letter to author and enclosures, 16 December 1995). In 1997, the rack rate for a double room in the Palace Hotel was 46,000 pesetas ($300); a double deluxe cost 50,000 ($325) a night.

507. *Anuarios Bailly-Baillière* (1923), 141, 168; *Anuarios Bailly-Baillière* (1930), 922. Cars were becoming such important commodities that Citroën, which in 1927 had two offices in Madrid, expanded into five offices by 1930, of which the Citroën-Palace was the main one.

508. Hemingway, *Selected Letters*, 303, 311.

509. Cossío (1943–97), "Pereira Palha, don José," I: 305. Father and son were

very closely associated and early on the father registered his holdings in his son's name. Because of this, Cossío does not provide a separate entry for the father, Antonio José Pereira Palha, the founder of the ranch.

510. *Toros y toreros en 1931*, 163.

511. Earlier bullfights were held in the central plaza (today called Plaza del Castillo). This was true for many Spanish cities, which simply erected wooden barriers to separate the spectators from the action.

512. Iribarren, *Hemingway y los sanfermines*, 147.

513. Portz, "Allusion and Structure," 32–34.

514. Portz, "Allusion and Structure," 32–34.

515. Beegel, *Hemingway's Craft of Omission*, 32–35.

516. Miura bulls were fought in Pamplona in 1922 and 1925. Since Hemingway saw his first bullfight in 1923, the earliest Miura corrida in Pamplona he could have seen would be the one of 8 July 1925.

517. Iribarren, *Hemingway y los sanfermines*, 58.

518. Although the bulls were a disappointment in the ring, they had provided plenty of excitement during the 6:00 A.M. *encierro*, when they almost gored two young runners on Calle Estafeta. The Miura corrida of 8 July 1925 was reviewed on the front page of *El pensamiento navarro*, 9 July 1925.

519. Cossío (1943–97), "Pastor y Durán (Vicente)," III: 714–17 and VI: 248–49; Bagüés, *Historia de los matadores*, 120–21; Tapia, *Breve historial del toreo*, 327–28.

520. *Encyclopaedia Britannica*, 11th ed., XX: 937.

521. "Patti, Adelina," *The Concise Oxford Dictionary of Music*, 482; *Encyclopedia Americana* XXI: 409; *Encyclopaedia Britannica*, 11th ed., XX: 937. The *Encyclopedia Americana* says she was Italian; *Collier's Encyclopedia* presents her as an "Italian-American coloratura soprano . . . born . . . of Italian parents in Madrid (XVIII: 502); and *Everyman's Encyclopedia* says she was French (IX: 512).

522. Cossío (1943–97), "Perea Rapel (Bonifacio), Boni," III: 720. Boni's son, Rafael Perea Cano (b. 1913), achieved the rank of *matador de toros* and was popular in Mexico: one of his beautiful verónicas is commemorated in a life-size statue on the perimeter wall of Mexico City's large bullring. He did not catch on in Spain, however, and never achieved the reputation and respect his father had enjoyed.

523. The Count of Santa Coloma and the Marquis of Albaserrada were brothers. Both of them bred excellent Vistahermosa stock. The two seed bulls were called Cristalino and Mesonero, the latter producing 1,150 offspring and deserving to be ranked with Diano (q.v.; Mira, *El toro bravo*, 65).

524. "Pérez Tabernero, D. Graciliano," *Toros y toreros en 1931*, 160–61. Cossío repeats the praise: "A nuestro juicio, y de todas las ganaderías del campo de Salamanca, que son muchas y casi todas de ellas muy bien atendidas y seleccionadas, ésta de don Graciliano es la que produce más finos toros" (in our judgment, of the many Salamancan ranches, almost all of which are carefully tended and selected, don Graciliano's produces the finest bulls; Cossío [1943–97] I: 288).

525. Cossío (1943–97), "Pérez, don Argimiro," I: 288; *Toros y toreros en 1931*, 168–69.

526. See Cossío (1943–97), "Pérez, don Antonio," I: 287; *Toros y toreros en 1931*, 165–66; Cossío (1943–97), "Pérez T. Sanchón, d. Alipio," I: 287–88; *Toros y toreros en 1931*, 166–67; Mira, *El toro bravo*, 166.

527. These alternate terms are supplied by Nieto Manjón, *Diccionario ilustrado* (235, 338), but they are not in common usage.

528. "Cuando un caballo tenga las tripas colgando de un modo repugnante al público, será retirado al patio, y . . . apuntillado en el acto" (When a horse's intestines hang out in a manner repugnant to the public, it will be removed to the stables and . . . killed immediately; *Artículo* 69 of the 1923 *Reglamento*).

529. The committee's first meeting, on 2 June 1926, included representatives from the bull-breeders' union, the matadors' union, the impresarios' union, the picadors' union, and the Society for the Protection of Animals, as well as a taurine critic and a matador (*La fiesta brava*, 17 June 1926, 3).

530. Nieto Manjón, "Peto," *Diccionario ilustrado de términos taurinos*, 322; Díaz-Cañabate, "Panorama del toreo hasta 1979," in Cossío (1943–97) V: 51; "Las inovaciones de la temporada: los petos," *El Clarín*, Almanaque 1929; "La prueba de petos," *El eco taurino*, 6 June 1927, 5; "¡Petos o puntilla!" *La fiesta brava*, 17 April 1926, unnumbered page 2; "Los petos y la sensibilidad," *La fiesta brava*, 19 June 1931; "Sobre la suerte de varas," *La fiesta brava*, 20 May 1926, 2–3; "Taller de reparaciones en traumas equinos," *La fiesta brava*, 17 June 1926, 3; "Sobre la suerte de varas: Las reformas del reglamento de toros," *La fiesta brava*, 14 October 1926, 6; "El primer tercio de la lidia: Variaciones sobre el mismo tema," *La fiesta brava*, 3 June 1926, 10–11. See also Cossío (1995), "Carácter y breve historia del tercio de varas," I: 142–47, which surveys the various aspects of pic-ing, from the time it was first differentiated from *rejoneo*, in the eighteenth century, until the introduction of the *peto*, which Cossío postdates to 1930 (the publication date of the new *Reglamento*, which was the first code to mandate the *peto*). Uno al Sesgo presented his revolutionary plan in his essay, "La modificación de la 'suerte de varas'," *Toros y toreros en 1926*, 50–64, and repeated it the next year, *Toros y toreros en 1927*, 51.

531. The *peto* was first used at a *novillada* in Madrid, on 6 March 1927. In April that year, at another Madrid *novillada*, the horses were kept out of the ring until it was time for the bull to be pic-ed (*Toros y toreros en 1927*, 233, 234); many innovations and experiments were performed that year. Sidney Franklin (q.v.) grandly and quite incorrectly proclaims that he was instrumental in designing both the *peto* itself and the laws requiring and governing its use; that he devoted the entire winter of 1929–30 to this issue (he neglects to note that by this time the *peto* had already been adopted); and that he and only he is to be credited with producing the "face-saving gesture" needed by Primo de Rivera who, in order to appease foreign sensibilities, had tried to outlaw bullfighting (Franklin, *Bullfighter from Brooklyn*, 187–88). In fact, Franklin's only association with the *peto* was his appearance in a

novillada in 1930 in which a new model of *peto* was tested, although by one of his fellow performers, not by himself.

532. The weight is legislated in *Artículo* 85 of the 1962 *Reglamento*, in *Artículo* 67 of 1992 *Reglamento*, and in *Artículo* 65 of the 1996 *Reglamento*. In practice, *petos* sometimes weigh considerably more: as one writer puts it, "the overweight protector was one of the chief abuses in the pic act," offering the horse great protection and making it increasingly unlikely that a horse would be killed in the bullring.

533. *Artículos* 19 and 74 of the 1930 *Reglamento*; for the 1947 commentary by Alberto Vera (Areva), see *Reglamento oficial para la celebración de espectáculos taurinos y de cuanto se relaciona con los mismos, notas y comentarios de Areva* (Madrid: Librería Beltrán, 1949), 93.

534. The number of horses is specified in *Artículo* 13 in Melchor Ordóñez's 1847 document; in *Artículo* 13 of the 1917 *Reglamento*; in *Artículos* 16 and 67 of the 1923 *Reglamento*; in *Artículos* 19 and 74 of the 1930 *Reglamento*; in *Artículo* 83 of the 1962 *Reglamento*; and in *Artículo* 62, section 4 of the 1992 *Reglamento*.

535. Baker, *A Life Story*, 142; Reynolds, *Paris Years*, 288; Kert, *Hemingway Women*, 155 *et passim*; Meyers, *Hemingway*, 346; Diliberto, *Hadley*, 189. For Virginia Pfeiffer's middle name, I am indebted to Ruth A. Hawkins, Director of the Hemingway-Pfeiffer Museum and Educational Center, Piggott, Arkansas.

536. Kamen, *Philip of Spain*, 226.

537. Uno al Sesgo, "Despejos," *Toros y toreros en 1931*, 7–8; Hernández San Román, "La tradición," 37–40. See also "Pius V," *Encyclopaedia Britannica*, 11th ed., XXI: 685; "Gregory XIII," *Encyclopaedia Britannica*, 11th ed., XII: 575; "Pius V, St.," *Collier's Encyclopedia* XIX: 91; "La iglesia ante las corridas de toros," *Gran enciclopedia Rialp* XXII: 600.

538. I am indebted to Anthony Brand, who found detailed descriptions of the outfit in del Campo, *Pamplona y los toros, siglo XVII*, 64; and in Nieto Manjón, *Historias de un alguacilillo*, 3.

539. "Pilar, Nuestra Señora del," *The Catholic Encyclopedia* XII: 83; Reynolds, *The 1930s*, 169; Kert, *Hemingway Women*, 184.

540. Baker, *A Life Story*, 213, 214.

541. Cossío (1943–97), "Pino (Manuel del), Niño del Matadero," III: 739 and VI: 281; *Toros y toreros en 1930*, 329; *Toros y toreros en 1931*, 311. The *novillo* that gored him on his debut was a Santa Coloma animal (*Toros y toreros en 1931*, 343). Manuel's brother Miguel (1921–92) was a *matador de toros* (Cossío [1943–97] IV: 653 and XII: 916).

542. "Pius V," *Encyclopaedia Britannica*, 11th ed., XXI: 685; "Pius V, St.," *Collier's Encyclopedia* XIX: 91.

543. "Gregory XIII," *Encyclopaedia Britannica*, 11th ed., XII: 575; "La iglesia ante las corridas de toros," *Gran enciclopedia Rialp* XXII: 600; Hernández San Román, "La tradición," 37.

544. *Anuarios Bailly-Baillière* (1923), 148; *Anuarios Bailly-Baillière* (1927), 150.

542 • NOTES

545. Colonel Enrico Pino, Stato Maggiore dell'esèrcito, Reparto Affari Generali, supplied a history and description of the "Sacrario di Pocol" (letter and enclosures, 26 April 1999).

546. Kahn, *Harvard*, 44; *The Harvard Book*, 1875 ed., available at <http://hbook.harvard.edu>.

547. Sánchez de Neira attributes the proverb to Fernando Gómez (q.v.): "En la suerte de matar, al que no hace la cruz se lo lleva el diablo" (*Gran diccionario taurómaco* II: 907). The proverb is also quoted in Abad Ojuel, *Estirpe y tauromaquia*, 335. Fernando Gómez's son-in-law, Ignacio Sánchez Mejías, explained that the bull is the devil (qtd. in Nieto Manjón, 143, s.v. *Cruz*).

548. There's another saying, attributed to Luis Miguel González (Dominguín, see in *DS*), to the effect that all of his *cornadas* carry a woman's name.

549. Cossío quotes el Espartero's famous proverb (Cossío [1943–97] III: 343 and Cossío [1995] II: 454).

550. Hotchner, *Papa Hemingway*, 129. A Quintana obituary describes him as "el primer arrendatario de la actual plaza de toros" (the first tenant of the current bullring [built in 1922]), *Diario de Navarra*, 29 January 1974, 8). Iribarren discusses Hemingway's relationship with Quintana in *Hemingway y los sanfermines*, 39–40, 63, 95–96, 137–38, 147–50.

551. Obituary, Luis Quintanilla, *Enciclopedia universal ilustrada*, *Suplemento 1977–78*, 909; more detail, including the addresses of his studios, can be found in the biographical sketch included in *Luis Quintanilla*, a catalogue prepared by the Salas de Exposiciones de la Dirección General del Patrimonio Artístico (Madrid, 1979) and made available to me by the Fundación Pablo Iglesias, Calle Zurbarán 18, Madrid.

552. Hemingway, blurb for the Quintanilla exhibit of etchings, Pierre Matisse Gallery, Baker Collection, Box 11, Folder 18, Manuscripts Division, Department of Rare Books and Special Collections, Princeton University Libraries.

553. Baker, *A Life Story*, 224.

554. The guide identifies Quintanilla as a "pintor histórico" (painter of historical or political subjects).

555. I am indebted to Anthony Brand for assistance in finding the street, determining angles of vision, and supplying historical perspective (interviews and field trip, October 2000).

556. Wiser, *Crazy Years*, 134–35; O'Rourke, letter to author, 20 August 1998, and unpublished article, " 'With Pascin at the Dome': A Reported or Invented Story?" presented at the Hemingway Centennial Conference, Oak Park, Illinois, 18–21 July 1999. Hemingway cracked a joke about Radiguet's bisexuality and Cocteau's homosexuality (*Selected Letters*, 368).

557. Klüver and Martin, *Kiki's Paris*, notes to pp. 116–17.

558. Wiser, *Crazy Years*, 134–35; O'Rourke, " 'With Pascin at the Dome': A Reported or Invented Story?"

559. Reynolds writes that Ruth Lowry "was a cousin, related to Ernest through

his Aunt Arabella White Hemingway who married his Uncle Tyler. In 1917, Tyler and the Whites' considerable name got Ernest his first job on the Kansas City *Star*, for Tyler always thought well of this nephew. When Tyler died, Arabella remarried a man named Shepard and moved in quite close to the Lowrys. Between aunt and cousin, the Hemingways were well taken care of in Kansas City, connecting quickly with Carlos Guffey, the doctor who would twice deliver Pauline. Spacious, comfortable, and with a well-stocked liquor cabinet, the Lowry house on Indian Lane was welcome relief for Hemingway . . . Ernest stopped by the convention center one morning, but did not stay long" (*American Homecoming*, 179–80). At the time, Hemingway was wrestling with the end of *A Farewell to Arms*.

560. According to Reynolds: "A Max Perkins-EH letter (June 26, 1928, JFK) confirms Hemingway's brief visit to the convention. At one time Hemingway planned to do a convention report for [Ezra] Pound's *Exile*, but with the novel running smoothly, he lost interest" (*American Homecoming*, 253, n. 32).

561. Domecq Díez, 69; Mira, *El toro bravo*, 93 (genealogical tree).

562. Cossío (1943–97), "Lozano, don Manuel," I: 280–81; Cossío (1943–97), "Comisario," I: 348–49; Carralero and Borge, *Toros célebres*, 92; *Toros y toreros en 1929*, 289.

563. Toplady published the words in *Gospel Magazine* (1776); Hastings published the words and music in a devotional songbook, *Spiritual Songs for Social Workshop* (1833). I quote the version published in 1918 in a hymnal published by Concordia Publishing House, St. Louis, Missouri. My thanks to James Brasch for the information (E-mail, 26 October 1999).

564. A banderillero, Genaro Martínez, was also known as Rodalito. Active in the 1930s, he performed only in his native Mexico, not in Spain, and is clearly not the Rodalito Hemingway discusses. See Cossío (1943–97), "Martínez (Genaro), Rodalito," VI: 57.

565. Durán Blázquez and Sánchez Vigil, both books, passim.

566. "Félix Rodríguez," *Toros y toreros en 1929*, 229.

567. Pepe Dominguín, qtd. in Benlloch and Sobrino, *Los grandes maestros del toreo valenciano*, 71. Although Rodríguez's syphilis was an open secret, the disease was not named in contemporary or even in later accounts. According to taurine historian Anthony Brand, Benlloch's 1999 book is the first to acknowledge it in print.

568. Cossío (1943–97) III: 787.

569. Qtd. in Abella, *Historia* II: 43.

570. Cossío (1943–97), "Rodríguez Ruiz (Félix)," III: 787–88 and IV: 680; Tapia, *Breve historial del toreo*, 415–16; Abella, *Historia* II: 42–43; Bagüés, *Historia de los matadores*, 193–94; *Toros y toreros en 1924*, 201; *Toros y toreros en 1929*, 229; *Toros y toreros en 1931*, 249; *El Clarín*, Almanacs for 1924–1929. There was another matador by this name, Félix Rodríguez Antón (known as Rodríguez II, b. 1910), but Hemingway's references to the matador's illness and birth place (200, 267) point to the older of these two matadors; the younger one

was not promoted to *matador de toros* until 1932. Thirty years later, he was still fighting, mostly in Ecuador and Colombia, where he also breeds bulls and manages other bullfighters.

571. The dates of Rodríguez's appearances are available in the annuals *Toros y toreros en 1927—Toros y toreros en 1931*. Hemingway attended the Pamplona and Valencia ferias in 1927, 1929, and 1931; ticket stubs also confirm his attendance at Rodríguez's performances elsewhere (JFK, Bullfighting Materials).

572. Hemingway doesn't mention that Cagancho was first signed on by Domingo González (Dominguín), who also managed Domingo Ortega. From the beginning, Dominguín saw to it that Cagancho was paid enormous fees. Cagancho and Ortega were Dominguín's two major discoveries.

573. "Los que han visitado el 'hule' en 1927," *El Clarín*, Almanac, 1928 (describing the season of 1927). The details about the Almagro fight of 25 August appear in *Toros y toreros en 1927*, 236; see also 184.

574. "Joaquín Rodríguez, Cagancho," *Toros y toreros en 1927*, 182.

575. It is a sign of Cagancho's talent that he was compared to Belmonte. But the same critics who made the comparison, flattering even when negative, would dismiss Cagancho as a flash in the pan when, as happened all too frequently, he was terrible. The critic known as Don Quijote argues that if the comparison is to be made at all, it should be between Cagancho and the younger Belmonte, who also had many failures, and not to the Belmonte of 1927. He claims that although Cagancho will probably never acquire the bravery with which Belmonte was born, he may, like Belmonte, develop into a more confident, skillful matador, able to dominate the bulls which frighten him now. Cagancho combines Belmonte's style with Rafael's psychology; he will probably always be uneven, but he can achieve lasting greatness ("En torno de Cagancho," *La fiesta brava*, 24 November 1927, 4).

576. Morla Lynch, for example, describes Cagancho's clothes and conversation at an elegant dinner party: he wore a "terno gris, camisa de seda blanca, corbata azul, calcetines del mismo color y zapatos de gamuza" (gray suit, white silk shirt, blue necktie, socks of the same color and suede shoes); he held his audience spellbound (*En España con Federico García Lorca*, 288).

577. Cossío (1943–97), "Rodríguez (Joaquín), Cagancho," III: 790–93, IV: 682, and VI: 360; Silva Aramburu, *Enciclopedia taurina*, 282; Bagüés, *Historia de los matadores*, 194–95; *El Clarín*, Almanacs for 1926–29; *Toros y toreros en 1926*, 243–45 (an unusually long write-up for a *novillero*); *Toros y toreros en 1927*, 182–84; *Toros y toreros en 1928*, 189; *Toros y toreros en 1931*, 230.

According to Cossío, Cagancho's son (Joaquín Rodríguez Sánchez, b. 1927) took his *alternativa* in San Feliú de Guixols, a pretty coastal town of absolutely no taurine importance, in 1960, in a ceremony at which Antonio Ordóñez (see in *DS*) officiated (Cossío [1995], II: 701). Ordóñez's presence may have been a tribute to Cagancho the father, and not to his son, who was already thirty-three and clearly not destined for greatness. After the 1960 ceremony, the younger Cagancho seems not to have fought in Spain again. It is interesting that Ordóñez's biographer, Abad

Ojuel, does not list the younger Cagancho among the "Alternativas concedidas por Antonio Ordóñez" (*Estirpe y tauromaquia*, 419), although the record for 1960 does indicate that on 24 July Ordóñez performed at San Feliú de Guixols with Rafael Jiménez (Chicuelo *hijo*) and Cagancho *hijo*.

578. Iribarren, *Hemingway y los sanfermines*, 102. Iribarren considers this corrida the climax of that year's Pamplona fiesta. He writes that Cagancho's *faena* with his first bull was "estupenda," but the killing was awkward and protracted. With his second, very difficult bull, Cagancho was superb throughout: "Recuerdo esta faena como una de las cuatro mejores que he visto en mi vida. Para la mayoría de los pamploneses de aquellos tiempos es la mejor que se ha realizado en nuestra plaza . . . Cagancho parecía transfigurado" (I remember this *faena* as one of the four best I have seen in my life. For most Pamplonese of those times, it was the best ever performed in our plaza . . . Cagancho seemed to be transported). Hemingway told Iribarren that he would never forget that performance (*Hemingway y los sanfermines*, 102–103).

579. Bagüés gives Costillares's full name as Joaquín Rodríguez y de Castro and his dates as 1748–1800 (*Historia de los matadores*, 29); Silva Aramburu gives the dates as 1729–1800 (*Enciclopedia taurina*, 232); the *Enciclopedia Universal, Suplemento 1953–1954* gives the birth year as 1746 and the investiture at age sixteen (637–38). Cossío cites legal and other documents to explain the variety of dates given for his birth and for his *alternativa*.

580. Cossío writes that Costillares' ill health manifested itself as general weakness and, later, a weakness in the left arm and a tumor on a hand ([1943–97] III: 798–99); Bagüés mentions a tumor on the right hand (*Historia de los matadores*, 29).

581. Costillares, like Romero and the other early greats of the bullfight, is discussed in practically every taurine history; I have relied most heavily on Cossío (1943–97), "Rodríguez (Joaquín), Costillares," III: 793–800.

582. Cossío credits Valencia II with thirty-eight corridas for 1924 ([1943–97] III: 816), but *El Clarín*'s almanac for 1924 and *Toros y toreros en 1924* (138–39) both cite the lower number.

583. One such performance was offered in October 1928, in benefit of the victims of the fire that destroyed the Madrid theater Novedades: Valencia was seriously gored. Cossío also recalls that, as a result of a political argument between Valencia and a taxicab driver, all taxis went on strike during the hours of Valencia's performance in the Madrid bullring, whose audience showed their support of him by giving him a long standing ovation when he entered the ring ([1943–97] III: 816). Hemingway, absent from Spain in 1928 and 1930, may not have been aware of these events. Cossío adds that Madrid credited Valencia with raising the level of bullfighting by infusing fellow performers with his spirit, goading or encouraging them to sacrifice safety for art.

584. Cossío (1943–97), "Roger y Serrano (Victoriano), Valencia II," III: 814–16; Bagüés, *Historia de los matadores*, 168; Tapia, *Breve historial del toreo*,

388–89; *Toros y toreros en 1924*, 137–39; Luján, *Historia del toreo*, 315–16; Abella, *Historia* II: 18.

585. On 30 June 1931, a Tovar bull gored Victoriano Roger in the thigh; the wound was described as "grave" (*Toros y toreros en 1931*, 347. Hemingway refers to this wound (*DIA*, 219).

586. *Toros y toreros en 1924-Toros y toreros en 1931*; *El Clarín*, Almanacs 1924–28; JFK, Bullfight Materials (ticket stubs).

587. It is interesting that in his text Hemingway presents a thorough evaluation of Victoriano Roger—he mentions his courage, cape and muleta work, and his badly sewn up wound—but then mentions him in Chapter Twenty, which is devoted to subjects the narrator was *not* able to include in the book. Chiquito's "girl's face" was similarly discussed in earlier chapters, unlike the other details alluded to on page 276 and throughout Chapter Twenty.

588. Cossío (1943–97), "Roger (José), Valencia," III: 813; short obituary, *Toros y toreros en 1924*, 236, s.v. 8 January 1924.

589. The numbers are: eight corridas in 1921, seven in 1922, nine in 1923, ten in 1924, eleven in 1925, six in 1926, three in 1927, six in 1928, and one in 1929.

590. Cossío (1943–97), "Roger y Serrano (José), Valencia," III: 813–14 and VI: 376; Cossío (1995) II: 705–706; Tapia, *Breve historial del toreo*, 367–68; Bagüés, *Historia de los matadores*, 159; *Toros y toreros en 1924*, 128–29; *Toros y toreros en 1925*, 151–52; *Toros y toreros en 1926*, 182; *Toros y toreros en 1927*, 152.

591. The Romeros were carpenters, the craft being passed down from generation to generation even after bullfight fever infected them. Francisco tried to dissuade his son Juan from becoming a bullfighter; Juan similarly insisted that his sons be carpenters. Once the younger generation convinced their elders, however, the older bullfighters trained and advised the young ones, each generation achieving greater fame than the preceding one.

Juan Romero (1722–1824) lived to be 102 years old; his wife, Mariana Martínez, died at age 105. Their famous son, Pedro Romero Martínez, was tall, strong, healthy, and still fighting bulls in his eighties. Their other four sons were also bullfighters. José (b. 1745), who did not get along with his brother Pedro, appeared frequently with Pedro's rivals Costillares and Pepe-Hillo. It was he who killed Barbudo, the bull which killed Pepe Hillo in 1801, and, although depressed by the loss of his friend and partner, he continued to fight for almost two more decades: he retired in August 1818, at age seventy-two.

Juan and Mariana's son Juan was a banderillero who died young. Their son Gaspar (1756-c. 1802) performed with Pedro in the early years but had a generally undistinguished career and seems to have retired early. And Antonio (1763–1802) was killed by a bull. There was a daughter as well: she married Jerónimo José Cándido, a well-known bullfighter who in his later years was associated with the taurine school of which Pedro Romero was the head. For information on the Romeros, see "La fiesta de toros," *Enciclopedia Universal, Suplemento 1953–1954*, 636–37; Silva Aramburu, *Enciclopedia taurina*, 232–35; Tapia, *Breve historial del toreo*,

17–30, 52–55; and the various entries for the brothers, all under "Romero Martínez," Cossío (1995) II: 712–14; see also the entry for "José Cándido" in Silva Aramburu, *Enciclopedia taurina*, 236–37.

592. Silva Aramburu describes Pedro Romero as "el coloso del siglo XVIII, el maestro insuperable de su época" (the colossus of the eighteenth century, the insuperable master of his period; *Enciclopedia taurina*, 233).

593. Romero's letter is quoted in Cossío (1943–97) III: 832.

594. Cossío (1943–97), "Romero (Pedro)," III: 825–34; Tapia, *Breve historial del toreo*, 30–52; Silva Aramburu, *Enciclopedia taurina*, 233–35. For the manuscript version of the passage on Pedro Romero, see JFK, Item 22, Folder 22–4, 161. Both in this manuscript and in the published version, Hemingway notes incorrectly that Romero was ninety-five when he died, but in the handwritten manuscript for an unpublished chapter, entitled "Cogidas," Hemingway notes more accurately that Pedro Romero died in Ronda in 1839, aged eighty-five, after killing 5,600 bulls during his forty years in the bullring (JFK, Item 39, Folder 57, 2). Another Goya portrait of Pedro Romero hangs in the museum of Sevilla's Maestranza bullring.

595. "La iglesia del Espíritu Santo se levantó en conmemoración de la toma de la ciudad por los Reyes Católicos el 12 de mayo de 1485 y en el mismo lugar donde Fernando V estableciera sus reales," *Enciclopedia universal ilustrada*, LII: 256.

596. The hotel seems to have been sold early in the Spanish Civil War. After that, it had various owners until, late in 1958 or early in 1959, it became the property of the Ayuntamiento (City Hall) of Ronda. The Ayuntamiento, wanting it to continue as a hotel, rejected a local school's offer to acquire the building and its extensive grounds, but did sell it in 1960 to the Caja de Ahorros de Ronda, an independent bank (now Unicaja), which enlarged the building twice, once in 1962 and again in 1972. Since 1985 the hotel has been leased to Hoteles Unidos S.A. (HUSA). Mrs. Ana López García, head receptionist, Hotel Reina Victoria, Ronda, supplied details about the hotel's history (interviews, 8 and 9 October 1995).

597. Martínez Salvatierra describes the 1924 wound in detail: the horn entered neatly, making only a small rip in the uniform but slicing open his abdomen and causing grave internal damage. When the pressure of the tight uniform was removed, most of his intestines popped out (*Los toros*, 187–88; see also *Toros y toreros en 1924*, 250). Rosa suffered this wound in Valencia.

598. Cossío (1943–97), "Rosa de la Garquén," III: 834–36; Bagüés, *Historia de los matadores*, 160; *Toros y toreros en 1924*, 129–30. Hemingway correctly reports that Marcial Lalanda "had been in the ring when Granero was killed" on 7 May 1922 (*DIA*, 74), but fails to add that Juan Luis de la Rosa was also on that afternoon's *cartel*. The fact emerges in *For Whom the Bell Tolls* (251–53).

I doubt that Hemingway ever saw Rosa perform. He could only have seen him on his first short trip to Spain, May-June 1923, but Rosa spent most of that year in military service: "la temporada que hizo . . . en 1923 fué breve; casi toda ella la pasó cumpliendo sus deberes militares y, por lo tanto, permaneció apartado de los ruedos" (his 1923 season was curtailed by military service; Minguet y Calderón de la Barca, *Desde la grada*, 116). Rosa did not perform in Pamplona in July 1923 or 1924.

599. "American Bohemians in Paris," 114.

600. Marco Miranda, *Las conspiraciones*, 30.

601. Marco Miranda, a fellow conspirator, identifies the plotters (*Las conspiraciones*, 30–31).

602. Qtd. in Cossío (1943–97) III: 838.

603. Cossío (1943–97), "Royo Turón (Francisco), Lagartito," III: 837–38 and VI: 394; "Francisco Royo, Lagartito," *Toros y toreros en 1924*, 196–97, 250; *Toros y toreros en 1925*, 208–209; *Toros y toreros en 1926*, 217–18; *Toros y toreros en 1927*, 179–80, 239–40; *Toros y toreros en 1929*, 228; *Toros y toreros en 1930*, 267; and Bagüés, "Francisco Royo y Turón (Lagartito), *Historia de los matadores*, 193. For his brothers, see Cossío (1943–97), "Royo Turón (José), Lagartito II," III: 838 and VI: 394; and "Royo Turón (Eduardo), Lagartito III," III: 837.

604. "Portrait of Three, or The Paella," JFK, Item 660, unnumbered page 2.

605. Cossío (1943–97), "Rubio Rubio (Rafael), Rodalito," III: 840 and VI: 751–52, 773–76; the name is corrected to Rafael Rubio Oltra in Cossío (1995) II: 718, which also supplies his death date. See also Bagüés, *Historia de los matadores*, 176–77; *Toros y toreros en 1924*, 155–56; *Toros y toreros en 1926*, 196–97; *Toros y toreros en 1927*, 164; *Toros y toreros en 1929*, 249.

606. *Toros y toreros en 1930*, 299 and 360. Rodalito did not perform in 1931.

607. Hoffman, Allen, and Ulrich, *The Little Magazine*, 85–86, 257–58. Hoffman, Allen, and Ulrich write that "Frank's place among the critics of the twenties was high; and this survey of his work [in *S 4 N*] is valuable . . . in indicating the high regard with which he was considered" (108). The success of his contemporaries did not sit well with Hemingway, and the attack on Frank may be aimed at those critics who praised him and who, Hemingway expects, will fail to appreciate *Death in the Afternoon* (*see* Narratee). Hemingway's copy of this issue of *S 4 N* is now in the Hemingway Collection, JFK.

608. Munson's "Herald of the Twenties: A Tribute to Waldo Frank," was published in *Forum* (1961) and reprinted in his *The Awakening Twenties: A Memoir-History of a Literary Period* (Baton Rouge: Louisiana State University Press, 1985).

609. Lewis, "The Making of *Death in the Afternoon*," 47, 48.

610. Cossío (1943–97), "Federico, doña Carmen de," I: 271; Vera, "Vistahermosa," *Orígenes e historial*, 20; Cossío (1943–97), "Indice alfabético de ganaderos y fecha en que, por primera vez a su nombre, se han corrido toros, como nuevos, en las plazas de Madrid, desde el año 1765," I: 313; a similar listing in Vera, arranged chronologically instead of alphabetically, also connects Arias de Saavedra to the date 17 July 1837. Mira reports the little-known sale to Idefonso Núñez de Prado (*El toro bravo*, 178) and displays the long-extinct Saavedra brand in his excellent genealogical diagrams (*El toro bravo*, 156, 166).

611. Cossío and Bagüés spell the name Sáinz; *El Clarín* and *Toros y toreros* prefer Hemingway's spelling.

612. Cossío (1943–97) III: 857 and *Toros y toreros en 1925*, 145: these two sources give different accounts of who were the preceding Saleris. *Toros y toreros en 1927* reiterates its earlier statement that Sáiz was really Saleri V (150).

613. Cossío announces thirty corridas, but *El Clarín*'s annual Almanac and *Toros y toreros en 1924* both claim three for 1924. Cossío's thirty seems a typographical error.

614. Cossío (1943–97), "Sáinz Martínez (Julián), Saleri II," III: 856–57 and IV: 702; Cossío (1995) II: 729–30; Bagüés, *Historia de los matadores*, 150–51; "Julián Sáiz, Saleri II," *Toros y toreros en 1924*, 121.

615. *Toros y toreros en 1926*, 178. This usually reserved annual publication is atypically hostile to Saleri, not only denying him past triumphs in the 1926 volume but using unusually strong language against him in 1927, when it remarked that his *toreo* is "incoloro, inodoro e insípido" (colorless, odorless, and insipid; *Toros y toreros en 1927*, 150).

616. Cossío (1943–97), "Las plazas de toros," I: 544–47. Anthony Brand supplied the details about the disappearance of the bullring (telephone interview, April 1998), and Pepe Dominguín announced the new one before it was inaugurated (interview, July 1998, Madrid).

617. "Sánchez, Sr. Hijo de Rodríguez, D. Andrés," *Toros y toreros en 1931*, 181–82; Cossío (1943–97), "Sánchez, don Francisco," I: 293; "Ruiz Yagüe (don Daniel)," *Unión de criadores de toros de lidia* (1995), 149.

618. Sánchez de Neira, *El toreo* (1879), qtd. in Cossío (1943–97) III: 895.

619. Qtd. in Cossío (1943–97) III: 900.

620. Cossío (1943–97), "Sánchez Povedano (Salvador), Frascuelo," III: 894–901; Bagüés, *Historia de los matadores*, 76–78; Silva Aramburu, *Enciclopedia taurina*, 247–49; Tapia, *Breve historial del toreo*, 253–59.

621. Hemingway writes that he didn't read much pre-1873 taurine history (*DIA*, 240), which explains why he didn't mention the other famous rivals or "pairs" of fighters of the nineteenth century: José Redondo (el Chiclanero, 1819–53) and Francisco Arjona (Cúchares, 1818–68); and Antonio Sánchez (el Tato, 1831–95) and Antonio Carmona (el Gordito, 1838–1920). Cúchares's long career enabled him to compete with Cayetano Sanz, the pupil of his erstwhile rival el Chiclanero; similarly, in the 1870s Sanz appeared in bullrings with Lagartijo and Frascuelo, though he offered very little competition to the younger bullfighters.

Taurine rivalries may be based on geography, style, or personal character, and often assume political and social overtones. They frequently overlap, with younger bullfighters inheriting the fans of a master with whom they share geographical or other bonds. The generations are tightly intertwined, which makes bullfighting history an extremely complex affair.

622. Peña y Goñi, author of *Lagartijo, Frascuelo y su tiempo*, described Frascuelo as short-waisted, long-legged, knock-kneed, skinny, stiffly muscle-bound, and very dark-skinned (qtd. in Silva Aramburu, *Enciclopedia taurina*, 248); Lagartijo was said to be perfectly proportioned and extremely elegant and graceful (Bagüés, *Historia de los matadores*, 74–75).

623. The obituary in *Toros y toreros en 1934* confirms that he was killed in his sixth corrida of that season.

624. Cossío (1943–97), "Sánchez Mejías (Ignacio)," III: 875–82 and VII: 659–60; Silva Aramburu, *Enciclopedia taurina*, 273–74; Tapia, *Breve historial del toro*, 349–53; *Toros y toreros en 1925*, 149–51; *Toros y toreros en 1926*, 180–82; *Toros y toreros en 1934*, 330–31 (obituary); Bagüés emphasizes his strong personality (*Historia de los matadores*, 158–59). Antonio García-Ramos and Francisco Narbona's biography, *Ignacio Sánchez Mejías*, is excellent.

As his defiance of his strong father indicates, Ignacio always liked to get his own way. Gregorio Corrochano describes a face-off between Ignacio and Mr. Salgueiro, the impresario of the Seville bullring: the impresario refused to contract Sánchez Mejías for that year's fiesta, and Sánchez Mejías retorted that whatever the impresario said or did, he would appear in the bullring that April. In the middle of one of the corridas, he suddenly jumped into the ring, approached the matador who was performing, and asked if he would permit him to place the banderillas. Of course the audience, which included the king, recognized the famous intruder, were aware of the impresario's ban against him, and gave him a standing ovation when he entered the ring. The acting matador handed him the banderillas, Sánchez Mejías approached the president, was granted permission to perform, and placed the banderillas with his usual grace: the audience was delirious (*¿Qué es torear?* 131–32). For Sánchez Mejías's presidency of the Unión de Matadores de Toros y de Novillos, see *Toros y toreros en 1924*, 246; for his confrontation with the Unión de Empresarios de Plazas de Toros, see *Toros y toreros en 1924*, 22; and *Toros y toreros en 1925*, 17–18. Corrochano spells the name Megías, Bagüés spells it Mejía, and Hemingway at one point spells it Mejeas (*DIA*, 201).

625. Sánchez Mejías's schedules are detailed in *Toros y toreros en 1924*, 128; *Toros y toreros en 1925*, 150–51; *Toros y toreros en 1926*, 181–82.

626. Alfredo Corrochano did train in Salamanca, as Hemingway claims: many bullfighters did and do, since Salamanca has huge bull-breeding ranches. I have found no reference to Sánchez Mejías's being Alfredo's mentor, nor is there any evidence that Gregorio Corrochano "attacked" Joselito. In *¿Qué es torear?* which is subtitled "Introducción a las tauromaquias de Joselito y de Domingo Ortega," Corrochano repeatedly praises Joselito as one of the all-time greats, a true artist and a master of the bullfight. Hemingway's dislike of Sánchez Mejías (and of other bullfighters) expresses itself in these unflattering "stretchers."

The charge that Sánchez Mejías liked attention and would fight in an uncouth manner in order to get publicity was made by Uno al Sesgo in the early 1920s, but by 1922 Sánchez Mejías's artistry convinced the critic to change his mind, and by 1924 Uno al Sesgo was a fan, impressed both by Ignacio's work and by his personality: "se impuso a todos y a todo . . . su figura ha ganado en prestigio y superioridad . . . ha sido la figura más interesante del año" (he has imposed his will on everyone and everything . . . he has gained in prestige and excellence . . . he has been the most interesting figure of the year; *Toros y toreros en 1924*, 126–28).

627. Greacen, *Chink*, 16–27. David Penn, of the Imperial War Museum, London, also supplied information about Dorman-Smith's family, education, and career. He writes that Dorman-Smith was educated at Uppingham and Sandhurst (letter to author, 18 January 1996). Mrs. M. I. L. de Lee, acting curator, Sandhurst Collection, The Royal Military Academy Sandhurst, confirmed Greacen's details about Chink's education; the Sandhurst records list him under Smith (letter to author, 9 October 1997).

628. The Count's name and death date were found by the indefatigable Anthony Brand in Ventura Bagüés, *Al hilo de las tablas*, 22–23. History of the herd: in the nineteenth century the breeder Manuel Suárez Cordero established a herd with stock acquired from Isabel Montemayor, viuda de (widow of) Lesaca, stock that can be traced back to the Varea-Martín-Lesaca branch of the Vistahermosa holdings. In 1850 the herd was inherited in equal lots by Manuel Suárez's heirs, his son Manuel and his daughter Manuela, the son also inheriting all the rights to the herd's brand, colors, and *antigüedad*. Soon after inheriting it, the son sold his share, with all its rights, to Dolores Monge viuda de Murube (q.v.), who expanded this herd with Saavedra stock. In 1884 she sold half of this herd to Eduardo Ibarra who, twenty years later, sold it to two other famous Sevillian breeders: Fernando Parladé and Manuel Fernández Peña. One year later, in 1905, the Count of Santa Coloma bought Fernández Peña's holdings.

629. Cossío's flattering appraisal appears in "Santa Coloma, Sr. Conde de," *Toros y toreros en 1931*, 183–84. See also Cossío (1943–97), "Buendía, don Joaquín," I: 264; and Vera, *Orígenes e historial*, "Buendía Peña (don Joaquín), 37–38. In *Orígenes e historial*, Vera gives the herd's *antigüedad* as 17 May 1908, but in *Toros y toreros en . . . ,* for which he prepared the entries on the bull breeders, he gives the date as 1908 in the 1924 annual, but 1906 in the 1931 annual. Cossío similarly gives two dates, 1906 and 1908 ([1943–97] I: 264 and 390). All agree that the day and month were 17 May. When the herd was sold in 1932, Buendía acquired the herd's *antigüedad*, listed in the U.C.T.L. as 17 May 1906.

The Count of Santa Coloma's brother, the Marquis of Albaserrada, acquired Santa Coloma stock in 1912. He presented them in Madrid on 29 May 1919 (the date of their *antigüedad*). That line of bulls, so closely related to the Santa Colomas, is now (as of 2000) the property of Victorino Martín Andrés.

630. Now known as the "Ganadería de Joaquín Buendía Peña," it is owned by José Luis Buendía Ramírez de Arellano (*Unión de criadores de toros de lidia* [2000], 59).

631. Reynolds, *Chronology*, 51, 58, 64–65.

632. Sanz's sober elegance was contrasted with the rougher art of Desperdicios, who was "torpón y desmañado . . . de un valor excepcional . . . Valiente hasta la exageración" (clumsy, unskilled . . . exceptionally brave . . . exaggeratedly brave; Silva Aramburu, *Enciclopedia taurina*, 244–45). Their contrasting styles and personalities exacerbated the rivalry between Madrid and Sevilla but did not arouse the same passion among their followers as did the next generation's pair, Rafael

Molina (Lagartijo) and Salvador Sánchez (Frascuelo): Lagartijo's Madrid supporters made life so miserable for Frascuelo that he absented himself from the Madrid ring in the late 1870s (*see* the entry for Sánchez, Salvador, in this volume; and Rivalry in *DS*).

633. El Tato and el Gordito were themselves frequently paired rivals and are usually discussed together in taurine histories.

634. Cossío (1943–97), "Sanz (Cayetano)," III: 906–08; Silva Aramburu, *Enciclopedia taurina*, 245; Bagüés, *Historia de los matadores*, 61–62; Tapia, *Breve historial del toreo*, 217–20. The date of Sanz's *alternativa* is given as 1848 by Tapia and Bagüés and as 1849 by Cossío ([1943–97] III: 907). Cossío (1995) amends the date to 1848.

635. Mott, *A History of American Magazines* IV: 671–716; "Magazines," *The Reader's Encyclopedia*, 687. The *Post* published many of F. Scott Fitzgerald's stories but rejected everything Hemingway submitted.

636. Franklin, *Bullfighter from Brooklyn*, 172.

637. *Selected Letters*, 17; Baker, *A Life Story*, 51.

638. Cossío gives the date of the *alternativa* as 23 October 1931, an obvious typographical error; *Toros y toreros en 1931* twice gives it as 29 October (26, 277), and Bagüés confirms that date (*Historia de los matadores*, 216).

639. Victoriano de la Serna is listed among those who fought in ten or fewer *novilladas* ("Han toreado de una a diez corridas los siguientes matadores de novillos," *Toros y toreros en 1930*, 332).

640. Serna's remark is qtd. in Abella, *Historia* II: 61.

641. Silva Aramburu, *Enciclopedia taurina*, 283. Néstor Luján, author of *Historia del toreo* (a book Hemingway owned), wrote of Victoriano de la Serna that his was a "pasión fría y cerebral por los toros. Buscó la belleza de un pase, de un momento plástico, sin preocuparse de nada más. Como personaje, es en la historia del toreo un ser extravagante y pintoresco. . . . Como estilista de la elegancia, fue una de las cumbres del toreo posbelmontino" (cold and cerebral passion for the bulls. He sought the beauty of the pass, of the sculptural moment, without caring about anything else. He is an extravagant, picturesque creature in the history of the bullfight. As an elegant stylist, he was one of the high points of the post-Belmonte era; qtd. in Abella, *Historia* II: 61).

642. For the highlights of his career, see Cossío (1943–97), "Serna y Gil (Victoriano de la)," III: 916–18 and IV: 716; Cossío (1995) II: 760; Abella, *Historia* II: 59–62; Bagüés, *Historia de los matadores*, 216–17; *Toros y toreros en 1931*, 26, 48, 277–78, 280, 319; and *Toros y toreros 1936 a 1940*, 310. The careers of his younger brothers Ramón and Rafael are discussed only in Cossío (1943–97) III: 916. Ramón died in 1990 (Cossío [1943–97] XII: 1062).

643. Cossío (1943–97) III: 917.

644. Hemingway, "The Friend of Spain," rpt. *By-Line*, 149.

645. Cossío (1943–97) III: 918.

646. Information on Dr. Serra was supplied by Ms. Vicenta Peiro Guerrero, ar-

chivist of the Colegio Oficial de Médicos, 20 Avenida de la Plata, Valencia (personal interview, 5 October 1995).

647. "El doctor Serra de Valencia entre nosotros," *La fiesta brava*, 13 October 1927, 15.

648. Serra, *Taurotraumatología*, 107–11; the quote is from 109. Jennifer Bell and Anthony Brand supplied dates and other information about penicillin (faxes, 11 October 1999).

649. Mandell and Sande, "Antimicrobial Agents," 1126.

650. Garrod and O'Grady, *Antibiotic and Chemotherapy*, 7. This remarkable antibiotic was discovered twice, in 1896 by a French medical student (no one paid any attention to it) and in 1928 by Alexander Fleming.

651. "The Dangerous Summer," *Life* (5 September 1960), 91. The typescript for *The Dangerous Summer* also reports a conversation with Juan Belmonte about the use of penicillin to cure and, hopefully, eradicate hoof and mouth disease in cattle (qtd. in DeFazio, "The HemHotch Letters," 1323).

652. Gómez Santos, *Mi ruedo ibérico*, 201.

653. Qtd. in DeFazio, "The HemHotch Letters," 1461.

654. "Evan B. Shipman, Racing Writer, 53," *New York Times*, 26 June 1957, 29; O'Rourke, letter to author, 20 August 1998. O'Rourke looked at the Shipman-Hemingway correspondence in the Hemingway Collection, JFK. He reports that in addition to running away from Salisbury, Shipman was expelled from Groton.

655. Herbert Channick, "Evan Shipman," informal biography written for Shipman's fiftieth reunion at Groton; O'Rourke, "Evan Shipman," 86–89; personal interview with O'Rourke, 28 August 1996, Boston. O'Rourke, who generously shared his materials with me, argues that Shipman was a historical prototype for the gambler in Hemingway's story "The Gambler, the Nun and the Radio," written 1931–32 ("Evan Shipman and 'The Gambler, the Nun, and the Radio'," 86–89).

656. Obituary, "Evan B. Shipman, Racing Writer, 53," *New York Times*, 25 June 1957, 29.

657. Thomas Gilcoyne, research librarian of the National Museum of Racing and Hall of Fame, Saratoga Springs, New York, provided information about the Evan Shipman Handicap (interview, 26 March 1998). In 1991, the stake was $88,000.

658. Josephson, "Evan Shipman: Poet and Horse-Player," 853.

659. The hero of Shipman's *Free for All* is Will Broderick, a horse trainer closely identified with the horses he tends. We first meet him in connection with "a big angular gelding" (4), seven years old, whose courage enables him to succeed in spite of the weakness of his legs. Stamina's broken leg marks the beginning of Will's descent into drink. Will becomes less and less reliable until his employer, Fred Dunbar, is forced to let him go. Will goes south, has various adventures, and ends up caring for Regal, another old horse. Will believes that Regal deserves a cushy retirement, but Regal's owner callously decides to sell the old racehorse to a milkman.

The novel describes Regal's pitiful condition, as he is about to be sent off with "nothing . . . but the halter . . . No blankets . . . an old halter" to the humiliation of a milk route (315). Will stands up for the horse, insults the owner, and thus wins the admiration of Dunbar, who offers him a job for the next season. The book ends with Will telling himself that "Maybe I'm not such an unlucky son-of-a-gun as I'm always making myself out to be. I'll get by" (318).

The pointedly named horses, Stamina and Regal, stand for qualities that need to be recognized and honored. Various subplots reinforce the theme that courage and commitment should be rewarded; one such plot reports the death of Pete, one of the two broken-down drunks whose love for the horses impels him to hang around the tracks and whose life and death Will glorifies.

660. Shipman obituary, *New York Times*, 25 June 1957, 29.

661. Brasch and Sigman, *Hemingway's Library*, 338. The second copy may have been intended for Howard Hawks, who "is going to make a trotting picture and I talked about Evan to him for a long time and I think I might get Evan a job as technical adviser for the picture and perhaps to do some of the writing. Hawks was very interested in him and I promised to get him a copy of the book" (Hemingway, *Selected Letters*, 529).

662. Tavernier-Courbin, *Ernest Hemingway's* A Moveable Feast, 96.

663. Hemingway, "Introduction," *Men at War*, xxv–xxvi.

664. *Newsweek*, 29 April 1991, 38.

665. In *The Best Times*, Dos Passos describes Hemingway as "a moody kind of fellow. . . . Sorry for himself . . . about not having been to college. I used to tell him he was damn lucky. Think of all the tripe he hadn't had to unlearn. Suppose he'd gone to Yale and been tapped for Bones like Don Stewart. He'd laugh and admit that would have been the ruination of him" (143). Dos Passos writes that Stewart had not only "made Bones at Yale" but also had "a certain obsession with social status" (*The Best Times*, 140).

666. Donnelly, *Sara & Gerald*, 24, 9, 128–29. Vaill also mentions Murphy's concern with what was proper to wear at the bullfight: "Finally he settled on a pearl gray gabardine suit and an old golf cap of his father's — 'I didn't want to wear a Panama hat,' he recalled — and, to his relief, won Ernest's approval" (*Everybody Was So Young*, 179). Hemingway reinstates the Panama hat (*DIA*, 34).

667. JFK, Item 22, Folder 26.

668. JFK, Incoming Correspondence. The letters date from 1918 to 1961.

669. Kenneth G. Johnston, " 'The Three Day Blow': Tragicomic Aftermath of a Summer Romance," 21.

670. *Selected Letters*, 149; Baker, *A Life Story*, 153; Reynolds, *Paris Years*, 269.

671. Under Walsh and Moorhead's editorship, *This Quarter* published Hemingway's "Big Two-Hearted River" (May 1925) and "The Undefeated" (Autumn-Winter 1925–26); Edward Titus, the next editor, published "The Sea Change" in *This Quarter*'s December 1931 issue. In *A Moveable Feast*, Hemingway mentions that *This Quarter* had published his work and that Walsh offered him a sizeable prize or grant that never materialized (*MF*, 125–29).

672. Smith dates the typescript to "late 1926 or early 1927" and argues that the piece was drafted "closer to 1925 than to 1930" (*Reader's Guide*, 189).

673. One of the poem's characters, "Our uncle," is described as "innocent of books" but "rich in lore of fields and brooks"—a natural historian. He is compared with the Reverend Gilbert White (q.v.), whom Hemingway also mentions at the beginning of his own "Natural History of the Dead" (q.v.). This uncle describes the activities of the partridge, the mink, and the woodchuck; the nephew is equally enthralled by all the stories. He remembers the uncle as

> A simple, guileless, childlike man,
> Content to live where life began,
> Strong only on his native grounds,
> The little world of sights and sounds
> Whose girdle was the parish bounds,
> Whereof his fondly partial pride
> The common features magnified,
> As Surrey hills to mountains grew
> In White of Selborne's loving view,
> He told how teal and loon he shot,
> And how the eagle's eggs he got,
> The feats on pond and river done,
> The prodigies of rod and gun;
> Till, warming with the tales he told,
> Forgotten was the outside cold
> (*Snow Bound*, ll.323–38)

674. Bradley *et al.*, *The American Tradition in Literature*, 787–88.

675. Lounsberry, "Hemingway's Celebration of Memory," 30; Lounsberry, "The Holograph Manuscript," 45, n. 7.

676. Hemingway's issues of *Sol y sombra* are at the Hemingway Collection, JFK.

677. "Jesús Solórzano," *Toros y toreros en 1931*, 264–66.

678. Cossío (1943–97), "Solórzano Dávalos (Jesus)," III: 927–28 and IV: 721; Cossío (1995) II: 767; Abella, *Historia* II: 46; Bagüés, *Historia de los matadores*, 210–11; Tapia, *Breve historial del toreo*, 422–24.

679. Cossío (1995), "Solórzano Dávalos (Eduardo)," II: 766–67; Bagüés, *Historia de los matadores*, 242; Abella, "Jesús Solórzano," *Historia* III: 297–98.

680. One of the joys of research is the impossibility of establishing basic facts. The capacity of Soria's bullring, for example, is variously reported as 3,589 (*Agenda-Guía del calendario fichero taurino*, 163), 4,100 (Cossío [1943–97] I: 554), 5,500 (Carmona González, *Consultor indicador taurino universal*, 273), and 6,313 (Pinto Maeso, *Plazas de toros*, 92). It was built either in 1852 or 1854.

681. Fermín Martín Alonso, with whom Sotomayor negotiated a complicated exchange, had recently inherited the Arauz herd from his father, also named Fermín

Martín. The Arauz herd, of Ibarra heritage, was held by two generations of the Martín family before coming to Sotomayor in 1931. Sotomayor was wealthy enough to be a selective breeder, and he wanted the Arauz stock badly enough to relinquish a good fraction of his herd, as well as its *antigüedad*, in order to acquire them. In their annual summary, *Toros y toreros en 1930* praised Sotomayor both for breeding so carefully and for selling only fine bulls to the bullrings; such selectivity and restraint are made possible only by a sizable fortune, which frees the owner to buy the best and to forego the profits he could obtain by selling more bulls. Sotomayor obviously withheld from the market those of his expensively bred bulls that did not meet his standards (*Toros y toreros en 1930*, 200–201). After the 1931 sale, in which he divested himself of his *antigüedad*, Sotomayor continued breeding bulls, but he did not present his new herd in Madrid and so it had no *antigüedad*. See Cossío (1943–97), "Sotomayor, don Florentino," I: 394–95; *Toros y toreros en 1918*, 77; *Toros y toreros en 1924*, 96–97; *Toros y toreros en 1925*, 103; *Toros y toreros en 1926*, 138; *Toros y toreros en 1927*, 112; *Toros y toreros en 1929*, 170–71; *Toros y toreros en 1930*, 200–201; "Martín Alonso, d. Fermín," *Toros y toreros en 1931*, 147. For the herd's modern history, see Vera, "Prieto de la Cal y Divildos (don Tomás)," *Orígenes e historial*, 242–44; "Prieto de la Cal (Don Tomás)," *Unión de criadores de toros de lidia* (1995), 145; *Unión de criadores de toros de lidia* (1997), 300; and *Unión de criadores de toros de lidia* (2000), 236. For the Sotomayor family's taurine activities after the 1931 sale of the Sotomayor *antigüedad*, see "Eduardo Sotomayor," *Toros y toreros 1936 a 1940*, 233; and Vera, "Vázquez de Troya (don Fernando)," *Orígenes e historial*, 153–54.

682. "Arctic Autopsy of the 1918 Flu Pandemic," *International Herald Tribune*, 21 August 1998, 1. The study of the human tissue found in Alaska did not yield the hoped-for explanation of the causes of the lethal flu virus. Such plagues spawn histrionic, gossipy books, such as Gina Kolata's *Flu: The Story of the Great Influenza Pandemic of 1918 and the Search for the Virus that Caused It* (Touchstone, 2000) and Pete Davies's *The Devil's Flu: The World's Deadliest Influenza Epidemic and the Scientific Hunt for the Virus that Caused It* (Owl, 2000).

683. Qtd. in Griffin, *Along with Youth*, 96.

684. Stanley, *A Familiar History of Birds*, 241.

685. Portz, "Allusion and Structure," 33–34.

686. Mellow, *A Life without Consequences*, 321; Stein, *The Autobiography of Alice B. Toklas*, 216.

687. Qtd. in Mellow, *A Life without Consequences*, 235.

688. "The first matador got the horns" is one of the six Hemingway sketches that Jane Heap published in the *Little Review* (Spring 1923) and that were later incorporated into *in our time* (1924; see Reynolds, *Chronology*, 31). As I document elsewhere, Hemingway saw his first bullfights in May and June 1923 (Mandel, "The Birth of Hemingway's *Afición*").

689. JFK, Item 22, Folder 26.

690. "Donald O. Stewart, Screenwriter, Dies," *New York Times*, 3 August 1980, 32: 1–2.

691. *Selected Letters*, 138, 214.

692. Stewart provides an account of his growing disenchantment with Hemingway: "On Bea's birthday in October [1926] I gave a party at Prunier's where I discovered to my dismay that Ernest's marriage to Hadley was breaking up. I also discovered at around this time a curious bitter streak in Ernest. This first displayed itself in *The Torrents of Spring*, a book I loathed both for its bitterness and for its inept attempts at humor. More serious, for me, was a viciously unfair and unfunny poem about Dorothy Parker which Ernest read at a party in Archie MacLeish's apartment. I told him what I thought of his poem and our friendship, to my lasting sorrow, came to an end. . . . Ernest was somebody you went along with, or else" (*By a Stroke of Luck*, 157, 131; Hemingway's poem "To a Tragic Poetess" mocks Parker's abortion, her suicide attempts, and her dislike of Spain). Sylvia Grinder, of the Association of Yale Alumni, Yale University, provided details about Stewart's education and first marriage (letter to author, 8 September 1995). Meyers identifies Stewart's birth date variously as 1894 and 1896 (*Hemingway*, 643, 150); Baker identifies his first wife as Beatrice and Bertha (*A Life Story*, 176, 694). The facts are that Stewart was born in 1896 and that he married Beatrice Ames in July 1926; they had two sons and were divorced in October 1938. Stewart married Ella Winter Steffens, the widow of Lincoln Steffens, in March 1939. For fuller discussion of the Stewart-Hemingway relationship, see Baker, *A Life Story*, 149–50, 176, 203; and Reynolds, *Paris Years*, 213, 301–303.

693. Fire Marshal's Report, on the Chicago Union Stock Yards Fire (Chicago History Web Site: Deaths, Disturbances, Disasters and Disorders in Chicago).

694. For another description of the fire, see Upton Sinclair, *The Jungle*, 1986 ed., 31–32. Hamlin Garland, Charles Dudley Warner, and Waldo Frank all commented upon Chicago's polluted skies. My thanks to Hilary K. Justice for bringing Sinclair to my attention (E-mail, 3 November 1999); and to Susan F. Beegel, who supplied additional descriptions and clarified details about atmospheric conditions (E-mail, 5 November 1999).

695. Cossío (1943–97), "Suárez (Luis), Magritas," III: 932–33 and IV: 723; *Toros y toreros en 1926*, 312.

696. Chaves was injured by a Miura bull named "Troyano," which ripped open his right forearm, exposing the bone, and also gored him in the chest (*Toros y toreros en 1926*, 323).

697. Cossío (1943–97), "Tamarit (Francisco), Chaves," III: 937–38, IV: 725, and VI: 508; Cossío (1995) II: 770; *Toros y toreros en 1925*, 190–91; *Toros y toreros en 1926*, 211–12, 323; *Toros y toreros en 1927*, 176; *Toros y toreros en 1929*, 227–28; *Toros y toreros en 1931*, 246; *El Clarín*, Almanacs for 1924–28; Bagüés, *Historia de los matadores*, 190. Cossío mistakenly reports that Chaves's promotion to *matador de toros* occurred in 1926; the error is not corrected in the 1995 edition. Francisco Tamarit's younger brother, Juan (Chaves II) became a *novillero* who, after three unsuccessful seasons, abandoned bullfighting.

698. *Selected Letters*, 341; Freiberg, *The French Press*, 31–33, 84–85.

699. Cossío (1943–97), "Tiebas (Cándido)," III: 940 and VI: 517; *Toros y tore-ros en 1925*, 212; *Toros y toreros en 1930*, 349–50; *El Clarín*, Almanacs for 1925–29.

700. Cossío (1943–97), "Todó de la Paz (Isidoro), Alcalareño," III: 941–42; *El Clarín*'s Almanacs, 1925–29; *Toros y toreros en 1925*, 205; *Toros y toreros en 1926*, 231; *Toros y toreros en 1927*, 200; *Toros y toreros en 1929*, 250; *Toros y toreros en 1930*, 300; *Toros y toreros en 1931*, 338. Cossío is remarkably inaccurate on this bullfighter, reporting his birth date as 1895, his Madrid debut as 1919, and his death date as 1930.

701. "En la plaza de toros de Madrid, el novillo Cartelero, de la ganadería de Conradi, causó la muerte a Isidoro Todó (Alcalareño II)," *El Clarín* (14 November 1931).

702. "Otra vez la muerta pasa" and "Entierro de Alacareño II," *El eco taurino*, 31 August 1931, 3–5.

703. "La trágica temporada madrileña," *La fiesta brava*, 2 October 1931, un-numbered page 5.

704. Cossío III: 942; *Toros y toreros en 1931*, 338; Tynan, *Bull Fever*, 53; inter-view with Ordóñez, 11 October 1995.

705. "Corto: Se dice del torero de escaso repertorio de suertes y limitados recur-sos de dominio para la lidia"; "Largo: Torero de copiosos recursos y extenso reper-torio de suertes para la lidia" (Nieto Manjón, *Diccionario ilustrado de términos taurinos*, 146, 254). Ramón de Lacadena Brualla (don Indalecio) discussed these terms at length in "Toreros largos y toreros cortos; toreros machos y toreros hem-bra" (Zaragoza: Industrias Gráficas Uriarte, 1930).

706. *Torerías* is listed in Cossío (1943–97) II: 585; and in "Revistas y periód-icos, en España," *Toros y toreros en 1924*, 266.

707. The journal is listed in the annual compendium *Toros y toreros en . . .* for all the years Hemingway visited Spain; see, for example, "La prensa taurom-áquica," *Toros y toreros en 1925*, 272; "Prensa taurina," *Toros y toreros en 1929*, 301; and "Bibliografía," *Toros y toreros en 1931*, 356. Madrid's Biblioteca Nacio-nal does not, unfortunately, carry this journal.

708. Brasch and Sigman, *Hemingway's Library*, 279–80; Cossío (1943–97), "Periódicos taurinos," II: 585 and VI: 1035. The annual *Toros y toreros en . . .* was compiled by Tomás Orts Ramos (Uno al Sesgo), who reported on the bullfighters; by Ventura Bagüés (don Ventura), who compiled the sections on the bulls and the bull breeders, until 1928; and, for a few years, by Dr. J. Vilar Jimenez (Doctor Vesalio), who kept track of injuries and deaths. Orts Ramos was succeeded by his son, Edmundo Orts Climent, known appropriately as Medio al Sesgo.

These invaluable annual publications gave complete schedules of *corridas de toros*, *corridas de novillos*, and other important taurine events, such as *corridas extraordinarias*, *alternativas*, openings of new plazas, deaths, taurine banquets and awards, and so on; they covered taurine events in Spain, Portugal, France, and those Central and South American countries that have important plazas or ranches. The books present statistics such as numbers of corridas per month, per plaza, per bull-fighter, per bull-breeding ranch, and so on. Important ranches, *matadores de toros*, and *matadores de novillos* are evaluated in hundreds of short, individual essays. Overview essays open each volume and a bibliography appears at the end. *Toros y toreros en* . . . was advertised and admiringly quoted in most of the taurine journals Hemingway read; for a sample of its evaluations, see the entry on Enrique Torres.

The Biblioteca Nacional, Madrid, carries *Toros y toreros en* . . . for the years 1904–16, 1918–22, 1924–50, and 1968.

709. Brasch and Sigman, 255; Reynolds, *Hemingway's Reading*, 159. Minguet's son, who called himself *Pensamientos hijo*, produced the later volumes.

710. Hemingway's copies of *Le Toril* from 1926, 1927, and 1928, as well as the receipt for his 1925 subscription, are in the Hemingway Collection, JFK. Most of the annuals are in his library at the Finca Vigía, Cuba.

711. Cossío (1943–97) II: 586; *Toros y toreros en 1924*, 265.

712. "Alternativa de Torón" and "De la alternativa de Torón," *La fiesta brava*, 18 July 1930; Lalanda had to kill Torón's second bull. The third matador that afternoon was Félix Rodríguez; the bulls were Concha y Sierra.

713. "Saturio Torón," *Toros y toreros en 1930*, 281–82; "Efemérides," *Toros y toreros en 1930*, 356, 358.

714. Among the injuries Torón suffered in 1930 were a goring during the *novillada* of 9 March, in Valencia, and another one just eleven days later, in Cádiz. These frequent injuries repel the public, who want to see art, not blood (*Toros y toreros en 1930*, 350, 352). On the afternoon of 9 March, another *novillero* was injured as well, and Torón's banderillero Cándido Tiebas (q.v.) died in the *callejón* of a sudden heart attack—a miserable afternoon indeed!

715. Cossío (1943–97), "Torón (Saturio)," III: 943–44 and VI: 521. *Toros y toreros en 1929*, 267–68; *Toros y toreros en 1931*, 261–62; Tapia, *Breve historial del toreo*, 387–88. Bagüés gives Torón's birth date as 1902 and says that even after his promotion to *matador de toros*, he never achieved a real understanding of bull-fighting ("No le entró el toreo en la cabeza"; Bagüés, *Historia de los matadores*, 208).

716. Cossío (1943–97), "Indice de toros célebres," I: 325–408; Cossío (1995), "Toros célebres," I: 515–78.

717. 1927 really did produce a good crop: Cagancho and Gitanillo de Triana, both Southerners, were also promoted that year. They were older (b. 1903).

718. Bagüés, "Enrique Torres y Herrero," *Historia de los matadores*, 197–98; Cossío (1943–97) III: 947–48 and IV: 728; Tapia, *Breve historial del toreo*, 428; Abella, *Historia* II: 53; *El Clarín*, Almanacs for 1924–29.

719. *Toros y toreros en 1926*, 246–47; *Toros y toreros en 1928*, 193. See also *Toros y toreros en 1927*, 189–90; *Toros y toreros en 1929*, 233–34; *Toros y toreros en 1930*, 271–72; and *Toros y toreros en 1931*, 254.

720. The nickname was bestowed by the taurine critic José de Loma (Don Modesto), in a review entitled "El Papa de la tauromaquia" (Mira, *Antonio Bienven-*

ida, 22). A few days later, Don Modesto nicknamed Manuel Mejías "el Papa Negro" (the Black Pope), i.e., second only to Bombita.

721. Cossío (1943–97), "Torres Reina (Ricardo), Bombita," III: 950–54 and IV: 730; Bagüés, *Historia de los matadores*, 109; Silva Aramburu, *Enciclopedia taurina*, 258; Tapia, *Breve historial del toreo*, 328–30. A Mexican bullfighter also called Ricardo Torres (1914–53) came to Spain in 1934, too late for Hemingway to have included him in *DIA*.

722. Cossío (1943–97), "Tovar, señores herederos del Duque de," I: 295; *Toros y toreros en 1931*, 188–89; "Veiga Teixeira (don Antonio José da)," *Unión de criadores de toros de lidia* (1995), 361.

723. In 1924 and 1926, while he owned the Arribas herd, the Duke sold bulls but not *novillos* to the Madrid bullring (*Toros y toreros en 1924*, 99–100; *Toros y toreros en 1926*, 140–41). In 1927, he sold a lot of five *novillos* to the Madrid bullring (*Toros y toreros en 1927*, 114). Thus, Hemingway could not have seen six Tovar *novillos* in Madrid those years.

In 1925 and 1929, the Duke did sell lots of six *novillos* each to the Madrid bullring. Of the 1925 lot, two of the six were good, three were satisfactory, and one required *banderillas de fuego* to encourage him to perform (*Toros y toreros en 1925*, 105–106). In 1929, they were all "mansurrones" (lacked spirit; *Toros y toreros en 1929*, 172); these were from the recently acquired Suárez herd. Hemingway was in Spain both in 1925 and 1929, and could have seen either lot. In 1930 Hemingway did not go to Spain, and in 1931, his last season in Spain before the publication of *Death in the Afternoon*, the Duke's heirs did not sell *novillos* to Madrid (*Toros y toreros en 1931*, 188–89). Thus Hemingway could have seen six Tovar *novillos* in Madrid on only two occasions: from the Arribas herd in 1925, or from the Suárez herd in 1929.

724. *Toros y toreros en 1925*, 253.

725. "Triana nació mora, no romana," *El correo de Andalucía*, 26 December 2000, 6–7.

726. Reynolds, *Hemingway's Reading*, 193.

727. Baker, *A Life Story*, 145; Reynolds, *Paris Years*, 288–89.

728. "Uncas," *Encyclopedia Americana*, 1961 ed., XXVII: 269.

729. There was also an Unca, foaled in 1877, whose sire was named Uncas. Information about these horses is sketchy.

730. Howard Bass, of Thoroughbred Racing Communications, supplied information about the two nineteenth-century horses named Uncas (letter to author, 21 September 1990; E-mail communication, 12 September 1995). For information on Uncas, Mr. Bass consulted the Jockey Club Information Systems' Equine Line (R), a computer data base. Information about the twentieth century Uncas was supplied by Louis Romanet, Direction des Relations Internationales, France Galop, Boulogne (fax, 30 January 1996).

In 1926, Uncas won five races, four of them in a period of about six weeks:

21 February: Prix Vaucouleurs, with a stake of 10,000 FF, and the betting at 19 to 10.

11 March: Prix du Grand Veneur, with a stake of 10,000 FF, and the betting at 6 to 10.

1 April: Prix de la Bigauderie, with a stake of 10,000 FF and the betting at 4 to 10.

4 April: Prix du Président de la République, with a stake of 100,000 FF, and the betting at 45 to 4. Betting on Uncas at this race would have been a very good thing indeed.

1 November: Prix de l'Anniversaire, 50,000 FF, with the betting at 44 to 10.

731. Baker, *A Life Story*, 593.

732. Cossío (1943–97), "Valera Jiménez (Rafael), Rafaelillo," III: 968–69 and IV: 735.

733. Vandel's photos appear in Durán Blázquez and Sánchez Vigil, both books, *passim*. "Suerte de varas en San Sebastián, 1921" appears in *Historia de la fotografía taurina*.

734. See Olano, *Dinastías*, 28; Varé is also called Varest and Vara.

735. Qtd. in Cossío (1943–97) III: 971.

736. Cossío (1943–97), "Varé García (Manuel), Varelito," III: 970–72; Tapia, *Breve historial del toreo*, 366–67. Bagüés gives his birth date as 1894 (*Historia de los matadores*, 157).

737. Varé "tenía el más elevado concepto de su responsabilidad, se creía obligado a lucir su especialidad con todos los toros, pundonor que le costó algunas cornadas" (Bagüés, *Historia de los matadores*, 157).

738. Qtd. in Cossío (1943–97) III: 972.

739. Cossío (1943–97) II: 970.

740. Vicente José Vázquez added stock from the herds of the Marquis of Casa-Ulloa, who bred a mixture of Cabrera and Vistahermosa stock, known for their nerve. He also acquired animals from the herds of Becker (also spelled Becquer); these were mostly of the Cabrera (q.v.) strain, famous for their size and strength. And he also bought Vistahermosa (q.v.) stock, known for their nobility. These strains or castes are defined in Cossío (1943–97), "Castas de toros y ganaderías," I: 251; Vera, *Orígenes e historial*, 21; "Toros: Ganaderías de toros de lidia," *Gran enciclopedia Rialp* XXII: 603–605.

741. Cossío (1943–97) III: 979.

742. Cossío (1943–97), "Vega de los Reyes (Francisco), Gitanillo de Triana," III: 978–80; *El Clarín*, Almanacs for 1926–29; Bagüés, *Historia de los matadores*, 195–96; Tapia, *Breve historial del toreo*, 407–408; "Gitanillo de Triana," *La fiesta brava*, 21 August 1931, unnumbered page 7. Cossío gives his birth date as 1903, Bagüés as 1904, and the obituary in *Toros y toreros en 1931* as 23 December 1904 (337); he was not yet twenty-seven when he died.

743. Bagüés, *Historia de los matadores*, 195.

744. Conrad, *Encyclopedia of Bullfighting*, 116.

745. *Toros y toreros en 1927*, 185–86; JFK, Bullfight Materials (ticket stubs). The narrator remarks that before the fatal afternoon of 31 May 1931, he had last seen Gitanillo in the year of the car crash, i.e., 1929.

746. "Veiga (Simão) da," *Enciclopedia Universal Ilustrada, Suplemento 1959–1960*, 534–35; Cossío (1943–97) III: 982; *Toros y toreros en 1924*, 220–21, 240–41. Both in 1924 and 1925, Veiga performed in Madrid in June; the 1925 performance was a benefit, in which Veiga was followed by Marcial Lalanda, who killed six bulls by himself. Cossío credits Veiga with popularizing *rejoneo* in Spain.

747. "Pamplona en Fiestas," *Zig Zag*, 19 July 1924, 11; *El eco taurino*, 15 August 1927, 2; Cossío calls him "Veiga Junior" ([1943–97] III: 982). Hemingway also saved *Sangre y arena*'s glowing review of Veiga's earlier performance in Madrid, on Corpus Christi, which described him as a "formidable caballista, estupendísimo torero de a caballo" (formidable as a horseman, stupendous as a mounted bullfighter; "Toros en Madrid," *Sangre y arena*, 25 June 1924, JFK, Periodicals).

748. For an interesting discussion of the self-reflexiveness of *For Whom the Bell Tolls*, see Robin Gajdusek, "Artists in Their Art: Hemingway and Velásquez—The Shared Worlds of *For Whom the Bell Tolls* and *Las Meninas*."

749. The Dukes of Veragua claim descent from Christopher Columbus.

750. Manuel Martín Alonso's brother, Fermín, was also a famous bull breeder; *see* the entry for Sotomayor, don Florentino.

751. "Veragua (Sr. Duque de)," *Toros y toreros en 1924*, 100–102; "Domecq-Villavicencio, D. Juan Pedro," *Toros y toreros en 1931*, 116–17; Vera, "Vistahermosa," *Orígenes e historial*, 20–21; Vera, "Domecq Díez (don Juan Pedro)," *Orígenes e historial*, 54–57; Cossío (1943–97), "Domecq-Villavicencio, don Juan Pedro," I: 269–70; "Domecq (don Juan Pedro)," *Unión de criadores de toros de lidia* (1995), 197; "La casta veragüeña," *La fiesta brava*, 24 November 1927, 6–7. Goya's painting of Pedro Romero was in the Duke of Veragua's private collection.

752. "Veronica, St.," *Encyclopaedia Britannica*, 11th ed., XXVII: 1037–38; "Veronica," *New Catholic Encyclopedia* XIV: 625; "Suertes del toreo: la verónica," *La fiesta brava*, 14 June 1929, unnumbered page 3.

753. Carralero and Borge, "Víbora," *Toros célebres*, 310.

754. Herwig and Heyman, "Victor Emmanuel III," *Biographical Dictionary of World War I*, 347–48; "Victor Emmanuel III," *Who Was Who in World War II*, 213–14.

755. Lewis notes that G. M. Trevelyan, author of *Scenes from Italy's Wars* (London: T. C. and E. C. Jack, 1919), mentions this fact: "They call the Carabinieri 'aeroplanes,' on account of their wide-winged hats." Lewis argues that Hemingway got many of his facts from Trevelyan ("Hemingway in Italy," 233). See "carabiniere," *Dizionario Enciclopedico Italiano* II: 759.

756. "Victoria Eugenia," *Enciclopedia universal* LXVIII: 630–33 and *Suplemento 1969–1970*, 316.

757. Uriarte consistently spells the name Serres (*Almanaques* for 1941–42 and 1943–44), as does Bagüés (*Historia de los matadores*, 173). Cossío spells it Serris ([1943–97] III: 995).

758. Cossío (1943–97) III: 996; Luján, *Historia del toreo*, 316–17; Bagüés, *Historia de los matadores*, 173–74.

759. For Hemingway's first exposure to Villalta, see Mandel, "The Birth of Hemingway's *Afición*," especially 141–42.

760. See also Cossío (1943–97), "Villalta y Serris (Nicanor)," III: 995–96 and IV: 752–53; Silva Aramburu, *Enciclopedia taurina*, 282; Tapia, *Breve historial del toro*, 384–85. Bagüés reports that on the birth certificate his last names were misspelled as Vilalta Serres and that he fought fifty corridas in 1926 and fifty-two in 1927 (*Historia de los matadores*, 173–74). Hemingway describes the first corrida he ever saw (Madrid 1923), saying of Villalta that "he was straight as a lance and walked like a young wolf" ("Bullfighting is Not a Sport," 340–46). In his report of Pamplona, Hemingway does not mention Villalta ("Pamplona in July," 347–54). On 6 July 1923, Villalta performed with Freg and Márquez (qq.v.); on 8 July with Márquez and Martín: all three performed badly with their first bulls and were whistled at by the crowd, but in the second half of the corrida Márquez cut one ear and Villalta cut two. The season's bullfight schedules are available in each year's *Toros y toreros en . . .*, which I consulted for the relevant years, checking Villalta's appearances against the bullfight tickets, programs, and schedules that Hemingway saved (JFK, Bullfight Materials) to ascertain when Hemingway saw this bullfighter.

761. The date 22 April 1921 is given by the U.C.T.L. *Toros y toreros en 1925* gives the *antigüedad* as 20 July 1919, but by the 1929 edition the date had been corrected to 22 April 1921.

762. Vera, "Villamarta (señor marqués de)," *Orígenes e historial*, 158–59; *Toros y toreros en 1924*, 104–105; *Toros y toreros en 1931*, 190–91; "Garcibravo, S. A. (Ganadería de)," *Unión de criadores de toros de lidia* (1995), 207.

763. Vera, "Vega-Villar," *Orígenes e historial*, 21. The Villar brothers' acquisition of the Vega herd was announced in "Nueva ganadería," *Palmas y pitos*, October 1915.

764. "Encinas Fernández del Campo, d. José," *Toros y toreros en 1931*, 117–18.

765. "Quinta y última de feria," *El pensamiento navarro*, 14 July 1923, 1, cols. 5–6. The newspaper's taurine critic signed himself "Jaleo."

766. Hemingway saw Francisco Villar's bulls in Pamplona for several consecutive years. On 11 July 1924 the Villar bulls were fought by Manuel García (Maera), Juan Anlló (Nacional II), and José García (Algabeño). The next year, on 7 July 1925, Antonio Márquez, Martín Agüero, and Cayetano Ordóñez (Niño de la Palma) fought the Villar corrida, and on 11 July 1926, eight Villar bulls were fought by Marcial Lalanda, Nicanor Villalta, Antonio de la Haba (Zurito), and Cayetano Ordóñez.

767. Uno al Sesgo, "Los toros en 1926," *Toros y toreros en 1926*, 45, 49. The criticism occurs twice: on page 45 the Villar bulls are defined as three-year-olds (i.e., *novillos*, not *toros de lidia*; the *toro* must be at least four years old), and on page 49 they are dismissed as *becerros* (even younger, not yet *novillos* and certainly not to be fought by *matadores de toros* at a formal corrida). In 1927, Uno al Sesgo complains again that too many underage and underweight bulls were fought. He explains that both bullfighters and bull breeders prefer to send younger animals

to corridas, the former because they are livelier and enable a showy *faena*, the latter because selling them earlier saves the breeder an expensive year of pasturage. Uno al Sesgo claims that in 1927, as in the previous year, even *utreros* were fought (*Toros y toreros en 1927*, 48). While this critic is willing to bend the rules occasionally, if the result is a beautiful, lively performance, he objects to making the undersized bull the norm.

Weight as well as age determines the fitness of bulls for battle. For an interesting discussion of the taurine terminology concerning weight of bulls, see Jean Cau, *Las orejas y el rabo*, 115–16. Writing for the French taurine public, whom the Spaniards consider as outsiders, Cau tells his readers that if they master the jargon they will be able to pass themselves off as real taurine insiders.

768. For Francisco Villar, see "Villar (D. Francisco)," *Toros y toreros en 1924*, 105; "Villar (D. Francisco)," *Toros y toreros en 1931*, 191 (the new herd, acquired in 1928 but not fought in any bullring); Cossío (1943–97), "Villar, don Francisco," I: 297; "Sánchez Cobaleda, d. Arturo," *Toros y toreros en 1931*, 180–81. I also consulted other issues of *Toros y toreros* for 1924–29, as well as the taurine reviews in *El pensamiento navarro* for the same years.

The complaint that followed Villar's sale to Sánchez Cobaleda appeared in "Compuesto y sin ganadería," *El eco taurino*, 14 January 1929, 3. Other reliable records, however, do not indicate that Villar's new herd, carrying the colors of green and crimson, supplied bulls or *novillos* in 1929, 1930, or 1931 (*Toros y toreros en 1929*, 175; *Toros y toreros en 1930*, 207; *Toros y toreros en 1931*, 191). Not having been fought in the Madrid ring, they lacked *antigüedad*, or seniority. In April 1931, six Sánchez Cobaleda bulls died when the truck transporting them to a corrida in Arles had an accident: it burst into flames and the bulls burned to death. All told, in 1931, Sánchez Cobaleda presented only twelve bulls to be fought: "no ha sido mucho ni bueno" (not very much and not very good).

769. Vindel's work is listed in *La fiesta taurina: Ensayo de bibliografía taurina*, compiled by the Biblioteca Nacional (Madrid, 1973). Brasch and Sigman list the two books as part of Hemingway's library (100, 385). Anthony Brand supplied the address of Vindel's shop (letter to author, April 1998).

770. Lewis, "The Making of *Death in the Afternoon*," 47. Baker lists several instances where Hemingway echoes Frank's opinions (*The Writer as Artist*, 150–52).

771. "Toros: Ganaderías de toros de lidia," *Gran enciclopedia Rialp* XXII: 603–605; Vera, "Vistahermosa," *Orígenes e historial*, 20.

772. Bagüés, "Ganaderías asociadas: los toros en 1925," *Toros y toreros en 1925*, 28–29.

773. "White, Gilbert," *Britannica Micropaedia*, 1990 ed. Because it was annotated, I used the 1900 edition of White's *The Natural History & Antiquities of Selborne & A Garden Kalendar*, ed. R. Bowdler Sharpe.

774. Gilbert White, *Natural History*, 175, n. 1; and 166, n. 1.

775. Baker, *A Life Story*, 110.

776. Mary Hemingway, *How It Was*, 332, 336.

777. Fitch, "Ernest Hemingway—c/o Shakespeare and Company," 177.

778. Woolf, "An Essay in Criticism," 9–15. For Hemingway's response, dated 1 November 1927, see *Selected Letters*, 264–65.

779. Biographical details about McAlmon were taken from Knoll's notes in the McAlmon anthology, *McAlmon and the Lost Generation*, 11, 39, 88–89; and Baker, *A Life Story*, 111.

780. All the McAlmon quotes are from "Let's Be Shadow-Boxers," first published in *Being Geniuses Together*; rpt. in *McAlmon and the Lost Generation*, 231–32.

781. McAlmon, *McAlmon and the Lost Generation*, 231–32.

782. McAlmon, *McAlmon and the Lost Generation*, 231–32.

783. Information about Yale in China was taken from Reuben Holden's carefully documented account, *Yale in China*; the two quotes are from pages 53 and 174. Yale University established another overseas campus, the Yale-Columbia Southern Station, at the University of Witwatersrand, Union of South Africa.

784. Reynolds, *Young Hemingway*, 22–23, 128.

785. For Anson Hemingway and the YMCA, see Reynolds, *Young Hemingway*, 3; and Nagel, *The Oak Park Legacy*, 9. For Ernest's membership in the YMCA, see JFK, Other Materials: Stubs and Membership cards; and Reynolds, *The 1930s*, 163. Anson was the only one of three brothers to survive the American Civil War (1860–64); this may have intensified his religious feelings and the desire to serve others. When he moved to Oak Park in 1870, Anson founded a successful real estate business.

786. "Mañana comienzan las fiestas," *Heraldo de Aragón*, 10 October 1926; Reynolds, *The American Homecoming*, 68. Special trains from the north brought the increased traffic to Zaragoza ("El segundo día de las fiestas del Pilar," *Heraldo de Aragón*, 13 October 1926).

787. The events of each day, and the schedules of events for subsequent days, were announced in the *Heraldo de Aragón*, 10–17 October 1926. The *Heraldo* had announced that all eight bulls for the corrida of 14 October would all be from the Encinas ranch, but substitutions were made on the day itself.

788. "Corridas celebradas en España," *Toros y toreros en 1926*, 244–25. My thanks to Beatriz Penas and Alberto Cabeza, of the University of Zaragoza, and Cruz Bespin, of the Biblioteca Pública de Zaragoza, who arranged for me to have microfilm prints of the *Heraldo de Aragón*, 10–21 October 1926 (including the special supplement for the fiesta).

789. *Heraldo de Aragón*, 12–21 October 1926.

790. My thanks to Beatriz Penas for up-to-date information about the *jota* contests, the Teatro Principal, the Campo del Iberia, and other details of modern-day Zaragoza (E-mail, 28 March 2001).

791. *Heraldo de Aragón*, 15 and 17 October 1926.

792. "*Zig Zag*," in "Revistas y periódicos," *Toros y toreros en 1924*, 267; and

in Cossío (1943–97) II: 585. Hemingway saved some copies of *Zig Zag* (JFK, Bull-fight Materials).

793. Cossío (1943–97) III: 129 and 462–63; "Efemérides," *Toros y toreros en 1932*, 348.

794. Cossío glowingly describes Zurito as the best picador of his time (Cossío [1943–97], "Haba Bejarano, (Manuel de la), Zurito," III: 428–29). For the picador José de la Haba, see Cossío (1943–97) III: 428, IV: 501, and V: 1062; for his brother Francisco, see Cossío (1943–97) IV: 501. For the third generation, see Cossío (1995), "Haba Vargas (Gabriel de la), Zurito," II: 509. The family is from Córdoba, a region that typically produces earnest, serious men.

Works Cited

Abad Ojuel, Antonio. *Estirpe y tauromaquia de Antonio Ordóñez.* 2nd ed. Madrid: Espasa-Calpe, 1988.

Abella, Carlos. *Historia del toreo.* Volume II: *De Luis Miguel Dominguín a "El Cordobés."* Volume III: *De "Niño de la Capea" a "Espartaco."* Madrid: Alianza Editorial, 1992.

———. *Luis Miguel Dominguín.* Madrid: Espasa-Calpe, 1995.

Abrams, M. H., et al., eds. *The Norton Anthology of English Literature.* 5th ed. 2 vols. New York: W. W. Norton, 1986.

Acebal, Edmundo G., ed. *Reglamento taurino.* Madrid: Gráficas Versal, 1967.

Acronyms, Initialisms, & Abbreviations Dictionary. 1960. 5th ed. 3 vols. Ed. Ellen T. Crowley. Detroit: Gale Research, 1976.

Agenda-guía del calendario fichero taurino para la temporada 1963. Madrid: Gráficas Versal, 1963.

Aguado, Paco. *El rey de los toreros: Joselito el Gallo.* Madrid: Espasa-Calpe, 1999.

Alameda, José. *El hilo del toreo.* Madrid: Espasa-Calpe, 1989.

Alderman, Taylor. "Fitzgerald, Hemingway, and *The Passing of the Great Race.*" *Fitzgerald-Hemingway Annual* (1977): 215–17.

Alinei, Tamara. "The Corrida and *For Whom the Bell Tolls.*" *Neophilologus* 56 (1972): 487–92.

American Authors 1600–1900: A Biographical Dictionary of American Literature. Ed. Stanley J. Kunitz and Howard Haycraft. New York: H. W. Wilson, 1938.

American Women: 1935–40: A Composite Biographical Dictionary. Detroit: Gale Research Company, 1981.

Annuaire de la Chronique du Turf. Paris: Éstablissements Chérie, 1920–35.

Antigüedad, Alfredo R. *Y el nombre se hizo renombre: La novela de Luis Miguel.* Madrid: Prensa Castellana, 1949.

Anuarios Bailly-Baillière y Riera Reunidos: Guía directorio de Madrid y su provincia (Guía comercial Bailly-Baillière-Riera). Madrid: Librería Bailly-Baillère, 1923–59.

Arlen, Michael J. *Exiles.* New York: Farrar, Straus & Giroux, 1970.

Aronowitz, Alfred, and Peter Hamill. *Ernest Hemingway: The Life and Death of a Man.* New York: Lancer Books, 1961.

Asch, Sholem. "Der Ochsen-Kampf" ("The Bullfight"). In "Mein Reize über Spanien," in Volume XIX of *The Collected Works of Sholem Asch*. Warsaw: Kultur-Liga, 1926. 5–15.

Aschan, Ulf. *The Man Whom Women Loved: The Life of Bror Blixen*. New York: St. Martin's Press, 1987.

Ashton, E. O. *Swahili Grammar*. 2nd ed. London: Longmans, 1947.

Atkins, John. *The Art of Ernest Hemingway: His Work and Personality*. London: Spring Books, 1952.

Auge, Claude, and Paul Auge, eds. *Nuevo pequeño Larousse ilustrado, Diccionario enciclopédico*. Trans. from the French by Miguel de Toro y Gisbert. Paris: Librairie Larousse, 1951.

August, Jo, comp. *Catalog of the Ernest Hemingway Collection at the John F. Kennedy Library*. 2 vols. Boston: G. K. Hall, 1982. Addendum (1983–92) prepared by Megan Floyd Desnoyers, Lisa Middents, and Stephen Plotkin; available at the Hemingway Room, J.F.K. Library.

Bagüés, Ventura (don Ventura). *Al hilo de las tablas*. Madrid: n.p., 1948.

———. *Domingo Ortega, el torero de la armonía*. Barcelona: Fiesta Brava, 1931.

———. *Historia de los matadores de toros*. Barcelona: Enciclopedias de Gassó, 1970.

Bailey, William G. *Americans in Paris: 1900–1930, A Selected, Annotated Bibliography*. New York: Greenwood, 1989.

Bailly-Bailliere, G. *Guía comercial de Madrid y su provincia publicada con datos del comercio*. Madrid: Librería editorial de D. Carlos Bailly-Bailliere, 1886–1959.

Baker, Carlos. *Ernest Hemingway: A Life Story*. 1969. New York: Collier/Macmillan, 1988.

———. *Hemingway: The Writer as Artist*. Princeton, N.J.: Princeton University Press, 1952; 4th ed., 1972.

———. "The Slopes of Kilimanjaro." *American Heritage* 19 (August 1968): 40, 42–43, 90–91.

———. "The Sun Rose Differently." *New York Times Book Review*, 18 March 1979, 7, 28.

Baker, Carlos, ed. *Ernest Hemingway: Critiques of Four Major Novels*. New York: Charles Scribner's Sons, 1962.

———, ed. *Ernest Hemingway: Selected Letters 1917–1961*. New York: Charles Scribner's Sons, 1981. Rpt. London: Panther Books, Granada Publishing, Ltd., 1985.

Bald, Wambly. *On the Left Bank 1929–1933*. Ed. Benjamin Franklin V. Athens, Ohio: Ohio University Press, 1987.

Barea, Arturo. "Not Spain but Hemingway." In *The Literary Reputation of Hemingway in Europe*. Ed. Roger Asselineau. New York: New York University Press, 1965. 197–210.

Barga Bensusán, Ramón. *El toro de lidia*. Madrid: Alianza Editorial, 1995.

Barnatán, Marcos Ricardo. *Diano.* Madrid: Júcar, 1982.

The Barnhart Dictionary of Etymology. H. W. Wilson, 1988 ed.

Barnils, Ramón. " 'L'artista i Mont-roig,' Mirant allò que Miró veia." *El temps* (Valencia), 23 August 1993, 52–56.

Bartlett, John. *A Complete Concordance or Verbal Index to Words, Phrases and Passages in the Dramatic Works of Shakespeare.* London: Macmillan, 1962.

———. *Familiar Quotations.* 15th ed. Ed. Emily Morison Beck. Boston: Little, Brown, 1980.

Bastin, Maril, Ghislain Pinckers, and Michel Teheux. *Dios cada día: Siguiendo el leccionario ferial.* 5 vols., 1982. Trans. Carlos López de la Rica. Vol. 2: *Adviento, Navidad, y santoral.* Santander: Editorial Sal Terrae, 1989.

Baudot, Marcel, et al., eds. *The Historical Encyclopedia of World War II.* Trans. from the French by Jesse Dilson. New York: Facts on File, 1980.

Beach, Sylvia. *Shakespeare and Company.* 1959; rpt. London: Plantin Paperbacks, 1987.

Beegel, Susan F. " 'A Lack of Passion': Its Background, Sources and Composition History." *The Hemingway Review* 9.2 (1990): 50–56.

———. "Ernest Hemingway's 'A Lack of Passion.' " In *Hemingway: Essays of Reassessment.* Ed. Frank Scafella. New York: Oxford University Press, 1991. 62–78.

———. *Hemingway's Craft of Omission: Four Manuscript Examples.* Ann Arbor: UMI Research Press, 1988.

Beegel, Susan F., ed. *Hemingway's Neglected Short Fiction: New Perspectives.* Ann Arbor: UMI Research Press, 1989.

———. "The Lack of Passion Papers." *The Hemingway Review* 9.2 (1990): 69–93.

Belmonte, Juan. *Juan Belmonte, Killer of Bulls: The Autobiography of a Matador,* as told to Manuel Chaves Nogales. Trans. from the Spanish by Leslie Charteris. Garden City, N.Y.: Doubleday, Doran, 1937.

Benlloch, José Luis, and Vicente Sobrino. *Los grandes maestros del toreo valenciano: Félix Rodríguez y José María Manzanares.* Valencia: Diputación de Valencia, 1999.

Benson, Jackson J. *Hemingway: The Writer's Art of Self-Defense.* Minneapolis: University of Minnesota Press, 1969.

Benstock, Shari. *Women of the Left Bank: Paris, 1900–1940.* Austin: University of Texas Press, 1986.

Bernier, Rosamond. "The Painter Miró, This Month 87, Is As lively As Ever," *Smithsonian* 11 (April 1980): 102–11.

Blanco, Carlos. *La dictadura y los procesos militares.* Madrid: Javier Morata, editor, 1931.

Blasco Ibáñez, Vicente. *Sangre y arena.* 1907. Madrid: Alianza Editorial, S. A. (Biblioteca Blasco Ibáñez), 1998.

Blashill, John. "Report from Valencia: Ordóñez vs. Dominguín." *Sports Illustrated,* 17 August 1959: 42–43.

Bleu, F. (Félix Borrell Vidal). *Antes y después del Guerra: Medio siglo de toreo.* 1914. Madrid: Espasa-Calpe, 1983.

Blixen-Finecke, Bror von. *African Hunter.* Trans. from the Swedish by F. H. Lyon. New York: Knopf, 1937; rpt. New York: St. Martin's Press, 1986.

The Bloodstock Breeders' Review: An Illustrated Annual Devoted to the British Thoroughbred. London: The British Bloodstock Agency, Ltd., 1920–35.

Bluefarb, Samuel. "The Sea—Mirror and Maker of Character in Fiction and Drama." *English Journal* 48 (1959): 501–10.

Blum, Daniel C. *Great Stars of the American Stage: A Pictorial Record.* New York: Greenberg, 1952.

The Book of the XV Brigade: Records of British, American, Canadian and Irish Volunteers the XV International Brigade in Spain 1936–1938. Pub. and with a preface by Frank Graham, 6 Queen's Terrace, Newcastle-Upon-Tyne, England, 1975.

Boreth, Craig. *The Hemingway Cookbook.* Chicago: Chicago Review Press, 1998.

Botsford, Keith. *Dominguín.* Chicago: Quadrangle Books, 1972.

Bradley, Sculley, Richmond Croom Beatty, E. Hudson Long, and George Perkins, eds. *The American Tradition in Literature.* 4th ed. New York: Grosset & Dunlap, 1974.

Brand, Anthony. Personal interviews and correspondence. 1995–2001.

Brasch, James Daniel. "Invention from Knowledge: The Hemingway-Cowley Correspondence." In *Ernest Hemingway: The Writer in Context.* Ed. James Nagel. Madison: University of Wisconsin Press, 1984. 201–36.

Brasch, James Daniel, and Joseph Sigman. *Hemingway's Library: A Composite Record.* New York: Garland, 1981.

Bredahl, A. Carl, Jr., and Susan Lynn Drake, with the assistance of William R. Robinson. *Hemingway's* Green Hills of Africa *as Evolutionary Narrative: Helix and Scimitar.* Studies in American Literature, Vol. 5. Lewiston, N.Y.: Edwin Mellen, 1990.

Bredendick, Nancy. "*Toros célebres*: Its Meaning in *Death in the Afternoon.*" *The Hemingway Review* 17.2 (1998): 64–73.

Brenner, Gerry. "Are We Going to Hemingway's *Feast*?" *American Literature* 54.4 (1982): 528–44.

———. *Concealments in Hemingway's Works.* Columbus: Ohio State University Press, 1983.

———. "Note on *Riruce* and Research," *Hemingway Newsletter* 9 (January 1985): Item 4.

———. *The Old Man and the Sea: Story of a Common Man.* Twayne's Masterwork Studies No. 80. New York: Twayne, 1991.

Brinnin, John Malcolm. *The Third Rose: Gertrude Stein and Her World.* Radcliffe Biography Series. Reading, Massachusetts: Addison-Wesley, 1987.

Bruccoli, Matthew J. *Fitzgerald and Hemingway: A Dangerous Friendship.* New York: Carroll & Graf, 1994.

———. *Scott and Ernest: The Authority of Failure and the Authority of Success.* New York: Random House, 1978.

———. *Some Sort of Epic Grandeur: The Life of F. Scott Fitzgerald.* New York: Harcourt Brace Jovanovich, 1981.

Bruccoli, Matthew J., ed., with the assistance of Judith S. Baughman. *F. Scott Fitzgerald: A Life in Letters.* New York: Charles Scribner's Sons, 1994.

Bruccoli, Matthew J., ed., with the assistance of Robert W. Trogdon. *The Only Thing That Counts: The Ernest Hemingway / Maxwell Perkins Correspondence 1925–1947.* New York: Charles Scribner's Sons, 1996.

Bruccoli, Matthew J., and C. E. Frazer Clark Jr., compilers, *Hemingway at Auction, 1930–1973.* Detroit: Gale Research, 1973.

Burke, W. J., and Will D. Howe. *American Authors and Books: 1640 to the Present Day.* 3rd rev. ed. New York: Crown, 1972.

Burke's Peerage and Baronetage. London: Burke's Peerage, 1975.

Burke's Royal Families of the World. London: Burke's Peerage, 1977.

Burns, Edward, ed. *The Letters of Gertrude Stein and Carl Van Vechten, 1913–1946.* New York: Columbia University Press, 1986.

Burwell, Rose Marie. *Hemingway: The Postwar Years and the Posthumous Novels.* Cambridge: Cambridge University Press, 1996.

Cairis, Nicholas T. *Cruise Ships of the World.* London: Pegasus, 1989.

Callaghan, Morley. *That Summer in Paris.* New York: Dell, 1963.

Calvache. Catalogue for the Exposition, "Antonio Calvache," Centro Cultural del Conde Duque. Madrid: Ediciones Artes Gráficas Luis Pérez, S. A., 1994.

Calvocoressi, Peter. *Who's Who in the Bible.* 1987. London: Penguin, 1988.

The Cambridge Guide to Literature in English. Ed. Ian Ousby. Cambridge: Cambridge University Press, 1988.

The Cambridge Guide to World Theatre. Ed. Martin Banham. Cambridge: Cambridge University Press, 1988.

Capellán, Angel. *Hemingway and the Hispanic World.* Ann Arbor: UMI Research Press, 1977, 1985.

Carabantes, Andrés, and Eusebio Cimorra. *Un mito llamado Pasionaria.* Barcelona: Editorial Planeta, 1982. Colección Documentos, Documento 76.

Carmona González, Angel, comp. *Consultor indicador taurino universal,* 4th ed. Madrid: n.p., 1949.

Carralero, José, and Gonzalo Borge. *Toros célebres.* Santoña: Imprenta de R. Meléndez, 1908.

Carralero Burgos, José. *Los toros de la muerte, o sea la ganadería de D. Eduardo Miura.* Madrid: Imprenta Gutenberg, Castro y Compañía, 1909.

Carrias, Eugene. *La Pensée Militaire Française.* Paris: Presses Universitaires de France, 1960.

El Cartel taurino: Quites entre sol y sombra. Ed. Begoña Torres González, Ministerio de Educación y Cultura. Madrid: Sociedad Editorial Electa España, S. A., 1998.

Cassell's Encyclopedia of World Literature. Ed. S. H. Steinberg. 2 vols. New York: Funk & Wagnalls, 1953.

Cassell's Encyclopedia of World Literature. Rev. and enlarged ed. General ed. J. Buchanan-Brown. 3 vols. New York: William Morrow, 1973.

Castells Peig, Andreu. *Las Brigadas Internacionales de la Guerra de España.* Barcelona: Editorial Ariel, 1974.

Catálogo de Periodistas Españoles del Siglo XX. Antonio López de Zuago Algar. Madrid, 1980–81.

Catalogue Collectif des Périodiques du Début de XVIIe Siècle a 1939. 5 vols. Paris: Bibliotéque Nationale, 1977–81.

The Catholic Encyclopedia. 15 vols. and Index. New York: Robert Appleton, 1907–14.

Cau, Jean. *Las orejas y el rabo* (1961). Spanish translation, Barcelona: Plaza & Janés, 1962.

Chambers's Encyclopedia. New rev. ed. London: International Learning Systems, 1973.

Charters, James (Jimmie the Barman) as told to Morrill Cody. *This Must Be the Place: Memoirs of Montparnasse.* Ed. with a preface by Hugh Ford. Introduction by Ernest Hemingway. London: Herbert Josephs, 1934; rpt. New York: Collier Books, 1989.

Chinn, George M. *The Machine Gun.* 3 vols. Washington, D.C.: U.S. Government Printing Office, 1951.

Claramunt López, Fernando. "Marismas de Vila Franca de Xira." *Clarín taurino: Revista cultural de la fiesta de los toros (Bilbao)* (August 1995): 15–19.

Clark, Sidney A. *Cuban Tapestry.* New York: Robert M. McBride, 1936.

Collier's Encyclopedia. Ed. in chief, Louis Shores. 24 vols. Crowell-Collier Educational Corp., 1968.

Columbia Dictionary of Modern European Literature. General ed. Horatio Smith. New York: Columbia University Press, 1947.

Concise Dictionary of American Biography. 3rd ed. New York: Charles Scribner's Sons, 1980.

Concise Dictionary of American Literature. Ed. Robert Fulton Richards. Paterson, N.J.: Littlefield, Adams, 1959.

The Concise Oxford Dictionary of Music. 3rd ed. Ed. Michael Kennedy. Oxford: Oxford University Press, 1980.

Connolly, Cyril. *Enemies of Promise.* London: Routledge, 1938; rev. ed., 1948; rpt. New York: Stanley Moss/Persea Books, 1983.

Conrad, Barnaby. "*The Dangerous Summer.*" *The Book Review, Los Angeles Times,* 23 June 1985, 1, 4.

———. *Encyclopedia of Bullfighting.* 1961. London: Michael Joseph, 1962.

———. *How to Fight a Bull.* Garden City, N.Y.: Doubleday, 1968.

———. *Matador.* Boston: Houghton Mifflin, 1952.

Cooper, Douglas. "Gertrude Stein and Juan Gris." In *Four Americans in Paris: The*

Collections of Gertrude Stein and Her Family. Catalogue of the Exhibition. New York: The Museum of Modern Art, 1970. 64–73.

Córdoba, José Luis de. *Córdoba en la historia del toreo*. Córdoba, 1989.

Corrochano, Gregorio. *Cuando suena el clarín*. Madrid: Revista de Occidente, 1961.

———. *La edad de oro del toreo*. Madrid: Espasa-Calpe, 1992.

———. *La edad de plata del toreo*. Madrid: Espasa-Calpe, 1993.

———. *¿Qué es torear? Introducción a la tauromaquia de Joselito*. Madrid: Góngora, 1953. Enlarged ed., *¿Qué es torear? Introducción a las tauromaquias de Joselito y de Domingo Ortega*. Madrid: Ediciones de la Revista de Occidente, 1966.

———. *Teoría de las corridas de toros*. Madrid: Revista de Occidente, 1962.

Cortada, James W. *Historical Dictionary of the Spanish Civil War, 1936–39*. Westport, Conn.: Greenwood Press, 1982.

Cossío y Martínez de Fortún, José María de. *Los toros: Tratado técnico e histórico*. 12 vols. Madrid: Espasa-Calpe, 1943–97.

———. *Los toros* (1995). 2 vols. Madrid: Espasa-Calpe, 1995.

Cowley, Malcolm. *Exile's Return: A Literary Odyssey of the 1920s*. 1934; rpt. New York: Compass Books, 1956.

Cowley, Malcolm, ed. *The Portable Hemingway*. New York: Viking Press, 1944.

Cullum, George W., comp. *Biographical Register of the Officers and Graduates of the U.S. Military Academy at West Point, New York, from Its Establishment in 1802, to 1890*. 3rd ed., rev. and extended. 3 vols. Boston: Houghton, Mifflin, 1891.

Cunningham, Patrick. *A River of Lions*. Santa Barbara, Calif.: Neville, 1991.

Daza, José. *Arte del toreo: Manuscrito inédito de 1778*. Madrid: Unión de Bibliófilos Taurinos, 1959.

de la Hiz Flores, María (Mahizflor). *Bienvenida: Dinastía torera*. Madrid: Espasa-Calpe, 1993.

de la Riestra Sanz, Mariano. *La fiesta de los toros: Memorias de un viejo aficionado*. Madrid: n.p., 1955.

de Miguel, Andrés, and José Ramón Márquez. *Adios, Madrid*. Madrid: Ediciones La Librería, 1998.

Debrett's Peerage and Baronetage. London: Debrett's Peerage, 1939, 1990.

DeFazio, Albert John. "The HemHotch Letters: The Correspondence and Relationship of Ernest Hemingway and A. E. Hotchner." Unpublished dissertation, University of Virginia, 1992.

del Campo, Luis. *Pamplona y los toros, siglo XVII*. Pamplona: Editorial Gráficas Navasal, 1975.

Derks, Scott, ed., *The Value of a Dollar: Prices and Incomes in the United States, 1860–1989*. Detroit: Gale Research Company, 1994.

DeVost, Nadine. "Hemingway's Girls: Unnaming and Renaming Hemingway's Female Characters." *The Hemingway Review* 14.1 (1994): 46–59.

Díaz Arquer, Graciano. *Libros y folletos de toros.* Madrid: Pedro Vindel, 1931.

Díaz Cañabate, Antonio. *La fábula de Domingo Ortega.* Madrid: Juan Valero, 1950.

———. *Historia de tres temporadas: 1958, 1959, 1960.* 2 vols. Madrid: Editorial Taurina Capela, 1961.

Diccionario de argot. Comp. Juan Manuel Oliver. Madrid: Sena Editorial, S. A., 1985.

Diccionario de autoridades médicas. Ed. José Alvarez Sierra. Madrid: Editora Nacional, 1963.

Diccionario de expresiones malsonantes del español: Léxico descriptivo. Jaime Martín Martín. Madrid: Ediciones Istmo, 1974, 1979.

Diccionario de la lengua española. 19th ed. 6 vols. Madrid: Real Academia Española, 1970, 1982.

Diccionario de la lengua española. 2 vols. Madrid: Real Academia Española, 1984.

Diccionario enciclopédico abreviado. Madrid: Espasa-Calpe, 1954.

Diccionario enciclopédico abreviado. 7th ed. 7 vols. Madrid: Espasa-Calpe, 1972.

Dictionary of American Biography. 1964 ed. 10 vols. New York: Charles Scribner's Sons, 1964.

Dictionary of American Naval Fighting Ships. Vol. 5. Washington, D.C.: Office of the Chief of Naval Operations, 1970.

Dictionary of Literary Biography. Vol IV: *American Writers in Paris, 1920–39.* Ed. Karen Lane Rood. Detroit: Gale Research Company, 1980.

Dictionary of National Biography. Founded in 1822 by George Smith. Eds. Sir Leslie Stephen and Sir Sidney Lee. 21 vols. plus Index and Supplements. Oxford: Oxford University Press, 1917–.

Dictionnaire de Biographie Française. Ed. Jo Balteau et al. Paris: Librairie Letorzey et Ane, 1939.

Dictionnaire des Marins Français. Comp. M. Taillemite. Paris: Editions maritimes et outre-mer, 1982.

Diliberto, Gioia. *Hadley.* New York: Ticknor & Fields, 1992.

Dizionario Biografico degli Italiani. Roma: Instituto della Enciclopedia Italiana, 1960–.

Dizionario Enciclopedico Italiano. 12 vols. Rome: Instituto della Enciclopedia Italiana, 1970.

Domecq y Díez, Alvaro. *El toro bravo: Teoría y práctica de la bravura.* 7th ed. Madrid: Espasa-Calpe, 1996.

Dominguín, Pepe (pseud. of José González Lucas). *Mi gente.* Madrid: Editorial Piesa, 1979.

———. With illustrations by Onésimo Anciones. *Toros en Las Ventas.* Madrid: O.I.A., 1981.

Donaldson, Scott. *By Force of Will: The Life and Art of Ernest Hemingway.* New York: Viking, 1977.

Donaldson, Scott, in collaboration with R. H. Winnick. *Archibald MacLeish: An American Life.* Boston: Houghton Mifflin, 1992.

Donnelly, Honoria Murphy, with Richard N. Billings. *Sara & Gerald: Villa America and After.* New York: Holt, Rinehart and Winston, 1984.

Dorman-Smith, Eric Edward. "A Bull Fight at Pamplona." *Royal Military College Magazine and Record.* London, Aldershot, Portsmouth: Gale & Polden, 1924: 19–29.

———. "Il Encierro." *Royal Military College Magazine and Record.* London, Aldershot, Portsmouth: Gale & Polden, January 1925: 87–92.

Dos Passos, John. *The Best Times: An Informal Memoir.* New York: The New American Library, 1966.

Drabeck, Bernard A., and Helen E. Ellis, eds. *Archibald MacLeish: Reflections.* Amherst: University of Massachusetts Press, 1986.

Dunning, John. *Tune in Yesterday.* New York: Prentice-Hall, 1976.

Durán Blázquez, Manuel, and Juan Miguel Sánchez Vigil. *Antología de la fotografía taurina, 1839–1939.* Madrid: Espasa-Calpe, 1999.

———. *Historia de la fotografía taurina.* Vol. I. Madrid: Espasa-Calpe, 1991.

Dydo, Ulla E., ed. *A Stein Reader.* Evanston, Ill.: Northwestern University Press, 1993.

Eliot, T. S. *The Complete Poems and Plays: 1909–1950.* New York: Harcourt Brace, 1952.

Ellman, Richard. *James Joyce.* New York: Oxford University Press, 1959.

Emmons, Frederick E. *American Passenger Ships.* Newark: University of Delaware Press, 1985.

Enciclopedia universal ilustrada europeo-americana. 70 vols. plus *Apéndices* (10 vols), Index, and annual *Suplementos* beginning 1936. Madrid: Espasa-Calpe, 1908–.

Encyclopaedia Britannica. 11th ed. 24 vols. New York: Encyclopaedia Britannica, 1910–11.

Encyclopaedia Britannica. 14th ed. 24 vols. Chicago: Encyclopaedia Britannica, 1973.

Encyclopaedia Britannica. 15th ed. 30 vols, including the Macropaedia (19 vols.), Micropaedia (10 vols.), and Propaedia (1 vol.). Chicago: Encyclopaedia Britannica, 1974, 1990.

Encyclopaedia Judaica. Vol. III. Jerusalem: Keter Publishing House, 1971.

Encyclopedia Americana. 30 vols. plus Annuals, 1962–78. New York: Americana Corporation, 1961.

Encyclopedia of Associations. 4 vols. Ed. Katherine Gruber. Detroit: Gale Research, 1985. Volume I: *National Organizations of the U.S.* Part I: Trade, Business, and Commercial Organizations.

Everyman's Encyclopedia. 5th ed. 12 vols. Ed. E. F. Bozman. London: Dent, 1967.

Ezell, Edward Clinton. *Small Arms of the World: A Basic Manual of Small Arms.* Harrisburg, Pa.: Stackpole, 1977.

Feiner, Muriel. *La mujer en el mundo del toro.* Madrid: Alianza Editorial, 1995.

Fergusson, Erna. *Cuba.* New York: Alfred A. Knopf, 1946.

576 • WORKS CITED

Fernández, Tomás-Ramón. *Reglamentación de las corridas de toros: Estudio histórico y crítico*. Madrid: Espasa-Calpe, 1987.

Fernández Ortiz, Celestino. *La Sevilla de Rafael el Gallo*. Dos Hermanas (Sevilla): Imprenta Sevillana, S. A., 1982.

Fernández Salcedo, Luis. *Diano, o el libro que se quedó sin escribir*. Madrid: Librería Merced, 1959; reissued Madrid: Agrícola Española, D. L., 1988.

First Time Ever: 650 Outstanding Songs. Melville, N.Y.: MCA/Mills, n.d.

Fisher, Clive. *Cyril Connolly: The Life and Times of England's Most Controversial Literary Critic*. New York: St. Martin's, 1995.

Fishkin, Shelley Fisher. *From Fact to Fiction: Journalism & Imaginative Writing in America*. Baltimore and London: The Johns Hopkins University Press, 1985.

Fitch, Noel Riley. "Ernest Hemingway—c/o Shakespeare and Company." *Fitzgerald-Hemingway Annual* (1977): 157–81.

———. *Sylvia Beach and the Lost Generation: A History of Literary Paris in the Twenties and Thirties*. New York: W. W. Norton, 1983.

———. *Walks in Hemingway's Paris: A Guide to Paris for the Literary Traveler*. New York: St. Martin's, 1989.

Fleischer, Nathaniel S., ed. *Nat Fleischer's All-Time Ring Record Book*. Norwalk, Conn.: C. J. O'Brien Suburban Press, 1941–.

Fleming, Robert E. *Ernest Hemingway: A Study of the Short Fiction*. Boston: Twayne, 1989.

———. *The Face in the Mirror: Hemingway's Writers*. Tuscaloosa and London: University of Alabama Press, 1994.

———. "Hemingway and Peele: Chapter 1 of *A Farewell to Arms*." *Studies in American Fiction* 11.1 (1983): 95–100.

———. "The Libel of Dos Passos in *To Have and Have Not*." *Journal of Modern Literature* 15.4 (1989): 597–601.

———. "Portrait of the Artist as a Bad Man: Hemingway's Career at the Crossroads." *North Dakota Quarterly* 55.1 (1987): 66–71.

Floría, Guillem B., ed. *Historia de España, Diccionario*. 4th ed. 6 vols. Barcelona: Playa & Janes, S. A., 1976.

Forbes, Patrick. *Champagne*. London: Gollancz, 1967.

Ford, Ford Madox. *It Was the Nightingale*. 1933; rpt. New York: the Ecco Press, 1984.

Ford, Hugh, ed. *The Left Bank Revisited: Selections from the Paris Tribune 1917–1934*. University Park: The Pennsylvania State University Press, 1972.

Ford, Richard. *Gatherings from Spain*. London, 1846. Rpt. in Rex Smith, ed., *Biography of the Bulls: An Anthology of Spanish Bullfighting*. New York: Rinehart & Company, 1957. 148–71.

Frank, Waldo. *Virgin Spain: Scenes from the Spiritual Drama of a Great People*. New York: Boni & Liveright, 1926; rev. ed., 1942.

Franklin, Sidney. *Bullfighter from Brooklyn: An Autobiography*. New York: Prentice-Hall, 1952.

Fratellini, Albert. *Nous, les Fratellini*. Paris: Grasset, 1955.

Freiberg, J. W. *The French Press: Class, State, and Ideology*. New York: Praeger, 1981.

Fuentes, Norberto. *Hemingway in Cuba*. Secaucus, N.J.: Lyle Stuart, 1984.

———. *Hemingway Rediscovered*. Photographs by Roberto Herrera Sotolongo. New York: Charles Scribner's Sons, 1988.

Fulton, John. *Bullfighting*. Sevilla: Quijote Classic Edition, 1992.

Fussell, Paul. *The Great War and Modern Memory*. London: Oxford University Press, 1975.

Gajdusek, Robin. "Artists in Their Art: Hemingway and Velásquez—The Shared Worlds of *For Whom the Bell Tolls* and *Las Meninas*." *Hemingway Repossessed*. Ed. Kenneth Rosen. Westport, Conn.: Praeger, 1994. 17–27.

———. "A Brief Safari into the Religious Terrain of *Green Hills of Africa*." *North Dakota Quarterly* 60.3 (1992): 26–40.

———. *Hemingway and Joyce: A Study in Debt and Payment*. Corte Madera, Calif.: Square Circle Press, 1984.

———. *Hemingway's Paris*. New York: Charles Scribner's Sons, 1978.

Gallup, Donald. *Ezra Pound: A Bibliography*. Charlottesville: University Press of Virginia, 1983.

Gandolfi, Luca. "The Outskirts of Literature: Uncovering the Munitions Factory in 'A Natural History of the Dead'." *The Hemingway Review* 19.2 (2000): 105–107.

García, Miguel Angel. Personal interviews. 20–24 August 1997.

García-Ramos, Antonio, and Francisco Narbona. *Ignacio Sánchez Mejías, dentro y fuera del ruedo*. Madrid: Espasa-Calpe, 1988.

Garrod, Lawrence P., and Francis O'Grady. *Antibiotic and Chemotherapy*. 3rd ed. Edinburgh and London: E & S Livingstone, 1971.

Gathorne-Hardy, Jonathan. *Gerald Brenan, The Interior Castle: A Biography*. New York: W. W. Norton, 1993.

Gerogiannis, Nicholas. "Hemingway's Poetry: Angry Notes of an Ambivalent Overman." 1981; rpt. in *Ernest Hemingway: Six Decades of Criticism*. Ed. Linda W. Wagner. East Lansing: Michigan State University Press, 1987. 257–72.

Gerogiannis, Nicholas, ed. *Complete Poems: Ernest Hemingway*. Rev. ed. Lincoln and London: University of Nebraska Press, 1979, 1992.

Gibson, Ian. *The Assassination of Federico García Lorca*. London: W. H. Allen, 1979.

Gide, André. *Corydon*. New York: Farrar, Straus and Giroux, 1950.

———. *If It Die . . . An Autobiography*. New York: Vintage Books, 1965.

Gilcoyne, Thomas. Personal interviews. 15 December 1997–26 March 1998.

Gómez Santos, Marino. "Antonio Ordóñez Cuenta su Vida," *El Pueblo*, 6–11 July 1959.

———. *Mi ruedo ibérico: De Vicente Pastor a Curro Romero*. Madrid: Espasa-Calpe, 1991.

Gran diccionario de la lengua española. Barcelona: Larousse Planeta, S. A., 1996.

Gran Enciclopèdia Catalana. 15 vols. Barcelona: Enciclopèdia Catalana, S. A., 1979.

Gran Enciclopedia de Andalucía. Gen. ed., José María Javierre. 10 vols. Sevilla: Promociones Culturales Andaluzas, Ediciones Ariel, 1979.

Gran Enciclopedia Navarra. Gen ed., Juan Luis Uranga Santebestan. 11 vols. Pamplona: Caja de Ahorros de Navarra, 1990.

Gran Enciclopedia Rialp. 24 vols. Madrid: Ediciones Rialp, 1971–1976.

Grand Dictionnaire Encyclopedique Larousse. 10 vols. Paris: Librairie Larousse, 1982–85.

Le Grande Encyclopédie. Paris: Larousse, 1974.

Graves, Robert. *Fairies and Fusiliers.* New York: Alfred A. Knopf, 1918.

Greacen, Lavinia. *Chink: A Biography.* London: Macmillan, 1989.

Great Soviet Encyclopedia. 3rd ed. Moscow: Sovetskaia Entsiklopediia Publishing House, 1970—. English translation, 31 volumes and Index. New York: Macmillan, 1973–83.

Greenclose, Barbara S. "Hemingway's 'The Revolutionist': An Aid to Interpretation." *Modern Fiction Studies* 17 (1971–72): 565–70.

Griffin, Peter. *Along with Youth: Hemingway, The Early Years.* New York: Oxford University Press, 1985.

———. *Less Than a Treason.* New York: Oxford University Press, 1990.

Der Grosse Brockhaus. 15th ed. 20 vols. Leipzig: F. A. Brockhaus, 1924–32.

Der Grosse Brockhaus. 16th ed. 12 vols. Wiesbaden: F. A. Brockhaus, 1952–55.

Guggenheim, Peggy, ed. *Art of This Century.* New York: Art of This Century, 1942.

Guía taurina: Directorio profesional del mundo de los toros, 1966. Comp. Salvador Heredia and Pedro Fraile. Madrid: Editorial Pentágono, S. A., 1966.

Hagemann, Meyly Chin. "Hemingway's Secret: Visual to Verbal Art." *Journal of Modern Art* 7.1 (1979): 87–112.

Hail, Marshall. *Knight in the Sun: Harper B. Lee, First Yankee Matador.* Boston: Little, Brown and Company, 1962.

Hamelman, William S. *The History of the Prussian Pour le Mérite Order.* Vol. III: *1888–1918.* Dallas: Matthaus, 1986.

Hammett, Dashiell. *Five Complete Novels: Red Harvest, The Dain Curse, The Maltese Falcon, The Glass Key, The Thin Man.* New York: Alfred A. Knopf, 1965; rpt. New York: Avenell Books, 1980.

Hanneman, Audre. *Ernest Hemingway: A Comprehensive Bibliography.* Princeton, N.J.: Princeton University Press, 1967.

———. *Supplement to* Ernest Hemingway: A Comprehensive Bibliography. Princeton, N.J.: Princeton University Press, 1975.

Hansen, Arlen J. *Expatriate Paris: A Cultural and Literary Guide to Paris of the 1920s.* New York: Arcade Publishing (Little, Brown), 1990.

Harrison, Charles Yale. *Generals Die in Bed.* 1928; rpt. Hamilton, Ontario: Potlatch Publications, 1975.

Hays, Peter L. *Ernest Hemingway.* New York: Continuum, 1990.

———. "Exchange between Rivals: Faulkner's Influence on *The Old Man and the Sea.*" In *The Writer in Context.* Ed James Nagel. Madison: University of Wisconsin Press, 1984. 147–64.

———. "Hemingway and Fitzgerald." *Hemingway In Our Time.* Ed. Richard Astro and Jackson J. Benson. Corvallis: Oregon State University Press, 1974. 87–97.

———. "Hemingway and the Fisher King." *The University Review* 32 (1965–66): 225–28.

Hemingway, Ernest. "African Journal." Edited and with an Introduction by Ray Cave. Illustrations by Jack Brusca. "Part One: Miss Mary's Lion," *Sports Illustrated* 35 (20 December 1971): 40–52, 57–66; "Part Two: Miss Mary's Lion," *Sports Illustrated* 36 (3 January 1972): 26–46; and "Part Three: Imperiled Flanks," *Sports Illustrated* 36 (10 January 1972): 22–30, 43–50.

———. "American Bohemians in Paris," *The Toronto Star Weekly,* 25 March 1922; rpt. in *Ernest Hemingway: Dateline: Toronto, The Complete Toronto Star Dispatches, 1920–1924.* Ed. William White. New York: Charles Scribner's Sons, 1985. 114–16.

———. "Bull Fighting Is Not a Sport—It Is a Tragedy." *The Toronto Star Weekly,* 20 October 1923; rpt. as "Bullfighting a Tragedy." *Ernest Hemingway: Dateline: Toronto, The Complete Toronto Star Dispatches, 1920–1924.* Ed. William White. New York: Charles Scribner's Sons, 1985. 340–46.

———. "Bullfighting, Sport and Industry." *Fortune* 1 (March 1930): 83–88, 139–46, 150.

———. *By-Line: Ernest Hemingway: Selected Articles and Dispatches of Four Decades.* Ed. William White. New York: Charles Scribner's Sons, 1967.

———. *Complete Poems: Ernest Hemingway.* Rev. ed. Ed. Nicholas Gerogiannis. Lincoln and London: University of Nebraska Press, 1979, 1992.

———. *The Dangerous Summer,* serialized in *Life.* Part I: "The Dangerous Summer" (5 September 1960): 78, 85–88, 91–92, 94, 96–100, 102, 104–105, 109; "Part II: The Pride of the Devil" (12 September 1960): 61–66, 68, 73, 75–76, 78–80, 82; and "Part III: An Appointment with Disaster" (19 September 1960): 74, 76, 78, 81, 83, 87–88, 90, 95–96.

———. *The Dangerous Summer.* New York: Charles Scribner's Sons, 1985.

———. *The Dangerous Summer* Manuscripts. Ernest Hemingway Collection, John F. Kennedy Library, Boston.

———. *Dateline: Toronto: The Complete* Toronto Star *Dispatches, 1920–1924.* Ed. William White. New York: Charles Scribner's Sons, 1985.

———. *Death in the Afternoon.* New York: Charles Scribner's Sons, 1932, 1960.

———. *Death in the Afternoon* Manuscripts. Ernest Hemingway Collection, John F. Kennedy Library, Boston.

———. *A Farewell to Arms.* New York: Charles Scribner's Sons, 1929, 1957.

———. "The Farm," *Cahiers d'Art* 9.1–4 (1934): 28–29 (JFK, Hageman Collection, Box 1, Hn-32).

———. "The Friend of Spain: A Spanish Letter." *Esquire*, January 1934; rpt. in *Ernest Hemingway, By-Line: Selected Articles and Dispatches of Four Decades.* Ed. William White. New York: Charles Scribner's Sons, 1967. 144–52.

———. *Green Hills of Africa.* New York: Charles Scribner's Sons, 1935, 1963.

———. "Introduction." *Men at War: The Best War Stories of All Time.* Ed. Ernest Hemingway. New York: Crown, 1942; rpt. New York: Bramhall House, 1979. xi–xxvii.

———. "Marlin Off Cuba." In *American Big Game Fishing.* Ed. Eugene V. Connett. New York: Derrydale Press, 1935. 55–81.

———. "A Matter of Wind." *Sports Illustrated* (17 August 1959): 43.

———. *A Moveable Feast.* New York: Charles Scribner's Sons, 1964.

———. "Pamplona in July: World's Series of Bullfighting a Mad, Whirling Carnival." *The Toronto Star Weekly*, 27 October 1923. rpt. as "Pamplona in July." *Ernest Hemingway: Dateline: Toronto, The Complete Toronto Star Dispatches, 1920–1924.* Ed. William White. New York: Charles Scribner's Sons, 1985. 347–54.

———. *Selected Letters, 1917–1961.* Ed. Carlos Baker. New York: Charles Scribner's Sons, 1981; rpt. London: Panther Books, Granada Publishing, 1985.

———. "A Silent, Ghastly Procession." *The Toronto Daily Star*, 20 October 1922; rpt. in *Ernest Hemingway: Dateline: Toronto, The Complete Toronto Star Dispatches, 1920–1924.* Ed. William White. New York: Charles Scribner's Sons, 1985. 232.

———. *The Sun Also Rises.* New York: Charles Scribner's Sons, 1926, 1954.

———. *El verano sangriento.* Serialized in *Life en español.* Trans. into Spanish by Angel Bonomini. Part I: "El verano sangriento" (3 October 1960): 43–47, 50–66; Part II: "Un orgullo demoníaco" (14 November 1960): 68–82; and Part III: "Cita con el desastre" (28 November 1960): 66–72, 74–76, 79–81.

———. *Winner Take Nothing.* 1933. New York: Charles Scribner's Sons, 1961.

Hemingway, Gregory H., M.D. *Papa: A Personal Memoir.* Boston: Houghton Mifflin, 1976.

Hemingway, Jack. *Misadventures of a Fly Fisherman: My Life with and without Papa.* Dallas, Tex.: Taylor Publishing, 1986.

Hemingway, Leicester. *My Brother, Ernest Hemingway.* Cleveland: World, 1962; rpt. New York: Crest, 1963.

Hemingway, Mary Welsh. "Hemingway's Spain." *Saturday Review* 50 (11 March 1967): 48–49, 102–104, 107.

———. "Holiday for a Wounded Torero." *Sports Illustrated* (17 August 1959): 46–51.

———. *How It Was.* New York: Knopf, distributed by Random House, 1976.

Hernaiz, Angel. *La última corrida de Joselito: Notas de un talaverano.* Toledo: Imprenta de la Editorial Católica Toledana, 1920.

Hernández Menéndez, Carlos. *Historia de las armas cortas.* Madrid: Editorial Nebrija, 1980.

Hernández Ramírez, Rafael (Rafael). *Historia de la plaza de toros de Madrid (1874–1934)*. Madrid: Prensa Castellana, 1955.

———. "Míster Ernest Hemingway, el amigo de España." *La Libertad* (23 September 1933): 7.

Hernández San Román, Felipe. "La tradición de los festejos taurinos: Ensayo histórico y marco legal." *Toro bravo* 7 (1966): 37–39.

Herrick, Robert. "What Is Dirt?" In *The Bookman* 70 (November 1929), 258–62; rpt. in Stephens, *Ernest Hemingway: The Critical Reception*, 86–89.

Hervey, John. *Racing in America, 1922–1936*. New York: The Jockey Club, privately printed at Scribner's, 1937.

Herwig, Holger H., and Neil M. Heyman, eds. *Biographical Dictionary of World War I*. Westport, Conn.: Greenwood Press, 1982.

Hinkle, James. "Hemingway's Iceberg." *The Hemingway Review* 2.2 (Spring 1983): 10.

The Historical Encyclopedia of World War II. Trans. from the French by Jesse Dilson. London: MacMillan, 1980.

Hiz Flores, María de la. *Bienvenida: Dinastía torera*. Madrid: Espasa-Calpe, 1993.

Hoffman, Frederick J., Charles Allen, and Carolyn F. Ulrich. *The Little Magazine: A History and a Bibliography*. Princeton, N.J.: Princeton University Press, 1946.

Holden, Reuben. *Yale in China: The Mainland 1901–1951*. New Haven, Conn.: The Yale in China Association, 1964.

Hotchner. A. E. *Papa Hemingway: A Personal Memoir*. New York: Random House, 1966.

Hoyt, J. K. *The Cyclopedia of Practical Quotations*. Rev. ed. New York: Funk & Wagnalls, 1896.

Hualde, Fernando. *Hemingway: Cien años y una huella*. Pamplona: Hotel Maisonnave, 1999.

Hutton, Virgil. "The Short Happy Life of Francis Macomber." *University Review* 30 (1964): 253–63; rpt. in *The Short Stories of Ernest Hemingway: Critical Essays*. Ed. Jackson J. Benson. Durham, N.C.: Duke University Press, 1975. 239–50.

Huxley, Aldous. "Foreheads Villainous Low." In his *Music at Night and Other Essays*. London: Chatto & Windus, 1931. 201–10.

Hyamson, Albert M. *A Dictionary of Universal Biography of All Ages and of All Peoples*. 2nd. ed. London: Routledge & Kegan Paul, 1951.

Iribarren, José María. *Hemingway y los sanfermines*. Pamplona: Gómez-Edyvel, D. L., 1984.

———. *El porqué de los dichos: Sentido, origen y anécdota de los dichos, modismos y frases proverbiales de España con otras muchas curiosidades*. Pamplona: Departamento de Educación y Cultura, 1994.

———. *Vocabulario taurino*. 1952. 2nd ed., rev. by Ricardo Ollaquindia. Pamplona: Comunidad Foral de Navarra, 1984.

Jalón, César. *Memorias de "Clarito."* Madrid: Guadarrama, 1972.

Jarvis, Nancy H., ed. *Historical Glimpses—Petoskey*. Petoskey, Michigan: Little Traverse Historical Society, 1986.

Jenkins, Alan. *The Thirties*. New York: Stein and Day, 1976.

Johnston, Kenneth G. "Hemingway and Freud: The Tip of the Iceberg." *Journal of Narrative Technique* 14.1 (1984): 68–73.

———. "Hemingway and Mantegna: The Bitter Nail Holes." *Journal of Narrative Technique* 1 (1971): 86–94.

———. " 'The Three Day Blow': Tragicomic Aftermath of a Summer Romance." *The Hemingway Review* 2 (1982): 21–25.

Johnston, Walter. *Brave Employment: The Myth and Reality of the Spanish Corrida*. London: Club Taurino of London, 1997.

Joost, Nicholas. *Ernest Hemingway and the Little Magazines: The Paris Years*. Barre, Mass.: Barre Publishers, 1968.

Joost, Nicholas, and Alan Brown, "T. S. Eliot and Ernest Hemingway: A Literary Relationship," *Papers on Language and Literature* 14.4 (1978): 425–49.

Josephs, F. Allen. "At the Heart of Madrid." *Atlantic* 244 (July 1979): 74–77.

———. "Hemingway's Poor Spanish: Chauvinism and Loss of Credulity in *For Whom the Bell Tolls*." In *Hemingway: A Revaluation*. Ed. Donald R. Noble. Troy, N.Y.: Whitston Publishing, 1983. 205–223.

Josephson, Matthew. "Evan Shipman: Poet and Horse-Player." *Southern Review* (Autumn 1978): 828–56.

Junkins, Donald. "Hemingway's Old Lady and the Aesthetics of *Pundonor*." *North Dakota Quarterly* 62.2 (1994–95): 195–204.

Kahn, E. J., Jr. *Harvard: Through Change and Through Storm*. New York: W. W. Norton, 1968.

Kamen, Henry. *Philip of Spain*. New Haven, Conn.: Yale University Press, 1997.

Kampis, Antal. *The History of Art in Hungary*. Trans Lili Halapy. London: Corvina in cooperation with Collet's Publishers, 1966.

Kearns, Cleo McNelly. *T. S. Eliot and Indic Traditions: A Study in Poetry and Belief*. Cambridge: Cambridge University Press, 1987.

Kennedy, J. Gerald. *Imagining Paris: Exile, Writing, and American Identity*. New Haven, Conn.: Yale University Press, 1993.

Kenner, Hugh. *The Pound Era*. Berkeley: University of California Press, 1971.

Kern, Robert W., ed. *Historical Dictionary of Modern Spain, 1700–1988*. Westport, Conn.: Greenwood Press, 1990.

Kert, Bernice. *The Hemingway Women*. New York: W. W. Norton, 1983.

Kipling, Rudyard. *Rudyard Kipling's Verse*. Volume II: *Inclusive Edition, 1885–1918*. London: Hodder & Stoughton, 1919.

Klüver, Billy, and Julie Martin. *Kiki's Paris: Artists and Lovers 1900–1930*. New York: Harry N. Abrams, 1989.

Lacadena Brualla, Ramón de (don Indalecio). "Toreros largos y toreros cortos; toreros machos y toreros hembra." Lecture delivered to the Peña Agüero, Bilbao, 12 April 1930. Zaragoza: Industrias Gráficas Uriarte, 1930.

Landis, Arthur H. *The Abraham Lincoln Brigade*. New York: Citadel, 1967.

Lanier, Doris. "The Bittersweet Taste of Absinthe in Hemingway's 'Hills Like White Elephants.' " *Studies in Short Fiction* 26.3 (1989): 279–88.

LaPrade, Douglas E. "The Reception of Hemingway in Spain." *The Hemingway Review* (Special European Issue, 1992): 42–50.

Laqueur, Walter, ed. *A Dictionary of Politics*. Rev. ed. New York: The Free Press, 1973.

Larson, Kelli A. *Ernest Hemingway: A Reference Guide 1974–1989*. Boston: G K. Hall, 1991.

Lax, Roger, and Frederick Smith. *The Great Song Thesaurus*. 2nd ed. New York: Oxford University Press, 1989.

Layman, Richard. "Hemingway's Library Cards at Shakespeare and Company." *Fitzgerald-Hemingway Annual* (1975): 191–207.

Leland, John. *A Guide to Hemingway's Paris*. Chapel Hill, N.C.: Algonquin Books, 1989.

Lewis, Robert W. A Farewell to Arms: *The War of the Words*. Twayne's Masterwork Studies No. 84. New York: Twayne Publishers, 1992.

———. "Hemingway in Italy: Making It Up." *Journal of Modern Literature* 9.2 (1981–82): 209–36.

———. *Hemingway on Love*. Austin: University of Texas Press, 1965.

———. "The Making of *Death in the Afternoon*." In *The Writer in Context*. Ed James Nagel. Madison: University of Wisconsin Press, 1984. 31–52.

———, ed., *Hemingway in Italy and Other Essays*. New York: Praeger, 1990.

Linares, Agustín. *Toreros mexicanos*. Mexico: Impresiones Modernas, S.A., 1958.

Lockridge, Ernest. "*Othello* as Key to Hemingway." *The Hemingway Review* 18.1 (1998): 68–77.

Loeb, Harold. *The Way It Was*. New York: Criterion Books, 1959.

López de Zuazo Algar, Antonio. *Catálogo de periodistas españoles del siglo XX*. Madrid: Universidad Complutense, 1980–81.

López García, Ana. Personal interviews. 8 and 9 October 1995.

Lottman, Herbert R. *The Left Bank: Writers, Artists, and Politics from the Popular Front to the Cold War*. Boston: Houghton Mifflin, 1982.

Lounsberry, Barbara. "*Green Hills of Africa*: Hemingway's Celebration of Memory." *The Hemingway Review* 2.2. (1983): 23–31.

———. "The Holograph Manuscript of *Green Hills of Africa*." *The Hemingway Review* 12.2 (1993): 36–45.

Lozano Sevilla, Manuel. *All about Bullfighting*. Trans. Betty Morris. Barcelona: Editorial Planeta, 1965.

Luca de Tena, Consuelo, and Manuel Mena. *Guide to the Prado*. Madrid: Silex, 1986.

Lugo, Santiago. *Nombres de personas: Santoral, significado, fiestas*. Barcelona: Editorial Irina, 1989.

Luján, Néstor. *Historia del toreo*. Barcelona: Ediciones Destino, S.L., 1954.

Lynn, Kenneth S. *Hemingway*. New York: Simon & Schuster, 1987.

MacLeish, Archibald. *New and Collected Poems, 1917–1976*. Boston: Houghton Mifflin, 1976.

Macnab, Angus. *The Bulls of Iberia: An Account of the Bullfight*. London: William Heinemann, 1957.

Madoz, Pascual. *Diccionario geográfico-estadístico-histórico de España y sus posesiones de ultramar*. 2nd ed. 16 vols. Madrid, 1846–50.

Mandel, Miriam B. "The Birth of Hemingway's *Afición*: Madrid and 'The First Bullfight I Ever Saw'." *Journal of Modern Literature* 23.1 (1999): 127–43.

———. "Index to Ernest Hemingway's *The Dangerous Summer*." *Resources for American Literary Study* 24.2 (1998): 235–69.

———. "Index to Ernest Hemingway's *Death in the Afternoon*." *Resources for American Literary Study* 23.1 (1997): 86–132.

———. *Reading Hemingway: The Facts in the Fictions*. Metuchen, N.J.: Scarecrow Press, 1995.

———. "Reading the Names Right." In *Hemingway Repossessed*. Ed. Kenneth Rosen. Westport, Conn.: Praeger, 1994. 131–41.

Mandell, Gerald L., and Merle A. Sande. "Antimicrobial Agents: Penicillins and Cephalosporins." In *The Pharmacological Basis of Therapeutics*. 6th ed. Eds. Alfred Goodman Gilman *et al.* New York: MacMillan, 1980. 1126–28.

Manual del librero hispanoamericano. 28 vols. plus 7 vols. of Index. Comp. Agustín Palau Claveras. Published simultaneously, Oxford: The Dolphin Book and Barcelona: Empuries, Palacete Palau Dulcet, 1948–. Vol. VI: *Tauromaquia* (1986).

Marco Miranda, Vicente. *Las conspiraciones contra la dictadura (Relato de un testigo)*. Madrid: Imprenta de los Hijos de Tomás Minuesa, 1930.

Marks, John. *To the Bullfight*. New York: Alfred A. Knopf, 1953.

Martin, John. "Hemingway's View of Emerson: A Note on His Reading." *The Hemingway Review* 11.1 (Fall 1991): 40–45.

Martin, Lawrence A. "Hemingway's Constructed Africa: *Green Hills of Africa* and the Conventions of Colonial Sporting Books." Paper read before the Hemingway Society's International Conference, Sun Valley, Idaho, 1996.

Martindale: The Extra Pharmacopoeia. 27th ed. Ed. Ainley Wade. London: The Pharmaceutical Press, 1977.

Martínez Kleiser, Luis, comp. *Refranero general, ideológico español*. Madrid: Real Academia Española, 1953.

Martínez Salvatierra, José. *Los toros: La fiesta nacional española*. Barcelona: Ediciones Sayma, 1961.

Maurois, Andre. *A History of France*. Trans. Henry L. Binsse. New York: Grove Press, 1960.

McAlmon, Robert. *Being Geniuses Together 1920–1930*. Revised with supplementary chapters by Kay Boyle. Garden City, N.Y.: Doubleday, 1968.

———. *McAlmon and the Lost Generation: A Self-Portrait*. Ed. Robert E. Knoll. Lincoln: University of Nebraska Press, 1962.

McEwen, W. A., and A. H. Lewis. *Encyclopedia of Nautical Knowledge*. Cambridge, Md.: Cornell Maritime Press, 1953.

McLendon, James. *Papa: Hemingway in Key West*. Miami: E. A. Seemann, 1972.

Mellow, James R. *Charmed Circle: Gertrude Stein & Company*. 1974. New York: Avon/Praeger, 1975.

———. *Hemingway: A Life without Consequences*. Boston: Houghton Mifflin Company, 1992.

Menke, Frank G., ed. *Encyclopedia of Sports*. 4th rev. ed. South Brunswick, N.J.: A. S. Barnes, 1969.

Meyers Enzyklopädisches Lexikon. 25 vols. Mannheim: Bibliographisches Institut, Lexiconverlag, 1974 ed.

Meyers, Jeffrey. *"For Whom the Bell Tolls* as Contemporary History." *Research and Creative Work* 1 (Fall 1988): 1–19.

———. *Hemingway: A Biography*. London: Grafton, 1985.

———. "Kipling and Hemingway: The Lesson of the Master." *American Literature* 56.1 (1984): 87–99.

Miller, Linda Patterson, ed. *Letters from the Lost Generation: Gerald and Sara Murphy and Friends*. New Brunswick, N.J.: Rutgers University Press, 1992.

Miller, Madelaine Hemingway. *Ernie: Hemingway's Sister "Sunny" Remembers*. New York: Crown, 1975.

Minguet y Calderón de la Barca, Enrique (Pensamientos). *Desde la grada: Anuario taurino de 1923*. Madrid: Imprenta Girada, 1923.

Mira, Filiberto. *Antonio Bienvenida: Historia de un torero*. Barcelona: I.G. Seix Barral Hnos, S. A., 1977.

———. Personal interview. 31 June 1998.

———. *El toro bravo: Hierros y encastes*. 1979. 2nd ed, rev. Sevilla: Ediciones Guadalquivir, S.L., 1981.

———. *Vida y tragedia de Manolete*. Valencia: Aplausos, D. L., 1984.

Moddelmog, Debra A. *Reading Desire: In Pursuit of Ernest Hemingway*. Ithaca and London: Cornell University Press, 1999.

Moliner, María. *Diccionario de uso del español*. Madrid: Editorial Gredos, 1983.

Monteiro, George. " 'Between Grief and Nothing': Hemingway and Faulkner." *Hemingway Notes* 1.1 (1971): 13–14.

———. "Hemingway and Faulkner," Unpublished paper, read at the Centennial Conference, Oak Park, Illinois, July 1999.

Montesinos, Rafael, ed. *Poesía taurina contemporánea*. Barcelona: Editorial RM, 1960.

Morla Lynch, Carlos. *En España con Federico García Lorca: Páginas de un diario íntimo, 1928–1936*. Madrid: Editorial Aguilar, 1957.

Morris, Richard B., ed. *Encyclopedia of American History, Bicentennial ed.* New York: Harper and Row, 1976.

Morrison, Ian. *Boxing: The Records*. Enfield, Middlesex: Guinness Superlatives, 1986.

Mott, Frank Luther. *American Journalism: A History: 1690–1960.* 3rd ed. New York: Macmillan, 1962.

——. *A History of American Magazines.* Vol. III: 1865–85. Cambridge, Mass.: Harvard University Press, 1938.

——. *A History of American Magazines.* Vol. IV: 1885–1905. Cambridge, Mass.: Harvard University Press, 1957.

Nagel, James, ed. *Ernest Hemingway: The Writer in Context.* Madison: University of Wisconsin Press, 1984.

——. *Ernest Hemingway: The Oak Park Legacy.* Tuscaloosa and London: University of Alabama Press, 1996.

National Cyclopaedia of American Biography. New York: James T. White, 1893–1984.

The National Union Catalog, Pre-1956 Imprints. London: Mansell, 1968–81.

Navajas Zubeldia, Carlos. *Ejército, estado y sociedad en España (1923–1930).* Logroño: Instituto de Estudios Riojanos, 1991.

New Catholic Encyclopedia. 14 vols. Washington, D.C.: The Catholic University of America, 1967.

The New Century Cyclopedia of Names. Ed. Clarence L. Barnhart. 3 vols. New York: Appleton-Century-Crofts, 1954.

The New Columbia Encyclopedia. Ed. William H. Harris and Judith S. Levey. New York: Columbia University Press, 1975.

The New Encyclopaedia Britannica. 15th ed. Chicago: Encyclopaedia Britannica, 1994.

The New Lexicon Webster's Dictionary of the English Language. Encyclopedic Edition. New York: Lexicon Publications, 1988.

New York Times Annual Obituaries: 1983. Chicago: St. James Press, 1984.

Nieto Manjón, Luis. *Diccionario ilustrado de términos taurinos.* Madrid: Espasa-Calpe, 1987.

——. *Historias de un alguacilillo (Colección de relatos taurinos).* Madrid: Editorial Fernando Plaza del Amo, 1993.

Nueva enciclopedia Larousse. 10 vols. Barcelona: Editorial Planeta, 1981, 1984.

Nuevo pequeño Larousse ilustrado: Diccionario enciclopédico. Paris: Librería Larousse, 1957.

Oag, Shay. *Antonio Ordóñez: In the Presence of Death.* London: Barrie & Rockliff, The Cresset Press, 1968.

Olano, Antonio D. *Dinastías: Dominguín, Ordóñez, Rivera.* Madrid: Promociones Ch.Ass, S. A., 1988.

Ordóñez, Antonio. "Hemingway and I." *Diario de Málaga,* special number, n.d. (probably 1961), n.p. JFK: Other Materials: Bullfight Materials, Clippings.

O'Rourke, Sean. "Evan Shipman and 'The Gambler, the Nun, and the Radio'." *The Hemingway Review* 13.1 (1993): 86–89.

——. "Evan Shipman and Hemingway's Farm." *Journal of Modern Literature* 21.1 (1997): 155–59.

————. " 'With Pascin at the Dome': A Reported or Invented Story?" Unpublished article, delivered at the Hemingway Centennial Conference, Oak Park, Illinois, 18–21 July 1999.

Ortega, Domingo. *El arte del toreo.* Madrid: Revista del Occidente, 1950.

Ortega y Gasset, Eduardo. *España encadenada: La verdad sobre la dictadura.* Paris: Juan Dura, 1925. Chapter XVIII, rpt. in *La dictadura de Primo de Rivera (1923–1930): Textos.* Ed. Jordi Cassasas Ymbert. Barcelona: Editorial del Hombre, 1983. 131–48.

Ortiz Blasco, Marceliano, and José María Sotomayor. *Tauromaquia A-Z.* 2 vols. Madrid: Espasa-Calpe, 1991.

Orts Ramos, Tomás (Uno al Sesgo), and Ventura Bagüés (don Ventura), eds. *Toros y toreros en . . .* Barcelona and Madrid, 1920–34.

Orwell, George. *Homage to Catalonia.* 1938. London: Martin Secker & Warburg, 1951, 1954.

The Oxford Companion to American Literature. 4th ed. Ed. James D. Hart. New York: Oxford University Press, 1965.

The Oxford Companion to American Literature. 5th ed. Ed. James D. Hart. New York: Oxford University, 1983.

The Oxford Companion to the Bible. Ed. Bruce M. Metzger and Michael D. Coogan. New York: Oxford University Press, 1993.

The Oxford Companion to English Literature. 3rd ed. Ed. Sir Paul Harvey. Oxford: Oxford University at the Clarendon Press, 1946.

The Oxford Companion to English Literature. 5th ed. Ed. Margaret Drabble. Oxford: Oxford University Press, 1985.

The Oxford Companion to Music. 9th ed. Ed. Percy A. Scholes. London: Oxford University Press, 1955.

The Oxford Companion to Sports and Games. Ed. John Arlott. London: Oxford University Press, 1975.

The Oxford Companion to the Theatre. 4th ed. Ed. Phyllis Hartnoll. Oxford: Oxford University Press, 1983.

The Oxford Dictionary of Quotations. London: Oxford University Press, 1941.

Pace, Mildred Mastin. *Kentucky Derby Champion.* Ashland, Ky.: The Jesse Stuart Foundation, 1993.

Padilla, Guillermo E. *Historia de la plaza El Toreo, Epoca de oro (1929–1946).* México, D.F.: Espectáculos Futuro, S. A. de C. V., 1989.

Palmer, Joe H., ed. *American Race Horses.* 1947. New York: Sagamore Press, 1948.

Park, Mungo. *Travels in the Interior Districts of Africa: Performed under the Direction and Patronage of the African Association in the Years 1795–1796, and 1797.* London: W. Bulmer, 1799.

Partridge, Eric. *Eric Partridge's Dictionary of Slang and Unconventional English.* 8th ed. Ed. Paul Beale. London: Routlege & Kegan Paul, 1984.

————. *Name into Word: Proper Names that Have Become Common Property: A Discursive Dictionary.* London: Secker and Warburg, 1949.

Peiro Guerrero, Vicenta. Personal interview. 5 October 1995.

The Penguin Companion to Literature: Britain and the Commonwealth. Ed. David Daiches. London: Penguin, 1971.

The Penguin Companion to Literature: Europe. Ed. Anthony Thorlby. London: Penguin, 1969.

Pérez Fernández de Velasco, Carmelo. *Juan Anlló "Nacional II."* Soria: Ingrabel II, S. A., 1996.

Pérez Maroto, Victoriano. *Estadística taurina de 1931.* Madrid: Editorial Ernesto Giménez Moreno, 1932.

Peterson, Richard K. *Hemingway Direct and Oblique.* The Hague: Mouton, 1969, 1974.

Peterson, Theodore. *Magazines in the Twentieth Century.* Urbana: University of Illinois Press, 1964.

Pinto Maeso, Luis. *Plazas de toros de España.* Madrid: Aro Artes Gráficas, S. A., 1981.

Plimpton, George. "The Art of Fiction XXI: Ernest Hemingway (Interview)." *The Paris Review* 18 (1958): 60–89.

Popelin, Claude. *El toro y su lidia.* 1952. Madrid: Calleja, 1956.

Portz, John. "Allusion and Structure in Hemingway's 'A Natural History of the Dead.' " *Tennessee Studies in Literature* 10 (1965): 27–41.

Preston, Paul. *Franco: A Biography.* London: Fontana/HarperCollins, 1993, 1995.

Qui est Qui en France: Dictionnaire biographique, 1988–89. 20th ed. Paris: Jacques Lafitte, 1988.

Quintanilla, Luis. *All the Brave.* New York: Modern Age Books, 1939.

The Quotation Dictionary. Ed. Robyn Hyman. New York: Macmillan, 1962.

Raeburn, John. *Fame Became of Him: Hemingway as Public Writer.* Bloomington: Indiana University Press, 1984.

Rao, E. Nageswara. "The Motif of Luck in Hemingway," *Journal of American Studies* 13.1 (1979): 29–35.

The Reader's Encyclopedia of American Literature. Ed. Max J. Herzberg. New York: Crowell, 1962; London: Methuen, 1963.

Reardon, John. "Hemingway's Esthetic and Ethical Sportsmen." In *Ernest Hemingway: Five Decades of Criticism.* Ed. Linda W. Wagner. East Lansing: Michigan State University Press, 1974. 131–44.

Reynolds, Michael S. *Hemingway: The American Homecoming*: Oxford: Blackwell, 1992.

———. *Hemingway, An Annotated Chronology: An Outline of the Author's Life and Career.* Detroit: Omnigraphics, 1991.

———. *Hemingway: The 1930s.* New York and London: W. W. Norton, 1997.

———. *Hemingway: The Paris Years.* Cambridge: Basil Blackwell, 1989.

———. *Hemingway's First War: The Making of* A Farewell to Arms. Cambridge: Basil Blackwell, 1987.

———. "Hemingway's 'My Old Man': Turf Days in Paris." In *Hemingway in Italy and Other Essays.* Ed. Robert W. Lewis. New York: Praeger, 1990. 101–106.

————. *Hemingway's Reading, 1910–1940: An Inventory*. Princeton, N.J.: Princeton University Press, 1981.

————. *The Sun Also Rises: A Novel of the Twenties*. Boston: Twayne, 1988.

————. "A Supplement to *Hemingway's Reading: 1910–1940*." *Studies in American Fiction* 14.1 (1986): 99–108.

————. *The Young Hemingway*. Cambridge: Basil Blackwell, 1986.

Richardson, R. Dan. *Comintern Army: The International Brigades and the Spanish Civil War*. Lexington: University Press of Kentucky, 1982.

Rigdon, Walter. *The Biographical Encyclopaedia & Who's Who of the American Theatre*. New York: James H. Heineman, 1966.

Roberts, W. Adolphe. *Havana: The Portrait of a City*. New York: Coward-McCann, 1953.

Robertson, Ian. *Blue Guide: Spain, The Mainland*. London: Ernest Benn, 1980.

Rodríguez, Mariano Alberto. *Armillita, el maestro: Recuerdos y vivencias*. Mexico: Unión Gráfica, S.A., 1984.

Rolfe, Edwin. *The Lincoln Battalion: The Story of the Americans Who Fought in Spain in the International Brigades*. New York: Random House, 1939.

Rosen, Kenneth, ed. *Hemingway Repossessed*. Westport, Conn.: Praeger, 1994.

Ross, Lillian. "How Do You Like It Now, Gentlemen?" *The New Yorker*, 13 May 1950; rpt. in *Hemingway: A Collection of Critical Essays*. Ed. Robert P. Weeks. Englewood Cliffs, N.J.: Prentice-Hall, 1962. 17–39.

————. *Portrait of Hemingway*. New York: Avon, 1961.

Rouch, John S. "Jake Barnes as Narrator." *Modern Fiction Studies* 11 (1965–66): 361–70.

Rovit, Earl. *Ernest Hemingway*. Boston: Twayne, 1963.

Rovit, Earl, and Gerry Brenner. *Ernest Hemingway*. Rev. ed. Boston: Twayne, 1986.

Rubio Cabeza, Manuel. *Diccionario de la guerra civil española*. 2 vols. Barcelona: Planeta, 1987.

Ruffner, Frederick G., Jr., and Robert C. Thomas, eds. *Code Names Dictionary: A Guide to Code Names, Slang, Nicknames, Journalese and Similar Terms*. Detroit: Gale Research, 1963.

Saintsbury, George. *A Last Scrap Book*. London: Macmillan, 1924.

Salvat Universal: Diccionario biográfico. 16th ed. 20 vols. Barcelona: Salvat Editores, 1986–88.

Sánchez Carrere, Adolfo. "Rafael Gómez (Gallo): El gitano calvo que torea al pelo." Number 8 in the series *Los triunfadores del ruedo*. Barcelona: Ediciones "Biblioteca Films," n. d.

Sánchez de Neira, José. *El toreo: Gran diccionario taurómaco*. 2 vols. Madrid: Guijarro, 1879. Rev. and expanded, Madrid: Velasco, 1896. Rpt. Madrid: Ediciones Giner, D. L., 1985.

Sánchez Robles, José, and Carlos Gutiérrez. *Samuel Flores, La pasión por el toro: 200 años de tradición ganadera en la historia de Albacete*. Albacete: Feria Taurina, C. B., 1996.

Sanfermines: 204 Hours of Fiesta. Pamplona: Larrión & Pimoul, 1992.

Sanford, Marcelline Hemingway. *At the Hemingways: A Family Portrait.* Boston: Little, Brown, 1962. Reissued as *At the Hemingways: With Fifty Years of Correspondence between Ernest and Marcelline Hemingway.* Moscow: University of Idaho Press, 1999.

Santainés Cirés, Antonio. *La dinastía de los Bienvenida: Un siglo de gloria y tragedia.* Zaragoza: Mira, D. L., 1988.

———. *Domingo Ortega: Ochenta años de vida y toros.* 2nd ed. Madrid: Espasa-Calpe, 1987.

———. "Estadísticas de las corridas y novilladas toreadas por Antonio Ordóñez en España, Portugal, Francia, México, Colombia, Venezuela, Perú, Ecuador, Argelia, Marruecos y Estados Unidos (1949–1962 y 1965–1981)." Appendix to Antonio Abad Ojuel, *Estirpe y tauromaquia de Antonio Ordóñez.* Madrid: Espasa-Calpe, 1988; unnumbered pages 353 ff.

Scafella, Frank, ed. *Hemingway: Essays of Reassessment.* New York: Oxford University Press, 1991.

Schneider, Daniel J. "Hemingway's *A Farewell to Arms*: The Novel as Pure Poetry." *Modern Fiction Studies* 14 (1968): 283–96.

Scholes, Robert, and Nancy R. Comley. *Hemingway's Genders: Rereading the Hemingway Text.* New Haven, Conn.: Yale University Press, 1994.

———. "Responsible Extravagance: Reading after Post-Structuralism." *Narrative* 1.1 (1993): 3–11.

Schulberg, Budd. *The Harder They Fall.* New York: Random House, 1947.

Sedgwick, Henry Dwight. *Ignatius Loyola: An Attempt at an Impartial Biography.* New York: MacMillan, 1923.

Serra Juan, Francisco de P. *Taurotraumatología, precedida de un diseño histórico sobre la fiesta de los toros.* Bilbao: FAESA, Fábrica española de productos químicos y farmacéuticos, S. A., 1945.

Serrano Labrador, Tiburcio. *La Caprichosa: Notas históricas de la plaza de toros de Talavera de la Reina.* Toledo: Ayuntamiento de Talavera, 1989.

"Sevilla, ayer y hoy." Insert 29, *ABC* (June 1998): 454–61.

Seville, Alfredo. *Abecedary.* New York: Hawthorn Books, 1966.

Shipman, David. *The Great Movie Stars: The Golden Years.* London: Hamlyn, 1970.

Shipman, Evan. *Free for All.* 1935; rpt. Freeport, New York: Books for Libraries Press, 1970.

———. "It'll be Trotters for Hemingway: Famous Writer Must Take Part in Action." *The Morning Telegraph* (8 April 1950).

———. *Mazeppa. The New Caravan.* Ed. Alfred Kreymborg. New York: W. W. Norton, 1936. 290–96.

Shubert, Adrian. *Death and Money in the Afternoon: A History of the Spanish Bullfight.* Oxford: Oxford University Press, 1999.

Siegel, Ben. *The Controversial Sholem Asch: An Introduction to His Fiction.* Bowling Green, Ohio: Bowling Green University Popular Press, 1976.

Sifakis, Carl, ed. *The Dictionary of Historic Nicknames*. New York: Facts on File Publications, 1984.

Silva Aramburu, José (Pepe Alegrías). *Enciclopedia taurina*. Barcelona: Editorial de Gassó Hnos., 1961.

Sinclair, Upton. *The Jungle*. 1906. New York: Penguin Classics, 1986.

Skelton, Barbara. *Tears before Bedtime*. London: Hamish Hamilton, 1987.

Smith, Paul. *A Reader's Guide to the Short Stories of Ernest Hemingway*. Boston: G. K. Hall, 1989.

Smoller, Sanford J. *Adrift among Geniuses: Robert McAlmon, Writer and Publisher of the Twenties*. University Park: The Pennsylvania State University Press, 1975.

Sokoloff, Alice Hunt. *Hadley: The First Mrs. Hemingway*. New York: Dodd, Mead, 1973.

Sopena Garreta, Juan. *Historia del armamento español*. Volume III: *Las armas de fuego, 1700–1977*. Barcelona, 1979; rpt. 1984.

Sotomayor, José María. *Miura: Siglo y medio de casta, 1842–1992*. Madrid: Espasa-Calpe, 1992.

Spilka, Mark. "Hemingway's Barbershop Quintet: *The Garden of Eden* Manuscript." *Novel* 21.1 (1987): 29–55.

———. *Hemingway's Quarrel with Androgyny*. Lincoln: University of Nebraska Press, 1990.

———. "A Source for the Macomber 'Accident': Marryat's *Percival Keene*." *The Hemingway Review* 3 (1984): 29–37.

Stanley, Edward. *A Familiar History of Birds*. 1840. New edition, London: Longmans, Green, 1865.

Stanton, Edward F. *Hemingway and Spain: A Pursuit*. Seattle: University of Washington Press, 1989.

Stearns, Harold. *The Confessions of a Harvard Man: The Street I Know Revisited*. 1935. Reissued with an Introduction by Hugh Ford and a Preface by Kay Boyle. Sutton West & Santa Barbara: The Paget Press, 1984.

Stein, Gertrude. *The Autobiography of Alice B. Toklas*. New York: Harcourt Brace, 1933; New York: Vintage Books, Random House, 1961.

Stephens, Robert O. *Hemingway's Non-Fiction: The Public Voice*. Chapel Hill: University of North Carolina Press, 1968.

———. "Hemingway's Old Man and the Iceberg." *Modern Fiction Studies* 7 (1961): 295–304.

———, ed. *Ernest Hemingway: The Critical Reception*. New York: Burt Franklin, 1977.

Stephenson, E. Roger. "Hemingway's Women: Cats Don't Live in the Mountains." In *Hemingway in Italy and Other Essays*. Ed. Robert W. Lewis. New York: Praeger, 1990. 35–46.

Stevenson, Burton, ed. *The Home Book of Quotations, Classical and Modern*. 6th ed. New York: Dodd, Mead, 1952.

Stewart, Donald Ogden. *By a Stroke of Luck! An Autobiography by Donald Ogden Stewart*. New York: Paddington Press, 1975.

Stock, Noel. *The Life of Ezra Pound* (an expanded edition). San Francisco: North Point Press, 1982.

Strater, Henry. "Portrait: Hemingway." *Art in America* 49.4 (1961): 84–85.

Strychacz, Thomas. "Trophy-Hunting as a Trope of Manhood in Ernest Hemingway's *Green Hills of Africa*." *The Hemingway Review* 13.1 (Fall 1993): 36–47.

Sureda Molina, Guillermo. *Conversaciones con Antonio Ordóñez*. Palma de Mallorca, 1962.

————. *El toreo contemporáneo* (1947–54). Palma de Mallorca, 1955.

Svoboda, Frederic Joseph. "Review of *The Dangerous Summer*." *The Hemingway Review* 5.2 (1986): 49–50.

————. *Hemingway and* The Sun Also Rises: *The Crafting of a Style*. Lawrence: University Press of Kansas, 1983.

Tapia, Daniel. *Breve historial del toreo* (1947); rpt. as *Historia del toreo, Vol. I: De Pedro Romero a Manolete*. Madrid: Alianza Editorial, S. A., 1992.

Tavernier-Courbin, Jacqueline. *Ernest Hemingway's* A Moveable Feast: *The Making of a Myth*. Boston: Northeastern University Press, 1991.

Toklas, Alice B. *What is Remembered*. London: Michael Joseph, 1963.

Toros y toreros en . . . Eds. Tomás Orts Ramos (Uno al Sesgo) and Ventura Bagüés (don Ventura). Barcelona and Madrid, 1920–34.

Torrente Fortuño, José Antonio. "Contar, recordar . . . Bolsa y periodismo: Memorias autobiográficas en desorden." Unpublished typescript, Biblioteca, Sociedad Rectora Bolsa de Madrid.

————. *Historia de la Bolsa de Madrid*. 4 vols. Madrid: Imprenta de la Bolsa, 1974.

Torres Martínez, Ricardo. *La predestinación de un hombre*. Monterrey, Mexico: Cigarrera La Moderna, 1993.

Trogdon, Robert W. " 'Forms of Combat': Hemingway, the Critics, and *Green Hills of Africa*." *The Hemingway Review* 15.2 (1996): 1–14.

————. "Hemingway and Scribners: The Professional Relationship." Unpublished dissertation, University of South Carolina, 1996.

Tynan, Kenneth. *Bull Fever: New Edition with Some Afterthoughts*. New York: Atheneum, 1966.

————. "The Testing of a Bullfighter," *The Atlantic* 231 (May 1973): 50–55.

Unión de criadores de toros de lidia: Temporada taurina de 1978. Madrid, 1978.

Unión de criadores de toros de lidia: Temporada taurina de 1982. Madrid, 1982.

Unión de criadores de toros de lidia: Temporada taurina de 1995. Vitoria: Diputación Foral de Alava, 1995.

Unión de criadores de toros de lidia: Temporada taurina de 1997. Madrid: Ediciones del Toro, 1997.

Unión de criadores de toros de lidia: Temporada taurina de 2000. Madrid: Ediciones del Toro, 2000.

Uriarte, Luis (Don Luis). *Toros y toreros en 1943 y 1944: Resumen estadístico, apreciación crítica, y notas gráficas de dichas temporadas*. Madrid: n.d.

Vaill, Amanda. *Everybody Was So Young: Gerald and Sara Murphy, A Lost Generation Love Story.* New York: Broadway Books, 1999.

Vera, Alberto (Areva). *Orígenes e historial de las ganaderías bravas*, 5th ed. Madrid: Artes Gráficas E.M.A., 1961.

Vera, Alberto (Areva)., ed. *Reglamento oficial para la celebración de espectáculos taurinos y de cuanto se relaciona con los mismos, notas y comentarios de Areva.* Madrid: Librería Beltrán, 1949.

———, ed. *Reglamento taurino comentado*, 3rd ed. Madrid: Librería Beltrán, 1949.

Vergara Martín, Gabriel María. *Refranero geográfico español.* 2nd ed. Madrid: Librería y casa editorial Hernando, S. A., 1986.

Viertel, Peter. *Dangerous Friends: Hemingway, Huston, and Others.* London: Penguin, 1991.

———. *Love Lies Bleeding.* Garden City, N.Y.: Doubleday, 1964; New York: Pocket Books, 1966.

———. "Luis Miguel Dominguín." *Gentlemen's Quarterly* 34 (April 1965), 72–73, 125–26, 128, 133. JFK: Hagemann Collection, Hn 155.

———. "The Passion of Luis Miguel." *Los Angeles Times West Magazine* (19 December 1971): 28–29, 31. JFK: Hagemann Collection, Hn 244.

Vila, Enrique. *Miuras: Cien años de gloria y de tragedia.* Sevilla: Talleres comerciales del diario Fé, 1941.

———. *Miuras: Más de cien años de tragedia y gloria.* Madrid: Escelicer, 1968.

Vila-San-Juan, José Luis. *La vida cotidiana en España durante la dictadura de Primo de Rivera.* Barcelona: Editorial Argos Vergara, S. A., 1984.

Villard, Henry S., and James Nagel. *Hemingway in Love and War: The Lost Diary of Agnes von Kurowsky.* 1989. London: Hodder and Stoughton, 1997.

Voss, Frederick, with Michael Reynolds. *Picturing Hemingway: A Writer in His Time.* New Haven and London: Yale University Press, 1999.

Wagner, Linda W., ed. *Ernest Hemingway: Five Decades of Criticism.* East Lansing: Michigan State University Press, 1974.

———, ed. *Ernest Hemingway: Six Decades of Criticism.* East Lansing: Michigan State University Press, 1987.

Waldhorn, Arthur. *A Reader's Guide to Ernest Hemingway.* New York: Farrar, Straus, and Giroux, 1972.

Walker, John, ed. *Halliwell's Film and Video Guide, 1997 Edition.* 12th ed. London: HarperCollins, 1997.

Watson, Milton H. *Flagships of the Line.* England: P. Stephens, 1988.

Watson, William Braasch. "Hemingway's Civil War Dispatches." *The Hemingway Review* 7.2 (1988): 4–92.

Watts, Emily Stipes. *Ernest Hemingway and the Arts.* Urbana: University of Illinois Press, 1971.

Way, Brian. "Hemingway the Intellectual: A Version of Modernism." *Ernest Hemingway: New Critical Essays.* Ed. A. Robert Lee. London: Vision Press, 1983. 151–71.

Weber, Ronald. *Hemingway's Art of Non-Fiction*. London: Macmillan, 1990.

Webster's American Biographies. Ed. Charles Van Doren. Springfield, Mass.: G & C Merriam, 1974.

Webster's American Military Biographies. Ed. Robert McHenry. New York: Dover Publications, 1978.

Webster's Biographical Dictionary. Springfield, Mass.: G & C Merriam, 1972.

Webster's Guide to American History. Springfield, Mass.: G & C Merriam, 1971.

Webster's New Twentieth Century Dictionary of the English Language. Unabridged. 2nd ed. Ed. in chief, Jean L. McKechnie. New York: World Publishing, 1956.

Webster's Third New International Dictionary of the English Language. Unabridged. Ed. in chief, Philip Babcock Gove. Springfield, Mass.: G & C Merriam, 1966.

Weeks, Robert P., ed. *Hemingway: A Collection of Critical Essays*. Englewood Cliffs, N.J.: Prentice-Hall, 1962.

Weir, Alison. *Britain's Royal Families: The Complete Genealogy*. London: Bodley Head, 1989.

Wentworth, Harold, and Stuart Berg Flexner, eds. *Dictionary of American Slang*. New York: Thomas Y. Crowell, 1960. 2nd supplemented ed., 1975.

White, Gilbert. *The Natural History & Antiquities of Selborne & A Garden Kalendar*. 1789. Annotated edition, ed. R. Bowdler Sharpe. London: S. T. Freemantle and Philadelphia: J. B. Lippincott, 1900.

White, William, ed. *Ernest Hemingway, Dateline: Toronto, The Complete Toronto Star Dispatches, 1920–1924*. New York: Charles Scribner's Sons, 1985.

———, ed. *Ernest Hemingway: By-Line, Selected Articles and Dispatches of Four Decades*. 1967. London: Grafton, 1989.

Who Was Who in America. 4 vols. Chicago: Marquis-Who's Who, 1968.

Who Was Who in World War II. Ed. John Keegan. New York: Crescent/Bison, 1984.

Who Was Who on Screen. 2nd ed. Ed. Evelyn Mack Truitt. New York: R. R. Bowker, 1977.

Who's News and Why. Ed. Anna Rothe. New York: H. H. Wilson, 1945.

Who's Who in the Bible. Ed. Peter Calvocoressi. Harmondsworth: Penguin, 1987.

Who's Who in Paris Anglo-American Colony. Paris: The American Register, 1905.

Wickes, George. *Americans in Paris*. Garden City, N.Y.: Doubleday, 1969; rpt. New York: Da Capo Press, 1980.

Williams, William Carlos. *The Autobiography of William Carlos Williams*. New York: Random House, 1951.

Wiser, William. *The Crazy Years: Paris in the Twenties*. New York: Atheneum, 1983.

Woolf, Virginia. "An Essay in Criticism," *New York Herald Tribune Books* 4 (9 October 1927): 1, 8; rpt. in Horst Weber, ed., *Hemingway*. Darmstadt: Wissenschaftliche Buchgesellschaft, 1980. 9–15. Also rpt. in Robert O. Stephens, ed. *Ernest Hemingway: The Critical Reception*. N.p.: Burt Franklin, 1977. 46–47, 53–54.

Wyden, Peter. *The Passionate War: The Narrative History of the Spanish Civil War, 1936–1939*. New York: Simon and Schuster, 1983.

Wylder, Delbert. *Hemingway's Heroes*. Albuquerque: University of New Mexico Press, 1969.

Young, Philip. *Ernest Hemingway: A Reconsideration*. University Park: Pennsylvania State University Press, 1966.

Yunck, John A. "The Natural History of a Dead Quarrel: Hemingway and the Humanists." *South Atlantic Quarterly* 62 (1963): 29–43.

Zabala, Vicente. *La ley de la fiesta*. Madrid: Editorial Prensa Española, 1971.

Zaragoza, Cristóbal. *Ejército popular y militares de la República, 1936–1939*. Barcelona: Planeta, 1983.

Index

Hernández Barrera, Félix, 217
Hernández Ramírez, Rafael, 68, 207–208, 239, 349
Hernandorena, Domingo, 208, 436
Héros XII (horse), 208–209
Hidalgo, Germán, 160
"Hills Like White Elephants" (Hemingway), 50
Historia de la plaza de toros de Madrid (Hernández Ramírez), 208
homosexuals, 209–210, 394; homosexual authors, 98, 145–46, 175, 464, 465; homosexual bullfighters, 154–55; story about, 305
Hoover, Herbert, 354
horse contractors, 70–71, 175, 339, 341
horses: horse racing, 210–11; killed in bullfights, 33–35. *See also* individual horses: Bess, Citation, Epinard, Exterminator, Goofy, Héros XII, Kzar, Man o' War, Master Bob, Pinky, Secretariat, Uncas
Host, 211. *See also* Roman Catholic
hotels: Pensión Aguilar (Madrid), 47, 53–54, 93, 248, 249, 333, 346, 356; Hotel Alfonso XIII (Seville), 46; Hotel Inglés (Madrid), 47; Hotel María Cristina (Algeciras), 46, 368; Hotel Palace (Madrid), 147, 329; Pensión Suiza (Madrid), 53; Hotel Quintana (Pamplona), 76, 207, 317–18; Hotel Reina Victoria (Ronda), 368; Hotel Valencia (Valencia), 211–12; Hotel Victoria (Madrid), 93
Hudson, W. H., 68, 212
Huelva (Andalucía), 90–91
humanism, 213–14
humor. *See* clowns
Hurón (bull), 215
Huxley, Aldous, 68, 215–16; reviews *A Farewell to Arms*, 141, 145, 172, 265, 269, 270; wife of, 342

Ibarra, Eduardo, 121, 216–17, 301, 377, 378, 390
iceberg theory, 217–18
Iglesias, Pablo, 350, 351
Ignatius of Loyola (saint), 246–47
Ildefonso (saint), 193
Imperio, Pastora. *See* Rojas Monje, Pastora
"In Another Country" (Hemingway), 256
in our time (Hemingway, 1924), 81, 130

In Our Time (Hemingway, 1930), 167, 315, 338, 405, 455
"Indian Camp" (Hemingway), 126
Indiano. *See* Diano
Indians. *See* Mexico
"Indignation of a High-Minded Spaniard" (Wordsworth), 352
Informaciones (newspaper), 207
Inglés. *See* cafés, in Spain; hotels
Instituto de Reforma Agraria, 51
international brigades, 401
International Exposition (1929), 311
International Herald Tribune (newspaper), 305
Isabel of Valois, 342
Isabella I (Isabela la Católica), 64, 143, 193, 218–19, 342
Isidro (saint), 30, 219, 365
Islands in the Stream (Hemingway), 203, 212, 394, 437; and painters, paintings, 94, 195, 282
Islero (bull), 285
Israel, 67, 149
Italy, 172; bullfights in, 374; and World War I, 1, 88, 129, 173–74, 297, 451. *See also* cafés, in Italy; kings and queens of

Jaime, James (saint), 344, 365
James, Henry, 68, 107, 219–20
Janeiro, Jesús (Jesulín de Ubrique), 492n43, 537n490
Jaqueta. *See* Giráldez, Antonio; Giráldez Díaz, José
Jeffries, James Jackson, 146, 154, 221–22, 229
Jerez de la Frontera (Cádiz), 26
Jijón, don José, 262
Jijona, 443, 456, 526–27n387; in various herds, 55, 177, 262, 328
Jiménez, Juan Ramón, 459
Jiménez, Manuel (Chicuelo father), 222, 476
Jiménez, Manuel (Chicuelo, Chicuelo II), 24, 44–45, 95, 222–29; bad press, 318; *cuadrilla* of, 55, 90, 132, 417, 440; and early promotion, 19–20; featured in articles, stories, 130, 233; height of, 424; long career, 21; mentioned, 155, 445; performances: in 1924, 62, 63, 157; in 1928, 444; in 1929, 313, 456; serves as witness to *alternativa*, 358
Jiménez, Manuel (el Niño del Matadero), 308

About the Author

Miriam B. Mandel taught at Douglass College (State University of New Jersey) and Clemson University before moving with her family to Israel in 1979. She is currently a senior lecturer in the English Department at Tel Aviv University. In addition to her work on Hemingway, Mandel has translated critical essays on the fiction of Ramón del Valle-Inclán and published articles on Jane Austen, Joseph Conrad, F. Scott Fitzgerald, A. E. Housman, and Katherine Mansfield. She has also read papers before learned societies in Australia, Canada, France, Spain, and the United States. The research for her book *Reading Hemingway: The Facts in the Fictions* (Scarecrow Press, 1995) was supported by the United States-Israel Educational Fund (USIEF-TAU) and the John F. Kennedy Library Foundation. *Hemingway's* Death in the Afternoon: *The Complete Annotations* and its companion volume, *Hemingway's* The Dangerous Summer: *The Complete Annotations*, were supported by a second grant from the John F. Kennedy Library Foundation and a generous three-year grant from the National Endowment for the Humanities.